CHURCH HISTORY IN THE FULNESS OF TIMES

The History of
The Church of Jesus Christ of Latter-day Saints

Prepared by the
Church Educational System

Published by
The Church of Jesus Christ of Latter-day Saints
Salt Lake City, Utah

Acknowledgment

We extend appreciation for the use of the visuals in this manual. Visuals that are not specifically identified were provided by Church Archives, the Museum of Church History and Art, Church Educational System College Curriculum, and the Church Visual Resources Library.

CONTENTS

PREFACE

IN THE LAST DAYS "shall the God of heaven set up a kingdom, which shall never be destroyed." This kingdom, as foreseen by Daniel, was likened unto a stone "cut out of the mountain without hands," which would roll forth and gain momentum until it eventually filled the whole earth (Daniel 2:44–45; see also D&C 65:2).

Elder Mark E. Petersen, of the Quorum of the Twelve Apostles, testified, "The Church to which you and I belong is that stone. It has been cut out of the mountain without hands, and your destiny and mine is to help roll it forth" (in Conference Report, Oct. 1960, p. 82).

From the days of Adam the prophets have looked forward to the time when the dispensation of the fulness of times would be ushered in and the Lord would "gather together in one all things in Christ, both which are in heaven, and which are on earth," which are necessary for his second coming and millennial reign (Ephesians 1:10).

The appointed hour foretold by all the holy prophets came in the spring of 1820 when God the Father and his Son Jesus Christ appeared to Joseph Smith. With this glorious vision the prophetic words of Isaiah began to be fulfilled, wherein he testified that the Lord would do "a marvellous work and a wonder" among the children of men (Isaiah 29:14).

Joseph Smith, called of God, laid the foundation that his successors have built upon. Through the inspiration of heaven, the Prophet translated the Book of Mormon, received the holy priesthood, and organized the Church of Jesus Christ once again among mortal man. Through him the keys of the priesthood were restored.

"And again, what do we hear? . . .

"The voice of Michael, the archangel; the voice of Gabriel, and of Raphael, and of divers angels, from Michael or Adam down to the present time, all declaring their dispensation, their rights, their keys, their honors, their majesty and glory, and the power of their priesthood; giving line upon line, precept upon precept; here a little, and there a little; giving us consolation by holding forth that which is to come, confirming our hope!" (D&C 128:20–21).

With the restoration of these keys Israel could now be gathered in from its long dispersion, and all saving ordinances of the gospel could now be administered for both the living and the dead.

Among the early commandments to the Church was the injunction that "Zion must increase in beauty, and in holiness; her borders must be enlarged; her stakes must be strengthened; yea, verily I say unto you, Zion must arise and put on her beautiful garments" (D&C 82:14).

Since those days the Church has survived exile from four states, harassment and continuous persecution of its leaders and members, an extermination order from a governor, martyrdom of its prophet, disenfranchisement by the government, and poverty of the Saints. This is what the Church endured and survived in the first century of its history; through such adversity, persecution, and impoverishment, the Church gained strength and matured.

By the time Joseph F. Smith, son of the Prophet Joseph's brother Hyrum, became President of the Church, he could say, "We have passed through the stages of infancy . . . and are indeed approaching the condition of manhood and womanhood in our experience in the Gospel" (in Conference Report, Apr. 1909, p. 2).

The missionary force brought a harvest of converts from all over the world. Seeds were planted abroad as missions became stakes. Zion's borders became enlarged. When Joseph Fielding Smith, son of President Joseph F. Smith, became President of the Church, he declared, "We are coming of age as a church and as a people. We have attained the stature and strength that are enabling us to fulfill the commission given us by the Lord through the Prophet Joseph Smith that we should carry the glad tidings of the restoration to every nation and to all people" (in Manchester England Area Conference 1971, p. 5).

Two years later, President Smith's successor, President Harold B. Lee, said:

"Today we are witnessing the demonstration of the Lord's hand even in the midst of his saints, the members of the Church. Never in this dispensation, and perhaps never before in any single period, has there been such a feeling of urgency among members of this church as today. Her boundaries are being enlarged, her stakes are being strengthened. . . .

"No longer might this church be thought of as the 'Utah church,' or as an 'American church,' but the membership of the Church is now distributed over the earth" (in Conference Report, Apr. 1973, p. 6; or *Ensign*, July 1973, pp. 4–5).

A "stone . . . cut out of the mountain without hands" by God's intervention (Daniel 2:45) is the metaphor used by the Lord to describe the expansion of the gospel to all the world. This stone is rolling forth and, indeed, will fill the earth. Then will the Lord's kingdom stand forever, and he will rule over the world and reign among the house of Israel, who have loved him and kept his commandments.

PRELUDE TO THE RESTORATION

◄ Second Coming *by Harry Anderson*

THE RESTORATION of the gospel of Jesus Christ and the establishment of Zion are the two great events in the history of mankind that precede the second coming of Jesus Christ. "The building up of Zion is a cause that has interested the people of God in every age," wrote the Prophet Joseph Smith. "It is a theme upon which prophets, priests and kings have dwelt with peculiar delight; they have looked forward with joyful anticipation to the day in which we live."¹ This latter-day restoration is the last act in God's divine drama for his children before the Millennium. This is the "dispensation of the fulness of times" (Ephesians 1:10) in which the "restitution of all things" would take place as the Lord promised through "all his holy prophets since the world began" (Acts 3:21).

The gospel is actually older than the earth itself. Its principles are eternal and were made known to God's children in the councils in heaven. The Father's plan centered on Jesus Christ, who was chosen to be the "Lamb slain from the foundation of the world" (Revelation 13:8). In those councils our Heavenly Father explained that the earth would provide a place of testing for his children, declaring, "And we will prove them herewith, to see if they will do all things whatsoever the Lord their God shall command them" (Abraham 3:25). Therefore, the Father granted his children the eternal principle of agency so that they might choose good over evil. Lucifer rebelled against the Father and his plan and was cast out of heaven. He became known as Satan, or the devil, the father of all lies, who on earth would deceive men and "lead them captive at his will, even as many as would not hearken unto [God's] voice" (Moses 4:4).

On the other hand, God has raised up prophets to teach his children the saving principles and ordinances of the gospel of Jesus Christ. From the beginning there has been a struggle between the kingdoms of God and Satan. The Church of Jesus Christ, the Lord's earthly organization, was established at times on the earth to gather the chosen and obedient children of God into a covenant society and to train them to fight evil. The true Church has the necessary principles and ordinances of the gospel of Jesus Christ that lead to eternal life.

A period when the Lord reveals his gospel doctrines, ordinances, and priesthood, is called a *dispensation*. For example, there were the dispensations of Adam, Enoch, Noah, Abraham, Moses, and of the Nephites. These dispensations gave the faithful and obedient the opportunity on earth to overcome the wicked world and prepare for eternal life by conforming to the principles and ordinances of the gospel of Jesus Christ.

Time after time the flowering of the true Church was followed by an apostasy, or a falling away from the truth. Thus in world history these flowerings and apostasies were cyclical. Each time the Lord's people fell into apostasy, there came a need for a restoration of the gospel. The Restoration discussed in this text is simply the last in the series of restorations that have occurred through the ages.

THE NEW TESTAMENT CHURCH

When the Lord Jesus Christ was born into mortality and ministered among Israel, he restored the gospel and the higher priesthood. He organized a church with a "foundation of the apostles and prophets" (Ephesians 2:20) to carry on the work after him. The Savior spent much of his ministry privately tutoring his Apostles, giving them the authority and keys to continue the work after his death. He chose Peter, James, and John to be the presiding Apostles. At his ascension he commissioned the Apostles to carry the message of salvation unto all the world.

The Church was small in numbers when the Apostles assumed its leadership. Just over a week after the Savior's ascension, the Holy Spirit was manifest in rich abundance on the Day of Pentecost as the Apostles taught the gospel and bore witness of the reality of the resurrected Lord. On this occasion three thousand people were baptized into the Church. The Apostles continued to minister with power and authority resulting in the conversion of additional thousands. So far, the gospel had been confined to the house of Israel. One day, however, as Peter was praying on the roof of a house in Joppa, he had a vision in which he learned that God is no respecter of persons, that no group should be regarded as unclean, and that the gospel should go to the Gentiles as well as to the Jews (see Acts 10:9–48).

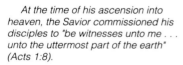

At the time of his ascension into heaven, the Savior commissioned his disciples to "be witnesses unto me . . . unto the uttermost part of the earth" (Acts 1:8).

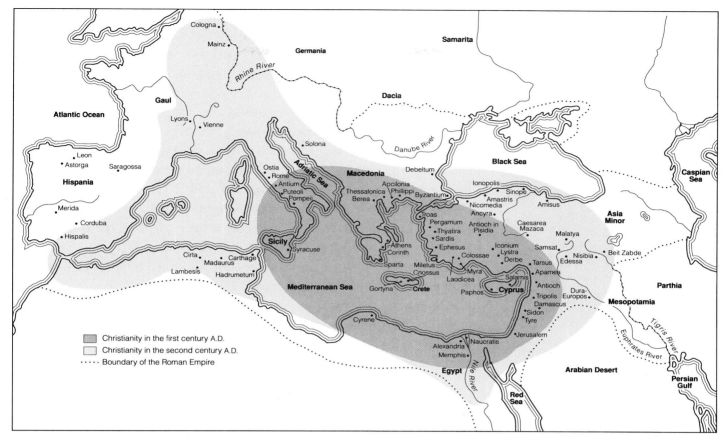

The spread of early Christianity. By the end of the first century A.D. the Apostles had taken the gospel north into Syria and Asia Minor; west to Macedonia, Greece, Italy, and the isles of the Mediterranean; then to northeastern Africa, and Egypt. A century later Christian communities existed in Gaul (France), Germany, and the Iberian Peninsula (Spain) as well as in northwestern Africa.

The conversion of Saul of Tarsus sometime later was of great significance to the growth of the Church. Saul, who had been persecuting the early believers, beheld the Savior in a bright light while on the road to Damascus. "I am Jesus whom thou persecutest" (Acts 9:5), proclaimed the risen Lord to the stricken Pharisee. And Saul, the agent of the Sanhedrin, became Paul the defender of the faith, a "chosen vessel" (Acts 9:15) to proclaim the name of Christ before gentiles and kings. Over the next thirty years this intrepid Apostle, along with many other devoted disciples who accompanied him, spread the gospel message and established branches of the Church throughout much of the Roman Empire. As growth continued and branches multiplied, elders, bishops, deacons, priests, teachers, and evangelists (patriarchs) were called and given proper authority by the Apostles.

THE GREAT APOSTASY

While the Apostles and other missionaries were courageously working to establish the Lord's kingdom on earth, the seeds of apostasy were already sprouting within the Church. Peter wrote that there were false teachers already among the people and that still others would come "who privily shall bring in damnable heresies, even denying the Lord that bought them, and bring upon themselves swift destruction" (2 Peter 2:1). Peter also predicted that "many shall follow their pernicious ways" (v. 2). Paul

Crucifixion of Peter

similarly testified that out of the congregation of believers would "men arise, speaking perverse things, to draw away disciples after them" (Acts 20:30).

But internal apostasy and disbelief were not the only challenges the early missionaries faced. While it was generally Roman policy to extend cultural and religious freedom to their subjects, there were intermittent periods when the Christians were severely persecuted, making it difficult for them to worship openly and proclaim the "good news" of the gospel. Naturally, at such times the Church leaders were especially targeted for imprisonment and death. The first notable Roman persecution occurred during the reign of Nero, who made the Christians the scapegoat for the burning of Rome in A.D. 64. Tradition says the Apostle Peter was crucified upside down and that later, in A.D. 67–68, the Apostle Paul was beheaded by the order of the emperor.

At first the Twelve perpetuated the apostolic office. For example, Matthias, who was not of the original Twelve, was called to be an Apostle. But through the spirit of prophecy, the leaders of the Church eventually recognized that an apostasy was not only inevitable but imminent. As the Apostles were killed, revelation to guide the Lord's church ceased, along with authority to operate it.

The years after the Apostles died provided ample evidence of the predicted demise of Christ's church. Principles of the gospel were corrupted by being mixed with prevailing pagan philosophies. Loss of the Holy Spirit was evidenced by a gradual disappearance of spiritual gifts. Changes were made in church organization and government, and essential ordinances of the gospel were modified.

According to President Joseph Fielding Smith the results of the Apostasy were devastating: "Satan in his wrath drove the [Church] into the wilderness, or from the earth; the power of the Priesthood was taken from among men, and after the Church with its authority and gifts disappeared from the earth, then in his anger the serpent continued his war upon all who had faith and sought the testimony of Jesus, desiring to worship God according to the dictates of conscience. So successful did he become that his dominion extended over all the known world."[2]

THE LONG, DARK NIGHT

The change from truth to error in the Church did not take place in a day. The Apostasy, hastened by the death of the Apostles in the latter half of the first century, gradually deepened during the years that followed. By the fourth century there was hardly a trace of the Church of Jesus Christ that was recognizable, and the "long, dark night" was well underway. With the Apostles gone, local church officers gradually assumed more authority. Bishops determined policy and doctrine for their local areas, claiming to be the proper successors to the Apostles. Gradually, a few bishops in key cities, such as Rome, Alexandria, Jerusalem, and Antioch gained supreme

Constantine the Great at the battle of Milvian Bridge in Rome. Constantine became the undisputed master of Rome and the western empire in A.D. 312. A year later Christianity secured toleration by his edict of Milan.

Victories in 324 brought him control of the eastern half of the empire, and the following year the Council of Nicaea was convened to begin the religious unification of the empire. In 330 he moved his capital to Constantinople to get away from Rome, the stronghold of paganism, and to facilitate making Christianity the state religion.

The dramatic moment of Constantine's conversion, when he claimed to see in vision a flaming cross in the noonday sky with the legend "By This Conquer," is captured in Gian Lorenzo Bernini's Constantine, now located in the Vatican.

authority in their entire regions. A great diversity of practices and dogma came as church leaders relied upon logic and rhetoric rather than upon revelation. "The compromising of truth and error, the assimilation of the gospel of Christ with the philosophies of men produced a new religion. This new religion was an appealing composite of New Testament Christianity, Jewish traditions, Greek philosophy, Graeco-Roman paganism, and the mystery religions."[3]

As the Christian church developed and spread, the Roman government changed its policy from mostly toleration to persecution. This was in part due to Christianity emerging as a group separate and distinct from Judaism, which had been allowed special privileges under Roman law. The Christians were considered antisocial in that they refused to hold political office, serve in the military, use the civil courts, or participate in public festivals. They were called atheists because there was no room in Christian monotheism for the Roman gods or for a deified emperor. For these reasons, and perhaps for others, the Romans sporadically launched attacks upon the church until the reign of Diocletian (A.D. 284–305). Diocletian determined to destroy everything that was not pagan as un-Roman. Churches were destroyed, scriptures burned, and Christians made to sacrifice or face torture. In an edict of 306 the persecution was ordered empire-wide.

It was perhaps inevitable that the empire would be forced to rescind its anti-Christian legislation. The church continued to grow, and the weakening condition of the empire called for unity, not disharmony. Constantine, at the Milvian Bridge in A.D. 312, utilized the cross as his symbol as he crushed his opponent Maxentius. The next year at Milan, Constantine issued his famous Edict of Toleration which granted to all people the right to worship as they pleased, revoking the measures which had meant to suppress Christianity.

Constantine himself did not become a Christian until he lay dying, but his acceptance and endorsement of Christianity placed the church in partnership with the aims of the empire. The desperate need to strengthen Roman unity is credited for Constantine's interest in the theological dispute within the church. To resolve a dispute over the nature of the Godhead, Constantine was instrumental in calling the Council of Nicaea, the first of the great ecumenical councils, in a city just south of his capital in A.D. 325. The creed that emerged from the council's deliberation, and was approved by the emperor, is a classic example of the way apostasy results when revelation is supplanted by argumentation and decree. As similar conflicts were resolved during the following centuries, a strong alliance developed between the state and the church, ensuring a growing secular influence upon the doctrines and practices of the church.

By the time of the barbarian invasion of Western Europe in the fifth century, many of the Germanic tribes already had been reached by various types of Christian missionaries. Therefore they took quickly to Roman culture and Catholicism. The sack of Rome in A.D. 410, however, was a clear signal that the empire was not invulnerable. The masses of Goths, Vandals, and Huns who crossed the imperial boundaries turned the unity of the West into a shambles, leaving behind the beginning of several nationalist states. Local political leaders exerted increased influence over the church in their areas at the expense of Rome. For the next several centuries, the churches in the various developing European countries became in effect the fiefs or feudal estates of the lords of the manors. Culture, education, and general morals retrogressed. It was a beginning of the time often referred to in history as the Dark Ages.

RENAISSANCE AND REFORMATION

By the fourteenth century, there was a renewed interest in classical Greece and Rome resulting in a flowering of literature, science, and art. It was, in effect, a period of "rebirth," or "renaissance," when men with confidence in themselves started to explore new ways of exploiting their environment. Artists turned from dreary mysticism to employ their skills using new techniques in sculpture, art, and literature. It was an age of naturalism—when the tools of science and art were applied to glorify the human body and to erect vast new cathedrals.

Men seemed to unshackle themselves from old ways. Gunpowder revolutionized warfare; the mariners' compass opened new vistas of travel and exploration; commerce was launched into the vast reaches of the Orient; and the Western Hemisphere was discovered. In the fifteenth century printing by movable type was greatly refined, and the whole field of printing gained new potential. This of course directly affected the rise of the universities and the dissemination of information.

The Renaissance was also a time of spiritual change. In their search for the classical past, men were introduced to the writings of the early church fathers and to copies of the scriptures in Hebrew and Greek. The scholars of the Renaissance began making these works available to the common people. Discovering the simplicity of the early church as opposed to the ritual and complexity of medieval Christianity led many to discover "anew" their original faith. These people founded or joined new religious orders, such as the Franciscans and Dominicans, as well as heretical movements, such as the Albigensians and Waldensians. In a sense, the effects of the Renaissance provided a setting for the Protestant reformation, which tore asunder the unity of Christendom once and for all.

The most famous of the Reformers was Martin Luther, who was born in Eisleben, Saxony, on 10 November 1483. When he was eighteen he was sent by his father, Hans Luther, to Erfurt to prepare for a career in law. In 1505, however, he abandoned his legal training to enter the monastery of the Augustinian Order of Eremites. In 1508 he was sent to Wittenberg to further his studies in theology and lecture on Aristotle's philosophy. From his earliest years, he seemed to have been tormented by the wide discrepancy

Martin Luther (1483–1546) was an Augustinian monk who challenged the doctrines and structure of the Roman Catholic church. He translated the New Testament into German and otherwise defied the traditions of the Roman church. He was excommunicated from the Roman church and led the German Reformation.

between the doctrines and teachings of the scriptures and the practices of Catholicism. During a journey to Rome in 1510, he was shocked at the corruption of the clergy and the religious apathy of the people. This did much to dispel the veneration in which he had held the papacy and armed him to challenge its authority. Luther's intensive study of the Bible led him to the doctrinal position that later came to mark the reform movement: that men are justified by faith alone (see Romans 3:28) and not by their good works.

That which most provoked Luther's direct opposition to the Church of Rome was the sale of indulgences by the agents of Pope Leo X. These indulgences were offered to repay Albert of Mainz his cost in acquiring the archbishopric of Mainz and to continue work on St. Peter's unfinished basilica. The purchase of indulgences granted individuals the remission of sin and punishment in purgatory and complete remission of all sins for the dead. On 31 October 1517, Luther nailed to the church door at Wittenberg his Ninety-Five Theses, which challenged the church to debate on the efficacy of indulgences and the church's sacramental practices.

Luther's theses were originally written to promote discussion among scholars, but the masses soon saw in him a champion and public hero. He defended himself against prelate and scholar and finally was even heard by the imperial diet (assembly) at Worms in 1521. By this time his movement had moved beyond the merely religious to the political, and the unity of the holy Roman Empire was threatened.

When Luther was ordered to give up his work, he boldly declared: "Unless I be refuted by Scriptural testimonies, or by clear arguments—for I believe neither the Pope nor the councils alone, since it is clear that they have often erred and contradicted one another—I am convinced by the passages of Scripture, which I have cited, and my conscience is bound in the word of God. I cannot and will not recant anything; since it is insecure and dangerous to act against conscience."[4]

Luther's resistance led to his excommunication from the church and to his being placed under the ban of the empire, which made him an outlaw. Luther was protected by German princes who sympathized with his ideas and who wanted more political autonomy from Rome. This protection enabled him to complete a German translation of the Bible in only eleven weeks. This translation was of transcendent importance in all of Europe because it was the first common language translation not based on Jerome's Latin Vulgate.

Gradually new forms of worship and doctrinal innovations advocated by Luther were introduced in many of the German states. When it was evident the Catholic church would not reform, Luther's followers founded the Lutheran church. Lutheranism became the religion of many of the northern and central German states but never succeeded in winning Bavaria and the states to the east. The faith spread northward, however, into Scandinavia and from there into Iceland. While it cannot be said that Luther brought religious freedom to Europe, the strength of his movement at least assured a pluralistic society where other religious groups could work for toleration.

Although Luther was the most famous of the Reformers, he was not the first. A century and a half earlier, in the 1300s, John Wycliffe in England denounced the corruption and abuses of the Catholic church and condemned the pope as anti-Christ. He translated the scriptures and circulated them among the common people. He was strongly condemned by the church, but his teachings were widely accepted among his countrymen. Thus, when Luther and other continental reformers began their work, many Englishmen sympathized with them.

The reformation in England was different than in other countries. King Henry VIII, who disapproved of Luther, insisted that the pope did not have the authority to deny Henry a divorce from his wife. A quarrel ensued in which the king rejected the pope's authority, and in 1533 the pope excommunicated the king. Henry then established the Church of England.

The two major reformers in Switzerland were Ulrich Zwingli and John Calvin. Zwingli convinced the citizens of Zurich that the Bible should be the only standard of religious truth. Using this standard Zwingli rejected life in a monastery, celibacy, the mass, and other Catholic practices.

John Calvin was even more influential. At Geneva, he attempted to create a holy city around the biblical models. Gradually Calvinism became predominant in many parts of Switzerland, and from there it spread to France, England, Scotland, Holland, and even, in a lesser degree, to Germany. John Knox, an early convert to Calvinism, helped refine and expand its teachings.

The Pilgrims and Puritans, two strict Calvinist groups who came to the New World, greatly influenced American values. For example, basic tenets of Calvinism prominent in early America included the absolute sovereignty of God, the election of man to grace, the idea that saved church members were to be instruments in God's hand in redeeming others, and the concept that the church was to be "a light on the hill" to influence the affairs of men in this world.

The Latter-day Saints believe the work of all these reformers was in preparation for the restoration of the gospel. President Joseph Fielding Smith has written:

"In preparation for this restoration the Lord raised up noble men, such as Luther, Calvin, Knox, and others whom we call reformers, and gave them power to break the shackles which bound the people and denied them the sacred right to worship God according to the dictates of conscience. . . .

"Latter-day Saints pay all honor to these great and fearless reformers, who shattered the fetters which bound the religious world. The Lord was their Protector in this mission, which was fraught with many perils. In that day, however, the time had not come for the restoration of the fulness of the gospel. The work of the reformers was of great importance, but it was a preparatory work."[5]

DISCOVERY AND COLONIZATION OF AMERICA

Another important preparation for the restoration of the gospel was the discovery and colonization of America. It had been preserved as a choice land from which the gospel would go to the nations of the earth in the last days. Moroni, an ancient American prophet, wrote: "Behold, this is a choice land, and whatsoever nation shall possess it shall be free from bondage, and from captivity, and from all other nations under heaven, if they will but serve the God of the land, who is Jesus Christ, who hath been manifested by the things which we have written" (Ether 2:12).

The arrival of Christopher Columbus was seen in vision by Nephi, also an ancient American prophet, over two thousand years before Columbus was born. "And I looked and beheld a man among the Gentiles, who was separated from the seed of my brethren [descendants of Lehi], by the many waters; and I beheld the Spirit of God, that it came down and wrought upon the man; and he went forth upon the many waters, even unto the seed of my brethren, who were in the promised land" (1 Nephi 13:12). Columbus himself confirmed in his writings that he felt inspired in his ventures as a mariner and in establishing religion among the Indians.[6]

Nephi continued his prophecy: "And it came to pass that I beheld the Spirit of God, that it wrought upon other Gentiles; and they went forth out of captivity, upon the many waters" (1 Nephi 13:13). Many people who settled the promised land were led there by the hand of God (see 2 Nephi 1:6).

Nephi foresaw many other events in America. He saw that the Lamanites (the Indians in North and South America) would be scattered throughout the land by the Gentiles, and that the Gentiles would humble themselves and call upon the Lord, and the Lord would be with them. Nephi beheld that the colonists in America would war against their "mother Gentiles" (in the American Revolution and the War of 1812) and would be delivered by the hand of the Lord (see 1 Nephi 13:14–19).

President Joseph Fielding Smith said, "The discovery [of America] was one of the most important factors in bringing to pass the purpose of the Almighty in the restoration of his Gospel and in its fulness for the salvation of men in the latter days."[7]

RELIGIOUS FREEDOM IN AMERICA

While many historians today insist that most early colonists came to America for economic reasons, many colonists were also seeking religious liberty. Among these were the Puritans, who established a powerful religious commonwealth in New England. They believed that they possessed the true faith and consequently did not tolerate any other religion.[8] This intolerance had to be overcome before there could be a restoration of Christ's church.

Certain dissenters among the Puritans, Roger Williams chief among them, argued that there ought to be a clear distinction between church and state and that no particular religion ought to be imposed upon the citizens. He also taught that all churches had fallen away from the true apostolic succession. Williams was banished from Massachusetts in 1635, and within a few years, he and others with similar ideas succeeded in obtaining a charter to establish the colony of Rhode Island, which allowed total toleration of all religions.

A courageous woman, Anne Hutchinson, who went to Massachusetts in 1634, disagreed with the local leaders on two theological issues: the role of good works in salvation and whether or not an individual may receive inspiration from the Holy Spirit. Mrs. Hutchinson was likewise banished from Massachusetts, and she sought refuge in Rhode Island in 1638. Despite the efforts of Roger Williams, Anne Hutchinson, and others, religious toleration was not achieved in New England for another century and a half.

Meanwhile, various religiously motivated groups established settlements throughout the rest of the American colonies. Each in its way contributed to the religious environment of America. Roman Catholics who settled Maryland passed the first toleration act in American history. Quakers in Pennsylvania also promoted religious tolerance and separation of church and state. The various colonists were of so many different faiths that it was impossible for any one denomination to predominate. This religious pluralism was a major reason for the religious liberties that became a unique feature of the United States.

Even though there were many different churches in America, most colonists did not claim membership in any particular denomination. An important movement in American religious history was the Great Awakening, which began about 1739 and continued for almost two decades. This first widespread revival in early American history was a fervent effort to restore righteousness and religious zeal. The Great Awakening swept throughout the length and breadth of the thirteen colonies. Evangelists and itinerate preachers held services in informal settings, including homes, barns, and even pastures. The Great Awakening kindled a religious commitment that had not been felt in America for years, and it promoted greater participation by both laymen and ministers in the affairs of organized religion. It also aroused within the colonial Americans a desire to unite in a democratic order.[9]

In spite of this zeal, complete religious freedom was not achieved in America until the American Revolution enhanced the climate for religious freedom. As colonists united against the British, they discovered that their religious differences were really not important to their cause and that they could agree on the essentials of their religious beliefs.[10] Furthermore,

Thomas Jefferson (1743–1826) wanted to be remembered for three things in his long and illustrious career as one of America's finest statesman. He wanted to be known as author of the Declaration of American Independence, the founding father of the University of Virginia, and the author of the statute of Virginia for religious freedom, which was adopted in 1785

The Constitution of the United States was signed by the Constitutional convention on 17 September 1787, and the new government was put into operation in 1789.

Thomas Jefferson was a fierce opponent of undue pressures upon government by organized religion. The Declaration of Independence, which he wrote, stated that man was capable of discovering correct political institutions for himself.

With the new feeling of freedom that followed the Revolutionary War, several states sought to protect basic human rights, including religious liberty. Virginia was the first in 1785 when it adopted Jefferson's Bill for Establishing Religious Freedom, which guaranteed that no person could be forced to attend or support any church or be discriminated against because of his religious preference.

After a few years as an unsuccessful confederation of states, the United States drafted a new constitution in 1787 that was ratified in 1789. This document, which was formed "by the hands of wise men whom [the Lord] raised up unto this very purpose" (D&C 101:80), embodied both the democratic impulse for freedom and the fundamental need for order. Freedom of religion was guaranteed in the first amendment to the Constitution.

The Prophet Joseph Smith stated that "the Constitution of the United States is a glorious standard; it is founded in the wisdom of God. It is a heavenly banner; it is to all those who are privileged with the sweets of liberty, like the cooling shades and refreshing waters of a great rock in a thirsty and weary land."[11] One reason this was true was because "under the Constitution the Lord could restore the gospel and reestablish his church. . . . Both were part of a greater whole. Both fit into his pattern for the latter days."[12]

Concurrent with the American Revolution and the establishment of the Constitution was a Second Awakening that brought about a reorientation of Christian thinking. Several new religious societies grew in strength and held a variety of beliefs: Unitarians, Universalists, Methodists, Baptists, and Disciples of Christ. Many beliefs were introduced in the new nation,

including the idea that there was a need for the restoration of New Testament Christianity. Those searching for this restoration were popularly known as *seekers*. Many of them were ripe for the divine Restoration and became its early converts.[13]

Almost concurrently with the Second Great Awakening, there arose a spirit of revivalism. Itinerate preachers held spirited camp meetings among new settlers in frontier areas of the growing United States. Lonely settlers from farms and villages gathered in huge crowds to enjoy the camp meetings. Noisy but gifted preachers lent a festive air to these religious gatherings while trying to win converts to their faith.[14]

The Second Great Awakening also influenced the formation of voluntary associations to promote missionary work, education, moral reform, and humanitarianism. Revivals brought religious emotions to a fever pitch and aided the growth of the popular denominations, particularly the Methodists and Baptists.[15] This religious awakening lasted for at least forty years, including the time of Joseph Smith's first vision.

The restoration of the gospel and of the Lord's true Church could not have taken place amidst the religious intolerance in Europe and early America. It was only possible in the setting of religious liberty, reevaluation of Christian thinking, and the spiritual awakening that had developed in early nineteenth-century America. The Lord's hand was evident in directing that the Restoration take place exactly when it did.

Noted American historian Gordon S. Wood acknowledges that there was a special timing to when the Restoration took place:

"Its timing in 1830 was providential. It appeared at precisely the right moment in American history; much earlier or later and the Church might not have taken hold. The Book of Mormon would probably not have been published in the eighteenth century, in that still largely oral world of folk beliefs prior to the great democratic revolution that underlay the religious tumult of the early Republic. In the eighteenth century, Mormonism might have been too easily stifled and dismissed by the dominant enlightened gentry culture as just another enthusiastic folk superstition. Yet if Mormonism had emerged later, after the consolidation of authority and the spread of science in the middle decades of the nineteenth century, it might have had problems of verifying its texts and revelations."[16]

God knows the end from the beginning and is the author of the grand design of human history. He directed the affairs of history so that America was appropriately fertile soil for the seed of the restored gospel to be planted and tended by his chosen seer, Joseph Smith.

ENDNOTES

1. *History of the Church*, 4:609.

2. Joseph Fielding Smith, *The Progress of Man* (Salt Lake City: Deseret News Press, 1952), p. 166.

3. Milton V. Backman, Jr., *American Religions and the Rise of Mormonism* (Salt Lake City: Deseret Book Co., 1965), p. 6.

4. Henry Eyster Jacobs, *Martin Luther: The Hero of the Reformation*, 1483–1546 (New York and London: G. P. Putnam's Sons, Knickerbocker Press, 1973), p. 192.

5. Joseph Fielding Smith, *Doctrines of Salvation*, comp. Bruce R. McConkie, 3 vols. (Salt Lake City: Bookcraft, 1954–56), 1:174–75.

6. See Samuel Eliot Morison, *Admiral of the Ocean Sea: A Life of Christopher Columbus* (Boston: Little, Brown, and Co., 1942), pp. 44–45, 279, 328.

7. Smith, *Progress of Man*, p. 258.

8. See Edwin Scott Gaustad, *A Religious History of America* (New York: Harper and Row, 1966), pp. 47–55; Sydney E. Ahlstrom, "The Holy Commonwealths of New England," *A Religious History of the American People* (New Haven, Conn.: Yale University Press, 1972), pp. 135–50.

9. See Alan Heimert, "The Great Awakening as Watershed," cited in John M. Mulder and John F. Wilson, eds., *Religion in American History: Interpretive Essays* (Englewood Cliffs, N.J.: Prentice-Hall, 1978), pp. 127–44.

10. See Sidney E. Mead, "American Protestantism during the Revolutionary Epoch," in Mulder and Wilson, eds., *Religion in American History*, pp. 162–76.

11. Joseph Smith, *Teachings of the Prophet Joseph Smith*, sel. Joseph Fielding Smith (Salt Lake City: Deseret Book Co., 1976), p. 147.

12. Mark E. Petersen, *The Great Prologue* (Salt Lake City: Deseret Book Co., 1975), p. 75.

13. See Backman, *American Religions and the Rise of Mormonism*, pp. 186–248.

14. See Martin E. Marty, *Pilgrims in Their Own Land: 500 Years of Religion in America* (Boston: Little, Brown, and Co., 1984), p. 168.

15. See Ahlstrom, *A Religious History of the American People*, pp. 415–28.

16. Gordon S. Wood, "Evangelical America and Early Mormonism," *New York History*, Oct. 1980, p. 381.

JOSEPH SMITH'S NEW ENGLAND HERITAGE

◄ *The birthplace of Joseph Smith was Sharon township, Vermont. The granite memorial to Joseph Smith was erected and the site dedicated on 23 December 1905 by President Joseph F. Smith in commemoration of the centennial of the Prophet's birth.*

The monument is 38 1/2 feet high, one foot for each year of his life. The Memorial Cottage (immediately left of the monument), which was used as a visitors' center, was completed and dedicated at the same time as the monument.

WE ARE ALL AFFECTED and influenced by our surroundings. We are nourished and nurtured by families and friends and respond to our environment. Joseph Smith grew up on the family farm and was almost exclusively under his family's influence. The things he learned at home were the most important legacy of his New England heritage. His parents emphasized hard work, patriotism, and personal religion. Joseph learned, listened well, and gleaned much from his heritage. During his formative years, Joseph Smith began to incorporate and manifest qualities that would help him fulfill his foreordained mission.

PATERNAL ANCESTRY OF JOSEPH SMITH

An examination of Joseph Smith's ancestry shows that his family possessed important character traits that were perpetuated in him. He developed strong family bonds, learned to work hard, to think for himself, to serve others, and to love liberty. He recalled, "Love of liberty was diffused into my soul by my grandfathers while they dandled me on their knees."[1]

The Ancestry of Joseph Smith

Joseph Smith
Born 23 December 1805
Place Sharon, Windsor Co., Vermont
Died 27 June 1844
Place Carthage, Hancock Co., Illinois

Joseph Smith, Sr.
Born 12 July 1771
Place Topsfield, Essex Co., Massachusetts
Died 14 September 1840
Place Nauvoo, Hancock Co., Illinois

Lucy Mack
Born 8 July 1776
Place Gilsum, Cheshire Co., New Hampshire
Died 14 May 1856
Place Nauvoo, Hancock Co., Illinois

Asael Smith
Born 7 March 1744
Place Topsfield, Essex Co., Massachusetts
Died 31 October 1830
Place Stockholm, St. Lawrence Co., New York

Mary Duty
Born 11 October 1743
Place Rowley, Essex Co., Massachusetts
Died 27 May 1836
Place Kirtland, Lake Co., Ohio

Solomon Mack
Born 15 September 1732
Place Lyme, New London Co., Connecticut
Died 23 August 1820

Lydia Gates
Born 3 September 1732
Place East Haddam, Middlesex Co., Connecticut
Died about 1817
Place Royalton, Windsor Co., Vermont

The Smith family marker in Pine Grove Cemetery in Topsfield, Massachusetts. Buried here are Samuel Smith; his wife, Rebecca; Samuel II; and his wife, Priscilla Gould. George A. Smith helped erect the monument to his ancestors in 1873.

Five generations of the Smith family lived in Topsfield: Robert Smith, Samuel Smith I, Samuel Smith II, Asael Smith, and Joseph Smith, Sr. Joseph Smith, Sr., was born in this house on 12 July 1771. The home was torn down in 1875.

Although not always affiliated with a church, generations of his ancestors sought to live by correct religious principles, and some anticipated that an important spiritual leader would be raised up among their posterity.

Among the rolling hills about twenty miles north of Boston, Massachusetts, is the small township of Topsfield, where many of the Prophet's ancestors lived. Five generations of Smiths lived in Topsfield. The first of these was Joseph Smith's third-great-grandfather, Robert Smith, who emigrated from Topsfield, England, to Boston in 1638 while still in his teens. Robert married Mary French and, after a brief stay in nearby Rowley, settled in Topsfield, Massachusetts. They were the parents of ten children. When Robert died in 1693 he left an estate valued at 189 pounds, a comparatively large sum for the era. Samuel Smith, a son of Robert and Mary, was born in 1666. He was listed on the town and county records as a "gentleman" and apparently held a public office. He married Rebecca Curtis, and they had nine children.

Samuel and Rebecca's first son was born in 1714. Samuel, Jr., was a distinguished community leader and a promoter of the American War of Independence. According to his obituary, "He was a sincere friend to the liberties of his country, and a strenuous advocate for the doctrines of Christianity."[2] Samuel, Jr., married Priscilla Gould, a descendant of the founder of Topsfield. Priscilla died after bearing five children, and Samuel married her cousin, also named Priscilla. She bore no children but reared those of Samuel's first wife, including Joseph Smith's grandfather, Asael, born in 1744.

Asael was affiliated with the established religion in New England, the Congregationalists, but he later became skeptical of organized religion. To his thinking the teachings of established churches were not reconcilable with scripture and common sense. At age twenty-three he married Mary Duty of

Joseph Smith's ancestry lived in New England.

Rowley, Massachusetts. At great sacrifice to himself and his family, Asael moved from Derryfield, New Hampshire, back to Topsfield where he worked for five years to liquidate the debts his father had been unable to pay before his death.

The Smiths remained in Topsfield until 1791 when Asael, Mary, and their eleven children moved briefly to Ipswich, Massachusetts, and then on to Tunbridge, Vermont, in quest of inexpensive, virgin land. At Tunbridge, Asael continued his community service, and during his thirty years there occupied nearly every elective office.

Asael's philosophy agreed with that of the Universalists, who believed in Jesus Christ as a god of love who would save all of his children. Like all Universalists, Asael was more comfortable with a god who was more interested in saving than in destroying mankind. He believed that life continued after death.

In an address to his family, Asael wrote: "The soul is immortal. . . . Do all to God in a serious manner. When you think of him, speak of him, pray to him, or in any way make your addresses to his great majesty, be in good earnest. . . . And as to religion, study the nature of religion, and see whether it consists in outward formalities, or in the hidden man of the heart. . . .

"Sure I am my Savior, Christ, is perfect, and never will fail in one circumstance. To him I commit your souls, bodies, estates, names, characters, lives, deaths and all—and myself, waiting when he shall change my vile body and make it like his own glorious body."[3]

Asael Smith also predicted that "God was going to raise up some branch of his family to be a great benefit to mankind."[4] Many years later when his son Joseph Smith, Sr., gave him a recently published Book of Mormon, he was vitally interested. George A. Smith recorded, "My grandfather Asael fully believed the Book of Mormon, which he read nearly through."[5] Asael died in the fall of 1830, confident that his grandson Joseph was the long-anticipated prophet and that he had heralded in a new religious age.

Mary Duty Smith outlived her husband Asael by six years. In 1836 Mary made an arduous journey of five hundred miles to join her descendants who by then had moved to Kirtland, Ohio. Elias Smith, a grandson, was with Mary when she was reunited with her children and grandchildren. "The meeting between the grandmother and her prophet descendant and his brother was most touching; Joseph blessed her and said she was the most honored woman on earth."[6] She completely accepted the testimony of her grandson and fully intended to be baptized. Unfortunately, her age and health prevented this. She died on 27 May 1836, just ten days after arriving in Kirtland.

THE MATERNAL ANCESTRY OF JOSEPH SMITH

Comparatively little is known about the Mack family through which Joseph's mother, Lucy Mack, came. John Mack, born in Inverness, Scotland, from a line of clergymen, arrived in New England in 1669. For a number of years he lived in Salisbury, Massachusetts. He and his wife moved to Lyme, Connecticut, in 1696. Their eighth child, Ebenezer, married Hannah Huntley, and they prospered for a time on the Mack estate. But prosperity was short-lived, and Solomon, born in 1732, was apprenticed to a neighboring farmer in Lyme at the age of four. He recalled, "I was treated by my master as his property and not as his fellow mortal."[7] He remained an apprentice until the age of twenty-one, but his master never taught or spoke to him about religion.

For most of the rest of his life, Solomon searched for the anchorage he never found as a youth. Having fulfilled his apprenticeship, he enlisted for service in the French and Indian War. In succeeding years Solomon was a merchant, land developer, shipmaster, mill operator, and farmer. Though he expended considerable effort, fortune did not favor him, and he was beset with accidents, hardships, and financial reverses.

This hearty adventurer did experience some good fortune in 1759. After a brief acquaintance, he married Lydia Gates, a trained and accomplished schoolteacher and eldest child of the respected and successful Congregationalist church deacon, Daniel Gates. Lydia had been a practicing Congregationalist from her early youth. Although Solomon and Lydia came from contrasting backgrounds, theirs was an enduring marriage. Lydia took charge of both the secular and religious educations of her eight sons and daughters. She probably taught her husband to read and write along with their children. Solomon believed that Lydia not only exhibited "the polish of education, but she also possessed that inestimable jewel which in a wife and mother of a family is truly a pearl of great price, namely, a pious and devotional character."[8]

Soon after their marriage, Solomon purchased sixteen hundred acres of wilderness land in northern New York. A leg injury prevented him from clearing the land as the contract stipulated, and he lost the property. In 1761 Solomon and Lydia settled with two young sons in Marlow, New Hampshire. They remained there for ten years and had four more children. In 1771 the Macks moved to Gilsum, New Hampshire, where two additional children were born. Lucy, the youngest, would become the mother of the Prophet Joseph Smith.

During the American Revolution, Solomon enlisted in an artillery company but soon took sick and was sent home to recover. He might have been safer with his unit, because in rapid succession Solomon was crushed by a tree, bruised on a waterwheel, and knocked unconscious by a falling tree limb. The last accident was particularly severe, and thereafter he was subject to periods of unconsciousness or "fits" as he called them.[9]

But Solomon Mack could never forego adventure for long. With his teenage sons, Jason and Stephen, Solomon signed on as a sailor on an American privateer. After four years and calamities which included a

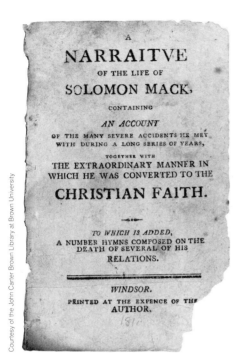

Title page of Solomon Mack's autobiography

This is Tunbridge's general store. It was still in use after 160 years. Traditionally, it is the place Joseph, Sr., and Lucy first met.

hurricane, a shipwreck, and illness, they returned empty-handed. Solomon found Lydia and the children homeless, having been swindled out of their property. "I did not care whether I lived or died," he wrote concerning this period of his life.[10] This despondency was only temporary though because through hard work Solomon was able to provide for his family again.

Solomon Mack had not been outwardly religious, though he was a God-fearing and good-hearted man. He showed little inclination toward scripture reading or church-going, but in 1810 rheumatism forced him to reassess his values. "After this I determined to follow phantoms no longer, but devote the rest of my life to the service of God and my family."[11] That winter he read the Bible and prayed earnestly; eventually he found peace of soul and mind. Until his death in 1820, Solomon spent much of his time telling others of his conversion and admonishing them to serve the Lord. He wrote an autobiography with the hope that others would not become enamored with material gain as he had. He enthusiastically shared his conviction with his grandchildren, among whom was young Joseph Smith, Jr. Solomon died just three weeks before his eighty-eighth birthday, several months after his grandson's remarkable vision of the Father and the Son of which he was probably unaware.

During the years of Solomon's mishaps and adventures, his wife, Lydia Gates, provided stability and direction for their children. All the children, especially Lucy, the youngest daughter, showed her influence. Lucy gave credit to her mother "for all the religious instructions as well as most of the educational privileges which I had ever received."[12]

Lucy, though intelligent, assertive, and reared amid pious surroundings, did not experience significant spiritual stirrings until age nineteen. She wondered if life had meaning and soon concluded she needed to revise her gloomy attitude. To avoid being labeled worldly, she decided to join a church but was frustrated at the rival claims put forth by various clergymen. She inquired, "How can I decide in such a case as this, seeing they are all unlike the Church of Christ, as it existed in former days!"[13]

Lucy did not find a satisfying answer to her spiritual dilemma. Seemingly convinced that existing churches could not fulfill her needs, she temporarily put aside her quest for a church, and gradually her anxiety dissipated. In less than two years she met and married Joseph Smith, Sr. Little did Lucy realize that from that union would come a prophet-son who would give solace and direction to all who, like herself, were seeking to find the Church of Jesus Christ.

PARENTS OF THE PROPHET

Lucy Mack met Joseph Smith, Sr., while visiting her brother Stephen at Tunbridge, Vermont. Joseph was twenty-five, over six feet tall, and powerfully built, like his father, Asael. After their marriage on 24 January 1796, they settled on one of the family farms in Tunbridge. They spent six years

Tunbridge Gore, Vermont, was the first home of Joseph and Lucy Smith. Hyrum Smith was born here on 9 February 1800.

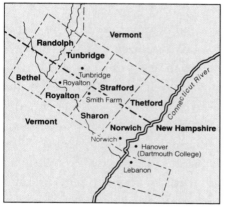

The Joseph Smith, Sr., family moved several times in New England. (1) Following Joseph and Lucy's marriage in 1796 they lived and farmed in Tunbridge, Vermont. (2) In 1802 they moved to Randolph and opened a mercantile establishment. (3) The next year they returned to Tunbridge. (4) Also in 1803, they sold the Tunbridge farm and moved to Royalton for a few months. (5) In 1804 they moved to Sharon township in Windsor County, where Joseph Smith, Jr., was born. (6) They moved back to Tunbridge, where Samuel Harrison was born. (7) In 1808 they again moved to Royalton, where Ephraim and William were born. (8) In 1811 they moved to West Lebanon, New Hampshire, where a typhoid epidemic struck the family. (9) In 1813 they moved to Norwich, Vermont, where they experienced three successive crop failures. (10) Crop failures forced a final move to the Palmyra vicinity in New York in 1816.

there, during which their first three children were born. Joseph and Lucy rented out their Tunbridge farm, possibly because of stony soil, and moved to Randolph in 1802, where they opened a mercantile establishment.

In Randolph Lucy fell ill. A physician diagnosed her condition as tuberculosis, the illness her older sisters, Lovisa and Lovina, had died from. Hearing that doctors said she would die, Lucy pleaded with the Lord to spare her life so that she might bring comfort to her children and husband.

Lucy wrote, "I made a solemn covenant with God that if He would let me live I would endeavor to serve him according to the best of my abilities. Shortly after this I heard a voice say to me, 'Seek, and ye shall find; knock, and it shall be opened unto you. Let your heart be comforted; ye believe in God, believe also in me.'

". . . As soon as I was able I made all diligence in endeavoring to find someone who was capable of instructing me more perfectly in the way of life and salvation. . . .

". . . I went from place to place for the purpose of getting information and finding, if it were possible, some congenial spirit who could enter into my feelings and thus be able to strengthen and assist me in carrying out my resolutions. . . .

". . . I said in my heart that there was not then upon earth the religion which I sought. I therefore determined to examine my Bible and, taking Jesus and His disciples for my guide, to endeavor to obtain from God that which man could neither give nor take away. . . .

"At length I considered it my duty to be baptized and, finding a minister who was willing to baptize me and leave me free in regard to joining any religious denomination, I stepped forward and yielded obedience to this ordinance."[14]

While Lucy was preoccupied with religion and salvation, her husband was embarking on an ill-fated economic venture. Learning that ginseng root,

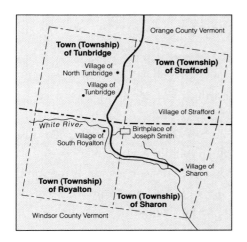

Joseph Smith was born in the township of Sharon in Windsor County, Vermont. This should not be confused with the village of Sharon southeast of the Smith farm. As the map shows, the farm was on the township line.

which grew wild in Vermont, was highly valued in China because of its supposed ability to heal and to enhance life, Joseph, who had experienced a series of financial setbacks, invested heavily in the herb. Having obtained a substantial quantity, he was offered three thousand dollars for it by a Mr. Stevens from Royalton, but he declined. When Joseph went to New York to arrange for shipment, Mr. Stevens followed him to find out which ship Joseph's cargo was on. Having some ginseng himself, he sent his son to represent himself and Joseph in selling the product. Young Stevens sold the ginseng at a good profit, but misrepresented the returns and gave Joseph Smith, Sr., only a chest of tea. When Stevens' dishonesty was discovered, he fled to Canada with the money, leaving Joseph and Lucy with an eighteen-hundred-dollar debt. Lucy recalled, "This farm, which was worth about fifteen hundred dollars, my husband sold for eight hundred dollars in order to make a speedy payment."[15] To this Lucy added the one thousand dollars she had received for a wedding present. They were out of debt, but penniless.

Joseph and Lucy moved to Royalton, Vermont, for a few months and then to Sharon in Windsor County. There Joseph rented Solomon Mack's farm. He farmed in the summer and taught school in the winter. While in Sharon, Joseph and Lucy had another son, born 23 December 1805, whom they named Joseph. Naming him this fulfilled a prophecy of Joseph in Egypt who had predicted that a "choice seer" would be raised up among his descendants. One of the keys by which this seer could be identified was that he would receive the name of the ancient patriarch Joseph, which would also be his father's name (see 2 Nephi 3:14–15).

Joseph Smith, Sr., and Lucy were dutiful parents and endeavored to teach their children religious precepts. Lucy especially encouraged her children to study the Bible. Their son William, born in 1811, recalled his mother's concern with religious matters: "My mother who was a very pious woman and much interested in the welfare of her children, both here and hereafter,

Children of Joseph Smith, Sr., and Lucy Mack Smith

Name	Birth Date	Place of Birth	Death Date
1. Child	about 1797	Tunbridge, Vermont	about 1797
2. Alvin	11 February 1798	Tunbridge, Vermont	19 November 1823
3. Hyrum	9 February 1800	Tunbridge, Vermont	27 June 1844
4. Sophronia	16 May 1803	Tunbridge, Vermont	1876
5. Joseph, Jr.	23 December 1805	Sharon, Vermont	27 June 1844
6. Samuel Harrison	13 March 1808	Tunbridge, Vermont	30 July 1844
7. Ephraim	13 March 1810	Royalton, Vermont	24 March 1810
8. William	13 March 1811	Royalton, Vermont	13 November 1893
9. Catherine	28 July 1812	Lebanon, New Hampshire	1 February 1900
10. Don Carlos	25 March 1816	Norwich, Vermont	7 August 1841
11. Lucy	18 July 1821	Palmyra, New York	9 December 1882

made use of every means which her parental love could suggest, to get us engaged in seeking for our souls' salvation."[16]

Joseph, Sr., was as gentle as he was big. Heber C. Kimball recalled he was "one of the most cheerful men I ever saw, and he was harmless as a child."[17] Lucy said he was "an affectionate companion and tender father as ever blessed the confidence of a family."[18]

Though less inclined to teaching his family, Joseph, Sr., was religious. William remembered: "My father's religious habits [were] strictly pious and moral."[19] Like his father, Asael, Joseph was suspicious of traditional churches but always retained a strong belief in God. Sometime in 1811, his "mind became much excited upon the subject of religion."[20] While in this state of agitation and concern, he had the first of a series of dreams which came within an eight-year period. In the first dream Joseph found himself traveling through a barren field of dead timber with a spirit who told him the field represented the world without religion. Joseph was told he would find a box of food which if eaten would make him wise. He tried to partake but was prevented from doing so by horned beasts. He told Lucy he awoke trembling but happy and that he was now convinced that even the religious knew nothing of the kingdom of God.

Later in 1811, Joseph, Sr., experienced a second profound dream that related to his family. It was much like Lehi's dream of the tree of life. He found himself following a path to a beautiful fruit tree. As he began to eat the delicious fruit, he realized that he must bring his wife and family to the tree so they could enjoy it together. He went and brought them, and they began to eat. He reported that "We were exceedingly happy, insomuch that our joy could not easily be expressed."[21]

His last dream took place in 1819 in New York, shortly before his son's first vision. A messenger said, "I have . . . always found you strictly honest in all your dealings. . . . I have now come to tell you that this is the last time I shall ever call on you, and that there is but one thing which you lack in order to secure your salvation."[22] He awoke before learning what he lacked. Because heavenly communications were part of Joseph, Sr.'s life, it was easy for him to accept his son's prophetic calling. Eventually he learned that he lacked the saving principles and ordinances of the gospel of Jesus Christ, which the Lord restored through his son Joseph.

JOSEPH SMITH'S EARLY BOYHOOD

During Joseph Smith's earliest years, his family moved frequently, trying to find fertile soil or a suitable livelihood. Their first move after his birth took them from Sharon to Tunbridge. In 1807, soon after Samuel was born, they moved to Royalton, Vermont, where two more sons were born. Shortly after William's birth in 1811 the Smiths moved to the small community of West Lebanon, New Hampshire, and began, according to Lucy, "to contemplate, with joy and satisfaction, the prosperity which had attended our recent exertions."[23] Her optimism gave way to despair when typhoid fever came into West Lebanon and "raged tremendously." It was part of an epidemic that swept the upper Connecticut valley leaving six thousand people dead. One by one the Smith children fell ill. Sophronia, afflicted for three months, was near death but began to recover when Joseph and Lucy beseeched the Lord to spare her.

Seven-year-old Joseph, Jr., was ill with the fever only two weeks but suffered complications which eventually required four surgeries. The most serious complication involved a swelling and infection in the tibia of his left leg, a condition that today would be called osteomyelitis. Joseph was in agony for over two weeks. Throughout the ordeal his older brother Hyrum showed him great tenderness. Lucy recorded: "Hyrum sat beside him, almost day and night for some considerable length of time, holding the affected part of his leg in his hands and pressing it between them, so that his afflicted brother might be enabled to endure the pain."[24]

The first two attempts to reduce the swelling and drain the infection in Joseph's leg failed. The chief surgeon recommended amputation, but Lucy refused and urged the doctors, "You will not, you must not, take off his leg, until you try once more."[25] Providentially, "the only physician in the United States who aggressively and successfully operated for osteomyelitis" in that era was Dr. Nathan Smith, a brilliant physician at Dartmouth Medical College in Hanover, New Hampshire.[26] He was the principal surgeon, or at least the chief adviser, in Joseph's case. In his treatment of the disease, Dr. Smith was generations ahead of his time.

Joseph insisted on enduring the operation without being bound or drinking brandy wine to dull his senses. He asked his mother to leave the room so she would not have to see him suffer. She consented, but when the physicians broke off part of the bone with forceps and Joseph screamed, she rushed back into the room. "Oh, mother, go back, go back," Joseph cried out. She did, but returned a second time only to be removed again.[27] After the ordeal Joseph went with his Uncle Jesse Smith to the seaport town of Salem, Massachusetts, hoping that the sea breezes would help his recovery. Due to the severity of the operation, his recovery was slow. He walked with crutches for three years and sometimes limped slightly thereafter, but he returned to health and led a robust life.

According to his mother, Joseph's operation may have been the only notable incident in his early boyhood.[28] About 1813 the family moved to Norwich, Vermont. There Joseph probably attended a common, or grammar, school for a brief period. He also received religious instruction and education in his home and likely engaged in the outdoor activities and games of his day. He was tall, athletic, and energetic, but was also contemplative and even-tempered. His mother said that Joseph "seemed much less inclined to the perusal of books than any of the rest of our children, but far more given to meditation and deep study."[29] In Norwich, the Smiths began to farm on

Nathan Smith, one of young Joseph Smith's physicians

the property of Esquire Murdock. It was their last attempt at wresting a livelihood from the Vermont soil. Lucy wrote, "The first year our crops failed; yet, by selling fruit which grew on the place, we succeeded in obtaining bread for the family."[30] The second-year crops were also a dismal failure.

The Smith's third-year crops were frozen along with nearly everyone else's in 1816, the infamous year without a summer. It was known as "eighteen hundred and froze to death." Mount Tambora in the Dutch East Indies (Indonesia) had exploded in a violent eruption in mid-April of 1815. It was considered the largest volcanic eruption in recorded history. It ejected an estimated twenty-five cubic miles of volcanic debris. Dust blew into the stratosphere obscuring the sun more severely than any volcano since 1600 and altering the weather pattern for an extended period.[31]

New England was hard hit. Four killing frosts struck between 6 June and 30 August, which destroyed all but the hardiest of crops. Unaware of the cause, but discouraged by successive crop failures, hundreds of people left New England—among them the Smiths of Norwich, Vermont. During the decade of 1810–20, there was a major exodus from Vermont. More than sixty Vermont towns experienced population losses.[32] Most Vermonters who left headed westward, stirred by newspaper advertisements of available lands in New York, Pennsylvania, and Ohio, lands that were said to be "well-timbered, well-watered, easily accessible and undeniably fertile—all to be had on long-term payments for only two or three dollars an acre."[33]

MOVE TO PALMYRA

In 1816, Joseph, Sr., went to Palmyra, Ontario County, New York, in the company of a Mr. Howard. Before departing he called on his creditors and debtors to settle existing accounts, but some of them neglected to bring their accounts to the settlement. Evidently their claims against him were satisfied either by payment of cash or by the transfer of claims Joseph had against his debtors. Believing that all accounts were settled, he proceeded to Palmyra and purchased land. He then sent a communication to Lucy instructing her to stow their belongings on a wagon and prepare to move. Joseph arranged with Caleb Howard, cousin of the Mr. Howard who had traveled with him to Palmyra, to drive the team and bring his family to New York. Before Lucy Smith left to join her husband, however, additional creditors appeared and presented their uncanceled accounts for payment. Lucy described this event: "I concluded it would be more to our advantage to pay their unjust claims than to hazard a lawsuit. Therefore, by making considerable exertion, I raised the required sum, which was one hundred and fifty dollars, and liquidated the demand." When well-meaning neighbors proposed to ease the burden by raising money through subscription, Lucy refused. "The idea of receiving assistance in such a way as this was indeed very repulsive to my feelings."[34]

The Appalachian Mountains formed a formidable barrier to western migration in the early history of the United States. Explorers eventually found three tolerable routes from the tidewater to the interior: the Great Genesee Road's Mohawk Turnpike in New York; the National Road in Maryland, Pennsylvania, and Ohio; and the Wilderness Road in North Carolina, Tennessee, and Kentucky.

The Smith family used the first of these routes to travel to the Palmyra, New York, region. The path came out of New England in Massachusetts to Albany in eastern New York and up the Mohawk River valley.

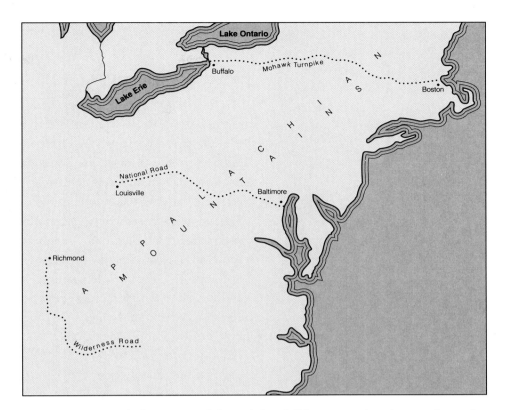

Accounts settled, Lucy and her eight children, ranging in age from the infant Don Carlos to seventeen-year-old Alvin, set out for New York with Caleb Howard. In South Royalton, Lucy's mother, Lydia, was injured by an overturning wagon. When Lydia was taken to her son's home in Tunbridge, mother and daughter tearfully exchanged good-byes. The aged Lydia admonished her daughter: "I beseech you to continue faithful in the service of God to the end of your days, that I may have the pleasure of embracing you in another and fairer world above."[35] Lydia died two years later in Royalton of the injuries she had received at that time.

As the Smith family continued their journey, it became apparent to Lucy that "Mr. Howard, our teamster, was an unprincipled and unfeeling wretch."[36] The money Joseph, Sr., paid Howard to gather the Smith family to New York was spent in drinking and gambling at inns along the way. Joseph, Jr., at the time a boy of ten, later remembered that even though he had not yet fully recovered from his leg operation, Howard made him walk "in my weak state through the snow 40 miles per day for several days, during which time I suffered the most excruciating weariness & pain."[37]

At Utica, several miles from their destination, Howard unloaded the Smith's belongings and was about to leave with their team when Lucy confronted him: "Sir, I now forbid you touching the team, or driving it one step further." The determined Lucy then reloaded the wagon and drove the team the rest of the way to Palmyra. She arrived with only two cents, but was "happy in once more having the society of my husband, and in throwing myself and children upon the care and affection of a tender companion and father."[38]

INFLUENCE OF NEW ENGLAND ON JOSEPH SMITH

The Smiths were but one of many New England families whose names are linked to the Restoration. Brigham Young, Joseph's successor; Heber C. Kimball, faithful Apostle; and numerous other Church leaders had New England roots. Among their ancestors were men and women who sailed on the *Mayflower* or served in the American Revolution.[39] These industrious and independent people who carved homes and societies out of the New England wilderness were remarkable people. They were patriotic, socially responsible, and religious. Joseph Smith had no need to apologize for his comparatively humble origins. His was an enduring moral legacy.

Many of the principles of Puritanism that shaped and molded Joseph's environment complemented revealed principles and doctrines he would later receive as a prophet. When Joseph learned by revelation that "Thou shalt not be idle" (D&C 42:42), this confirmed the appropriateness of the frugal and resourceful New England life. When the Lord told him to seek learning out of the best books "even by study and also by faith" (D&C 88:118), it reaffirmed the Puritan emphasis on education. When Joseph later promulgated the concept of an ideal theocratic society, he espoused a principle with which Puritan New England could readily identify.

But Joseph Smith was not bound by his New England heritage. In his lifetime he introduced gospel doctrines and ordinances that directly opposed his Puritan background, but exceeded any previous theological formulation of any other religious leader in their scope and clarity. For example, his concept of a personal and caring god opposed the Calvinistic idea of a stern god of justice. Revelations declaring the Godhead to be three separate and distinct personages directly contradicted traditional Calvinistic trinitarian theology.

But more than any environmental influence it was God who shaped the ideas of Joseph Smith. Indeed, it is part of Latter-day Saint theology that the Lord knew and prepared Joseph Smith in a previous sphere of existence to assume his pivotal role in restoring God's church upon the earth. Joseph spoke of his foreordination when he said: "Every man who has a calling to minister to the inhabitants of the world was ordained to that very purpose in the Grand Council of heaven before this world was. I suppose that I was ordained to this very office in that Grand Council."[40]

Brigham Young said of Joseph Smith: "It was decreed in the counsels of eternity, long before the foundations of the earth were laid, that he should be the man, in the last dispensation of this world, to bring forth the word of God to the people, and receive the fulness of the keys and power of the Priesthood of the Son of God. The Lord had his eye upon him, and upon his father, and upon his father's father, and upon their progenitors clear back to Abraham, and from Abraham to the flood, from the flood to Enoch, and from Enoch to Adam. He has watched that family and that blood as it has circulated from its fountain to the birth of that man. He was foreordained in eternity to preside over this last dispensation."[41]

ENDNOTES

1. In *History of the Church*, 5:498.

2. *Salem Gazette*, 22 Nov. 1785, cited in Richard Lloyd Anderson, *Joseph Smith's New England Heritage* (Salt Lake City: Deseret Book Co., 1971), pp. 89, 91.

3. Cited in Anderson, *Joseph Smith's New England Heritage*, pp. 124–25, 129; see also pp. 130–40.

4. George A. Smith, "Memoirs of George A. Smith," p. 2, cited in Anderson, *Joseph Smith's New England Heritage*, p. 112; see also *History of the Church*, 2:443.

5. Smith, "Memoirs," p. 2, cited in Anderson, *Joseph Smith's New England Heritage*, pp. 112–13.

6. Edward W. Tullidge, *History of Salt Lake City* (Salt Lake City: Star Printing Co., 1886), p. 157.

7. Solomon Mack, *A Narrative Life of Solomon Mack* (Windsor, Vt.: [1811]), p. 4.

8. Lucy Mack Smith, preliminary manuscript of *Biographical Sketches of Joseph Smith*, cited in Anderson, *Joseph Smith's New England Heritage*, p. 27.

9. See Mack, *A Narrative Life of Solomon Mack*, pp. 11–12, 17.

10. Mack, *A Narrative Life of Solomon Mack*, p. 17.

11. In Lucy Mack Smith, *History of Joseph Smith*, ed. Preston Nibley (Salt Lake City: Bookcraft, 1958), pp. 7–8.

12. Smith, *Biographical Sketches*, p. 68, cited in Anderson, *Joseph Smith's New England Heritage*, p. 29.

13. Smith, *History of Joseph Smith*, p. 31.

14. Smith, *History of Joseph Smith*, pp. 34–36.

15. Smith, *History of Joseph Smith*, p. 40.

16. William Smith, *William Smith on Mormonism* (Lamoni, Iowa: Herald Steam Book and Job Office, 1883), p. 6.

17. In *Journal of Discourses*, 8:351.

18. Smith, *History of Joseph Smith*, p. 182.

19. William Smith, cited in Richard Lloyd Anderson, "Joseph Smith's Home Environment," *Ensign*, July 1971, p. 58.

20. Smith, *History of Joseph Smith*, p. 46.

21. In Smith, *History of Joseph Smith*, p. 49; see also pp. 48–50.

22. In Smith, *History of Joseph Smith*, p. 68.

23. Smith, *History of Joseph Smith*, p. 51.

24. Smith, *History of Joseph Smith*, p. 55.

25. Smith, *History of Joseph Smith*, p. 56.

26. LeRoy S. Wirthlin, "Nathan Smith (1762–1828) Surgical Consultant to Joseph Smith," *Brigham Young University Studies*, Spring 1977, p. 337; see also LeRoy S. Wirthlin, "Joseph Smith's Boyhood Operation: An 1813 Surgical Success," in *Sidney B. Sperry Symposium*, 26 Jan. 1980, pp. 328–47.

27. In Smith, *History of Joseph Smith*, p. 57.

28. See Smith, *History of Joseph Smith*, p. 67.

29. Smith, *History of Joseph Smith*, p. 82.

30. Smith, *History of Joseph Smith*, p. 59.

31. Henry Stommel and Elizabeth Stommel, *Volcano Weather* (Newport, R.I.: Henry and Elizabeth Stommel, 1983), pp. 3, 11–12.

32. Larry C. Porter, "A Study of the Origins of The Church of Jesus Christ of Latter-day Saints in the States of New York and Pennsylvania, 1816–1831," Ph.D. diss., Brigham Young University, 1971, p. 30.

33. Lewis D. Stilwell, "Migration from Vermont (1776–1860)," cited in *Proceedings of the Vermont Historical Society* (Montpelier, Vt.: Vermont Historical Society, 1937), p. 135.

34. Smith, *History of Joseph Smith*, p. 61.

35. Smith, *History of Joseph Smith*, p. 62.

36. Smith, *History of Joseph Smith*, p. 62.

37. Manuscript History of the Church, cited in Dean C. Jessee, ed., *The Personal Writings of Joseph Smith* (Salt Lake City: Deseret Book Co., 1984), p. 666; spelling standardized.

38. Smith, *History of Joseph Smith*, p. 63.

39. See Gustive O. Larson, "New England Leadership in the Rise and Progress of the Church," *Improvement Era*, Aug. 1968, p. 81.

40. *History of the Church*, 6:364.

41. In *Journal of Discourses*, 7:289–90.

CHAPTER THREE

THE FIRST VISION

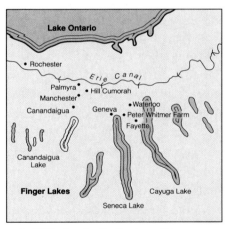

In 1816 when the Smiths moved to Palmyra, it was a village of about six hundred people. In 1818 or 1819 they began to clear a one-hundred-acre farm nearby in Farmington township (later Manchester township).

◄ This stained glass window depicting the First Vision was donated to the Salt Lake City Seventeenth Ward in 1907 by Annie D. Watkins. It was made by professional glass artists in Belgium.

FOR CENTURIES THE WORLD was in spiritual darkness because of the rejection of the Lord's Apostles. Except for a few glimmers of light, such as those seen by the Reformers, the heavens were closed. A young boy's experience in a grove in upstate New York in the spring of 1820 changed all of this. A day of spiritual enlightenment dawned.

President Spencer W. Kimball explained: "That new day dawned when another soul with passionate yearning prayed for divine guidance. A spot of hidden solitude was found, knees were bent, a heart was humbled, pleadings were voiced, and a light brighter than the noonday sun illuminated the world—the curtain never to be closed again.

". . . Heaven kissed the earth, light dissipated the darkness, and God again spoke to man."[1]

SETTING IN WESTERN NEW YORK

Joseph Smith, Sr., chose to settle in Palmyra, a small village in the Finger Lakes area of New York state. The region bore this name because the lakes resembled fingers. Sparsely inhabited at the turn of the nineteenth century, the population of the Finger Lakes area grew rapidly. By 1820 there were many communities along the shores.

Fertile soil and heavily wooded land contributed greatly to the territory's growth. The Erie Canal, a vital inland waterway designed to transport goods and persons across New York State from Albany to the Great Lakes, contributed much to the area's growth. Completed mostly by hand in 1825 at a cost of more than seven million dollars, this 363-mile watercourse reduced transportation time across the state from three weeks to six days and cut expenses by millions of dollars. The canal passed within a block of Palmyra's main street.

Joseph Smith, Sr., the father of a family of ten—eleven by 1821, worked hard for a living. After two years in Palmyra, he accumulated enough money for a down payment on one hundred acres of wooded land in the nearby township of Farmington. During the first year he and his sons cleared thirty acres of heavy timber, prepared the ground for cultivation, and planted wheat.[2] Clearing land meant not only felling trees with handsaws and axes but also removing stumps and roots by sheer physical toil of man and beast. Young Joseph later recalled that "it required the exertions of all that were able to render any assistance for the support of the Family."[3] Eventually the

Ground for the Erie Canal was broken on 4 July 1817.

A Methodist circuit rider, drawing by A. R. Waud

township of Farmington was divided, and in 1822 the Smith farm became part of the newly created township of Manchester.

At this time Joseph's opportunities for schooling were extremely limited. He attributed this to the "indigent circumstances" he was raised under. "We were deprived of the benefit of an education. Suffice it to say, I was merely instructed in reading, writing, and the ground rules of arithmetic which constituted my whole literary acquirements."[4]

As more and more Americans crossed the Catskill and Adirondack mountains to settle in the Finger Lakes area of western New York, they tended to lose contact with established churches in their former homes. These "unchurched," settlers worried religious leaders of the main denominations, principally the Baptists, Methodists, and Presbyterians who established proselyting programs for their disadvantaged brothers in the West.

The Methodists and Baptists were particularly zealous in their efforts to bring religion to those without its benefits. The Methodists employed circuit riders. These were traveling ministers who rode horseback from town to town throughout a given region, or circuit, ministering to the religious needs of the people. The Baptists used the farmer-preacher system. In this system a local man earned his living by farming but occupied a nearby pulpit on the Sabbath. These efforts were bolstered by the enthusiasm of the Second Great Awakening which was then sweeping the United States.

Nearly all churches in upstate New York conducted revivals. These were evangelistic gatherings designed to awaken the religiously inert. Revivals were often in the form of camp meetings held on the edge of a grove of trees or in a small clearing in the forest. Participants often traveled many miles over dusty or rut-filled roads to pitch their tents or park their wagons on the outskirts of the encampment. Camp meetings frequently lasted several days with some sessions lasting nearly all day and into the night. Ministers rotated, but it was not uncommon to find two or three ministers exhorting their listeners simultaneously.[5] So fervent and enthusiastic was the religious zeal in western New York in the early 1800s that the region came to be known as the Burned-Over District. Because the Finger Lakes area was set figuratively ablaze with evangelistic fire, it is not surprising that young Joseph Smith and his family were caught up in the fervor.

JOSEPH'S PERSONAL QUEST

Farmington (later Manchester township) was one of several settlements in its district affected by this religious enthusiasm. In later years Lucy Mack Smith remembered it as "a great revival in religion, which extended to all the denominations of Christians in the surrounding country in which we resided. Many of the world's people, becoming concerned about the salvation of their souls, came forward and presented themselves as seekers after religion."[6] Most folks wanted to join some church but were undecided on which one to adopt. The Prophet Joseph recalled that about two years after

A typical camp meeting about 1830-35, drawing by A. Rider

Courtesy of the Library of Congress

they moved to the farm there was "an unusual excitement on the subject of religion. It commenced with the Methodists, but soon became general among all the sects in that region of country. Indeed, the whole district of country seemed affected by it, and great multitudes united themselves to the different religious parties, which created no small stir and division amongst the people" (Joseph Smith—History 1:5).

Revivals and camp meetings affected young Joseph. He wrote in his personal history that "at about the age of twelve years, my mind became seriously impressed with regard to the all important concerns for the welfare of my immortal soul."[7] This, in turn, led him to search the scriptures and seek for forgiveness of his sins. As for the claims put forth by the various teachers of religion, he said, "I knew not who was right or who was wrong, but considered it of the first importance to me that I should be right, in matters . . . involving eternal consequences."[8] Joseph said, "I attended their several meetings as often as occasion would permit. . . . It was impossible for a person young as I was, and so unacquainted with men and things, to come to any certain conclusion who was right and who was wrong" (Joseph Smith—History 1:8).

Joseph was also confused by the bitterness and hypocrisy he witnessed among ministers and fellow Christians. He said, "My intimate acquaintance with those of different denominations led me to marvel exceedingly, for I discovered that they did not adorn their profession by a holy walk and Godly conversation agreeable to what I found contained in that sacred

31

depository [the holy scriptures]. This was a grief to my soul."⁹ When the converts began to join first one church and then another, he saw that the "seemingly good feelings of both the priests and the converts were more pretended than real for a scene of great confusion and bad feeling ensued—priest contending against priest, and convert against convert; so that all their good feelings one for another, if they ever had any, were entirely lost in a strife of words and a contest about opinions" (Joseph Smith—History 1:6).

One can only imagine the impact such conditions had on Joseph's youthful, searching mind. The very men he thought could point the way to God "understood the same passages of scripture so differently as to destroy all confidence in settling the question by an appeal to the Bible" (v. 12). Joseph explained, "In the midst of this war of words and tumult of opinions, I often said to myself: What is to be done? Who of all these parties are right; or, are they all wrong together? If any one of them be right, which is it, and how shall I know it?" (v. 10).

Joseph Smith came from a religious family. His mother, a sister, and two brothers had joined the Presbyterian faith, but that system of belief did not satisfy him. Nevertheless, his parents had instructed him in the Christian religion from childhood. One of the existing churches must be right, he reasoned, but which one was it? In his search for the correct church, Joseph did not intend to start his own church, nor did he think that truth was not on the earth. He simply did not know where to find the truth, but, trained to believe the scriptures, he turned there for his answer.

Like many other frontier families, the Smiths owned a Bible. Seeds planted by "goodly parents," were nurtured by the Holy Spirit. How many days and nights he pondered, searched, and prayed for light he does not say. Nor does he tell us whether he confided his secret feelings and desires to his family. His years of preparation and his time, effort, and meditation were rewarded. He found a possible solution to his problem at age fourteen while reading this passage in the Bible: "If any of you lack wisdom, let him ask of God, that giveth to all men liberally, and upbraideth not; and it shall be given him" (James 1:5).

This passage had a profound impact on Joseph. "Never did any passage of scripture come with more power to the heart of man than this did at this time to mine. It seemed to enter with great force into every feeling of my heart. I reflected on it again and again, knowing that if any person needed wisdom from God, I did; for how to act I did not know, and unless I could get more wisdom than I then had, I would never know" (Joseph Smith—History 1:12).

The Bible did not tell Joseph which church was true, but it told him that prayer could solve his problem. He reflected on this idea.

"At length I came to the conclusion that I must either remain in darkness and confusion, or else I must do as James directs, that is, ask of God. . . .

The exact location where Joseph Smith experienced his first vision is unknown. The grove across the street from the family home is assumed to be the most likely spot.

"So, in accordance with this, my determination to ask of God, I retired to the woods to make the attempt. It was on the morning of a beautiful, clear day, early in the spring of eighteen hundred and twenty" (vv. 13–14). It was the first time he had ever tried to pray vocally (see v. 14).

What happened next set Joseph Smith apart from his contemporaries for ever after. God the Eternal Father and his Son Jesus Christ appeared to him. The word *theophany* is used to describe a vision of deity. The Bible confirms that theophanies are real. At Peniel, Jacob rejoiced, saying, "for I have seen God face to face, and my life is preserved" (Genesis 32:30). With Moses, God spoke "face to face, as a man speaketh unto his friend" (Exodus 33:11; see also Numbers 12:8). And Isaiah wrote, "Mine eyes have seen the King, the Lord of hosts" (Isaiah 6:5).

God the Father and his Son Jesus Christ appeared together to the fourteen-year-old Joseph Smith. Not since the resurrection of Jesus Christ had there been such a threat to the devil's kingdom. Little wonder, then, that Satan was present that morning.

Like Moses (see Moses 1:12–22), Joseph experienced direct opposition from Satan: "After I had retired to the place where I had previously designed to go, having looked around me, and finding myself alone, I kneeled down and began to offer up the desires of my heart to God. I had scarcely done so, when immediately I was seized upon by some power which entirely overcame me, and had such an astonishing influence over me as to bind my tongue so that I could not speak. Thick darkness gathered around me, and it seemed to me for a time as if I were doomed to sudden destruction" (Joseph Smith—History 1:15).

The powers of darkness were terrible, but greater powers brought deliverance. Joseph exerted all his strength to call upon God to deliver him from the enemy that had seized him. Joseph described this experience:

"At the very moment when I was ready to sink into despair and abandon myself to destruction . . . , I saw a pillar of light exactly over my head, above the brightness of the sun, which descended gradually until it fell upon me.

"It no sooner appeared than I found myself delivered from the enemy which held me bound. When the light rested upon me I saw two Personages, whose brightness and glory defy all description, standing above me in the air. One of them spake unto me, calling me by name and said, pointing to the other—*This is My Beloved Son. Hear Him!*" (vv. 16–17).

Satan and his power were banished. In his place stood the Father and the Son in immortal glory. As soon as he was able to speak, Joseph asked the Personages which of the sects was right and which he should join. He reported:

"I was answered that I must join none of them, for they were all wrong; and the Personage who addressed me said that all their creeds were an abomination in his sight; that those professors were all corrupt; that: 'they draw near to me with their lips, but their hearts are far from me, they teach for doctrines the commandments of men, having a form of godliness, but they deny the power thereof.'

"He again forbade me to join with any of them. . . . When I came to myself again, I found myself lying on my back, looking up into heaven" (vv. 19–20). He was weak from the presence of Deity, and it was some time before he regained his strength and returned home.

Joseph was profoundly affected by the heavenly vision. In addition to being given the answer to his question about which church was right, he was told that his sins were forgiven[10] and that "the fullness of the Gospel should at some future time be made known unto [him]."[11] The effects of this experience influenced the Prophet throughout his life. In later years he remembered its impact vividly: "My soul was filled with love, and for many days I could rejoice with great joy, and the Lord was with me."[12]

REACTION TO JOSEPH'S VISION

Shortly after he arrived home, his mother, perhaps noticing his weakened condition, asked him what was wrong. He replied, "Never mind, all is well—I am well enough off. . . . I have learned for myself that Presbyterianism is not true " (Joseph Smith—History 1:20). Joseph did not say whether or not he told his mother more at this time. Eventually he confided his theophany to other family members. His brother William affirmed, "We all had the most implicit confidence in what he said. He was a truthful boy. Father and Mother believed him, why should not the children?"[13] The momentous occurrence answered Joseph's question, but it did not do so for others. He reported, "I soon found, however, that my telling the story had excited a great deal of prejudice against me among professors of religion, and was the cause of great persecution, which continued to increase" (Joseph Smith—History 1:22).

One of the first outside the family to hear Joseph's account of what happened to him was "one of the Methodist preachers, who was very active in the before mentioned religious excitement." Joseph naively believed that the minister would welcome this great news from heaven. Joseph wrote, however: "I was greatly surprised at his behavior; he treated my communication not only lightly, but with great contempt, saying it was all of the devil, that there were no such things as visions or revelations in these days; that all such things had ceased with the apostles, and that there would never be any more of them" (v. 21).

Such an attitude was commonplace in the sectarian world. It was unthinkable that Almighty God would condescend to make himself known to a fourteen-year-old boy in 1820 the way he had made himself known to ancient prophets. Joseph's sacred experience brought on bitter persecution. The hatred of those who professed Christianity was difficult for him to understand. As he put it, "I was an obscure boy, only between fourteen and fifteen years of age, and my circumstances in life such as to make a boy of no

The Reverend George Lane (1784-1859) was a Methodist minister who lived at the time of Joseph Smith. Smith family tradition linked Lane with the Palmyra revival.

consequence in the world, yet men of high standing would take notice sufficient to excite the public mind against me. It was often the cause of great sorrow" (vv. 22–23). William Smith later reflected: "We never knew we were bad folks until Joseph told his vision. We were considered respectable till then, but at once people began to circulate falsehoods and stories in a wonderful way."[14]

The reality of what Joseph Smith experienced enabled him to endure the increasing persecution. He compared himself to Paul the Apostle who saw the risen Lord and heard his voice. Very few people believed Paul, and some even claimed he was dishonest or mentally deranged. Yet this did not destroy the reality of what Paul knew he had experienced. Joseph declared, "So it was with me. I had actually seen a light, and in the midst of that light I saw two Personages, and they did in reality speak to me; and though I was hated and persecuted for saying that I had seen a vision, yet it was true" (Joseph Smith—History 1:25).

Joseph felt much like the child who has been wrongly accused and punished. He said, "I was led to say in my heart: Why persecute me for telling the truth? I have actually seen a vision; and who am I that I can withstand God, or why does the world think to make me deny what I have actually seen? For I had seen a vision; I knew it, and I knew that God knew it, and I could not deny it" (v. 25). To deny it would place him under condemnation, and he dared not risk offending God.

SIGNIFICANCE OF THE FIRST VISION

The First Vision was a pivotal event in the rise of the kingdom of God on the earth in the last days. Joseph Smith, although only an unlettered youth, learned profound truths that have become the foundation of the faith of the Latter-day Saints. He had actually seen and spoken with God the Father and his Son Jesus Christ. Therefore, he learned that the promise in James is true. God will answer sincere prayer of inquiry and not chastise. To Joseph, God became an approachable reality, a vital source of truth, and a loving Heavenly Father. Joseph Smith's belief in the reality of God was no longer a matter of faith; it was based on personal experience. Thus, he was qualified, as was the Apostle Peter, to be a witness who was chosen of God and commanded to preach and testify of Jesus Christ (see Acts 10:39–43). He could also testify that the Father and Son were separate and distinct glorious beings in whose literal image man is made.

Joseph Smith now also knew of the reality of Satan, a being who possessed formidable power and a foe determined to destroy the work of God. Satan failed in the Sacred Grove, but the conflict had just begun. Joseph would fight many battles with this adversary of righteousness before his work was done. Moreover, the Lord's answer to his question about which church was true, was a sweeping indictment of nineteenth century Christianity, for no church then on earth had divine approval. Just as the

Savior warned his disciples against the doctrinal "leaven" of the Pharisees and Sadducees (see Matthew 16:6–12), he taught Joseph Smith that the existing churches taught the "commandments of men" (Joseph Smith—History 1:19). Therefore, he was to join none of them.

Joseph F. Smith, nephew of the Prophet and sixth President of the Church, elaborated on the importance of the First Vision: "The greatest event that has ever occurred in the world, since the resurrection of the Son of God from the tomb and his ascension on high, was the coming of the Father and of the Son to that boy Joseph Smith, to prepare the way for the laying of the foundation of his kingdom—not the kingdom of man—never more to cease nor to be overturned. Having accepted this truth, I find it easy to accept of every other truth that he enunciated and declared during his mission of fourteen years in the world."[15]

ENDNOTES

1. Spencer W. Kimball, in Conference Report, Apr. 1977, p. 114; or *Ensign*, May 1977, p. 77.

2. See Lucy Mack Smith, *History of Joseph Smith*, ed. Preston Nibley (Salt Lake City: Bookcraft, 1958), pp. 63–64.

3. "History of Joseph Smith By Himself," 1832 (written in Kirtland, Ohio, between 20 July and 27 Nov. 1832), LDS Historical Department, Salt Lake City, p. 1; see also Dean C. Jessee, ed., *The Personal Writings of Joseph Smith* (Salt Lake City: Deseret Book Co., 1984), p. 4 (contains a printing of all the known holographic writings of Joseph Smith).

4. "History of Joseph Smith By Himself," p. 1; spelling, punctuation, and capitalization standardized; Jessee, *Personal Writings of Joseph Smith*, p. 4.

5. See Milton V. Backman, Jr., *Joseph Smith's First Vision*, 2d ed. (Salt Lake City: Bookcraft, 1980), pp. 72–74.

6. Smith, *History of Joseph Smith*, p. 68.

7. "History of Joseph Smith By Himself," pp. 1–2; spelling, punctuation, and capitalization standardized; Jessee, *Personal Writings of Joseph Smith*, pp. 4–5.

8. Joseph Smith, "History A-1," Nov. 1835, LDS Historical Department, Salt Lake City, p. 120.

9. "History of Joseph Smith By Himself," p. 2; spelling, punctuation, and capitalization standardized; Jessee, *Personal Writings of Joseph Smith*, p. 5.

10. See "History of Joseph Smith By Himself," p. 3; Jessee, *Personal Writings of Joseph Smith*, p. 6.

11. *History of the Church*, 4:536. This statement is part of a reply written by Joseph Smith to Mr. John C. Wentworth, editor of the *Chicago Democrat*. Mr. Wentworth had written in behalf of a friend of his, Mr. Bastow (his actual name was George Barstow), who was writing a history of New Hampshire and wished to include "correct information" respecting the rise and progress of The Church of Jesus Christ of Latter-day Saints.

12. "History of Joseph Smith By Himself," p. 3; spelling, punctuation, and capitalization standardized; Jessee, *Personal Writings of Joseph Smith*, p. 6.

13. In J. W. Peterson, "Another Testimony, Statement of William Smith, Concerning Joseph the Prophet," *Deseret Evening News*, 20 Jan. 1894, p. 11.

14. In Peterson, "Another Testimony," p. 11.

15. Joseph F. Smith, *Gospel Doctrine*, 5th ed. (Salt Lake City: Deseret Book Co., 1939), pp. 495–96.

A PERIOD OF PREPARATION, 1823–29

Archaeological investigations in the summer of 1982 verified the location of the log house as stated in an 1820 street survey. Although the shallow foundation had been destroyed by field plows over the years, archaeologists found three areas below the plow zone, including a well and a shallow cellar, that yielded numerous artifacts from the period.[1]

It was while the Smith family was living in the log home that Joseph Smith received his first vision in 1820. In September 1823, Angel Moroni appeared to Joseph in this home.

WHEN JOSEPH SMITH walked out of the grove of trees that beautiful spring morning in 1820, he would never be the same again. He knew the Father and the Son lived, and he would testify of this truth throughout his life. It was three years, however, after he experienced his great vision of God before Joseph received further instructions concerning the important work he had been called to.

During this period Joseph passed through his mid-teens, a time when sympathetic teachers and a congenial community could have strengthened him. But Joseph had little formal education, and as we have seen, his testimony aroused hostility. Even some trusted friends turned against him; however, Joseph continually had the loving support of his family.

Joseph acknowledged that during this period he "frequently fell into many foolish errors, and displayed the weakness of youth" (Joseph Smith —History 1:28). His native cheery temperament was one reason he gave for sometimes associating with jovial company and being guilty of levity, which he considered inconsistent with the character of one called of God (see v. 28). He was not, however, guilty of any "great or malignant sins" (v. 28). According to his mother, little of importance took place during this period. Joseph labored as usual with his father on the family farm working in the fields, clearing trees, or tapping sugar maples; occasionally he had an odd job, such as digging a building foundation or working in the corn fields for Martin Harris. This three-year interval gave young Joseph the time to grow, mature, gain experience, and receive further nurturing.

FIRST APPEARANCE OF MORONI

In 1822, Joseph began helping his older brother Alvin build a new frame house for the family. By September of 1823, it was two stories high but without a roof. The family continued to live in their small log house. Here late in the evening on Sunday, 21 September 1823, seventeen-year-old Joseph retired for the night. Concerned about his standing before the Lord, he earnestly prayed for forgiveness of his sins. He was confident that he would again receive a divine manifestation. Suddenly his room filled with light and a heavenly messenger stood by his bedside in partial fulfillment of the great prophecy of John the Apostle (see Revelation 14:6–7). Joseph described this resurrected being:

By 1818–19 the Smith family had negotiated to purchase about one hundred acres in Farmington (later Manchester) township, and they began building a small log home (approximately twenty-four feet by thirty feet), which they completed in 1818–19. The Smiths lived in the log house until 1825, when they built a larger and nicer home, where they lived until 1829.

Financial difficulties led to the loss of the home, so they moved back into the log house. In 1830, Joseph Smith, Sr., moved his remaining family to the village of Waterloo in Seneca County, New York.[2]

"He had on a loose robe of most exquisite whiteness. It was a whiteness beyond anything earthly I had ever seen; nor do I believe that any earthly thing could be made to appear so exceedingly white and brilliant. His hands were naked, and his arms also, a little above the wrist; so, also, were his feet naked, as were his legs, a little above the ankles. His head and neck were also bare. I could discover that he had no other clothing on but this robe, as it was open, so that I could see into his bosom.

"Not only was his robe exceedingly white, but his whole person was glorious beyond description, and his countenance truly like lightning. The room was exceedingly light, but not so very bright as immediately around his person. When I first looked upon him, I was afraid; but the fear soon left

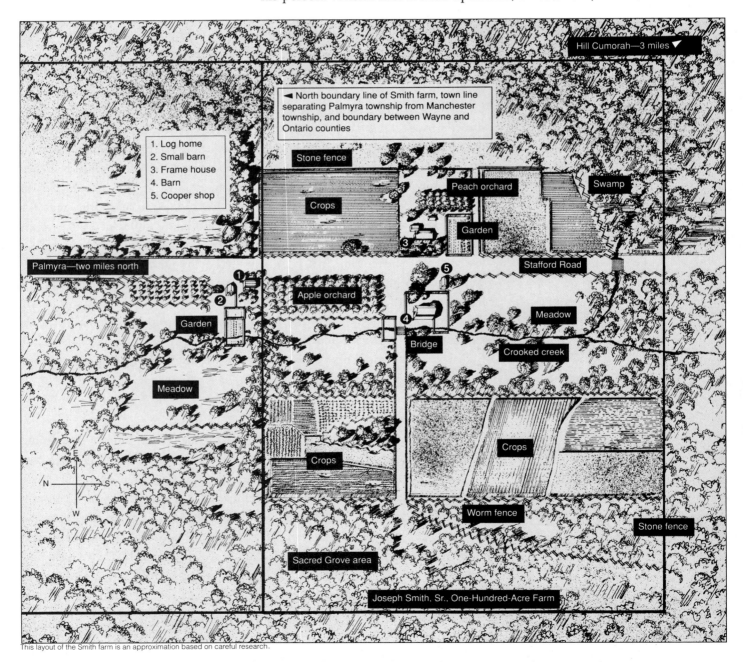

This layout of the Smith farm is an approximation based on careful research.

President Heber J. Grant presided at a special meeting held in the Sacred Grove on 23 September 1923 in commemoration of the one hundreth anniversary of the appearance of Moroni.

Pictured in this photo are (from left) John Harris Taylor, Elder Joseph Fielding Smith, Elder Rudger Clawson, President Grant, Sister Augusta W. Grant, Elder James E. Talmage, and Elder Brigham H. Roberts, president of the Eastern States Mission.

me" (Joseph Smith—History 1:31–32).

The messenger introduced himself as Moroni, a prophet who had lived on the American continent. As holder of the keys of the "stick of Ephraim" (see D&C 27:5), Moroni came at the appointed hour to reveal the existence of a record written on gold plates which had lain hidden in the ground for fourteen centuries. It was "an account of the former inhabitants of this continent. . . . He also said that the fulness of the everlasting Gospel was contained in it, as delivered by the Savior to the ancient inhabitants" (Joseph Smith—History 1:34). Joseph was to translate the record and publish it; because of this and other things he would be called to do, his name would be known for good and evil among all people (see v. 33).

Moroni cited several passages from the Bible quoting prophets such as Malachi, Isaiah, Joel, and Peter concerning the preparations to be made in the last days for the millennial reign of Christ. This commenced the gospel tutorship of Joseph Smith by Moroni.

So important was Moroni's message and the need to impress it on the mind of the young Prophet that Moroni returned twice more that night and repeated the same instructions, adding information each time. During the first "interview" Joseph saw in vision the location of the plates (see v. 42). They were buried in a hillside about three miles from his home. In the second visit, Joseph was told of judgments which were coming upon the earth (see v. 45). At the end of the third visit, Moroni warned Joseph that Satan would try to tempt him to get the plates for their temporal value because of his family's poverty. Moroni directed seventeen-year-old Joseph that he was to have only one purpose for obtaining the plates and that was to glorify God. Only *one* motive should influence him, and that was to build God's kingdom (see v. 46). Through subsequent events the Prophet learned why Moroni had given such admonitions and directions. Joseph's interviews with Moroni occupied most of the night, for at the end of the third visit he heard a rooster crow. Indeed, a new day of spiritual light was about to dawn. Isaiah spoke of this day as a time when a "marvellous work and a wonder" would come forth (Isaiah 29:14).

THE FIRST VISIT TO CUMORAH

That morning Joseph went to work as usual with his father and brothers in the field. Lack of sleep and having been in the presence of a glorified, resurrected being most of the night weakened him so that he had trouble working. Noticing his son's condition and thinking he was ill, Joseph's father told him to go back to the house. On the way home Joseph collapsed. The next thing he knew someone was calling him by name. As he became aware of his surroundings, to his surprise Moroni again stood before him.[3] He then repeated the same message he had given Joseph before and further commanded him to inform his father of the vision and commandments he had received.

Palmyra and Hill Cumorah area

The Hill Cumorah is a drumlin, a long hill with steep sides and a sloping end formed under an advancing continental ice sheet. Drumlins in this region run north and south. Oliver Cowdery, who visited the hill in 1830, described it:

"The north end rose suddenly from the plain, forming a promontory without timber, but covered with grass. As you passed to the south you soon came to scattering timber, the surface having been cleared by art or by wind; and a short distance further left, you are surrounded with the common forest of the country. . . . It was at the second mentioned place where the record was found to be deposited, on the west side of the hill, not far from the top down its side."4

Joseph returned and explained the whole matter to his father, who assured him it was from God and instructed him to do as he had been commanded. Joseph related, "I left the field, and went to the place where the messenger had told me the plates were deposited; and owing to the distinctness of the vision which I had had concerning it, I knew the place the instant that I arrived there" (Joseph Smith—History 1:50). Near the top of the hill Joseph found a large stone, "thick and rounding in the middle on the upper side, and thinner towards the edges" (v. 51). It was the lid of a stone box. We can only imagine his excitement as he opened the box. There, having laid hidden for centuries, were the plates, the Urim and Thummim, and the breastplate just as Moroni had explained.

"The box in which they lay was formed by laying stones together in some kind of cement. In the bottom of the box were laid two stones crossways of the box, and on these stones lay the plates and the other things with them" (Joseph Smith—History 1:52).

While in mortality Moroni had prophesied that the plates could not be used for temporal gain because of the commandment of God, but would one day be of "great worth" to future generations in bringing them to a knowledge of God (Mormon 8:14–15).

As Joseph approached the Hill Cumorah, he had thoughts about the poverty of his family and the possibility that the plates or the popularity of the translation would produce enough wealth to "raise him above a level with the common earthly fortunes of his fellow men, and relieve his family from want."5 When he reached down for the plates he received a shock and was thus prevented from taking them out of the box. Twice more he tried and was thrown back. In frustration he cried out, "Why can I not obtain this book?" Moroni appeared and told him it was because he had not kept the commandments but had yielded to the temptations of Satan to obtain the plates for riches instead of having his eye single to the glory of God as he had been commanded.6

Repentant, Joseph humbly sought the Lord in prayer and was filled with the Spirit. A vision was opened to him, and the "glory of the Lord shone round about and rested upon him. . . . He beheld the prince of darkness. . . . The heavenly messenger [Moroni] said, 'All this is shown, the good and the evil, the holy and impure, the glory of God and the power of darkness, that you may know hereafter the two powers and never be influenced or overcome by that wicked one.' . . . You now see why you could not obtain this record; that the commandment was strict, and that if ever these sacred things are obtained they must be by prayer and faithfulness in obeying the Lord. They are not deposited here for the sake of accumulating gain and wealth for the glory of this world: they were sealed by the prayer of faith, and because of the knowledge which they contain they are of no worth among the children of men, only for their knowledge."[7] Moroni concluded by warning Joseph that he would not be allowed to obtain the plates "until he had learned to keep the commandments of God—*not only till he was willing but able to do it.* . . .

"The ensuing evening, when the family were altogether, Joseph made known to them all that he had communicated to his father in the field, and also of his finding the record, as well as what passed between him and the angel while he was at the place where the plates were deposited."[8]

JOSEPH'S PREPARATION CONTINUES

The monumental work of bringing forth the Book of Mormon was foretold by ancient prophets (see Isaiah 29, Ezekiel 37:15–20, Moses 7:62). A work of such magnitude requires careful preparation. In this instance, it required four years of tutoring. During that time Joseph met annually with Moroni at the Hill Cumorah to receive instructions in preparation for receiving the plates. Other Nephite prophets who had a vital interest in the coming forth of the Book of Mormon also played a significant role in Joseph's preparation. Nephi, Alma, the twelve Apostles chosen by the Savior in America, and Mormon all instructed Joseph.[9] His education was intense during this period.

His mother, Lucy, describes their evening conversations: "Joseph would occasionally give us some of the most amusing [interesting] recitals that could be imagined. He would describe the ancient inhabitants of this continent, their dress, mode of traveling, and the animals upon which they rode; their cities, their buildings, with every particular; their mode of warfare; and also their religious worship. This he would do with as much ease, seemingly, as if he had spent his whole life among them."[10]

INTERIM EVENTS

Between Moroni's first appearance and when Joseph received the plates, several significant events occurred in his life. In November of 1823, tragedy struck the Smith home. Alvin, Joseph's oldest brother, became ill; Father

Alvin Smith's gravestone. "In memory of Alvin, son of Joseph and Lucy Smith, who died Nov. 19, 1823, in his 25th year of his life."

The distance from the Smith farm in Palmyra to Harmony, Pennsylvania, is approximately 130 miles.

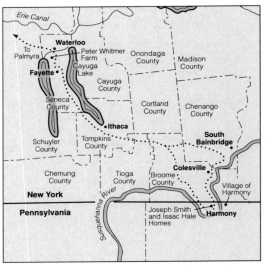

Smith was unable to find their family physician. The doctor who finally came administered calomel (mercurous chloride), a laxative, which at the time was used as a remedy for many ailments. But the medicine lodged in Alvin's stomach, creating greater suffering. He died 19 November 1823 after four days of illness. Alvin was a faithful and serious young man, and Joseph idolized him. Joseph saw in him a guileless person who lived an upright life. Alvin loved Joseph, too, and was greatly interested in the sacred record. As death neared he counseled Joseph: "I want you to be a good boy, and do everything that lies in your power to obtain the Record. Be faithful in receiving instruction, and in keeping every commandment that is given you."[11] Joseph learned by revelation years later that Alvin was an heir to the celestial kingdom (see D&C 137:1–6).

Following Alvin's death the Smiths experienced economic difficulties. Joseph and his brothers hired out by the day at whatever work was available. Treasure hunting, or "money-digging" as it was then called, was a craze in the United States at this time. In October 1825, Josiah Stowell, from South Bainbridge, New York, a farmer, lumber mill owner, and deacon in the Presbyterian church, came to ask Joseph to help him in such a venture. Stowell had relatives in Palmyra and probably heard of Joseph from them. Stowell was looking for a legendary lost silver mine that was thought to have been opened by Spaniards in northern Pennsylvania. Stowell was one of many men of character and substance in his day who were convinced that treasures were buried in various places in America and who spent money and effort searching for them. Stowell had heard that Joseph was able to discern invisible things and desired his assistance in the project. The Prophet was reluctant, but Stowell persisted, and since Joseph's family was in need, he and his father together with other neighbors agreed to go. It was a decision that would have great importance to Joseph's life and the future of the Church.

Joseph and his associates boarded with Isaac Hale in Harmony township in Pennsylvania. The village of Harmony was several miles away where a bend of the Susquehanna River dips into northeastern Pennsylvania, not far from the supposed mine site. While boarding with the Hales, Joseph was attracted to Isaac's dark-haired daughter Emma. She was also attracted to him, although she was Joseph's senior by a year and a half. The budding

Emma Hale was the seventh of nine children. "Emma was a tall, attractive young woman with comely features. Dark-complexioned, with brown eyes and black hair, she possessed a singular, regal beauty of form and of character."[12]

Home of Squire Tarbell. Joseph and Emma were married 18 January 1827 in South Bainbridge (later Afton), Chenango County, New York, by Zachariah Tarbell. The home has since been torn down.

romance, however, was frowned upon by Emma's father who disliked money digging and disdained Joseph's lack of education. His cultured daughter was a schoolteacher, and he wanted better for her. Meanwhile, the search for the silver mine was unproductive. After nearly a month's work, Joseph was able to persuade Josiah Stowell that his efforts were in vain, and the pursuit of the mine in Harmony was abandoned.

Since the time of this episode Joseph's detractors have used what they call his "money digging" to attack his character, to question his motives, and to cast doubt upon the validity of the church he organized. The circumstances are best understood in the context of their time and place. In New England and western New York, such activities were not frowned upon the way they came to be later. Years later, Joseph candidly acknowledged his participation in the venture but pointed out that it was insignificant.[13]

While working in the borderlands of New York and Pennsylvania, Joseph made another contact that became important to him and to the early Church in New York. Joseph Knight, Sr., a friend of Josiah Stowell, was a humble farmer and miller who lived in Colesville, Broome County, New York. Joseph Smith also worked for him for a time and in the process developed close friendships with him and his sons, Joseph, Jr., and Newel. They accepted the testimony of the young Prophet as he recounted his sacred experiences to them.

Between working for Josiah Stowell, Joseph Knight, Sr., and visiting his own family in Manchester, Joseph continued to court Emma Hale. Because of her father's strong opposition to the marriage, Joseph and Emma eloped. They were married by a justice of the peace in South Bainbridge, New York, on 18 January 1827. Immediately afterward, Joseph moved his new bride to the family home in Manchester, where he spent the succeeding summer farming with his father. Emma was well received by Joseph's family, and a close relationship developed between Emma and Lucy Mack Smith.

JOSEPH ENTRUSTED WITH THE PLATES

Little is known of Joseph's visits with Moroni between 1824 and 1827, but sometime before the fall of 1827, Joseph returned home one evening later than usual. His family was concerned, but he told them he had been delayed because he had just received a severe chastisement from Moroni. He said that as he passed by the Hill Cumorah, "The angel met me and said that I had not been engaged enough in the work of the Lord; that the time had come for the record to be brought forth; and that I must be up and doing and set myself about the things which God had commanded me to do."[14]

Much must have transpired in Joseph's four years of preparation. He passed through his teens largely untainted by the precepts of men. He enjoyed the emotional support of his family, and he took on the responsibilities associated with marriage. Angels prepared him to translate a divinely inspired record and taught him the necessity of self-discipline and obedience.

Moroni Delivers the Plates, *by L. A. Ramsey*

Museum of Church History and Art

This is the wooden box the Prophet hid the plates in. The inside measurement of the box is 14" x 16". The depth is 6 1/4" sloping to 4". The wood is 3/4" thick.

The lid and bottom are walnut, and the sides are made from boxwood. The box was used as a lap desk, which explains the sloped top.

The box is in the possession of Patriarch Eldred G. Smith.

He was undoubtedly anxious to begin translating the Book of Mormon. At this time Joseph Knight and Josiah Stowell were in Manchester visiting with the Smith family. This might have been in anticipation of Joseph's receiving the plates.

Long before sunrise on 22 September 1827, Joseph and his wife hitched Joseph Knight's horse to Josiah Stowell's spring wagon and drove the three miles to the Hill Cumorah. Leaving Emma at the base, Joseph climbed the hill for his final interview with Moroni. Moroni gave him the plates, the Urim and Thummim, and the breastplate. He also gave Joseph a specific warning and promise concerning his responsibilities. Joseph was now responsible for these sacred objects, and if he was careless or negligent and lost them he would be cut off. On the other hand, if he used all his efforts to preserve them until Moroni returned for them, he was assured that they would be protected (see Joseph Smith—History 1:59).

For the first time in over fourteen hundred years the precious records were entrusted to a mortal. Joseph carefully hid the plates in a hollow log

Except for Joseph Smith, no man played a more varied role in the coming forth of the Book of Mormon than Martin Harris. He provided financial support so the Prophet could move from Manchester, New York, to Harmony, Pennsylvania, in December 1827, helping to fulfill an ancient prophecy (see Isaiah 29:11–12). He also served as scribe, became a witness of the coming forth of the Book of Mormon, financially assisted in its publication, and testified of the truthfulness of the book throughout his life.

ISAIAH 29:1–14

10 For the LORD hath poured out upon you the spirit of deep ᵃsleep, and hath closed your ᵇeyes: the ᶜprophets and your rulers, the ᵈseers hath he ᵉcovered.
11 And the vision of all is become unto you as the words of a ᵃbook that is ᵇsealed, which *men* deliver to one that is learned, saying, Read this, I pray thee: and he saith, I cannot; for it *is* sealed:
12 And the book is delivered to ᵃhim that is not learned, saying, Read this, I pray thee: and he saith, I am not learned.
13 ¶ Wherefore the Lord said, Forasmuch as this people ᵃdraw near *me* with their ᵇmouth, and with their

This ancient prophecy of Isaiah has mystified students of the Bible for generations. Martin Harris and Joseph Smith understood it as pertaining to the Book of Mormon. This was verified by an expanded version of Isaiah's prophecy in 2 Nephi 27.

near his home. The Prophet's friends were not the only ones who eagerly anticipated his receiving the plates. Others in the neighborhood had heard that Joseph was going to bring home valuable metal plates. Some of them may have also been involved in searching for the silver mine and now felt that they should have a share in any treasure. Joseph soon learned why Moroni had strictly charged him to protect the plates. "Every stratagem that could be invented" was used to get them from him (v. 60). For example, Willard Chase, a neighboring farmer, along with other treasure seekers, sent for a sorcerer to come and find the place where the plates were hidden. When the Smiths learned of the plot they sent Emma to get Joseph, who was working in Macedon a few miles west of Palmyra. He returned immediately and retrieved the plates. Wrapping them in a linen frock, he started through the woods, thinking it might be safer than the traveled road. But just as he jumped over a log, he was struck from behind with a gun. Joseph, however, was able to knock his assailant down and flee. Half a mile later he was assaulted again but managed to escape, and before he arrived home he was accosted a third time. His mother said that when he reached home he was "altogether speechless from fright and the fatigue of running."15

Efforts to steal the plates intensified, but Moroni's promise of protection was also fulfilled. Joseph often moved the plates from their hiding place just minutes before the treasure seekers arrived. Once he hid them under the hearthstone of the fireplace of his home. A large group of men gathered in front of the house, but they scattered when Joseph and his brothers faked a counterattack by running out the front door screaming and yelling as if a large company of men were assisting them. Joseph then hid the chest under the wooden floor of the cooper shop on the Smith farm, but he was prompted to conceal the records themselves under the flax in the loft. That night his enemies tore up the floor of the cooper shop, but the plates remained safe.

PROPHECY OF ISAIAH FULFILLED

During this period Joseph's life was in danger, so he decided to take Emma back to Harmony where he hoped to begin the translation in peace. Before they left, Martin Harris, a prominent citizen of Palmyra who would later play a great role in the Restoration, stepped forward and offered help. He was a prosperous weaver, businessman, and farmer who had met the Smiths when they first settled in Palmyra and had hired various family members to work for him over the years. He provided money so Joseph and Emma could liquidate their debts and also gave them fifty dollars for their trip. With the plates hidden in a barrel of beans in the back of the wagon, they drove out of town on a wintry day in December of 1827 headed for Harmony. Prior arrangements had been made to board temporarily with Emma's parents.

Samuel Latham Mitchill (1764–1831) was born in Long Island, New York. He served in the state legislature and in the United States House of Representatives and Senate. He was known for his work as a historian, linguist, ichthyologist, botanist, geologist, editor, chemist, physician, and surgeon.

Following a brief stay with the Hales, the couple purchased a house from Emma's eldest brother, Jesse. It was a small two-story home on a thirteen-acre farm bordering the Susquehanna River. For the first time in weeks Joseph was able to work in relative peace. Between December 1827 and February 1828, he copied many of the characters from the plates and translated some of them by using the Urim and Thummim. In the early stages of the work, Joseph spent considerable time and effort becoming familiar with the language of the plates and learning how to translate.

According to previous arrangement, Martin Harris visited Joseph in Harmony sometime in February of 1828. By then the Lord had prepared Martin to assist Joseph in his mission. According to his own testimony, Martin was instructed by the Lord in 1818 not to join any church until the words of Isaiah were fulfilled. Sometime later it was revealed to Martin that the Lord had a work for him to do. In 1827 several manifestations convinced Martin Harris that Joseph Smith was a prophet and that he should assist Joseph in bringing the Book of Mormon to this generation. Therefore, Martin went to Harmony to obtain a copy of some of the characters from the plates to show several noted linguists of the time, which fulfilled the prophecy of Isaiah 29:11–12 to help convince an unbelieving world.[16]

Martin visited at least three men with reputations as able linguists. In Albany, New York, he talked with Luther Bradish, a diplomat, statesman, world traveler, and student of languages. In New York City he visited Dr. Samuel Mitchill, vice president of Rutgers Medical College. He also visited a man who knew four languages including Hebrew and Babylonian. This was Professor Charles Anthon of Columbia College in New York City, who was perhaps the most qualified of Martin's contacts to judge the characters on the document. He was among the leading classical scholars of his day. At the time of Martin Harris's visit, Charles Anthon was adjunct professor of Greek and Latin. He knew French, German, Greek, and Latin, and was familiar, if books in his library are evidence, with the latest discoveries pertaining to the Egyptian language including the early work of Champollion.[17]

According to Martin Harris, Professor Anthon examined the characters and their translation and willingly gave him a certificate stating to the citizens of Palmyra that the writings were authentic. Anthon further told Martin the characters resembled Egyptian, Chaldean, Assyrian, and Arabic, and expressed his opinion that the translation was correct. Martin put the certificate in his pocket and was about to leave when Anthon called him back and asked how Joseph Smith found the gold plates in the hill. Martin explained that an angel of God revealed the location to Joseph, whereupon Charles Anthon asked for the certificate, which Martin gave to him. "He took it and tore it to pieces, saying, that there was no such thing now as ministering of angels, and that if I [Martin] would bring the plates to him, he would translate them. I informed him that part of the plates were sealed,

Charles Anthon was a professor of classical studies at Columbia College (now Columbia University) in New York for forty-seven years.

and that I was forbidden to bring them. He replied, 'I cannot read a sealed book.' "[18]

Martin Harris's trip was significant for several reasons. First, it showed that scholars had an interest in the characters and were willing to give them serious consideration as long as an angel was not part of their story. Second, it was, in the view of Martin and Joseph, the direct fulfillment of prophecy relative to the Book of Mormon. Third, it was a demonstration that translating the record would require the assistance of God; intellect alone was insufficient (see Isaiah 29:11–12; 2 Nephi 27:15–20). Finally, it built up Martin's own faith. He returned to New York confident that he had evidence to convince his neighbors of Joseph Smith's work. He was now ready to wholeheartedly commit himself and his means to the bringing forth of the Book of Mormon.

THE LOST MANUSCRIPT

Martin could not foresee the difficulties that awaited him in Palmyra. His wife, Lucy, was angry that he had gone to the East without her. She was afraid the Smiths were trying to defraud him, and she resented the time he spent with Joseph and away from her. Her bitterness was made evident when Martin returned. She was the kind of person who demanded positive proof, so when Martin prepared to leave for Pennsylvania again, she insisted on accompanying him. He agreed to take her for a few days. In Harmony, her first priority was to see the plates. She ransacked the house, forcing Joseph to hide them outside. She thought she had found where they were buried, but when she stooped down to look, she was frightened away by a large, black snake. Angered by failing to find the plates, she told anyone who would listen that her husband had been duped by a "grand imposter." After two weeks, Martin took her home. Despite her attempts to dissuade him, he returned to Harmony. In Martin's absence, Lucy continued her criticism in Palmyra.[19]

In Pennsylvania, Joseph and Martin labored together on the translation until 14 June 1828. By that time the translation filled 116 foolscap pages (roughly legal-size), and Martin asked if he could take this manuscript home to show his wife and friends. He hoped this would convince Lucy that the work was legitimate and stop her opposition. Through the Urim and Thummim, Joseph inquired of the Lord. The answer was no. Martin, not satisfied, persisted until Joseph again asked the Lord; still the answer was no. Martin's pleadings and solicitations continued. Joseph wanted to satisfy his benefactor. He was young and inexperienced, and he relied upon the age and maturity of Martin. Moreover, Martin was the only one Joseph knew who was willing to work as scribe and finance the publication of the book. These considerations moved him to ask again. Finally, the Lord granted a conditional permission. Martin agreed in writing to show the manuscript to only four or five people, including his wife; his brother, Preserved Harris; his father; his mother; and Lucy's sister, Mrs. Polly Cobb. Martin then left for Palmyra with the only copy of the manuscript.

Shortly after Martin's departure, Emma Smith bore a son, Alvin, who died the day he was born. Emma nearly died herself, and for two weeks Joseph was constantly at her bedside. When she improved, his attention returned to the manuscript. By this time Martin had been gone for three weeks, and they had heard nothing from him. Martin had not been totally irresponsible. He had spent time with his wife, taken care of business in Palmyra, and served on a jury.

Emma encouraged Joseph to catch a stage to Palmyra and check on the matter. After traveling from Harmony to the Palmyra area and walking the last twenty miles during the night, Joseph finally arrived at his parents' home in Manchester. He immediately sent for Martin. Martin usually came quickly, so breakfast was prepared for him and the Smiths. Several hours passed before Martin finally plodded up the walk with head hung down. He climbed on the fence and sat there with his hat down over his eyes. Finally he came in and sat down at the breakfast table, but he could not eat. Lucy Mack Smith, the Prophet's mother, recorded: "He took up his knife and fork as if he were going to use them, but immediately dropped them. Hyrum, observing this, said 'Martin, why do you not eat; are you sick?' Upon which Mr. Harris pressed his hands upon his temples, and cried out in a tone of deep anguish, 'Oh, I have lost my soul! I have lost my soul!'

"Joseph who had not expressed his fears till now, sprang from the table, exclaiming, 'Martin, have you lost that manuscript? Have you broken your oath, and brought down condemnation upon my head as well as your own?'

" 'Yes; it is gone,' replied Martin, 'and I know not where.' "

Self-condemnation and fear beset the Prophet. He exclaimed, " 'All is lost! all is lost! What shall I do? I have sinned—it is I who tempted the wrath of God. I should have been satisfied with the first answer which I received from the Lord; for he told me that it was not safe to let the writing go out of my possession.' He wept and groaned, and walked the floor continually.

"At length he told Martin to go back and search again.

" 'No'; said Martin, 'it is all in vain; for I have ripped open beds and pillows [looking for the manuscript]; and I know it is not there.'

" 'Then must I,' said Joseph, 'return with such a tale as this? I dare not do it. And how shall I appear before the Lord? Of what rebuke am I not worthy from the angel of the Most High?' . . .

"The next morning, he set out for home. We parted with heavy hearts, for it now appeared that all which we had so fondly anticipated, and which had been the source of so much secret gratification, had in a moment fled, and fled forever."[20]

Upon returning to Harmony without the 116 pages of manuscript, Joseph immediately began to pray for the Lord to forgive him for acting contrary to his will. Moroni appeared to Joseph and required him to return the plates

TO THE READER—

As many false reports have been circulated respecting the following work, and also many unlawful measures taken by evil designing persons to destroy me, and also the work, I would inform you that I translated, by the gift and power of God, and caused to be written, one hundred and sixteen pages, the which I took from the Book of Lehi, which was an account abridged from the plates of Lehi, by the hand of Mormon; which said account, some person or persons have stolen and kept from me, notwithstanding my utmost exertions to recover it again—and being commanded of the Lord that I should not translate the same over again, for Satan had put it into their hearts to tempt the Lord their God, by altering the words, that they did read contrary from that which I translated and caused to be written; and if I should bring forth the same words again, or, in other words, if I should translate the same over again, they would publish that which they had stolen, and Satan would stir up the hearts of this generation, that they might not receive this work: but behold, the Lord said unto me, I will not suffer that Satan shall accomplish his evil design in this thing: therefore thou shalt translate from the plates of Nephi, until ye come to that which ye have translated, which ye have retained; and

Joseph Smith explained that the lost 116 pages of manuscript had come from the book of Lehi, which was part of the large plates of Nephi. Scholars believe that after the loss of the manuscript, when he was permitted to translate again, the Prophet continued from Mosiah on using the large plates. Later he translated the small plates of Nephi, which is 1 Nephi to Mosiah. A study of the handwriting in the extant portions of the original manuscript of the Book of Mormon supports this view.

and the Urim and Thummim, but promised that he could receive them back if he were humble and penitent. Some time later he received a revelation which chastised him for negligence and for "setting at naught the counsels of God" but also comforted him that he was still chosen to perform the work of translation if he repented (see D&C 3:4–10). Joseph did repent and again received the plates and the Urim and Thummim, along with a promise that the Lord would send a scribe to assist him in the translation. There was a special message: "The angel seemed pleased with me . . . , and he told me that the Lord loved me, for my faithfulness and humility."[21]

With his divine gift restored, Joseph learned by revelation that wicked men, intending to entrap him, had altered the words of the manuscript. If he translated the same material again and published it, they would say he was unable to do it the same way twice, and therefore the work must not be inspired (see D&C 10). God, however, had prepared for this circumstance. The lost document was the book of Lehi taken from Mormon's abridgment of the large plates of Nephi. But Mormon had been inspired to attach the small plates of Nephi to his record for "a wise purpose," which at the time he did not understand (see Words of Mormon 1:3–7). These smaller plates contained an account similar to that in the book of Lehi. Joseph was instructed not to retranslate, but to continue on and at the appropriate time to include the material from the small plates of Nephi. These records were the account of Nephi which the Lord said was "more particular concerning the things which, in my wisdom, I would bring to the knowledge of the people" (D&C 10:40).

THE PROPHET'S PREPARATION

The five and one half years between September 1823 and April 1829 were important in Joseph Smith's preparation for translating the Book of Mormon and leading the Church in the dispensation of the fulness of times. He was now twenty-three years old. He was tall and strong; he worked on the farm, in the fields, and at odd jobs. Although he had had little formal schooling, Joseph had a hungry and curious mind. He liked to discover things for himself and to seek his answers from the scriptures (see Joseph Smith—History 1:11–12). This thirst for knowledge, especially spiritual knowledge, never left him.

In June of 1843, Joseph told the Saints: "I am a rough stone. The sound of the hammer and chisel was never heard on me until the Lord took me in hand."[22] Courage, optimism, and faith were hallmarks of his personality. He had shown great courage at an early age, when he endured a painful leg operation. He later faced moblike neighbors who were trying to get the plates from him. Despite his poverty and lack of education, he was optimistic about himself and life. Rebuked by the Lord and corrected by Moroni, he was always submissive, repentant, and energetic. He faced despair when the 116 pages were lost, but from that experience he learned obedience and was later able to say, "I made this my rule: *When the Lord commands, do it.*"[23] He also learned valuable lessons about controlling his motives and purposes and was, therefore, able to keep his "eye single to the glory of God" (D&C 4:5) and channel his energies and thoughts toward building the kingdom.

By this time Joseph Smith had gained considerable experience with various means of revelation. He had communed with God and his Son and with angelic messengers. He had seen visions, felt the promptings of the Spirit, and grown in skill in using the Urim and Thummim. We should not conclude that revelation came easy to him, for another lesson he learned during this time was the price in faith, diligence, persistence, worthiness, and obedience he had to pay to receive communication from God.

TERMINOLOGY HELPFUL IN UNDERSTANDING THE EASTERN UNITED STATES

The names of places connected with the early history of the Church in the eastern United States often confuse modern readers. This is because many people are not familiar with the political subdivisions of most eastern states and the different meanings of common words pertaining to them. If we understand the terminology used in the eastern United States, this confusion is cleared up and the reading of Church history becomes more understandable.

The word *town* does not mean a village, hamlet, or city. Rather, it is the shortened form of the word *township,* which refers to a subsection of a county. A county may be subdivided into many townships. For example, Windsor County, Vermont, is composed of twenty-four townships, one called Sharon. When we read in Church histories that Joseph Smith was born in the "town" of Sharon in Windsor County, Vermont, it does not mean the village or community of Sharon, but the township of Sharon.

The names of these towns (townships) were and are often used in such legal documents as deeds and wills. These towns also have their own local governments and elected officials, which are distinctly different from government officials of villages and communities in the township.

Often villages or small communities have the same name as their township, which can add to the confusion. In some cases, however, communities in a state have the same name as a township but are not in that township. Thus, if we assume that Joseph and Emma lived in the community of Harmony, Pennsylvania, and look for it on a map, we would find it in Butler County in the western end of the state. But this was not the location of their home. They lived in the "town," or township, of Harmony, which is in Susquehanna County, in the northeastern corner of Pennsylvania.

One of the ways easterners have avoided confusion of the two meanings of the word *town* is to be specific in reference to communities. When a community is too small to have a local organization, it is usually called a hamlet. When it is incorporated, it is called a village (or, in Pennsylvania, a borough). It remains a village until it has a population of about ten thousand; then it becomes a city.

With this background, it may be helpful to review some of the significant locations of Church history mentioned in these early chapters. The maps in these chapters will also help clarify these points.

1. Joseph Smith's progenitors did not live in the village of Topsfield, Massachusetts, but in the township of Topsfield.

2. Joseph Smith was born in the township of Sharon in Windsor County, Vermont. The home was located some distance from the village of Sharon and straddled the township line. It is believed that he was born in the township of Sharon only because the bedroom where he was born was on the Sharon side of the line.

3. The Joseph Smith farm and the Sacred Grove are in the township of Manchester, Ontario County, New York, and not in the village of Palmyra. The post office address, however, is and always has been Palmyra, Wayne County, New York.

4. There was no hamlet of Oakland in the days of Isaac Hale and Joseph Smith, but there was a village of Harmony in what was then the township of Harmony. The community of Oakland developed later. Oakland township was then divided off from the old township of Harmony. The village of Harmony has since disappeared and is no longer identifiable.

5. The Joseph Knight farm was not in a village or hamlet called Colesville, Broome County, New York. Rather, it was in the township of Colesville and was some distance from the hamlets of North and West Colesville, the closest village being that of Nineveh.

6. Joseph and Emma were married at the home of Squire Tarbell in the village of South Bainbridge (now Afton) in the township of Bainbridge, Chenango County, New York.

7. The Church was not organized in the hamlet of Fayette, Seneca County, New York. The organization took place in the log cabin of Peter Whitmer in the township of Fayette.

ENDNOTES

1. See Dale L. Berge, "Archaelogical Work at the Smith Log House," *Ensign,* Aug. 1985, pp. 24–26.

2. Information for the layout of the Smith farm was obtained from Donald E. Enders, Joseph Smith, Sr., Family in Palmyra/Manchester, New York, research file, Museum of Church History and Art, Salt Lake City, Utah, 1989.

3. See Lucy Mack Smith, *History of Joseph Smith,* ed. Preston Nibley (Salt Lake City: Bookcraft, 1958), p. 79.

4. In *Latter Day Saints' Messenger and Advocate,* Oct. 1835, pp. 195–96.

5. Oliver Cowdery, in *Messenger and Advocate,* July 1835, p. 157.

6. Cowdery, in *Messenger and Advocate,* Oct. 1835, p. 198.

7. Cowdery, in *Messenger and Advocate,* Oct. 1835, p. 198.

8. In Smith, *History of Joseph Smith,* p. 81; emphasis added.

9. See *History of the Church,* 4:537; George Q. Cannon, in *Journal of Discourses,* 13:47; John Taylor, in *Journal of Discourses,* 17:374; 21:94.

10. Smith, *History of Joseph Smith,* p. 83.

11. In Smith, *History of Joseph Smith,* p. 87.

12. Buddy Youngreen, *Reflections of Emma, Joseph Smith's Wife* (Orem, Utah: Grandin Book Co., 1982), p. 4.

13. See *History of the Church,* 3:29.

14. In Smith, *History of Joseph Smith,* pp. 100–101.

15. Smith, *History of Joseph Smith,* p. 108.

16. See Smith, *History of Joseph Smith,* p. 114; Joseph Smith 1832 History, Joseph Smith Letterbook, cited in Dean C. Jessee, ed., *The Personal Writings of Joseph Smith* (Salt Lake City: Deseret Book Co., 1984), pp. 7–8.

17. See Stanley B. Kimball, "I Cannot Read a Sealed Book," *Improvement Era,* Feb. 1957, pp. 80–82, 104, 106; "Charles Anthon and the Egyptian Language," *Improvement Era,* Oct. 1960, pp. 708–10, 765; "The Anthon Transcript: People, Primary Sources, and Problems," *Brigham Young University Studies,* Spring 1970, pp. 325–52.

18. In *History of the Church,* 1:20.

19. See Smith, *History of Joseph Smith,* pp. 119–23.

20. Smith, *History of Joseph Smith,* pp. 128–29.

21. In Smith, *History of Joseph Smith,* p. 135.

22. In *History of the Church,* 5:423.

23. *History of the Church,* 2:170.

CHAPTER FIVE

COMING FORTH OF THE BOOK OF MORMON AND RESTORATION OF THE PRIESTHOOD

THE YOUNG PROPHET and the Church he was to restore faced an important year in 1829. At the end of 1828, Moroni returned the plates and the Urim and Thummim and promised a new scribe to assist in the translation. That fall Joseph's parents, who had worried about him, came to Harmony and were pleased to find him in good spirits and learn that the plates and the Urim and Thummim were safe in Emma's red morocco trunk. When his father and mother left for home they were "relieved of a burden which was almost insupportable, and . . . joy far overbalanced all [their] former grief."[1] The Lord's promise to send a scribe was fulfilled in the spring of 1829 when Oliver Cowdery arrived in Harmony. He and Joseph labored diligently to complete the translation. In the process they learned important gospel principles, some that were the catalyst for new spiritual experiences and for the restoration of the priesthood. The way was being prepared for the organization of the Church of Jesus Christ the following year.

OLIVER COWDERY'S ARRIVAL

During the winter of 1828–29, Joseph Smith periodically worked on the translation with the help of Emma and her brother, but earning a living left little time for translating. Emma's father, Isaac Hale, was suspicious of Joseph's claims about the plates and showed little sympathy. Hence, in March of 1829, Joseph said, "I had not where to go and I cried unto the Lord that he would provide for me to accomplish the work whereunto he had commanded me."[2] The Lord told him to stop for the present and wait "until I command thee, and I will provide means whereby thou mayest accomplish the thing which I have commanded thee" (D&C 5:34). Confidently the Prophet awaited the arrival of a new scribe, and on 5 April, Oliver Cowdery came.

Oliver Cowdery was born 3 October 1806 in Wells, Rutland County, Vermont. He was the youngest of eight children. As he grew up he received an education consisting of reading, writing, and the basic rules of arithmetic. Several of the elder Cowdery brothers had found that business opportunities were limited in Vermont and had moved to western New York. In 1825 Oliver followed and took employment as a clerk in a village general store. He also engaged in blacksmithing and farming. Oliver was slight of build, about five feet five inches tall, with dark, wavy hair and piercing dark eyes.

Oliver Cowdery (1806-50)

Early in 1829 one of Oliver's older brothers, Lyman Cowdery, was hired to teach at the village school in Manchester township close to where Joseph Smith's family lived. Lyman was unable to fulfill his commitment and suggested that the trustees hire his brother Oliver. Approved by the trustees, one of whom was Hyrum Smith, Oliver commenced teaching and was invited to board at the home of Joseph Smith, Sr. Lucy Smith related that almost immediately "he began to hear from all quarters concerning the plates, and as soon began to importune Mr. Smith upon the subject, but for a considerable length of time did not succeed in eliciting any information."[3] The Smiths were reluctant to share their experiences because they had been ridiculed by neighbors in the past.

When Oliver gained the trust of the Smiths, Joseph Smith, Sr., told him about the plates. Oliver prayed privately and meditated upon the subject, even confiding in Joseph Smith, Sr., that he felt impressed that he would have the privilege of writing for Joseph, who he had not yet met. He told the family that it was the "will of the Lord" that he go with Samuel to visit Joseph in the spring following the school term. He said, "If there is a work for me to do in this thing, I am determined to attend to it."[4] Accordingly, in the first part of April, Samuel Smith and Oliver Cowdery left for Harmony, Pennsylvania. The wet and disagreeable weather would have discouraged most people, but Oliver was not to be deterred from meeting and speaking with Joseph Smith.

Before meeting the Smiths in Manchester, Oliver Cowdery had met and become close friends with David Whitmer of Fayette, New York. En route to Harmony, Oliver and Samuel stopped to see David, who asked Oliver to write to him about his impression on whether Joseph really had the ancient records. This friendship with the Whitmer family later had significant impact on the coming forth of the Book of Mormon and the establishment of the Church.

When Oliver arrived in Harmony on Sunday, 5 April, Joseph Smith recognized him as the assistance the Lord had promised. They sat down together and discussed Joseph's experiences until late in the evening. The next day they attended to some business, and on Tuesday, 7 April, they commenced the work of translation in earnest.

THE TRANSLATION ACCELERATED

Joseph and Oliver labored "with little cessation" on the translation throughout April. With Oliver's help, Joseph proceeded faster than ever before. During the next three months Joseph and Oliver completed the amazing task of translating approximately five hundred printed pages. This was a glorious period in their lives. Oliver wrote: "These were days never to be forgotten—to sit under the sound of a voice dictated by the *inspiration* of heaven. . . . Day after day I continued, uninterrupted, to write from his mouth, as he translated, with the *Urim* and *Thummim* . . . the history, or record, called 'The Book of Mormon.' "[5]

Painting by Earl Jones of Joseph and Oliver translating

Joseph and Emma Smith's home in Harmony, Pennsylvania. The center portion is the original home. This is where Emma gave birth to their first child, Alvin, who died the same day, 15 June 1828.

Here Joseph Smith translated a large portion of the Book of Mormon. While living in Harmony, the Prophet received several revelations (see D&C 3–13, 24–27).

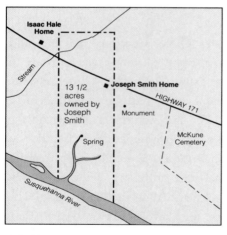

In Harmony, Joseph and Emma resided with her parents until Isaac Hale became angry because Joseph would not let him see the plates. Joseph and Emma then purchased a home with 13 1/2 acres of land from Emma's father, Isaac Hale, for two hundred dollars. It was a long narrow strip that ran south to the Susquehanna River.

The Aaronic Priesthood was likely restored on the banks of the river somewhere on the Smith property or nearby. Between 1947–56 the Church purchased three parcels of land in this area to obtain as much of the original site as possible. In 1960 a monument was erected near the Joseph Smith homestead commemorating the restoration of the Aaronic Priesthood.

During April significant revelations came to Oliver Cowdery through Joseph Smith. The first one (now D&C 6) commended Oliver for his righteous desires in calling upon the Lord and reminded him that "as often as thou hast inquired thou hast received instruction of my Spirit. If it had not been so, thou wouldst not have come to the place where thou art at this time" (v. 14). Apparently, however, Oliver desired a further witness of the truthfulness of the work, so the Lord told him:

"Cast your mind upon the night that you cried unto me in your heart, that you might know concerning the truth of these things.

"Did I not speak peace to your mind concerning the matter? What greater witness can you have than from God?" (D&C 6:22–23). Only after this revelation did Oliver tell Joseph that one night while boarding with the Smith family he had called upon God in prayer to know if Joseph Smith was a prophet and had received the peaceful assurance that he was.

While the two continued working together, Oliver desired the power to translate. This blessing was granted and he translated a few words, but he had not followed the necessary process of spiritual preparation and mental exertion. The Lord explained:

"You must study it out in your mind; then you must ask me if it be right, and if it is right I will cause that your bosom shall burn within you; therefore, you shall feel that it is right.

"But if it be not right you shall have no such feelings, but you shall have a stupor of thought that shall cause you to forget the thing which is wrong; therefore, you cannot write that which is sacred save it be given you from me" (D&C 9:8–9).

About this time an old friend, Joseph Knight, Sr., came from Colesville, New York, a distance of twenty-eight miles, with provisions, including potatoes, mackerel, and several bushels of grain. He also brought lined paper and money to purchase more. Knight's visit was important in keeping the work moving because Joseph and Oliver, being in great need, had recently been looking for employment. If they were forced to work, even

Emma's parents, Isaac and Elizabeth Hale, are buried in McKune Cemetery. Joseph and Emma's first son, Alvin, is also buried here.

Isaac Hale's tombstone reads, "ISAAC HALE died Jan. 11, 1839, age 75 yrs. 10 mo. & 10 ds.

"The body of Isaac Hale, the Hunter, like the cover of an old book, its contents torn out, and stript of its lettering and guilding, lies here food for worms, yet the work itself shall not be lost for it will as he believed: appear once more in a new and more beautiful edition, corrected and ammended."

Elizabeth Hale's tombstone reads, "ELIZABETH, wife of Isaac Hale Died Feb. 16, 1842, aged 75 years 2 mo. & 28 ds."

temporarily, the translation would be delayed. Therefore, they were deeply grateful for the timely assistance, which they considered a gift from heaven.

RESTORATION OF THE PRIESTHOOD AND BAPTISM

Joseph and Oliver were thrilled as such doctrines as the resurrected Savior's visit to the inhabitants of the Western Hemisphere and his teachings about baptism were unfolded during the translation (see 3 Nephi 11:18–38). At this point their souls were driven to mighty prayer to learn how they could obtain the blessing of baptism. On 15 May 1829, Joseph and Oliver went into the nearby woods along the Susquehanna River to pray. Oliver described the scene that followed: "On a sudden, as from the midst of eternity, the voice of the Redeemer spake peace to us, while the veil was parted and the angel of God came down clothed with glory, and delivered the anxiously looked for message, and the keys of the gospel of repentance!—What joy! what wonder! what amazement! While the world were racked and distracted . . . our eyes beheld—our ears heard."[6]

The angel introduced himself as John (John the Baptist in the New Testament) and told them that he was acting under the direction of the Apostles Peter, James, and John. He laid his hands upon Joseph and Oliver and said, "Upon you my fellow servants, in the name of Messiah, I confer the Priesthood of Aaron, which holds the keys of the ministering of angels, and of the gospel of repentance, and of baptism by immersion for the remission of sins" (Joseph Smith—History 1:69; see also D&C 13:1). John explained that the Melchizedek Priesthood would be bestowed upon them at a later time. For the first time in centuries, the priesthood was again on the earth.

John directed that Joseph should baptize Oliver, and Oliver should then baptize Joseph. They were then to confer the Aaronic Priesthood upon each other. As they came out of the water from their baptisms, they were filled with the spirit of prophecy. Oliver predicted "many things which should shortly come to pass," and Joseph prophesied "concerning the rise of this Church, and many other things connected with the Church, and this generation of the children of men" (Joseph Smith—History 1:73). Filled with the Holy Ghost, they rejoiced in the God of their salvation and their minds were enlightened with previously unexperienced insight into the meaning of the scriptures. They were, however, forced to keep these things secret because of persecution from local religious leaders. Isaac Hale, Joseph's father-in-law, had stepped in to provide protection, but his ability to control the situation waned.

During this time, Joseph received some visitors in Harmony. The first was his younger brother, Samuel. Joseph and Oliver eagerly told Samuel about their recent experiences, informed him of what the Lord was about to do, and showed him what had thus far been translated from the plates. Samuel was not easily persuaded, even after Joseph and Oliver had reasoned with him from the Bible concerning the gospel of Jesus Christ. He retired to the woods to try to resolve his doubts through prayer. Joseph reported, "The result was that he obtained revelation for himself sufficient to convince him of the truth of our assertions to him; and on the twenty-fifth day of that same month in which we had been baptized and ordained, Oliver Cowdery baptized him; and he returned to his father's house, greatly glorifying and praising God, being filled with the Holy Spirit."[7]

Joseph's older brother Hyrum was the next to arrive. At Hyrum's request, Joseph asked the Lord through the Urim and Thummim to ascertain the Lord's will concerning him. The Lord told Hyrum he would be the means of accomplishing much good in this generation, but that he should be patient and study the scriptures, including the Book of Mormon which was then being translated, and prepare himself for the day when he would be called to preach the gospel of repentance (see D&C 11).

Soon afterward Joseph and Oliver went to Colesville. On their return trip, the Lord's chief Apostles, Peter, James, and John, appeared to them on the banks of the Susquehanna River (see D&C 128:20). The angelic visitors conferred upon Joseph and Oliver the holy Melchizedek Priesthood and the keys of the apostleship (see D&C 27:12). Joseph and Oliver now had the authority to act as legal agents for the Lord in building the kingdom of God upon the earth.

COMPLETION OF THE TRANSLATION

Shortly after beginning to assist Joseph Smith with the work of translation, Oliver wrote to David Whitmer in Fayette township. He enthusiastically testified that Joseph Smith had the ancient records and that the work was divine. Soon he sent a few lines of the translation and bore witness that he knew the plates contained a record of the people who once inhabited this continent. David Whitmer, then twenty-four years of age, eagerly showed these letters to his parents and brothers and sisters. Persecution began to intensify in the Harmony area, so late in May, Oliver communicated with David about the possibility of Joseph and Oliver going to stay with the Whitmers in Fayette. In response Peter Whitmer, Sr., David's father, invited Joseph to stay at his farm home as long as was needed to finish the work of translation. David's brother John offered to help as Joseph's scribe. Many people in the Fayette area were anxious to hear more about the work.[8]

A late May planting was essential for successful fall crops; therefore, David Whitmer had to plow and prepare the soil before he could take his two-horse wagon to pick up Joseph Smith and Oliver Cowdery. At the end of a day of plowing he found he had accomplished in one day what normally would have taken two days to do. David's father was likewise impressed by this apparent miracle. Peter Whitmer, Sr., said, "There must be an overruling hand in this, and I think you would better go down to Pennsylvania as soon as your plaster of paris is sown."[9] (Plaster of paris was used to reduce the acidity of the soil.) The next day David went to the fields to sow the plaster, but to his surprise he found the work had been done. His sister, who lived near the field, said that her children

David Whitmer (1805-88) was one of the three witnesses of the Book of Mormon. He died in Richmond, Missouri, at the age of eighty-four.

had called her to watch three strangers the day before spread the plaster with remarkable skill. She assumed they were men David had hired.[10]

Grateful for this divine intervention, David Whitmer hurried off on the three-day journey to Harmony. Joseph Smith and Oliver Cowdery met him as he approached the town. Although David had not told them exactly when he was coming, Joseph had seen in vision the details of David's trip to Harmony.[11] These three miracles witnessed by David Whitmer exemplified the Prophet's seership and the Lord's intervention for the successful inauguration of the Restoration.

This was the first meeting between Joseph Smith and David Whitmer. As had happened with Oliver Cowdery, David and Joseph quickly became friends. Soon they were on their way to Fayette, some one hundred miles away. On this occasion Moroni took the plates to avoid danger while transporting them. Another unusual event occurred en route. It happened while they were riding along in the wagon. David Whitmer described the event:

"A very pleasant, nice-looking old man suddenly appeared by the side of our wagon and saluted us with, 'good morning, it is very warm,' at the same time wiping his face or forehead with his hand. We returned the salutation, and, by a sign from Joseph, I invited him to ride if he was going our way. But he said very pleasantly, 'No, I am going to Cumorah.' This name was something new to me, I did not know what Cumorah meant. We all gazed at him and at each other, and as I looked around enquiringly of Joseph, the old man instantly disappeared. . . .

". . . It was the messenger who had the plates, who had taken them from Joseph just prior to our starting from Harmony."[12]

The group arrived in Fayette about the first of June. Emma, who had remained behind to care for the house in Harmony, soon joined her husband in Fayette. Meanwhile, the translating resumed at once. The Whitmer family was most gracious in providing for the needs of Joseph, Emma, and Oliver Cowdery.

While the translation progressed, the gospel was being taught in Seneca County, and Hyrum Smith, David Whitmer, and Peter Whitmer, Jr., were baptized in June for the remission of sins. Peter Whitmer's three sons, David, John, and Peter, Jr., became zealous assistants in the work. Anxious to learn of their respective duties, Joseph sought the Lord, and a revelation was granted to each of them. Each was told to help in building the kingdom of God by declaring repentance (see D&C 14–16). All these activities were not easy on Peter and Mary Whitmer, who were hosting the Smiths and Oliver Cowdery in their home. Their son, David, said that this added burden greatly increased the anxiety of his mother. She did not complain, but she felt overwhelmed. David later related what happened one day as his mother went to the barn to milk the cows: "She was met out near the yard by the same old man [seen earlier by David] (judging by her description of him) who said to her: 'You have been very faithful and diligent in your labors, but you are tired because of the increase of your toil; it is proper therefore that you should receive a witness that your faith may be strengthened.' Thereupon he showed her the plates."[13] This event strengthened Mary Whitmer and her family as they continued to support Joseph Smith and the important work he was engaged in.

PROCESS OF TRANSLATION

Little is known about the actual process of translating the record, primarily because those who knew the most about the translation, Joseph Smith and Oliver Cowdery, said the least about it. Moreover, Martin Harris, David Whitmer, and Emma Smith, who assisted Joseph, left no contemporary descriptions. The sketchy accounts they recorded much later in life were often contradictory.

The Prophet was reluctant to give the details about the translation. In a Church conference held 25–26 October 1831 in Orange, Ohio, Hyrum requested that a firsthand account of the coming forth of the Book of Mormon be given. But the Prophet said, "It was not intended to tell the world all the particulars of the coming forth of the Book of Mormon."[14] Joseph explained in an open letter to a newspaper editor in 1833 the heart of the matter, but he gave few particulars, stating that the Book of Mormon was "found through the ministration of an holy angel, and translated into our own language by the gift and power of God."[15] His explanation is consistent with the Doctrine and Covenants, which says that he was granted "power to translate through the mercy of God, by the power of God, the Book of Mormon" (D&C 1:29) and that the Lord "gave him power from on high, by the means which were before prepared, to translate the Book of Mormon" (D&C 20:8).

This is a portion of the Book of Mormon manuscript in the handwriting of John Whitmer. He was one of the people who served as a scribe to the Prophet during the Book of Mormon translation.

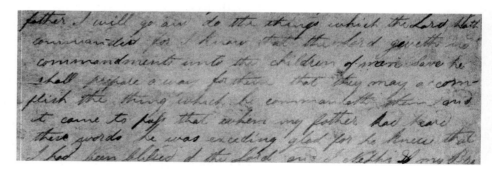

Clearly the most important feature of the translation, as the title page of the Book of Mormon states, is "the interpretation thereof by the gift of God." Moroni, the last custodian of the ancient text, challenged every reader of the Book of Mormon to learn through prayer the truthfulness of the book; he promised that by the power of the Holy Ghost all people could know that it was true (see Moroni 10:4–5). The Lord's own testimony of the Book of Mormon is that Joseph Smith "has translated the book, even that part which I have commanded him, and as your Lord and your God liveth it is true" (D&C 17:6).

Some critics have suggested that Sidney Rigdon was a principal author of the Book of Mormon. They say that he used a romance by Solomon Spaulding called either *Manuscript Found* or *Manuscript Story* as a guide for the historical portions of this work. There is no evidence, however, that Sidney Rigdon knew Joseph Smith before the Book of Mormon was published. Elder Rigdon's own testimony is that the first time he heard of the book was in October 1830 when a copy was handed to him by Parley P. Pratt (see pages 80–81 of this text). Solomon Spaulding's manuscript was discovered in the 1880s, and it bears no resemblance to the Book of Mormon. This obviously fabricated yet widely-propounded Spaulding-Rigdon theory is an attempt by Satan to discredit the word of God.

When Joseph Smith began translating in 1827, he evidently started with the book of Lehi from Mormon's abridgment of the large plates of Nephi (see heading to D&C 10). After the loss of the 116 pages of manuscript, Joseph apparently started with the book of Mosiah, also found on the large plates. He had just begun the book of Mosiah when Oliver Cowdery was sent to him in early April of 1829. Five weeks later, 15 May 1829, they were on 3 Nephi and the Savior's sermon on baptism to the Nephites. Not until arriving at the Whitmer residence in Fayette did Joseph translate the small plates of Nephi, which contain 1 Nephi through the Words of Mormon. The Prophet was commanded to translate the small plates to replace the 116 lost pages (see D&C 10:43–45). In the original manuscript of the Book of Mormon, John Whitmer's work as a scribe only dealt with material from the small plates, thus substantiating this conclusion.[16]

WITNESSES TO THE BOOK OF MORMON

Almost immediately after Joseph Smith translated Nephi's writings about the need for witnesses (see 2 Nephi 27:12–14; Ether 5), Martin Harris went to Fayette from Palmyra to inquire about the progress of the work. Martin along with Oliver Cowdery and David Whitmer asked Joseph to pray and ask the Lord if they could be the promised witnesses. He did so and obtained a revelation in which they were told that if they exercised faith and full purpose of heart they would be granted the privilege of beholding the sacred plates and of viewing the breastplate, the sword of Laban, the Urim and Thummim used by the brother of Jared, and the Liahona—the miraculous director given to Lehi in the wilderness (see D&C 17). The Lord declared, "It is by your faith that you shall obtain a view of them, even by that faith which was had by the prophets of old" (D&C 17:2). The Lord also told them that after viewing these items, they would be bound to testify of them to the world.

As soon as the translation was completed, Joseph Smith sent word to his parents in Manchester to come to the Whitmer home in Fayette. When they arrived, bringing Martin Harris, they spent a joyful evening reading from the manuscript. The next morning the prospective witnesses and the others who were staying with the Whitmers gathered in their usual morning devotional to read the scriptures and to sing and pray. Lucy Smith wrote, "Joseph arose from his knees, and approaching Martin Harris with a solemnity that thrills through my veins to this day, when it occurs to my recollection, said, 'Martin Harris, you have got to humble yourself before God this day, that you may obtain a forgiveness of your sins. If you do, it is the will of God that you should look upon the plates, in company with Oliver Cowdery and David Whitmer.' "[17]

Thereafter the four men retired to the woods and sought for the promised fulfillment of the revelation. After two unsuccessful attempts, however, Martin Harris felt that his presence was the reason for their failure to receive an answer. He withdrew a distance and offered his private prayers. The other three had no sooner resumed their prayers when Moroni appeared in glory holding the plates in his hands. Joseph recorded, "He turned over the leaves one by one, so that we could see them, and discern the engravings thereon distinctly. . . . We heard a voice from out of the bright light above us, saying, 'These plates have been revealed by the power of God, and they have been translated by the power of God. The translation of them which you have seen is correct, and I command you to bear record of what you now see and hear.'

"I now left David and Oliver, and went in pursuit of Martin Harris, whom I found at a considerable distance, fervently engaged in prayer. He soon told me, however, that he had not yet prevailed with the Lord, and earnestly requested me to join him in prayer, that he might also realize the same blessings which we had just received. We accordingly joined in prayer, and ultimately obtained our desires, for before we had yet finished, the same vision was opened to our view, at least it was again opened to me, and I once more beheld and heard the same things; whilst at the same moment, Martin Harris cried out, apparently in an ecstasy of joy, ' 'Tis enough; 'tis enough; mine eyes have beheld; mine eyes have beheld.' "[18]

When Joseph returned to the Whitmer home, he told his parents of his relief that others had now seen the angel and the plates and would have to bear witness of these truths, saying, "Now they know for themselves, that I do not go about to deceive the people, and I feel as if I was relieved of a burden which was almost too heavy for me to bear, and it rejoices my soul, that I am not any longer to be entirely alone in the world."[19] The Three Witnesses testified of their experience: "We, through the grace of God the Father, and our Lord Jesus Christ, have seen the plates which contain this record. . . . And we also know that they have been translated by the gift and power of God, for his voice hath declared it unto us; wherefore we know of a surety that the work is true."[20] They went on to testify that the angel showed them the engravings on the plates. Their testimony has been included in each edition of the Book of Mormon since that time.

A few days later eight additional witnesses—faithful men who were close to the Prophet during the translation were also chosen to see the plates. These eight men were Joseph Smith's father, Joseph Smith, Sr.; Joseph's brothers, Hyrum and Samuel; four of the Whitmer brothers—Christian, Jacob, Peter, and John; and a brother-in-law to the Whitmers, Hiram Page. Joseph was permitted to show them the plates near the Smith residence in Manchester when he was making arrangements for the printing of the book.[21] The Eight Witnesses testified that they handled and lifted the plates and saw the engravings on the individual leaves. Their testimony is also contained in all published editions of the Book of Mormon. Thus, according to the divine law of witnesses, the truth of the Book of Mormon is further substantiated and the inhabitants of the earth are held accountable for what is contained in it.

Each of the eleven special witnesses to the Book of Mormon plates went on to serve in important ecclesiastical positions in the restored Church. Five of them, the three Smiths and Christian and Peter Whitmer, Jr., died while they were actively involved in Church service. But each of the Three Witnesses—Martin Harris, Oliver Cowdery, and David Whitmer—later turned away from the Church. John and Jacob Whitmer and Hiram Page of the Eight Witnesses also fell away from the faith. None of these six, however, ever denied his witness, although they had many opportunities to do so. Each pointedly maintained the truthfulness of his testimony whenever asked about it. Oliver Cowdery and Martin Harris eventually returned to the Church and died in full fellowship.

The Eight Witnesses of the Book of Mormon Plates

Name	Date of Birth	Place of Birth	Age When Shown Plates	Occupation	Death
Christian Whitmer	18 January 1798	Harrisburg, Pennsylvania	31 years	Shoemaker	27 November 1835 Clay County, Missouri Remained faithful
Jacob Whitmer	27 January 1800	Harrisburg, Pennsylvania	29 years	Shoemaker	21 April 1856 Richmond, Missouri
Peter Whitmer, Jr.	27 September 1809	Fayette, New York	19 years	Tailor Farmer	22 September 1836 Liberty, Clay County, Missouri Remained faithful
John Whitmer	27 August 1802	Harrisburg, Pennsylvania	26 years	Farmer	11 July 1878 Far West, Missouri
Hiram Page	1800	Vermont	29 years	Physician Farmer	12 August 1852 Excelsior Springs, Missouri
Joseph Smith, Sr.	12 July 1771	Topsfield, Essex County, Massachusetts	57 years	Farmer	14 September 1840 Nauvoo, Illinois Remained faithful
Hyrum Smith	9 February 1800	Tunbridge, Vermont	29 years	Farmer	27 June 1844 Carthage, Illinois Remained faithful
Samuel H. Smith	13 March 1808	Tunbridge, Vermont	21 years	Farmer	30 July 1844 Nauvoo, Illinois Remained faithful

PUBLICATION OF THE BOOK OF MORMON

A few days after Joseph Smith and Oliver Cowdery arrived in Fayette in June of 1829, Joseph felt he was far enough along in the translation that he should apply for a copyright. Accordingly, on 11 June, Joseph Smith filed for and was granted a copyright for the Book of Mormon by the Northern District of New York.[22] This secured the book from plagiarism.

As the work of translation drew to a close in late June, the Prophet turned his attention to the publication of the book. Repeated negotiations were held with Egbert B. Grandin, a twenty-three-year-old printer in Palmyra. A few sheets of the manuscript with the title page were submitted to him for an estimate of the cost. Grandin and his businessmen friends were reluctant to undertake the project of printing the "golden Bible," as they called it. So Joseph and his companions went to Rochester where they

Original manuscript copyright of the Book of Mormon. Richard R. Lansing, clerk of the federal district court, prepared two copies of the application for the copyright of the Book of Mormon. One is housed in the Church archives and the second in the Library of Congress.

Egbert Bratt Grandin (1806–45). At the age of eighteen, Grandin had begun to learn the printing trade at Palmyra's weekly newspaper, the Wayne Sentinel. By the time the Book of Mormon manuscript was taken to him for publication, he was well acquainted with the printing business. This is an 1843 portrait by Alonzo Parks.

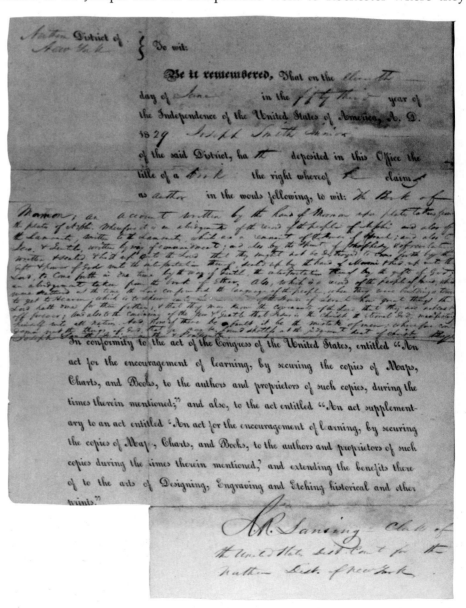

This is an excerpt from E. B. Grandin's journal begun in January 1831. This entry, dated 14 July 1831, records that he "spent most of day in moving Gold Bibles from Mr. [Luther] Howard's Bindery to my Bookstore."

contacted a prominent citizen and printer, Thurlow Weed, who turned them down because he did not believe Joseph's account of the translation. They then visited Elihu F. Marshall also of Rochester who was willing to print and bind the manuscript, but his price was exorbitant. The brethren returned to Grandin and finally persuaded him to print the book if Martin Harris would sign a mortgage agreement guaranteeing payment for the printing through the sale of part of his Palmyra farm if necessary. By then the Prophet had received another bid from a Rochester printer, so Grandin agreed to publish. An agreement was made on 17 August 1829 to print five thousand copies for three thousand dollars.[23] This was an extremely large number of copies in those days, especially for a small local printer.

Joseph had learned an important lesson from the loss of the 116 pages of manuscript. He assigned Oliver Cowdery and Hyrum Smith to supervise the printing while he returned to Harmony to be with Emma and care for his temporal concerns. He also left them with strict instructions to produce a second manuscript for the printer and to keep the original at the Smith home for security. Accordingly, Oliver prepared a printer's copy of the manuscript.[24] For security reasons this manuscript was taken piecemeal to

The Grandin shop is identifiable by the two carriages parked in front. The Book of Mormon was printed on the third floor.

Grandin's printshop as the work proceeded. For several months Hyrum made almost daily trips to the printer's shop to oversee the work.

With such a process it is understandable how a few transcribing and printing errors could creep into the book. Moreover, the original manuscripts contained no punctuation or paragraphing. With the permission of Hyrum Smith, Grandin's typesetter, John H. Gilbert, provided the punctuation and paragraphing. The 1837 edition, prepared by Parley P. Pratt, and the 1840 edition, carefully prepared by the Prophet himself, corrected most of the early printing errors and revised some of Gilbert's work.

During the printing of the Book of Mormon, Oliver Cowdery "learned the printing business in the office of E. B. Grandin, setting much of the type for the book by his own hands."[26]

Opposition to the new scripture surfaced even before the printing was completed. Abner Cole used Grandin's building and press on Sundays and evenings to publish his Palmyra *Reflector* under the pseudonym Obediah Dogberry. He considered the Book of Mormon rubbish; and with his access to the printer's manuscript, he pilfered a few pages and began to publish

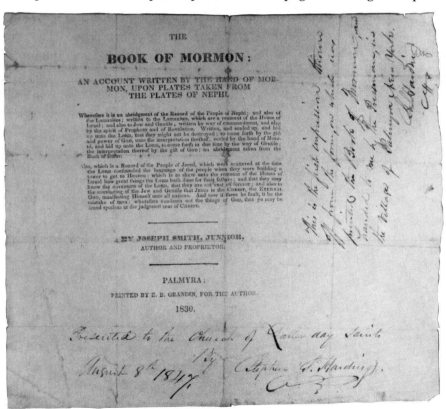

John Hulburd Gilbert, Jr. (1802–95), typesetter for the Book of Mormon. Since there was very little punctuation in the original manuscript, Gilbert punctuated a major portion of the book during the printing process. Once Gilbert gained the confidence of Hyrum and Oliver, he was allowed to take the printer's manuscript home with him for several nights and punctuate it with his pencil.

This photo was taken in 1892 when Gilbert was ninety years old.

In this agreement, signed 16 January 1830, Joseph Smith, Sr., agreed that the first profits from the sale of the Book of Mormon were to go to Martin Harris toward payment of the printer, thus relieving him of the full burden of payment. Nevertheless, Martin had to sell 151 acres of land in 1831 to meet the debt.

them. One Sunday in December, Hyrum and Oliver felt uneasy and went into town to the printing office where they found Cole feverishly working on an extract from the Book of Mormon.

They ordered him to desist because they held a legal copyright, but he defied them and published extracts in the *Reflector*. Joseph Smith, Sr., immediately went to tell the Prophet and bring him back to Palmyra. Upon his arrival Joseph demanded that Cole stop his literary piracy. Cole wanted to fist fight, but the Prophet remained levelheaded, and reason prevailed. The last installment appeared in the 22 January 1830 issue.[27]

Cole's mockery reflected the general feeling in Palmyra at the time. A number of people held a meeting and passed resolutions not to purchase the book when it came from the press. When Grandin grew nervous, Joseph returned to Palmyra to reassure him that the printing costs would be paid.[28] Martin Harris, fearing that he might lose his farm if the Book of Mormon did not sell, approached the Prophet and requested guidance. By revelation Martin was commanded not to "covet" his own property, but to "impart it freely" for the purpose of covering the costs of printing the Book of Mormon (see D&C 19:26). One hundred and fifty-one acres of Martin Harris's farm were sold at a public auction in April 1831 to pay off Mr. Grandin. This sacrifice made the printing of the Book of Mormon possible.[29] The *Wayne Sentinel* announced that the first copies of the Book of Mormon would be available for public sale on 26 March 1830.

The Book of Mormon represents the mind and will of God for the people of these last days. Our generation is privileged to have the Lord's own assessment of this great book:

The Book of Mormon "contains a record of a fallen people, and the fulness of the gospel of Jesus Christ to the Gentiles and to the Jews also;

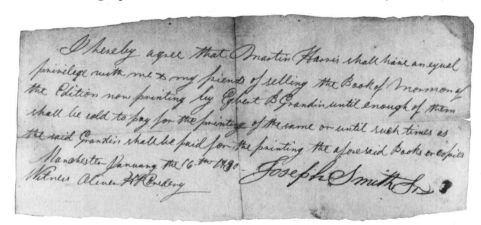

"Which was given by inspiration, and is confirmed to others by the ministering of angels, and is declared unto the world by them—

"Proving to the world that the holy scriptures [the Holy Bible] are true, and that God does inspire men and call them to his holy work in this age and generation, as well as in generations of old" (D&C 20:9–11).

THE BOOK OF MORMON:

AN account written by the hand of Mormon, upon plates, taken from the plates of Nephi. Wherefore it is an abridgment of the Record of the People of Nephi, and also of the Lamanites; written to the Lamanites, which are a remnant of the House of Israel; and also to Jew and Gentile; written by way of commandment, and also by the spirit of Prophecy and of Revelation. Written, and sealed up, and hid up unto the Lord, that they might not be destroyed; to come forth by the gift and power of God unto the interpretation thereof; sealed by the hand of Moroni, and hid up unto the Lord, to come forth in due time by the way of Gentile; the interpretation thereof by the gift of God; an abridgment taken from the Book of Ether.

Also, which is a Record of the People of Jared, which were scattered at the time the Lord confounded the language of the people when they were building a tower to get to Heaven: Which is to shew unto the remnant of the House of Israel how great things the Lord hath done for their fathers; and that they may know the covenants of the Lord, that they are not cast off forever; and also to the convincing of the Jew and Gentile that Jesus is the Christ, the Eternal God, manifesting Himself unto all nations. And now if there be fault, it be the mistake of men; wherefore condemn not the things of God, that ye may be found spotless at the judgement seat of Christ. BY JOSEPH SMITH, JUNIOR, Author and Proprietor.

The above work, containing about 600 pages, large Duodecimo, is now for sale, wholesale and retail, at the Palmyra Bookstore, by HOWARD & GRANDIN.

Palmyra, March 26, 1830. 339

On 19 March 1830 the Wayne Sentinel in Palmyra ran an advertisement that said, "We are requested to announce that the 'Book of Mormon' will be ready for sale in the course of a week." On 26 March 1830 another advertisement appeared in the same newspaper indicating when the Book of Mormon went on sale.

EVENTS ASSOCIATED WITH THE PUBLICATION OF THE BOOK OF MORMON

11 June 1829. Copyright for the Book of Mormon was obtained.

1 July 1829. Translation of the Book of Mormon was completed.

July 1829. Oliver Cowdery began making the printer's manuscript of the Book of Mormon.

17 August 1829. Joseph Smith and Martin Harris contracted with Egbert Grandin to publish five thousand copies of the Book of Mormon.

August 1829. Oliver Cowdery delivered the first pages of manuscript to the printer. Typesetting commenced and the first uncut sheets came off the press. Stephen Harding was given the first title page.

25 August 1829. Martin Harris mortgaged his farm for three thousand dollars to pay for the printing.

October 1829. Joseph Smith returned to Harmony, Pennsylvania.

6 November 1829. Oliver wrote to Joseph explaining that the printing was delayed because of sickness and because Grandin was waiting for additional type. Oliver was up to Alma 36 in the printer's manuscript.

16 January 1830. Joseph Smith, Sr., and Martin Harris entered an agreement that they would have equal privilege in selling the Book of Mormon until Grandin was paid.

December 1829–January 1830. Abner Cole illegally published extracts of the Book of Mormon in his *Reflector* newspaper.

January 1830. Grandin stopped printing because of a threatened boycott of the Book of Mormon. Joseph returned to Palmyra from Harmony to deal with Cole and to convince Grandin to complete the printing.

19 March 1830. Wayne Sentinel advertised that the Book of Mormon would be ready for sale in a week.

26 March 1830. Wayne Sentinel advertised that the Book of Mormon was for sale.

ENDNOTES

1. Lucy Mack Smith, *History of Joseph Smith*, ed. Preston Nibley (Salt Lake City: Bookcraft, 1958), p. 137.

2. Joseph Smith, 1832 History, p. 5, cited in Dean C. Jessee, ed., *The Personal Writings of Joseph Smith* (Salt Lake City: Deseret Book Co., 1984), p. 8; punctuation standardized.

3. Smith, *History of Joseph Smith*, p. 138.

4. In Smith, *History of Joseph Smith*, p. 139.

5. *Latter Day Saints' Messenger and Advocate*, Oct. 1834, p. 14; capitalization standardized; see also Joseph Smith—History 1:71n (LDS edition).

6. In *Messenger and Advocate*, Oct. 1834, p. 15; spelling standardized; see also Joseph Smith—History 1:71n (LDS edition).

7. *History of the Church*, 1:44.

8. See *History of the Church*, 1:48–49; *Millennial Star*, 9 Dec. 1878, p. 772; *Millennial Star*, 4 July 1881, pp. 422–23.

9. In Lucy Mack Smith, *History of Joseph Smith*, p. 148.

10. See Lucy Mack Smith, *History of Joseph Smith*, pp. 148–49.

11. See "Report of Elders Orson Pratt and Joseph F. Smith," *Millennial Star*, 9 Dec. 1878, p. 772.

12. "Report of Elders Orson Pratt and Joseph F. Smith," p. 772.

13. "Report of Elders Orson Pratt and Joseph F. Smith," pp. 772–73; spelling standardized.

14. Donald Q. Cannon and Lyndon W. Cook, eds., *Far West Record: Minutes of The Church of Jesus Christ of Latter-day Saints, 1830–1844* (Salt Lake City: Deseret Book Co., 1983), p. 23; capitalization standardized.

15. *History of the Church*, 1:315.

16. See Stan Larson, " 'A Most Sacred Possession': The Original Manuscript of the Book of Mormon," *Ensign*, Sept. 1977, p. 90.

17. Lucy Mack Smith, *History of Joseph Smith*, pp. 151–52.

18. *History of the Church*, 1:54–55.

19. In Lucy Mack Smith, *History of Joseph Smith*, p. 152.

20. *History of the Church*, 1:56–57.

21. See "The Testimony of Eight Witnesses" in the Book of Mormon.

22. See *History of the Church*, 1:58.

23. See *History of the Church*, 1:71.

24. See "Historic Discoveries at the Grandin Building," *Ensign*, July 1980, pp. 49–50.

25. See Lucy Mack Smith, *History of Joseph Smith*, p. 157.

26. *Wayne County Journal*, Lyons, New York, 6 May 1875; information obtained from Donald E. Enders, Joseph Smith, Sr., Family in Palmyra/Manchester, New York, research file, Museum of Church History and Art, Salt Lake City, Utah, 1989; spelling standardized.

27. See Lucy Mack Smith, *History of Joseph Smith*, pp. 164–66; Richard L. Bushman, *Joseph Smith and the Beginnings of Mormonism* (Chicago: University of Illinois Press, 1984), pp. 108–9; Russell R. Rich, "The Dogberry Papers and the Book of Mormon," *Brigham Young University Studies*, Spring 1970, pp. 315–20.

28. See Lucy Mack Smith, *History of Joseph Smith*, pp. 166–67.

29. See Wayne C. Gunnell, "Martin Harris—Witness and Benefactor to the Book of Mormon," Master's thesis, Brigham Young University, 1955, pp. 37–40.

ORGANIZATION OF THE CHURCH OF JESUS CHRIST

THE DATE OF 6 APRIL 1830 is significant to Latter-day Saints. The Church of Jesus Christ of Latter-day Saints was organized on that day. The organization of the Church climaxed a decade of preparation for the Prophet Joseph Smith, as Elder Gordon B. Hinckley pointed out:

"This day of organization was, in effect, a day of commencement, the graduation for Joseph from ten years of remarkable schooling. It had begun with the incomparable vision in the grove in the spring of 1820, when the Father and the Son appeared to the fourteen-year-old boy. It had continued with the tutoring from Moroni, with both warnings and instructions given on multiple occasions. Then there was the translation of the ancient record, and the inspiration, the knowledge, the revelation that came from that experience. There was the bestowal of divine authority, the ancient priesthood again conferred upon men by those who were its rightful possessors—John the Baptist in the case of the Aaronic Priesthood, and Peter, James, and John in the case of the Melchizedek. There were revelations, a number of them, in which the voice of God was heard again, and the channel of communication opened between man and the Creator. All of these were preliminary to that historic April 6."[1]

A DAY TO BE REMEMBERED

Shortly after Joseph Smith and Oliver Cowdery received the priesthood from heavenly messengers in 1829, they were shown in revelation "the precise day upon which, according to [God's] will and commandment, we should proceed to organize his church once again, here upon the earth."[2] Peter Whitmer, Sr., offered the use of his home for the organization meeting that was scheduled for Tuesday, 6 April, according to the revelation. At the appointed hour, close to sixty people assembled to witness the formal organization of the Church of Jesus Christ. Approximately twenty of these people had come from Colesville, a distance of approximately one hundred miles, to participate in the events of this sacred occasion.[3]

The meeting was simple. Joseph Smith, then twenty-four years old, called the group to order and designated five associates—Oliver Cowdery, Hyrum Smith, Peter Whitmer, Jr., Samuel H. Smith, and David Whitmer—to join him to meet New York's legal requirements for incorporating a religious society.[4] After kneeling in solemn prayer, Joseph asked those present if they were willing to accept him and Oliver as their teachers and spiritual

The reconstructed log home of Peter Whitmer in Fayette township, New York. Many important events took place in the Whitmer home: the testimony of the Three Witnesses was signed here, the Book of Mormon translation was completed here, the Church was organized here, and the Doctrine and Covenants records twenty revelations that were received here.

advisers. Everyone raised their hands in the affirmative. Although they had previously received the Melchizedek Priesthood, Joseph Smith and Oliver Cowdery then ordained each other to the office of elder. They did this to signify that they were elders in the newly organized church. The sacrament of the Lord's supper was administered next. The prayers used had been received through revelation (see D&C 20:75–79). Joseph and Oliver then confirmed those who had previously been baptized as members of the Church of Jesus Christ and bestowed upon them the gift of the Holy Ghost.

In a revelation received on this historic day, Joseph was designated "a seer, a translator, a prophet, an apostle of Jesus Christ" (D&C 21:1). The Lord instructed members of the infant Church to receive Joseph's word "as if from mine own mouth, in all patience and faith" (D&C 21:5).

The organization of the Church of Jesus Christ was an unforgettable occasion for those present. Joseph reported that "after a happy time spent in witnessing and feeling for ourselves the powers and blessings of the Holy Ghost, through the grace of God bestowed upon us, we dismissed with the pleasing knowledge that we were now individually members of, and acknowledged of God, 'The Church of Jesus Christ,' organized in accordance with commandments and revelations given by Him to ourselves in these last days, as well as according to the order of the Church as recorded in the New Testament."[5] Joseph also took opportunity to teach the Saints and bear his own testimony. Several individuals were baptized on that eventful day, including Orrin Porter Rockwell, Martin Harris, and Joseph Smith's parents. It was a time of joy and happiness in the life of the Prophet, who exclaimed, "Praise to my God! that I lived to see my own father baptized into the true Church of Jesus Christ!"[6]

On Sunday, 11 April, Oliver Cowdery delivered the Church's first public discourse in the Whitmer's Fayette home. Many people attended, and that same day six people were baptized. A week later seven more joined. Joseph Smith also received a revelation answering the question of the necessity of being baptized again when an individual has previously been baptized in another Church. The answer was: "Although a man should be baptized an hundred times it availeth him nothing, for you cannot enter in at the strait gate by the law of Moses, neither by your dead works" (D&C 22:2). The Lord affirmed that authority was essential to perform a valid baptism. The Church, then as now, provided all sincere believers in Christ and his gospel the organizational structure for receiving the saving ordinances, enjoying fellowship with other believers, being taught more perfectly in the principles of the gospel, and assisting in the saving of others.

THE PROPHET'S MINISTRY IN COLESVILLE

Later in the month of April, Joseph Smith visited Joseph Knight, Sr., in Colesville. The Knights were willing to reason with Joseph on religious matters and were quick to defend him against enemies. While in the Colesville area, Joseph held several meetings that were attended by many friends. Joseph related that "many began to pray fervently to Almighty God, that He would give them wisdom to understand the truth."

One of the people who regularly attended the meetings was Newel Knight, a close friend of the Prophet. Newel Knight was afraid to pray vocally, but he finally accepted the persuasive challenge of the Prophet to do so in the next meeting. When the moment arrived, Newel declined, promising that he would pray later in private. The next morning he went into the woods where he tried to pray, but he failed because he felt guilty for refusing to pray publicly. He began to feel uneasy and to grow ill, and he returned home, where his wife was alarmed by his appearance. Newel asked her to send for Joseph. When the Prophet arrived, Newel was "suffering very much in his mind, and his body acted upon in a very strange manner; his visage and limbs distorted and twisted in every shape and appearance possible to imagine; and finally he was caught up off the floor of the apartment [room], and tossed about most fearfully."

Neighbors and relatives gathered to witness the frightful scene. Joseph finally caught hold of Newel's hand. Newel said he knew he was possessed of the devil and he also knew that Joseph had the power to cast him out. Acting on Newel's faith as well as his own, Joseph commanded the devil to depart in the name of Jesus Christ. Newel immediately declared that he saw the devil leave him and vanish. This was regarded as the first miracle performed in the Church. Joseph affirmed that "it was done not by man, nor by the power of man, but it was done by God, and by the power of godliness."[7] Newel Knight's facial expressions returned to normal, and the distortions of his body ceased.

The three centers of the Church in New York in June of 1830: (1) Manchester township, (2) Fayette township, and (3) the Colesville area

The Spirit of the Lord came over Newel so that the visions of eternity were opened to him. In his weakened condition he was placed on his bed, but he said he felt himself "attracted upward, and remained for some time enwrapt in contemplation, insomuch that I knew not what was going on in the room." In this state his body was elevated until he felt the ceiling beams pressing against his shoulder and head.

Many of the people who saw these events were convinced of the power of God and later joined the Church. Joseph soon returned to Fayette. A few weeks later, Newel Knight came to Fayette and was baptized by David Whitmer.[8]

FIRST CONFERENCE OF THE CHURCH

By June 1830 the Saints in New York were located primarily in Manchester, Fayette, and Colesville. The membership of the Church at this point was about thirty people. Following revealed instructions (see D&C 20:75), the Prophet called them together for the first conference of the Church on 9 June, at Fayette. Many people attended who were either believers or were anxious to learn. Those assembled partook of the sacrament, and several recent converts were confirmed. Samuel H. Smith was ordained an elder, and Joseph Smith, Sr., and Hyrum were ordained priests. Ten brethren received "licenses," which were small documents certifying they were authorized to represent the Church (see D&C 20:64–65). Oliver

Joseph Smith, Sr., certificate of ordination as a priest signed by Joseph Smith, Jr., and Oliver Cowdery

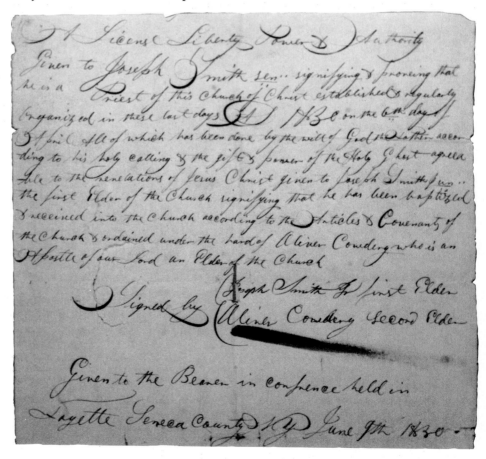

Cowdery kept the minutes of this meeting and was appointed by the conference to keep the official Church records.

Joseph Smith read to the congregation the "Articles and Covenants of the Church of Christ" (most of sections 20 and 22 of the Doctrine and Covenants), which contain significant instructions pertaining to the order of the Church.[9]

Joseph Smith wrote, "Much exhortation and instruction was given, and the Holy Ghost was poured out upon us in a miraculous manner—many of our number prophesied, whilst others had the heavens opened to their view." Newel Knight was filled with unspeakable love and peace. He saw a vision of the Savior and learned that he would someday be admitted into the presence of the Lord.

"Such scenes as these were calculated to inspire our hearts with joy unspeakable, and fill us with awe and reverence for that Almighty Being. . . . To find ourselves engaged in the very same order of things as observed by the holy Apostles of old; to realize the importance and solemnity of such proceedings; and to witness and feel with our own natural senses, the like glorious manifestations of the powers of the Priesthood, the gifts and blessings of the Holy Ghost, and the goodness and condescension of a merciful God unto such as obey the everlasting Gospel of our Lord Jesus Christ, combined to create within us sensations of rapturous gratitude, and inspire us with fresh zeal and energy in the cause of truth."[10]

Shortly after this conference twelve people were baptized in Seneca Lake by David Whitmer. They included Joseph Smith's sister Katherine and his brothers William and Don Carlos.

TRIBULATION AND JOY IN COLESVILLE

Immediately after the conference, Joseph Smith returned to his home in Harmony, Pennsylvania. In the latter part of June 1830, the Prophet, accompanied by his wife, Oliver Cowdery, and John and David Whitmer, visited the Knight family in Colesville, New York. Joseph Knight, Sr., who had read the Book of Mormon and was satisfied it was true, and a number of others in the area desired baptism. On Saturday, 26 June, the brethren dammed a stream to make a pond suitable for baptisms. That night a mob, incited by leaders of some area churches who feared losing members, demolished the dam. On Sunday the brethren proceeded with the meeting. Oliver preached and others bore witness of the truthfulness of the Book of Mormon and the doctrines of repentance, baptism for the remission of sins, and the laying on of hands for the gift of the Holy Ghost. Some members of the mob attended the meeting and afterward harassed those in attendance.

Early the next day, 28 June, the brethren repaired the dam and held the baptismal service. Thirteen people were baptized, including Emma Smith. Many neighbors mocked them, asking if they "had been washing sheep."[11] Quietly the Saints returned to Joseph Knight's residence and then to the home of Newel Knight, but their enemies followed them hurling insults and threatening to harm the new converts. A meeting was to be held that evening to confirm those who had been baptized, but before it could begin, Joseph Smith was arrested and taken to South Bainbridge in Chenango County for trial as a disorderly person. Mobs tried to intercept Joseph and the constable, but the officer succeeded in protecting the Prophet.

Joseph Knight, Sr., arranged for two neighbors, James Davidson and John Reid, men known for their integrity, to defend Joseph Smith in court the next day. The circulation of scandalous falsehoods about the Prophet attracted many boisterous spectators to the trial. Nevertheless, the testimonies of Josiah Stowell and two of his daughters were instrumental in achieving Joseph's acquittal. But the trial was no sooner over than a constable from Broome County arrested him again on the same charge.

Joseph reported: "The constable who served this second warrant upon me had no sooner arrested me than he began to abuse and insult me; and so unfeeling was he with me, that although I had been kept all the day in court without anything to eat since the morning, yet he hurried me off to Broome county, a distance of about fifteen miles, before he allowed me any kind of food whatever. He took me to a tavern, and gathered in a number of men, who used every means to abuse, ridicule and insult me. They spit upon me, pointed their fingers at me, saying, 'Prophesy, prophesy!' and thus did they imitate those who crucified the Savior of mankind, not knowing what they did."

In the trial the next morning, many witnesses swore to falsehoods against the Prophet, often contradicting themselves. When Newel Knight took the stand, Mr. Seymour, a prosecutor who was anxious to defy Mormonism, questioned Newel about the incident of the devil being cast out of him:

" 'And had not Joe Smith some hand in its being done?'

" 'Yes, sir.'

" 'And did not he cast him out of you?'

" 'No, sir; it was done by the power of God, and Joseph Smith was the instrument in the hands of God, on the occasion. He commanded him to come out of me in the name of Jesus Christ.'

" 'And are you sure that it was the devil?'

" 'Yes, sir.'

" 'Did you see him after he was cast out of you?'

" 'Yes, sir! I saw him.'

" 'Pray, what did he look like?'

". . . The witness replied:

" 'I believe I need not answer your last question, but I will do it, provided I be allowed to ask you one question first, and you answer me, viz., Do you, Mr. Seymour, understand the things of the spirit?'

" 'No,' answered Mr. Seymour, 'I do not pretend to such big things.'

" 'Well, then,' replied Knight, 'it would be of no use to tell you what the devil looked like, for it was a spiritual sight, and spiritually discerned; and of course you would not understand it were I to tell you of it.'

"The lawyer dropped his head, whilst the loud laugh of the audience proclaimed his discomfiture. . . .

". . . These men [James Davidson and John Reid], although not regular lawyers, were upon this occasion able to put to silence their opponents, and convince the court that I was innocent. They spoke like men inspired of God."[12] The Prophet was again acquitted, but mobs harassed him until he found safety at his wife's sister's house and later at his home in Harmony.

A few days later Joseph Smith returned to Colesville with Oliver Cowdery to confirm those who had been baptized; they had scarcely arrived when a mob began to gather. They thought it best to leave, without even taking time to rest. Joseph and Oliver barely escaped the mob that pursued them throughout the night. Joseph said, "Thus were we persecuted on account of our religious faith—in a country the Constitution of which guarantees to every man the indefeasible right to worship God according to the dictates of his own conscience—and by men, too, who were professors of religion, and who were not backward to maintain the right of religious liberty for themselves, though they could thus wantonly deny it to us."[13]

Meanwhile the Saints in Colesville prayed that Joseph and Oliver would again come to visit them. The Prophet's return to Colesville in early August involved a miracle. Because hostile feelings persisted, Joseph and Hyrum Smith and John and David Whitmer prayed mightily before their journey, and as Newel Knight declared, "their prayers were not in vain. A little distance from my house they encountered a large company of men at work upon the public road, amongst whom were some of our most bitter enemies who looked earnestly at the brethren but not knowing them, the brethren passed on unmolested."[14] The confirmations that followed and the partaking of the sacrament together was a joyful interlude between troubles.

Throughout these tribulations, the Lord sustained the Prophet and revealed fundamental truths of Latter-day Saint theology and practice. Among these truths were the "visions of Moses," comprising chapter 1 of the book of Moses in the Pearl of Great Price, which set forth the nature and extent of God's work (see Moses 1:33, 39) and exposed Satan as the source of opposition to righteousness. Throughout the summer Joseph studied the book of Genesis in the Old Testament. This study formed the basis for the book of Moses and much of his "inspired translation" of the Bible, which is now known as the Joseph Smith Translation.[15]

Other revelations were received during July telling Joseph to be patient in his afflictions and instructing him to continue in prayer and "in writing the things which shall be given thee by the Comforter, and expounding all scriptures unto the church. . . .

"For thou shalt devote all thy service in Zion; and in this thou shalt have strength. . . .

"And in temporal affairs thou shalt not have strength" (D&C 24:5, 7, 9). Joseph's calling was as a prophet; he was not to be directly concerned about providing for his own temporal needs. This was not an easy sacrifice for him or his family. He was also counseled to let his "time be devoted to the study-ing of the scriptures [an allusion to his inspired translation of the Bible], and to preaching, and to confirming the church at Colesville, and to performing your labors on the land, such as is required, until after you shall go to the west to hold the next conference; and then it shall be made known what you shall do" (D&C 26:1). This conference would take place in September in Fayette.

In July, Joseph received a revelation for his wife, Emma (see D&C 25). She was designated "an elect lady" (v. 1) and comforted in her afflictions. She was also directed to compile the first hymnbook for the Church. The hymns she compiled, and others written since that time, represent an impor-tant expression of faith for the Latter-day Saints. Speaking of the importance of music in our dispensation, the Lord said, "my soul delighteth in the song of the heart; yea, the song of the righteous is a prayer unto me, and it shall be answered with a blessing upon their heads" (v. 12).

When the Prophet returned to Harmony in August, he received an important revelation concerning sacramental emblems. Newel Knight and his wife, Sally, had gone to Harmony to visit Joseph and Emma. Neither of the women had been confirmed members of the Church, so the two couples, together with John Whitmer, decided to attend to this ordinance and to partake of the sacrament. Joseph went to obtain some wine for the occasion, but he had gone only a short distance when he was met by a heavenly messenger. The angel told him that it did not matter what was eaten or drunk in the sacrament as long as the ordinance was performed with an eye single to the glory of God. Joseph was also warned not to purchase wine from enemies (see D&C 27:2–4). In obedience to this charge, the small group used some wine of their own making and held a meeting. They spent the evening in "a glorious manner," as the Spirit was abundantly poured out upon them.[16]

EARLY MISSIONARY LABORS AND CONVERSIONS

While these events transpired in Colesville and Harmony during the summer of 1830, missionary work was also underway in other parts of New York State. People had shared the gospel with family, friends, and neighbors even before the Church was organized. More than one aspiring missionary had been told through revelation: "Behold, the field is white already to harvest; therefore, whoso desireth to reap, let him thrust in his sickle with his might, and reap while the day lasts, that he may treasure up for his soul everlasting salvation in the kingdom of God" (D&C 6:3; see also 4:4; 11:3; 12:3; 14:3).

Once printing of the Book of Mormon started, public interest in Joseph Smith and Mormonism increased. Rumors flourished about the gold book being printed in Palmyra. One man who heard the rumors was Thomas B. Marsh of Boston, who later became the first president of the Quorum of the Twelve Apostles. His curiosity led him to Grandin's print shop; there he met

Brigham Young and his brother Phineas. John P. Greene and Phineas Young joined the Church as a result of Samuel Smith's missionary labors. Samuel was also indirectly responsible for the conversion of Brigham Young and Heber C. Kimball through the copy of the Book of Mormon given to Phineas Young.

Martin Harris, who gave him proof sheets of the first sixteen printed pages of the Book of Mormon and then accompanied him to the Smith home in Manchester. Oliver Cowdery spent portions of two days telling him about Joseph and the Restoration. Thomas returned to Massachusetts and taught his family about the new work. When he heard the Church had been organized, he moved his family to Palmyra. In September 1830 he was baptized and called on a mission (see D&C 31).

Samuel H. Smith, the Prophet's younger brother, was ordained an elder at the first conference of the Church on 9 June 1830 and was soon taking summer trips into neighboring counties, alone or with his parents, to sell the Book of Mormon. He was often discouraged because his efforts were for the most part rejected. He did, however, leave one copy of the Book of Mormon with a Reverend John P. Greene, who, although not interested in reading it himself, said he would ask his parishioners whether they would like to buy a copy. Three weeks later Samuel went again to see Reverend Greene, but he had not returned from his circuit tour. His wife, Rhoda, said that the book had not sold but that she had read the book and liked it. Samuel left the book with her, and later her husband read it and was converted.

Phineas Young, a brother of Rhoda Young Greene, had bought a copy of the Book of Mormon from Samuel earlier in April 1830 when he met Samuel returning from Lima, New York, where he had been preaching. He gave the Book of Mormon to Brigham Young, who gave it to his sister, Fanny Young Murray, the mother-in-law of Heber C. Kimball. After intense study these men and their families were baptized into the Church. Brigham Young spent two years in study and comparison before he was baptized in April 1832. Hence, Samuel Smith's early missionary labors resulted in some of the most influential converts of the early Church. He was a dedicated missionary who labored in New York, New England, Ohio, and Missouri converting scores of people and organizing several branches of the Church.

Joseph Smith, Sr., also thrust his sickle into "ripe fields" that first summer. With his fourteen-year-old son, Don Carlos, he preached to his father's family in St. Lawrence County, and his message was received with joy. Asael's son John, brother of Joseph, Sr., also accepted the gospel, as did John's son George A. Smith, who later became one of the twelve Apostles. Thus, three generations were united in the faith of the Restoration.

Twenty-three-year-old Parley P. Pratt was another New York convert that summer. Parley had settled in the wilderness of northeastern Ohio, and there he joined a group of restorationists (disciples or Campbellites) under Sidney Rigdon's leadership. In the summer of 1830, as Parley journeyed by canal through New York to visit relatives, the Spirit prompted him to send his wife, Thankful, on ahead so he could stop to preach his religious ideas near Palmyra at the village of Newark. A Baptist deacon told him about the Book of Mormon and let him read it. With eagerness he read the title page and the testimony of the witnesses and began to read the text. He recounted the following:

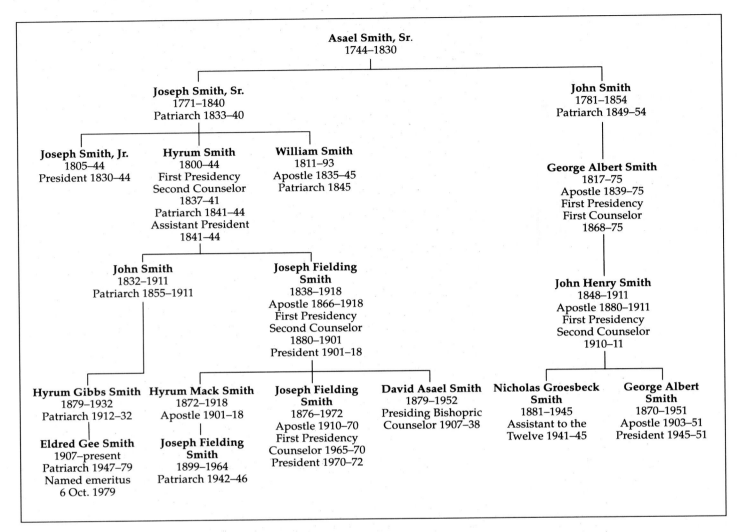

Asael Smith, Sr.
1744–1830

Joseph Smith, Sr.
1771–1840
Patriarch 1833–40

John Smith
1781–1854
Patriarch 1849–54

Joseph Smith, Jr.
1805–44
President 1830–44

Hyrum Smith
1800–44
First Presidency
Second Counselor
1837–41
Patriarch 1841–44
Assistant President
1841–44

William Smith
1811–93
Apostle 1835–45
Patriarch 1845

George Albert Smith
1817–75
Apostle 1839–75
First Presidency
First Counselor
1868–75

John Smith
1832–1911
Patriarch 1855–1911

Joseph Fielding Smith
1838–1918
Apostle 1866–1918
First Presidency
Second Counselor
1880–1901
President 1901–18

John Henry Smith
1848–1911
Apostle 1880–1911
First Presidency
Second Counselor
1910–11

Hyrum Gibbs Smith
1879–1932
Patriarch 1912–32

Eldred Gee Smith
1907–present
Patriarch 1947–79
Named emeritus
6 Oct. 1979

Hyrum Mack Smith
1872–1918
Apostle 1901–18

Joseph Fielding Smith
1899–1964
Patriarch 1942–46

Joseph Fielding Smith
1876–1972
Apostle 1910–70
First Presidency
Counselor 1965–70
President 1970–72

David Asael Smith
1879–1952
Presiding Bishopric
Counselor 1907–38

Nicholas Groesbeck Smith
1881–1945
Assistant to the
Twelve 1941–45

George Albert Smith
1870–1951
Apostle 1903–51
President 1945–51

Asael Smith's family, showing subsequent leaders of the Church

"I read all day; eating was a burden, I had no desire for food; sleep was a burden when the night came, for I preferred reading to sleep.

"As I read, the spirit of the Lord was upon me, and I knew and comprehended that the book was true, as plainly and manifestly as a man comprehends and knows that he exists. My joy was now full, as it were, and I rejoiced sufficiently to more than pay me for all the sorrows, sacrifices and toils of my life. I soon determined to see the young man who had been the instrument of its discovery and translation.

"I accordingly visited the village of Palmyra, and inquired for the residence of Mr. Joseph Smith. I found it some two or three miles from the village. As I approached the house at the close of the day I overtook a man who was driving some cows. . . . It was Hyrum Smith. I informed him of the interest I felt in the Book of Mormon, and of my desire to learn more about it. He welcomed me to his house. . . . We conversed most of the night, during which I unfolded to him much of my experience in my search after truth, and my success so far; together with that which I felt was lacking, viz. a commissioned priesthood, or apostleship to minister in the ordinances of God."[17]

Parley P. Pratt (1807–57), converted through the Book of Mormon, became one of the Church's leading theologians and a member of the first Quorum of the Twelve Apostles. He was assassinated in Arkansas in 1857.

Orson Pratt (1811–81)—missionary, scholar, Church historian, and Apostle

Hyrum continued to teach Parley, and they soon journeyed to Fayette to meet the Whitmers and other members of the growing branch of the Church. Parley was baptized and ordained an elder by Oliver Cowdery in September 1830. Invested with authority, Parley traveled to his boyhood home in Columbia County, New York, where he addressed large audiences each day, but only his brother Orson accepted the message. Orson was baptized on his nineteenth birthday and left within two weeks to meet the Prophet Joseph Smith in Fayette.

THE PROPHET'S MOVE TO FAYETTE

Meanwhile in Harmony, Joseph Smith, assisted by John Whitmer, began to arrange and copy the revelations Joseph had received. While engaged in this project, Joseph received a letter from Oliver Cowdery that grieved him. Oliver said he had discovered the following error of language in one of the revelations: "and truly manifest by their works that they have received of the Spirit of Christ unto the remission of their sins" (D&C 20:37). Believing that his position as the second elder in the Church authorized him to do so, Oliver wrote to Joseph. Joseph reported:

"The . . . quotation, he said, was erroneous, and added: 'I command you in the name of God to erase those words, that no priestcraft be amongst us!'

"I immediately wrote to him in reply, in which I asked him by what authority he took upon him to command me to alter or erase, to add to or diminish from, a revelation or commandment from Almighty God."

About this time a Methodist minister convinced Isaac Hale of many falsehoods about his son-in-law. As a result, life became unbearable for Joseph and his family in Harmony. Therefore, Joseph began to make preparations to permanently move to Fayette where he had been invited to live with Peter Whitmer, Sr., again. In late August, Newel Knight took his team and wagon to Harmony to move Joseph and his family to Fayette. Upon arriving there, Joseph discovered that the Whitmers agreed with Oliver Cowdery about the supposed error in the revelation. Joseph noted, "It was not without both labor and perseverance that I could prevail with any of them to reason calmly on the subject. However, Christian Whitmer at length became convinced that the sentence was reasonable, and according to Scripture; and finally, with his assistance, I succeeded in bringing, not only the Whitmer family, but also Oliver Cowdery to acknowledge that they had been in error, and that the sentence in dispute was in accordance with the rest of the commandment."[18]

In Fayette Joseph encountered another serious problem regarding revelation. Hiram Page, one of the Eight Witnesses and a brother-in-law to the Whitmers, possessed a certain stone through which he received what he called revelations about the building of Zion and the order of the Church. Joseph insisted that these claims "were entirely at variance with the order of God's house, as laid down in the New Testament, as well as in our late revelations."[19] Since a conference was scheduled for 26 September, the

Prophet decided not to do more than talk with the brethren about the subject until the conference met. Many people, especially Oliver Cowdery and the Whitmers, believed in the claims of Hiram Page.

The Prophet turned to the Lord in prayer and received a revelation directed to Oliver Cowdery in which he was charged not to command Joseph Smith, the leader of the Church. The Lord made it clear that only the President of the Church has the right to receive revelations for the Church (see D&C 28:2). He also was told that the location of the city of Zion had not yet been revealed, but would be in due time (see v. 9). Furthermore, Oliver was instructed to go to Hiram Page and convince him that the stone and the purported revelations came from Satan (see v. 11). At the scheduled September conference, Hiram Page's stone was discussed; those present, including Hiram, renounced it and the "revelations" received through it as false. The conference also voted that Joseph Smith was to "receive and write Revelations & Commandments for this Church."[20] In all, the conference lasted three days. Joseph testified that "much of the power of God manifested amongst us; the Holy Ghost came upon us, and filled us with joy unspeakable; and peace, and faith, and hope, and charity abounded in our midst."[21]

ENDNOTES

1. "150-Year Drama: A Personal View of Our History," *Ensign*, Apr. 1980, pp. 11–12.

2. "History of Joseph Smith," *Times and Seasons*, 1 Oct. 1842, pp. 928–29.

3. See letter from Edward Stevenson to F. D. Richards, 10 Jan. 1887, cited in *Journal of Edward Stevenson*, 1886, vol. 3, LDS Historical Department, Salt Lake City.

4. See Larry C. Porter, "A Study of the Origins of The Church of Jesus Christ of Latter-day Saints in the States of New York and Pennsylvania, 1816–1831," Ph.D. diss., Brigham Young University, 1971, pp. 374–86.

5. *History of the Church*, 1:79.

6. In Lucy Mack Smith, *History of Joseph Smith*, ed. Preston Nibley (Salt Lake City: Bookcraft, 1958), p. 168; see also *History of the Church*, 1:79.

7. *History of the Church*, 1:81–83.

8. *History of the Church*, 1:83–84.

9. See Donald Q. Cannon and Lyndon W. Cook, eds., *Far West Record: Minutes of The Church of Jesus Christ of Latter-day Saints, 1830–1844* (Salt Lake City: Deseret Book Co., 1983), pp. 1–3.

10. *History of the Church*, 1:84–86.

11. Joseph Knight, Jr., "Joseph Knight's Incidents of History from 1827 to 1844," comp. Thomas Bullock, from loose sheets in Joseph Knight's possession, LDS Historical Department, Salt Lake City, p. 2; see also *History of the Church*, 1:87–88.

12. *History of the Church*, 1:91–94.

13. *History of the Church*, 1:97.

14. Newel Knight's Journal, typescript, LDS Historical Department, Salt Lake City, p. 11; see also Larry C. Porter, "The Joseph Knight Family," *Ensign*, Oct. 1978, p. 42.

15. See Robert J. Matthews, "A Plainer Translation," *Joseph Smith's Translation of the Bible: A History and Commentary* (Provo: Brigham Young University Press, 1975), pp. 25–26.

16. See *History of the Church*, 1:108.

17. Parley P. Pratt, ed., *Autobiography of Parley P. Pratt*, Classics in Mormon Literature series (Salt Lake City: Deseret Book Co., 1985), pp. 20–22.

18. *History of the Church*, 1:105.

19. *History of the Church*, 1:110.

20. In Cannon and Cook, *Far West Record*, p. 3; see also Doctrine and Covenants 21.

21. *History of the Church*, 1:115.

THE INFANT CHURCH EXPANDS

Indian territory at the time of the first Lamanite mission. Several of these "reservations" were created and occupied prior to President Andrew Jackson's 1830 Indian Removal Act.

S INCE EARLY 1830 the Latter-day Saints have acknowledged the American Indian as a remnant of the house of Israel, who great promises have been extended to. Referring to these people as "Lamanites," a Book of Mormon prophet declared, "At some period of time they will be brought to believe in his [God's] word, and to know of the incorrectness of the traditions of their fathers; and many of them will be saved" (Alma 9:17). The 1830 Saints believed these promises and were moved since the early days of the Church to bring to pass their fulfillment.

CALL TO TEACH THE LAMANITES

The Church was barely six months old when Oliver Cowdery was called by revelation to go to the Lamanites and preach the gospel (see D&C 28:8). Subsequently Peter Whitmer, Jr., Ziba Peterson, and Parley P. Pratt were called to assist him (see D&C 30:5; 32:1–3). The destination of the missionaries was "the borders by the Lamanites" (D&C 28:9). This phrase was

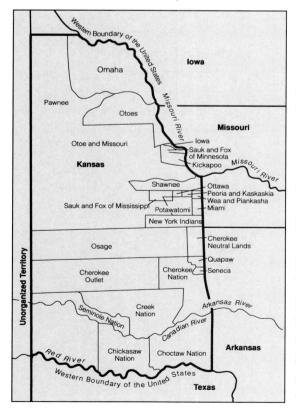

understood to refer to the line between Missouri and the Indian territory to the west. For more than twenty years many Americans had agitated for the removal of Indians from the Eastern States to a permanent Indian frontier in the plains beyond. As a result of this agitation, less than four months before the call of the missionaries, President Andrew Jackson signed into law the "Indian Removal Act." The Shawnee and Delaware Indians from Ohio, anticipating these developments, made the move on their own as early as 1828–29. Both tribes settled near the Kansas River just west of the Missouri border.

time, that thou shalt go, until the time that thou shalt
return, what thou shalt do; and thou must open thy
mouth at all times, declaring my Gospel with the
sound of rejoicing.—Amen.

MANCHESTER, Oct. 17, 1830.

I, Oliver, being commanded of the Lord God, to go
forth unto the Lamanites, to proclaim glad tidings of
great joy unto them, by presenting unto them the fulness of the Gospel, of the only begotten son of God;
and also, to rear up a pillar as a witness where the
Temple of God shall be built, in the glorious New-Je-
rusalem; and having certain brothers with me, who
are called of God to assist me, whose names are Parley, Peter and Ziba, do therefore most solemnly covenant before God, that I will walk humbly before
him, and do this business, and this glorious work according as he shall direct me by the Holy Ghost; ever praying for mine and their prosperity, and deliverance from bonds, and from imprisonments, and whatsoever may befal us, with all patience and faith.—
Amen.   OLIVER COWDERY.

We, the undersigned, being called and commanded
of the Lord God, to accompany our Brother Oliver
Cowdery, to go to the Lamanites, and to assist in the
above mentioned glorious work and business. We
do, therefore, most solemnly covenant before God, that
we will assist him faithfully in this thing, by giving
heed unto all his words and advice, which is, or shall
be given him by the spirit of truth, ever praying with
all prayer and supplication, for our and his prosperity, and our deliverance from bonds, and imprisonments, and whatsoever may come upon us, with all
patience and faith.—Amen.

Signed in presence of

JOSEPH SMITH, Jun.
DAVID WHITMER,
P. P. PRATT,
ZIBA PETERSON,
PETER WHITMER.

*Shortly after their call, the missionar-
ies to the Lamanites signed a covenant
of cooperation before leaving New York.
The original has not been found, but
scholars believe that this transcription
printed in the Ravenna, Ohio Star, on
8 December 1831 is an accurate representation of the agreement.*

*Missionaries to the Lamanites trudg-
ing through the snow*

Following the second conference of the Church, preparations for the
missionary journey began in earnest. Emma Smith and several other sisters
made arrangements to furnish the missionaries with necessary clothing.
Even though Emma was not well, she spent many hours sewing suitable
clothing for each missionary. Saints in the Fayette, New York, area generously furnished food, and Martin Harris supplied copies of the Book of
Mormon for distribution. Before departing, the missionaries bound
themselves in writing to give "heed unto all [the] words and advice" of
Oliver Cowdery. They pledged to proclaim the "fulness of the Gospel" to
their brethren, the Lamanites.[1] On 18 October they began their fifteen-
hundred-mile westward trek.

EARLY SUCCESS ON THE WESTERN RESERVE

The missionaries visited a friendly tribe of Seneca Indians on the
Cattaraugus Reservation near Buffalo, New York, where they paused just
long enough to introduce the Book of Mormon as a record of their forgotten
ancestors. "We were kindly received, and much interest was manifested
by them on hearing this news," Parley reported.[2] Leaving two copies of
the book, the missionaries journeyed onward. So far as is known, these were
the first American Indians to hear the message of the Restoration in this
dispensation.

When the elders arrived in northeastern Ohio, they reached an area
popularly known as the Western Reserve because in colonial times it was
allotted to Connecticut as a "western reserve." Parley P. Pratt was familiar
with this country, having lived at Amherst, fifty miles west of Kirtland, for
about four years before his conversion to the Church. Parley had studied
under Sidney Rigdon, a prominent minister in the area who presided over a
group of *seekers* (people seeking a return to New Testament Christianity). At
one time Sidney merged his interests with those of another seeker,
Alexander Campbell, and helped found the church called the Disciples of
Christ, also known as the Campbellites. But Rigdon disagreed with
Campbell on certain doctrinal practices and formed his own group, the
Reformed Baptist Society. Because of his former close associations with
Rigdon, Elder Pratt convinced his companions to visit Sidney in Mentor,

Some colonial charters allowed the colonies to claim extensive tracts of western land. As pointed out in the text, Ohio's "Western Reserve" derived its name from the fact that it was part of Connecticut's claim in the West. It consisted of eight northeastern Ohio counties.

John Murdock (1792–1871) was a missionary, bishop, pioneer of 1847, member of Salt Lake high council, and patriarch.

Ohio, where he testified to his former teacher that the Restoration had occurred, including the restoration of divine authority. Oliver Cowdery, an eyewitness to the restoration of the priesthood, bore firsthand testimony of that event.

Although Sidney treated the missionaries cordially and with respect, his was no instantaneous conversion. He told the elders, "I will read your book, and see what claims it has upon my faith." The elders then asked to present their message in Rigdon's church. Consent was given, "the appointment was accordingly published, and a large and respectable congregation assembled." At the end of the meeting, Rigdon, with commendable open-mindedness, told his listeners that the message they had just heard "was of an extraordinary character, and certainly demanded their most serious consideration." He reminded the congregation of the Apostle Paul's advice to "prove all things; hold fast that which is good" (1 Thessalonians 5:21).[3]

Meanwhile, the elders were not idle. Less than five miles from Rigdon's home in Mentor was the village of Kirtland, where numerous members of Sidney's congregation lived. The missionaries preached from house to house, likewise receiving respectful attention. Soon some residents were convinced that no one among them possessed the divine authority necessary to administer gospel ordinances and that they had not been authoritatively baptized themselves. After much study and prayer, many people, including Sidney Rigdon, requested baptism at the hands of the missionaries. News of their teachings spread rapidly. Parley reported, "The people thronged us night and day, insomuch that we had no time for rest and retirement. Meetings were convened in different neighborhoods, and multitudes came together soliciting our attendance; while thousands flocked about us daily; some to be taught, some for curiosity, some to obey the gospel, and some to dispute or resist it."[4]

Within three weeks of the missionaries' arrival, 127 persons were baptized. Prominent among the number were Isaac Morley, Levi Hancock, Lyman Wight, and John Murdock, well-known residents of the area who were destined to play an important role in future Church affairs. In reminiscing later about his own baptism and its affect upon him, John Murdock wrote that "the Spirit of the Lord sensibly attended the ministration, and I came out of the water rejoicing and singing praises to God, and the Lamb."[5]

Another early Ohio convert, Philo Dibble, who lived about five miles east of Kirtland, was told of a "golden Bible." Curious, he sought out the missionaries and, after hearing Oliver Cowdery speak, believed and presented himself for baptism. His description of the spiritual power attending his reception of the Holy Ghost may be a clue to why so many early Saints found joy in the Restoration:

"When I came out of the water, I knew that I had been born of water and of the spirit, for my mind was illuminated with the Holy Ghost.

". . . While in bed that night I felt what appeared to be a hand upon my left

Frederick G. Williams (1787–1842) was the Prophet Joseph Smith's family physician, counselor, and friend. He was always very liberal in his contributions to the Church. After his death, his wife, son, and daughter-in-law emigrated to Utah with the Saints.

shoulder and a sensation like fibers of fire immediately enveloped my body. . . . I was enveloped in a heavenly influence, and could not sleep for joy."[6]

The brief stopover the missionaries made in the Western Reserve that November bore immediate and lasting fruits. These Ohio conversions more than doubled Church membership in only three weeks. It was as the Lord had promised the Saints by revelation: "For behold the field is white already to harvest; and lo, he that thrusteth in his sickle with his might, the same layeth up in store that he perisheth not, but bringeth salvation to his soul" (D&C 4:4; see also 11:3; 12:3). The missionaries ordained Sidney Rigdon and a few others and left them in charge of the ministry. In company with Frederick G. Williams, who had practiced medicine in Kirtland prior to his conversion, they continued their westward journey toward the "border of the Lamanites."

A VISIT TO THE PROPHET IN NEW YORK

Shortly after the missionaries left Kirtland, Sidney Rigdon and a close associate, Edward Partridge, decided to go to New York "to inquire further" into the origins of the restored gospel that had just been introduced to them. Lydia Partridge wrote, "My husband partly believed, but he had to take a journey to New York State and see the Prophet" before he could be satisfied.[7] According to Philo Dibble, Partridge also went in behalf of others. He was told by a neighbor, "We have sent a man down to York State to find out the truth of this work, and he is a man who will not lie."[8]

Arriving in Manchester, New York, in December 1830, Sidney and Edward learned that Joseph was living with the Whitmers in Fayette township, twenty miles away. Upon inquiring among the neighbors concerning the Smith family, they found that their reputation had been impeccable until Joseph had made known his discovery of the Book of Mormon. They also noted the good order and evident industry of the family farm. Edward and Sidney found the Prophet at his parents' place in Waterloo, where Edward asked Joseph Smith to baptize him.[9] Four days later Edward was ordained an elder by Sidney Rigdon, his friend and traveling companion.

Joseph Smith was impressed with Sidney and Edward from the first. He referred to the latter as "a pattern of piety, and one of the Lord's great men."[10] Shortly after Edward's baptism, the Prophet received revelations setting forth the duties and callings of both men. Because of his influence upon his followers, the Lord compared Sidney to John the Baptist, who had prepared the way for Jesus Christ. Sidney's new assignment was to serve as scribe for Joseph Smith (see D&C 35:4, 20). Edward was called to preach the gospel "as with the voice of a trump" (D&C 36:1). Joseph Smith and Sidney Rigdon were admonished to strengthen the Church wherever it was found, but "more especially in Colesville; for, behold, they pray unto me in much faith" (D&C 37:2).

The faith of the Colesville Saints was rewarded with a visit from the Prophet and his new associate, Sidney Rigdon. Here Sidney's oratorical gifts were first evidenced in the Church as he obeyed the command he had received by revelation to "preach my gospel and call on the holy prophets to prove his words" (D&C 35:23). He delivered an effective and powerful sermon.

The New York Saints were also blessed by important doctrinal revelations given to Joseph Smith. Between June and October 1830 he worked on an inspired revision of the book of Genesis. Joseph said that at the time "much conjecture and conversation frequently occurred among the Saints, concerning the books mentioned, and referred to, in various places in the Old and New Testaments, which were now nowhere to be found. The common remark was, 'They are *lost books*'; but it seems the Apostolic Church had some of these writings, as Jude mentions or quotes the Prophecy of Enoch, the seventh from Adam."[11] To the joy of the Church, which now numbered about seventy in New York, the Lord revealed a portion of the ancient book of Enoch, which included a lengthy prophecy about the future. Through this account, now found in Moses 7 in the Pearl of Great Price, the Lord "encouraged and strengthened the faith of His little flock . . . by giving some more extended information upon the Scriptures" than was previously known.[12]

Journey to Missouri

Meanwhile, the five missionaries to the Indians continued to preach to all people as they proceeded westward. Parley P. Pratt wrote, "Some wished to learn and obey the fulness of the gospel. . . . Others were filled with envy, rage and lying."[13]

Fifty miles west of Kirtland, Parley was arrested on a frivolous charge, tried, found guilty, and ordered to pay a fine. Because he could not pay, Parley spent the night locked in a public inn. The next morning, he was visited briefly by his companions and urged them to move ahead on their journey, promising to soon rejoin them. Parley reported: "After sitting awhile by the fire in charge of the officer, I requested to step out. I walked out into the public square accompanied by him. Said I, 'Mr. Peabody, are you good at a race?' 'No,' said he, 'but my big bull dog is, and he has been trained to assist me in my office these several years; he will take any man down at my bidding.' 'Well, Mr. Peabody, you compelled me to go a mile, I have gone with you two miles. You have given me an opportunity to preach, sing, and have also entertained me with lodging and breakfast. I must now go on my journey; if you are good at a race you can accompany me. I thank you for all your kindness—good day, sir.'

"I then started on my journey, while he stood amazed and not able to step one foot before the other. . . . He did not awake from his astonishment sufficiently to start in pursuit till I had gained, perhaps, two hundred yards.

. . . He now came hallooing after me, and shouting to his dog to seize me. The dog, being one of the largest I ever saw, came close on my footsteps with all his fury; the officer behind still in pursuit, clapping his hands and hallooing, 'stu-boy, stu-boy—take him—watch—lay hold of him, I say—down with him,' and pointing his finger in the direction I was running. The dog was fast overtaking me, and in the act of leaping upon me, when, quick as lightning, the thought struck me, to assist the officer, in sending the dog with all fury to the forest a little distance before me. I pointed my finger in that direction,

The missionaries traveled approximately fifteen hundred miles during the fall and winter of 1830–31 to bring the gospel to the Lamanites who had been relocated west of Missouri. The trip was made on foot, except for a steamboat ride between Cincinnati, Ohio, and Cairo, Illinois.

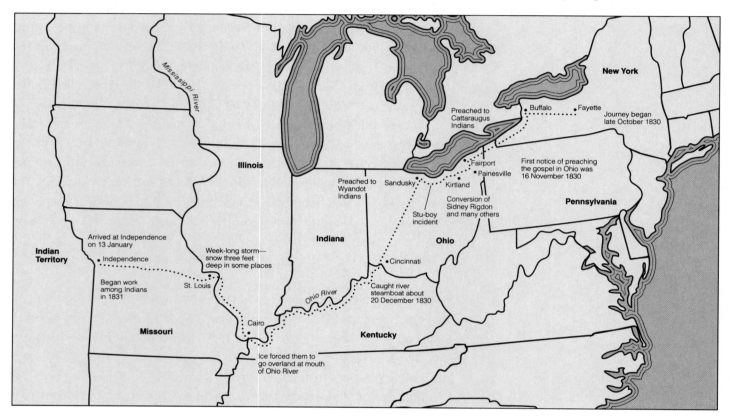

clapped my hands, and shouted in imitation of the officer. The dog hastened past me with redoubled speed towards the forest; being urged by the officer and myself, and both of us running in the same direction."

Having eluded both the dog and the officer, Elder Pratt rejoined his companions via an alternate route. Parley later learned that Simeon Carter, who he had left a Book of Mormon with, along with about sixty others in that area had joined the Church and formed a branch.[14]

The missionaries had not forgotten their charge to teach the gospel to Native Americans. At Sandusky, Ohio, they stopped for several days among the Wyandot Indians. Parley wrote, "They rejoiced in the tidings, bid us God speed, and desired us to write to them in relation to our success among the tribes further west."[15]

It was winter when the intrepid missionaries left Sandusky for Cincinnati, and they walked all the way. The winter of 1830–31 is known in midwest annals as the winter of the deep snow. The latter part of December 1830 was "bitter cold, a blinding, swirling blur of snow, and leaden, lowering skies, combined to make this storm a thing to paralyze that prairie country. It seems to have continued for days, unabated—a wonder, at first, then a terror, a benumbing horror as it became a menace to [the] life of men and animals."[16] In Cincinnati, Ohio, five days before Christmas, the elders boarded a steamboat bound for St. Louis. Ice floes, however, choked the Ohio River, compelling them to disembark in Cairo, Illinois, and continue on foot. Twenty miles from St. Louis, a howling storm of rain and snow forced a week's delay and left snow nearly three feet deep in some places.

Slowly they pressed westward, trudging through the knee-deep snow for whole days without a house or a fire, "the bleak northwest wind always blowing in our faces with a keenness which would almost take the skin off," wrote Parley. The cold was so intense that the snow did not melt, even at midday on the south side of the houses, for nearly six weeks. For three hundred miles they carried their clothes, books, and food in knapsacks on their backs. All they had to eat was frozen corn bread and raw pork. Parley said the bread was "so frozen that we could not bite or penetrate any part of it but the outside crust." For a month and a half they endured fatigue and suffering as they traveled from Kirtland to Independence. On 13 January 1831 the missionaries arrived in Independence, Missouri, the extreme western frontier of the United States.[17]

TEACHING THE GOSPEL

Nearing their destination, the missionaries took up residence in the home of Colonel Robert Patterson on the western boundary of Missouri while waiting for the weather to moderate. About 1 February, Peter Whitmer and Ziba Peterson set up a tailor shop in Independence to earn needed funds while Oliver Cowdery, Parley P. Pratt, and Frederick G. Williams entered Indian lands to preach and introduce the Book of Mormon.[18]

They found a listener in William Anderson, the aged chief of the Delawares, son of a Scandinavian father and an Indian mother. The chief had been unwilling to listen to other Christians, but he was finally persuaded to hear the missionaries. With about forty tribal leaders comfortably seated in the chief's lodge, Oliver Cowdery was invited to speak. He quickly gained their confidence as he recounted the long and difficult trip from the East to bring news of the Book of Mormon to them. He acknowledged the Indians' present plight: once they were many, now they were few; once their possessions were great, now they were small. Skillfully he wove the Book of Mormon story into his narrative: "Thousands of moons ago, when the red men's forefathers dwelt in peace and possessed this whole land, the Great Spirit talked with them, and revealed His law and His will, and much knowledge to their wise men and prophets." Oliver told them that this, their

William Clark (1770–1838). After returning from his epic exploration of the Louisiana Purchase with Meriweather Lewis, William Clark was made Indian agent for the tribes of the Louisiana Territory by President Thomas Jefferson. Clark spent most of the rest of his life as a government Indian official. He became Superintendent of Indian Affairs in 1822 and was in this position when Oliver Cowdery wrote to him.

history, and prophecies of the "things which should befall their children in the latter days" were written in a book. He promised that if they would receive and follow this book, their "Great Father" would make them prosperous again and return them to their former greatness. He explained that he and his companions had come to bring them copies of the book, which held the key to their future success. Chief Anderson expressed his gratitude for the white men's kindness:

" 'It makes us glad in here'—placing his hand on his heart.

" 'It is now winter, we are new settlers in this place; the snow is deep, our cattle and horses are dying, our wigwams are poor; we have much to do in the spring—to build houses, and fence and make farms; but we will build a council house, and meet together, and you shall read to us and teach us more concerning the Book of our fathers and the will of the Great Spirit.' "

The elders "continued for several days to instruct the old chief and many of his tribe." Their hosts' desire to learn more about the Book of Mormon grew each day, and the elders, finding several people who could read, distributed copies among them, and the readers helped spread the word.[19]

Government Indian agents were in control of the area, and unfortunately the missionaries had not obtained the required permit to enter Indian lands and teach the gospel. The local Indian agent immediately informed them that they were in violation of the law and ordered them to desist until they had secured permission from General William Clark, Superintendent of Indian Affairs in St. Louis.[20] Parley P. Pratt stated, however, that when news of the missionaries' success reached the frontier settlements of Missouri it "stirred up the jealousy and envy of the Indian agents and sectarian missionaries to that degree that we were soon ordered out of the Indian country as disturbers of the peace; and even threatened with the military in case of non-compliance."[21]

In a letter dated 14 February 1831, Oliver Cowdery wrote to General Clark explaining that he represented a religious society centered in New York State and wished to establish "schools for the instruction of [the Indian] children and also teaching [their elders] the Christian religion." This they would do, he said, "without intruding or interfering with any other Mission now established."[22] It is not known if Clark ever responded to their request or granted permission. The missionaries settled in Independence and preached the gospel to interested settlers there.

Meanwhile Parley P. Pratt was selected to return to the East and report the mission and to obtain more copies of the Book of Mormon. After he left, the other missionaries' interest in the Indians increased as they learned of the existence of the Navajos, a large, industrious tribe living about three hundred miles west of Santa Fe.[23] Circumstances forced the missionaries to abandon any further attempts to take the gospel to any other Indian tribes.

Oliver Cowdery's 14 February 1831 letter to William Clark proposing to establish schools for Indian children

ASSESSMENT OF THE MISSIONARY JOURNEY

Although the "Lamanite mission" was not very successful in proselyting native Americans, it did have a significant impact on the subsequent history of the Church. It not only introduced the gospel for the first time to this remnant of the house of Israel, but it created an awareness of how important these people were in the eyes of the Lord.

In terms of conversions and immediate impact, the mission was most successful among the white settlers in the Western Reserve. Many people who would have a significant impact on the growing Church were drawn into the gospel net in Ohio. Within months there were more members in Ohio than in New York, so when conditions in New York required a move, Ohio was designated by the Lord as the gathering place and headquarters of the Church.

In another sense the mission demonstrated the motivating power of the Book of Mormon as a means of conversion and as a test of the strength conversion brought. This book of scripture was the means of redirecting the course of many lives.

The Lamanite mission also paved the way for future revelation respecting the land of Zion, although it was not so recognized right away. The precise location of the center of Zion was not yet revealed, although the Lord had already indicated to the Saints that Zion would be "on the borders by the Lamanites" (D&C 28:9). Five stalwart members of the Church now had experience in that area and could witness that this was a goodly land.

ENDNOTES

1. Letter dated 17 Oct. 1830, in *Ohio Star*, 8 Dec. 1831, p. 1.

2. Parley P. Pratt, ed., *Autobiography of Parley P. Pratt*, Classics in Mormon Literature series (Salt Lake City: Deseret Book Co., 1985), p. 35.

3. *History of the Church*, 1:124; "History of Joseph Smith," *Times and Seasons*, 15 Aug. 1843, pp. 289–90.

4. Pratt, *Autobiography of Parley P. Pratt*, pp. 35–36.

5. John Murdock, "An Abridged Record of the Life of John Murdock Taken from His Journals by Himself," LDS Historical Department, Salt Lake City, p. 16.

6. Philo Dibble, "Philo Dibble's Narrative," *Early Scenes in Church History* (Salt Lake City: Juvenile Instructor Office, 1882), pp. 75–76.

7. Account of Lydia Partridge, cited in Edward Partridge genealogical record, 1878, LDS Historical Department, Salt Lake City, p. 5.

8. Dibble, "Philo Dibble's Narrative," p. 77.

9. See Lucy Mack Smith, *History of Joseph Smith*, ed. Preston Nibley (Salt Lake City: Bookcraft, 1958), pp. 191–92.

10. *History of the Church*, 1:128.

11. *History of the Church*, 1:132; punctuation standardized.

12. *History of the Church*, 1:131–33.

13. Pratt, *Autobiography of Parley P. Pratt*, p. 36.

14. Pratt, *Autobiography of Parley P. Pratt*, pp. 36, 38–39.

15. Pratt, *Autobiography of Parley P. Pratt*, p. 39.

16. Eleanor Atkinson, "The Winter of the Deep Snow," *Transactions of the Illinois State Historical Society for the Year 1909*, p. 49.

17. Pratt, *Autobiography of Parley P. Pratt*, p. 40.

18. See Warren A. Jenning, "Zion Is Fled: The Expulsion of the Mormons from Jackson County, Missouri," Ph.D. diss., University of Florida, 1962, pp. 6–7; interview of A. W. Doniphan, in *Kansas City Journal*, 24 June 1881, cited in *Saint's Herald*, 1 Aug. 1881.

19. Pratt, *Autobiography of Parley P. Pratt*, pp. 42–44.

20. See letter from Major Richard Cummins to General William Clark, 13 Feb. 1831, *William Clark Letter Book* (Topeka, Kans.: Kansas State Historical Society, n.d.) roll 2, vol. 6, pp. 113–14.

21. Pratt, *Autobiography of Parley P. Pratt*, p. 44.

22. Letter from Oliver Cowdery to General William Clark, 14 Feb. 1831, *William Clark Letter Book*, p. 103.

23. See Oliver Cowdery, in *History of the Church*, 1:182.

GATHERING TO OHIO

WHEN THE YEAR 1831 arrived, most members of the Church were thinking of gathering to Ohio. Sometime in December of 1830 the Lord commanded his people to move to Ohio (see D&C 37:3). Because of this Joseph and his scribe, Sidney Rigdon, temporarily stopped the translation of the scriptures. On New Year's Day the Prophet and his associates in Fayette completed preparations for the third general conference of the Church, which was scheduled to consider the move to Ohio.

THE SAINTS INSTRUCTED TO GATHER

On 2 January 1831 the Saints from the various branches throughout New York met in the home of Peter Whitmer, Sr. After transacting some Church business, Joseph Smith "addressed the congregation and exhorted them to stand fast, looking forward considering the end of their salvation."[1] Following his remarks, several Church members inquired about the commandment to move to Ohio. In the presence of the congregation, Joseph Smith prayed to the Lord and received a revelation (see D&C 38). It promised the Latter-day Saints "greater riches, even a land of promise, a land flowing with milk and honey, upon which there shall be no curse when the Lord cometh;

"And I will give it unto you for the land of your inheritance, if you seek it with all your hearts" (D&C 38:18–19). The precise location of Zion, however, was not revealed. For the present, the Saints were to go to Ohio, where the Lord promised to reveal to them his "law," endow them with power, and give further instructions pertaining to the growth of the Church (see D&C 38:32–33).

Not everyone at the conference was in harmony with this revelation. A few people claimed that Joseph Smith invented it to deceive the people and to enrich himself. John Whitmer wrote in his history that this claim arose because the hearts of the Saints "were not right in the sight of the Lord, for they wanted to serve [both] God and man."[2] In addition, some people were reluctant to leave farms and comfortable circumstances for the uncertainties of the Western Reserve in Ohio. There was the prospect that many would lose money and some might even be unable to sell their property (see D&C 38:37). Most of the New York Saints, however, reconciled themselves to the commandment and made preparations to leave.

John Whitmer (1802–78) was the first presiding elder of the Kirtland Saints until Joseph Smith arrived in February 1831.

Newel K. Whitney (1795–1850) was a successful businessman as well as prominent in civic affairs. In 1844 he was sustained as the First Bishop of the Church, and in 1847 as Presiding Bishop.

Following the conference, Joseph Smith and Sidney Rigdon went to Colesville to strengthen the members of the Colesville branch and to preach for the last time to nonmembers in the vicinity. Threats on their lives prevented them from extended proselyting. Upon their return to Fayette, the Prophet sent John Whitmer to Ohio with copies of several of the revelations to comfort and strengthen the Saints. Brother Whitmer was also assigned to be their presiding elder until the arrival of the Prophet. By the time he arrived in Kirtland, the membership of the Church in Geauga and Cuyahoga counties in Ohio had swelled to about three hundred, more than twice the number reported only two months earlier.[3] Since the departure of the missionaries to the Lamanites, proselyting in the area had continued unabated. One of the most successful missionaries was the former restorationist preacher, John Murdock. Between November 1830 and March 1831, he baptized over seventy settlers living in Cuyahoga County.[4] Other missionaries fared equally well in their labors in Ohio.

GATHERING TO OHIO BEGINS

Moving to Ohio was advantageous to the young Church. By leaving New York the Saints hoped to leave behind religious persecution, particularly in the Colesville area. In addition, there were more Church members in Ohio than anywhere else, and gathering in one place enabled everyone to receive instructions from the Prophet, thus maintaining doctrinal and organizational uniformity. Ohio's available waterways also provided a gateway to the rest of the country for missionary work. But, most important, the move to Ohio was a step closer to "the borders by the Lamanites," where Zion would be established (D&C 28:9). In Ohio many principles pertaining to the building of Zion could be implemented.

Joseph Smith was eager to meet with the Saints in Ohio, and John Whitmer wrote urging him to come right away. Joseph sought the Lord's will and was told to leave immediately, but the prospect of moving seemed grim to Emma. She had moved seven times in the first four years of marriage and was just recovering from a month-long illness in addition to being six months pregnant. Under such conditions the three-hundred mile trip to Ohio in the dead of winter was arduous at best. Joseph Knight graciously provided a sleigh to make traveling less strenuous for her. At the end of January 1831, Joseph and Emma Smith, Sidney Rigdon, and Edward Partridge set out for Kirtland.

About the first of February the sleigh pulled up in front of Newel K. Whitney's store in Kirtland. Joseph sprang from the sleigh and entered the store. " 'Newel K. Whitney! Thou art the man.' he exclaimed, extending his hand cordially, as if to an old and familiar acquaintance. 'You have the advantage of me,' replied the merchant, . . . 'I could not call you by name as you have me.' 'I am Joseph the Prophet,' said the stranger smiling. 'You've prayed me here, now what do you want of me?' " Joseph explained to the

The Newel K. Whitney store, located at the four corners area in Kirtland, was built between 1826 and 1827. Many important things took place there, including the following:

1. Joseph and Emma Smith lived there beginning in the fall of 1832.

2. The store became the headquarters of the Church.

3. Joseph Smith III was born there on 6 November 1832.

4. The School of the Prophets, which commenced on 24 January 1833 and ended sometime in April, was held there.

5. Many revelations were given there to the Prophet Joseph Smith, including Doctrine and Covenants 84, 87–89, 95, and 98.

6. For a time the store was used as the bishops' storehouse.

7. Joseph Smith completed much of the translation of the Bible there.

In 1979 the Church acquired the Newel K. Whitney store and soon after began to restore it. The building was dedicated 25 August 1984 by President Gordon B. Hinckley.

amazed merchant that back in New York he had seen Newel in a vision praying for him to come to Kirtland.[5] The Whitneys received Joseph and Emma Smith with kindness and invited them to live temporarily with them. During the next several weeks the Smiths "received every kindness and attention which could be expected, and especially from Sister Whitney."[6]

Between the end of January and the middle of May 1831, most of the New York Saints sold their possessions, packed their most precious material goods, and migrated to Kirtland and the adjacent areas. Joseph Smith and a few others went early and were followed by three separate companies—the Colesville Saints, members from Fayette and surrounding locations in Seneca County, and those from Palmyra-Manchester. A few others came later in the year.

The Colesville branch was the first group to leave. They arrived in Buffalo on 1 May to find that bitter lake winds had blown ice into the Buffalo harbor, which delayed them for eleven dreary days. They finally arrived in Fairport, Ohio, on 14 May. Over two hundred people went to Ohio, some by sleigh and stage coach, but most by canal barges to Buffalo and then by steamboats and schooners on Lake Erie.

Meanwhile Church members in the Fayette vicinity also prepared for migration. With her older sons and husband already gone, Lucy Smith, a natural leader in her own right, organized a party of about fifty people (twenty adults and thirty children) to occupy a barge on the Cayuga and Seneca Canal. Another group of about thirty, organized by Thomas B. Marsh, took passage on an accompanying barge, and together the two boats traveled to Buffalo.

En route, Lucy "called the brethren and sisters together, and reminded them that we were traveling by the commandment of the Lord, as much as Father Lehi was, when he left Jerusalem; and, if faithful, we had the same

Lucy Mack Smith (1776–1856)

reasons to expect the blessings of God."[7] Although they suffered from hunger because some had brought clothing rather than food, they sang and prayed as they journeyed and left a favorable impression on the captain. Lucy took charge of the situation and prevented greater suffering.

When they arrived in Buffalo, they met the icebound Colesville Saints. After several anxious days in Buffalo, a number of the children had become sick, and many of the group were hungry and discouraged. They took deck passage on a boat, put their things on board, and obtained temporary shelter for the women and children until early the next morning. When they were back on board, Lucy persuaded the still murmuring group to ask the Lord to break the twenty-foot clogs of ice that jammed the harbor. She explained, "A noise was heard, like bursting thunder. The captain cried, 'Every man to his post.' The ice parted, leaving barely a passage for the boat, and so narrow that as the boat passed through the buckets of the waterwheel were torn off with a crash. . . . We had barely passed through the avenue when the ice closed together again." The Colesville group followed a few days later.[8]

As these New York Saints were arriving in Ohio, a third party of about fifty people left Palmyra, New York, under the direction of Martin Harris. With their arrival in Ohio, the first phase of the westward movement of the Latter-day Saints ended. In contrast to many Americans who migrated westward at the same time seeking free or inexpensive land, adventure, or escape from creditors, these humble people moved in response to a commandment of God.

EARLY CHALLENGES IN OHIO

During the three months Joseph Smith was in Kirtland before the Saints from New York began to arrive, he faced many challenges arising from the rapid growth of the Church there. The first problem was the manifestation of "strange notions and false spirits" among the members of the branch.[9] Because they lacked the guidance of Church authorities in northern Ohio, some new members entertained "wild enthusiastic notions" about the effects of the Holy Spirit upon the converted. John Corrill, an early Ohio convert, was disturbed by the bizarre actions of some of the young people who claimed they saw visions: "They conducted themselves in a strange manner, sometimes imitating Indians in their maneuvers, sometimes running out into the fields, getting on stumps of trees and there preaching as though surrounded by a congregation,—all the while so completely absorbed in visions as to be apparently insensible to all that was passing around them."[10] Satan's inroads in the Church were due to the credulity and gullibility of these new Saints who brought some of their previous ways with them and were without priesthood direction for a few months.

Only a few members behaved in this manner, however. "The more substantial minded looked upon it with astonishment, and were suspicious that it was from an evil source."[11] Distressed by what he saw, Joseph felt that these excesses were "calculated to bring disgrace upon the church of God; to cause the spirit of God to be withdrawn; and to uproot and destroy those glorious principles which had been developed for the salvation of the human family."[12] "With a little caution and some wisdom" and the guidance of several revelations, he succeeded in overcoming these problems.[13]

Still, in late February 1831, some individuals continued to claim they had received revelations. This was not a new problem; Hiram Page had done the same thing in Fayette the previous fall (see D&C 28). One of these so-called "revelators" was a professed prophetess named Hubble, who claimed she should be allowed to become a teacher in the Church. According to John Whitmer, she "appeared to be very sanctimonious and deceived some who were not able to detect her in her hypocrisy." Many saw through her false claims, however, and "her follies and abominations were made manifest."[14] The Prophet inquired of the Lord about her stratagems. In a revelation directed to the elders of the Church, the Lord declared "that there is none other appointed unto you to receive commandments and revelations until [Joseph Smith] be taken, if he abide in me" (D&C 43:3). So-called revelations through others for the guidance of the Church were not of God (see D&C 43:4–6).

Shortly thereafter another revelation called the elders to go forth by twos in all directions to preach the gospel (see D&C 44:1–3; 42:6–7). Soon many elders were seen going into villages and towns throughout Ohio. For example, John Corrill recounted that he and Solomon Hancock "went to New London, about one hundred miles from Kirtland, where we built up a church [branch] of thirty-six members in about three weeks time, though we were bitterly opposed by other preachers."[15] That spring the Church in Ohio increased by several hundred converts.

The growing Church did not go unnoticed in northern Ohio. Joseph Smith wrote that in the spring of 1831, "many false reports, lies, and foolish stories, were published in the newspapers, and circulated in every direction, to prevent people from investigating the work, or embracing the faith."[16] For example, a devastating earthquake struck near Peking, China, which a young Mormon girl had predicted six weeks earlier. This event convinced Simonds Ryder, a well-known Campbellite preacher who had been perplexed over Mormonism for some time, to join the Church. His conversion caused quite a disturbance in the vicinity, and the earthquake was heralded in the newspapers as Mormonism in China. "But to the joy of the Saints who had to struggle against everything that prejudice and wickedness could invent," the Prophet received a revelation that identified numerous signs that will precede the second coming of the Lord.[17] In it the Saints were commanded to "stand in holy places" and take "the Holy Spirit for their guide," and they were promised that they would be rewarded for this with the establishment of the "New Jerusalem" (D&C 45:32, 57, 66).

Also in the spring of 1831 a Methodist preacher named Ezra Booth brought a party to Kirtland, which included a well-to-do farmer named John

Johnson and his wife, Elsa, from Hiram, Ohio. Elsa's arm was partially paralyzed from rheumatism, and she could not raise it above her head. As they talked with the Prophet, one of the visitors asked if there was anyone on earth who had the power to cure Elsa's lame arm. When the conversation turned to another subject, Joseph went up to Mrs. Johnson, took her by the hand, and with calm assurance said, "Woman, in the name of the Lord Jesus Christ I command thee to be whole." As Joseph went from the room, leaving everyone astonished and speechless, she raised her arm. The next day she hung out her first wash in over six years without any pain. Ezra Booth and some members of the Johnson family joined the Church as a result of the healing. The miracle also attracted wide acclaim throughout northern Ohio.[18]

That same spring Parley P. Pratt returned to Kirtland with a report on the mission to the Lamanites and was delighted to see the tremendous growth of the Church. He was especially happy that Joseph had moved to Ohio. Parley was soon called to go on a mission to a religious group called the Shakers in northern Ohio.

The Shakers (United Society of Believers in Christ's Second Coming) originated in England and came to America in 1774 because of persecution. They derived their name from their manner of worship, which involved singing, dancing, and clapping hands to music, but their dress and manner were similar to those of the Quakers, so they were sometimes called the Shaking Quakers. The Shaking Quakers were led by Ann Lee from 1754 to 1784. She had claimed to be the Messiah returned to earth in female form. She taught that men and women were equals and that there should be no marriage among the believers. Leman Copley, a former Shaker, had converted to Mormonism but still believed that the Shakers were correct in many of their doctrines, so he asked Joseph for guidance on the matter.[19] The revelation Joseph Smith received repudiated the Shaker doctrines of celibacy, abstaining from meat, and God appearing in the form of a woman. Sidney Rigdon, Parley P. Pratt, and Leman Copley were also called to take the gospel to the Shakers (see D&C 49). The trio visited a settlement of Shakers near Cleveland, Ohio, but according to Parley, "they utterly refused to hear or obey the gospel."[20]

Elder Pratt then visited a number of branches of the Latter-day Saints in the Western Reserve, where he found the same spiritual fanaticism among the members that Joseph Smith had encountered when he arrived in Kirtland in February. Other elders were also disheartened by what they saw. John Whitmer related, "Some would fancy to themselves that they had the sword of Laban, and would wield it as expert as a light dragoon, some would act like an Indian in the act of scalping, some would slide or scoot on the floor, with the rapidity of a serpent, which termed sailing in the boat to the Lamanites, preaching the gospel, and many other vain and foolish maneuvers, that are unmeaning and unprofitable to mention. Thus the devil blinded the eyes of some good and honest disciples."[21] Parley Pratt concurred that "a false and lying spirit seemed to be creeping into the Church."[22]

Uncertain how to handle these spiritual phenomena, the brethren joined with the Prophet in prayer in his translating room in Kirtland. Joseph then dictated a revelation (see D&C 50). Elder Pratt remembered the sublime experience of observing a revelation in process: "Each sentence was uttered slowly and very distinctly, and with a pause between each, sufficiently long for it to be recorded, by an ordinary writer, in long hand."[23]

The Lord began by acknowledging that there were many "false spirits, which have gone forth in the earth, deceiving the world" (D&C 50:2–3) and that Satan was seeking to deceive the people that he might overthrow them. Therefore the Lord gave the brethren a key by which they could detect and deal with evil spirits:

"Wherefore, it shall come to pass, that if you behold a spirit manifested that you cannot understand, and you receive not that spirit, ye shall ask of the Father in the name of Jesus; and if he give not unto you that spirit, then you may know that it is not of God.

"And it shall be given unto you, power over that spirit; and you shall proclaim against that spirit with a loud voice that it is not of God" (D&C 50:31–32).

THE LAW OF CONSECRATION

Now settled in Kirtland, the Prophet was eager to know the Lord's will concerning the economic salvation of the Saints, many of whom were impoverished, particularly those who had left their homes in New York. His interest in the Lord's economic program was aroused when he arrived in Ohio and discovered a group of about fifty people who had established a cooperative venture based on their interpretation of statements in the book of Acts, describing the early Saints as having all things in common (see Acts 2:44–45; 4:32). This group, known as "the family," formerly followers of Sidney Rigdon, were members of the Church living on Isaac Morley's farm near the village of Kirtland. When John Whitmer arrived in mid-January, he noted that what they were doing created many problems. For example, Heman Bassett took a pocket watch belonging to Levi Hancock and sold it. When asked why, Heman replied, "Oh, I thought it was all in the family." Levi responded that he did not like such "family doing" and would not endure it any longer.[24]

The Prophet Joseph, however, realized the need to establish a more perfect system to meet the growing economic needs of the Church. Revenue was required to finance various Church undertakings, such as publishing revelations and missionary tracts. The Prophet was without a home for his family; Sidney Rigdon had lost his pastoral home and the economic support he had previously received from his congregation. Money, goods, and property were needed to help the poor and to assist immigrants who were sacrificing much to gather to Ohio, so Joseph inquired of the Lord.

In 1831 the Church purchased the Peter French farm, which eventually became the center of the Church in Kirtland, as the close up and enlarged views show.

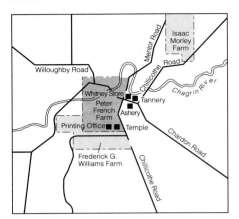

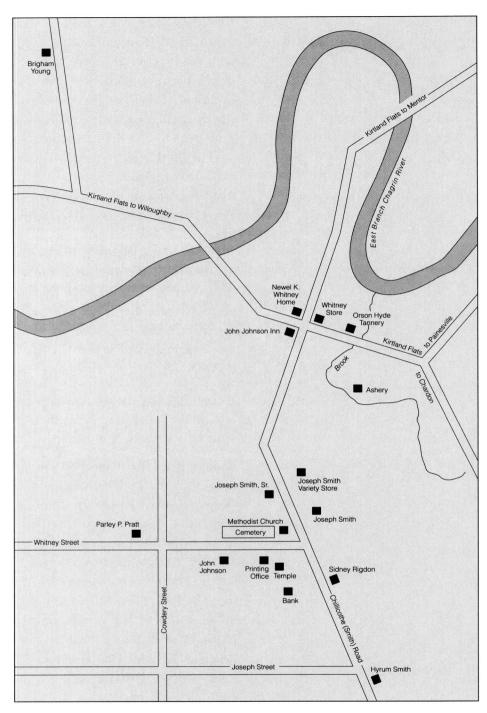

On 4 February 1831 the Prophet received a revelation calling for Edward Partridge to serve as the first bishop of the Church, with instructions for him to devote his time to this calling (see D&C 41:9). Five days later another important revelation was received, embracing the law of the Church. It gave Bishop Partridge further instruction on his responsibilities and outlined the new economic system (see D&C 42).

One of the underlying principles of this new economic system was that the earth and everything on it belonged to the Lord, and man was a steward

A consecration deed of October 1832

(see Psalm 24:1; D&C 104:13–14). Under the law of consecration members of the Church were asked to consecrate, or deed, all their property, both real and personal, to the bishop of the Church. He would then grant an "inheritance," or stewardship, to an individual from the properties received. The size of the stewardship depended on the circumstances, wants, and needs of the family, as determined jointly by the bishop and the prospective steward (see D&C 42:32–33; 51:3). The family then administered its stewardship to the best of their ability. If they were industrious and successful, then at the

Significant Revelations about the Law of Consecration and the United Order

Date	Where Received	Where Recorded	Content
4 Feb. 1831	Kirtland, Ohio	D&C 41:9	Edward Partridge appointed as first bishop.
9 Feb. 1831	Kirtland, Ohio	D&C 42:30–34	Law of consecration explained.
Feb. 1831	Kirtland, Ohio	D&C 44:6	Saints to administer to the poor according to law.
7 Mar. 1831	Kirtland, Ohio	D&C 45:64–75	Call to gather Zion: prospect of New Jerusalem.
Mar. 1831	Kirtland, Ohio	D&C 48	Saints who settled in Ohio to save money for inheritance in Zion.
May 1831	Thompson, Ohio	D&C 51:3ff	Bishop Partridge to appoint portions (stewardships) according to family size, circumstances, wants, and needs. Storehouse to be established.
June 1831	Kirtland, Ohio	D&C 56:16–20	Rich and poor commanded to repent.
20 July 1831	Jackson County, Missouri	D&C 57	Missouri appointed and consecrated as the land of inheritance and center place for Zion.
1 Aug. 1831	Jackson County, Missouri	D&C 58:1–9, 50–57	Zion to come after much tribulation. Early immigrants honored to lay foundation of Zion. Lands to be purchased in Independence.
Aug. 1831	Kirtland, Ohio	D&C 63:27–31	Saints commanded to purchase lands with money and forbidden to obtain lands by blood.
12 Nov. 1831	Kirtland, Ohio	D&C 70:1–8	Elders appointed stewards over revelations. Surpluses to be consecrated to the Church.
4 Dec. 1831	Kirtland, Ohio	D&C 72	Newel K. Whitney appointed as second bishop of the Church in Kirtland. Further duties of bishop made known.
Mar. 1832	Hiram, Ohio	D&C 78	Saints commanded to establish storehouses in Zion and to further organize so Church would be independent.
26 Apr. 1832	Jackson County, Missouri	D&C 82:11–12	United order to be established to manage affairs in Zion and Kirtland.
30 Apr. 1832	Independence, Missouri	D&C 83	Widows and orphans to be provided for by consecration of the Church to storehouses.
27 Nov. 1832	Kirtland, Ohio	D&C 85	To receive an inheritance in Zion a person must be willing to live the law of consecration.
25 June 1833	Kirtland, Ohio	History of the Church, 1:364–65	Letter from the Prophet to Bishop Edward Partridge on the size of a member's stewardship.
2 Aug. 1833	Kirtland, Ohio	D&C 97:10–21	House in Zion (Jackson County) commanded. Zion is pure in heart.
6 Aug. 1833	Kirtland, Ohio	D&C 98	Saints commanded to follow the Constitution. Law of war and law of forgiveness given to Saints.
12 Oct. 1833	Perrysburg, New York	D&C 100:13–17	Chastened Zion to be redeemed.
10 Dec. 1833	Kirtland, Ohio	History of the Church, 1:453–56	Letter from the Prophet to retain lands: petition to God to return Saints to land of inheritances.
16 Dec. 1833	Kirtland, Ohio	D&C 101	Reasons given for Saints' expulsion from Jackson County. Zion not to be moved out of her place. Saints to rely on constitutional process.
24 Feb. 1834	Kirtland, Ohio	D&C 103	Saints to redeem Zion after tribulation. Zion to be redeemed by power.
23 Apr. 1834	Kirtland, Ohio	D&C 104:47–66	Separation of united order in Kirtland and Zion. Sacred treasury provided for.
22 June 1834	Fishing River, Missouri	D&C 105	Redemption of Zion postponed until Saints are prepared, endowed, and numerous. United order dissolved until after Zion's redemption.
1 Sept. 1835	Kirtland, Ohio	History of the Church, 2:254	Prophet's letter to elders of the Church relating his June 1831 vision to go to western Missouri.

(Adapted from William O. Nelson, *Ensign*, Jan. 1979, p. 23.)

year's end they would have a net gain called a surplus (profit). Any surplus remaining beyond the wants and needs of the family was to be turned over to the storehouse to be used by the bishop to "administer to the poor and needy" (D&C 42:34). The law of consecration was designed to bring about relative economic equality and eliminate greed and poverty.

The Church gradually learned more about the law of consecration as additional revelations were given. For example, the Prophet asked the Lord how the Church should acquire lands for the settlement of the incoming Saints. Those with property in Kirtland were commanded to impart freely of their lands. Other funds were to be consecrated to buy more land (see D&C 48:2–3). The bedraggled New York Saints began arriving in May, and it was necessary to get them settled. The responsibility rested with Bishop Partridge, so he sought direction from the Prophet. The bishop was instructed to begin apportioning stewardships to the immigrants (see D&C 51:3). "And let every man deal honestly, and be alike among this people, and receive alike, that ye may be one, even as I have commanded you" (v. 9).

Joseph Smith directed the Colesville immigrants to settle in Thompson, Ohio, a few miles east of Kirtland, on property owned by Leman Copley. The Saints in Seneca County were assigned to live on the Isaac Morley farm, where they erected log cabins and planted crops. Although Bishop Partridge tried to inaugurate the law of consecration in Thompson, conflicts prevented its full implementation. Leman Copley broke his contract agreeing to let Latter-day Saints occupy his farmland and ordered them off his property. When informed of the difficulties, the Prophet sought and obtained a revelation instructing Newel Knight, president of the Colesville branch, and others living on the Copley farm to "repent of all their sins, and . . . journey into the regions westward, unto the land of Missouri, unto the borders of the Lamanites" (D&C 54:3, 8). Shortly thereafter, at least fourteen families under Newel Knight's direction left for the Missouri frontier.[25]

In the February revelation calling Edward Partridge to be bishop, the Lord had directed Joseph and Sidney to resume the translation of the scriptures. "And again, it is meet that my servant Joseph Smith, Jun., should have a house built, in which to live and translate" (D&C 41:7). Five days later the Prophet received the following instruction:

"Thou shalt ask, and my scriptures shall be given as I have appointed, and they shall be preserved in safety;

"And it is expedient that thou shouldst hold thy peace concerning them, and not teach them until ye have received them in full" (D&C 42:56–57). The pair diligently continued their work almost daily throughout the spring in a small house constructed for Joseph and Emma on Isaac Morley's farm.

At this time Emma went into labor. She had not yet recovered from her illness and the arduous midwinter journey from New York. On 30 April she delivered twins, but they only lived three hours. She and Joseph had now lost all three children born to them. Coincidentally, twins were born on 1 May to

Cemetery across the street to the north of the Kirtland Temple. Louisa and Thaddeus, the twins born to Joseph and Emma Smith, are buried in this cemetery. Jerusha Smith (Hyrum's wife) and Mary Duty Smith (grandmother of the Prophet) are also buried here.

Julia Murdock, but she died following their birth. Elder John Murdock was leaving on a mission about this time and gladly consented when Joseph asked if he and Emma could adopt the children. Emma's grief was eased, and she willingly took the infants—a girl named Julia and a boy named Joseph—to raise as her own.

GENERAL CONFERENCE IN OHIO

The fourth general conference of the Church convened in a schoolhouse just outside Kirtland on Friday, 3 June 1831. Many missionaries in Ohio returned for the meetings. Minutes record that sixty-three priesthood holders were in attendance.[26] In Joseph Smith's words, "The Lord displayed His power to the most perfect satisfaction of the Saints" at the conference.[27] After the opening business, Joseph announced that the Lord wanted worthy elders "ordained to the high priesthood."[28] These were the first ordinations to the office of high priest in this dispensation. The Prophet ordained five brethren high priests; one of them, Lyman Wight, ordained several more in the same meeting. John Corrill and Isaac Morley were called to be counselors to Bishop Edward Partridge and were set apart to that calling by Lyman Wight.[29]

During the conference the Spirit was with the Prophet in an "unusual manner. And [he] prophesied that John the Revelator was then among the ten tribes of Israel . . . to prepare them for their return from their long dispersion."[30] The spirit of prophecy also rested upon Lyman Wight: "He said the coming of the Savior should be like the sun rising in the east, and will cover the whole earth." He predicted that some of the brethren would suffer martyrdom for the sake of their religion and would seal their testimony of Christ with their blood.[31] The Prophet Joseph, Harvey Whitlock, and Lyman Wight saw the heavens open and Jesus Christ sitting on the right hand of the Father. Lyman testified that he saw the Son of God making intercession for the Saints.[32]

Not all that happened at the conference was good. As it had happened in previous months, a manifestation of evil spirits appeared. Church historian John Whitmer related that "the devil took a notion, to make known his power."[33] Horrid noises shrieked through the meeting, and several men were thrown around violently by evil spirits. Harvey Green was thrown on the floor in convulsions. The Prophet laid hands upon him and cast out an evil spirit. Harvey Whitlock and John Murdock were bound so they could not speak. Joseph Smith said that all of this was a fulfillment of the scriptures stating that the "man of sin" would be revealed (see 2 Thessalonians 2:3). The Prophet saw the design of Satan and commanded him in the name of Christ to depart, which he did to the "joy and comfort" of those present.[34] These early experiences in Kirtland served as a warning to all Saints to avoid tampering with evil spirits and to avoid excessive spiritual zeal.

Thus ended the first critical months of gathering the New York Saints to Ohio and establishing the headquarters of the Church there. While members experienced several encounters with evil spirits, they also received valuable instructions and saw the power of God overcome the power of the evil one. Joseph Smith and Sidney Rigdon resumed work on the inspired translation of the Bible. The eternal principles of the law of consecration were revealed, and further foundations were laid for the great latter-day missionary work.

ENDNOTES

1. In F. Mark McKiernan and Roger D. Launius, eds., *An Early Latter Day Saint History: The Book of John Whitmer* (Independence, Mo.: Herald Publishing House, 1980), p. 32.

2. In McKiernan and Launius, *An Early Latter Day Saint History*, p. 35.

3. See McKiernan and Launius, *An Early Latter Day Saint History*, p. 36.

4. See "Journal of John Murdock," Nov. 1830–July 1859, LDS Historical Department, Salt Lake City.

5. In *History of the Church*, 1:146.

6. *History of the Church*, 1:146.

7. Lucy Mack Smith, *History of Joseph Smith*, ed. Preston Nibley (Salt Lake City: Bookcraft, 1958), p. 196.

8. Smith, *History of Joseph Smith*, pp. 200–205.

9. *History of the Church*, 1:146.

10. John Corrill, *Brief History of the Church of Christ of Latter Day Saints* (St. Louis: John Corrill, 1839), p. 13; see also Joseph Smith, "Try the Spirits," *Times and Seasons*, 1 Apr. 1842, p. 747.

11. Corrill, *Brief History of the Church*, p. 13.

12. In *Times and Seasons*, 1 Apr. 1842, p. 747; spelling standardized.

13. *History of the Church*, 1:146.

14. In McKiernan and Launius, *An Early Latter Day Saint History*, p. 42; spelling standardized.

15. Corrill, *Brief History of the Church*, p. 13.

16. *History of the Church*, 1:158.

17. *History of the Church*, 1:158.

18. In *History of the Church*, 1:215–16; see also *Millennial Star*, 31 Dec. 1864, p. 834.

19. See *History of the Church*, 1:167.

20. Parley P. Pratt, ed., *Autobiography of Parley P. Pratt*, Classics in Mormon Literature series (Salt Lake City: Deseret Book Co., 1985), p. 47.

21. In McKiernan and Launius, *An Early Latter Day Saint History*, p. 62; spelling and punctuation standardized.

22. Pratt, *Autobiography of Parley P. Pratt*, p. 48; spelling, punctuation, and capitalization standardized.

23. Pratt, *Autobiography of Parley P. Pratt*, p. 48.

24. Levi W. Hancock, "Levi Hancock Journal," LDS Historical Department, Salt Lake City, p. 81.

25. See Larry C. Porter, "A Study of the Origins of The Church of Jesus Christ of Latter-day Saints in the States of New York and Pennsylvania, 1816–1831," Ph.D. diss., Brigham Young University, 1971, pp. 299–303.

26. See Donald Q. Cannon and Lyndon W. Cook, eds., *Far West Record: Minutes of The Church of Jesus Christ of Latter-day Saints, 1830–1844* (Salt Lake City: Deseret Book Co., 1983), pp. 6–7.

27. *History of the Church*, 1:175.

28. In McKiernan and Launius, *An Early Latter Day Saint History*, p. 66; punctuation and capitalization standardized.

29. See Cannon and Cook, *Far West Record*, p. 7.

30. In McKiernan and Launius, *An Early Latter Day Saint History*, p. 66; punctuation and capitalization standardized.

31. In McKiernan and Launius, *An Early Latter Day Saint History*, p. 67; punctuation standardized.

32. In McKiernan and Launius, *An Early Latter Day Saint History*, p. 67; see also "Levi Hancock Journal," LDS Historical Department, Salt Lake City, pp. 91–92.

33. In McKiernan and Launius, *An Early Latter Day Saint History*, p. 71.

34. In McKiernan and Launius, *An Early Latter Day Saint History*, p. 71; see also *History of the Church*, 1:175.

GATHERING TO THE LAND OF ZION

ZION! THE HOLY CITY! The New Jerusalem! Enoch built a Zion (see Moses 7:19–21), Isaiah predicted a future Zion (see Isaiah 33:20; 52:1, 8), and John the Revelator envisioned Zion's descent from heaven (see Revelation 21:2). The publication of the Book of Mormon helped clarify this dream because it said that America would be the place of the New Jerusalem (see Ether 13:2–3; 3 Nephi 20:22). The Book of Mormon thus fired the Saints with a zeal to know the time and place for the establishment of Zion. Only in Zion, the Saints believed, could they find protection from the desolation and tribulation soon to descend upon the wicked (see D&C 29:7–9; 45:65–71). In the writings of Enoch, revealed in December of 1830, the Saints found a concrete example in the righteous achievements of Enoch and his city: "And the Lord called his people ZION, because they were of one heart and one mind, and dwelt in righteousness; and there was no poor among them" (Moses 7:18).

JOURNEYS TO MISSOURI

Locating and establishing Zion became one of the prime objectives of the Latter-day Saints. In early 1831 curiosity about the location of the land of Zion began to grow. On the day following the fourth general conference of the Church (held 3 June 1831) a revelation directed Joseph Smith and other Church leaders to go to Missouri where the land of their inheritance would be revealed. In addition, thirteen pairs of missionaries were called to travel two by two, each pair taking a different route to Missouri, and to preach along the way (see D&C 52:3–8, 22–33; 56:5–7). Excitement reigned in and around Kirtland the next two weeks as the leaders and the elders prepared to leave. After all, the Lord gave them a promise:

"If ye are faithful ye shall assemble yourselves together to rejoice upon the land of Missouri, which is the land of your inheritance, which is now the land of your enemies.

"But, behold, I, the Lord, will hasten the city [the New Jerusalem] in its time, and will crown the faithful with joy and with rejoicing" (D&C 52:42–43).

It was during this period that Newel Knight asked the Prophet about the problem that had arisen on the consecrated lands in Thompson, Ohio. The Colesville branch members were directed to "take [their] journey into the regions westward, unto the land of Missouri, unto the borders of the

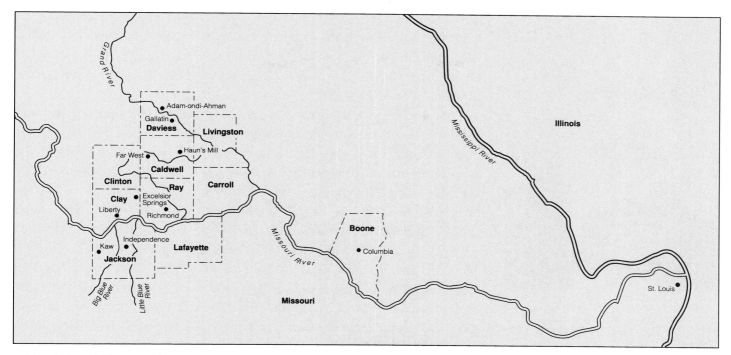

Map of Missouri (Kaw township, Kansas City, Missouri, was located in Jackson County. It embraced all that part of Jackson County lying west of the Big Blue River.)

William Wines Phelps (1792–1872) was born in Hanover, New Jersey, and died in Salt Lake City, Utah.

An active man with varied gifts and talents, he was an editor, a lawyer, a composer of hymns, a missionary, an educator, a legislator, a chaplain, and an ordinance worker in the Endowment House on Temple Square in Salt Lake City.

Lamanites" (D&C 54:8). Hence, three different groups prepared to travel to Missouri and to meet at the western borders of that state—Joseph Smith's party, the Colesville branch, and the missionaries.

While preparations went forward for the journey, a man who subsequently played an important role while the Church was in Missouri and afterward, William Wines Phelps, arrived from Canandaigua, New York, with his wife, Sally, and their children. Brother Phelps was thirty-nine years old and was a man of ability. As an editor of a partisan political newspaper, he was an experienced writer and printer. At one time he had been a candidate for the office of lieutenant governor of New York. He was converted to the gospel after purchasing a copy of the Book of Mormon. "By that book I found a key to the holy prophets; and by that book began to unfold the mysteries of God, and I was made glad. Who can tell his goodness, or estimate the worth of such a book?" he later wrote of the Book of Mormon in his conversion.[1] Brother Phelps said he came to Kirtland to do the will of the Lord. A revelation directed to him said he was "called and chosen," but first he was to be baptized and ordained, and then he was to accompany Joseph Smith and Sidney Rigdon to Missouri. Once in Missouri he was to assist Oliver Cowdery with the printing and with selecting and writing books for children to be used in the schools of the Church (see D&C 55:1–5).

On 19 June, Joseph Smith, Sidney Rigdon, Edward Partridge, Martin Harris, Joseph Coe, William W. Phelps, and Sidney Gilbert and his wife Elizabeth finally began their nearly nine-hundred-mile journey from Kirtland to the western border of Missouri. At last they were fulfilling their long-awaited hope and were bound for the land of Zion, although they did

Zebedee Coltrin (1804–87) was called and ordained as one of the seven presidents of the First Quorum of the Seventy when it was organized on 28 February 1835.

not know at this point exactly where it was located. Journeying to Cincinnati, the Prophet's company booked passage on a steamer headed down the Ohio River to its junction with the Mississippi and then on up into St. Louis. En route, they were joined by the Colesville branch under the direction of Newel Knight.[2]

The journey to Missouri was not an easy one. This was particularly true for the Colesville Saints who left Thompson, Ohio, carrying their belongings and provisions in twenty-four wagons.[3] At Wellsville, Ohio, they left the wagons and traveled by steamboat down the Ohio River to the junction of the Mississippi River. They then traveled up the Mississippi River to St. Louis. At St. Louis, Newel Knight and his company and some of the Prophet's companions elected to journey by steamboat on the Missouri River. This necessitated a wait of several days before passage could be secured. The Prophet and the others set out on foot and arrived in Independence about the middle of July,[4] approximately ten days before those on the steamer arrived. Joseph described the journey as "long and tedious" and said they arrived only after "suffering many privations and hardships."[5] Newel Knight said the task of leading the Colesville Saints "required all the wisdom" he possessed.[6]

Almost every pair of elders was ready to leave Kirtland within two weeks of their call. Each set chose a different route, because they had been commanded to "not build upon another's foundation, neither journey in another's track" (D&C 52:33). Some pairs of elders enjoyed greater success than others did. Parley P. Pratt, who had returned from Missouri only a few months before, and his brother Orson spent most of the summer of 1831 preaching in Missouri, Ohio, Indiana, and Illinois. Although they "suffered the hardships incident to a new and, in many places, unsettled country," they baptized many people and organized branches in the states they passed through. They did not arrive in western Missouri until September.[7]

Two others who enjoyed success were Zebedee Coltrin and Levi Hancock. After leaving Kirtland, they headed south and west along the National Road toward Indianapolis, Indiana. Baptisms came slowly at first, but when they reached Winchester, Indiana, they found ready listeners. Levi wrote, "We continued to preach here and in the regions round about until we had raised a large branch of the Church." They enjoyed similar results in Ward township, and "in a short time we had in both places about one hundred members." Their presence aroused a group of local men who accosted them and ordered them to leave the area by ten o'clock the next morning.

The elders decided to stay and keep an eleven o'clock appointment. Some of the men who appeared for the meeting were among the ones who had threatened the missionaries. In his sermon Levi said that his father had fought in the Revolutionary War for the freedom his listeners then enjoyed

Levi Hancock (1803–82) was called and ordained as one of the seven presidents of the First Quorum of the Seventy when it was organized on 28 February 1835.

and that his relative, John Hancock, was the first signer of the Declaration of Independence. Levi recorded, "After the meeting we went to the water and baptized seventeen out of that crowd who the day before were going to mob us." The brethren expressed gratitude for God's protection and help on that occasion. They arrived in Missouri sometime later, Zebedee in October, and Levi, compelled to lay over because of illness, in November.[8]

Typical of the profound but unrealized impact missionaries often have was that of the journey across southern Indiana made by twenty-three-year-old Samuel Smith and forty-one-year-old Reynolds Cahoon. They spent three days in Green County among Cahoon's relatives, and on their return trip two and a half months later the pair stopped again in the area for over two weeks. Among the many who were converted at the time was John Patten, who had a twenty-four-year-old brother, David, living in Michigan. John wrote to David the following spring telling him of the restored gospel and saying that he had received the gift of the Holy Ghost. David related, "This caused my heart to leap for joy, and I resolved to go immediately and see for myself."[9] He was baptized by his brother in June of 1832 and three years later was called to be one of the Twelve Apostles in this dispensation.

Several elders made the journey more quickly. Lyman Wight and John Corrill, for example, completed the trip on foot in two months—from 14 June to 13 August.[10] Few of the missionaries, however, arrived in time to participate in the conference held by the Prophet. Upon arrival in Independence, some of the single elders established themselves as permanent residents, while those with families in the East returned home. With this missionary labor, many people between Kirtland, Ohio, and Independence, Missouri, became acquainted with the Latter-day Saints and what they believed. Future missionaries would reap where these earliest elders had sown.

The case of Polly Knight illustrates the strong feelings of many members of the Church. Sister Knight, mother of Newel and a member of the Colesville branch, risked her life making the trip to Zion. Polly's health had been failing for some time, but her anxiety to see the promised land was so great that she refused to be left behind in Ohio. Nor would she remain with friends along the route for rest and recuperation. Her son wrote, "Her only, or her greatest desire, was to set her feet upon the land of Zion, and to have her body interred in that land." Fearing that she might die at any time on the journey, Newel left the boat on one occasion and went ashore to purchase lumber for a coffin. He later reported that "the Lord gave her the desire of her heart, and she lived to stand upon that land."[11] Polly died within two weeks of her arrival in the land of Zion and was the first Latter-day Saint to be buried in Missouri. But the Lord gave these consoling words: "Those that live shall inherit the earth, and those that die shall rest from all their labors, and their works shall follow them; and they shall receive a crown in the mansions of my Father, which I have prepared for them" (D&C 59:2).

IDENTIFYING THE LAND OF ZION

The Prophet and his brethren knew that the glorious New Jerusalem would one day stand somewhere near their stopping place because revelation said that Zion would be "on the borders by the Lamanites" (D&C 28:9) and be located in Missouri (see D&C 52:2, 42). But where? Missouri's western border was approximately three hundred miles long. "When will Zion be built up in her glory, and where will Thy temple stand?" the Prophet asked.[12] The Lord's reply, given 20 July 1831, was simple and direct:

"This land, which is the land of Missouri . . . is the land which I have appointed and consecrated for the gathering of the saints. . . .

". . . Behold, the place which is now called Independence is the center place; and a spot for the temple is lying westward, upon a lot which is not far from the courthouse" (D&C 57:1, 3). Joseph Smith and the gathering Saints were elated that at last the exact location of the promised city of Zion was revealed to them.

The gathering Saints learned that the countryside in Jackson County was beautiful with rolling hills and valleys. The climate was invigorating, the air and water clean and healthful, and the vegetation lush and green. Two clearwater streams, the Big Blue and Little Blue rivers, drained the central highlands as they flowed quietly into the Missouri River on the north. Black walnut, hickory, elm, cherry, and oak trees fronted streambeds, and an attractive carpet of bluegrass on the prairie was ideal for raising stock. This region was still largely unsettled, with the county seat, Independence, having been established four years previous. The Prophet Joseph Smith was exuberant about the prospects for the area. He taught that Jackson County, Missouri, was the location of the Garden of Eden.[13]

The temple lot in Independence, Missouri, was dedicated by Joseph Smith on 3 August 1831. The ground where the Prophet stood to dedicate the temple lot is now owned by the Church of Christ (Temple Lot), or Hedrickites. Other portions of the original temple lot are owned by the LDS and RLDS faiths.

The building in the northeast corner of the temple lot is the headquarters of the Church of Christ (Temple Lot). In the lower left corner of the picture is the tabernacle of the Reorganized Church of Jesus Christ of Latter Day Saints, and in the bottom right corner is our Latter-day Saint visitors' center.

The price of land and its ready availability also attracted the Saints. In 1831 whole sections of this undeveloped country could be purchased for $1.25 per acre. The Lord directed the brethren to purchase as much land as they were able (see D&C 57:3–5; 58:37, 49–52; 63:27), and Sidney Rigdon was appointed to "write a description of the land of Zion" (D&C 58:50) to be circulated among eastern Saints in a quest for funds. Sidney Gilbert was appointed "an agent unto the Church" to receive money from contributors and buy lands (D&C 57:6). Edward Partridge, already serving as a bishop, was commanded to divide the purchased land among the gathering Saints as "their inheritance" (D&C 57:7). The Lord also cautioned regarding Zion, "Let all these things be done in order. . . . And let the work of the gathering be not in haste, nor by flight" (D&C 58:55–56).

DEDICATION OF THE LAND OF ZION AND ITS TEMPLE SITE

Two important items required Joseph Smith's attention in Missouri before he returned to Ohio: the dedication of the land as a place of gathering for the Saints and the dedication of the temple site itself. Both events were presided over by the Prophet Joseph Smith. At a special service on 2 August 1831, twelve men, five of them from the Colesville branch (in honor of the twelve tribes of Israel), laid the first log "as a foundation of Zion in Kaw township, twelve miles west of Independence."[14] Sidney Rigdon consecrated and dedicated the land unto the Lord. As part of the service he asked his listeners, "Do you pledge yourselves to keep the laws of God on this land, which you never have kept in your own lands? [The audience responded,] we do. Do you pledge yourselves to see that others of your brethren who shall come hither do keep the laws of God? [Those present again said,] we do. After [the dedicatory] prayer [Elder Rigdon] arose and said, I now pronounce this land consecrated and dedicated to the Lord for a possession and inheritance for the Saints (in the name of Jesus Christ having authority from him). And for all the faithful servants of the Lord to the remotest ages of time. Amen."[15]

The dedication of the temple site in Independence took place the next day; again the services were simple but inspiring. Following the reading of Psalm 87, which extols the glory and majesty of Zion, a single stone, marking the southeast corner, was laid in place. Joseph Smith then dedicated the temple site by prayer. He reported that "the scene was solemn and impressive."[16]

According to previous commandment (see D&C 52:2), the brethren convened a conference on 4 August in Kaw township, and the Prophet presided. Sidney Rigdon admonished the Saints to obey every requirement of heaven, and other business of the Church was transacted before the brethren disbanded and returned to Ohio.[17]

RETURN TO OHIO

The return journey (by canoe on the Missouri River) began on 9 August 1831. The company stopped the first night at Fort Osage, a government-maintained outpost that provided protection from marauding Indians. On the third day, W. W. Phelps saw a vision of "the destroyer in his most horrible power" riding upon the water. Other people present heard the noise of the evil one.[18] This encounter left a strong impression on the travelers, some of whom feared for their safety.

The next morning Joseph received a revelation informing the elders that it was not necessary for the entire company to return to their homes in haste, particularly with many people on either side of the river "perishing in unbelief" (D&C 61:3). The waters, especially "these waters" (Missouri River), were declared to hold particular dangers for travelers; nevertheless, the Lord revealed, "It mattereth not unto me, after a little, if it so be that they fill their mission, whether they go by water or by land" (D&C 61:5, 22). The elders were to travel two by two and "declare the word among the congregations of the wicked" (D&C 61:33). The next day the brethren had a joyful meeting with several elders who were still on their way to the land of Zion. Joseph Smith received a revelation in their behalf urging them to continue on to Zion and to hold a meeting of rejoicing there (see D&C 62:1–4).

Joseph Smith and the others arrived in Kirtland late in August. He noted that their efforts to preach the gospel along the way were hindered because Satan had blinded the eyes of the people.[19] He also reported to the Saints in Ohio the glorious events he and his brethren experienced in locating the land of Zion. At this time the Lord promised that the members in Ohio who contributed to the Saints in Zion would "receive an inheritance in this world, . . . and also a reward in the world to come" (D&C 63:48).

CONTINUED DEVELOPMENTS IN ZION

Settling a frontier land was a new experience for most of the Saints who arrived from the East. Timber needed to be cut; ferries, bridges, mills, and dams had to be built; homes, out-buildings, and fences had to be constructed. Remembering the fall of 1831, Newel Knight wrote, "We were not accustomed to a frontier life, so things around us seemed new and strange and the work we had to do was of a different nature to that which had been done in the East. Yet we took hold with cheerful hearts, and a determination to do our best, and with all diligence went to work to secure food and prepare for the coming winter."[20] Parley P. Pratt commended the industry and optimism of a group of the Missouri Saints:

"They had arrived late in the summer, and cut some hay for their cattle, sowed a little grain, and prepared some ground for cultivation, and were engaged during the fall and winter in building log cabins, etc. The winter was cold, and for some time about ten families lived in one log cabin, which was open and unfinished, while the frozen ground served for a floor. Our food consisted of beef and a little bread made of corn, which had been grated into coarse meal by rubbing the ears on a tin grater. This was rather an inconvenient way of living for a sick person; but it was for the gospel's sake, and all were very cheerful and happy. . . .

". . . There was a spirit of peace and union, and love and good will manifested in this little Church in the wilderness, the memory of which will be ever dear to my heart." Plainly it was not what Zion was but what it could become that buoyed up the Saints and lifted sagging spirits.[21]

Gradually funds began arriving from the East. By January 1832, Bishop Edward Partridge had received $2,694.70 and expended $2,677.83.[22] He bought more land and superintended the establishment of a storehouse to receive and distribute the consecrations of the Saints. Church leaders in Missouri also began a printing enterprise as they had been commanded (see D&C 58:37). W. W. Phelps, who was called to be the printer and newspaper editor in Zion (see D&C 57:11–12), prepared to publish the Church's first periodical, the *Evening and Morning Star.*

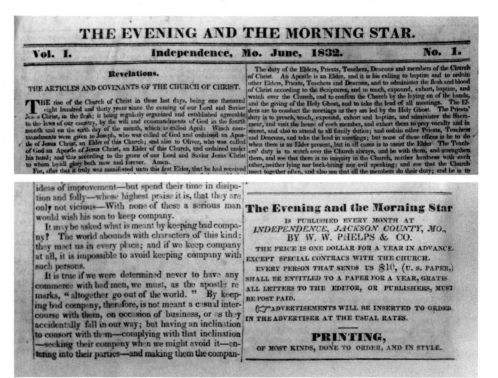

The Evening and the Morning Star *was a monthly newspaper first issued in* Independence, Missouri, in June 1832. *Fourteen issues were printed by William W. Phelps. The printing press was destroyed on 20 July 1833, stopping the publication.*

During the spring and summer of 1832, three to four hundred more Saints arrived in Missouri, where they received their inheritances from the bishop and began developing the land. An observer reported the intensity of their efforts and industry: "It was a strange sight indeed, to see four or five yoke of oxen turning up the rich soil. Fencing and other improvements went on in rapid succession. Cabins were built and prepared for families as fast as time, money and labor could accomplish the work; and our homes in this new country presented a prosperous appearance—almost equal to Paradise itself—and our peace and happiness, as we flattered ourselves, were not in a great degree deficient to that of our first parents in the garden of Eden, as no labor or painstaking was spared in the cultivation of flowers and shrubbery of a choice selection."[23]

But if land was plentiful, skilled artisans and builders were scarce. The majority of residents in Zion were farmers and common laborers. What was needed were wheelwrights, blacksmiths, brick masons, and carpenters. A revelation specifying the need to send for workmen "of all kinds unto this land, to labor for the saints of God" did not bring swift response (D&C 58:54). Levi Hancock, a carpenter and resident of Zion, had more work than he could handle. His first project was building a combined home and printing office for W. W. Phelps.[24]

On 29 May 1832 a conference was held in the newly completed printing office for the purpose of dedicating the facility. Remarks were given by Oliver Cowdery and W. W. Phelps, and then Bishop Edward Partridge offered the dedicatory prayer.[25]

In June 1832, Elder Phelps began publishing the *Evening and Morning Star*. Over the next year, the *Star* published numerous revelations given to Joseph Smith that later were included in the Doctrine and Covenants. Since it was the only newspaper in the county and printed both national and international news, it was read by non-Mormons as well as by members of the Church. But the paper performed its greatest service for the Saints. Considerable attention was devoted in every issue to urging members to faithfulness in performing religious and family duties. In the first edition, W. W. Phelps urged the Saints: "The disciples should lose no time in preparing schools for their children, that they may be taught as is pleasing unto the Lord, and brought up in the way of holiness. Those appointed to select and prepare books for the use of schools, will attend to that subject, as soon as more weighty matters are finished. But the parents and guardians in the Church of Christ need not wait—it is all important that children, to become good should be taught so."[26] In the fall of 1832, a school, known as the Colesville School, was started near a large spring in Kaw township; Parley P. Pratt was the first teacher. Later that same year a second school was opened in Independence in a log schoolhouse erected for that purpose near the temple lot.[27]

Proper observance of the Lord's Day received special emphasis in the *Star*. One of the first revelations received by Joseph Smith in Zion admonished the Saints to "go to the house of prayer and offer up thy sacraments upon my holy day . . . , and to pay thy devotions unto the Most High" (D&C 59:9–10).

Setting Sunday apart from other days and acknowledging it as a holy day was not the custom of the other residents of Jackson County. Reinforcing the message of this revelation, the *Star* offered this advice to the Saints: "Observe the Sabbath day to keep it holy. The Lord is not well pleased with a disciple that does any thing on that holy day that should be done on a laboring day. Nor should a disciple go to meeting one Sabbath here, and another there; let all that can, be strict to attend meeting in their own place. . . . Neither should the children be allowed to slip off and play, rather than meet where they may be trained up in the way they should go to be saved. We are the children of God, and let us not put off his law. When a saint works on the Sabbath, the world can reply: So do we. When the saints travel to do business on the Sabbath, the world can reply: So do we. When the saints go from one meeting to another to see and be seen, the world can reply: So do we. When the children of the saints play on the Sabbath, the world can reply: So do ours. Brethren, watch, that you may enter into the Lord's sacred rest."[28]

But the subject of the gathering received the most attention in the pages of the *Star*, and many articles were printed dealing with the matter. In July, Elder Phelps reminded migrating Saints that they were to bring a recommend from the bishop in Ohio or from three elders. They were also advised not to proceed to Zion without being told by one of the bishops that preparations had been made for them. Failure to observe this caution, he warned, "would produce pestilence" and cause confusion. "Moreover by being in haste, and forcing the sale of property, unreasonable sacrifices have been made, and although this is a day of sacrifice and tithing, yet to make lavish and unreasonable sacrifices, is not well pleasing in the sight of the Lord."[29] Later, Saints traveling to Zion were counseled to keep God's commandments "in every point" and set such a good example that others would "be constrained to say: They act like the children of God."[30]

By November 1832 there were 810 Saints in Missouri. Up to this point Zion was able to absorb its immigrants, and the Saints were pleased with the results. Editorials in the *Star* reflected their optimism, as future prospects for Zion appeared bright and promising.

ENDNOTES

1. In *Latter Day Saints' Messenger and Advocate*, Sept. 1835, p. 178.

2. See *History of the Church*, 1:188; Emily M. Austin, *Mormonism; or, Life among the Mormons* (Madison, Wis.: M. J. Cantwell, 1882), pp. 63–64.

3. See Austin, *Mormonism*, p. 63.

4. See *History of the Church*, 1:188.

5. In *Messenger and Advocate*, Sept. 1835, p. 179; punctuation and capitalization standardized.

6. *Scraps of Biography* (Salt Lake City: Juvenile Instructor Office, 1883), p. 70.

7. Parley P. Pratt, ed., *Autobiography of Parley P. Pratt*, Classics in Mormon Literature series (Salt Lake City: Deseret Book Co., 1985), p. 54.

8. "The Life of Levi Hancock," unpublished manuscript, Brigham Young University, Special Collections, Provo, pp. 54–64.

9. In "History of David W. Patten," *Millennial Star*, 25 June 1864, p. 407.

10. In letter from Lyman Wight to Wilford Woodruff, 24 Aug. 1857, Lyman Wight papers, LDS Historical Department, Salt Lake City.

11. *Scraps of Biography*, p. 70.

12. *History of the Church*, 1:189.

13. See George Q. Cannon, in *Journal of Discourses*, 11:336–37; Brigham Young, in *Journal of Discourses*, 8:195.

14. In *History of the Church*, 1:196.

15. In F. Mark McKiernan and Roger D. Launius, eds., *An Early Latter Day Saint*

History: The Book of John Whitmer (Independence, Mo.: Herald Publishing House, 1980), p. 79; punctuation and capitalization standardized.

16. *History of the Church*, 1:199.

17. In *History of the Church*, 1:199; Journal History of The Church of Jesus Christ of Latter-day Saints, 4 Aug. 1831, Historical Department, Salt Lake City.

18. In *History of the Church*, 1:203.

19. See *History of the Church*, 1:206.

20. *Scraps of Biography*, p. 72.

21. Pratt, *Autobiography of Parley P. Pratt*, p. 56.

22. See Journal History of the Church, 27 Jan. 1832.

23. Austin, *Mormonism*, p. 67.

24. See Dennis A. Clegg, "Levi Ward Hancock, Pioneer, Soldier, Political and Religious Leader of Early Utah," Master's thesis, Brigham Young University, 1966, p. 20; Levi Hancock Diary, typescript, Brigham Young University Special Collections, Harold B. Lee Library, Brigham Young University, Provo, p. 67.

25. See Journal History of the Church, 29 May 1832.

26. "Common Schools," *The Evening and the Morning Star*, June 1832, p. 6; spelling and punctuation standardized.

27. See H. S. Salisbury, "History of Education in The Church of Jesus Christ of Latter Day Saints," *Journal of History*, July 1922 (Independence, Mo.: Herald Publishing House, 1922), p. 259.

28. "To the Saints in the Land of Zion, and Abroad," *The Evening and the Morning Star*, Oct. 1832, p. 5.

29. "The Elders in the Land of Zion to the Church of Christ Scattered Abroad," *The Evening and the Morning Star*, July 1832, p. 5.

30. "The Way of Journeying for the Saints of the Church of Christ," *The Evening and the Morning Star*, Dec. 1832, p. 5.

DEVELOPMENT OF THE CHURCH IN OHIO, 1831–34

The northeastern Ohio area

THE EARLY KIRTLAND YEARS were one of the most significant periods in the history of the Church, although at the time few members comprehended the importance of what they were experiencing. Wilford Woodruff recounted that in April 1834 the Prophet Joseph Smith told a group of priesthood holders: "You know no more concerning the destinies of this Church and kingdom than a babe upon its mother's lap. You don't comprehend it. . . . It is only a little handful of Priesthood you see here tonight, but this Church will fill North and South America—it will fill the world."[1] Even so, the limited vision they possessed fired the Saints' souls, and the infant Church grew, developed, and matured.

Not only was Joseph concerned about establishing the Church, but like other Saints he and his wife, Emma, were struggling to set up a regular household. In fact they would not have a permanent home during their first two years in Ohio. In September 1831, just two weeks after Joseph returned from his journey to Missouri, he moved his family to Hiram, Ohio, about thirty miles southeast of Kirtland. The Prophet and his family stayed with the John Johnson family in Hiram for about six months. During that time he made rapid progress on the translation of the Bible with the able assistance of Sidney Rigdon.

OPPOSITION AND APOSTASY

From the outset the Church had an unpopular public image that was added to by apostates and nurtured by the circulation of negative stories and articles in the press. People gave many reasons for apostatizing. For example, Norman Brown left the Church because his horse died on the trip to Zion. Joseph Wakefield withdrew after he saw Joseph Smith playing with children upon coming down from his translating room. Simonds Ryder denied Joseph's inspiration when Ryder's name was misspelled in his commission to preach. Others left the Church because they experienced economic difficulties.

Ezra Booth, a former Methodist minister, was an influential apostate during this period. He joined the Church in May 1831 when he saw the Prophet heal the lame arm of Elsa Johnson. Booth, along with other missionaries, was called and sent to Missouri in the summer of 1831 (see D&C 52:3, 23). Upset about having to walk and preach the entire journey, he began to criticize and find fault with the leadership of the Church. He was

The John Johnson home located in Hiram, Ohio. The Prophet Joseph Smith received many revelations here. One of the greatest doctrinal revelations given in this dispensation, known as the Vision (D&C 76), was received in this home.

disappointed to arrive in Missouri and not experience manifestations of the Spirit, such as miracles and the gift of tongues, which he expected would increase his religious fervor. He returned to Hiram, Ohio, full of suspicion and faultfinding. The Prophet observed that Booth had become disappointed "when he actually learned that faith, humility, patience, and tribulation go before blessing, and that . . . he must become all things to all men, that he might peradventure save some."[2] Booth arrived in Hiram on 1 September, and was excommunicated five days later. Soon he and Simonds Ryder publicly renounced their faith at a Methodist camp meeting at Shalersville, a few miles southwest of Hiram.

Hoping to impede the progress of the Latter-day Saints in Ohio, critics in Portage County sought to capitalize on Booth's influence and encouraged him to publicize his criticisms. Booth believed that his conversion had influenced others to accept the gospel, and he wanted to reverse that affect as well as dissuade others from joining the Church. He published nine letters in the *Ohio Star* in Ravenna, from 13 October to 8 December 1831, detailing his objections to the Church.

These letters posed a challenge to the Church. They were circulated extensively and later became a major section of the first anti-Mormon book, Eber D. Howe's *Mormonism Unvailed,* published in 1834. Late in 1831 a number of missionaries were called to counteract Booth's influence, and in December the Lord called Joseph Smith and Sidney Rigdon to join the effort. They were to meet their enemies "both in public and in private," and the Lord promised them that "no weapon that is formed against you shall prosper" (D&C 71:7, 9). The two men labored about five weeks, and Joseph reported that their work "did much towards allaying the excited feelings which were growing out of the scandalous letters then being published."[3]

Tarring and Feathering of Joseph Smith by C.C.A. Christensen, a pioneer artist

Nevertheless, the negative influence of Booth and Ryder continued. Violence erupted in Hiram on the night of 24 March 1832 when a mob of twenty-five or thirty, under the influence of whiskey, attacked the households of Joseph Smith and Sidney Rigdon. Having stayed up late to care for his adopted infant son, who was sick with the measles, Joseph had finally fallen asleep on a trundle bed. The next thing he knew he was being dragged out the door, amid Emma's screams. He struggled but was overpowered. The mob ridiculed him, choked him, stripped him, and tried to force a vial of acid into his mouth, which chipped one of his teeth, causing him thereafter to speak with a slight whistle. One man scratched him with "his nails like a mad cat and then muttered out: 'G—d—ye, that's the way the Holy Ghost falls on folks!' " They daubed tar all over his body, covered him with feathers, and left him suffering. When Joseph finally made his way back to the house, Emma fainted at the sight of the tar, which she mistook for blood. Friends spent the night cleaning off the tar, and the next day, Sunday, Joseph preached a sermon and baptized three people.[4]

During the night of the incident, the door to the Johnson home was left open; the infant, Joseph Murdock Smith, caught cold and died five days later. During that same night Elder Rigdon was dragged by his heels from his home, and his head was severely lacerated by the rough, frozen ground. He was delirious for several days.[5]

VISIT TO MISSOURI IN 1832

Shortly after the mobbing, the Lord instructed the Prophet to return again to Missouri (see D&C 78:9). Some of the Jackson County Saints were jealous because Joseph Smith lived in Ohio rather than on the frontier. The Lord explained that Joseph should go to Missouri and counsel with the Saints because Satan was seeking to use the situation to "turn their hearts away" (D&C 78:10). Another reason for visiting Missouri was to coordinate the operation of the Church's storehouses in Kirtland and Independence. In March 1832 a revelation established that there were to be storehouses in both of these areas (see D&C 78). The profits of the Independence store were to assist the migrating Saints. One of the items of business in Missouri was to unite the two firms and consolidate the economic activities of the Church.

The stay in Missouri was short but productive. On 26 April, a "general council" sustained Joseph as President of the High Priesthood, as he had been ordained at a similar conference at Amherst, Ohio, on 25 January 1832. In the afternoon session, Joseph was instructed in a revelation (D&C 82) to combine the economic orders in Kirtland and Independence into the United Firm so they could be "independent of every encumbrance beneath the celestial kingdom, by bonds and covenants of mutual friendship, and mutual love."[6] The leaders agreed that the firm would regulate the business of the Church and authorized Newel K. Whitney, the bishop in Ohio, to negotiate a fifteen thousand dollar loan to purchase goods for the company. Joseph said that

Watch the Prophet
Joseph Smith gave to
Newel K. Whitney and a
letter opener he gave to
Newel K. and Elizabeth
Whitney

when he and his party arrived in Kaw township, the Saints received them with "a welcome only known by brethren and sisters united as one in the same faith. . . . It is good to rejoice with the people of God."[7]

Joseph Smith, Newel K. Whitney, and Sidney Rigdon left for home by stagecoach early in May. Near Greenville, Indiana, the horses were frightened and broke and ran. Bishop Whitney jumped from the coach, but his coat tangled and his foot caught in one of the wheels, breaking his leg in several places. Joseph and Sidney leaped from the stagecoach unhurt. The Prophet remained with Bishop Whitney a month in Greenville while Sidney traveled on to Kirtland with the news. During this time Joseph often enjoyed the solitude of walking in the woods. He wrote to Emma that he visited a grove outside of town nearly every day to pray and meditate: "I have called to mind all the past moments of my life and am left to mourn and shed tears of sorrow for my folly in suffering the adversary of my soul to have so much power over me as he has had in times past, but God is merciful and has forgiven my sins."[8]

After dinner one day, the Prophet took sick and vomited so severely that he dislocated his jaw. Bishop Whitney administered to him, and he was healed immediately, although the effects of the poison caused him to lose some of his hair. The Prophet decided it was best to move on, assuring Bishop Whitney that their journey would proceed smoothly. Joseph explained: I "told him if he would agree to start for home in the morning, we would take a wagon to the river, about four miles, and there would be a ferry-boat in waiting which would take us quickly across, where we would find a hack which would take us directly to the landing, where we should find a boat, in waiting, and we would be going up the river before ten o'clock."[9] The pair traveled just as Joseph had predicted and arrived in Kirtland early in June.

For the next several months, the Prophet again occupied most of his time on the inspired translation of the Bible, except for a hurried journey in the fall with Bishop Whitney to Albany, New York City, and Boston, where they took care of business as well as warning the inhabitants to repent and accept the gospel (see D&C 84:114–15). They arrived back in Kirtland on 6 November 1832, just hours after Emma had given birth to her fourth and first surviving child, Joseph Smith III.[10]

Soon thereafter Brigham Young and Heber C. Kimball arrived in Kirtland from upstate New York; they had recently joined the Church and were anxious to meet the Prophet. In a gathering that evening, Brigham spoke in tongues while praying. While answering questions about the gift, Joseph Smith prophesied that one day Brigham Young would preside over the Church.[11]

During the spring and summer of 1833 the Prophet devoted much of his time to translating the Bible, teaching the School of the Prophets, and beginning construction on the Kirtland Temple.

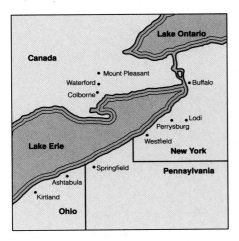

Church history sites in Upper Canada

JOSEPH SMITH'S MISSION TO CANADA

In the fall of 1833, Joseph Smith and Sidney Rigdon went to Upper Canada at the urging of Freeman Nickerson, a recent convert, who convinced the brethren that his sons who lived there would be receptive to the gospel. The journey was historic. While it was not the first time missionaries had been in Canada (brief excursions had been made in 1830, 1832, and 1833), Joseph's visit gave the work there considerable spark. The Prophet developed such a love for the Canadians that he visited them again in 1837 and saw to it that missionary work there continued throughout his life.

In Mount Pleasant, Joseph Smith and Sidney Rigdon baptized twelve people, including the sons of Elder Nickerson and their families, who became the nucleus of the branch there.

Lydia Bailey was one of those in the Eleazer Freeman Nickerson household in Mount Pleasant who responded to the gospel with all of her heart. She was raised in Massachusetts and New York and at age sixteen married Calvin Bailey. Because he drank, her life with him was unhappy. After three years of marriage, he abandoned her, her daughter, and the child she was expecting. Her son died at birth, and less than a year later her daughter also died. At age twenty Lydia went to Canada with the Nickersons to recover her emotional health. There she met Joseph Smith, and he told her, "You shall yet be a savior to your father's house." Lydia later moved to Kirtland, where she met and married Newel Knight, a widower. Many years later, in Utah, Lydia did the ordinance work for seven hundred of her kindred dead in the St. George Temple, thus fulfilling Joseph's prophecy.[12]

Joseph's journal of this mission gives us a glimpse into his character. Like other missionaries, he worried about his family and alternately faced disappointments and successes. Joseph frequently recorded brief prayers in his journal. For example, as he began the trip on 14 October 1833, he wrote, "Lord, be with us on our journey." In his record of 22 October he noted, "We hope that great good may yet be done in Canada which, O Lord, grant for thy name's sake." On 23 October, as he referred to the superstitious people they preached to, he prayed, "Oh God, establish thy word among this people."[13]

The Upper Canadian mission was one of fourteen missions undertaken by Joseph Smith during the Kirtland era. He left Ohio at least once each year between 1831 and 1838 to labor as a full-time missionary while serving as President of the Church.

THE JOSEPH SMITH TRANSLATION OF THE BIBLE

Joseph Smith's inspired translation of the Bible was one of the pivotal developments of his work as a prophet and has had a profound influence on the Church. Joseph's knowledge about the principles of the gospel and God's work with his ancient prophets and people increased immensely through this project. He considered it an important "branch" of his calling and

Flyleaf of Joseph Smith's King James Version of the Bible. It contains the following information in Joseph Smith's handwriting:

"The Book of the Jews And the property of Joseph Smith Junior and Oliver Cowdery
"Bought October the 8th 1829, at Egbert B. Grandins Book Store Palmyra Wayne County New York
"Price $3.75
"Holiness to the Lord"

labored diligently at it. When he and Sidney Rigdon were at home in Ohio, this was their major preoccupation. The frequency with which the "translation" is referred to in the revelations and historical documents of the period underscores the importance of this project. The Prophet first began this work in New York in 1830. When he arrived in Ohio in February 1831, he continued his work in the Old Testament with the help of his scribe, Elder Rigdon. But early in March, Joseph was commanded to work on the translation of the New Testament (see D&C 45:60–61). During the next two years Joseph and Sidney continued their work on both the New and the Old Testaments. They optimistically pronounced their work finished on 2 July 1833.[14]

In addition to the great legacy left to the Church in the Joseph Smith Translation (JST) itself, numerous revelations now recorded in the Doctrine and Covenants came to the Prophet while he worked on the inspired translation. The study of the Bible stimulated him to inquire of the Lord about significant doctrinal and organizational matters. Doctrine and Covenants sections 76, 77, and 91 have direct links with the translation effort, "and probably much of the information in sections 74, 84, 86, 88, 93, 102, 104, 107, 113, and 132." It is probable that many others are indirectly connected.[15]

ORIGINS OF THE DOCTRINE AND COVENANTS

The revelations the Prophet Joseph Smith received contained timely instruction from the Lord concerning the doctrines and government of the Church. Three months after the organization of the Church, the Prophet and John Whitmer arranged and copied the revelations received up to that time. Occasionally Joseph gave copies to friends, missionaries, and other Church members, but most people did not have access to the revelations. The establishment of a printing press in Missouri in 1831, however, provided the opportunity to publish them. This matter was the principal subject at a series of conferences in Hiram, Ohio, in early November 1831. By then more than sixty revelations had been recorded. On 1 November it was agreed to have William W. Phelps print ten thousand copies of the revelations in book form. (The number of copies to be printed was later reduced to three thousand.) The title of the book, the Book of Commandments, was derived from a revelation given in the same conference. The Lord designated the revelation as a "preface unto the book of my commandments" (D&C 1:6).

Later that day a few brethren made negative comments about the language and style of the revelations. Therefore, the Lord in a revelation challenged the critics to select the "least" of the commandments and to have the wisest man among them try to write a better one (see D&C 67:4–9). William E. McLellin, a schoolteacher and recent convert, presumptuously accepted the challenge. The Prophet said that McLellin, "as the wisest man, in his own estimation, having more learning than sense, endeavored to write a commandment like unto one of the least of the Lord's, but failed; it was an awful responsibility to write in the name of the Lord." This experience renewed the brethren's faith in the revelations, and they agreed "to bear testimony of their truth to all the world."[16] Subsequently, the Prophet wrote that the revelations were "the foundation of the Church in these last days."[17]

Further conference sessions completed the details preparatory to the publication of the book. On 3 November 1831 an "appendix" (later D&C 133) was added to the revelations. Another session on 8 November directed Joseph Smith, under the direction of the Holy Ghost, to correct the errors he discovered in the written copy of the revelations. On 12 November the Lord called John Whitmer, the Church historian and recorder, to accompany Oliver Cowdery who had been commanded to carry the manuscripts to Missouri for printing (see D&C 69). Another revelation given that day called six brethren "to be stewards over the revelations and commandments" (D&C 70:3). This group became known as the "Literary Firm."[18]

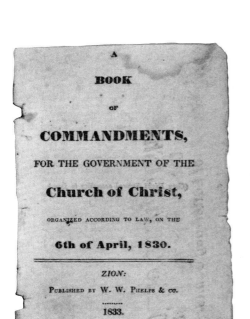

The Book of Commandments

On 20 November 1831, Oliver and John started for Missouri. They arrived in Independence on 5 January 1832 after a long, cold journey. In June, Elder Phelps began publishing extracts from the revelations in the *Evening and Morning Star* and setting the type for the Book of Commandments.

DEVELOPMENTS IN CHURCH ORGANIZATION

The rapid growth of the infant Church required a substantial expansion of its organization. In keeping with the principle of giving revelation "line upon line, precept upon precept" (D&C 98:12), the Lord directed the establishment of Church government as required. Immediately after the Church was organized in 1830, men were called to serve in the ministry and were ordained to one of four priesthood offices: deacon, teacher, priest, or elder. Other priesthood offices were added the following year.

Edward Partridge (1793–1840). The Lord compared Edward to Nathanael of old (see D&C 41:11).

The first new office to be added was that of bishop. Edward Partridge was appointed to this calling in February of 1831 (see D&C 41:9). His duties, however, were not revealed all at once. The earliest revelations pertaining to the office of bishop gave him responsibility for implementing the law of consecration. Specifically he was to receive consecrations, assign stewardships, and maintain a storehouse for the relief of the poor. He was also to be responsible for buying land and for building houses of worship (see D&C 42:30–35; 51:1–3). As these duties grew, agents were called to assist the bishop in receiving monies, purchasing property, and conducting secular business (see D&C 51:8; 53:4; 58:49; 84:113).

Further revelations also assigned judicial responsibilities to the bishop. At first elders' courts handled Church discipline, with the bishop present if possible (see D&C 42:82). By August 1831, the bishop's assignment as common judge in Israel was made more specific. The bishop was "to judge his people by the testimony of the just, and by the assistance of his counselors, according to the laws of the kingdom which are given by the prophets of God" (D&C 58:18). Even so, elders' courts, and later high councils, carried much of the judicial load in Kirtland. To this point the bishop did not have the pastoral duties, which later became an important part of a bishop's responsibilities.

After Edward Partridge moved to Missouri, a second bishop, Newel K. Whitney, was called in December 1831. He was to determine the worthiness of members living in Ohio and to provide certificates to the bishop in Zion attesting that they had been members in good standing before they moved to Missouri.

The roles of the President of the Church and later the First Presidency were defined in the early Kirtland years. At the meeting where the Church was organized, Joseph Smith was called by revelation "a seer, a translator, a prophet, an apostle of Jesus Christ, an elder of the church" (D&C 21:1), and the Lord specified that he was the only one authorized to receive revelations for the whole Church (see D&C 28:1–6). At the conference of 3–6 June 1831

Bishop's certificate of Edward Partridge

[Handwritten document — Bishop's certificate of Edward Partridge, with signatures of Elders including William E. McLellin, Harvey Whitlock, David Whitmer, John Corrill, Samuel Dollinger, Peter Dustin, Asa Dodds, Orson Pratt, John Whitmer, Sidney Rigdon, Joseph Smith, Oliver Cowdery, William W. Phelps, Martin Harris, Isaac Morley, Peter Whitmer Jr., Sidney Gilbert, Joseph Coe, Simeon Carter, Hyrum Smith]

several brethren were ordained to the office of high priest for the first time. Subsequently on 25 January 1832 at a conference in Amherst, Ohio, Joseph was ordained "President of the High Priesthood."[19]

For nearly two years Joseph presided over the Church without counselors. Early in March 1832 he was authorized to appoint counselors for the first time. On 8 March, Joseph selected Jesse Gause and Sidney Rigdon from among the recently ordained high priests. On 15 March a revelation announced that this Presidency held the "keys of the kingdom" (D&C 81:2). Jesse Gause fell away from the Church in 1832, so the First Presidency was reorganized on 18 March 1833, and Frederick G. Williams was called as the new counselor.

The calling of Patriarch to the Church eliminated one of Joseph Smith's responsibilities. Frequently individuals wanted him personally to ask the

Joseph Smith, Sr. (1771–1840)

Lord for a revelation for them, but as the Church grew, this became impractical. On 18 December 1833, while giving blessings to his family, the Prophet was inspired to call and ordain his father as the first Patriarch to the Church. From that time until his death in 1840, Joseph Smith, Sr., traveled among the branches, holding special blessing meetings where he gave many faithful Saints their patriarchal blessings. In addition to providing revelation to individuals, the patriarchal blessings also identified the person's lineage in the house of Israel.

The first stake of Zion was organized in Kirtland on 17 February 1834. Initially the three members of the First Presidency were appointed to serve as the presidency of this stake. With the organization of the high council in Kirtland at the same time, a second level of Church judiciary was initiated. According to the minutes, the high council's purpose was to settle "important difficulties which might arise in the church, which could not be settled by the church or the bishop's council" (D&C 102:2). It was to be a court of original jurisdiction on difficult cases and an appellate court. Decisions of the high council could also be appealed to the First Presidency. A second high council was organized in Clay County, Missouri, on 3 July 1834.

DOCTRINAL REVELATIONS

Nearly one-third of the revelations in the Doctrine and Covenants were received between August 1831 and April 1834. The revelations opened new vistas of gospel understanding and provided the Saints with valuable guidelines for their daily conduct. On 16 February 1832, for example, Joseph Smith and Sidney Rigdon received a revelation in direct answer to a question that had arisen during their work on the Bible. A vision of the Father and the Son, Satan's fall, the sons of perdition, and the kingdoms of glory enormously expanded their understanding of the plan of salvation.

During the fall of 1832, when a number of missionaries had returned from their labors and were enjoying a conference, the Lord gave an important revelation on the priesthood (D&C 84). It began with a statement that the New Jerusalem and the temple would be built in Missouri. In addition to giving a brief history of the descent of the priesthood through the ancient patriarchs and prophets, the Lord explained that the greater, or Melchizedek, priesthood has the authority to administer the gospel ordinances (see v. 19) and that the lesser, or Aaronic, priesthood administered the ordinances of the "preparatory gospel" (see v. 26). The revelation went on to explain that recipients of the priesthood received it by the "oath and covenant" (v. 40), which if adhered to faithfully would bring eternal life. Information was also given about the light of Christ and the signs that follow the preaching of the gospel. Instructions to missionaries and other ministers of the gospel completed the revelation.

The Lord also spoke on war and peace. On Christmas day of 1832, he gave a revelation that contained the famous prophecy of the American Civil

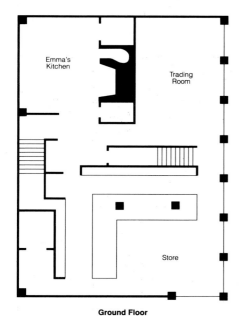

Ground Floor

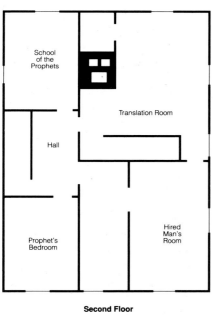

Second Floor

Floor plan of the Newel K. Whitney store

War. It was to be the beginning of wars that would "shortly come to pass" and would eventually be "poured out upon all nations" (D&C 87:1–2). Saints were warned that as war engulfed the globe they would be safe only if they would "stand ye in holy places, and be not moved" (v. 8). Two days later Joseph Smith received a revelation. He called it "the Olive Leaf which we have plucked from the tree of Paradise, the Lord's message of peace to us."[20] This revelation was not an explanation, however, of how men could solve their domestic and international difficulties. Rather, it diverted the Saints' attention from their petty concerns and focused it on such eternal matters as preparing for the Lord's coming and living the law leading to exaltation in the celestial kingdom.

This revelation also directed the formation of a "school of the prophets" to prepare the brethren to better serve one another (see D&C 88:118–41). The school began meeting the end of January 1833 in an upstairs room above the Whitney store. These meetings provided the setting for many remarkable spiritual experiences and in-depth discussions of gospel principles.

Dietary matters were a concern during the early years of the Church. For example, a nearby Shaker colony adhered to an unusually stringent dietary code forbidding the eating of meat. In March 1831 the Lord told Joseph that this Shaker doctrine was not ordained of God because "the beasts of the field and the fowls of the air, and that which cometh of the earth, is ordained for the use of man for food and for raiment" (D&C 49:19). A revelation given in Missouri during August of the same year added the caution that men were to use these things "with judgment, not to excess" (D&C 59:20).

During the winter of 1833, the School of the Prophets frequently met to discuss the affairs of the Church; as was the custom of the time, many of the brethren chewed or smoked tobacco. As Brigham Young recalled, Joseph Smith became concerned at having to instruct the school "in a cloud of tobacco smoke," and Emma complained at having to clean the room after the brethren. This caused the Prophet to inquire of the Lord concerning the use of tobacco. In answer he received the revelation now known as the Word of Wisdom (see D&C 89).[21] The revelation forbade the use of tobacco, wine, strong drink, and "hot drinks," which were understood to be coffee and tea; it also stressed the use of wholesome vegetables, fruits, and grains. The Saints were promised if they followed this Word of Wisdom, they would have health and strength, "find wisdom and great treasures of knowledge," and "the destroying angel shall pass by them" (D&C 89:19, 21).

In 1833 the Lord also molded Latter-day Saint political thought, especially regarding the nature of the Constitution of the United States. Two principles were fundamental. The Constitution was an inspired document written "by the hands of wise men . . . raised up unto this very purpose" (D&C 101:80). It also had global application. The Lord explained that constitutional law, which guarantees rights and freedoms, "belongs to all mankind, and is justifiable before me" (D&C 98:5). He reaffirmed that it was established to maintain the "rights and protection of all flesh, according to just and holy principles; That every man may act in doctrine and principle . . . according to the moral agency which I have given unto him, that every man may be accountable for his own sins in the day of judgment" (D&C 101:77–78). Joseph Smith best expressed the Saints' attitudes toward the Constitution when he said it is "a glorious standard; it is founded in the wisdom of God. It is a heavenly banner. . . . It is like a great tree under whose branches men from every clime can be shielded from the burning rays of the sun."[22]

KIRTLAND, THE HUB OF MISSIONARY WORK

As the headquarters of the Church, Kirtland was the center of missionary work during this period. It was near the main routes of transportation and contained the largest concentration of Church membership. Kirtland was the point of departure for missions to Canada, the Northeast, the Mid-Atlantic States, the Midwest, and the South. The state of Ohio itself was saturated with missionaries who crossed the state on their way to or from other fields of labor. Frequently those unable to go on longer missions or those home during the winter months visited local communities.

Typically missionaries proselyted among their relatives or in the communities they had migrated to Ohio from. Missions ranged in length from a few days to a year or more, although most were fairly short. Normally there was a rhythmic pattern as missionaries went out for a few weeks or months to preach, returned to Kirtland for rest and recuperation, and then went out again on another mission.[23] Often, as was the case with Orson Pratt, Orson Hyde, Erastus Snow, Brigham Young, and others, this pattern repeated itself many times during the first decade of their lives in the Church.

Before the organization of the Quorum of the Twelve and the First Quorum of the Seventy in 1835, the direction of missionary work rested with the local priesthood quorums, the high council, or the Presidency of the Church. Some effort was made to improve the training of the missionaries. The School of the Prophets and the School of the Elders played a key role in this training. In the School of the Elders, Joseph Smith and Sidney Rigdon presented lectures on faith, and the missionaries were encouraged to memorize them so they could teach the precepts of the gospel logically and systematically. A revelation commanded the brethren to study geography, geology, history, prophecy, culture, war, and language—all "that ye may be prepared in all things when I shall send you again to magnify the calling whereunto I have called you, and the mission with which I have commissioned you" (D&C 88:80).

Although going from door to door was a common practice, missionaries often found their best success in small groups in the homes of the receptive. Many missionaries preferred public meetings. They used any available space where they could preach, such as a barn, school, church, home, or courthouse. They spoke about prophecy, the Book of Mormon, the signs of the times, spiritual gifts, the Apostasy, and the Restoration, but the missionaries were cautioned to avoid the mysteries of the gospel in their teaching. Ordinarily an elder preached and then gave "liberty" to anyone who desired to respond to his message. This technique put the local clergy on the spot because silence on their part would be interpreted as consent or defeat. Therefore, it frequently generated discussions or debates on the gospel. The missionary companion then exhorted the congregation to accept baptism.

Missionaries often encountered rejection, hostility, or indifference. Their disappointment was particularly poignant when a disbeliever was a member of the missionary's family. In 1832, Orson Hyde visited his relatives in New York and New Hampshire to teach them the gospel. His brother Asahel remained unmoved by the gospel message, and Orson recorded that they separated "with hearts full of grief." Three months later he tried with his sister and her husband, but they too rejected his message. He wrote, "We took our things and left them, and tears from all eyes freely ran, . . . but it was like piercing my heart; and all I can say is 'The Will of the Lord Be Done.' "[24]

The clergy were particularly vehement and sometimes ingenious in their opposition to the missionaries. In 1835 a Baptist deacon passed a pop-gun and ammunition through a window to a friend listening to a missionary sermon by Elder George A. Smith. Elder Smith wrote that the man shot "wads of tow [short broken fiber from flax that is used for yarn] at me all the time I was preaching. He was an excellent shot with the pop-gun, [and] most of the wads hit me in the face. I caught several of them in my hands. Many of them [the audience] were tickled, but some of them paid good attention. I finished my discourse without noticing the insult."[25]

Despite the harassment, these early missionaries, inspired by faith and testimony, were remarkably successful. They remained undaunted by constant doses of opposition, heckling, and criticism, and the work prospered and set a pattern of continuous and fast-paced growth. Had not the Lord declared that the field was "white already to harvest"? (D&C 4:4).

Letters from outlying branches published in Church periodicals, the *Evening and Morning Star* and the *Latter-day Saints' Messenger and Advocate*, frequently pleaded for more missionaries. These publications also communicated instructions, decisions of authorities, information about developments throughout the Church, and explanations of gospel doctrines.

Most conferences and meetings, both in Kirtland and in the outlying branches, were devoted to missionary matters. The charge to take the restored gospel to the whole earth received an early impetus in the Kirtland headquarters of the Church. But at the same time the Church was prospering in Ohio, serious problems were developing in Zion between the Saints and their Jackson County, Missouri, neighbors.

ENDNOTES

1. In *Conference Report*, Apr. 1898, p. 57; spelling standardized.

2. *History of the Church*, 1:216.

3. *History of the Church*, 1:241.

4. In *History of the Church*, 1:261–64.

5. See *History of the Church*, 1:265.

6. *History of the Church*, 1:269; spelling standardized.

7. *History of the Church*, 1:269.

8. Letter from Joseph Smith to Emma Smith, 6 June 1832, cited in Dean C. Jessee, ed., *The Personal Writings of Joseph Smith* (Salt Lake City: Deseret Book Co., 1984), p. 238; spelling, punctuation, and capitalization standardized.

9. *History of the Church*, 1:272.

10. See *History of the Church*, 1:295.

11. See Brigham Young, "History of Brigham Young," *Millennial Star,* 11 July 1863, p. 439.

12. In *Lydia Knight's History* (Salt Lake City: Juvenile Instructor Office, 1883), pp. 10–13, 23, 101.

13. Cited in Jessee, *Personal Writings of Joseph Smith*, pp. 18–19; spelling, punctuation, and capitalization standardized.

14. See *History of the Church*, 1:368.

15. Robert J. Matthews, *"A Plainer Translation,"* Joseph Smith's Translation of the Bible: A History and Commentary (Provo: Brigham Young University Press, 1975), p. 256; see also pp. 264–65.

16. *History of the Church*, 1:226; spelling standardized.

17. *History of the Church*, 1:235.

18. See *History of the Church*, 2:482–83.

19. In *History of the Church*, 1:267.

20. In B. H. Roberts, *The Missouri Persecutions* (Salt Lake City: Bookcraft, 1965), p. 61.

21. In *Journal of Discourses*, 12:158.

22. *History of the Church*, 3:304.

23. See Davis Bitton, "Kirtland as a Center of Missionary Activity, 1830–1838," *Brigham Young University Studies,* Summer 1971, pp. 499–500.

24. Mission Journal of Orson Hyde, typescript, 1832, Brigham Young University, Special Collections, Provo, pp. 14–15, 31.

25. George A. Smith, "My Journal," *Instructor,* Oct. 1946, p. 462.

EXPULSION FROM JACKSON COUNTY

Expulsion from Jackson County by C.C.A. Christensen

THE PROPHET JOSEPH and those who accompanied him to Missouri in the summer of 1831 were joyful to learn that Jackson County was the location of the latter-day Zion. They did not realize that within two years the Saints would be driven from their homes in western Missouri. Although Church members were unaware of the persecutions that were before them, the Lord had told them that the glory of Zion would come only "after much tribulation" (D&C 58:4).

The year 1833 was one of tribulation for the Saints in Jackson County, Missouri. Irreconcilable conflicts developed with their neighbors over several issues, causing some citizens to take decisive action against the members of the Church. The conflict began during the summer, and in November organized mobs mercilessly drove the Saints from their homes and across the Missouri River under the worst of conditions.

A NEED TO REPENT

By the end of 1832 there were over eight hundred Saints gathered into five branches in Jackson County. New people were arriving almost every week to establish their homes. Seven high priests—Oliver Cowdery, William W.

Phelps, John Whitmer, Sidney Gilbert, Edward Partridge, Isaac Morley, and John Corrill—were appointed by Joseph Smith to preside over the affairs of the rapidly expanding Church in Zion. These brethren called other elders to preside over individual branches.

Some members, however, tried to circumvent the Church leaders in Missouri by ignoring their authority to preside; therefore, making it difficult to set some of the branches in order. Others "sought to obtain inheritances in some other way than according to the laws of consecration and steward-ship."[1] Elder Phelps wrote a letter to Joseph Smith in Kirtland about the dilemma and received a prompt reply containing revealed instructions. The Lord warned those who had evaded the revealed laws that they were not worthy to "have their names enrolled with the people of God" or "written in the book of the law of God" (D&C 85:3, 5). As Church historian, John Whitmer was directed to keep a record of those who received their inheritances "legally" from Bishop Edward Partridge as well as those who subsequently apostatized (see D&C 85:1–2).

Other difficulties arose in Zion. Petty jealousies, covetousness, light-mindedness, unbelief, and general neglect in keeping the commandments of God came to the attention of the Prophet. Some people in Zion even charged Joseph Smith with "seeking after monarchial power and authority" and said that he was purposely putting off settling in Zion.[2]

The Prophet wrote back in the spirit of peace and sent a copy of the "Olive Leaf" (D&C 88): "Though our brethren in Zion indulge in feelings towards us, which are not according to the requirements of the new covenant, yet, we have the satisfaction of knowing that the Lord approves of us, and has accepted us, and established His name in Kirtland for the salvation of the nations; . . . if Zion will not purify herself, He will seek another people. . . . Repent, repent, is the voice of God to Zion."[3]

At the same time a council in Kirtland appointed Hyrum Smith and Orson Hyde to write a letter of reproof to the Church in Missouri. The letter was a stern warning to "repent, repent, or Zion must suffer, for the scourge and judgment must come upon her." It went on to plead with the Saints to read and obey the scriptures and humble themselves before God. "They have not come up to Zion to sit down in idleness, neglecting the things of God, but they are to be diligent and faithful in obeying the new covenant."[4]

Following receipt of the Olive Leaf revelation, a council of high priests met on 26 February 1833 and called for solemn assemblies to be held in each of the branches (see D&C 88:70). David Pettigrew wrote in his journal that Bishop Partridge appointed them "as a day of confession and repentance."[5] Elders Oliver Cowdery, William W. Phelps, and John Corrill also wrote to the authorities in Kirtland in behalf of the Saints in Zion expressing their desire to keep the commandments in the future.[6] The Lord was pleased with this new spirit and revealed to the Prophet that "the angels rejoice" over the Saints in Missouri (D&C 90:34).

OPTIMISTIC OUTLOOK FOR THE FUTURE

The migration of new Saints to Missouri in the spring and early summer of 1833 exceeded that of the previous season. Parley P. Pratt remembered that as new arrivals purchased land, built homes, and cultivated the land, "peace and plenty had crowned their labors, and the wilderness became a fruitful field, and the solitary place began to bud and blossom as the rose." The Saints assembled each Sunday in their branches to worship. Harmony prevailed among them during these early days in June. Parley said, "There has seldom, if ever, been a happier people upon the earth than the Church of the Saints now were."[7]

During the summer a school for the elders was organized in Zion that was modeled after the School of the Prophets in Kirtland. Parley P. Pratt was called to preside and to teach a class of about sixty elders, who met in shady groves. Elder Pratt fondly remembered: "Here great blessings were poured

School in Zion monument at Troost Park in Kansas City, Missouri. It was dedicated 14 September 1963 by Joseph Fielding Smith. The monument commemorates the location of the school in Zion, established by the Church in Kaw township in 1831 and the first schoolhouse to be erected within the boundaries of Kansas City.

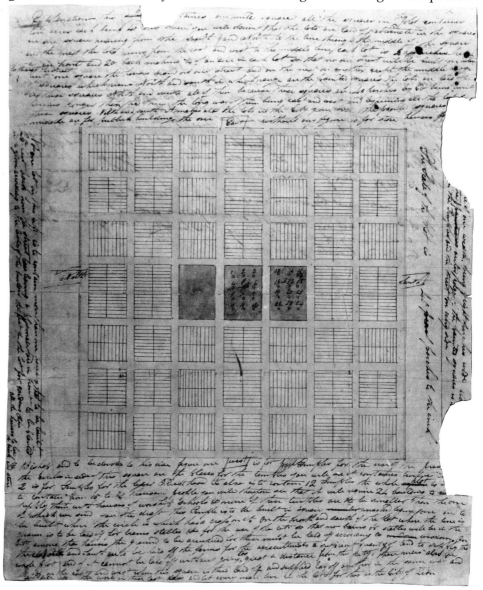

Edward Partridge purchased 63.43 acres from Jones Hoy Flournoy on 19 December 1831. This included the ground previously dedicated for the temple site. On 25 June 1833 the Prophet sent this plat to the brethren in Missouri.

The plat is one mile square with each square in the plat representing ten acres.[8]

out, and many great and marvelous things were manifested and taught. The Lord gave me great wisdom, and enabled me to teach and edify the Elders."[9] Some of the brethren experienced the gift of tongues in these meetings. Meanwhile, W. W. Phelps continued to prepare the *Book of Commandments* for publication, and he also edited the *Evening and Morning Star,* which appeared monthly.

Late in June 1833 the Prophet sent a plan for the building up of the city of Zion and its accompanying temple to the Saints in Missouri. The city was designed for fifteen to twenty thousand people and was to be one mile square with ten-acre blocks divided into one-half-acre lots, one house per lot. A complex of twenty-four temples was to be built and used as houses of worship. The schools were to be located on two central city blocks. Lands on the north and south of the city were to be used for barns, stables, and farms. The farmer, as well as the merchant and mechanic, was to live in the city to enjoy all the social, cultural, and educational advantages.[10] Unfortunately, mob interference prevented the implementation of this plan, although many of its basic ideas were later used by the Latter-day Saints in northern Missouri, Nauvoo, Illinois, and in hundreds of other settlements in the West.

CAUSES OF THE CONFLICT IN JACKSON COUNTY

The happy and favorable circumstances of the Saints in Jackson County ended suddenly in July of 1833. The original inhabitants of the area became increasingly suspicious as the number of Church members in Jackson County grew rapidly. Many people feared they would soon be outnumbered by the new religiously-motivated pilgrims from the East. The "old settlers" were from a different background than the incoming Latter-day Saints, and it was natural that cultural, political, religious, and economic differences arose.

Jackson County's residents were a rough-and-ready group who had come from the mountainous regions of several southern states to the western edge of the United States to find freedom from societal restraints. Most of them were uneducated and lacked the cultural refinement that was more common in New England and the East. Many of them indulged in profanity, Sabbath-breaking, horse-racing, cock-fighting, idleness, drunkenness, gambling, and violence. Following his first visit to Jackson County, the Prophet Joseph Smith reflected on "how natural it was to observe the degradation, leanness of intellect, ferocity, and jealousy of a people that were nearly a century behind the times, and to feel for those who roamed about without the benefit of civilization, refinement, or religion."[11]

The old settlers viewed the growing body of Saints as a political threat, even though members of the Church did not run for office or vote as a bloc during their short stay in Jackson County. By July 1833 the Mormon population in the county was almost twelve hundred, with more arriving each month. Some members boasted that thousands more were coming to live in the county. "By sheer arithmetic a few hundred additional Mormons could have wrested political control from those who had established the city and county."[12] Local citizens were naturally apprehensive of a religious zeal that predicted that all "gentiles" (non-Mormons) would be cut off when the millennial kingdom was established in Jackson County.

Protestant ministers also resented the Mormon intrusion into the county. Latter-day Saints were labeled fanatics and knaves and were denounced as gullible and ignorant because they believed in and frequently experienced miracles, prophecy, healings, and speaking in tongues. Jealousy and fear of losing some from their flocks added to the antagonism of the ministers. The Reverend Finis Ewing of the Cumberland Presbyterian Church asserted, "The 'Mormons' are the common enemies of mankind and ought to be destroyed." A reverend of the Missionary Society (sent to Christianize the American Indians) went "from house to house, seeking to destroy the Church by spreading slanderous falsehoods, to incite the people to acts of violence against the saints."[13]

In addition, Mormon merchants and tradesmen successfully took over a portion of the lucrative Santa Fe Trail trade previously dominated by the Missourians. Some of the old settlers feared that the Church members were determined to take over their lands and businesses. Moreover, the Saints "did not purchase goods from the local merchants, as they had no money, but traded among themselves at the Church storehouse. . . . Some of the old settlers were selling their property to the Mormons and moving away. This meant fewer and fewer customers in the stores, and future financial ruin" for the remaining old settlers.

To complicate matters, in the spring of 1833 the Missouri flooded, destroyed the landing at Independence, and shifted the channel of the river away from the community. A new town, Westport, with a better landing, was established farther upstream, and the business in Independence declined. Entrepreneurs in Independence blamed the Mormons for this situation.[14] Foreseeing what the future might bring, some of the old settlers offered to sell out to the Saints. Members of the Church wanted to buy the farms and possessions, but did not have enough capital to do so. This exasperated the Missourians, and soon they were spreading tales of how poverty-stricken the Mormons were.

The Missouri frontiersmen feared and hated the Indians. Their antipathy increased in the 1830s as the government began to resettle eastern tribes on lands just west of Independence. After the 1832 Black Hawk War, citizens of western Missouri petitioned Congress to establish a line of military posts for their protection. The first Mormon missionaries came into this tense atmosphere declaring the prophetic destiny of the native Americans. The old settlers were afraid the Saints would use the Indians to help them conquer the area for their New Jerusalem. Matters were further complicated by Protestant ministers who were jealous of Latter-day Saint proselyting efforts among the Indians.

Both the Santa Fe and Oregon trails began in Independence, Missouri. Here fur traders, pioneers, and adventurers of all types were outfitted for the trek west.

The conflict between the Saints and the old settlers came to a head over the slavery issue. Missouri had come into the Union as a slave state under the famous Compromise of 1820. Slaveholding was limited, however. The old settlers prized their right to hold slaves and despised abolitionism. Some of the Saints brought abolitionist sentiments from the North and East, and the possibility of a black rebellion was a fear throughout the South at this time. In 1831 Nat Turner's slave uprising in Virginia had resulted in the death of over seventy whites and one hundred slaves. An irrational fear of revolts swept over the slave states. Therefore, Missourians were highly aroused early in 1832 by rumors that the Saints were trying to persuade slaves to disobey their masters or run away.

To squelch the rumors, the July 1833 *Evening and Morning Star* ran an article cautioning the missionaries about proselyting among slaves and among former slaves, known as "free people of color." Unfortunately the local Missourians misinterpreted this advice to mean that Brother Phelps was inviting free blacks to join the Mormons in Jackson County. The article caused such a furor that Phelps issued an "Extra" explaining that the Church had no intention of inviting free blacks to Missouri, but his denials were to no avail.

During the summer of 1833, the many differences between the Saints and the old settlers combined to set the stage for violence. A mob atmosphere had been developing since April; in early July hundreds of people, including prominent citizens, signed a manifesto known as the "secret constitution," denouncing the Mormons and calling for a meeting on 20 July. The manifesto accused the Mormons of tampering with slaves, encouraging sedition, and inviting free Negroes and mulattoes to join the Church and immigrate to Missouri. It declared the intent of the signers to remove the Mormons "peaceably if we can, forcibly if we must."[15]

MOBS THREATEN THE SAINTS

On Saturday, 20 July, four or five hundred disgruntled citizens met at the Independence courthouse. They chose officers and selected a committee to draft a document outlining their demands of the Mormons. The officers and committee members were some of the leading citizens of Jackson County: "In the main they were the county officers—the county judge, the constables, clerks of the court and justices of the peace."[16] The lieutenant governor of Missouri, Lilburn W. Boggs, a resident and large landholder in the county, also attended the meeting and encouraged the anti-Mormon activity.

The "secret constitution" was read at the meeting, and the committee drafted the bitter ultimatum that no Latter-day Saints would be allowed to move to or settle in Jackson County, and those that were already there must pledge to leave within a reasonable time. The Church newspaper was also to cease publication. A committee of twelve was appointed to present these demands to the Saints. The brethren, startled by the request and realizing

The flight of the Mormons from Jackson County, Missouri, by C.C.A. Christensen

that they should not forsake Zion, asked for three months to consider the proposition and to consult with Church leaders in Ohio. This was denied them. They asked for ten days, but the committee allowed them only fifteen minutes and returned to the meeting at the courthouse.

The meeting quickly turned into a mob that decided to destroy the printing office and the press. They surrounded the printing office and residence of W. W. Phelps, threw the furniture into the street and garden, broke the press and hauled it away, scattered the type, and destroyed nearly all the printed work, including most of the unbound sheets of the Book of Commandments. They soon leveled the two-story printing office. Next the mob decided to destroy the goods of the Gilbert and Whitney Store. Only when Sidney Gilbert promised that he would pack the goods in three days were they dissuaded.

With loud cursings, the mob then searched for the leading elders of the Church. Men, women, and children ran in all directions. The mob took Bishop Edward Partridge from his home and dragged him to the public square. Charles Allen, a twenty-seven-year-old convert from Pennsylvania, was also taken to the public square. The mob demanded that they renounce the Book of Mormon or leave the county. The two men refused to do either, so the mob prepared tar and feathers. Bishop Partridge calmly declared that he was willing to suffer for the sake of Christ as the Saints in former ages had done. The two bore the cruel indignity of tarring and feathering with so much resignation and meekness, that the crowd, which had been shouting vile oaths, dispersed in silence.[17]

A small number of copies of the Book of Commandments, which contained revelations received by the Prophet Joseph Smith, were providentially preserved. Two sisters, Mary Elizabeth and Caroline Rollins, ages

In 1828, at the age of ten, Mary Elizabeth Rollins moved with her family to Kirtland. She was baptized in October 1830 after hearing the testimonies of Oliver Cowdery, Peter Whitmer, and Ziba Peterson.

She married Adam Lightner in August 1835, and they became the parents of ten children. She died in Minersville, Utah, on 17 December 1913 at the age of ninety-five.

Isaac Morley (1786–1865) served as first counselor to Bishop Edward Partridge for nine years. During the last ten years of his life he was a patriarch in Sanpete County, Utah.

fourteen and twelve, watched the mob throw the large, unbound sheets out onto the ground outside the printing office. Determined to save some of the copies, the girls grabbed as many sheets as they could carry in their arms and ran behind the building. Mobbers shouted at them to stop, but the girls escaped through a gap in a wooden fence and ran into a cornfield. For a long time they heard the men searching for them as they laid quietly on the ground.

When the mobbers left, Mary and Caroline found Sister Phelps and her family hidden in an old stable. Sister Phelps took charge of the sheets, and later the few preserved copies were bound. Each of the girls received a copy of the Book of Commandments, which they prized for the rest of their lives. A young man, twenty-year-old John Taylor (not the future President of the Church), risked his life by reaching between the logs of the print shop to retrieve a few sheets, and he also miraculously escaped from the mob as they tried to stone him.[18]

The mob appeared again on 23 July with rifles, pistols, whips, and clubs. They searched for Church leaders, cursing and profaning as they went. They set fire to haystacks and grain fields and destroyed several homes, barns, and businesses. The mob eventually confronted six leaders of the Church who, seeing the property and lives of the Saints in jeopardy, offered their lives as a ransom. Their names—Edward Partridge, Isaac Morley, John Corrill, John Whitmer, W. W. Phelps, and Sidney Gilbert—are held in honorable remembrance by the Church.

Rejecting this offer, the mob leaders threatened that every man, woman, and child would be whipped unless they consented to leave the county. Under duress the brethren signed an agreement to leave the county—the leaders by 1 January 1834 and the members themselves by 1 April. John Corrill and Sidney Gilbert were allowed to remain as agents to sell the property of the Saints. Corrill wrote that the members of the Church up to this time "had not so much as lifted a finger, even in their own defense, so tenacious were they for the precepts of the gospel,—'turn the other cheek.'"[19]

SEEKING REDRESS

After the agreement was signed, Oliver Cowdery was sent to Ohio to confer with Church authorities on the plight of the Saints in Missouri. A council in Kirtland met on 21 August and sent elders Orson Hyde and John Gould to Jackson County as special messengers. They instructed the Saints not to dispose of their lands or property nor to move from the county, unless they had specifically signed the agreement to do so. This message did not arrive in western Missouri until 28 September.

Meanwhile a few Church members attempted to settle in Van Buren County, but the citizens there also drew up an agreement to drive the Mormons out, so they returned again to their former homes. Throughout the summer, the mobs broke into the Mormon homes daily and continued their violence to the Jackson County inhabitants, even though they had agreed to refrain from harassing the Saints.

In August, the *Western Monitor*, a newspaper in Fayette, Missouri, ran a series of articles censuring the mob action in Jackson County and suggesting that the Saints seek redress from state authorities for the wrongs they had suffered. Thereupon Church leaders wrote up a petition detailing their grievances and denying the false accusations of the old settlers of Jackson County: "Influenced by the precepts of our beloved Savior when we have been smitten on the one cheek, we have turned the other also; . . . we have borne the above outrages without murmuring; but we cannot patiently bear them any longer; according to the laws of God and man, we have borne enough."[20] In early October, W. W. Phelps and the Church representative from Ohio, Orson Hyde, went to Jefferson City, the state capital, and presented the petition to Governor Daniel Dunklin. They asked him to raise troops to defend them in their rights, to give them permission to sue for damaged and lost property, and to bring the mob element to justice.

After a few days of consultation with the attorney general, the governor replied that he felt force would not be necessary to carry out the laws. He advised the Church representatives to seek redress and protection under the laws through petitioning the circuit judge and justices of the peace in Jackson County. If this effort failed, he promised to use other means to enforce the law.[21]

His advice proved ineffective. Samuel D. Lucas, the county judge for Jackson County, and two of the justices of the peace in the county, were among those who were trying to drive the Mormons out. Nevertheless, following the governor's instructions, Church leaders engaged the services of four prominent lawyers in Clay County. These lawyers became friends of the Saints and defended them against their oppressors throughout the rest of the decade in Missouri. Two of them, Alexander Doniphan and David Atchison, attained state and national prominence between 1845 and 1865.

In addition to seeking legal redress, Church leaders ended their policy of passive resistance and counseled the members to arm themselves for the defense of their families and homes. A delegation to Clay County purchased powder and lead, and Church officials announced on 20 October 1833 their intent to defend themselves against any physical attack.

SAINTS DRIVEN FROM JACKSON COUNTY

When the old settlers saw that the Saints' intended to defend themselves, they renewed their acts of violence and circulated rumors about the blasphemy of the Mormons' doctrines and their supposed intentions to take possession of Jackson County by force. Within a week the mood of the county was at a fevered pitch. On the night of Thursday, 31 October, a mob of about fifty horsemen attacked the Whitmer Settlement on the Big Blue River, west of Independence. They unroofed thirteen houses and nearly whipped to death several men, including Hiram Page, one of the eight witnesses of the Book of Mormon. These depredations continued for the next two nights in Independence, in Blue township, in Kaw township, and again in the Whitmer Settlement. Men were beaten, and women and children were terrorized. When Church leaders were unable to obtain a warrant against the raiders, the elders posted guards at each of their settlements to defend themselves.

Not all of the citizens of Jackson County were against the Saints. Some of those who were friendly toward the members of the Church had no sympathy with the rioters or with the lawlessness of the mob. Unfortunately little was done by these sympathizers to prevent the violence inflicted upon the religious newcomers.

Monday, 4 November, became known as the "bloody day" of the conflict. Several Missourians captured a Mormon ferry on the Big Blue River, and soon thirty or forty armed men from each side confronted each other in the corn fields. The mob fired first, wounding Philo Dibble in the stomach, but he was miraculously healed through a priesthood blessing by Newel Knight. Andrew Barber was mortally wounded. The Mormons returned fire and killed two Missourians and a few horses. That same day several Church leaders had been arrested in Independence and brought to trial. As their trial was in progress in the courthouse, altered news of the battle reached the town accusing the Mormons of entering the house of a citizen and shooting his son. This enraged the crowd, which threatened to kill the prisoners. The prisoners, however, were quickly taken to the jail and locked up for their safety. Throughout the night citizens collected arms and ammunition in preparation for a general massacre of the Saints the next day. Rumors also circulated that the Mormons were going to bring in Indians to fight with them. Meanwhile the jailed prisoners, hearing of these preparations, informed the sheriff that they intended to leave the county and to urge all other Church members to do the same.

At the instigation of Lieutenant Governor Boggs, a unit of the state militia, under the command of avowed anti-Mormon Colonel Thomas Pitcher, was called in to drive the Mormons out of the county. Meanwhile, Lyman Wight, hearing of the imprisonment of Church leaders, gathered about two hundred armed brethren and marched toward the jail. About a mile outside Independence, they learned that the militia had been called in. Boggs negotiated an agreement that both camps would give up their arms and that the Saints would leave the county within ten days. The Saints surrendered their weapons with the understanding that the weapons would be returned once the Saints had moved to Clay County. The militia retained their arms, however, and the Saints never saw theirs again.

True to their pledge, as soon as they were released, the prisoners made plans for a quick retreat of the Saints across the Missouri River. A number of marauders, however, rode through the countryside the next three days harassing the Mormon settlers, including a group of about 130 women and children who had been left alone while their men hunted for wagons. At least two women died while the Saints were fleeing the county.

The shores of the Missouri near the ferry were lined with refugees on both sides. Some were fortunate enough to escape with their household goods, but many of them lost everything. Parley P. Pratt wrote: "When night again closed upon us the cottonwood bottom had much the appearance of a camp meeting. Hundreds of people were seen in every direction, some in tents and some in the open air around their fires, while the rain descended in torrents. Husbands were inquiring for their wives, wives for their husbands; parents for children, and children for parents. . . . The scene was indescribable, and, I am sure, would have melted the hearts of any people on the earth, except our blind oppressors."[22]

The mob in Jackson County continued tormenting the few remaining members of the Church until all of them were driven out of the county. Lyman Wight reported, "I saw one hundred and ninety women and children driven thirty miles across the prairie, with three decrepit men only in their company, in the month of November, the ground thinly crusted with sleet; and I could easily follow on their trail by the *blood that flowed from their lacerated feet* on the stubble of the burnt prairie!"[23] Early in the spring of 1834 the Missourians learned of the approach of Mormons from Ohio and burned the remainder of the houses belonging to the Saints in an attempt to discourage the return of the exiles.

AFTERMATH OF THE EXPULSION

Most of the exiled Saints found temporary quarters in Clay County, although a few sought refuge in other nearby counties. The citizens of Liberty, the county seat of Clay County, charitably offered shelter, work, and provisions. The refugees moved into abandoned slave cabins, built crude huts, pitched tents, and lived on a meager subsistence until the arrival of spring. Some men found work splitting rails, building houses, and grubbing brush. Several of the sisters worked in the households of well-to-do farmers, while others taught school. In the spring some were able to rent land and plant crops. Although most of the citizens of Clay County were friendly, they considered the settlement of the Saints in their midst as only temporary. Hostile elements in Jackson County dubbed these sympathizers "Jack-Mormons," a term applied in the nineteenth century to friendly non-Mormons.

Meanwhile from Kirtland Joseph Smith followed the events in western Missouri. Upon hearing of the July troubles he wrote to the Church in Zion: "Brethren if I were with you I should take an active part in your sufferings, and although nature shrinks, yet my spirit would not let me forsake you unto death, God helping me."[24] In October 1833 the Lord revealed to Joseph that "Zion shall be redeemed, although she is chastened for a little season.

. . . Let your hearts be comforted; for all things shall work together for good to them that walk uprightly, and to the sanctification of the church" (D&C 100:13, 15).

Elders Hyde and Gould, emissaries from Kirtland to Missouri, returned to Ohio on 25 November with "the melancholy intelligence of the mob in Jackson county persecuting the brethren."[25] This deeply distressed the Prophet. He wrote, "I cannot learn from any communication by the Spirit to me, that Zion has forfeited her claim to a celestial crown, notwithstanding the Lord has caused her to be thus afflicted. . . . I know that Zion, in the due time of the Lord, will be redeemed; but how many will be the days of her purification, tribulation, and affliction, the Lord has kept hid from my eyes; and when I inquire concerning this subject, the voice of the Lord is: Be still, and know that I am God! All those who suffer for my name shall reign with me, and he that layeth down his life for my sake shall find it again."[26]

A few days later the Lord explained that the Saints in Missouri suffered affliction "in consequence of their transgressions. . . . There were jarrings, and contentions, and envyings, and strifes, and lustful and covetous desires among them; therefore by these things they pollute their inheritances" (D&C 101:2, 6).

The Saints in Missouri wondered whether they should establish permanent or temporary settlements in Clay County since there was little hope of returning to their homes in Jackson County. At a conference on 1 January 1834 they decided to send two elders to Kirtland to counsel with the Prophet and arrange for relief for the Missouri Saints. Lyman Wight and Parley P. Pratt volunteered. They lacked the means to make the trip, however. Parley wrote, "I was at this time entirely destitute of proper clothing for the journey; and I had neither horse, saddle, bridle, money nor provisions to take with me; or to leave with my wife, who lay sick and helpless most of the time."[27] These noble brethren were outfitted with the aid of other members. They proceeded by horseback as rapidly as possible, but inclement weather delayed their arrival until the early spring.

While awaiting instructions from their Prophet, Church leaders in Missouri sought reparation from the Missouri state government. A court of inquiry held in Liberty in December called for the arrest of Colonel Thomas Pitcher of the state militia. It soon became evident, however, that public opinion in Jackson County against the Saints was so strong that criminal prosecution was impossible. Church leaders decided to abandon the effort. Governor Dunklin ordered the arms of the Church members to be returned, but his order was defied.

The Saints kept the subject of their wrongs constantly before the state authorities. At the same time they petitioned Andrew Jackson, president of the United States, and enclosed with their petition the reply of Governor Dunklin to their petition to him. The governor claimed that the law did not authorize him to keep a military force in Jackson County to protect the

Mormons after they were returned to their homes. The Saints asked the president to restore them to their homes and possessions and to ensure their protection. Unfortunately this request came during one of the great debates in American history over the question of sovereign rights of states. The general feeling in America was that the federal government had no authority to intervene in a state's internal affairs, such as those occurring in Jackson County, unless the governor declared a state of insurrection. In May 1834 the federal government denied the Saints' petition, arguing that the offenses listed were violations of state, not federal, law. Meanwhile Governor Dunklin also hesitated to take action. Lawyers for the Church argued the Saints' case before the state legislature, but that body also refused to help.

July 1833 to July 1834 was a period of the "refiner's fire" for the Latter-day Saints in western Missouri. Members of the Church throughout the United States were profoundly disappointed that the land of Zion had to be abandoned. Their only recourse was to wait patiently upon the Lord for deliverance and direction.

ENDNOTES

1. B. H. Roberts, *The Missouri Persecutions* (Salt Lake City: Bookcraft, 1965), p. 61.

2. *History of the Church*, 1:318–19.

3. *History of the Church*, 1:316.

4. *History of the Church*, 1:320.

5. In Donald Q. Cannon and Lyndon W. Cook, eds., *Far West Record: Minutes of The Church of Jesus Christ of Latter-day Saints, 1830–1844* (Salt Lake City: Deseret Book Co., 1983), p. 61n; see also *History of the Church*, 1:327.

6. See *History of the Church*, 1:327; Roberts, *Missouri Persecutions*, p. 68.

7. Parley P. Pratt, ed., *Autobiography of Parley P. Pratt*, Classics in Mormon Literature series (Salt Lake City: Deseret Book Co., 1985) p. 75; see also "The Season," *The Evening and the Morning Star*, June 1833, p. 102.

8. For detailed information on the plat, see *History of the Church*, 1:357–59.

9. Pratt, *Autobiography of Parley P. Pratt*, pp. 75–76.

10. See *History of the Church*, 1:357–58.

11. *History of the Church*, 1:189.

12. T. Edgar Lyon, "Independence, Missouri, and the Mormons, 1827–1833," *Brigham Young University Studies*, Autumn 1972, p. 17.

13. In Roberts, *Missouri Persecutions*, pp. 73–74.

14. Lyon, "Independence, Missouri, and the Mormons," pp. 17–18.

15. *History of the Church*, 1:374.

16. Roberts, *Missouri Persecutions*, p. 87.

17. See Roberts, *Missouri Persecutions*, pp. 84–86.

18. See Gerry Avant, "Book's History: A Tale of Mobs, Heroic Rescues," *Church News*, 30 Dec. 1984, p. 6.

19. John Corrill, *A Brief History of the Church of Christ of Latter Day Saints* (St. Louis: John Corrill, 1839), p. 19; spelling standardized.

20. *History of the Church*, 1:414–15.

21. See *History of the Church*, 1:423–24.

22. Pratt, *Autobiography of Parley P. Pratt*, p. 82.

23. In *History of the Church*, 3:439.

24. In Dean C. Jessee, ed., *The Personal Writings of Joseph Smith* (Salt Lake City: Deseret Book Co., 1984), p. 283.

25. *History of the Church*, 1:446.

26. *History of the Church*, 1:453–54; capitalization standardized.

27. Pratt, *Autobiography of Parley P. Pratt*, p. 87.

ZION'S CAMP

D URING THE WINTER of 1833–34 the Saints still hoped that Governor Daniel Dunklin would assist them in regaining their homes in Jackson County. On 16 December 1833, however, Joseph Smith received a revelation that raised ominous possibilities. The Lord set forth various means by which the Saints were to settle the Missouri dispute, but they were warned that if all peaceful remedies failed they might have to occupy their rightful lands by force (see D&C 101). As events unfolded, the Lord instructed the brethren in Kirtland to raise an army and go to Missouri. What was called Zion's Camp became a reality.

ZION'S CAMP ORGANIZED

After an arduous journey, Parley P. Pratt and Lyman Wight arrived in Kirtland from Missouri on 22 February 1834. The high council in Kirtland, which had been organized less than a week (see D&C 102 section heading), assembled in Joseph Smith's home two days afterward to hear the pair's report and consider the Missouri brethren's requests for help. At the conclusion of the meeting, Joseph Smith announced that he was going to Zion to help redeem it. He asked for a vote of the high council to sanction his decision. He was supported unanimously. The Prophet then asked for volunteers to go with him. Thirty to forty of the men present volunteered, and Joseph was selected to be the "commander-in-chief of the armies of Israel."[1]

That same day Joseph Smith received a revelation concerning the recruitment and size of this army. Eight men, including the Prophet, were called to help gather young and middle-aged members for Zion's Camp and to raise money to help the oppressed members in Missouri. They were to recruit a company of five hundred men if possible—but no fewer than one hundred—to march to Missouri to redeem and restore Zion (see D&C 103:11, 15, 22, 29–40).

Beginning in late February these eight missionaries traveling two by two visited the branches of the Church throughout the eastern United States gathering contributions and recruiting for Zion's Camp. The Prophet was not pleased with the number of volunteers they recruited. In April he suggested that the brethren in the East volunteer to go to Missouri with Zion's Camp, or lose the chance to "better themselves by obtaining so goodly a land, . . . and stand against that wicked mob. . . .

◄ Zion's Camp by C.C.A. Christensen

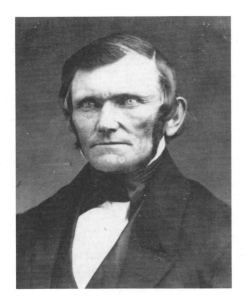

Wilford Woodruff (1807–98) was an avid student of the scriptures, a missionary, Apostle, Church historian, and President of the Church.

Hosea Stout (1810–89) joined the Church in 1838 while living in Far West, Missouri. He was a schoolteacher, an officer in the Nauvoo Legion, chief of the Nauvoo police force, a seventy, a lawyer, a missionary, and a colonizer.

". . . If this Church, which is essaying to be the Church of Christ will not help us, when they can do it without sacrifice, . . . God shall take away their talent, and give it to those who have no talent, and shall prevent them from ever obtaining a place of refuge, or an inheritance upon the land of Zion."[2]

Nevertheless, few in the East volunteered for the camp. One who did was a recent convert, twenty-seven-year-old Wilford Woodruff of Connecticut. Wilford was impressed with Parley P. Pratt's impassioned appeal for volunteers, but he was hesitant to go because of his business affairs. Wilford Woodruff recorded in his journal, "I told Brother Parley our circumstances. He told me it was my duty to try to prepare myself and go up to Zion. And accordingly I used every exertion to settle my accounts, arrange my affairs, and prepare myself to join my brethren to go to Missouri."[3] By 25 April, Wilford was living at Joseph Smith's home in Kirtland helping prepare others for the camp.

On 21 April, Hyrum Smith and Lyman Wight went northwest from Kirtland to seek out more recruits. They were to lead those who joined them to meet Joseph's company at the Salt River in eastern Missouri. They visited branches of the Church in northern Ohio, Michigan, and Illinois, and eventually recruited more than twenty volunteers, over half of them from Pontiac, Michigan. Hosea Stout, who later played key roles in the Church, had not yet become a member in 1834 when Hyrum and Lyman went to his hometown in Michigan. Hosea later wrote, "The effect of their preaching was powerful on me, and when I considered that they were going up to Zion to fight for their lost inheritances under the special directions of God it was all that I could do to refrain from going."[4]

Recruitment efforts in Kirtland were less disappointing. Many able-bodied priesthood holders in that community volunteered to march to Zion. Thirty-two-year-old Brigham Young stepped forward and tried to convince his older brother Joseph to go too. Joseph Smith declared to the two brothers, "Brother Brigham and brother Joseph, if you will go with me in the camp to Missouri and keep my counsel, I promise you, in the name of the Almighty, that I will lead you there and back again, and not a hair of your heads shall be harmed." Hearing this Joseph Young agreed to participate, and the three men clasped hands in confirmation of this promise.[5]

Many of the men in Zion's Camp left families with little or no money and no source of income. To prevent undue hardships, members of the Church planted gardens so the women and children could harvest corn and other crops during the army's absence. The volunteers also gathered supplies and teams for their journey, as well as clothing, bedding, food, and arms for the Saints in Missouri. A few elders, including Oliver Cowdery and Sidney Rigdon, were left behind to supervise the ongoing construction of the temple and to direct the other affairs of the Church in Kirtland.

THE MARCH TOWARD ZION

On 1 May, the day appointed to begin the one-thousand-mile march, only twenty people were ready to go. Joseph Smith sent them fifty miles south to New Portage, where they were to wait for the others to join them. By Sunday, 4 May, over eighty volunteers assembled in Kirtland. Nearly all of them were young men. Some were fearful of what lay ahead. Heber C. Kimball said, "I took leave of my wife and children and friends, not knowing whether I would see them again in the flesh."[6] That day the Prophet spoke to the Kirtland Saints before departing. George A. Smith wrote: "He impressed upon them the necessity of being humble, exercising faith and patience and living in obedience to the commands of the Almighty. . . . He bore testimony of the truth of the work which God had revealed through him and promised the brethren that if they all would live as they should, before the Lord, keeping his commandments, . . . they should all safely return."[7]

The next day Joseph Smith assumed his role as commander-in-chief of the army. The eighty men joined the twenty brethren in New Portage late Tuesday evening, 6 May 1834. There the Prophet organized the camp. He divided it into companies of tens and fifties and instructed each group to elect a captain, who was to assign each man his responsibilities. One recruit, Joseph Holbrook, reported that the camp was organized "according to the ancient order of Israel."[8] The men also consolidated their money into a general fund, which was managed by Frederick G. Williams, second counselor in the First Presidency, who was appointed paymaster. The average age of the recruits was twenty-nine, the age of their leader, Joseph Smith. George A. Smith, cousin of the Prophet, was the youngest at age sixteen, and Samuel Baker was the oldest at seventy-nine.

On 8 May the army of Israel resumed its long march west. Throughout its journey the camp was gradually strengthened with additional volunteers, arms, supplies, and money. Officers continued to recruit help from Latter-day Saints living in Ohio, Indiana, and Illinois. By the time Zion's Camp crossed the Mississippi River into Missouri, it numbered 185 individuals. On 8 June at the Salt River in Missouri, where Joseph Smith had arranged to meet Hyrum Smith's company, the army reached its maximum numerical strength: 207 men, 11 women, 11 children, and 25 baggage wagons.

In many respects the daily routine of Zion's Camp was similar to that of other armies. Most able-bodied men walked beside the heavily loaded wagons along the muddy and dusty trails. Many of them carried knapsacks and held guns. It was not unusual for them to march thirty-five miles a day, despite blistered feet, oppressive heat, heavy rains, high humidity, hunger, and thirst. Armed guards were posted around the camp at night. At 4:00 A.M. the trumpeter roused the weary men with reveille on an old, battered French horn. Each company gathered for prayer, then went to work at their respective assignments. Some members of the company gathered firewood, others

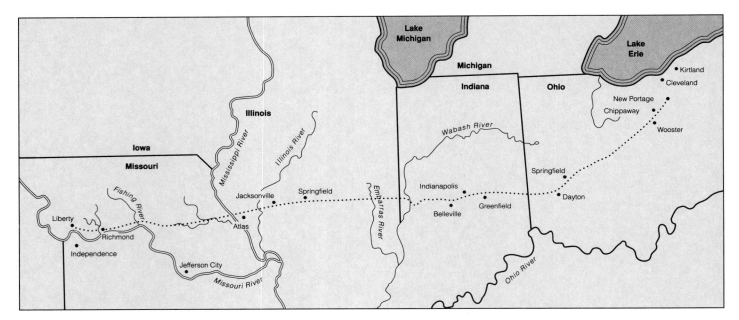

The journey of Zion's Camp

carried water, cooked breakfast, and took down tents. Wagon wheels had to be greased and horses fed and groomed before being hitched up for the day's journey.

Feeding the camp was one of the most persistent problems. The men were often required to eat limited portions of coarse bread, rancid butter, cornmeal mush, strong honey, raw pork, rotten ham, and maggot-infested bacon and cheese. George A. Smith wrote that he was frequently hungry: "I was so weary, hungry and sleepy that I dreamed while walking along the road of seeing a beautiful stream of water by a pleasant shade and a nice loaf of bread and a bottle of milk laid out on a cloth by the side of the spring."[9]

On occasion the men strained swamp water to remove wigglers (mosquito larvae), before drinking it. Milk and butter was often obtained from local farmers under unsanitary conditions, which raised fears among the camp of milk sickness, puking fever, or even death. But Joseph Smith advised them that unless they were told the milk was contaminated, "use all they could get from friend or enemy, it should do them good, and none be sick in consequence of it; and although we passed through neighborhoods where many of the people and cattle were infected with the sickness, yet my words were fulfilled."[10]

On a number of occasions, Joseph Smith taught those in the camp to conserve natural resources and to avoid killing. One afternoon while preparing to pitch his tent Joseph and others discovered three rattlesnakes. As the men prepared to kill them, the Prophet said, "Let them alone—don't hurt them! How will the serpent ever lose his venom, while the servants of God possess the same disposition, and continue to make war upon it? Men must become harmless, before the brute creation." The snakes were carefully carried across a creek on sticks and released. Joseph instructed the camp to refrain from killing any animal unless it was necessary to avoid starvation.[11]

Unlike most armies, Zion's Camp placed great emphasis upon spirituality. Besides company prayers the men were admonished to pray privately morning and evening. On Sundays the camp rested, held meetings, and partook of the sacrament. They were often privileged to hear the Prophet teach the doctrines of the kingdom. Those in the camp had faith that the Lord was accompanying them. The Prophet recalled, "God was with us, and His angels went before us, and the faith of our little band was unwavering. We know that angels were our companions, for we saw them."[12]

On 2 June 1834 the army crossed the Illinois River at Phillips Ferry. The Prophet and a few others walked along the bluffs and found a huge mound with human bones scattered about and what appeared to be the remains of three ancient altars. A hole was dug and a large human skeleton was discovered with a stone arrowhead between its ribs. As the brethren left the hill, the Prophet inquired of the Lord and learned in an open vision that the remains were those of a man named Zelph, a former Lamanite warrior-chieftain who was killed "during the last great struggle of the Lamanites and Nephites."[13]

The Lord also blessed the camp to travel safely through sometimes threatening circumstances. Members of the camp generally tried to conceal their identity and objectives as they marched. Occasionally the army appeared larger or smaller than it actually was to those who tried to determine its strength. Near Dayton, Ohio, a dozen men entered the camp and concluded there were six hundred soldiers. As the camp crossed the Illinois River, the ferryman thought there were five hundred in the company. When they faced opposition at Indianapolis, Joseph assured the brethren that they would pass through the city without anyone being aware of their doing so. He divided them into small groups which dispersed, taking different routes through the community undetected.

Potential enemies notwithstanding, quarreling and contention within the camp became its most vexing problem. Several men feared possible dangers, some complained about changes in their life-style, and a few questioned the decisions of their leaders. For forty-five days they marched together, and the inevitable personality clashes were exacerbated by the harsh conditions they encountered. Grumblers often blamed Joseph Smith for their discomfort.

Sylvester Smith (no relation to the Prophet), a sharp-tongued group captain, frequently led the dissension. He complained that the food was poor, preparations for the journey were inadequate, and Joseph's watchdog kept him awake at night. On the evening of 17 May, Joseph was called upon to settle a dispute among some of the brethren. He said that he found a "rebellious spirit in Sylvester Smith, and to some extent in others. I told them they would meet with misfortunes, difficulties and hindrances, and said, 'and you will know it before you leave this place,' exhorting them to humble themselves before the Lord and become united, that they might not be scourged."[14] The following day the prophecy was fulfilled: nearly every horse was sick or lame. The Prophet promised if they would humble

"Hark! Listen to the Trumpeters" was a march hymn sung by those in Zion's Camp as they traveled to Missouri. Occasionally Brigham Young and Joseph Young sang the hymn for the benefit of the camp.

Hark! Listen to the Trumpeters

Hark! listen to the trumpeters
    They call for volunteers;
On Zion's bright and flow'ry mount
    Behold the officers.

Their horses white, their armours bright,
    With courage bold they stand,
Enlisting soldiers for their King,
    To march to Zion's land.

It sets my heart all in a flame
    A soldier for to be;
I will enlist, gird on my arms,
    And fight for liberty.

We want no cowards in our bands
    That will our colours fly;
We call for valiant–hearted men,
    Who're not afraid to die.

To see our armies on parade,
    How martial they appear;
All arm'd and drest in uniform,
    They look like men of war.

They follow their great General,
    The great eternal Lamb,
His garments stain'd in his own blood,
    King Jesus is his name.

The trumpets sound, the armies shout,
    They drive the hosts of hell:
How dreadful is our God t'adore!
    The great Emmanuel!

Sinners, enlist with Jesus Christ,
    The eternal Son of God;
And march with us to Zion's land,
    Beyond the swelling flood.

There, on a green and flow'ry mount,
    Where fruits immortal grow,
With angels all arrayed in white,
    And our Redeemer know.

We'll shout and sing for evermore
    In that eternal world;
While Satan and his army too
    Shall down to hell be hurl'd.

Lift up your heads, ye soldiers bold,
    Redemption's drawing nigh;
We soon shall hear the trumpet sound
    That shakes the earth and sky.

In fiery chariots we shall rise,
    And leave the world on fire,
And all surround the throne of love,
    And join the heav'nly choir.[16]

themselves and overcome their discord, their animals would immediately be restored to health. By noon the horses were nimble once again, with the exception of Sylvester Smith's mount, which soon died.

Contention soon arose again when Sylvester Smith threatened to kill Joseph's dog. On 3 June a frustrated Joseph Smith stood on a wagon wheel and scolded the men for their lack of humility, their murmuring and fault-finding: "I said the Lord had revealed to me that a scourge would come upon the camp in consequence of the fractious and unruly spirits that appeared among them, and they should die like sheep with the rot; still, if they would repent and humble themselves before the Lord, the scourge, in a great measure, might be turned away; but, as the Lord lives, the members of this camp will suffer for giving way to their unruly temper."[15] This sad prophecy would be fulfilled within a few weeks.

EFFORTS TO ACHIEVE PEACE

The anti-Mormons in Jackson County learned of the advancing army in June when the postmaster in Chagrin, Ohio, wrote to his counterpart in Independence: "The Mormons in this region are organizing an army to restore Zion, that is to take it by force of arms."[17] Believing that a Mormon invasion was imminent, Jackson County troops began to drill, and sentries were posted at all ferries along the Missouri River. In a vindictive spirit, hoping perhaps to discourage the return of the Saints, mobbers burned 150 homes belonging to the Mormons who lived in the county. Members of Zion's Camp suspected that spies from Missouri had followed them for hundreds of miles. One night a Missourian went into camp and swore that he knew their destination was Jackson County and that they would never cross the Mississippi River alive.

At the same time, Church leaders in Clay County continued to petition Governor Daniel Dunklin for assurance that he would support the Saints in returning to their homes, regaining their property, and living in peace in Jackson County. The governor acknowledged that the Saints had been wronged by being driven from their homes, and he sought to have the arms returned that were taken from the Saints when they were expelled from Jackson County the previous November. Furthermore, he recognized that an armed force sent by the state would be necessary to restore the Mormons to their lands and protect them while the courts decided the legal issues involved.

Once Zion's Camp was in Missouri, Joseph Smith sent Elders Orson Hyde and Parley P. Pratt to Jefferson City, the state capital, to ascertain whether Governor Dunklin was still willing to honor his promise to reinstate the Saints in Jackson County with the assistance of the state militia. The interview was a bitter disappointment. Dunklin claimed that calling out the militia would probably plunge the state into open war. He advised the brethren that they could avoid bloodshed by relinquishing their rights, selling their lands, and settling elsewhere. This was unacceptable to the Church. The governor then advised an appeal to the courts, but the brethren felt that he knew this was not practical. Officers of the court were among the anti-Mormons in the county, so it was like referring them to a band of thieves to sue for the recovery of stolen property.[18] Parley was also convinced that the governor was a coward and was morally obligated to resign for failing to live up to the obligations of his office.

Elder Pratt and Elder Hyde rejoined the approaching Zion's Camp. Their report dashed any hopes that the Missouri Saints would be allowed to return to their homes peacefully. The brethren also realized that the anti-Mormons were waiting to destroy all Mormons who attempted to settle in Jackson County. The Prophet called upon God to witness the justice of the Saints' cause and the sincerity of their vows. Angered and frustrated by the governor's decision, Zion's Camp resumed marching.

Meanwhile Judge John J. Ryland of Clay County arranged a meeting for 16 June at the courthouse in Liberty. A committee of citizens from Jackson County and representatives of the Saints in Clay County were to meet in an effort to resolve the dispute. A large, unruly, belligerent crowd gathered at the meeting. The non-Mormons proposed to purchase within thirty days all property owned by the Saints in Jackson County at prices determined by three disinterested arbiters or to have the Mormons do likewise and buy all their property within the same time period. This proposal was unrealistic. The Saints did not have enough funds to purchase even a fraction of the land owned by the non-Mormons, and they could not sell their land in Zion because they had been commanded by the Lord to purchase and settle it. These facts, of course, were all known by the anti-Mormons. Tempers flared as Jackson County representative Samuel Owens swore that the Missourians would fight for every inch of ground rather than let the Saints return.

"A Baptist priest . . . said, 'The Mormons have lived long enough in Clay county; and they must either clear out, or be cleared out.'

"Mr. Turnham, the moderator of the meeting, answered in a masterly manner; saying, 'Let us be republicans; let us honor our country, and not disgrace it like Jackson county. For God's sake don't disfranchise or drive away the Mormons. They are better citizens than many of the old inhabitants.' "[19]

The Mormon committee prepared a statement specifying that the Saints would not commence hostilities, and they promised to respond to the Jackson County proposition within a week. Soon thereafter the Saints prepared a counterproposal suggesting that a neutral committee determine the value of the property of those in Jackson County who refused to live with the Latter-day Saints, and that the Saints buy that property within a year. Moreover, the Saints promised to stay out of Jackson County until full payment was made. These negotiations unfortunately proved futile.

EVENTS AT FISHING RIVER

By 18 June, Zion's Camp arrived within a mile of Richmond, the county seat of Ray County. As the army encamped, the Prophet had a premonition of danger. He went into the woods and prayed for safety, and he was assured that the Lord would protect them. He had the camp roused in the early morning hours, and they left without prayers or breakfast. As they marched through Richmond, a black slave woman agitatedly told Luke Johnson, "There is a company of men lying in wait here, who are calculating to kill you this morning as you pass through." They met no resistance, although they were able to make only nine miles, being slowed down by broken wagon wheels.

Instead of reaching their intended destination of Liberty, they camped just inside Clay County on a hill between two branches of the Fishing River. When Joseph learned that mobs were preparing to attack, he knelt and prayed again for divine protection. Joseph's fears were confirmed when five armed Missourians rode into camp, cursing, and swore that the Mormons would "see hell before morning." They boasted that nearly four hundred men had joined forces from Ray, Lafayette, Clay, and Jackson counties and were then preparing to cross the Missouri River at Williams Ferry and utterly destroy the Mormons.[20] Sounds of gunfire were heard, and some of the men wanted to fight, but the Prophet promised that the Lord would protect them. He declared, "Stand still and see the salvation of God."[21]

A few minutes after the Missourians left, a small black cloud appeared in the clear western sky. It moved eastward, unrolling like a scroll, filling the heavens with darkness. As the first ferry load of mobbers crossed the Missouri River to the south, a sudden squall made it nearly impossible for the boat to return to pick up another load. The storm was so intense that Zion's Camp abandoned their tents and found shelter in an old Baptist meetinghouse nearby. When Joseph Smith came in, he exclaimed, "Boys, there is some meaning to this. God is in this storm."[22] It was impossible for anyone to sleep, so the group sang hymns and rested on the rough benches. One camp member recorded that "during this time the whole canopy of the wide horizen was in one complete blaze with terrifying claps of thunder."[23]

Elsewhere the beleaguered mobbers sought any refuge they could. The furious storm broke branches from trees and destroyed crops. It soaked and made the mobbers' ammunition useless, frightened and scattered their horses, and raised the level of the Fishing River, preventing them from attacking Zion's Camp. The Prophet recalled, "It seemed as if the mandate of vengeance had gone forth from the God of battles, to protect His servants from the destruction of their enemies."[24]

Two days later, on 21 June, Colonel John Sconce and two associates of the Ray County militia rode into Zion's Camp to learn of the Mormons' intentions. "I see that there is an Almighty power that protects this people," Sconce admitted.[25] The Prophet explained that the only purpose of Zion's Camp was to help their brethren be reinstated on their lands and that their intent was not to injure anyone. He said, "The evil reports circulated about us were false, and got up by our enemies to procure our destruction."[26] Sconce and his companions were so affected by the stories of the unjust trials and suffering of the Saints that they promised to use their influence to offset feelings against the Mormons.

The next day, 22 June, Joseph received a revelation communicating the Lord's dissatisfaction with the members of the Church for their disobedience and selfishness:

They "do not impart of their substance, as becometh saints, to the poor and afflicted among them;

"And are not united according to the union required by the law of the celestial kingdom" (D&C 105:3–4).

This chastisement was directed specifically to members of the branches who were slow in sharing themselves and their means for the cause of Zion (see vv. 7–8). The Saints had to learn their duty and gain more experience before Zion could be redeemed (see vv. 9–10). Thus the Lord said, "it is expedient in me that mine elders should wait for a little season, for the redemption of Zion" (v. 13). He promised the obedient that they would receive an endowment from on high if they continued faithful (see vv. 11–12). If Zion's Camp did not succeed in its military objectives, it did succeed in serving the purposes of the Lord. Speaking of the men in the camp he said, "I have heard their prayers, and will accept their offering; and it is expedient in me that they should be brought thus far for a trial of their faith" (v. 19).

For a few of the Saints, the Lord's command not to do battle was the final trial of their faith. Disappointed and angry, they apostatized. As a result of their insurrection the Prophet again warned the camp that the Lord would send a devastating scourge upon them as a consequence of their unrighteous complaints. The day before the revelation was given two men contracted cholera. Three days later several more were struck with the dreaded disease, which was carried in contaminated water. The epidemic spread, causing severe diarrhea, vomiting, and cramps. Before it ended, about sixty-eight people, including Joseph Smith, were stricken by the disease, and fourteen members of the camp died, one of whom was a woman named Betsy Parrish. On 2 July, Joseph Smith told the camp that "if they would humble themselves before the Lord and covenant to keep His commandments and obey my counsel, the plague should be stayed from that hour, and there should not be another case of the cholera among them. The brethren covenanted to that effect with uplifted hands, and the plague was stayed."[27]

CHURCH HISTORY IN THE FULNESS OF TIMES

DISBANDING THE CAMP AND REORGANIZING THE SAINTS

On 25 June, during the height of the cholera attack, Joseph Smith divided Zion's Camp into several small groups to demonstrate the Saints' peaceful intent to the Missourians. Ten days later formal written discharges were prepared for each faithful member of the camp. Lyman Wight reported that the Prophet "said that he was now willing to return home, that he was fully satisfied that he had done the will of God, and that the Lord had accepted our sacrifice and offering, even as he had Abraham's when he offered his son Isaac; and in his benediction asked the heavenly Father to bless us with eternal life and salvation."[28]

The camp dispersed after being released by the Prophet. Some people remained in Missouri in accordance with the Fishing River revelation (see D&C 105:20), and some returned to the mission field, but most of them returned to their families in the East. On that same day, 3 July, the Prophet organized a presidency and high council in Missouri to help Bishop Edward Partridge administer the affairs of the Church in that area. Joseph Smith discouraged the Missouri Saints from holding Church meetings, however, in an attempt to allay the fears of local citizens.

Life in Clay County was easier for the Saints throughout the rest of 1834 and during 1835. This period was relatively free from persecution, and the Saints enjoyed some prosperity. Most of the non-Mormons in Clay County were cordial. The spirit of good will, however, began to change when Saints continued to migrate to Missouri in anticipation of returning to Jackson County and when some members of the Church bought property in Clay County. Unfortunately, a few of the members had not learned from the persecutions of Jackson County, and they incited the old settlers with talk that their lands would eventually belong to the Saints. Collectively the members failed to observe the Lord's counsel:

"Talk not of judgments, neither boast of faith nor of mighty works, but carefully gather together, as much in one region as can be, consistently with the feelings of the people;

"And behold, I will give unto you favor and grace in their eyes, that you may rest in peace and safety" (D&C 105:24–25).

Joseph Smith and a few other leaders of Zion's Camp arrived back in Kirtland in early August, to the relief of the Saints in Kirtland who had worried about reports that Joseph Smith had been killed in Missouri. Later in the month a high council court heard the complaints of Sylvester Smith and others who were still bitter over Zion's Camp. Ten men who had participated in Zion's Camp disputed the charges of Sylvester Smith and testified that Joseph Smith was not guilty of improper conduct. After reviewing the evidence, Sylvester admitted that he was in error and had behaved improperly.

Zion's Camp failed to help the Missouri Saints regain their lands and was marred by some dissension, apostasy, and unfavorable publicity, but a number of positive results came from the journey. By volunteering, the members demonstrated their faith in the Lord and his prophet and their earnest desire to comply with latter-day revelation. They showed their concern for the exiled Saints in Missouri by their willingness to lay down their lives if necessary to assist them.

This rugged journey served as a test to determine who was worthy to serve in positions of leadership and trust and to receive an endowment in the Kirtland Temple. The Prophet later explained: "God did not want you to fight. He could not organize his kingdom with twelve men to open the gospel door to the nations of the earth, and with seventy men under their direction to follow in their tracks, unless he took them from a body of men who had offered their lives, and who had made as great a sacrifice as did Abraham."[29] In February 1835 the Quorum of the Twelve Apostles and the First Quorum of the Seventy were organized. Nine of the original Apostles, all seven presidents of the Seventy's quorum, and all sixty-three other members of that quorum had served in the army of Israel that marched to western Missouri in 1834.

Zion's Camp chastened, polished, and spiritually refined many of the Lord's servants. The observant and dedicated received invaluable practical training and spiritual experience that served them well in later struggles for the Church. The hardships and challenges experienced over its thousand miles provided invaluable training for Brigham Young, Heber C. Kimball, and others who led the exiled Saints from Missouri to Illinois and from Nauvoo across the plains to the Rocky Mountains. When a skeptic asked what he had gained from his journey, Brigham Young promptly replied, "I would not exchange the knowledge I have received this season for the whole of Geauga County."[30]

ENDNOTES

1. In *History of the Church*, 2:39.

2. *History of the Church*, 2:48.

3. Wilford Woodruff Journals, 11 Apr. 1834, LDS Historical Department, Salt Lake City; spelling, punctuation, and capitalization standardized.

4. Reed A. Stout, ed., "Autobiography of Hosea Stout, 1810 to 1835," *Utah Historical Quarterly*, 1962, pp. 259–60; spelling and punctuation standardized.

5. "History of Brigham Young," *Millennial Star*, 18 July 1863, p. 455; or Elden Jay Watson, *Manuscript History of Brigham Young*, 1801–1844 (Salt Lake City: Elden Jay Watson, 1968), p. 8.

6. In Orson F. Whitney, *Life of Heber C. Kimball*, 3d ed. (Salt Lake City: Bookcraft, 1967), p. 40.

7. George A. Smith, "Memoirs of George A. Smith," 4 May 1834, LDS Historical Department, Salt Lake City, p. 13.

8. Joseph Holbrook, "History of Joseph Holbrook, 1806–1885," LDS Historical Department, Salt Lake City, p. 15.

9. Smith, "Memoirs of George A. Smith," p. 15.

10. *History of the Church*, 2:66–67.

11. *History of the Church*, 2:71–72.

12. *History of the Church*, 2:73.

13. *History of the Church*, 2:80.

14. *History of the Church*, 2:68; punctuation standardized.

15. *History of the Church*, 2:80.

16. *Sacred Hymns*, 1840, pp. 283–85.

17. Letter from J. M. Henderson to Independence postmaster, cited in Pearl Wilcox, *The Latter Day Saints on the Missouri Frontier* (Independence, Mo.: Pearl G. Wilcox, 1972), p. 121.

18. See Parley P. Pratt, ed., *Autobiography of Parley P. Pratt,* Classics in Mormon Literature series (Salt Lake City: Deseret Book Co., 1985), p. 94.

19. *History of the Church,* 2:97–98.

20. In *History of the Church,* 2:102–3.

21. "History of Joseph Holbrook," p. 17.

22. Wilford Woodruff, in *History of the Church,* 2:104n.

23. Journal of Moses Martin, LDS Historical Department, Salt Lake City, n.p.; spelling standardized; see also *History of the Church,* 2:104–5.

24. *History of the Church,* 2:105.

25. In *History of the Church,* 2:106.

26. *History of the Church,* 2:106.

27. *History of the Church,* 2:120.

28. Lyman Wight, in *The History of the Reorganized Church of Jesus Christ of Latter Day Saints* (Independence, Mo.: Herald Publishing House, 1896), 1:515–16.

29. Joseph Young, *History of the Organization of the Seventies* (Salt Lake City: Deseret News, 1878), p. 14; or *History of the Church,* 2:182n.

30. In *Journal of Discourses,* 2:10.

GLORIOUS DAYS IN KIRTLAND, 1834–36

BY AUGUST 1834 Joseph Smith and most of his associates in Zion's Camp had returned home. With the attempt to help the Missouri Saints behind them, the members in Ohio again turned their attention to building the kingdom of God in their own area. The two years following the return of Zion's Camp were a time of relative peace for these Ohio Saints. This period brought a number of significant and particularly far-reaching developments affecting Church organization, doctrine, scriptures, and temple activity.

FURTHER EXPANSION OF CHURCH ORGANIZATION

On 5 December 1834 the Prophet Joseph Smith ordained Oliver Cowdery as Assistant President of the Church.[1] He had been with the Prophet when the Aaronic and Melchizedek Priesthoods were restored. When the Church of Jesus Christ was organized in 1830, Oliver as "second elder" stood next to Joseph in authority (see Joseph Smith—History 1:68–73; D&C 110).[2] Thus, whenever priesthood authority or keys were restored, Oliver was with the Prophet Joseph. "It was necessary according to the divine law of witnesses for Joseph Smith to have a companion holding those keys."[3] Oliver Cowdery was not only to assist Joseph Smith in presiding over the Church, but he was also to stand with the Prophet as a second witness of the Restoration. By 1838 Oliver Cowdery had lost his office of Assistant President through apostasy and excommunication, but in 1841 the Lord called Hyrum Smith to fill this office (see D&C 124:94–96). The President and the Assistant President, or the first and second witnesses, would seal their testimonies with their blood at the Carthage Jail.

One of the most important events in the restoration of the Savior's church was the formation of the Quorum of the Twelve Apostles. Even before the Church was organized, the members had anticipated this significant step. Joseph Smith and Oliver Cowdery had received the authority of the apostleship (see D&C 20:2–3) probably as early as 1829. During that same year, a revelation directed Oliver Cowdery and David Whitmer to search out the twelve who would be "called to go into all the world to preach my gospel unto every creature" (D&C 18:28). Later Martin Harris was also called to assist in this selection. This meant that the three witnesses to the Book of Mormon, under the direction and consent of the First Presidency, would choose the Twelve Apostles who were to serve as special witnesses of the

Savior in this dispensation. The Prophet Joseph Smith invited the veterans of Zion's Camp and others to attend a special conference on Saturday, 14 February 1835. The minutes of the meeting reflect those events:

"He then gave a relation of some of the circumstances attending us while journeying to Zion—our trials, sufferings: and said God had not designed all this for nothing, but He had it in remembrance yet; and it was the will of God that those who went to Zion, with a determination to lay down their lives, if necessary, should be ordained to the ministry, and go forth to prune the vineyard for the last time, or the coming of the Lord, which was nigh. . . .

". . . Even the smallest and weakest among us, shall be powerful and mighty, and great things shall be accomplished by you from this hour; and you shall begin to feel the whisperings of the Spirit of God; and the work of God shall begin to break forth from this time; and you shall be endowed with power from on high." Following the Prophet's remarks, the meeting was adjourned for an hour. As the meeting reconvened, the Three Witnesses prayed and were blessed by the First Presidency. The witnesses then proceeded to select the Twelve Apostles.[4] Because they were all called at the same time, the Apostles' seniority in the quorum was set according to age.

THE ORIGINAL TWELVE OF THIS DISPENSATION

One week after their selection, the Twelve received an apostolic charge from Oliver Cowdery similar to the one the Savior gave the New Testament Apostles (see Matthew 10; 28:19–20; Acts 1:8). He warned them that they would have to face unprecedented difficulties.

"You will have to combat all the prejudices of all nations.

"He then read the revelation [D&C 18]. . . .

". . . I therefore warn you to cultivate great humility; for I know the pride of the human heart. Beware, lest the flatterers of the world lift you up; beware, lest your affections be captivated by worldly objects. Let your ministry be first. . . .

". . . It is necessary that you receive a testimony from heaven for yourselves; so that you can bear testimony to the truth. . . .

". . . You are to bear this message to those who consider themselves wise; and such may persecute you—they may seek your life. The adversary has always sought the life of the servants of God; you are therefore to be prepared at all times to make a sacrifice of your lives, should God require them in the advancement and building up of His cause. . . .

"He then took them separately by the hand, and said, 'Do you with full purpose of heart take part in this ministry, to proclaim the Gospel with all diligence, with these your brethren, according to the tenor and intent of the charge you have received?' Each answered in the affirmative."[5]

Two weeks later at a special conference, the Prophet organized another key priesthood quorum—the Seventy—from those who had been in Zion's Camp (see D&C 107:93). To accommodate their unique role as a "traveling"

Seniority in the first Quorum of the Twelve

Name	Age at Call
Thomas B. Marsh*	35
David W. Patten	35
Brigham Young	33
Heber C. Kimball	33
Orson Hyde	30
William E. McLellin	29
Parley P. Pratt	27
Luke S. Johnson	27
William B. Smith	23
Orson Pratt	23
John F. Boynton	23
Lyman E. Johnson	23

*Thomas was in his thirty-fifth year but did not turn thirty-five until 1 November 1835. At the time, David Patten did not know his age; however, subsequent records show he was actually older than Thomas, having been born 14 November 1799.

quorum with responsibility to preach the gospel worldwide, they were presided over by seven presidents. This was according to a vision of Church organization given to the Prophet.[6] Joseph Young, Hazen Aldrich, Levi Hancock, Leonard Rich, Zebedee Coltrin, Lyman Sherman, and Sylvester Smith were the original presidents of this quorum.

A month later the Lord revealed additional information concerning priesthood and Church government. The Twelve, who were preparing to depart on missions, felt they had not fully accepted the weighty responsibilities of their calling. In a spirit of repentance, they petitioned the Prophet to ask the Lord for further guidance. In response the Lord instructed the Twelve and the Seventy on their respective responsibilities. The Twelve were to be "special witnesses of the name of Christ" and serve under the direction of the First Presidency to "build up the church, and regulate all the affairs of the same in all nations" (D&C 107:23, 33). The Seventy were to serve under the direction of the Twelve and accomplish the same purpose. Together with the First Presidency, these quorums constituted the presiding councils of the Church. The revelation also outlined the duties of those who preside over the various quorums of the priesthood, and it closed with this admonition:

"Wherefore, now let every man learn his duty, and to act in the office in which he is appointed, in all diligence.

"He that is slothful shall not be counted worthy to stand" (D&C 107:99–100). In compliance with instructions given in the revelation, the first Aaronic Priesthood quorums were formed in 1835 in Kirtland. They were made up of mature men. There were no set ages for worthy candidates to advance from one office to another.[7]

In the light of instructions in Doctrine and Covenants 107, the "standing" stake high councils assumed an increasingly important role during the mid-1830s, particularly in the capacity of Church courts. Questions soon arose concerning the status and jurisdiction of the high councils and of the Twelve who were referred to as "a Traveling Presiding High Council" (D&C 107:33). The Prophet responded that the authority of the standing high councils was limited to the stakes, while the Twelve had jurisdiction over the Church abroad.[8] This raised the additional question about the jurisdiction of the Twelve in local matters. The Prophet assured them that since they stood next to the First Presidency in authority, they were not subject to any other body. Brigham Young later looked back on these months of discussion as a time of trial when the Twelve had to prove their willingness " 'to be everybody's servant for Christ's sake. . . .' This was necessary, according to Young, for only 'true servants' may receive the power."[9]

REACHING OUT TO SHARE THE GOSPEL

Organized proselyting had been temporarily interrupted by Zion's Camp in the summer of 1834. During the fall, however, missionary work resumed as Church leaders called more and more men to fill missions. Some of them labored for only a few weeks in nearby communities. Others spent longer periods proclaiming the gospel in distant areas. Many of the missionaries served more than one mission, often leaving home at times that were personally inconvenient. In 1836 William W. Phelps wrote, "The Elders are constantly coming and going."[10]

Missionary certificate of Edward Partridge and Isaac Morley

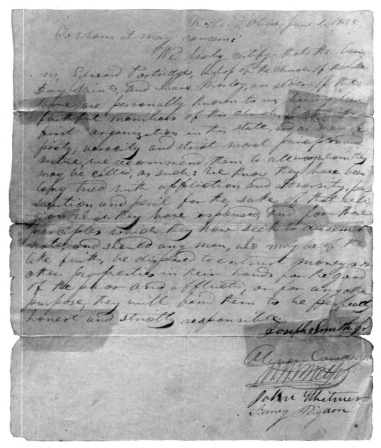

Formal missions were supplemented by the efforts of enthusiastic converts eager to share their newly-found treasure with family and friends. New convert Caroline Crosby exclaimed, "How often while listening to the voice of the prophet have I wished, Oh that my friends, parents, brothers, and sisters, could hear the things that I have heard, and their hearts be made to rejoice in them, as mine did."[11]

Many leaders of the Church were also involved in missionary service. The Prophet Joseph Smith went to Michigan in 1834 and 1835. But perhaps the most important effort was the five-month mission of the Quorum of the Twelve to the East in 1835. From May to September they traveled hundreds of miles throughout New York, New England, and Canada. Besides doing missionary work and regulating and strengthening local congregations, their assignments included gathering funds for temple construction, for purchase of lands in Zion, and for the printing endeavors of the Church. Traveling without purse or scrip they experienced typical problems of persecution, rejection, fatigue, and hunger; however, at one large meeting they counted 144 carriages and estimated that from two to three thousand people attended.

This mission is significant in Church history because it is the only time that all twelve members of the Quorum undertook a mission together. Upon their return to Kirtland, Heber C. Kimball reported that they had felt God's power and were able to heal the sick and cast out devils.[12] In this same season the Quorum of the Seventy also filled missions, primarily in the eastern states.

During the mid-1830s many Church leaders also served numerous individual missions. Elder Parley P. Pratt's Canadian mission is a notable example. In April 1836 fellow Apostle Heber C. Kimball blessed Parley and prophesied that he would go to Toronto and there "find a people prepared for the fulness of the gospel, and they shall receive thee, . . . and it shall spread thence into the regions round about . . . ; and from the things growing out of this mission, shall the fulness of the gospel spread into England, and cause a great work to be done in that land."[13] While Parley was in Hamilton en route to Toronto, a stranger gave him a letter of introduction to John Taylor, a Methodist lay preacher in Toronto. Taylor was affiliated with a group who believed existing churches did not correspond with New Testament Christianity. For two years this group had met several times a week for the "purpose of seeking truth, independent of any sectarian organization." In Toronto, Elder Pratt was courteously received by the Taylors, but they were not at first enthusiastic about his message.[14]

John Taylor (1808–87) was born in England and then emigrated to Canada, where he was converted to the gospel. A few of his many labors included serving as a publisher, missionary, Apostle, and President of the Church.

Discouraged at being unable to secure a place to preach, Parley decided to leave Toronto. Before going he stopped at the Taylors to get some of his luggage and to say goodbye. While he was there, Leonora Taylor told her friend Mrs. Isabella Walton about Parley's problem and said she was sorry he was leaving. "He may be a man of God," she said. Mrs. Walton replied that she had been inspired by the Spirit to visit the Taylors that morning because she was willing to let Elder Pratt stay at her home and preach. He did so and was eventually invited to attend a meeting of John Taylor's group, in which John read the New Testament account of Philip's preaching in Samaria. " 'Now,' said he, 'where is our Philip? Where is our receiving the Word with joy, and being baptized *when we believed?* Where is our Peter and John? Our apostles? Where is our Holy Ghost by the laying on of hands? . . .' "[15] When Parley was invited to speak, he declared that he had answers to John Taylor's questions.

For three weeks John Taylor attended Elder Pratt's meetings making detailed notes of his sermons and carefully comparing them with the scriptures. Gradually he became convinced that the true gospel of Jesus Christ was restored. He and his wife, Leonora, were baptized on 9 May 1836. Soon thereafter John Taylor was ordained an elder and became an active missionary. The work spread so rapidly that Orson Hyde was sent from Kirtland to assist Parley, while Orson Pratt and Freeman Nickerson, who

Mary Fielding Smith (1801–52)

Elder's certificate (front and back) of Wilford Woodruff, signed by Joseph Smith in 1836

were already in Canada, joined Parley in Toronto. When the missionaries left Toronto, John Taylor was set apart to preside over the congregations these elders had established.

The Fielding family, who also became important in the history of the Church, was part of this Canadian harvest. Mary Fielding married Hyrum Smith and became the mother of the sixth and grandmother of the tenth Presidents of the Church—Joseph F. Smith and Joseph Fielding Smith, respectively. A year after his baptism, Mary's brother Joseph joined the first missionaries to Britain and played a key role in establishing the work there.

Missionaries in other areas also enjoyed rich spiritual experiences. Wilford Woodruff, for example, went to Missouri in 1834 at the age of twenty-seven. That fall he was ordained a priest and sent to Arkansas and Tennessee as one of the earliest missionaries to carry the gospel to those regions. In later years he frequently testified that "in all his life he never had enjoyed more of the spirit and power of God than when he was a priest doing missionary work in the Southern States."[16]

Gradually congregations sprang up throughout the Northeast, the Midwest, and eastern Canada, and eventually the gospel spread into West Virginia, Kentucky, and Tennessee. At first local groups were called *churches*,

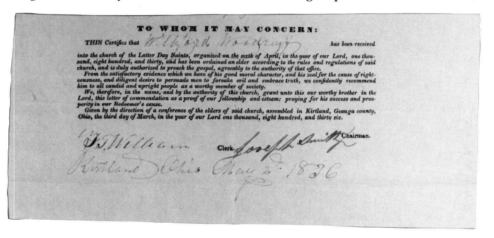

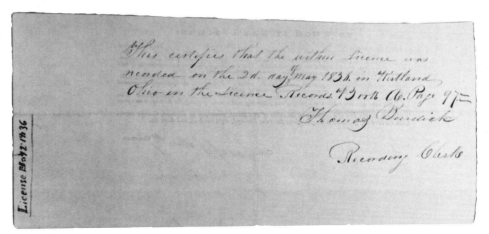

but by 1835 the term *branch* was common. This designation symbolized how the members in one locality extended the good news to friends living nearby who formed a new congregation, which was literally a branch of the parent group. Customarily several branches joined together for periodic conferences, and in 1835 the Twelve organized them into districts, called *conferences*, each having definite boundaries like modern stakes.[17]

DEVELOPMENTS IN SCRIPTURE

In a tomb on the west bank of the Nile River across from the ancient Egyptian city of Thebes (now called Luxor), Antonio Lebolo, a French-speaking explorer from the Piedmont (a region of northwestern Italy), discovered several mummies and along with them some papyrus scrolls. Following the death of Lebolo in 1830, the mummies and papyri were shipped to the United States, where Michael H. Chandler, who identified himself as Lebolo's nephew, came into possession of them in 1833. In 1835 Chandler displayed his artifacts in several eastern cities.

When he came to Kirtland at the end of June, the Saints showed great interest in the mummies and papyri. Chandler had heard that Joseph Smith claimed he could translate ancient records. He asked Joseph if he could translate the papyri. Orson Pratt recalled, "The Prophet took them and repaired to his room and inquired of the Lord concerning them. The Lord told him they were sacred records" and revealed the translation of some of the characters. Chandler had previously submitted a few characters from the records to scholars in order to determine their probable meaning. Upon receiving the Prophet's translation, he provided a signed testimonial that it corresponded in the most minute matters with those of the scholars.[18]

Greatly interested in their content, the Saints purchased the mummies and scrolls for twenty-four hundred dollars. Joseph immediately began working with the scrolls and found that they contained the writings of Abraham and the writings of Joseph who was sold into Egypt. "Truly we can say, the Lord is beginning to reveal the abundance of peace and truth."[19] During the rest of his time in Kirtland he maintained an active interest in working with these ancient writings. The fruit of his efforts, the book of Abraham, was not printed, however, until 1842 after more translating was completed in Nauvoo. In February 1843 the Prophet promised to supply more of the translation of the book of Abraham, but his demanding schedule did not allow him time to complete the work before he was assassinated.

In 1835 another standard work of the Church was published. The Missouri persecutions had disrupted the publication of the Book of Commandments in 1833. Steps were taken in Ohio to publish an expanded compilation of the revelations. In September 1834 the First Presidency was appointed to select the revelations to be published, and the Prophet revised some of them to correct printing errors and to add information revealed since 1833. The committee's work was completed the following summer, and

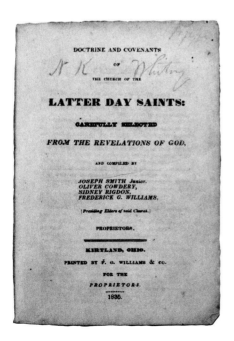

Title page of the 1835 Doctrine and Covenants

a solemn assembly was convened on 17 August 1835 to vote on the new book of scripture to be called the Doctrine and Covenants.

The book's title referred to its two major divisions. The first part, designated "doctrine," contained seven lectures on faith delivered in the School of the Elders the previous winter. The second section, entitled "Covenants and Commandments," included forty-five revelations in addition to those found in the Book of Commandments.[20] The volume's preface pointed out the differences between the theological lectures and the Lord's revelations.[21] This distinction became the basis for a decision in 1921 to publish the revelations without the *Lectures on Faith* to avoid confusing readers about the status of the lectures.

EVERYDAY LIFE IN KIRTLAND

During the middle 1830s Kirtland increasingly became a Latter-day Saint community. While the number of nonmembers there remained relatively constant at about twelve to thirteen hundred, the number of Saints almost tripled, growing from nearly five hundred to about fifteen hundred between 1834 and 1837. Thus the Church and its activities gradually exerted more influence on community life. This sometimes led to tensions between the two ideologically different groups of people.[22]

While most of the Saints were grateful for such momentous events as the calling of the Twelve Apostles and the publication of the Doctrine and Covenants, their day-to-day life centered on earning a living on the farm or in town. Despite long hours of hard physical work, the Saints found time for recreation, education, and worship.

Although leisure time was limited, the Kirtland Saints enjoyed hunting, fishing, swimming, and horseback riding. Wintertime favorites included ice skating and sleigh riding. Family associations were especially important to the Saints. After a long day's work, parents and children often enjoyed the evening together singing, playing, studying, and discussing topics of common interest. Holidays were infrequent and generally went almost unnoticed. Journals of the time seldom mention any special holiday activities, even on Christmas day. One Latter-day Saint girl was surprised during a trip to New York City to learn that other children received visits from Santa Claus, who filled their stockings with gifts and treats.[23]

The Saints considered education essential, and the home was the setting for most of the learning. Private tutors, such as Eliza R. Snow, who lived with Joseph Smith's family tutoring his children, were common. Occasionally teachers offered their services for private classes in a home or community building.

Following the early efforts of the School of the Prophets in 1833, the School of the Elders met during the next two winters, when the men were not so busy with farming or missionary assignments. It convened in a thirty-by-thirty-eight-foot room on the main floor of the printing building just west

The account book for the Newel K. Whitney store (November 1836–April 1837)

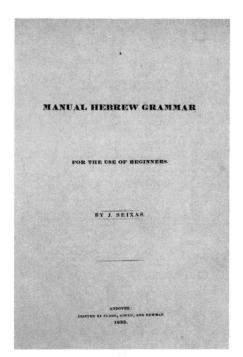

Title page of Joshua Seixas's Hebrew grammar book. Prior to being employed by the Prophet to teach Hebrew in Kirtland, Joshua Seixas had taught Hebrew at Oberlin College, where Lorenzo Snow was one of his students.

of the temple. Its purpose was to prepare the men who were about to go forth as missionaries or to serve in other Church callings. The curriculum included English grammar, writing, philosophy, government, literature, geography, and ancient as well as modern history. Theology, however, received the major emphasis.

An important outgrowth of the School of the Elders was a Hebrew school conducted from January to April of 1836 under the direction of a young Hebrew instructor, Joshua Seixas. He was contracted for $320 to teach forty students for seven weeks. Interest was greater than expected, so two additional classes were organized. After Seixas left, interest in Hebrew continued. William W. Phelps, for example, often shared his translations from the Hebrew Bible with his friends.[24] The Prophet Joseph Smith was particularly enthusiastic about his study of Hebrew. He declared, "My soul delights in reading the word of the Lord in the original."[25]

One young nonmember, Lorenzo Snow from nearby Mantua, Ohio, attended the Hebrew school. One day, while on his way to Oberlin College, Lorenzo met Elder David W. Patten. Their conversation turned to religion, and Elder Patten's sincerity and testimony made a lasting impression on Lorenzo. He was therefore receptive when his sister Eliza, a recent convert, invited him to attend the school. While there Lorenzo became acquainted with Joseph Smith and other Church leaders and was baptized in June 1836.

Sabbath worship was central in the lives of the early Latter-day Saints. Many people gathered enough firewood and completed other chores on Saturday so they could devote Sunday to spiritual matters. They met in homes and later in schools for their services, but during warm weather they gathered outdoors. Sunday meetings were simple. The morning meeting typically began at 10:00 with a hymn and prayer followed by one or two sermons. The afternoon service was similar, but usually included the administration of the sacrament. Occasionally confirmations and marriages were performed during these gatherings.

The first Thursday of each month was fast day. In meetings that often lasted six hours, the Saints sang, prayed, bore their testimonies describing divine manifestations in their lives, and exhorted each other to live the gospel. Eliza R. Snow fondly remembered these gatherings as "hallowed and interesting beyond the power of language to describe. Many, many were the pentecostal seasons of the outpouring of the spirit of God on those days, manifesting the gifts of the Gospel and the power of healing, prophesying, speaking in tongues, the interpretation of tongues, etc."[26] Weeknights were also filled with priesthood quorum meetings, preaching services, or meetings where patriarchal blessings were given.

Music has always been an important part in the Saints' worship. In July 1830 a revelation directed Emma Smith to compile a hymnbook for the Church. This small volume finally appeared in 1835. It included the words for ninety hymns, thirty-four that were written by Church members and bore testimony of the Restoration. The remainder of the hymns were drawn from popular contemporary hymnals. No music was printed in the hymnal. The Saints sang the hymns to popular tunes of the time, and frequently branches and choirs used different melodies for the same hymns. Several of the hymns selected by Emma Smith, with the assistance of William W. Phelps, are still in our present hymnbook.

BUILDING THE LORD'S HOUSE

For about three years the time and energies of the Kirtland Saints were devoted to building the first temple of this dispensation. This endeavor began in December 1832 when the Lord commanded them to "establish a house, even a house of prayer, a house of fasting, a house of faith, a house of learning, a house of glory, a house of order, a house of God" (D&C 88:119). Five months later the Lord chastised the Church for their delay and admonished them to move forward with the building of the temple (see D&C 95). The Saints then faithfully devoted themselves to the task.

The Prophet once asked a conference of high priests how the temple should be constructed. Some favored building it of logs. Others preferred a frame structure. " 'Shall we, brethren,' said he, 'build a house for our God, of logs? No, I have a better plan than that. I have a plan of the house of the Lord, given by himself; and you will soon see by this, the difference between our calculations and his idea of things.' "27 Truman O. Angell, one of the construction supervisors, testified that the Lord's promise to show the Prophet the building's design was literally fulfilled. He said that when the

Architectural drawing of the Kirtland Temple

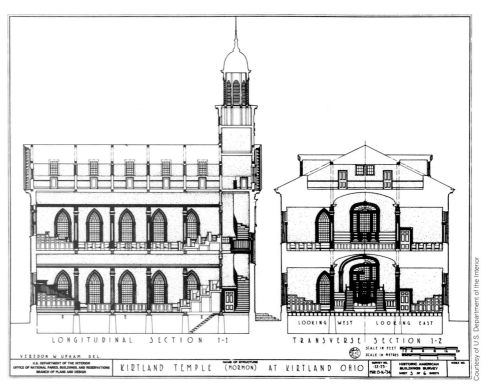

LONGITUDINAL SECTION 1-1

TRANSVERSE SECTION 1-2

LOOKING WEST   LOOKING EAST

VEREDON W UPHAM DEL.

U.S. DEPARTMENT OF THE INTERIOR
OFFICE OF NATIONAL PARKS, BUILDINGS, AND RESERVATIONS
BRANCH OF PLANS AND DESIGN

KIRTLAND TEMPLE (MORMON) AT KIRTLAND OHIO

First Presidency knelt in prayer, "the Building appeared within viewing distance." Later, while speaking in the completed temple, Frederick G. Williams said that the hall in which they met coincided in every detail with the vision given to them.[28]

The temple's exterior looked like a typical New England meetinghouse, but its interior was unique. The Lord had specified that the building should include two large rooms, one above the other, each measuring fifty-five by sixty-five feet. The lower hall was to be the chapel, for praying, preaching, and administering the sacrament. The upper hall was for educational purposes (see D&C 95:8, 13-17).

Construction on the temple began 6 June 1833. In response to the Lord's admonition, a committee was directed to procure materials for the work. A stone quarry was located two miles south of the building site, and a wagon load of stone was immediately quarried. Hyrum Smith and Reynolds Cahoon started digging a trench for the foundation. But the Saints were so poor, an early member recalled, that "there was not a scraper and hardly a plow that could be obtained among the Saints."[29] Nevertheless, "unity, harmony and charity abounded to strengthen" them to fulfill the commandment to build the temple.[30] On 23 July 1833, the cornerstones were laid "after the order of the Holy Priesthood."[31]

Almost all able-bodied men who were not away on missions worked on the temple. Joseph Smith served as foreman in the quarry. On Saturdays men brought teams and wagons and hauled enough quarried rock to the site to keep the masons busy during the coming week. Under Emma Smith's direction, the women "made stockings, pantaloons and jackets" for the temple workmen. Heber C. Kimball recalled, "Our wives were all the time knitting, spinning and sewing . . . ; they were just as busy as any of us."[32]

The work on the temple was not without difficulty. Mobs threatened to destroy the temple, and those who worked on it by day guarded it at night. Night after night for weeks, Heber C. Kimball said, we "were not permitted to take off our clothes, and were obliged to lay with our fire locks in our arms."[33] With the Church in constant financial distress during this period, the Saints in the United States and Canada were invited to make contributions, and many did so at great personal sacrifice. Vienna Jacques was one of the first to donate, giving much of her material resources. John Tanner loaned money to pay for the temple site and then sold his twenty-two-hundred-acre farm in New York in order to give three thousand dollars to buy supplies. He continued to give until he had given almost all he owned.[34]

Zion's Camp also interrupted the work during the summer of 1834, since few workmen were available and funds were diverted to aid the distressed Missouri Saints. When the brethren returned from Zion's Camp, work progressed more rapidly. That fall Joseph Smith wrote, "Great exertions were made to expedite the work of the Lord's house, and notwithstanding it was commenced almost with nothing, as to means, yet the way opened as we

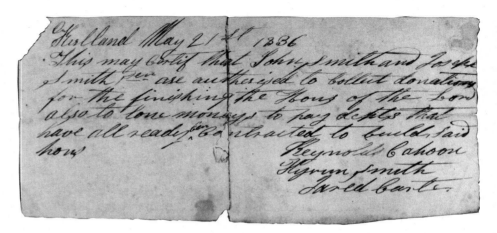

proceeded, and the Saints rejoiced."[35] The walls were about four feet high in the fall of 1834, but rose quickly during the winter. By November 1835 the exterior plastering commenced; crushed glassware was mixed with the stucco to make the walls glisten. Under Brigham Young's direction, the interior was finished during February of 1836. The sisters made the curtains and carpets.

A PENTECOSTAL SEASON

In addition to their great personal efforts, the Saints spent from forty to sixty thousand dollars on the temple. Because they were so willing to sacrifice in building the temple, the Lord poured out great blessings upon them. From 21 January to 1 May 1836 "probably more Latter-day Saints beheld visions and witnessed other unusual spiritual manifestations than during any other era in the history of the Church."[36] Members of the Church saw heavenly messengers in at least ten different meetings, and at five of these gatherings different individuals testified that they had beheld the Savior himself. Many experienced visions, some prophesied, and others spoke in tongues.

One of the most important meetings held in the Kirtland Temple was on Thursday, 21 January 1836. The Prophet recorded the incident:

In the evening "at early candle-light I met with the presidency at the west school room, in the Temple, to attend to the ordinance of anointing our heads with holy oil. . . .

"We then laid our hands upon our aged Father Smith, and invoked the blessings of heaven. . . . The heavens were opened upon us, and I beheld the celestial kingdom of God, and the glory thereof. . . . I saw . . . the blazing throne of God. . . . I saw the beautiful streets of that kingdom, which had the appearance of being paved with gold." Joseph Smith also saw many prophets in the celestial kingdom before the scene of his vision shifted (see D&C 137:1, 3–5). He then saw the recently appointed Twelve "standing together in a circle, much fatigued, with their clothes tattered and feet swollen, . . . and

Jesus standing in their midst, and they did not behold Him. . . .

"Many of my brethren who received the ordinance [of washing and anointing] with me saw glorious visions also. Angels ministered unto them as well as to myself, and the power of the Highest rested upon us. The house was filled with the glory of God, and we shouted Hosanna to God and the Lamb. . . .

". . . Some of them saw the face of the Savior, . . . for we all communed with the heavenly host."[37]

Joseph Smith saw his brother Alvin in the celestial kingdom and marvelled because Alvin had died before the gospel was restored. Also with the vision the Lord revealed the principle of mercy: "All who have died without a knowledge of this gospel, who would have received it if they had been permitted to tarry, shall be heirs of the celestial kingdom of God" (D&C 137:7). The Prophet also learned that all children who die before the age of accountability "are saved in the celestial kingdom of heaven" (D&C 137:10).

Some of the most memorable spiritual experiences occurred on the day the temple was dedicated—Sunday, 27 March 1836. Hundreds of Latter-day Saints came to Kirtland anticipating the great blessings the Lord had promised to bestow upon them. Early on the morning of the temple dedication, hundreds of people gathered outside the temple hoping to attend the dedicatory service. The doors were opened at 8:00 A.M., and the First Presidency assisted in seating the congregation of nearly a thousand people, but many were left outside. When the leaders of the Church were seated at the elevated pulpits and benches at each end of the hall and when all the available seats in the temple were filled, the doors were closed. This left hundreds of people still outside, including many who had sacrificed tremendously for the temple's construction and had come long distances to attend the dedication. Sensing their disappointment, the Prophet directed them to hold an overflow meeting in the schoolhouse just to the west. The dedicatory service was repeated a second time the following Thursday for their benefit.

After the choir's opening number, President Sidney Rigdon spoke for two and a half hours declaring that the temple was unique among all the buildings of the world because it was built by divine revelation. After a brief intermission, the officers of the Church were sustained. The climax of the day was the dedicatory prayer, which had previously been given to the Prophet by revelation. He expressed gratitude for God's blessings and asked the Lord to accept the temple which was built "through great tribulation . . . that the Son of Man might have a place to manifest himself to his people" (D&C 109:5). He petitioned that the blessings promised in the Lord's initial command to build the temple (see D&C 88:117–21) might now be realized, and he prayed that Church leaders, members, and the leaders of nations would be blessed, and that the promised gathering of the scattered remnants of Israel would be accomplished (see D&C 109:60–67). This prayer became a pattern for other temple dedicatory prayers.

Kirtland Temple

Following the prayer, the choir sang the hymn "The Spirit of God." It had been written especially for the dedication by W. W. Phelps. The sacrament was then administered and passed to the congregation. Joseph Smith and others testified that they saw heavenly messengers at the service. The congregation concluded the seven-hour service by standing and rendering the sacred "Hosanna Shout": "Hosanna, hosanna, hosanna to God and the Lamb, amen, amen, and amen," repeated three times. Eliza R. Snow said the shout was given "with such power as seemed almost sufficient to raise the roof from the building."[38]

That evening over four hundred priesthood bearers met in the temple. While George A. Smith was speaking, "a noise was heard like the sound of a rushing mighty wind which filled the Temple, and all the congregation simultaneously arose, being moved upon by an invisible power; many began to speak in tongues and prophesy; others saw glorious visions; and I beheld the Temple was filled with angels."[39] "David Whitmer bore testimony that he saw three angels passing up the south aisle."[40] "The people of the neighborhood came running together (hearing an unusual sound within, and seeing a bright light like a pillar of fire resting upon the Temple)." Others saw angels hovering over the temple and heard heavenly singing.[41]

The most transcendent spiritual manifestation of all occurred a week after the dedication. After the afternoon worship service, Joseph Smith and Oliver Cowdery retired to the Melchizedek Priesthood pulpits in the west end of the lower room of the temple. The canvas partition, called a *veil*, was lowered so that they could pray in private. As they prayed, "the veil was taken from our minds, and the eyes of our understanding were opened" (D&C 110:1). They saw a series of remarkable visions. The Lord Jesus Christ appeared, accepted the temple, and promised to manifest himself therein "if my people will keep my commandments, and do not pollute this holy house" (D&C 110:8; see also vv. 2–9).

Moses next appeared and restored "the keys of the gathering of Israel from the four parts of the earth, and the leading of the ten tribes from the land of the north" (v. 11). Elias then conferred "the dispensation of the gospel of Abraham" (v. 12). Finally, in fulfillment of Malachi's prophecy (see Malachi 4:5–6) and Moroni's promise (see D&C 2) to "turn the hearts of the fathers to the children, and the children to the fathers" (D&C 110:15), Elijah appeared to the Prophet and Oliver testifying that "the keys of this dispensation are committed into your hands" in preparation for "the great and dreadful day of the Lord" (v. 16). Through the sealing keys that were restored by Elijah, Latter-day Saints could now perform saving priesthood ordinances in behalf of their kindred dead as well as for the living. These sacred ordinances for the dead were not introduced to the members of the Church until the Nauvoo era.

This great day of visions and revelation occurred on Easter Sunday, 3 April 1836. What better day in the dispensation of the fulness of times to reconfirm the reality of the Resurrection? That weekend was also the Jewish Passover. For centuries Jewish families have left an empty chair at their Passover feasts, anticipating Elijah's return. Elijah has returned—not to a Passover feast, but to the Lord's temple in Kirtland.

The period from the fall of 1834 through the summer of 1836 was one of glorious progress for the Church, and it looked as if the momentum would continue. Dark and dreary days were still ahead for the Kirtland Saints, however, as forces from both within and without threatened the Church's advancement.

ENDNOTES

1. See *History of the Church,* 2:176.

2. See *History of the Church,* 1:39–43.

3. Joseph Fielding Smith, *Doctrines of Salvation,* comp. Bruce R. McConkie, 3 vols. (Salt Lake City: Bookcraft, 1954–56), 1:211.

4. In *History of the Church,* 2:182; see also pp. 181–89.

5. *History of the Church,* 2:195–96, 198.

6. See *History of the Church,* 2:181n., 201–2; Joseph Young, *History of the Organization of the Seventies* (Salt Lake City: Deseret News, 1878), pp. 1–2, 14.

7. See Milton V. Backman, Jr., *The Heavens Resound* (Salt Lake City: Deseret Book Co., 1983), pp. 253–55.

8. See *History of the Church,* 2:220.

9. In Ronald K. Esplin, "The Emergence of Brigham Young and the Twelve to Mormon Leadership, 1830–1841," Ph.D. diss., Brigham Young University, 1981, p. 170; spelling and punctuation standardized; see also Ronald K. Esplin, "Joseph, Brigham and the Twelve: A Succession of Continuity," *Brigham Young University Studies,* Summer 1981, pp. 308–9.

10. Journal History of The Church of Jesus Christ of Latter-day Saints, 2 June 1835, Historical Department, Salt Lake City; see also Backman, *Heavens Resound,* p. 112.

11. Caroline Crosby Journal, LDS Historical Department, Salt Lake City; spelling standardized; see also Kenneth W. Godfrey, Audrey M. Godfrey, and Jill Mulvay Derr, *Women's Voices* (Salt Lake City: Deseret Book Co., 1982), pp. 49–50.

12. See Ronald K. Esplin, "The Emergence of Brigham Young and the Twelve to Mormon Leadership," pp. 161–65; see also *History of the Church,* 2:222–26.

13. Parley P. Pratt, ed., *Autobiography of Parley P. Pratt,* Classics in Mormon Literature series (Salt Lake City: Deseret Book Co., 1985), p. 110.

14. See Pratt, *Autobiography of Parley P. Pratt,* pp. 113–19; B. H. Roberts, *The Life of John Taylor* (Salt Lake City: Bookcraft, 1963), pp. 31–38.

15. Parley P. Pratt, *Autobiography of Parley P. Pratt,* p. 119.

16. In Matthias F. Cowley, *Wilford Woodruff* (Salt Lake City: Bookcraft, 1964), p. 62.

17. See Samuel George Ellsworth, "A History of Mormon Missions in the United States and Canada, 1830–1860," Ph.D. diss., University of California, 1951, pp. 147–54.

18. Orson Pratt, in *Journal of Discourses,* 20:65; see also *History of the Church,* 2:235.

19. *History of the Church,* 2:236.

20. See Doctrine and Covenants, 1835 ed., pp. 5, 75.

21. See *History of the Church,* 2:250–51.

22. See Milton V. Backman, Jr., comp., *A Profile of Latter-day Saints in Kirtland, Ohio, and Members of Zion's Camp, 1830–1839: Vital Statistics and Sources* (Provo: Brigham Young University Religious Studies Center, 1983), p. 83.

23. See Mary Ann Stearns, "An Autobiographical Sketch of the Life of the Late Mary Ann Stearns Winters, Daughter of Mary Ann Stearns Pratt," LDS Historical Department, Salt Lake City, p. 6.

24. See *History of the Church,* 2:355–56; Backman, *Heavens Resound,* pp. 268–72.

25. *History of the Church,* 2:396.

26. Nicholas G. Morgan, comp., *Eliza R. Snow, an Immortal: Selected Writings of Eliza R. Snow* (Salt Lake City: Nicholas G. Morgan, Sr., Foundation, 1957), p. 63.

27. Lucy Mack Smith, *History of Joseph Smith,* ed. Preston Nibley (Salt Lake City: Bookcraft, 1958), p. 230; see also *History of the Church,* 1:352.

28. Autobiography of Truman O. Angell, LDS Historical Department, Salt Lake City; Kate B. Carter, comp., *Our Pioneer Heritage,* 19 vols. (Salt Lake City: Daughters of Utah Pioneers, 1967–76), 10:198.

29. Benjamin F. Johnson, *My Life's Review* (Independence, Mo.: Zion's Printing and Publishing Co., 1947), p. 16.

30. *History of the Church,* 1:349.

31. *History of the Church,* 1:400.

32. Heber C. Kimball, in *Journal of Discourses,* 10:165.

33. "Elder Kimball's Journal," *Times and Seasons,* 15 Jan. 1845, p. 771; or *History of the Church,* 2:2.

34. See Backman, *Heavens Resound,* pp. 151–53.

35. *History of the Church,* 2:167.

36. Backman, *Heavens Resound,* p. 285.

37. *History of the Church,* 2:379–82; punctuation and capitalization standardized.

38. Morgan, *Eliza R. Snow,* p. 62.

39. *History of the Church,* 2:428.

40. George A. Smith, in *Journal of Discourses,* 11:10.

41. *History of the Church,* 2:428; Backman, *Heavens Resound,* p. 300.

THE APOSTASY IN KIRTLAND, 1836–38

O N 6 J U L Y 1 8 3 8 a mile-long wagon train moved slowly southward along the old Chillicothe Road in northern Ohio. Over five hundred disheartened Saints were leaving homes, businesses, and a beautiful temple to embark on an arduous three-month journey to join the Prophet and the Saints in northern Missouri. One of the Saints recalled, "We turned the key and locked the door of our homes, leaving our property and all we possessed in the hands of enemies and strangers, never receiving a cent for anything we owned."[1]

It had only been two years since the Kirtland Temple dedication, and the Saints had enjoyed a great spiritual outpouring and had looked forward to a bright future. What crushed these hopes and forced the Saints to leave Kirtland?

DEALING WITH POVERTY

The gathering of new converts to the Kirtland area continued unabated following the dedication of the temple in March of 1836. Most of these Saints were hard-working, committed people, but, as Benjamin F. Johnson observed, most were of the "poorer class."[2] Unfortunately some of them arrived hoping to be cared for by the funds of the Church or the generosity of the members. The increasing number of Mormons living in poverty alarmed the old-time citizens of Kirtland, who banded together as early as 1835 and warned the poor to leave the city. Acknowledging the problem, the Prophet Joseph Smith advised the branches not to send penniless families to Kirtland. "The Saints have neglected the necessary preparation beforehand; . . . the rich have generally stayed back and withheld their money, while the poor have gone first and without money. Under these circumstances what could be expected but the appalling scene that now presents itself?"[3] Part of what contributed to the appalling scene was the many small and poorly-constructed homes that Church members built haphazardly along the Chagrin River and immediately south of the temple.

Regardless of these problems, a spirit of optimism began to fill Kirtland after the temple dedication, as ambitious Church members attempted to correct the impoverished conditions. The rapid influx of Saints into Kirtland, however, accelerated the demand for property, homes, and goods. Warren Cowdery observed in the *Messenger and Advocate* that "the noise and bustle of teams with lumber, brick, stone, lime or merchandise, were heard from the early dawn of morning till the grey twilight of evening. . . . The starting up, as if by magic, of buildings in every direction around us, [was] evincive to us of buoyant hope, lively anticipation, and a firm confidence that our days of pinching adversity had passed by, that the set time of the Lord to favor Zion had come."[4]

Even though the Saints' fortunes began to increase, the Church was still substantially in debt. Capital, such as gold and silver, remained in short supply. Furthermore, funds were needed to purchase property for settling the Saints in Kirtland and in northern Missouri. Church leaders sought anxiously for ways to relieve the debt and increase the amount of usable money.

In July of 1836 a Brother Burgess arrived in Kirtland and told Joseph Smith that he knew where a large sum of money was hidden in the cellar of a certain house in Salem, Massachusetts. He claimed to be the only person living who knew of the treasure and the location of the house. Salem was a prosperous seaport with a world trade, so it was plausible that treasure would be located there. Hunting for buried treasure, especially that left by Spanish pirates, was still widespread among Americans in that area. Persuaded by Burgess, the Prophet, with Sidney Rigdon, Hyrum Smith, and Oliver Cowdery, left Kirtland in late July for New York City. After arriving there they spent four days consulting with creditors about their debts. Oliver Cowdery also inquired about printing notes for a prospective Church-sponsored bank. From New York the party sailed to Boston and from there they traveled by rail to Salem to meet Burgess and to find out more about some money hidden in that city.

This was not Joseph Smith's first visit to Salem. When he was seven years old he had gone there with his Uncle Jesse to recover from a serious leg operation. Even with the help of Burgess, the brethren searched in vain for the house with the supposed treasure. Burgess soon departed, explaining that Salem had changed so much since he was last there that he could not find the house. The brethren persisted in looking, however. They eventually rented a dwelling matching Burgess's description, but they did not find any money.[5]

In a revelation given in Salem on 6 August 1836, the Lord said "I, the Lord your God, am not displeased with your coming this journey, notwithstanding your follies" (D&C 111:1). The Lord also told the brethren that in Salem he had "much treasure . . . and many people in this city, whom I will gather out in due time for the benefit of Zion" (v. 2). Five years later in Philadelphia, Hyrum Smith gave elders Erastus Snow and Benjamin Winchester a copy of the revelation and asked them to go to Salem to fulfill it. At first Elder Snow was reluctant because he was anxious to return home, but he prayed for guidance and received the assurance that he should go. Benjamin Winchester also went but only remained a short time. Although progress was slow at first, in 1842 Elder Snow organized a branch in Salem

Erastus Snow was a member of the Quorum of the Twelve from 1849 until his death in 1888. In October 1849 he was appointed to go to Denmark to introduce the gospel there.

with 120 members. After spending over a year there he left in February 1843. Thus Erastus Snow fulfilled the promise that "many people" would be gathered out of the city.[6]

THE KIRTLAND SAFETY SOCIETY

The number of banks in the United States had nearly doubled during the 1830s as the demand for credit and money increased. Banks provided loans, paper currency, a medium of exchange, and a safe depository for money. In Kirtland, Joseph Smith and other Church leaders pursued the idea of establishing a bank. With legal assistance, an article of agreement was drafted to incorporate a bank in Kirtland, which would be called the Kirtland Safety Society. In November 1836, Orson Hyde went to the capital of Ohio with a petition to the legislature requesting that they approve the proposal to incorporate the bank. At the same time, Oliver Cowdery went to Philadelphia to purchase plates for printing currency. He succeeded, but Orson returned from Columbus with discouraging news. The timing of the request was bad, and the legislature, after listening to the petition, refused to grant a charter for the requested bank. "Hard-money" Democrats who opposed an expansion of banks in Ohio had gained control of the legislature and were turning down nearly all requests for new banks.

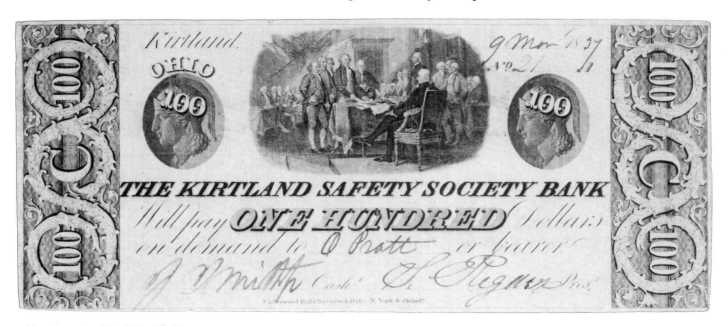

A banking note of the Kirtland Safety Society

The brethren were disappointed, but they decided to create a private joint-stock company to be called the Kirtland Safety Society Anti-Banking Company. Since other unchartered or unauthorized banks were organized in Ohio, they assumed that individuals had a legal right to organize a private company that engaged in banking activities. Many people in the Western Reserve, both members of the Church and nonmembers alike, initially supported the formation of the society with Joseph Smith as its treasurer and

Sidney Rigdon as secretary. The Kirtland Safety Society opened for business on 2 January 1837.

Serious problems soon arose to undermine the success of the bank. A lot of the other banks refused to accept the Safety Society's notes as legal tender, and the anti-Mormon newspapers branded the currency as worthless. Furthermore, the society's capital was primarily in the form of land; it did not possess much *specie* (hard currency, such as gold and silver) for satisfying any large demands for redemption of its paper currency. Enemies of the Church obtained enough notes to initiate a run on the bank, forcing the society to suspend payment in specie to its customers a few weeks after the first notes were issued. Lack of a charter also hindered the company's credibility. As a result, Joseph Smith and Sidney Rigdon were charged with violating the banking statutes of Ohio and brought to trial.

In the spring of 1837 the Saints' economic problems were compounded by a panic (later known as the Panic of 1837) that spread west from New York into other parts of the nation. By May there was a general suspension of payment in specie by all banks in Ohio. Money was scarce during the panic, and many creditors were unable to extend credit or had to postpone due dates. Joseph Smith did all he could to persuade investors to invest more funds to sustain the bank, but he finally turned its operation over to others. This failed to solve the problem, however, because of inept management and rumors that some of them were embezzling the society's funds.

A growing spirit of speculation in Kirtland also added to the Church's economic problems. With the availability of supposed money, which they borrowed from the bank, many people went into debt to purchase land for resale at a substantial profit. Warren Cowdery observed in the *Messenger and Advocate* that not a few members were "guilty of wild speculation and visionary dreams of wealth and worldly grandeur, as if gold and silver were their gods, and houses, farms and merchandize their only bliss or their passport to it."[7] In the fall of 1836, Heber C. Kimball returned from a mission and was amazed at the results of such speculation. He wrote, "When we left Kirtland a city lot was worth about $150; but on our return, to our astonishment, the same lot was said to be worth from $500 to $1000, according to location; and some men, who, when I left, could hardly get food to eat, I found on my return to be men of supposed great wealth; in fact everything in the place seemed to be moving in great prosperity, and all seemed determined to become rich."[8]

As the Kirtland Safety Society overextended itself, it was finally forced to close its doors in November 1837. The two hundred individuals who invested in the bank lost nearly everything they had invested. Joseph Smith's losses from the failure of the company were greater than anyone else's. While seeking to achieve success with the bank and, at the same time, to purchase land in Kirtland and goods for his store, he accumulated debts amounting to approximately one hundred thousand dollars. Although he had assets in land

and goods that were of greater value in some respects than his debts, he was unable to immediately transform these assets into a form that could be used to pay his creditors. As a result the Prophet endured seventeen lawsuits during 1837 in Geauga County for debts involving claims of more than thirty thousand dollars. Unfortunately, few people correctly understood the causes of their economic difficulties. Many Saints spoke against the Prophet and accused him of being responsible for all of their problems.

THE SPREADING APOSTASY

Many members of the Church apostatized during this dark period of economic distress. Eliza R. Snow observed that, following the temple dedication in 1836, a number of members of the Church felt that "prosperity was dawning upon them . . . , and many who had been humble and faithful . . . were getting haughty in their spirits, and lifted up in the pride of their hearts. As the Saints drank in the love and spirit of the world, the Spirit of the Lord withdrew from their hearts, and they were filled with pride and hatred toward those who maintained their integrity."[9]

Wilford Woodruff also remembered that the members were warned by their leaders that unless they humbled themselves and repented of their pride, a scourge awaited them as in the days of the ancient Nephites.[10] The Kirtland paper, the *Messenger and Advocate,* reported that some unscrupulous brethren were taking advantage of newcomers to the community by describing unusual investment opportunities to them, taking their money, and then deserting them.[11]

Backbiting against Joseph Smith was common during the spring and summer of 1837 in Kirtland, particularly when he was away on business or on missions. Some men who held positions of trust in the Church rejected his leadership and declared that he was no longer a true prophet. When Elder Parley P. Pratt returned from a Canadian mission the apostasy was well under way. He was temporarily caught up in these difficulties and left a candid account of his involvement.

"There were also envyings, lyings, strifes and divisions, which caused much trouble and sorrow. By such spirits I was also accused, misrepresented and abused. And at one time, I also was overcome by the same spirit in a great measure, and it seemed as if the very powers of darkness which war against the Saints were let loose upon me. But the Lord knew my faith, my zeal, my integrity of purpose, and he gave me the victory.

"I went to brother Joseph Smith in tears, and, with a broken heart and contrite spirit, confessed wherein I had erred in spirit, murmured, or done or said amiss. He frankly forgave me, prayed for me and blessed me. Thus, by experience, I learned more fully to discern and to contrast the two spirits, and to resist the one and cleave to the other."[12]

On several occasions stalwarts such as Brigham Young and Heber C. Kimball defended the Prophet in various meetings, even though they were endangered. In February 1837 several elders called a meeting in the temple for all those who considered Joseph Smith to be a fallen Prophet. They intended to appoint David Whitmer as the new Church leader. Brigham Young, Heber C. Kimball, and other faithful members attended the meeting. After listening to the arguments against the Prophet, Brigham arose and testified, "Joseph was a Prophet, and I knew it, and that they might rail and slander him as much as they pleased; they could not destroy the appointment of the Prophet of God, they could only destroy their own authority, cut the thread that bound them to the Prophet and to God, and sink themselves to hell."[13] In the Kirtland Temple on 19 February the Prophet spoke for several hours with the power of God. The complainers were silenced and the Saints were strengthened in their support of the Lord's chosen servant.[14]

MISSION TO GREAT BRITAIN

During this period of grave crisis, the Lord revealed to Joseph Smith that "something new must be done for the salvation of His Church."[15] On Sunday, 4 June 1837, the Prophet approached Heber C. Kimball in the temple and whispered to him, "Brother Heber, the Spirit of the Lord has whispered to me: 'Let my servant Heber go to England and proclaim my Gospel, and open the door of salvation to that nation.' " Heber was overwhelmed by his call to England because he lacked education and refinement. He prayed almost daily in an upper room of the temple for protection and power that he might fulfill an honorable mission. His family was near poverty, yet he was determined to serve. He said, "I felt that the cause of truth, the Gospel of Christ, outweighed every other consideration."[16]

Heber C. Kimball wanted his close friend and fellow Apostle Brigham Young to be his companion, but the Prophet needed Brigham to help with matters in troubled Kirtland. While Heber was being set apart for his mission, Orson Hyde walked into the room. Upon hearing what was happening, Orson was moved to repent, for he had been among the leaders of the Church caught up in the spirit of speculation and criticism of Joseph Smith. He acknowledged his faults, asked forgiveness, and offered to accompany Heber on his mission. The Prophet accepted his repentance and also set him apart to go to England.[17] Five others were also set apart to assist the two Apostles: Willard Richards, a Church member of only six months; Joseph Fielding, a native of Bedfordshire, England, who had emigrated to Canada in 1832; and three other Canadians, John Goodson, Isaac Russell, and John Snider, who all had relatives and friends in England they corresponded with. These last four had been converted to the gospel at the same time as John Taylor—during Parley P. Pratt's mission to Canada the year before.

Joseph Fielding's brother James, an Independent (formerly Methodist) minister in Preston, England, wrote to his brother in Canada and invited him to come and preach his new religion in his chapel. So, upon arriving in Britain the missionaries went to Preston, thirty miles north of the port city of

In this house, located on St. Wilfred Street in Preston, England, the missionaries were attacked by evil spirits who tried to stop the work from spreading in that land.

Courtesy of Daughters of Utah Pioneers, Salt Lake City

George D. Watt was the first convert baptized in England. He was baptized 30 July 1837. Having learned shorthand, which at the time was called phonography, George recorded the sermons of the leaders of the Church from 1851 to 1870.

Liverpool, to preach to James's congregation. Some people in that congregation had exercised such great faith and prayer that they had seen these American missionaries in dreams before their arrival in England. Beginning 23 July the brethren preached before three overflow crowds in Reverend Fielding's church, the Vauxhall Chapel. As soon as several parishioners requested baptism, however, Reverend Fielding denied the brethren the use of his chapel any longer. He later lamented, "Kimball bored the holes, Goodson drove the nails, and Hyde clinched them."[18]

Undaunted, the elders soon gained audiences in private houses that had been licensed for preaching and on street corners. Aware of the poverty and illiteracy of most of their listeners, the missionaries spoke on the level of their audience, acted as common men, wore no distinguishing garb, and did not teach for hire. They quickly extended the hand of fellowship and brotherhood, making all the people feel equal before God. The obvious sincerity of the missionaries was a dramatic contrast to the lordly attitude of the English clerics of the day. Soon many people applied for baptism.

On the morning of 30 July, the day the first baptisms were to be performed, the missionaries were attacked by Satan and his hosts. Elder Russell came to Elder Kimball, seeking relief from the torment of evil spirits. As Elders Hyde and Kimball laid their hands on him to bless him, Elder Kimball was knocked senseless to the floor by an invisible power. As he regained consciousness, he saw his brethren praying for him.

"I then arose and sat up on the bed, when a vision was opened to our minds, and we could distinctly see the evil spirits, who foamed and gnashed their teeth at us. We gazed upon them about an hour and a half. . . . I shall never forget the vindictive malignity depicted on their countenances as they looked me in the eye; and any attempt to paint the scene which then presented itself, or portray their malice and enmity, would be vain. . . .

"Years later, narrating the experience of that awful morning to the Prophet Joseph, Heber asked him . . . whether there was anything wrong with him that he should have such a manifestation.

" 'No, Brother Heber,' he replied, 'at that time you were nigh unto the Lord; there was only a veil between you and Him, but you could not see Him. When I heard of it, it gave me great joy, for I then knew that the work of God had taken root in that land. It was this that caused the devil to make a struggle to kill you.'

". . . 'The nearer a person approaches the Lord, a greater power will be manifested by the adversary to prevent the accomplishment of His purposes.' "[19]

Despite the terrors presented by Satan and his host, the baptisms in the River Ribble went on as scheduled. George D. Watt won a foot race to the river, which determined the honor of being the first to be baptized in England. These baptisms began a flood of English converts. The missionaries went on to the villages of Chatburn and Downham, approximately twenty

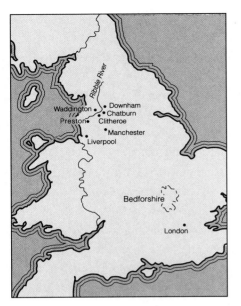

Sites of early missionary work in England

miles northeast of Preston in the Ribble Valley. In Chatburn Heber baptized twenty-five people the first night he preached there. During the next five days, with the assistance of his companion, Joseph Fielding, Heber baptized about one hundred and ten people and organized branches in Downham, Chatburn, Waddington, and Clithero.

As Heber walked the streets of Chatburn one day, children went before him "singing the songs of Zion, while their parents gazed upon the scene with delight, and poured their blessings upon our heads, and praised the God of heaven for sending us to unfold the principles of truth and the plan of salvation to them."[20] Heber explained:

"I went through the streets of that town feeling as I never before felt in my life. My hair would rise on my head as I walked through the streets, and I did not then know what was the matter with me. I pulled off my hat, and felt that I wanted to pull off my shoes, and I did not know what to think of it.

"When I returned, I mentioned the circumstance to brother Joseph, who said, '. . . some of the old Prophets travelled and dedicated that land [England], and their blessing fell upon you.' "[21]

Within eight months two thousand individuals had joined the Church, and twenty-six branches had been organized. Heber C. Kimball remembered that when he was set apart he was promised "that God would make me mighty in that nation in winning souls unto Him; angels should accompany me and bear me up, that my feet should never slip; that I should be mightily blessed and prove a source of salvation to thousands, not only in England but America."[22] This first mission to England set the stage for an even greater effort between the years 1839 and 1841 by the Quorum of the Twelve and for a continuous missionary harvest in the British Isles throughout most of the nineteenth century. The success of the British mission served as an important counterbalance to the Ohio apostasy and the Missouri persecution. The thousands of British converts who emigrated to America immensely strengthened the Church during crucial periods. By the 1850s and 1860s the majority of the families in Utah were headed by parents who had come from Great Britain.

A "GREAT APOSTASY"

As the British mission grew in numbers and strength, apostasy continued to weaken the Church in Kirtland. Caroline Barnes Crosby sadly noted:

"Many of our most intimate associates were among the apostates.

". . . These were some of our nighest neighbors and friends. We had taken sweet counsel together, and walked to the house of God as friends."[23]

In August 1837, while Joseph Smith and most of the Quorum of the Twelve were away on missions, Warren Parrish, a former scribe for the Prophet and an officer of the Kirtland Safety Society, and John Boynton, a member of the Twelve, led a group armed with pistols and bowie knives in an attempted takeover of the temple. In panic and terror, several people jumped out of the temple windows. The police managed to quell the disturbance and eject the men. When the Prophet returned, these men were disfellowshipped for their actions. Those who showed sincere contrition were reinstated.

In the fall, however, when Joseph Smith and Sidney Rigdon left for Missouri, troubles flared up again. Warren Parrish, John F. Boynton, Luke Johnson, and thirty other leading citizens organized a group called the Old Standard, or the Church of Christ. They considered themselves reformers, insisting that Joseph Smith was a fallen prophet who, with other Church authorities, had departed from the true faith. The group sought to overthrow the Church, take over the temple, and still teach most of the Church's doctrines, while rejecting the Book of Mormon and discrediting Joseph Smith and the priesthood. They encountered opposition from Martin Harris, who, though in a state of apostasy himself, bore witness that the Book of Mormon was true and that those who rejected it would be damned.

As a result of this apostasy fifty leading members of the Church were excommunicated under the direction of Joseph Smith, but the problems continued to fester. Several apostates tormented the faithful members with lawsuits and threatened loss of property. Anti-Mormons added their part by boycotting, ostracizing, and denying employment to those who were true to the Prophet and the Church. Hepzibah Richards, sister to Willard Richards, wrote the following:

"For the last three months we as a people have been tempest tossed, and at times the waves have well nigh overwhelmed us. . . .

"A dreadful spirit reigns in the breasts of those who are opposed to this Church. They are above law and beneath whatever is laudable. Their leading object seems to be to get all the property of the Church for little or nothing, and drive them [the Saints] out of the place."[24]

"Between November 1837 and June 1838, possibly two or three hundred Kirtland Saints withdrew from the Church, representing from 10 to 15 percent of the membership there."[25] The "great apostasy" also carried over somewhat to Missouri. In a nine month period, the Three Witnesses, a member of the First Presidency (Frederick G. Williams), four members of the Twelve Apostles, and several members of the First Quorum of the Seventy left the Church. Because he continued to boldly defend the Prophet, Brigham Young was threatened and forced to flee on horseback to Missouri.

In January 1838, Luke Johnson, an apostate himself but still sympathetic to Joseph Smith, warned the Prophet of an assassination plot. While the mob was nearby, Joseph was placed inside a box and taken out of town on an ox cart. When he was safely out of the reach of the mob, he mounted his horse and rode westward with Sidney Rigdon. Their enemies followed them for two hundred miles and were sometimes so near that the brethren could hear cursing and threats in an adjoining room. Emma Smith and their children joined Joseph en route, and after a severely trying journey, they were heartily welcomed by the Missouri Saints in March 1838. Sidney Rigdon arrived a few days later, having separated from the Prophet at Dublin, Indiana.

KIRTLAND CAMP

In the same month that Joseph Smith fled from Kirtland, the lives of the members of the high council were also threatened, and most of the faithful decided to follow their leader to Missouri. Hepzibah Richards wrote of this drastic situation: "All our friends design leaving this place soon as possible. . . . The feeling seems to be that Kirtland must be trodden down by the wicked for a season. . . . Probably several hundred families will leave within a few weeks."[26] But before most of the faithful could leave Kirtland, enemies began ransacking homes of the Saints and starting fires in basements.

Early in March the seventies began planning ways to help the poorest Saints move to Missouri. One of the presidents of the quorum, James Foster, had a vision of an orderly company of about five hundred Saints traveling to

Under the direction of Hyrum Smith, Presidents of the Seventies formulated the Kirtland Camp constitution. The document included nine articles to help govern the camp in their move to Missouri in 1838.

Missouri and camping by the way. Directed by vision and prophecy, the seventies drew up a constitution, formed a camp of those willing to abide by it, and designated leaders to preside over companies. Captains were to encourage their companies to keep the commandments and observe the Word of Wisdom.

The trek was delayed for several weeks as the Saints struggled to settle their debts, sell their property, and purchase wagons, teams, and equipment. They finally left Kirtland on 6 July 1838 with over five hundred Saints, 27 tents, 59 wagons, 97 horses, 22 oxen, 69 cows, and 1 bull. Benjamin Johnson wrote, "All means for defraying expenses were put together, and so all were to fare alike, and did so long as they remained in camp together."[27] Even so the travelers had to pause occasionally to earn money for supplies and equipment.

The Kirtland Camp was also dogged by persecution along the trail. Many people were suspicious of the bedraggled travelers who passed through towns and cities. "As we passed along the road in the morning, molesting no one, some of the company were saluted in modern style by having eggs thrown at them by some ruffians."[28] Ridicule was sometimes combined with threats of violence. In Missouri the citizens of one community placed "artillery" in the street to prevent the camp from passing through. They were only allowed to proceed when one of the seventies soothed the citizens' anxious feelings, and even then several of the camp's leaders were jailed overnight. Many forces contributed to the suffering in the Kirtland Camp.

"Accidents and illness constantly afflicted the pioneers. Some persons were crushed under wagon wheels; others succumbed to disease. . . . They perspired by day and slept on cold and sometimes damp terrain by night. They forded streams, climbed up and down inclines, and followed rutted roads and trails, continually weakened by fatigue, a meager and changing diet, and polluted drinking water.

"In the midst of their suffering and afflictions, they turned to their Heavenly Father for help. Throughout the journey, elders administered to the sick and the injured; and diarists reported that through the power of the priesthood, many of the afflicted were instantly healed."[29]

When the camp arrived at the Mississippi River in September, they were informed that war had broken out in western Missouri between the Mormons and their enemies, that all Mormons would soon be driven from the state, and that if they continued their journey, they would be attacked and would suffer a similar fate. Several members of the camp refused to enter Missouri as a result of these threats. But most of them pressed on, finally joining the Prophet in Far West, Missouri, on 2 October 1838. Two days later they arrived at Adam-ondi-Ahman, where they were to settle. They would soon discover that their problems had not been left behind in Ohio. Within weeks they would face worse persecutions in Missouri.

ENDNOTES

1. Stella Cahoon Shurtleff and Brent Farrington Cahoon, comps., *Reynolds Cahoon and His Stalwart Sons* (n.p.: Stella Cahoon Shurtleff, 1960), p. 28.

2. Benjamin F. Johnson, *My Life's Review* (Independence, Mo.: Zion's Printing and Publishing Co., 1947), p. 15.

3. *Latter Day Saints' Messenger and Advocate,* Sept. 1836, p. 379; spelling standardized.

4. *Messenger and Advocate,* June 1837, p. 520.

5. See Robert L. Millet and Kent P. Jackson, eds., *Studies in Scripture: Volume One, the Doctrine and Covenants* (Sandy, Utah: Randall Book Co., 1984), pp. 432–36.

6. See Andrew Karl Larson, *Erastus Snow: The Life of a Missionary and Pioneer for the Early Mormon Church* (Salt Lake City: University of Utah Press, 1971), pp. 67–74.

7. *Messenger and Advocate,* June 1837, p. 509.

8. In Orson F. Whitney, *Life of Heber C. Kimball,* 3d ed. (Salt Lake City: Bookcraft, 1967), p. 99.

9. Eliza R. Snow, comp., *Biography and Family Record of Lorenzo Snow* (Salt Lake City: Deseret News Co., 1884), p. 20.

10. Wilford Woodruff Journals, 17 Jan. 1837, LDS Historical Department, Salt Lake City.

11. *Messenger and Advocate,* May 1837, pp. 505–10.

12. Parley P. Pratt, ed., *Autobiography of Parley P. Pratt,* Classics in Mormon Literature series (Salt Lake City: Deseret Book Co., 1985), p. 144.

13. "History of Brigham Young," *Deseret News,* 10 Feb. 1858, p. 386.

14. See Dean C. Jessee, "The Kirtland Diary of Wilford Woodruff," *Brigham Young University Studies,* Summer 1972, p. 385.

15. *History of the Church,* 2:489.

16. In Whitney, *Life of Heber C. Kimball,* p. 104.

17. See *History of the Church,* 2:489–90.

18. In Whitney, *Life of Heber C. Kimball,* p. 125.

19. In Whitney, *Life of Heber C. Kimball,* pp. 130–31.

20. Whitney, *Life of Heber C. Kimball,* p. 172.

21. Heber C. Kimball, in *Journal of Discourses,* 5:22; see also Whitney, *Life of Heber C. Kimball,* pp. 170–73.

22. In Whitney, *Life of Heber C. Kimball,* p. 105.

23. In Kenneth W. Godfrey, Audrey M. Godfrey, and Jill Mulvay Derr, *Women's Voices* (Salt Lake City: Deseret Book Co., 1982), p. 56.

24. In Godfrey, Godfrey, and Derr, *Women's Voices,* p. 76.

25. Milton V. Backman, Jr., *The Heavens Resound* (Salt Lake City: Deseret Book Co., 1983), p. 328.

26. Typescript of letter from Hepzibah Richards to Willard Richards, 22 Jan. 1838, LDS Historical Department, Salt Lake City.

27. Johnson, *My Life's Review,* pp. 32–33.

28. *History of the Church,* 3:112.

29. Backman, *Heavens Resound,* pp. 359–60.

THE CHURCH IN NORTHERN MISSOURI, 1836–38

THE PROPHET AND other leaders of the Church left Kirtland in January 1838. Most other members followed later in the year. There was no decision to abandon Kirtland, but clearly the focal point of the Church was switching to northern Missouri. Perhaps a few members recalled the revelation given in 1831: "I, the Lord, will to retain a strong hold in the land of Kirtland, for the space of five years" (D&C 64:21). By early 1838 the years of Kirtland's glory had passed. The members in northern Missouri were already establishing new headquarters—Far West. Other scattered Saints in the United States and Canada were preparing to gather there. Latter-day Saints were eager to find a season of peace after the disastrous year of apostasy in 1837.

REQUEST FOR MORMONS TO LEAVE CLAY COUNTY

Following their expulsion from Jackson County in late 1833, the Missouri Saints lived in relative peace with the original inhabitants of Clay County. But the leaders of the Church never intended this arrangement to be permanent; they consistently petitioned government authorities for assistance to re-enter Jackson County and regain their property, but all their attempts proved futile. Meanwhile, Latter-day Saints continued to arrive, reinforcing the fear among Clay County residents that the Mormon settlements would become permanent.

Realizing these concerns, Bishop Edward Partridge and William W. Phelps went on two exploring expeditions in the spring of 1836 hoping to find potential sites for Mormon settlements in northern Missouri, a region commonly referred to as the "Far West." Most of this territory was prairie, covered by tall grass, with timber only along the streams and rivers. At that time only forested land was considered good for settlement. W. W. Phelps reported that "nearly every skirt of timber to the state line on the north . . . has some one in it." But the brethren found an uninhabited area in northern Ray County along Shoal Creek, although they feared there was not enough timber available to support a large population.[1] Nevertheless, the brethren began purchasing land in the Shoal Creek area on 3 May.

On 29 June 1836 a mass meeting was held in the Clay County courthouse in Liberty to discuss objections to the Mormons remaining in the area. Some were concerned that the "crisis" would erupt into a civil war. Opponents gave five reasons for their objection to the Saints: (1) They were poor.

(2) Their religious differences stirred up prejudice. (3) Their Eastern customs and dialect were alien to the Missourians. (4) They opposed slavery. (5) They believed the Indians were God's chosen people destined to inherit the land of Missouri with them. The citizens also reminded the Mormons of their pledge to leave the county and suggested that they consider moving to Wisconsin in the slave-free North where there were many areas suitable for settlement. These Clay County leaders promised to control any violence toward the Mormons until they could leave the area.

Confident that they would soon begin moving to Shoal Creek, Church leaders found no objection to the petition for a covenant of peace and called a public meeting on 1 July to draft a reply. Resolutions were passed expressing the Saints' gratitude for the kindness the citizens of Clay County had extended to the Saints and their desire for a peaceful resolution to the crisis. Leaders pledged to lead the Saints out of the county and to halt the tide of immigration. The following day Clay County leaders accepted the reply and began forming committees to help the Saints in their move.

In Ohio, the First Presidency having learned of these developments, wrote separate letters to leaders of the Church and to the Clay County committee. They urged members of the Church to preserve the peace but not to settle in Wisconsin. They informed the Clay County committee that they had advised the Saints to avoid bloodshed and to move from the county.

On 7 July the Church leaders in Missouri wrote Governor Daniel Dunklin of their intentions to move to the sixteen hundred acres they had purchased in northern Ray County and requested his assistance in breaking up potential mobs. In 1836 the "Mormon problem" was not as prominent in Missouri politics as it had been in 1833–34; and since it was an election year the governor was less inclined to help the Saints. Moreover, many voters in Ray County opposed the move of the Saints into their county, even the uninhabited northern prairies. Governor Dunklin replied on 18 July that, while he sympathized with the plight of the Saints, "public sentiment may become paramount law; and when one man or society of men become so obnoxious to that sentiment as to determine the people to be rid of him or them, it is useless to run counter to it.

". . . The consequences will be the same . . . unless you can, by your conduct and arguments, convince them [the people of Missouri] of your innocence. If you cannot do this, all I can say to you is that in this Republic the *vox populi* is the *vox Dei* [the voice of the people is the voice of God]."[2]

CREATION OF CALDWELL COUNTY AND FOUNDING OF FAR WEST

Conditions for the Saints were critical. Without assurance of protection from the governor and with hostility in both Clay and Ray counties, the stake presidency and the high council met in an emergency session on 25 July. To complicate matters further, the brethren had just learned that approximately one hundred families of immigrating Saints were camped on the Crooked River in lower Ray County. Many of them were ill, and most of them were without funds to purchase either provisions or land. Citizens in Ray County threatened them with violence if they did not leave. Furthermore, another hundred impoverished families were en route from the Mississippi River. "To prevent mobbing and confusion, and pestilence and death," Church leaders advised the immigrants to scatter among the people in the settlements and find temporary lodgings and work. Thomas B. Marsh and Elisha H. Groves, a convert from Kentucky, were sent to branches of the Church in other states to collect money to benefit "Poor Bleeding Zion," while W. W. Phelps, John Whitmer, Edward Partridge, Isaac Morley, and John Corrill were assigned to locate more land for settlement.[3]

Church leaders also assured the citizens of Ray County that the Saints intended to settle only in the prairies to the north and to apply for a new county, which the citizens readily agreed to. A proposal was also accepted to establish a six-mile buffer zone, three miles on each side of the dividing line between the counties, as a "no-man's land" where neither Mormon nor non-Mormon could settle.

Meanwhile, early in August, W. W. Phelps and John Whitmer located a site for a city, which they designated Far West, in northern Ray County. It was twelve miles west of Haun's Mill, a small Mormon settlement established by Jacob Haun on Shoal Creek a year earlier. The Saints began gathering in the late summer and fall, and soon Far West and numerous smaller settlements sprang into existence.

Alexander W. Doniphan, friend to the Saints and a state legislator, introduced a bill into the December 1836 legislative session to create two small counties out of the sparsely settled regions of northern Ray County. Doniphan named the new counties Daviess and Caldwell after two famous Indian fighters from Kentucky, where he was also born and raised. Caldwell County, the location of the Far West and Shoal Creek settlements, was to be exclusively for Mormons, and they would be allowed to send representatives to the state legislature. This segregation of the Latter-day Saints was considered an excellent solution to the "Mormon problem." Newly elected Governor Lilburn W. Boggs signed the bill creating the two new counties on 29 December 1836.

Internal difficulties were brewing as the Saints poured into Caldwell County, where they constructed log houses and prepared the soil for spring planting. Thomas Marsh and Elisha Groves returned early in 1837 from their fund-raising mission in Kentucky and Tennessee and turned $1450 over to W. W. Phelps and John Whitmer, counselors in the stake presidency, since President David Whitmer was in Ohio. The counselors used the money to buy more land, but they purchased it in their own names and then sold it to the Saints at a small profit, which they retained. Several members of the Church immediately protested, and some of the high council complained

Alexander W. Doniphan (1808–87) was born in Kentucky. At age eighteen he graduated from Augusta College in Kentucky. Later he studied law and passed the requirements to practice law in Ohio and Missouri.

He married Elizabeth Jane Thornton on 21 December 1837, and they had two sons, who both died in their youth. Alexander W. Doniphan died in Richmond, Missouri, and was buried in Liberty, which had been his home for many years.

that the counselors were also making decisions regarding Far West without consulting them. At a series of meetings in Far West in April, these brethren acknowledged their wrongs, and reconciliation was achieved. It was decided that Bishop Edward Partridge, acting with the counsel of the stake presidency, the high council, and two Apostles who were in Missouri—Thomas B. Marsh and David Patten—would distribute the lands.

A month later, however, Phelps and Whitmer again offended the high council and the Apostles with further attempts to profit from land deals. When the Prophet learned of this conflict, he sought and obtained guidance from the Lord and was told, "Verily thus saith the Lord unto you my servant Joseph—my servants John Whitmer and William W. Phelps have done those things which are not pleasing in my sight, therefore if they repent not they shall be removed out of their places."[4] Nevertheless, this conflict continued until November 1837.

A conference in Kirtland on 17 September 1837 resolved to send Joseph Smith and Sidney Rigdon to Missouri to seek other locations for stakes of Zion "so that the poor may have a place of refuge."[5] Also in response to the conference, Bishop Newel K. Whitney sent a letter on 18 September to branches of the Church scattered throughout the United States asking them to send tithing in gold and silver for the relief of Kirtland and the building of Zion in Missouri.

The Prophet and several other brethren arrived in Far West early in November and spent approximately ten days there holding meetings. It was determined that there were resources and space in northern Missouri for the gathering of the Saints, and a committee was chosen to locate sites for new stakes. Joseph decided to postpone the building of a temple in Far West until he received further direction from the Lord, but the size of Far West was enlarged from one square mile to two. The problems associated with the activities of the stake presidency in Missouri were temporarily resolved, and the stake presidency were sustained in their callings. At a conference of elders held 7 November 1837 in Far West, Frederick G. Williams was rejected as second counselor in the First Presidency and Hyrum Smith was sustained in his place.

During the winter new discord arose between the stake presidency and the high council in Missouri. Oliver Cowdery and Frederick G. Williams, who had been out of harmony with the Prophet in Kirtland, had now moved to Far West and, together with the stake presidency, decided to sell some Church lands in Jackson County held in their names. Selling lands in Zion violated the Lord's direction that the Saints should continue to hold claim upon their lands in Jackson County (see D&C 101:99).

Early in February 1838 the high council tried John Whitmer and W. W. Phelps for misusing Church funds and David Whitmer for willfully breaking the Word of Wisdom. Despite some feeling that the high council was not authorized to try the presidency, a majority voted to reject them, and a

Plat of Far West on sheepskin

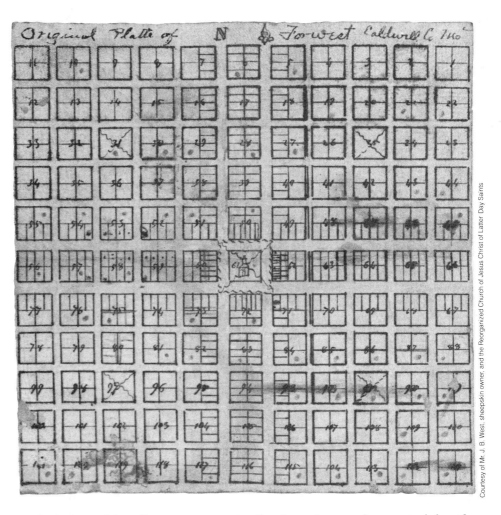

resolution to this effect was sent to the branches and accepted by the Saints. When the presidency claimed that the trial was illegal and that they had not been present to defend themselves, the high council was convinced that they were "endeavoring to palm themselves off upon the Church, as her Presidents" after they had been properly removed.[6] Therefore, on 10 February the high council, with the assistance of two Apostles, excommunicated W. W. Phelps and John Whitmer and sustained Thomas B. Marsh and David W. Patten as acting presidents until the expected arrival of Joseph Smith. Additional action against David Whitmer, Oliver Cowdery, and Lyman Johnson, an Apostle who had joined the dissenters, was postponed pending the Prophet's arrival.

In a letter to Joseph Smith, Elder Marsh explained, "Had we not taken the above measures, we think that nothing could have prevented a rebellion against the whole high council and bishop; so great was the disaffection against the presidents, that the people began to be jealous, that the whole authorities were inclined to uphold these men in wickedness, and in a little time the church, undoubtedly, would have gone, every man to his own way, like sheep without a shepherd."[7]

THE PROPHET SETTLES IN FAR WEST

The Prophet Joseph was still in Ohio; news of persecution and the unsettled state of the Church in Missouri disheartened him. On 12 January 1838, he received a revelation explaining that only the First Presidency could form a stake.[8] This revelation meant the creation of the Far West stake was invalid. Hence, he went to Missouri not only to escape his enemies, but to set the Church in Far West in order. The journey was difficult, but when Joseph and Emma, who was six months pregnant, arrived in Missouri in March, many Saints met them to accompany them to Far West. Eight miles from town another eager escort gladdened their hearts. After so many difficulties in the East, the Prophet was encouraged by the support of the Missouri Saints, and they were equally glad to have him settle among them.

While in Far West Joseph approved the removal of the stake presidency. By the end of March he was optimistic about the unity in Far West, despite the arrival of several letters from Kirtland apostates, which spread falsehood among a few. Joseph wrote back to Kirtland that "peace and love prevail throughout; in a word, heaven smiles upon the Saints in Caldwell."[9] Two days before April general conference they were heartened when Sidney Rigdon and his party arrived after a long and difficult journey.

At the conference the Prophet called the three senior members of the Quorum of Twelve Apostles—Thomas B. Marsh, David W. Patten, and Brigham Young—as the new stake presidency in Missouri. This, however, was only a temporary solution. Nine days later he received a revelation instructing Elder Patten to arrange his affairs so that he and others of the Twelve could leave in the spring of 1839 for a new mission abroad (see D&C 114). In a later session David Patten reviewed the status of the Quorum of the Twelve, not all of whom were in Missouri. He commended six of his brethren as being "men of God. . . . He spoke somewhat doubtful of William Smith, . . . William E. McLellin, Luke S. Johnson, Lyman E. Johnson, and John F. Boynton, as being men whom he could not recommend to the conference."[10] It became apparent that four of the men would have to be replaced. During the sessions on 7–8 April, additional action was taken to put the Church in Missouri in order.

After the conference the new stake presidency dealt with the cases of former leaders who had apostatized. They wrote to John Whitmer, who had been both the Church historian and a member of the stake presidency in Missouri, asking him to give his historical notes and writings to the Church. He did not comply. Only recently has his history been published in its entirety.

A much more serious matter was the case of Oliver Cowdery. He was charged by the high council for persecuting Church leaders with vexatious lawsuits, seeking to destroy the character of Joseph Smith, not abiding ecclesiastical authority in temporal affairs, selling lands in Jackson County, and leaving his calling as Assistant President of the Church and turning to the practice of law. Oliver refused to appear before the council, but he answered by letter. He denied the Church's right to dictate how he should conduct his life and asked that his fellowship with the Church be ended. The high council excommunicated him 12 April 1838. He spent a decade outside the Church, but later humbly submitted himself for rebaptism in October 1848 in Kanesville, Iowa.

The high council also excommunicated David Whitmer, another of the three witnesses to the Book of Mormon, on charges of usurping too much authority, writing letters of dissension to apostates, and breaking the Word of Wisdom. David never returned to the Church, although to his death he maintained his testimony that he saw the angel and the gold plates. Lyman Johnson of the Twelve was also excommunicated at the same time. Even though excommunicating such former stalwarts was painful, Church leaders felt it was necessary to cleanse the Church.

In the latter part of April 1838 the Prophet received a revelation regarding the building up of Far West. It first designated the correct name of the Church as "The Church of Jesus Christ of Latter-day Saints" (D&C 115:4). This settled confusion on the issue; the Church had been called the Church of Christ, the Church of the Latter Day Saints, and the Church of Christ of Latter Day Saints. The Lord also commanded the building of a temple. "Let the city, Far West, be a holy and consecrated land unto me; and it shall be called most holy, for the ground upon which thou standest is holy" (v. 7). But the First Presidency was told not to incur debt for this temple as had been done in Kirtland. The Lord also directed the brethren to establish stakes in the surrounding regions. This was to be done so "that the gathering together upon the land of Zion, and upon her stakes, may be for a defense, and for a refuge from the storm, and from wrath when it shall be poured out without mixture upon the whole earth" (v. 6).

The Prophet spent the next three weeks visiting with the Saints in Caldwell County and teaching them principles of the gospel. Then, with the assistance of Sidney Rigdon, he embarked on the ambitious project of writing the history of the Church from its beginning. The history written by John Whitmer, the first Church historian, had been incomplete and, in any event, was now unavailable. The history of Joseph Smith and the early events of the Restoration now found in the Pearl of Great Price were a product of this project begun in April 1838.

EXPANSION IN NORTHERN MISSOURI

Having set the affairs of the Church in order in Caldwell County, the Prophet Joseph Smith turned his attention to locating places of settlement for the Saints in Ohio and other eastern states who would come to Missouri in the spring and summer of 1838. In 1837 a few Latter-day Saints had settled north of Caldwell County in the newly-created county of Daviess. They did so in accordance with the gentleman's agreement that they obtain permission from the "gentile" inhabitants to settle. The most prominent Mormon to settle in Daviess County was Lyman Wight, who founded Wight's Settlement on a beautiful hillside overlooking the Grand River.

In mid-May 1838, Joseph Smith and others headed northward in an exploring expedition. When they reached Wight's Ferry on the Grand River, the Prophet directed the laying out of a city at that location. He also received a revelation that this was the site of Adam-ondi-Ahman. In 1835 the Lord revealed that three years before Adam died he had called his righteous posterity together "into the valley of Adam-ondi-Ahman, and there bestowed upon them his last blessing" (D&C 107:53; see also 78:15–16). Orson Pratt said the name means "Valley of God, where Adam dwelt. It is in the original language spoken by Adam."[11] Adam-ondi-Ahman will yet be

Lyman Wight's second cabin in the valley of Adam-ondi-Ahman. Lyman Wight was born 9 May 1796 in Fairfield, New York. He fought in the War of 1812.

He was baptized by Oliver Cowdery in 1830. Lyman served as a counselor to John Smith, president of the stake at Adam-ondi-Ahman. Lyman was ordained an Apostle in 1841, but through disobedience he lost his Church membership in 1848.

the location of a very important meeting for selected righteous people to greet the Savior. In the words of the revelation, "It is the place where Adam shall come to visit his people, or the Ancient of Days shall sit, as spoken of by Daniel the prophet" (D&C 116:1). This knowledge so thrilled the brethren that plans were discussed to create a stake at Adam-ondi-Ahman.

The explorers sought out other sites for settlement along the heavily timbered and navigable Grand River. With the explorations finished, Joseph Smith returned to Far West, realizing that Emma was soon to deliver another child. She gave birth to a son on 2 June 1838. They named him Alexander Hale Smith.

Before long Joseph was back in Adam-ondi-Ahman surveying the new city and building houses. He designated the community as a gathering place for the Kirtland Saints still in Ohio or en route to Missouri. When his uncle John Smith and family arrived in Far West, the Prophet counseled him to settle in Adam-ondi-Ahman. A conference was held on 28 June in the community, affectionately nicknamed "Di-Ahman," and John Smith was sustained as the president of the stake, with Reynolds Cahoon and Lyman Wight as his counselors. A high council was also organized. Vinson Knight was called as acting bishop until the arrival of Bishop Newel K. Whitney from Kirtland (see D&C 117:11).

Latter-day Saint immigrants poured into Adam-ondi-Ahman throughout the summer of 1838. They considered themselves greatly blessed to live in the land where Adam dwelt. An article in the August issue of the *Elders' Journal* portrays their excitement:

"The immense immigration . . . encourages the Saints, and induces us to believe that God is about to bring to pass his strange acts, of which he has spoken by his ancient Prophets.

"The immense growth of corn and other produce, this season . . . has not to our knowledge, had a parallel in this generation; and if the Lord should continue to bless, as he has now set his hand to do, there must soon be a surplus."[12] Indeed, a plentiful harvest that fall helped provide for the impoverished members of the Kirtland Camp when they arrived in Missouri and settled in Di-Ahman in early October.

About the time Di-Ahman was being settled the Saints also began to establish themselves in DeWitt, located in Carroll County near where the Grand River entered the Missouri River. This benefited the Church because the members established a steamboat landing that immigrants could move to from the other LDS settlements. John Murdock and George M. Hinkle, members of the Far West high council, were authorized to purchase property in DeWitt and begin a settlement. DeWitt grew rapidly. A housing shortage developed in the fall when a large group of Saints from Canada arrived, making the Mormon city of DeWitt largely a tent city.

By far the most prosperous of the Latter-day Saint communities was Far West. By the summer of 1838 the population of Caldwell County approached five thousand, and over half of them lived in Far West proper. The Saints built more than one hundred fifty homes, four dry goods stores, three family grocery stores, several blacksmith shops, two hotels, a printing shop, and a large schoolhouse that doubled as a church and courthouse.[13]

Due to persecution, the Elders' Journal *was published only twice in 1837 in Kirtland, Ohio. It was then moved to Far West, Missouri, where it was also published twice. The last issue was August 1838.*

The Saints were busy planting crops and building log houses, but they paused to worship and study the gospel. Twenty-four-year-old Sarah Rich was a new bride when she and her husband, Charles, settled in a "cozy and happy" log house four miles from Far West, "religion being first with us in all things," she declared. Each Sunday they rode horseback to town to attend meeting, "often listening to the Prophet Joseph Smith preach and instruct the people, a privilege we both appreciated very much."[14]

During the summer of 1838 the Prophet turned to the important matters of filling the vacancies in the Quorum of the Twelve Apostles. He reaffirmed their responsibilities and counseled the Saints on the financing of the Lord's kingdom. There was great sadness in the Church over the loss of four of the original Twelve. Elizabeth Barlow reflected, "We all felt more sorrowful at seeing Apostles leave the Church than we did over our trials and persecutions."[15]

Despite the grief, Joseph Smith began replacing these four Apostles and preparing the Twelve for their assignment to take the gospel to the world. In the fall of 1837, prior to his visit to Far West, he sent word to John Taylor, a stalwart convert from Toronto, of his future call to the apostleship.[16] At the time Elder Taylor was not presented before the membership of the Church for a sustaining vote. The following July the Prophet prayed, "Show unto us thy will O Lord concerning the Twelve."[17] The revelation that followed had a profound impact on the history of the Church. First the Lord directed that "men be appointed to supply the place of those who are fallen" (D&C 118:1). John Taylor, John E. Page, Wilford Woodruff, and Willard Richards were called.

As a missionary in Canada for two years, Elder John E. Page had traveled more than five thousand miles and baptized over six hundred converts. When this revelation was given, he was en route to Missouri with a company of Canadian Saints. They arrived in DeWitt in October. Elders Taylor and Page were ordained Apostles 19 December 1838 in Far West by Brigham Young and Heber C. Kimball. Elder Woodruff was a missionary in Maine when he received his call in a letter. He led a group of New England converts toward Missouri, but the Saints were driven from the state before they arrived, so he settled them in Illinois. Wilford Woodruff was ordained an Apostle in Far West on 26 April 1839 when he accompanied other members of the Twelve there to fulfill the commandment that the Twelve were to take up their mission to England from Far West (see D&C 118:4–5). Elder Richards, an English convert, was a missionary and priesthood leader in Great Britain and was not ordained until members of the Twelve arrived there in 1840.

The revelation concerning the Twelve also instructed Thomas B. Marsh to continue publishing the Lord's word (in the *Elders' Journal*) in Far West and directed the others to preach "in all lowliness of heart, in meekness and humility, and long-suffering" (v. 3). The Lord further charged the Twelve to prepare to depart 26 April 1839 from Far West "to go over the great waters, and there promulgate my gospel" (v. 4).

On the day the revelation to the Twelve was given, Joseph Smith also read two revelations concerning Church revenue to the Saints. With the Church deeply mired in economic difficulties, the Prophet had sought clarification on how the law of consecration should be applied. The Lord modified the original law given in 1831 when he replied:

"I require all their surplus property to be put into the hands of the bishop of my church in Zion,

"For the building of mine house, and for the laying of the foundation of Zion and for the priesthood, and for the debts of the Presidency of my Church.

"And this shall be the beginning of the tithing of my people.

"And after that, those who have thus been tithed shall pay one-tenth of all their interest [income] annually; and this shall be a standing law unto them forever" (D&C 119:1–4). The second revelation assigned a committee of General Authorities the responsibility of expending the tithes (see D&C 120).

Although the Saints in northern Missouri were optimistic, there was reason for apprehension. The Saints, having endured persecution and malcontent for seven years, were understandably impatient with dissenters who resided in Far West. These dissenters harassed them with lawsuits and condemned Church leaders. In June, Sidney Rigdon burst forth in a heated oration commonly referred to as the Salt Sermon. He drew his text from the scripture, "Ye are the salt of the earth: but if the salt have lost his savour, . . . it is thenceforth good for nothing, but to be cast out, and to be trodden under foot of men" (Matthew 5:13). The implication was that the dissenters should be cast out from among the Saints.

Soon afterward an unauthorized document appeared, addressed to Oliver Cowdery, David and John Whitmer, W. W. Phelps, and Lyman E. Johnson, the leading dissenters. The document was signed by eighty-four Church members, and it pointedly ordered the apostates to leave the county or face serious consequences. The sermon and letter had the desired effect; the dissenters fled in haste and were soon followed by their families. This extreme behavior on the part of a few horrified some people in the Church, and murmuring arose. Most unfortunately, it also reinforced the growing anti-Mormon hostility in northern Missouri.

Also contributing to the conflict with the gentiles was Sampson Avard's formation of an underground society called the *Danites*. This was an oath-bound group with secret identification and warning signs. Avard convinced his followers that they operated with the approval of the Presidency of the Church and that they were authorized to avenge themselves against the Church's enemies by robbery, lying, and murder if necessary. Danite depredations, both real and imagined, intensified hostilities and gave Missouri officials a reason to indict Joseph Smith and other leaders for crimes against the state.

Sidney Rigdon's Independence Day speech in 1838 added more fuel to the Mormon-gentile conflict. As the Saints in Far West celebrated the nation's birthday and laid the cornerstones of the temple, Sidney Rigdon's oratory whipped them into high emotion. He thundered out the Saints' own declaration of independence from any further mob violence or illegal activity. He warned potential mobs that the Church would no longer meekly bear persecution but would defend itself to the death. "It shall be between us and them a war of extermination, for we will follow them, till the last drop of their blood is spilled, or else they will have to exterminate us."[18] Copies of this inflammatory speech were imprudently published and circulated. Some copies reached the hands of Missouri officials and eventually provided the basis for charges of treason and violence against the Saints.

Thus the stage was set for the frightful conflict and terrible loss of life and property that followed. The Saints would have to pass through still more of the "refiner's fire" before they could find peace.

ENDNOTES

1. In *History of the Church*, 2:445.

2. In *History of the Church*, 2:462.

3. Donald Q. Cannon and Lyndon W. Cook, eds., *Far West Record: Minutes of The Church of Jesus Christ of Latter-day Saints, 1830–1844* (Salt Lake City: Deseret Book Co., 1983), p. 105.

4. *History of the Church*, 2:511.

5. In *History of the Church*, 2:516.

6. In *History of the Church*, 3:7.

7. *Elders' Journal*, July 1838, p. 45.

8. See "The Scriptory Book of Joseph Smith," LDS Historical Department, Salt Lake City, pp. 52–53.

9. *History of the Church*, 3:11.

10. In *History of the Church*, 3:14.

11. In *Journal of Discourses*, 18:343; see also Bruce R. McConkie, *Mormon Doctrine*, 2d ed. (Salt Lake City: Bookcraft, 1966), pp. 19–21.

12. *Elders' Journal*, Aug. 1838, p. 52; spelling and capitalization standardized.

13. See B. H. Roberts, *A Comprehensive History of The Church of Jesus Christ of Latter-day Saints, Century One,* 6 vols. (Salt Lake City: The Church of Jesus Christ of Latter-day Saints, 1930), 1:425.

14. Sarah DeArmon Pea Rich, holograph autobiography, LDS Historical Department, Salt Lake City, p. 36; spelling, punctuation, and capitalization standardized; or Kenneth W. Godfrey, Audrey M. Godfrey, and Jill Mulvay Derr, *Women's Voices* (Salt Lake City: Deseret Book Co., 1982), p. 98.

15. Elizabeth Haven Barlow, "Mother of Eight," in Kate B. Carter, comp., *Our Pioneer Heritage,* 19 vols. (Salt Lake City: Daughters of Utah Pioneers, 1967–76), 19:321; or Leonard J. Arrington and Susan Arrington Madsen, *Sunbonnet Sisters* (Salt Lake City: Bookcraft, 1984), p. 24.

16. See B. H. Roberts, *The Life of John Taylor* (Salt Lake City: Bookcraft, 1963), p. 47.

17. *History of the Church*, 3:46.

18. *Oration Delivered by Mr. S. Rigdon on the 4th of July 1838* (Far West: Journal Office, 1838), LDS Historical Department, Salt Lake City, p. 12.

MISSOURI PERSECUTIONS AND EXPULSION

Northwest Missouri

D URING THE HOT summer months of 1838, relations between the Latter-day Saints and their northern Missouri neighbors continued to deteriorate rapidly. Elder Parley P. Pratt, who had arrived in Far West in May after returning from missionary service in the East, described the tense situation that existed by July 1838. He said, "War clouds began again to lower with dark and threatening aspect. Those who had combined against the laws in the adjoining counties, had long watched our increasing power and prosperity with jealousy, and with greedy and avaricious eyes. It was a common boast that, as soon as we had completed our extensive improvements, and made a plentiful crop, they would drive us from the State, and once more enrich themselves with the spoils."[1] For these and other reasons, violence erupted which eventually resulted in the expulsion of the entire Church from the state of Missouri.

ELECTION DAY BATTLE AT GALLATIN

In 1831 a family named Peniston had become the first white settlers in what was to become Daviess County. The next year they built a mill on the Grand River to grind flour and meal for incoming settlers. They developed the village of Millport. When the county was created in 1836, there were still fewer than a hundred settlers. The town of Gallatin was platted to serve as the county seat, and as it grew, Millport, three miles to the east, declined.

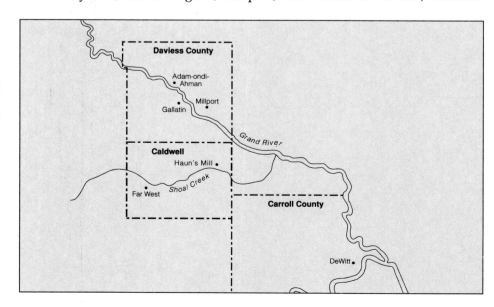

The Saints poured into Diahman, some four miles north of Gallatin, in the summer of 1838. They quickly began to outnumber the gentiles in Daviess County.

The year 1838 was an election year. The original settlers naturally wanted to elect a state legislator who was one of their own. William Peniston, a staunch foe of the Saints, was a candidate. He was afraid that with the rapid influx of Mormons, he would not win the election because most Church members supported John A. Williams. About two weeks before the election, Judge Joseph Morin of Millport advised two elders of the Church to go to the polls prepared for an attack by mobbers determined to prevent Mormons from voting. The election was to be held on Monday, 6 August, in Gallatin, which was at that time merely a straggling row of "ten houses, three of which were saloons."[2]

Hoping that the judge's prediction would prove false, a number of Mormon men went unarmed to Gallatin to vote. At 11 A.M., William Peniston addressed the crowd of voters, hoping to excite them against the Mormons: "The Mormon leaders are a set of horse thieves, liars, counterfeiters, and you know they profess to heal the sick, and cast out devils, and you all know that is a lie."[3] Election days in the West were rarely orderly, but with Peniston's inflammatory speech, and with some of the crowd filled with whiskey, a fight was inevitable. Dick Welding, the mob bully, punched one of the Saints and knocked him down. A fight ensued. Even though outnumbered, one of the Mormons, John L. Butler, grabbed an oak stake from a nearby woodpile and began to strike the Missourians with strength that surprised himself. The Missourians armed themselves with clapboards or anything that came to hand; during the brawl that followed, several persons on both sides were seriously hurt. Although few Mormons voted that day, Peniston still lost the election.

Distorted reports of the fight reached Church leaders in Far West the next morning. Hearing that two or three of the brethren had been killed, the First Presidency and about twenty others left immediately for Daviess County on Wednesday, 8 August. They armed themselves for their own protection and were joined en route by Church members from different parts of Daviess, some of whom had been attacked by the election mob. They arrived that evening at Diahman and were relieved to learn that none of the Saints had been killed.

While in that vicinity the Prophet determined that it would be wise to ride around the region with some of the other brethren to determine political conditions and to calm fear that had arisen in the county. They visited several of the old settlers in the vicinity, including Adam Black, the justice of the peace and newly-elected judge for Daviess County. Knowing that Black had participated in the anti-Mormon activities, they asked him if he would administer the law justly and if he would sign an agreement of peace. According to Joseph Smith, after Black signed an affidavit certifying that he would disassociate himself from the mob, the brethren returned to Adam-ondi-Ahman.[4] The next day a council composed of prominent Mormons and non-Mormons "entered into a covenant of peace, to preserve each other's rights, and stand in each other's defense; that if men did wrong, neither party would uphold them or endeavor to screen them from justice, but deliver up all offenders to be dealt with according to law and justice."[5]

The goodwill lasted less than twenty-four hours. On 10 August, William Peniston swore out an affidavit in Richmond, Ray County, before the circuit judge, Austin A. King, stating that Joseph Smith and Lyman Wight had organized an army of five hundred men and had threatened death to "all the old settlers and citizens of Daviess county."[6] Upon hearing this information, Joseph waited at home in Far West for further developments. When the sheriff learned that Joseph was willing to submit to arrest if he could be tried in Daviess County, he declined serving the writ and went to Richmond to consult with Judge King.

For about two weeks the tensions increased in Daviess and Carroll counties. Adam Black falsely claimed that 154 Mormons had threatened him with death unless he signed the agreement of peace. The Prophet responded that Black's statement "shows him in his true light—a detestable, unprincipled mobocrat and *perjured man*."[7] Civil war appeared imminent as rumors and exaggerated stories circulated throughout Missouri and false reports of a Mormon uprising reached Governor Lilburn W. Boggs.

THE STAGE SET FOR WAR

In September the Prophet reflected upon the deteriorating circumstances and outlined the Church's course of action. He made the following statement:

"There is great excitement at present among the Missourians, who are seeking if possible an occasion against us. They are continually chafing us, and provoking us to anger if possible, one sign of threatening after another, but we do not fear them, for the Lord God, the Eternal Father is our God, and Jesus . . . is our strength and confidence. . . .

". . . Their father the devil, is hourly calling upon them to be up and doing, and they, like willing and obedient children, need not the second admonition; but in the name of Jesus Christ . . . we will endure it no longer, if the great God will arm us with courage, with strength and with power, to resist them in their persecutions. We will not act on the offensive, but always on the defensive."[8]

The next day Joseph Smith asked Major General David Atchison and Brigadier General Alexander Doniphan of the Missouri state militia for advice on how to end the hostilities in Daviess County. Both had been lawyers for the Saints during the Jackson County troubles in 1833–34 and continued friendly toward the Church. General Atchison promised he would do all within his power as a military officer to disperse the mob. They advised the Prophet and Lyman Wight, who was also present, to volunteer to be tried in Daviess County. Accordingly a trial was held on 7 September just north of the county line at the home of a non-Mormon farmer. Wary of possible mob activity, Joseph Smith stationed a company of men at the county line "so as to be ready at a minute's warning, if there should be any difficulty at the trial."[9] No incriminating evidence against the two leaders was presented, but bowing to pressures, Judge King ordered them to stand trial before the circuit court and released them on five hundred dollars bond.

Unfortunately this did nothing to quell the mob spirit. Enemies of the Church, including many from other counties, prepared to attack Adam-ondi-Ahman. Lyman Wight held a colonel's commission in the fifty-ninth regiment of the Missouri Regiment, which was directed by the state under General H. G. Parks. Lyman directed the arming of over 150 men, part of the state militia, to defend the town against the mobs. Both Mormons and mobbers sent scouts throughout the countryside, occasionally took prisoners, and generally insulted each other. Only the prudent actions of generals Atchison and Doniphan prevented violence. Late in September, General Atchison wrote to the governor: "Things are not so bad in that county [Daviess] as represented by rumor, and, in fact, from affidavits I have no doubt your Excellency has been deceived by the exaggerated statements of designing or half crazy men. I have found there is no cause of alarm on account of the Mormons; they are not to be feared; they are very much alarmed."[10]

About this same time a committee of "old citizens" in Daviess County agreed to sell their property to the Saints. Joseph Smith immediately sent messengers to the East and South to try and raise the necessary funds, but the rapidly escalating conflict made this tentative agreement impossible to fulfill.

SIEGE OF DEWITT

During these conflicts, equally ominous events occurred between the Saints and their neighbors in DeWitt, Carroll County. A few Mormons had been welcomed earlier when they began settling in DeWitt in June 1838, but by July it was obvious to the citizens of Carroll County that the Latter-day Saints would soon outnumber them. As in Jackson, Clay, and Daviess counties, the fear of losing political control motivated the "old settlers" to believe the false reports about the "deluded Mormons" and to develop a pretext for driving them out. Three separate meetings were held in July to unify the citizens to expel the Mormons.

When approached with the ultimatum telling them to leave, George M. Hinkle, leader of the Saints and a colonel in the Missouri state militia, defiantly declared that the Saints would defend their rights to remain in DeWitt. Conditions throughout September remained at a standoff. Violence was avoided partly because many Carroll militiamen were away fighting in

Daviess County during September. Late in September, the Saints at DeWitt sent a letter to Governor Lilburn W. Boggs asking for assistance in defending themselves against "a lawless mob" from Carroll and other counties, but they received no response.

Meanwhile the non-Mormon forces in DeWitt continued to increase as troops from Ray, Howard, and Clay counties arrived almost daily. The Latter-day Saints also received reinforcements and began building barricades.

The first week in October was a fearful one for the Saints because fighting broke out between the two camps. John Murdock recorded: "We were continually employed day and night guarding [the Saints]. . . . One night . . . I traveled all night from one sentinel to another to keep them to their duty."[11] The need for food and shelter became critical. The anti-Mormon forces considered this siege "a war of extermination."[12]

While exploring for a new settlement, the Prophet Joseph Smith was met by a harried emissary headed for Far West to inform the brethren of the situation in DeWitt. Disappointed, the Prophet said, "I had hoped that the good sense of the majority of the people, and their respect for the Constitution, would have put down any spirit of persecution which might have been manifested in that neighborhood."[13] Changing his plans, Joseph traveled secretly by unfrequented roads to avoid enemy guards and slipped into DeWitt, where he found a handful of defenders opposing the large mob. The Prophet found that the Saints were experiencing systematic starvation and grievous privations.

Church leaders decided to appeal once again to the governor for assistance. They obtained affidavits from sympathetic non-Mormons about the treatment of the Saints and their perilous situation. On 9 October they received the governor's reply that " 'The quarrel was between the Mormons and the mob,' and that 'we might fight it out.' "[14] This blasted whatever hopes the Saints may have still entertained for executive relief.

Under these circumstances the earliest Mormon settlers of DeWitt urged their brethren to leave in peace. The Saints, Joseph Smith included, gathered up seventy wagons and sadly abandoned DeWitt on 11 October. That evening a woman who had recently given birth died from exposure suffered by having to travel before her strength would allow. She was buried without a coffin in a grove of trees. The mob continually harassed and threatened the traveling Saints, and several more of them died from fatigue and privation.[15]

GROWING DISTRESS IN CALDWELL AND DAVIESS COUNTIES

Encouraged by their success against the Saints in DeWitt and emboldened by the noninterference of the governor, the anti-Mormon forces marched toward Daviess County to remove the Mormons from there. News that eight hundred men were advancing on Adam-ondi-Ahman and that a large force was being raised to move against Caldwell County alarmed Church leaders. General Doniphan, who was in Far West when the message was received, ordered Colonel Hinkle to muster a militia from among the local residents to protect the Saints. Since the anti-Mormons were technically also members of various other militia units, an ironic conflict of militia versus militia developed.

On the Sabbath the Prophet spoke to the Saints using as his text a saying from the Savior: "Greater love hath no man than this, that he lay down his life for his brethren." He concluded by asking volunteers to join him in the public square the next morning. A company of about one hundred men, authorized by General Doniphan as state militia from Caldwell County, left for Diahman on Monday.[16]

Meanwhile the opposition was at work in Daviess County. John D. Lee reported that several settlers were "tied to trees and fearfully whipped with hickory withes, some of them being horribly mangled by the mob."[17] A number of houses were burned, and livestock was driven off. In addition, many of the scattered families were forced to flee to Adam-ondi-Ahman for safety and shelter amid a heavy snowstorm on 17 and 18 October. Joseph Smith remembered, "My feelings were such as I cannot describe when I saw them flock into the village, almost entirely destitute of clothes, and only escaping with their lives."[18]

General H. G. Parks, commanding officer of the Missouri militia in Daviess County, who witnessed these events, informed General David Atchison of the worsening situation. General Atchison, commander of the militia in northern Missouri, appealed to Governor Boggs warning him that the Missourians intended to drive the Mormons from Daviess and Caldwell counties, and he strongly urged the governor to visit the scene of trouble. This was Atchison's third futile appeal to the governor, but, as with others to follow, it was ignored. Governor Boggs never appeared willing to hear the Saints' side of the story, even from trustworthy sources such as General Atchison, but instead he chose to believe inflammatory anti-Mormon reports.

As hostilities in Daviess County increased, General Parks authorized Lyman Wight, a colonel in the militia, to organize a force of Mormon men and use them to disperse all mobs found in Daviess County. General Parks addressed the assembled troops: "I have visited your place frequently, [and] find you to be an industrious and thriving people, willing to abide the laws of the land; and I deeply regret that you could not live in peace and enjoy the privileges of freedom."[19]

Guerrilla warfare raged between Mormon and anti-Mormon forces for two days as both sides plundered and burned. Members of the Church considered taking from the gentiles to be a necessity laid upon them because their own goods had been stolen. A young Mormon militia officer, Benjamin F. Johnson, said, "We were being hemmed in on all sides by our enemies and were without food. All the grain, cattle, hogs, and supplies of every kind were left in the country, or so far from home they could not be obtained except with a strong guard. So our only possible chance was to go out in foraging companies and bring in whatever we could find, without regard to ownership."[20] This matter was magnified by the non-Mormons in the court proceedings that followed the Mormon War. For their part, the anti-Mormons often set fire to their own haystacks and property and then blamed it on the Saints. Rumors soon spread to the rest of Missouri that the Mormons were either stealing or destroying all the property of their neighbors.

In Far West the Saints were warned that two notorious anti-Mormons, Cornelius Gilliam and Samuel Bogart, officers in the militia, were planning assaults on the Caldwell County settlements. Meetings were held where the Saints covenanted to defend themselves and not desert the cause. Residents of the outlying settlements were instructed to gather to Far West, and the city hastened its preparations for defense.

Tragically, two members of the Quorum of the Twelve Apostles, Thomas B. Marsh and Orson Hyde, deserted the cause of the Church on 18 October and joined with the enemy at Richmond. Marsh swore out an affidavit, which was also mostly endorsed by Hyde, stating that "the Prophet inculcates the notion, and it is believed by every true Mormon, that Smith's prophecies are superior to the laws of the land. I have heard the Prophet say that he would yet tread down his enemies, and walk over their dead bodies; and if he was not let alone, he would be a second Mohammed to this generation."[21] This statement further justified the actions of the anti-Mormons in their own minds.

Regarding this treachery, Joseph Smith remarked that Thomas B. Marsh "had been lifted up in pride by his exaltation to office and the revelations of heaven concerning him, until he was ready to be overthrown by the first adverse wind that should cross his track, and now he has fallen, lied and sworn falsely, and is ready to take the lives of his best friends. Let all men take warning by him, and learn that he who exalteth himself, God will abase."[22] Thomas Marsh was excommunicated 17 March 1839, while Orson Hyde was relieved of his duties in the Council of the Twelve. On 4 May 1839 Orson Hyde was officially suspended from exercising the functions of his office until he met with the general conference of the Church and explained his actions.[23] On 27 June, after repenting and confessing his error, he was restored to the Quorum of the Twelve. After years of misery, Brother Marsh returned to the Church in 1857.

BATTLE OF CROOKED RIVER

A turning point in the "Mormon War" in Missouri was the Battle of Crooked River, which took place at dawn on Thursday, 25 October 1838. A principal cause of this tragedy was the provocative actions of Captain

Samuel Bogart from Jackson County, an enemy of the Saints. For days Bogart ranged the line between Caldwell and Ray counties, allegedly trying to prevent a Mormon attack. But instead of merely conducting their assigned patrols, Bogart's men twice entered Caldwell County and attacked the homes of the Saints, ordering the members to leave the state and taking three Mormon men prisoners. When word reached Far West, Elias Higbee, the Caldwell County judge and highest civil authority in the area, ordered Colonel Hinkle, the highest officer in command in Far West, to send out a company to disperse "the mob" and rescue the prisoners, who they expected to be murdered that night.

Members of the militia had been waiting several days for a call to arms. When the drums beat at midnight calling them to the public square, seventy-five men were mobilized into two companies commanded by David W. Patten and Charles C. Rich. As dawn approached they arrived at a ford on the banks of the Crooked River, twenty miles from Far West. Patten's patrol approached the crossing, unaware of Bogart's concealed position along the banks of the river. Suddenly one of Bogart's guards opened fire. Elder Patten ordered a charge, but silhouetted by the dawn, his men made good targets. In the quick, hard-fought skirmish, several men on each side were wounded. One of the wounded was Elder Patten of the Council of the Twelve. Young Gideon Carter was fatally shot through the head and left lying on the ground, defaced so badly that the brethren did not recognize him.

The brethren freed the three prisoners, one of them was also wounded, drove the enemy across the river, and then turned to care for their wounded. Elder Patten was carried to the home of Stephen Winchester near Far West, where he died several hours later. He thus became the first martyred Apostle in this dispensation. His faith in the restored gospel was such that he had once expressed to the Prophet Joseph Smith the desire to die the death of a martyr. "The Prophet, greatly moved, expressed extreme sorrow, 'for,' said he to David, 'when a man of your faith asks the Lord for anything, he generally gets it.' "[24] At his funeral in Far West two days after the battle, Joseph Smith eulogized him: "There lies a man that has done just as he said he would—he has laid down his life for his friends."[25]

Patrick O'Bannion also later died from his wounds. James Hendricks, another of the critically injured, was temporarily paralyzed from his waist down and had to be carried about on a stretcher. The entire responsibility for his family fell to his wife, Drusilla, who endured the additional dangers in Missouri and the arduous trek to Illinois with strength of character and deep faith.

Exaggerated accounts of the battle soon reached Governor Boggs in Jefferson City. One rumor was that Bogart's entire force was massacred or imprisoned and that the Mormons intended to sack and burn Richmond. These reports provided Boggs with the excuse he needed to order an all-out war against the Saints.

EXTERMINATION ORDER AND HAUN'S MILL MASSACRE

Northern Missouri was in an uproar the last week of October as "mobs were heard in every direction."[26] The mobs burned houses and crops, rustled cattle, detained prisoners, and threatened the Saints with death. General Atchison again urged Governor Boggs to come to the area. But instead, on 27 October, he ordered his militia to war. Relying solely upon the false reports of a Mormon insurrection, Boggs asserted that the Saints had defied the laws and initiated hostilities. Therefore, he wrote, "The Mormons must be treated as enemies and *must be exterminated* or driven from the state, if necessary for the public good. Their outrages are beyond all description."[27] By this time public opinion was so strong against the Saints that even those who knew the truth would not side openly with them. Governor Boggs's "extermination order" was an outgrowth and expression of the popular will.

General Atchison was in charge of the state troops but was dismissed by the governor prior to the surrender of Far West. The command was given to General John B. Clark. General Clark did not arrive at Far West until a few days after the surrender. General Samuel D. Lucas, a long-time anti-Mormon from Jackson County, was left in temporary command of the militia that was rapidly gathering from all sides to encircle Far West. By 31 October over two thousand men surrounded Far West, and most of them were determined to fulfill the governor's order.

It was at Haun's Mill that violence again erupted. This small settlement twelve miles east of Far West was founded by Jacob Haun, a convert from Green Bay, Wisconsin. He had moved to Shoal Creek in 1835, hoping to avoid the persecutions his fellow Saints were experiencing elsewhere in Missouri. Haun's Mill consisted of a mill, a blacksmith shop, a few houses, and a population of about twenty to thirty families at the mill itself and one hundred families in the greater neighborhood. On 30 October nine wagons with immigrants from Kirtland had arrived at the site. They had decided to rest a few days before traveling to Far West.

Immediately after the battle of Crooked River, the Prophet Joseph Smith advised all Saints in outlying areas to move to Far West or Adam-ondi-Ahman. Unwilling to abandon his property, Jacob Haun disregarded the Prophet's counsel and instructed the small community to remain. This unwise decision proved fatal. Haun's group planned to use the blacksmith shop as a fort in the event of an enemy attack. Guards were posted to protect the mill and the settlement.

On Sunday, 28 October, Colonel Thomas Jennings of the Livingston County militia sent one of his men to the settlement to conclude a peace treaty. Both sides pledged not to attack each other. The non-Mormons, however, did not disband as promised. On Monday a group of Missourians in Livingston County decided to attack Haun's Mill, probably intending to

Extermination order

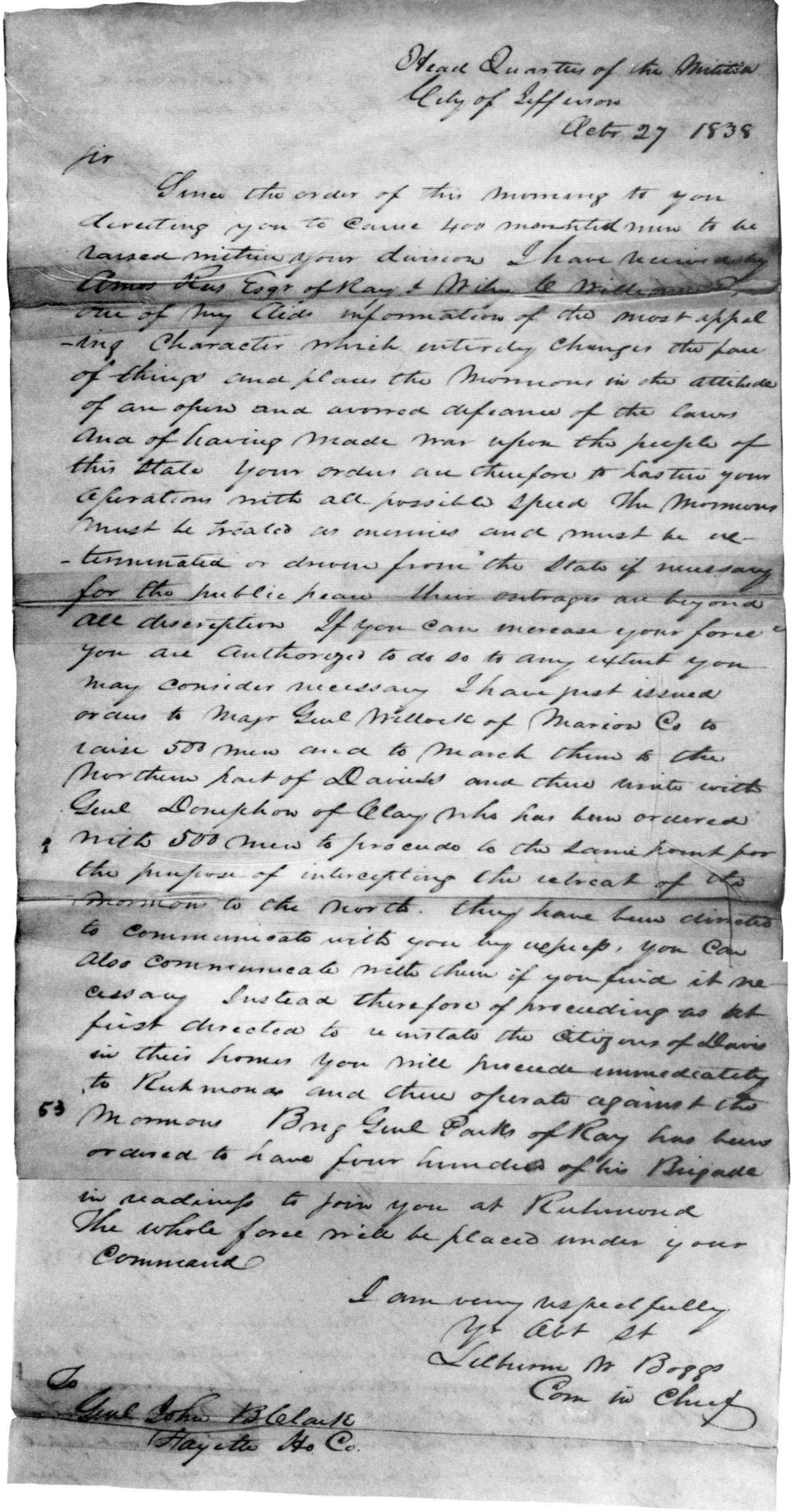

Head Quarters of the Militia
City of Jefferson
Octr 27 1838

Sir

Since the order of this morning to you directing you to cause 400 mounted men to be raised within your division I have received by Amos Rees Esqr of Ray & Wiley C Williams one of my Aids information of the most appaling Character which entirely changes the face of things and places the Mormons in the attitude of an open and avowed defiance of the laws and of having made war upon the people of this State Your orders are therefore to hasten your operations with all possible speed The Mormons must be treated as enemies and must be exterminated or driven from the State if necessary for the public peace their outrages are beyond all description If you can increase your force you are authorized to do so to any extent you may consider necessary I have just issued orders to Major Genl Willock of Marion Co to raise 500 men and to march them to the Northern part of Daviess and there unite with Genl Doniphon of Clay who has been ordered with 500 men to proceed to the same point for the purpose of intercepting the retreat of the Mormons to the North. they have been directed to communicate with you by express, you can also communicate with them if you find it necessary Instead therefore of proceeding as at first directed to reinstate the Citizens of Daviess in their homes you will proceed immediately to Richmond and there operate against the Mormons Brig Genl Parks of Ray has been ordered to have four hundred of his Brigade in readiness to join you at Richmond The whole force will be placed under your Command

I am very respectfully
Yr Obt St
Lilburn W Boggs
Com in Chief

To
Genl John B Clark
Fayette Ho Co.

carry out the governor's order. On Tuesday afternoon, 30 October, approximately 240 men approached Haun's Mill. Joseph Young, Sr., a member of the seven presidents of Seventy and a recent arrival at Haun's Mill, described the late afternoon setting: "The banks of Shoal creek on either side teemed with children sporting and playing, while their mothers were engaged in domestic employments, and their fathers employed in guarding the mills and other property, while others were engaged in gathering in their crops for their winter consumption. The weather was very pleasant, the sun shone clear, all was tranquil, and no one expressed any apprehension of the awful crisis that was near us—even at our doors."[28]

At about 4:00 P.M. the mob approached Haun's Mill. The women and children fled into the woods, while the men sought protection in the blacksmith shop. David Evans, the military leader of the Saints, swung his hat and cried for peace. The sound of a hundred rifles answered him, most of them aimed at the blacksmith shop. The mobbers shot mercilessly at everyone in sight, including women, elderly men, and children. Amanda Smith seized her two little girls and ran with Mary Stedwell across the millpond on a walkway. Amanda recalled, "Yet though we were women, with tender children, in flight for our lives, the demons poured volley after volley to kill us."[29]

The rabble entered the blacksmith shop and found ten-year-old Sardius Smith, son of Amanda Smith, hiding under the blacksmith's bellows. One ruffian put the muzzle of his gun against the boy's skull and blew off the upper part of his head. The man later explained, "Nits will make lice, and if he had lived he would have become a Mormon."[30] Alma Smith, Sardius's seven-year-old brother, witnessed the murder of his father and brother and was himself shot in the hip. He was not discovered by the mob and was later miraculously healed through prayer and faith. Thomas McBride was hacked

Haun's Mill *by C.C.A. Christensen*

to death with a corn knife. Although a few men along with women and children escaped across the river into the hills, at least seventeen people were killed, and about thirteen were wounded.[31] Jacob Haun was among the wounded, but he recovered. Years later the Prophet remarked, "At Hauns' Mill the brethren went contrary to my counsel; if they had not, their lives would have been spared."[32]

The survivors hid throughout the evening and night, fearing another attack. The next day a few able-bodied men buried the dead in a dry hole that had been dug for a well. Joseph Young had become so closely attached to young Sardius Smith during their trip from Kirtland that he broke down and could not lower the boy's body into the common grave. Amanda and her eldest son buried Sardius the following day.

The devastated survivors left Missouri during the winter and following spring along with other Church members. The mob continued to persecute some of the widows before they left, but the Lord helped them. Amanda Smith remembered the reassurance she received from the Lord as she crept into a cornfield to pray aloud.

"It was as the temple of the Lord to me at that moment. I prayed aloud and most fervently.

"When I emerged from the corn a voice spoke to me. It was a voice as plain as I ever heard one. It was no silent, strong impression of the spirit, but a *voice,* repeating a verse of the Saints' hymn:
'That soul who on Jesus hath leaned for repose
I will not, I cannot, desert to his foes;
That soul, though all hell should endeavor to shake,
I'll never, no never, no never forsake!'

"From that moment I had no more fear. I felt that nothing could hurt me."[33]

SIEGE OF FAR WEST

Meanwhile the anti-Mormon militia forces continued to gather around Far West in preparation for an attack. The militia of Far West barricaded the city with wagons and timber, but by Wednesday, 31 October, the anti-Mormon forces outnumbered those of the Saints by five to one. Neither side was eager to begin the battle, and the day was spent in a standoff, with each side trying to decide what to do. In the evening General Lucas sent a flag of truce, which was met by Colonel Hinkle, the leading officer for the Saints. Colonel Hinkle secretly agreed to Lucas's demands that certain leaders surrender for trial and punishment, Mormon property be confiscated to pay for damages, and the balance of the Saints surrender their arms and leave the state.

Returning to Far West, Hinkle convinced Joseph Smith, Sidney Rigdon, Lyman Wight, Parley P. Pratt, and George W. Robinson that Lucas wanted to talk to them in a peace conference. The brethren were shocked when Hinkle

Missouri state militia at Far West

turned them over to Lucas as prisoners. Parley P. Pratt described this tragic scene: "The haughty general [Lucas] rode up, and, without speaking to us, instantly ordered his guard to surround us. They did so very abruptly, and we were marched into camp surrounded by thousands of savage looking beings, many of whom were dressed and painted like Indian warriors. These all set up a constant yell, like so many bloodhounds let loose upon their prey, as if they had achieved one of the most miraculous victories that ever graced the annals of the world."[34]

The shrieking continued throughout the night, terrorizing the citizens of Far West, who feared that their Prophet may have already been murdered. Most Saints spent the night in prayer. In the enemy camp the brethren were forced to lie on the ground in a cold rain and listen to a constant tirade of mockery and vulgarity from their guards. "They blasphemed God; mocked Jesus Christ; swore the most dreadful oaths; taunted brother Joseph and others; demanded miracles; wanted signs, such as: 'Come, Mr. Smith, show us an angel.' 'Give us one of your revelations.' 'Show us a miracle.' "[35]

In a secret and illegal court-martial held during the night, the prisoners were sentenced to be executed the next morning on the public square in Far West. When General Alexander Doniphan received the order from General Lucas, he was indignant at the brutality and injustice of the affair and replied, "It is cold-blooded murder. I will not obey your order. My brigade shall march for Liberty tomorrow morning, at 8 o'clock; and if you execute these men, I will hold you responsible before an earthly tribunal, so help me God."[36] Intimidated by Doniphan's courageous response, Lucas lost his nerve. The prayers of the Saints were answered.

The same night word reached Far West that the enemy intended to arrest the remaining participants of the Battle of Crooked River. So before dawn about twenty brethren slipped out of Far West and headed northeast toward Iowa territory. Hyrum Smith and Amasa Lyman were not so fortunate. They were arrested and joined the other prisoners.

On the morning of 1 November, as George Hinkle marched the Mormon troops out of Far West, the Missouri militia entered the city. While searching for arms they vandalized the town, plundered valuable possessions, raped some of the women, and compelled the leading elders at bayonet point to sign promises to pay the expenses of the militia. Many prominent men were arrested and taken as prisoners to Richmond. The rest of the Saints were told to leave the state.

Plans were made to take the Church leaders to Independence for public display and trial. Thinking they might yet be executed, Joseph Smith and his fellow prisoners begged to see their families one last time, and they returned to Far West on 2 November. Joseph found his wife and children in tears because they thought he had been shot. "When I entered my house, they clung to my garments, their eyes streaming with tears, while mingled emotions of joy and sorrow were manifested in their countenances," he wrote. He was denied the privilege of a few private moments with them, but Emma wept and his children clung to him until "they were thrust from me by the swords of the guards."[37] The other prisoners suffered similarly as they bade farewell to their loved ones.

Lucy Smith, Joseph and Hyrum's mother, hurried to the wagon where they were kept under guard and was barely able to touch their outstretched hands before the wagon departed. After several hours of grief, she was comforted by the Spirit and blessed with the gift of prophecy: "Let your heart be comforted concerning your children, they shall not be harmed by their enemies."[38] A similar revelation came to the Prophet Joseph Smith. The next morning as the prisoners began their march, Joseph spoke to his companions in a low, but hopeful tone. "Be of good cheer, brethren; the word of the Lord came to me last night that our lives should be given us, and that whatever we may suffer during this captivity, not one of our lives should be taken."[39]

Meanwhile, General John B. Clark, the governor's designated commanding officer for the Mormon War, arrived in Far West. He ordered everyone to stay in the city, and the starving Saints were forced to live on parched corn. On 6 November he addressed the suffering citizens and indicated that he would not force them out of the state in the depths of winter. He said, "for *this* lenity you are indebted to *my* clemency. I do not say that you shall go now, but you must not think of staying here another season, or of putting in crops. . . . As for your leaders, do not once think—do not imagine for a moment—do not let it enter your mind that they will be delivered, or that you will see their faces again, for their *fate is fixed—their die is cast—their doom is sealed*."[40]

Another contingent of militia surrounded the Saints who had fled to Adam-ondi-Ahman for safety. After a three-day board of inquiry, all Mormons were ordered out of Daviess County, but permission was granted for them to go to Far West until spring.

While preparing for their exodus, the Saints again sought relief from the Missouri legislature. Although their grievances were clearly defined and considerable sympathy was shown by many members of the legislature and newspapers in Missouri, an official investigation was never launched. Instead, the legislature appropriated a meager two thousand dollars for the relief of the citizens of Caldwell County.

IN PRISON BONDS

Joseph Smith and a few other prisoners were taken to Independence and placed on public display. They were then transferred to Richmond, where they were chained together under guard in an old vacant house for over two weeks. In mid-November a thirteen-day trial began, presided over by circuit judge Austin A. King. The evidence was stacked against the Church leaders. Sampson Avard, the first witness, hypocritically accused the Prophet of responsibility for the wrongs of the Danites; other witnesses were equally bitter. When the prisoners submitted a list of defense witnesses, the witnesses were systematically jailed or driven from the county. Alexander Doniphan, counsel for the Saints, said that "if a cohort of angels were to come down, and declare we were innocent, it would all be the same; for he (King) had determined from the beginning to cast us into prison."[41]

For two horrible weeks, the prisoners were abused by the guards. One November night the brethren listened for several hours to "obscene jests, the horrid oaths, the dreadful blasphemies and filthy language" as the guards rehearsed the atrocities they had inflicted on the Saints. Parley P. Pratt lay next to the Prophet and listened until he could scarcely refrain from speaking out. Suddenly Joseph Smith rose to his feet shackled and unarmed and

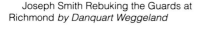

Joseph Smith Rebuking the Guards at Richmond *by Danquart Weggeland*

Museum of Church History and Art

Liberty Jail in Liberty, Missouri. The outside dimensions of the building are 22 1/2 feet long, 22 feet wide, and 12 feet high to the square. The building was used as a prison until 1856, when it was considered unsafe.

spoke in a voice of thunder: " 'SILENCE, ye fiends of the infernal pit. In the name of Jesus Christ I rebuke you, and command you to be still; I will not live another minute and bear such language. Cease such talk, or you or I die THIS INSTANT!'

"He ceased to speak. He stood erect in terrible majesty. Chained and without a weapon; calm, unruffled and dignified as an angel, he looked upon the quailing guards, whose weapons were lowered or dropped to the ground; whose knees smote together, and who, shrinking into a corner, or crouching at his feet, begged his pardon, and remained quiet till a change of guards."[42]

At the end of the trial, Judge King bound Joseph Smith and five others over for further prosecution and ordered them placed in Liberty Jail in Clay County. Parley P. Pratt and several others were to remain confined in Richmond, and most of the other prisoners were released.

In reality the two-story, twenty-two-foot square stone jail in Liberty was a dungeon. Small, barred windows opened into the upper level, and there was little heat. A hole in the floor was the only access to the lower level, where a man could not stand upright. For four winter months the Prophet and his companions suffered from cold, filthy conditions, smoke inhalation, loneliness, and filthy food. Perhaps worst of all, they were unable to accompany the faithful Saints, who were being driven from the state. Yet these were months of special significance to Joseph Smith and the Church. In the Prophet's absence, Brigham Young, Heber C. Kimball, and John Taylor demonstrated superior leadership ability and commitment. In his despair, Joseph Smith received priceless spiritual instructions from the Lord. Because of the things revealed there, Liberty Jail could be called a temple-prison.

Public opinion in Missouri was turning against Governor Boggs and the mob as Joseph Smith and his colleagues languished in jail waiting for state officials to determine what to do with them. Toward the end of March 1839, the Prophet wrote a long letter to the Church, parts of which now appear as sections 121, 122, and 123 of the Doctrine and Covenants. After reviewing the wrongs perpetrated upon the Saints, the Prophet had appealed to the Lord:

"Oh God, where art thou? And where is the pavilion that covereth thy hiding place?

"How long shall thy hand be stayed, and thine eye, yea thy pure eye, behold from the eternal heavens the wrongs of thy people and of thy servants, and thine ear be penetrated with their cries?

"Yea, O Lord, how long shall they suffer these wrongs and unlawful oppressions, before thine heart shall be softened toward them, and thy bowels be moved with compassion toward them?" (D&C 121:1–3).

The Prophet then inserted the Lord's response to his plea:

"My son, peace be unto thy soul; thine adversity and thine afflictions shall be but a small moment;

"And then, if thou endure it well, God shall exalt thee on high; thou shalt triumph over all thy foes.

"Thy friends do stand by thee, and they shall hail thee again with warm hearts and friendly hands" (D&C 121:7–9).

By April the prisoners in Liberty were sent to Daviess County for trial. A grand jury brought in a bill against them for "murder, treason, burglary, arson, larceny, theft, and stealing."[43] A change of venue was obtained, but while en route to Boone County for trial, the prisoners were allowed by the sheriff and other guards to escape to Illinois because some officials had concluded that the prisoners could not be successfully prosecuted. Later in the summer Parley P. Pratt and Morris Phelps also escaped from the Richmond Jail and made their way to Nauvoo. King Follett, a fellow prisoner, was recaptured but finally released in October 1839, being the last of the Saints held in bond.

For the fifth time in less than ten years many of the Latter-day Saints had left their homes and began anew to build a place of refuge. Though the last several months were marred by financial disaster, bitter persecution, apostasy, and expulsion from Missouri, most Church members did not lose sight of their divine destiny. As Joseph said in his letter to the Saints: "As well might man stretch forth his puny arm to stop the Missouri river in its decreed course, or to turn it up stream, as to hinder the Almighty from pouring down knowledge from heaven upon the heads of the Latter-day Saints" (D&C 121:33).

ENDNOTES

1. Parley P. Pratt, ed., *Autobiography of Parley P. Pratt,* Classics in Mormon Literature series (Salt Lake City: Deseret Book Co., 1985), p. 150.

2. In *Missouri: A Guide to the "Show Me" State,* rev. ed. (New York: Hastings House, 1954), p. 510.

3. In *History of the Church,* 3:57.

4. See *History of the Church,* 3:59–60.

5. *History of the Church,* 3:60.

6. In *History of the Church,* 3:61.

7. *History of the Church,* 3:65.

8. *History of the Church,* 3:67–68.

9. *History of the Church,* 3:73.

10. In *History of the Church,* 3:85.

11. "Journal of John Murdock," 1 Oct. 1838, LDS Historical Department, Salt Lake City, p. 101; spelling standardized.

12. Leland Homer Gentry, "A History of the Latter-Day Saints in Northern Missouri from 1836–1839," Ph.D. diss., Brigham Young University, 1965, p. 201.

13. *History of the Church,* 3:152.

14. *History of the Church,* 3:157.

15. See *History of the Church,* 3:159–60.

16. *History of the Church,* 3:162.

17. John D. Lee, *Mormonism Unveiled* (Philadelphia: Scammell and Co., 1882), p. 68. A *withe* is a tough flexible branch or twig of willows often used for binding.

18. *History of the Church,* 3:163.

19. Lyman Wight, in *History of the Church,* 3:443–44.

20. Benjamin F. Johnson, *My Life's Review* (Independence, Mo.: Zion's Printing and Publishing Co., 1947), p. 37.

21. In *History of the Church,* 3:167.

22. *History of the Church,* 3:167.

23. See *History of the Church,* 3:345

24. Lycurgus A. Wilson, *Life of David W. Patten* (Salt Lake City: Deseret News, 1900), p. 58.

25. In *History of the Church,* 3:175.

26. *History of the Church,* 3:175–76.

27. In *History of the Church,* 3:175.

28. In *History of the Church*, 3:184.

29. Andrew Jenson, *The Historical Record*, July 1886, p. 84.

30. In Jenson, *Historical Record*, Dec. 1888, p. 673.

31. See *History of the Church*, 3:326.

32. *History of the Church*, 5:137.

33. In Jenson, *Historical Record*, July 1886, p. 87.

34. Pratt, *Autobiography of Parley P. Pratt*, pp. 159–60.

35. Pratt, *Autobiography of Parley P. Pratt*, p. 160.

36. In *History of the Church*, 3:190–91.

37. *History of the Church*, 3:193.

38. In Lucy Mack Smith, *History of Joseph Smith*, ed. Preston Nibley (Salt Lake City: Bookcraft, 1958), p. 291.

39. In Pratt, *Autobiography of Parley P. Pratt*, p. 164.

40. In *History of the Church*, 3:203.

41. *History of the Church*, 3:213.

42. Pratt, *Autobiography of Parley P. Pratt*, pp. 179–80.

43. In *History of the Church*, 3:315.

REFUGE IN ILLINOIS

► *Options were limited as the Saints were driven from Missouri from the fall of 1838 into the spring of 1839. The most attractive possibility was to return east. For economic, political, and humanitarian reasons, Illinois initially welcomed the refugees.*

SOME PEOPLE SAW the flight from Missouri as evidence that the Lord had forsaken the Saints. The Prophet Joseph was in Liberty Jail with no prospect of release. Whatever hope the Saints had of regaining political rights and property in Missouri or establishing the city of Zion was dimmed. Even some Church members questioned the wisdom of gathering the Saints again into one location.

Where were the Church members to go for refuge? The vast Indian tracts to the west were not open to settlers. Iowa to the north was sparsely settled but offered little timber upon its vast, rolling plains. Going south meant traveling through hostile Missouri communities. The route east was most familiar and reassuring to Church members. Many of the Saints had traveled it only months before in exile from Kirtland. Now some of them were considering a return to Ohio. Crossing the Mississippi and pausing in some of the small Illinois communities along its bank, however, provided the respite necessary for the Saints to receive new direction from Church leaders.

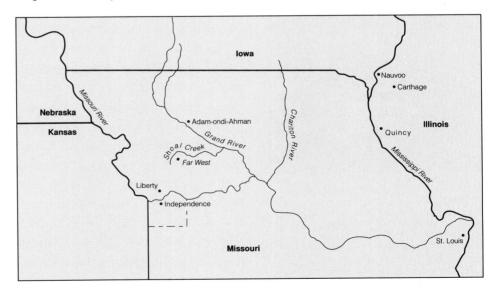

RESETTLEMENT OF THE SAINTS

The months following the surrender of Far West severely tested the leadership of the Church. The entire First Presidency—Joseph Smith, Sidney Rigdon, and Hyrum Smith—were in jail. The ranks of the Quorum of the Twelve had been thinned. David W. Patten had been killed in the Battle of

Crooked River, Parley P. Pratt was in Richmond Jail, and his brother Orson was with a group of Saints in St. Louis. Thomas B. Marsh, William Smith, and Orson Hyde were disaffected with the Church and consequently were of no help. Therefore the responsibility of overseeing the needs of the Church during the winter of 1838–39 and throughout the exodus from Missouri to Illinois fell mostly upon Brigham Young and Heber C. Kimball. John Taylor was called to the apostleship in December 1838. Wilford Woodruff and George A. Smith were added the following April; both of these men were able to provide valuable assistance during this critical time.

Church leaders delayed as long as possible the decision to leave Missouri, hoping that the legislature would revoke Governor Boggs's extermination order. They sent numerous petitions to state officials and to the legislature requesting them to let the Saints remain in their homes, but their pleas were ignored.

Meanwhile the Missourians grew impatient with the lingering Saints. In early 1839 Church leaders became convinced that their people could no longer hope to remain in Missouri. On 26 January, Brigham Young had created the Committee on Removal to facilitate the exodus. Throughout the winter and spring this committee arranged to feed, clothe, and transport the poor. By formal resolution nearly four hundred Latter-day Saints covenanted to place all of their available property at the disposal of the committee "for the purpose of providing means for the removing from this state of the poor and destitute who shall be considered worthy, till there shall not be one left who desires to remove from the state."[1] Even Joseph Smith somehow sent one hundred dollars from Liberty Jail to assist the effort.

By mid-February conditions were such that a large scale migration of the Saints began. Wagons and teams, although not of the best quality, had been acquired; food reserves were in place along the migration route; and there was a temporary break in the weather. Nevertheless, leaving Missouri was not easy for the refugees. Many people sold precious possessions and lands at unreasonably low prices to obtain means to flee the state. One Missourian bought forty acres of good land from a Church member for a "blind mare and a clock." Some other tracts of land sold for only fifty cents per acre.[2] Some people with oxen teams made several trips between Caldwell County and the Mississippi River, two hundred miles to the east, to convey friends and relatives out of danger. Amanda Smith, widowed at Haun's Mill, and her five children left Far West by ox team. Once her family was beyond the reach of the Missouri mobs she sent her team back to help other Saints in their trek eastward.

Charles C. Rich fled Missouri sometime in November to avoid arrest for his involvement in the Battle of Crooked River. He left behind his twenty-three-year-old wife, Sarah, who finally was able to leave Far West with the help of her father, John Pea. Her health was poor, and she was confined to a wagon bed for the entire journey to the Mississippi. She was accompanied

Charles C. Rich (1809–83) joined the Church in 1832. He assumed command at the Battle of Crooked River when David W. Patten was mortally wounded. He was a military and Church leader during the Nauvoo period. Brigham Young assigned him to preside over the temporary settlement of Mount Pisgah in Iowa in the winter of 1846–47.

He was ordained an Apostle on 12 February 1849. In the spring of 1864 he became one of the first settlers in Bear Lake Valley (Idaho and Utah) and was responsible for the settlement of that region. He was known for his goodness, generosity, and physical strength. He often carried the mail across the mountains to Salt Lake City during the winter when roads were blocked.

by Hosea Stout's wife, Samantha. Once there they found the ice breaking up and the crossing extremely hazardous. George Grant voluntarily braved the ice floes to carry a message to their husbands. As he neared the Illinois shore, he fell through what had appeared to be solid ice. He was, however, rescued.

Charles C. Rich and Hosea Stout, upon hearing that their wives had arrived, crossed the river in a canoe to meet them. The next morning they decided it would be best to bring Sarah, who was about to have her first child, and two other women to the Illinois side. They were forced by lack of space to leave Sarah's father to wait for the ferry. On the return journey huge blocks of ice threatened to crush the small canoe. Occasionally the men jumped onto the ice to push the craft out of danger. Meanwhile, Sarah's father, watching with tear-filled eyes, saw the party's safe arrival on the Illinois side.[3]

For Emma Smith, the months after Joseph's arrest were especially trying. In February 1839 a neighbor, Jonathan Holman, helped her place her four children and her meager belongings into a straw-lined wagon pulled by two horses. On the evening prior to her departure she received from Miss Ann Scott the priceless manuscripts of her husband's "translation" of the Bible. James Mulholland, the Prophet's secretary, had given the papers to Ann for safekeeping thinking that the mob might not search a woman. Ann had made two cotton bags to hold the documents. Emma used these same cotton bags to carry the manuscripts from Missouri to Illinois, tying them under her long skirt.

When the party arrived at the Mississippi they found the river frozen over. Rather than risk the weight of the wagon, Emma walked across the ice holding two children, with the other clinging to her skirt. They finally arrived safely at the outskirts of the village of Quincy, Illinois, where Emma lived until Joseph's release.

Arrival in Quincy

Until mid-spring 1839 Church leaders who were not in jail had no definite plan for where the Saints should settle. Word reached the leaders that the citizens of Illinois were sympathetic to their plight and would welcome the Saints. Many people in Illinois believed that a large influx of Mormons would help their struggling economy. The state's politicians also encouraged immigration because Illinois was nearly equally divided between the Whigs and Democrats. Each party hoped to attract the large Mormon vote.

Benevolent residents in Quincy, a community of twelve hundred, were generous and sympathetic to the plight of the exiles. Many of them opened their homes and provided jobs. They collected money, food, clothing, and other necessities on more than one occasion. The Democratic Association of Quincy was particularly instrumental in assisting the Saints. It convened three times during the week of 25 February to consider ways of helping the homeless exiles. Sidney Rigdon was invited to report on the condition of the Saints; collections were taken up, and resolutions were passed condemning Missouri's treatment of the Mormons. The association resolved that the people of Quincy should "observe a becoming decorum and delicacy [around the Saints] and be particularly careful not to indulge in any conversation or expressions calculated to wound their feelings, or in any way to reflect upon those, who by every law of humanity, are entitled to our sympathy and commiseration."[4] The leaders of the association also tried to help the Church gain redress from Missouri.

Peaceful relations with the people of Quincy and the Democratic party were threatened, however, by the unwise conduct of Lyman Wight. In a series of letters published in the local newspaper, he blamed the Missouri outrages on the national Democratic party. Quincy Democrats were understandably upset by his accusations and asked Church leaders whether this reflected the official view of the Church. On 17 May the First Presidency wrote a letter disavowing Wight's accusations. They also asked Elder Wight, if he continued to write against a political party, to make it clear that he was representing his own views and not those of the Church.

Throughout the late winter and spring, thousands of Latter-day Saints arrived at the western bank of the Mississippi across from Quincy. Elizabeth Haven wrote that in late February "about 12 families cross the river into Quincy every day and about 30 are constantly at the other side waiting to cross; it is slow and grimy; there is only one ferry boat to cross in."[5] Moderating weather caused dangerous ice floes to further inhibit progress of the crossings. When another cold spell set in and the river again froze over, scores of Saints hurried to cross on the ice.

As Quincy filled with hundreds of refugees, the living conditions there deteriorated. The Saints, most of whom were almost entirely destitute, suffered from hunger in the cold, rain, and mud.[6] Even so they kept up their religious observances. For a time the Saints were more numerous than any other religious denomination in the community. Non-Mormon Wandle Mace took in many Saints and was eventually converted himself. His home was used as a meeting and council house and as a shelter for the destitute. He reported that "Very many nights the floors, upstairs and down, were covered with beds so closely it was impossible to set a foot anywhere without stepping on a bed."[7]

The story of Drusilla Hendricks is typical of the Quincy experience. Her husband, James, had been shot in the neck in the Battle of Crooked River and had to be carried about on a stretcher. The family arrived in Quincy on 1 April and secured a room "partly underground and partly on top of the ground." Within two weeks they were on the verge of starving, having only one spoonful of sugar and a saucer full of corn meal to eat. Drusilla made mush out of it. Thinking they would eventually starve, she washed every-

James and Drusilla Dorris Hendricks were married in 1825. Their faith and sacrifice were typical of many early Missouri refugees. They arrived in Utah in 1847 in the Jedediah Grant Company. James served as bishop of the Nineteenth Ward from 1850–57.

Isaac Galland (1791–1858) was a land speculator in eastern Iowa and western Illinois. In 1839 he sold large parcels of land to the Church. He was later baptized and for a while acted as the Church land agent in trying to pay Church debts. His efforts produced little financial relief for the Church. In 1841–42 he fell away from the Church, although he apparently remained friendly toward it.

thing, cleaned their little room thoroughly, and waited for the worst. That afternoon Rubin Alred came by and told her he had had a feeling they were out of food, so on his way into town he had a sack of grain ground into meal for them. Two weeks later they were again without food. Drusilla remembered, "I felt awful, but the same voice that gave me comfort before was there to comfort me again and it said, hold on, the Lord will provide for his Saints." This time Alexander Williams arrived at the back door with two bushels of meal on his shoulder. He told her he had been extremely busy but the Spirit had whispered to him that "Brother Hendricks' family is suffering, so I dropped everything and came by."[8]

Eight to ten thousand Latter-day Saints migrated to western Illinois that season. The community of Quincy could not accommodate all the new arrivals. During the spring and summer of 1839 many people were forced into surrounding farmlands and adjoining counties wherever they could find a place to stay.

SETTLING NAUVOO

While the Saints were scattering across eastern Missouri and into Illinois, Joseph Smith was confined in Liberty Jail. Soon after the fall of Far West a group of veterans from the Battle of Crooked River became lost as they were escaping from their oppressors and ended up at the Des Moines River just north of where it joined the Mississippi. There they met Isaac Galland, one of the largest land speculators in the area. After hearing the plight of the Saints, Galland offered to sell the Church large parcels of land in Iowa and Illinois. In February the men took this information to the Church leaders in Quincy who were meeting to decide what to do next.

Sidney Rigdon, Edward Partridge, and a few others questioned the wisdom of gathering to one place again; they felt that this had been the major source of their problems in Missouri and Ohio. On the other hand, Brigham Young counseled the Saints to gather so they could better help each other. Uncertain how to act, the brethren wrote to the Prophet asking his advice. On 22 March the Prophet advised the brethren to buy the property and not to scatter.

In April, Joseph and Hyrum Smith and their fellow prisoners were allowed to escape from Missouri. They arrived in Quincy on 22 April 1839. The Prophet felt that it was the prayers of the brethren that had helped him escape. As Joseph arrived at the Quincy ferry, Dimick B. Huntington recognized him: "He was dressed in an old pair of boots full of holes, pants torn, tucked inside of boots, blue cloak with collar turned up, wide brim black hat, rim sopped down, not been shaved for some time, looked pale and haggard."[9] Since the Prophet wanted his arrival to be unnoticed, they took the back streets of the city to the Cleveland home four miles away from town where Emma was staying. She recognized her husband as he climbed off his horse and met him joyfully halfway to the gate.

Since the spring planting season was approaching, the Prophet wasted no time in moving the Church into action. Two days after his arrival a council meeting decided to send him and several others upstream to Iowa "for the purpose of making a location for the Church."[10] The next day the Prophet examined lands on both sides of the Mississippi River.

Once the decision was made to gather and relocate the Saints, the Church leaders moved vigorously to procure the necessary land. By the end of the summer of 1839 four major land transactions were completed to provide the Church the area it needed. The largest parcel was nearly twenty thousand acres of land purchased from Isaac Galland on the Iowa side of the river, as well as a small portion in Illinois. The other three purchases, totalling over six hundred acres, were across from the Iowa bank on a horseshoe-shaped bend in the river in Illinois. Two small towns, Commerce and Commerce City, had been platted on this land, but they had only a handful of dwellings between them. Some of the flatlands near the river were swampy because of a high water table and springs that flowed from the foot of the bluffs to the east and were consequently unhealthy. But Joseph Smith and the brethren were certain that they could make the area a suitable place of habitation for the Saints.

Since both the refugees and the Church in general had little cash, the land was purchased largely on credit. Reasonable interest rates and long term payments were attractive at the time, but given the indigent circumstances of the Saints, they became a heavy burden on the Church's resources throughout the Nauvoo period. For the next several years Joseph Smith solicited funds from Church members to help with the payments. Properties

Although the largest tracts of land the Church purchased were in Iowa, the most important Latter-day Saint communities were in Illinois.

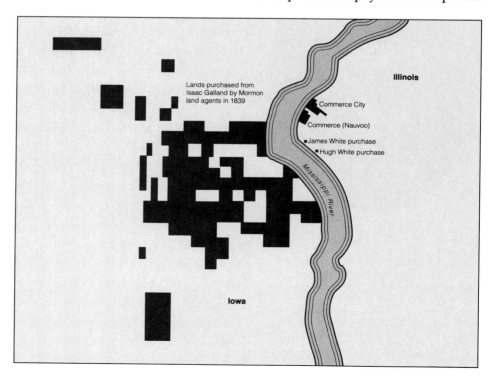

Lands purchased from Isaac Galland by Mormon land agents in 1839

Illinois

Commerce City

Commerce (Nauvoo)

James White purchase

Hugh White purchase

Mississippi River

Iowa

The Joseph Smith homestead in Nauvoo. The Prophet and his family lived here from 1839 to 1843. The north ell was added by the Prophet Joseph Smith about 1840. In about 1856 the Prophet's son Joseph Smith III added the larger addition to the west.

were sold in Nauvoo, but the Saints could rarely pay with cash. Consequently the payment for the properties on both sides of the river was never totally resolved during the period the Church was in that region.

After making the original land purchases on 30 April 1839, the Prophet and his associates returned to Quincy to complete preparations for the migration northward. A conference was held near Quincy on 4–5 May. At this time the body of the Church sanctioned the land acquisition and resolved that the next conference would be held in Commerce the first week in October. By 10 May the Prophet had returned to Commerce with his family and taken up residence in a small log house known as the Homestead close to the river on the southern end of the peninsula. While land was being cleared, surveyed, and platted, and the swamp drained, most arriving Saints lived in wagons, tents, or dugouts. Joseph and Emma took many of them into their own meager quarters. Across the river in Montrose, several families, including those of Brigham Young, John Taylor, Wilford Woodruff, and Orson Pratt, lived in empty military barracks left from the Black Hawk War.

In a public letter on 1 July, Joseph Smith called upon all Saints everywhere to migrate to the new site. Thousands responded to his call. During this same time Joseph was occupied with dictating his personal history and teaching the members of the Quorum of the Twelve, who were soon to leave on missions to Great Britain.

Sometime during these busy weeks the Prophet named the new Illinois site *Nauvoo,* a Hebrew word meaning "beautiful." The first formal use of the name Nauvoo was to place it on the official plat of the city on 30 August 1839. The United States post office adopted the name change in April of 1840, and in March of that year the city council passed an ordinance incorporating the sites of Commerce and Commerce City into Nauvoo. Once the success of this gathering place seemed assured and the Saints began swarming into the area, other landholders saw advantages in creating subdivisions which were attached to Nauvoo as "additions."

SICKNESS AND A DAY OF GOD'S POWER

In the summer of 1839 the swamp area on the Nauvoo peninsula had not yet been drained. While the Saints gathered, cleared, drained, built, and planted, they were oblivious to the danger of the Anopheles mosquito. This tiny insect, which bred profusely in the swampland and along the Mississippi riverbank, transmitted parasites to the red blood cells of humans by its bite. The disease this caused, characterized by periodic attacks of chills and fever, is now known as malaria, but people in the nineteenth century called it and diseases with similar symptoms the *ague* (pronounced `a gyu).

Scores of Church members on both sides of the river fell ill. The residents of the temporary tent city surrounding the Prophet's home were stricken by the disease as were the Saints staying in his home. Emma nursed the people night and day, while Joseph's six-year-old son carried water for the sick until he also caught the disease. The pestilence was indiscriminate, affecting all ages and classes. One of the early fatalities in the city was Oliver Huntington's mother, Zina. The Prophet Joseph invited Oliver to bring his family, who were all ill to his home for needed care. The Whitney family was in a similar situation. Elizabeth Ann reported that they "were only just barely able to crawl around and wait upon each other."[11] In those circumstances Elizabeth gave birth to her ninth child. When Joseph learned of their plight he insisted that the family move in with him. They accepted his offer and took up residence in a small cottage in Joseph's yard. By 12 July, Joseph Smith, Sr., was so ill he was near death.

Eventually Joseph Smith also became ill, but after several days confinement he was prompted to arise and extend help to others. The day of 22 July was, in the words of Wilford Woodruff, "a day of God's power" in Nauvoo and Montrose.[12] That morning the Prophet arose and, being filled with the Spirit of the Lord, administered to the sick in his house and in the yard outside. More sick people were down by the river, and there too he administered with great power to the faithful. One such, Henry G. Sherwood, was near death. Joseph stepped to the door of Brother Sherwood's tent and commanded him to rise and come out; he obeyed and was healed. Elder Heber C. Kimball and others accompanied the Prophet across the river to Montrose. One by one they visited the homes of the Twelve and administered to those who needed a blessing. Brigham Young, Wilford Woodruff, Orson Pratt, and John Taylor then joined Joseph in his mission of mercy.

One of the most memorable of the healings in Montrose was that of Elijah Fordham. When the brethren arrived he was lying in bed unable to speak.

"Brother Joseph walked up to Brother Fordham, and took him by the right hand. . . .

"He saw that Brother Fordham's eyes were glazed, and that he was speechless and unconscious.

"After taking hold of his hand, he looked down into the dying man's face and said: 'Brother Fordham, do you not know me?' At first he made no reply; but we could all see the effect of the Spirit of God resting upon him.

"He again said: 'Elijah, do you not know me?'

"With a low whisper, Brother Fordham answered, 'Yes!'

"The Prophet then said, 'Have you not faith to be healed?'

"The answer, which was a little plainer than before, was: 'I am afraid it is too late. If you had come sooner, I think it might have been.'

"He had the appearance of a man waking from sleep. It was the sleep of death.

"Joseph then said: 'Do you believe that Jesus is the Christ?'

" 'I do, Brother Joseph,' was the response.

"Then the Prophet of God spoke with a loud voice, as in the majesty of

Elijah Fordham (1798–1879) accepted the gospel in 1833 in Michigan. In 1835 he was ordained a seventy by Joseph Smith in Kirtland. Following his miraculous healing at the hands of Joseph Smith in Montrose, Iowa, Elijah moved to Nauvoo and worked on the temple until the Saints were forced from Illinois in 1846. He went to Utah in 1850 and continued faithful in the gospel the remainder of his life.

Elizabeth Haven (1811–92), a cousin of Brigham Young and Willard Richards, accepted the gospel in 1837. After the expulsion from Missouri she nursed many sick Saints in Quincy, Illinois. Her letters are a valuable source of information on this period of Church history. While in Quincy she met and married Israel Barlow. They migrated to Utah and settled in Bountiful. She died Christmas Day 1892.

the Godhead: 'Elijah, I command you, in the name of Jesus of Nazareth, to arise and be made whole!'

"The words of the Prophet were not like the words of man, but like the voice of God. It seemed to me that the house shook from its foundation.

"Elijah Fordham leaped from his bed like a man raised from the dead. A healthy color came to his face, and life was manifested in every act."[13]

They next visited Joseph B. Noble, who was also healed. Wilford Woodruff remembered this as the "greatest day for the manifestation of the power of God through the gift of healing since the organization of the Church."[14]

As the brethren were at the river bank preparing to cross back to Nauvoo, a nonmember who had heard of the miracles that day asked the Prophet if he would come and administer to his dying twin babies about two miles from Montrose. Joseph said he could not go, but he gave Wilford Woodruff a red silk handkerchief and told him to administer to them, promising that when he wiped their faces with it they would be healed. The Prophet also promised that the handkerchief would remain a bond between them as long as Wilford kept it. Obedient to the charge, Wilford testified that the children were healed. He treasured the keepsake the rest of his life.[15]

Despite this unusual demonstration of faith and power, sickness raged among the Saints in Nauvoo throughout the summer and into the fall. Only as winter approached did the outbreak begin to subside. In October, Elizabeth Haven reported from the general conference held in Nauvoo, which she attended. She wrote home to New England: "The Prophet says it is a sickly place, but is made known to him that it shall be sanctified and be a place of gathering."[16]

The illnesses were not confined to Nauvoo. Many Latter-day Saints in Quincy also suffered between February and September of 1839. In Commerce many people were sick, but there were few deaths. In Quincy, however, death caused great "havoc among the Saints." Elizabeth Haven wrote to her family, "O my friends, you know nothing about the ague, how it prostrates and bewilders the mind and impairs the health." Some families suffered the loss of two or three of their loved ones. The Goddard family, living across the street from Elizabeth, lost both parents and a sixteen-year-old daughter. Five children survived, but at one time four of them were sick. Providentially, Elizabeth did not contract the disease. She spent the summer and fall nursing others. So great was the need for nursing care that she did not get to a Sabbath meeting between June and October. She considered the trials of Far West small compared to "what they have been of late."[17]

SEEKING REDRESS FOR MISSOURI GRIEVANCES

While the Prophet and others suffered in Liberty Jail in 1838–39, they had discussed how to obtain redress from the state of Missouri for the land and property lost by the Saints during the persecutions of 1833 and 1838–39. In

1833 the Lord directed the brethren to petition the local and state governments. If this failed they were to seek help from the federal government (see D&C 101:81–91). This approach had been used first in 1834 when the Church unsuccessfully appealed to President Andrew Jackson. In March 1839, while in the Liberty Jail, the Prophet received a revelation that the Church should again appeal to the United States government for redress of the wrongs the Saints had suffered in Missouri. The members of the Church were charged to gather "up a knowledge of all the facts, and sufferings and abuses put upon them by the people of this State [Missouri]." This would be "the last effort which is enjoined on us by our Heavenly Father, before we can fully and completely claim that promise which shall call him forth from his hiding place" (D&C 123:1, 6).

Because of ill health Sidney Rigdon had been released from prison before the other members of the First Presidency. In Illinois he met with Governor Thomas Carlin and related the plight of the Saints. He also developed a plan to obtain redress based on a statement in the United States Constitution that "the general government shall give to each State a republican form of government." Sidney Rigdon felt that such a government did not exist in Missouri, so he planned to present the story of the persecutions to the governors of the respective states and their legislatures, hoping to induce as many as possible to pass a resolution to "impeach" the state of Missouri. He proposed sending Church representatives to each state capitol to lobby for the Church. The plan got as far as the appointment of his son-in-law, George W. Robinson, to collect the affidavits and general information on the subject; Sidney secured a letter of introduction to the governors and the president from Governor Carlin.[18]

It became obvious that it was useless to petition the officials of Missouri for help. The impracticality of Rigdon's plan was also soon evident. In May 1839 a conference appointed Sidney Rigdon to take the Latter-day Saint grievances directly to Washington, D.C. His delays, however, led to the additional appointment of Joseph Smith and Elias Higbee at the October conference in Commerce to approach President Martin Van Buren. Orrin Porter Rockwell was also invited to accompany them. They left Nauvoo on 29 October 1839 and were joined en route to Springfield by a new convert, Dr. Robert D. Foster. In Springfield the Prophet wrote to his wife, "It will be a long and lonesome time during my absence from you and nothing but a sense of humanity could have urged me on to so great a sacrifice, but shall I see so many perish and [not] seek redress? No, I will try this once in the [name] of the Lord."[19]

Because of illness Sidney Rigdon was left at the home of John Snyder in Springfield. The Prophet left him in the care of Dr. Foster and Orrin Porter Rockwell and then proceeded with Elias Higbee to the nation's capital, arriving on 28 November. The next day they scheduled an interview with a very reluctant President Van Buren. He was not impressed with their letters

Martin Van Buren (1782–1862), eighth president of the United States, served from 1837 to 1841. He would not support the cause of Joseph Smith and others for redress of the Saints' grievances arising from the Missouri persecutions.

of introduction and tried to turn them away, but Joseph's insistence led to an audience with the president. When Van Buren asked the Prophet how his religion differed from other Christian denominations of the day, Joseph said that the "mode of baptism, and the gift of the Holy Ghost by the laying on of hands" were the essential differences. "We considered that all other considerations were contained in the gift of the Holy Ghost."[20]

The president, responding to the states rights political philosophy of the day and being anxious not to offend his political allies, realized the Mormon-Missouri conflict was a touchy issue. He was therefore unsympathetic to the pleadings of the brethren. Joseph later asserted: "I had an interview with Martin Van Buren, the President, who treated me very insolently, and it was with great reluctance he listened to our message, which, when he had heard, he said: '*Gentlemen, your cause is just, but I can do nothing for you.*' "[21] The Prophet also tried convincing leading senator John C. Calhoun of his concerns, but was rebuffed.

The Prophet and Elder Higbee then contacted various other senators and representatives. The Illinois delegation treated them especially well, and Illinois Senator Richard M. Young promised to introduce their petition to Congress. The lengthy petition detailed the difficulties the Saints had endured since 1833 in Missouri and concluded: "We make our appeal as *American Citizens*, as *Christians*, and as *Men*—believing that the high sense of justice which exists in your honorable body, will not allow such oppression to be practiced upon any portion of the citizens of this vast republic with impunity; but that some measures which your wisdom may dictate, may be taken, so that the great body of people who have been thus abused, may have redress for the wrongs which they have suffered."[22]

Meanwhile the brethren wrote home asking the Saints to gather and send as many certificates and affidavits as possible verifying the persecutions and proving their ownership of Missouri land. In all the Prophet said he submitted the claims of about 491 individuals against the state of Missouri.[23] At the same time the embarrassed Missouri congressional delegation began building its own defense, based on transcripts of a hearing held in Richmond, Missouri, where numerous anti-Mormons and ex-Mormons testified.

While he was still in the East, the Prophet visited various branches of the Church. In Philadelphia, he spoke to a congregation of about three thousand Saints. He also spent several days with Elder Parley P. Pratt who was in Philadelphia arranging for the publication of several books. Parley P. Pratt remembered:

"During these interviews he taught me many great and glorious principles concerning God and the heavenly order of eternity. It was at this time that I received from him the first idea of eternal family organization. . . .

"It was from him that I learned that the wife of my bosom might be secured to me for time and all eternity." These blessed personal encounters with the Prophet affected Parley for the rest of his life.

"I had loved before, but I knew not why. But now I loved—with a pureness—an intensity of elevated, exalted feeling, which would lift my soul from the transitory things of this grovelling sphere and expand it as the ocean."[24]

The prevailing view in the nation, especially among southern politicians, was that questions like those raised by the Latter-day Saints were clearly state concerns. It was felt that the Constitution provided no authority for national intervention. These views clearly reflected the national debate over the sovereignty of the states that would culminate two decades later in the American Civil War.

Joseph Smith left Elias Higbee in Washington to await the results of the petition to Congress, and he returned to Nauvoo. On 4 March 1840 the Senate committee announced that Congress would do nothing; they recommended that the Church seek redress in the state or federal courts in America, a course that the Saints had found totally useless. In the April general conference of the Church the Saints voted that "if all hopes of obtaining satisfaction for the injuries done us be entirely blasted, that they then appeal our case to the Court of Heaven, believing that the Great Jehovah, who rules over the destiny of nations, and who notices the falling sparrows, will undoubtedly redress our wrongs, and ere long avenge us of our adversaries."[25]

NAUVOO CHARTER

The new gathering place for the Saints included not only Nauvoo, Illinois, and Montrose, Iowa, but also several neighboring locations on both sides of the river. Members of the Church settled in established communities such as Carthage—the Hancock County seat—La Harpe, and Fountain Green. And they established small settlements of their own at Ramus, Lima, and Yelrome (the name of Isaac Morley, the settlement's founder, spelled backward). There were also numerous suburbs surrounding Nauvoo itself. But clearly Nauvoo was the center place, and within a few months it gained political and economic influence in western Illinois.

Following Joseph Smith's return from the East, serious discussions began about the form of government that Nauvoo should have. The arrival of a prominent Springfield citizen, John C. Bennett, in Nauvoo in June 1840 prompted decisive action on this issue. The ambitious and energetic Bennett had quickly gained acceptance in military, medical, and political circles in the state capital. Governor Thomas Carlin had named him the state militia's quartermaster general. Before going to Nauvoo, Bennett wrote to the Prophet expressing indignation at the injustices Missouri had inflicted upon the Latter-day Saints and offering his assistance. Soon after he arrived he accepted the gospel and was baptized. His acquaintance with numerous government officials made him the logical person to lobby for a charter

Several communities of Saints grew up in Hancock County, Illinois, and Lee County, Iowa, during the Nauvoo era. Population estimates for the area totaled between fifteen and twenty thousand people by the time of the exodus from Illinois in 1846.

government for Nauvoo. At the October general conference, Joseph Smith, Robert B. Thompson, and John C. Bennett were nominated to draft a proposal and carry it to Springfield.

Bennett's lobbying efforts with both political parties were successful, and the Nauvoo charter became law on 16 December 1840. It was similar to the charters granted to Chicago and Alton in 1837, Galena in 1839, and Springfield and Quincy in 1840. It granted the right to establish a local militia, a municipal court, and a university. Church leaders were elated with its broad and liberal provisions, which seemed to ensure that government officials would no longer be able to take advantage of the Saints as they had in Missouri. Nauvoo's legislative and executive powers resided in the mayor, four aldermen, and nine councilors. The mayor and aldermen also served as judges of the municipal court, a change from the pattern of other chartered cities. This meant that five men controlled the legislative, executive, and judicial branches of the local government.

John C. Bennett was elected Nauvoo's first mayor on 1 February 1841. Other Church leaders, including Joseph Smith, Sidney Rigdon, and Hyrum Smith, were elected aldermen, ensuring a local government that would be friendly to the Saints. Immediately the city council created a militia unit, the Nauvoo Legion, which gradually grew to three thousand enlistees. Also, according to Nauvoo charter provisions, the Nauvoo Legion was under the control of Joseph Smith and other civic leaders, although it was technically part of the state militia. Once again jealous anti-Mormon observers became apprehensive about the unabated growth of Mormon influence and power in their area.

For the first time in a decade, the Saints felt some security. The Lord had again led them to find a refuge. The Apostles were able to go on their appointed mission to Great Britain. Their prophet was safe and well and leading the Church. Peace abounded, and opportunities to extend the gospel of Jesus Christ seemed readily available.

ENDNOTES

1. In *History of the Church*, 3:251.

2. *History of Caldwell and Livingston Counties, Missouri* (St. Louis: National Historical Co., 1886), p. 142.

3. See Kenneth W. Godfrey, Audrey M. Godfrey, and Jill Mulvay Derr, *Women's Voices* (Salt Lake City: Deseret Book Co., 1982), pp. 103–5.

4. In *History of the Church*, 3:269.

5. Letter from Elizabeth Haven to Elizabeth Howe Bullard, 24 Feb. 1839, in Ora H. Barlow, *The Israel Barlow Story and Mormon Mores* (Salt Lake City: Ora H. Barlow, 1968), p. 143.

6. See Wilford Woodruff Journals, 18 Mar. 1839, LDS Historical Department, Salt Lake City.

7. In Barlow, *Israel Barlow Story*, p. 156.

8. Drusilla Doris Hendricks, "Historical Sketch of James Hendricks and Drusilla Dorris Hendricks," typescript, LDS Historical Department, Salt Lake City, pp. 22–23.

9. In David E. and Della S. Miller, *Nauvoo: The City of Joseph* (Salt Lake City: Peregrine Smith, 1974), p. 26; spelling standardized.

10. In *History of the Church*, 3:336.

11. "A Leaf from an Autobiography," *Woman's Exponent*, 15 Nov. 1878, p. 91.

12. Wilford Woodruff Journals, 22 July 1839; punctuation standardized.

13. Wilford Woodruff, *Leaves from My Journal*, 2d ed. (Salt Lake City: Juvenile Instructor Office, 1882), p. 63.

14. Woodruff, *Leaves from My Journal*, p. 65.

15. See Woodruff, *Leaves from My Journal*, p. 65.

16. In Barlow, *Israel Barlow Story*, p. 163.

17. Letter from Haven to Bullard, 30 Sept. 1839, in Barlow, *Israel Barlow Story*, pp. 158, 160–61.

18. Andrew Jenson, *The Historical Record*, Mar. 1889, p. 738.

19. In Dean C. Jessee, ed., *The Personal Writings of Joseph Smith* (Salt Lake City: Deseret Book Co., 1984), p. 448; spelling and punctuation standardized.

20. In *History of the Church*, 4:42.

21. *History of the Church*, 4:80.

22. In *History of the Church*, 4:38.

23. *History of the Church*, 4:74. Additional appeals were made by the Church in 1842–43. A total of 703 petitioners filed individual affidavits; see Clark V. Johnson, "The Missouri Redress Petitions: A Reappraisal of Mormon Persecutions in Missouri, *Brigham Young University Studies*, Spring 1986, pp. 31–44.

24. Parley P. Pratt, ed., *Autobiography of Parley P. Pratt*, Classics in Mormon Literature series (Salt Lake City: Deseret Book Co., 1985), pp. 259–60.

25. In *History of the Church*, 4:108.

THE MISSION OF THE TWELVE

► Herefordshire Beacon, the most prominent hill in the region was the site of an old British fort that had been overrun by the Romans.

Wilford Woodruff, Brigham Young, and Willard Richards retired to this ancient and revered British landmark to pray and counsel together regarding the publishing of the Book of Mormon and a hymnbook for the use of the British Saints. After receiving a confirmation to proceed, they used three hundred pounds that they received from John Benbow and Thomas Kington to accomplish the project.

A S THE SAINTS were settling Nauvoo, the Prophet Joseph Smith was planning further overseas expansion of the Church. This expansion had begun with the call of Elders Heber C. Kimball and Orson Hyde to England in 1837. As early as 1835 the Lord had instructed members of the Quorum of the Twelve that they were to be "special witnesses of the name of Christ in all the world" and that they were to "build up the church, and regulate all the affairs of the same in all nations." They were given the keys "to open the door by the proclamation of the gospel of Jesus Christ" to all the world (D&C 107:23, 33, 35). The Twelve were further promised that "in whatsoever place ye shall proclaim my name an effectual door shall be opened unto you, that they may receive my word" (D&C 112:19). This promise was fulfilled the very day it was revealed, 23 July 1837, when Elder Heber C. Kimball and his companions were invited to preach in the Vauxhall Chapel in Preston, England, an invitation resulting in the first baptisms in the British Isles. As the work went forward in that land with great success, even more participation from the Apostles was anticipated.

On 26 April 1838 the Lord directed Joseph Smith to build a temple in Far West, Missouri. The cornerstones were laid on 4 July 1838, and the site was dedicated by Brigham Young. The Twelve left from there for their mission to England on 26 April 1839 in fulfillment of the command of the Lord in Doctrine and Covenants 118:3–6.

The Church now owns the property and in 1968 landscaped it, erected monuments and markers, and preserved the cornerstones.

THE TWELVE CALLED TO BRITAIN

Shortly after Joseph Smith settled in Far West, Missouri, in March 1838, he had begun preparing for an expanded missionary effort by the Twelve to Great Britain. One of the Apostles, David W. Patten, was instructed by revelation to prepare for a mission the next year (see D&C 114:1). On 8 July 1838 another revelation called John Taylor, John E. Page, Wilford Woodruff, and Willard Richards to the Twelve. The Apostles were charged "to go over the great waters, and there promulgate my gospel, the fulness thereof, and bear record of my name" (D&C 118:4). The Lord also told them the exact day, 26 April 1839, they were to leave Far West to depart for England.

When the revelation was received, the brethren anticipated little difficulty in fulfilling these directions, but the subsequent persecutions and the expulsion of the Saints from Missouri made an April departure from Far West extremely dangerous. Many mobsters harassed the remaining Church members in Missouri and openly boasted that the revelation would not be fulfilled. But Brigham Young urged his colleagues to go to Far West as the Lord had directed and promised that the Lord would protect them.

Shortly after midnight on 26 April, Elders Brigham Young, Heber C. Kimball, Orson Pratt, John E. Page, John Taylor, Wilford Woodruff, and George A. Smith gathered under moonlight with about twenty other Saints at the Far West temple site. In peril of their lives, they recommenced laying the foundation of the Lord's house by rolling up a large stone near the southeast corner. Brigham Young reported, "Thus was this revelation fulfilled, concerning which our enemies said, if all other revelations of Joseph Smith were fulfilled that one should not, as it had day and date to it."[1] In the early morning hours Theodore Turley, one of the Saints who had been at Far West with the Twelve, went to the home of apostate Isaac Russell to bid him farewell. Russell was astounded that his friend was in Far West with members of the Twelve and speechless upon learning that the prophecy was fulfilled.

There were no further preparations for the mission to Great Britain until the Saints had found a gathering place at Commerce (Nauvoo). On 27 June 1839 the First Presidency and the Twelve met in a special conference. After making a humble confession of his follies and sins, Orson Hyde was restored to fellowship with the Twelve. The Prophet Joseph Smith instructed the brethren about the basic principles of the gospel to better prepare them to fulfill their missions. A week later in Montrose, Iowa, following additional instructions, the First Presidency blessed each Apostle and his wife individually. Concerning those who were blessed, Wilford Woodruff recorded that "if we were faithful we had the promise of again returning to the bosom of our families and being blessed on our mission and having many souls as seals of our ministry." After the blessings, Joseph Smith instructed them that they were "not sent out to be taught but to teach—let every man be sober, be

This primitive painting of Phoebe Carter Woodruff, wife of Wilford Woodruff, and her son Joseph Woodruff is attributed to Thomas Ward, an LDS immigrant from Liverpool, England. This picture was probably painted in Nauvoo about 1845.

vigilant, and let all his words be seasoned with grace, and keep in mind that it is a day of warning and not of many words."[2]

On Sunday, 7 July, the Twelve spoke at a farewell meeting held in their behalf. Each one bore powerful witness of the work they were engaged in. Clearly, they were anxious to be on their way to England; unfortunately, they were not able to leave immediately. The next week a malaria epidemic hit the Nauvoo vicinity. The Apostles were stricken, and their mission was temporarily postponed. But after the day of God's power on 22 July, "All of the Twelve were . . . determined, 'sick or not,' to fulfill their mission. On Sunday, August 4, a day of fasting and prayer, the Prophet renewed his instruction to 'go forth without purse or scrip, according to the revelations of Jesus Christ.' "[3]

THE MISSIONARIES DEPART

John Taylor and Wilford Woodruff, still sick from malaria, determined to depart immediately. Wilford Woodruff wrote, "Early upon the morning of the 8th of August, I arose from my bed of sickness, laid my hands upon the head of my sick wife, Phoebe, and blessed her. I then departed from the embrace of my companion, and left her almost without food or the necessaries of life. She suffered my departure with the fortitude that becomes a saint, realizing the responsibilities of her companion. . . .

"Although feeble, I walked to the banks of the Mississippi River. There President Young took me in a canoe . . . and paddled me across the river. When we landed, I lay down on a side of sole leather, by the postoffice, to rest. Brother Joseph, the Prophet of God, came along and looked at me. 'Well, Brother Woodruff,' said he, 'you have started upon your mission.' 'Yes,' said I, 'but I feel and look more like a subject for the dissecting room than a missionary.' Joseph replied: 'What did you say that for? Get up, and go along; all will be right with you.' "[4]

John Taylor and Wilford Woodruff struggled on their journey to the east coast. In Indiana, John Taylor became deathly ill, and Wilford had to leave him behind, committing him into the hands of the Lord. After a miraculous recovery, Elder Taylor continued on his journey. He was stricken again, but finally met Elder Woodruff in New York.

The departures of the other brethren were similarly difficult. Brigham Young was prepared to leave on 14 September, just shortly after his wife, Mary Ann, had given birth to a daughter. When he left Montrose, however, he was so ill that he could not walk the thirty rods (about five hundred feet) to the river without assistance. Three days later, Mary Ann, still weak from childbirth, arranged to cross the river and care for her husband who was staying at the home of Heber C. Kimball in Nauvoo. On 18 September, Brigham and Heber decided it was time to start on their appointed mission. Both men were so ill that they had to be helped into a wagon. All of the Kimball household were bedridden except four-year-old Heber Parley, who could just manage to carry water to the sick.

As the men drove off, Heber said he felt that "my very inmost parts would melt within me at leaving my family in such a condition, as it were almost in the arms of death. I felt as though I could not endure it. I asked the teamster to stop, and said to Brother Brigham, 'This is pretty tough, isn't it; let's rise up and give them a cheer.' We arose, and swinging our hats three times over our heads, shouted: 'Hurrah, hurrah for Israel.' Vilate, hearing the noise, arose from her bed and came to the door. She had a smile on her face. Vilate and Mary Anne Young cried out to us: 'Goodbye, God bless you.' "[5]

Elders Young and Kimball were joined en route by George A. Smith. As they traveled Brigham reached into his trunk and always found just enough money for the next stage coach fare. He thought Heber was replenishing the fund, but later discovered that he had not. The brethren had started their trip with $13.50 in donations, yet they spent more than $87 on coach fares. They had no idea how the additional money had gotten into the trunk "except by some unseen agent from the Heavenly world to forward the promulgation of the Gospel."[6] The brethren stayed a few weeks in upstate New York due to sickness. Brigham Young became sick in Moravia, New York, and was nursed to health by the Caleb Haight and William Van Orden families. Brother Van Orden also made an overcoat for George A. Smith, who had only a quilt around his shoulders to keep him warm.

Seven of the Apostles arrived in New York City during the winter. There they preached the gospel, conducted other Church business, and obtained funds for their passage to England. Parley P. Pratt remembered, "During the few days that we were together in New York we held many precious meetings in which the Saints were filled with joy, and the people more and more convinced of the truth of our message. Near forty persons were baptized and added to the Church in that city during the few days of our brethren's stay there."[7] Wilford Woodruff, John Taylor, and Theodore Turley were the first to sail for England, leaving 19 December 1839 and arriving twenty-three days later. The others left in March and arrived in Liverpool on 6 April 1840, the tenth anniversary of the Church's organization.

The need for the Twelve in Britain was soon apparent. After the first mission there in 1837 many members had fallen into apostasy and had left the Church due to persecution and lack of mature local direction. Attacks on the Church in local newspapers grew in number and intensity, and ministers of various denominations aroused opposition through sermons and lectures. Within the Church, some had challenged the authority of the mission presidency—Joseph Fielding, Willard Richards, and William Clayton—and had led small factions of the Saints astray, slowing missionary success.

Elder Heber C. Kimball had written several encouraging letters from America that buoyed up the Saints and identified those disrupting the progress of the work in England. But if the Church was to remain in Britain, there was a pressing need for strong preachers and teachers who were firmly grounded in the doctrine of the restored gospel and for mature and experienced leaders who could set the branches in order.

During the mission of the Twelve to England, many parts of Great Britain were introduced to the gospel.

Edinburgh, Scotland. The first missionaries arrived here in December 1839. Elder Orson Pratt arrived on 18 May 1840; the following morning, at Arthur's Seat, a prominent hill overlooking the city, he dedicated Scotland for the preaching of the gospel.

Bishopton, Scotland. Here, on 14 January 1840, Alexander and Jessie Hay became the first converts baptized in Scotland.

Castle Frome, England. Wilford Woodruff preached here and at the Hill Farm between March and July 1840. He baptized many of the members of the United Brethren, including John and Jane Benbow.

Douglas, Isle of Man. John Taylor dedicated this island in 1840 and held a celebrated debate with a local minister. He preached to relatives of his wife, Leonora Cannon Taylor, aunt of George Q. Cannon.

Herefordshire Beacon, England. Here on 20 May 1840, with Elder Brigham Young presiding, a council decided to publish the Book of Mormon and an LDS hymnbook in Britain.

Liverpool, England. The first LDS missionaries landed here in 1837. As the headquarters of the Church in Britain from 1842 to 1929, Liverpool housed the mission, emigration, and printing offices. The Millennial Star was published here, as were other important Church publications. By 1900, eighty-five thousand Latter-day Saints had emigrated to America through Liverpool.

London, England. Missionary work started here on 18 August 1840. London was the birthplace of several General Authorities, including Charles W. Penrose, George Teasdale, and George Reynolds.

Loughbrickland, Ireland. John Taylor baptized the first Irish convert, Thomas Tait, here on 31 July 1840.

Milnthorpe, England. This was the birthplace of President John Taylor.

New Chapel, England. Site of the London Temple, which was dedicated by President David O. McKay on 7 September 1958.

Manchester, England. This city was the headquarters of the Church in Britain from 1840–42. Elder Brigham Young served most of his mission here. The first stake in Great Britain was organized by Elder Harold B. Lee on 27 March 1960, and the first area conference of the Church convened here in August 1971.

Preston, England. Heber C. Kimball preached the first gospel sermon here on 23 July 1837. A branch was organized that August. Preston served as Church headquarters from 1837–40. Willard Richards was ordained an Apostle at a conference held here in April 1840.

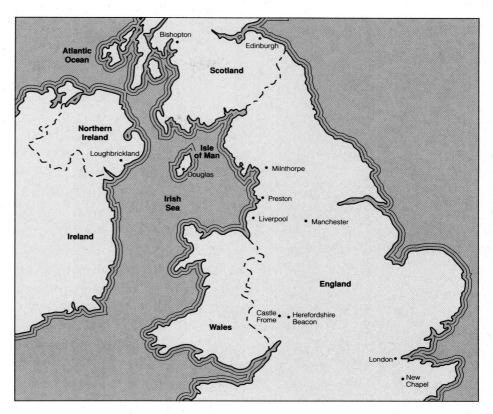

The British Isles were ripe for the coming of the members of the Twelve as missionaries. Most British subjects shared language, culture, and heritage with the missionaries from America. Freedom of religion was a strong tradition in Britain. There was not the strong reliance upon clergy typical on the European continent. The people loved to read the Bible, taking pride in the King James translation that the Apostles used in their preaching. England also had a strong central government that ensured uniform application of the laws respecting the practice of religion. This meant that the missionaries were legally equal with other ministers wherever they went in the country. Moreover, the industrial revolution had shattered the social standing of the lower classes and left them feeling they had been abandoned by their ministers. Many were seeking spiritual and temporal satisfaction and support in their lives.

This was the preparation the Lord provided to take the gospel to Great Britain.

THE TWELVE IN GREAT BRITAIN

Wilford Woodruff and John Taylor, the first of the Twelve to arrive in England, hastened to Church headquarters in Preston to meet with the mission presidency. There they decided to separate; Elder Taylor returned to Liverpool with Joseph Fielding, and Elder Woodruff traveled south with Theodore Turley to the Staffordshire Potteries, so called because of the industry carried on there.

A synopsis of Wilford Woodruff's travels and labors in 1840.8

Traveled	4,469 miles
Held	230 meetings
Established preaching	53 places
Planted which included	47 churches 1,500 Saints 28 elders 110 priests 24 teachers 10 deacons
Attended conferences	14
Baptized which included	336 persons 57 preachers 2 clerks of the Church of England
Assisted in the baptism	86 others
Confirmed	420
Assisted in confirmation	50 others
Ordained	18 elders 97 priests 34 teachers 1 deacon
Blessed	120 children
Administered unto	120 sick persons
Assisted in procuring	1,000 pounds sterling for printing Millennial Star, three thousand copies of Latter-day Saints hymns, and five thousand copies of the Book of Mormon
Assisted in emigrating to America	200 Saints
Wrote	200 letters
Received	112 letters
Mobs came against me	4

Elders Taylor and Fielding began working in Liverpool on 23 January and baptized their first converts on 4 February. Also in February they baptized the entire family of George Cannon, brother of John Taylor's wife, Leonora. George Q. Cannon, then but a boy of twelve, would become a noted missionary in the Hawaiian Islands, a member of the Twelve Apostles, and a counselor to four Presidents of the Church, including his uncle John Taylor. The work in Liverpool grew steadily, and by the time the remaining members of the Twelve arrived in England in April, a branch of the Church was functioning in that port city.

In the Potteries, Elder Woodruff successfully organized several branches in the small towns of the area and placed Elder Turley in charge of them. In March, Wilford was inspired to go further south to Herefordshire, accompanied by one of his converts, William Benbow. They contacted William's brother and sister-in-law, John and Jane Benbow, and a group of six hundred people who had formed their own religious society called the United Brethren. Eventually the leader of the group, Thomas Kington, and all but one of the six hundred members accepted the restored gospel and were baptized. Hundreds of others in the vicinity also joined the Church.

Although the work prospered, success did not come without opposition. A local constable was sent to arrest Elder Woodruff for preaching without a license, but instead he was baptized following an inspiring sermon. On another occasion, two clerks sent to discover what Wilford was teaching were both baptized. The clergy in the area finally wrote to the archbishop of Canterbury, head of the Church of England, requesting that he use his influence to ban the Mormons from Britain. Recognizing the laws of religious tolerance in the nation, the archbishop counseled the ministers to solve the problem themselves by becoming more dedicated pastors. Instead the clergy preached anti-Mormon sermons and agitated the local press to harass the Latter-day Saints.

Opposition grew as the Church prospered in the area. While preaching in the village of Hawcross, Wilford Woodruff was surrounded by a hostile mob. When some of the villagers requested baptism, Wilford told them that if they had faith enough to be baptized, he had sufficient faith to administer the ordinance, in spite of the threatened physical violence. The small group walked down to a pond and was soon surrounded by a mob armed with stones. Wilford Woodruff reported, "I walked into the water with my mind stayed on God and baptized five persons while they were pelting my body with stones, one of which hit me on the head and came very near knocking me down."9

On another occasion the minister in the village of Dymock led a mob of over fifty men in stoning the house where the Saints were holding a prayer meeting. Although such experiences were relatively rare in Britain, they reminded Elder Woodruff that there was strong opposition to the restored gospel.

The first issue of the Millennial Star came off the press 27 May 1840 in Manchester, England. It began as a monthly publication edited by Parley P. Pratt. Over the years it changed to a semi-monthly, then to a weekly, and finally back to a monthly.

In 1842 the Church headquarters in Britain was moved to Liverpool, and the Star was published there until 1933 when it began to be published in London. Until its cessation in 1970 it was the oldest continuous publication in the Church. For much of its history it was edited by the president of the British mission.

This building, located at 42 Islington Street in Liverpool, served as the headquarters for the British Mission and office for the Millennial Star from 1855–1904.

Through the efforts of Wilford Woodruff and others, some eighteen hundred people were converted in the three-county area of Hereford, Worcester, and Gloucester. Visiting the market town of Ledbury, Elder Woodruff was invited by the Baptist minister to preach to his congregation. Afterward the minister and several of the congregation requested baptism. On another occasion, while he was baptizing, some ministers rode up in a wagon, gratefully accepted baptism, and went on their way rejoicing. Reflecting on this extraordinary period of his life, Wilford Woodruff wrote, "The whole history of this Herefordshire mission shows the importance of listening to the still small voice of the spirit of God, and the revelations of the Holy Ghost. The people were praying for light and truth, and the Lord sent me to them."[10]

In April 1840, when the other Apostles arrived in the British Isles, Brigham Young, who had assumed leadership of the Church in the British Mission, summoned the brethren to Preston for a general conference of the Church. Nearly sixteen hundred members, representing thirty-three branches, came to the conference. The first order of business was the ordination of Willard Richards to the apostleship in accordance with the 1838 revelation. Brigham Young was also presented and sustained as President of the Quorum of the Twelve. There were now eight members of the Twelve in the British Isles, namely Brigham Young, Heber C. Kimball, Parley P. Pratt, Orson Pratt, John Taylor, Wilford Woodruff, George A. Smith, and Willard Richards. Two others, William Smith and John E. Page, did not fulfill missions in Britain. Orson Hyde arrived later, labored with his brethren for several months in England, and then proceeded to Palestine to dedicate that land for the return of the Jews. One vacancy in the Twelve still remained open at that time.

At the conference President Young's proposal to publish the Book of Mormon, a hymnbook, and a monthly periodical for the English Saints was also approved. At Elder Woodruff's suggestion, the new publication was to be called the *Latter-day Saints' Millennial Star*. Elder Parley P. Pratt was chosen as its editor. The Twelve concluded the conference by encouraging the Saints to emigrate to Nauvoo.

Brigham Young demonstrated great spiritual and administrative ability in his leadership of the Church in Great Britain. While visiting Wilford Woodruff and the converted United Brethren in the South, he exercised his priesthood power in a notable healing. Mary Pitt, an invalid for eleven years and the sister of musician William Pitt, requested a blessing. The Pitts had been baptized just the day before. Wilford Woodruff recorded, "We prayed for her and laid hands upon her. Brother Young was mouth, and commanded her to be made whole. She laid down her crutch and never used it after, and the next day she walked three miles."[11] Mary Pitt was one of the many Saints in England healed through the power of priesthood blessings given by Brigham Young.

Parley and Orson Pratt were both active in publishing tracts and a newspaper to promote the gospel message in Great Britain over a period of several years. Here is a list of their publications while in Britain:

Parley P. Pratt

An Address by a Minister of The Church of Jesus Christ of Latter-day Saints to the People of England

Key to the Science of Theology

A Letter to the Queen, Touching the Signs of the Times and the Political Destiny of the World

Marriage and Morals in Utah

Reply to Mr. Thomas Taylor's "Complete Failure," and Mr. Richard Livesey's "Mormonism Exposed"

The World Turned Upside Down; or, Heaven on Earth

Orson Pratt

Divine Authority; or, The Question, Was Joseph Smith Sent of God?

The Kingdom of God, Parts 1–4

Remarkable Visions

New Jerusalem; or, The Fulfillment of Modern Prophecy

Divine Authenticity of the Book of Mormon, Numbers 1–6

Reply to a Pamphlet Printed at Glasgow, with the "Approbation of Clergymen of Different Denominations" Entitled "Remarks on Mormonism"

Absurdities of Immaterialism

Great First Cause; or, The Self-Moving Forces of the Universe

The Holy Spirit

Latter-day Kingdom; or, The Preparations for the Second Advent

Necessity for Miracles

True Faith

True Repentance

Water Baptism

Spiritual Gifts

Universal Apostasy

New and Easy Solution of the Cubic and Biquadratic Equations

President Young also expanded the missionary work in the British Isles. Under his direction, Heber C. Kimball visited the branches in northern England where he had labored in 1837–38. He strengthened those who had remained faithful during the interim and worked to reconvert many who had fallen away due to persecution. Willard Richards was sent to assist Wilford Woodruff in southern England. John Taylor, having had some success in Liverpool with Irish immigrants, sailed with three Irish companions to Ireland to introduce the gospel there. Although they had little success, they laid an important groundwork. Returning to Liverpool, Elder Taylor felt impressed to expand the work to the Isle of Man in the Irish Sea where many relatives of his wife, Leonora, lived. Soon he had baptized several people and organized a branch on the island.

Orson Pratt was assigned to take the gospel to Scotland. There he built upon the work of two native Scottish converts—Samuel Mulliner and Alexander Wright—who in 1839 had returned from Canada to their homeland to share the gospel with their families and friends; they had a group of twenty converts before he arrived. Elder Pratt organized the first Scottish branch in Paisley, a few miles from Glasgow, on 8 May 1840. Late in May he dedicated Scotland for the preaching of the gospel and asked the Lord for two hundred converts. The work in the capital, Edinburgh, was slow at first, with only eighteen people being baptized by August. But Orson, a vigorous missionary, worked hard for ten months, often holding as many as seven street meetings in one day. He published a pamphlet called *A Interesting Account of Several Remarkable Visions,* which contained the first published account of the Prophet Joseph Smith's first vision. Elder Pratt spent nearly his entire mission in Scotland, and by the time he left in March 1841 his dedicatory prayer was answered—the membership of the Church in the Edinburgh conference numbered 226.

In August 1840, Elder George A. Smith accompanied Elders Kimball and Woodruff to London, one of the world's largest cities. They were denied the opportunity to preach in the Temperance Hall, and so turned to the famous open-air Smithfield Market. Informed that they could not preach there either, they were led by a local watchmaker to Tabernacle Square, just outside the city limits. There Elder Smith gave a sermon to a boisterous but interested audience. When a local minister informed the crowd that George A. Smith was a Mormon and they should not listen to him, British sympathy for the underdog asserted itself. The crowd gave increased attention, but none were willing to be baptized.

After several days of proselyting without success, the Apostles were finally rewarded when Henry Connor, the watchmaker who had befriended them, embraced the gospel. But the Church grew slowly in London. In reporting to Brigham Young, the brethren wrote, "In our travels, either in America or Europe, we have never before found a people, from whose minds we have had to remove a greater multiplicity of objections, or combination of obstacles, in order to excite an interest in the subject and prepare the heart for the reception of the word of God, than in the city of London."[12] Brigham Young visited London in December 1840 to lend support to the missionary work there, and by 14 February 1841, enough members had been baptized to organize a conference of the Church with a newly-arrived young missionary from America, Lorenzo Snow, as its president. During the three years Elder Snow remained in London he brought several hundred new members into the Church and presented two beautifully bound copies of the Book of Mormon to Queen Victoria and Prince Albert.

Parley P. Pratt's ministry in Britain focused mainly on the writing and editing of Church literature that was vital to the success of the missionary effort then taking place. He also wrote several tracts and edited the monthly *Millennial Star*, which provided the Saints in England with the first published material on Joseph Smith's revelations and his history. It contained general news from the Church in the United States as well, thus linking the English Saints with their American counterparts. Throughout the rest of the nineteenth century, the *Millennial Star* was a leading periodical in the Church. It was replete with historical documents and addresses by Church authorities.

IMPACT OF THE TWELVE'S MISSION TO BRITAIN

Under the able and inspired leadership of Brigham Young and the Twelve, the Church experienced phenomenal growth during 1840. At the October general conference held in Manchester, "ordinations were performed, disciplinary cases were acted upon, a fund was established to support missionaries with insufficient means [many of them native Britons], and missionaries were assigned to their places of labor. Total membership was reported to be up 1,115 since July, and there were 70 churches and 1,007 members at Herefordshire."[13]

Emigration of British Saints to America had commenced prior to the conference in Manchester. On 1 June 1840, Brigham Young and Heber C. Kimball met with approximately forty-six Saints and organized them for their journey to Nauvoo. John Moon, a faithful member converted during Elder Kimball's previous mission, was appointed en route to preside. When these Saints arrived in Nauvoo, they wrote encouraging letters back to their friends, supporting the gathering and contradicting the negative comments in the British papers about traveling to such a distant place.

Most of the English Saints needed no urging to emigrate. Even before the Apostles mentioned the gathering, they wanted to go to America to see the Prophet and to live among their fellow Saints. Brigham Young wrote to his brother Joseph, "They have so much of the spirit of gathering that they would go if they knew they would die as soon as they got there or if they knew that the mob would be upon them and drive them as soon as they got there."[14] Approximately one thousand Saints emigrated early in 1841, and a

► *The* Britannia, *a six hundred ton square-rigged packet ship, carried the first organized company of Latter-day Saints to emigrate to America. Forty members left Liverpool on 6 June 1840 under the direction of Elder John Moon, whose family had accepted the gospel message from Heber C. Kimball in 1837. The Moon family formed the core of this company, which arrived in New York harbor 20 July 1840 after a forty-one day journey where they encountered three storms and considerable sickness.*

The journey from New York to St. Louis via steamboat and train required nine months, including a winter layover near Pittsburgh. From St. Louis they took a river-steamer to Montrose, Iowa, arriving 16 April 1841. Two more companies left England in 1840. The last of these went via New Orleans, a more direct and less expensive all-water route.

When Joseph Smith called Heber C. Kimball to be the first missionary to Great Britain in 1837, he said it was because the Spirit had whispered to him that something must be done to save the Church. The following chart graphically illustrates the meaning of that statement.

Over twelve thousand converts joined the Church in the British Isles from 1837–47. More than four thousand of them went to Nauvoo in at least thirty-six companies. This accounted for approximately one third to one fourth of Nauvoo's population before the exodus.

These converts brought spirituality, enthusiasm, and leadership to the Church during this critical period. By 1850 there were over thirty thousand members in Great Britain, and as their immigration to the United States increased during the pioneer period, so did their impact on the Church.

British Emigrants to Nauvoo

M. Hamlin Cannon reported the following numbers of immigrants to Nauvoo from Great Britain, which was one third of the Nauvoo population.[15]

1840	240
1841	1,135
1842	1,614
1843	769
1844	623
1845	302
1846	50
Total	**4,733**

shipping agency was soon established to oversee travel arrangements. Homes in Liverpool were purchased to house the members waiting to leave, and the *Millennial Star* began publishing detailed instructions to help the Saints prepare for the long journey. During the next decade, over ten thousand British Saints sailed to America. By 1870 there were twenty-eight thousand more, and the majority of the adult Saints in Utah were former natives of the British Isles.

The Prophet Joseph Smith wrote to the Twelve in early 1841 and instructed them to return to Nauvoo in the spring. As the time for their departure drew near, the Apostles visited the regions where they had worked to strengthen the Saints. They held a series of meetings in Manchester in early April and culminated with a general conference on 6 April. Much joy was expressed at the conference because of the bounteous harvest the Lord had blessed them with. The membership was 5,864, up nearly 2,200 since the October conference and more than 4,300 since their first conference one year earlier. This did not include those who had already emigrated. Most of the Apostles departed from England in late April and arrived in Nauvoo in July. Parley P. Pratt remained to preside over the mission and to edit the *Millennial Star*.

This mission was an important time of training and maturing for the Quorum of the Twelve Apostles. Brigham Young was able to strengthen the leadership skills that he would soon be called upon to exercise in Nauvoo, particularly following the martyrdom of Joseph Smith. Through trials and sacrifices in Britain, as well as laboring for a common goal, the Twelve were united in a way that assured the Church strong leadership in the years ahead. With the addition of Lorenzo Snow in London, four future Presidents of the Church—Presidents Young, Taylor, Woodruff, and Snow—worked together in the British Mission. Furthermore, British converts who emigrated to Nauvoo provided vital support to the Twelve following the death of Joseph Smith.

The Prophet recognized both the leadership experience gained by the Apostles and the sacrifice that they and their families had made as a result of the Twelve's mission to Britain. He recorded: "Perhaps no men ever undertook such an important mission under such peculiarly distressing and unpropitious circumstances. . . . However, notwithstanding their afflictions and trials, the Lord always interposed in their behalf, and did not suffer them to sink in the arms of death. Some way or other was made for their escape—friends rose up when they most needed them and relieved their necessities; and thus they were enabled to pursue their journey and rejoice in the Holy One of Israel. They, truly, 'went forth weeping, bearing precious seed,' but have 'returned with rejoicing, bearing their sheaves with them.' "16

Missionary work to other parts of the world was also furthered as a result of the work in Britain. The British Empire became the avenue the gospel went through into many parts of the world when British converts emigrated or traveled on business or military duty.

ORSON HYDE'S MISSION TO PALESTINE

Elder Orson Hyde had not recovered sufficiently from malaria to accompany his brethren of the Twelve in 1839 on their mission to Britain. Although he tried to do some missionary work in the United States, he could not shake off the fever and chills. He reported, "I took the ague, which lasted me for months, and which came well nigh killing me and also my family. At the April Conference in 1840, [I was] reduced to a mere skeleton."17

At that conference Orson announced that for some time the Spirit had been prompting him to proceed with a mission to the Jews that the Prophet Joseph Smith had foretold nine years earlier. He referred to a vision he had received about a month earlier wherein he had seen London, Amsterdam, Constantinople, and Jerusalem. The Spirit had said to him, "Here are many of the children of Abraham whom I will gather to the land that I gave to their fathers; and here also is the field of your labors." The Prophet Joseph called Elder Hyde and fellow Apostle, John E. Page, to go to the Jewish people in Europe and then to Palestine to dedicate the Holy Land for the return of the Jews.18

As Elders Hyde and Page traveled to the East they preached and collected funds for their mission, including money to translate the Book of Mormon and other Church literature into German, since they contemplated meeting German-speaking European Jews. Elder Page lingered somewhat in Pennsylvania, so Elder Hyde, who felt a strong urgency for the mission, continued on to New York alone. In this he was vindicated, when on 15 January 1841, Joseph Smith wrote in the *Times and Seasons* that "the

Orson Hyde (1805–78) was one of eleven children. He accepted the gospel in 1831 in Kirtland, Ohio. He was a faithful missionary during his first years in the Church and was ordained an Apostle in 1835.

He was called to go to Jerusalem in 1840. After an arduous and lengthy journey he dedicated the Holy Land from the Mount of Olives on 24 October 1841.

For a time Orson Hyde edited the Millennial Star *in England and later the* Frontier Guardian *in Iowa. After settling in Salt Lake City he participated in the colonization effort and in territorial government.*

Orson Hyde's mission to Palestine was one of the great missionary journeys of modern times. Leaving Nauvoo on 15 April 1840, Elder Hyde worked, preached, wrote, and published on three continents for nearly three years before his return 7 December 1842.

1. *Nauvoo, Illinois*
2. *Lima, Illinois*
3. *Quincy, Illinois*
4. *Columbus, Illinois*
5. *Jacksonville, Illinois*
6. *Springfield, Illinois*
7. *Indianapolis, Indiana*
8. *Dayton, Ohio*
9. *Franklin, Ohio*
10. *Cincinnati, Ohio*
11. *Wellsburgh, West Virginia*
12. *Pittsburgh, Pennsylvania*
13. *Philadelphia, Pennsylvania*
14. *New York City, New York (4 Dec. 1840)*
15. *Left New York City on ship (13 Feb. 1841)*
16. *Liverpool, England (labored in England for four months) (3 Mar. 1841)*
17. *Preston, England*
18. *Manchester, England*
19. *London, England*
20. *Left for Rotterdam, Holland (20 June 1841)*
21. *Arnhem, Germany (later became Holland)*
22. *Mainz, Germany*
23. *Frankfurt, Germany*
24. *Regensburg, Germany*
25. *Entered Black Sea from Galati*
26. *Constantinople, Turkey*
27. *Aegean Sea; boat docked at Smyrna (later Izmir, Turkey)*
28. *Beirut (now in Lebanon)*
29. *Jaffa (now part of Tel Aviv, Israel) (19 Oct. 1841)*
30. *Prayer on Mount of Olives at Jerusalem (24 Oct. 1841)*
31. *East branch of the Nile River*
32. *Dumyat, Egypt*
33. *Cairo, Egypt*
34. *West branch of the Nile River*
35. *Alexandria (Egypt)*
36. *Arrived at harbor of Trieste, Italy (21 Dec. 1841)*
37. *Over the Alps to Munich (Germany) then Regensburg (Germany)*
38. *England, undoubtedly London (Sept. 1842)*
39. *Sailed from Liverpool, England (25 Sept. 1842)*
40. *Arrived in New Orleans, Louisiana (13 Nov. 1842)*
41. *Arrived in Nauvoo, Illinois (7 Dec. 1842)*

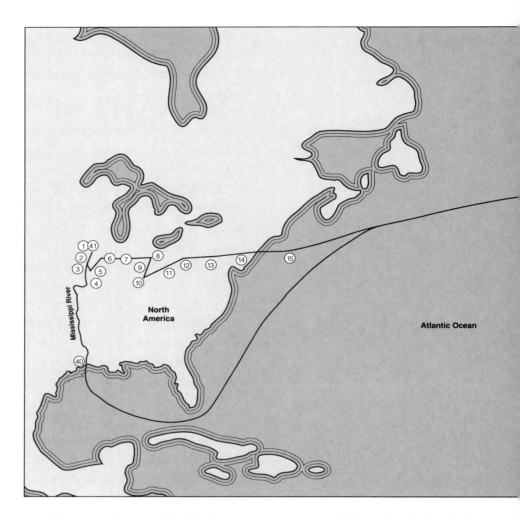

Lord is not well pleased with them in consequence of delaying their mission, (Elder John E. Page in particular,) and they are requested by the First Presidency to hasten their journey."[19] Elder Page did not respond to this message, leaving Elder Hyde no alternative but to leave for Europe without him, which he did on 13 February.

Orson Hyde spent three and a half months in England with the Twelve, and after most of them had returned to America, he wrote a brief history of the origin of the Church. While in England he contacted Jewish leaders in London. In June he visited Rotterdam, Amsterdam, and Frankfurt distributing copies of an address to the Jews before he sailed on the Danube River to the Black Sea. The trip from western Turkey to Beirut was extremely unpleasant. With only a week's worth of provisions, the ship was forced to remain at sea for nineteen days. Elder Hyde recorded, "A number of days I ate snails gathered from the rocks, while our vessel was becalmed in the midst of several small and uninhabited islands, but the greatest difficulty was, I could not get enough of them."[20] He was so weak and exhausted that he could hardly make it from the boat to the shore at Jaffa.

Elder Hyde arrived in Jerusalem on 21 October 1841. When he first

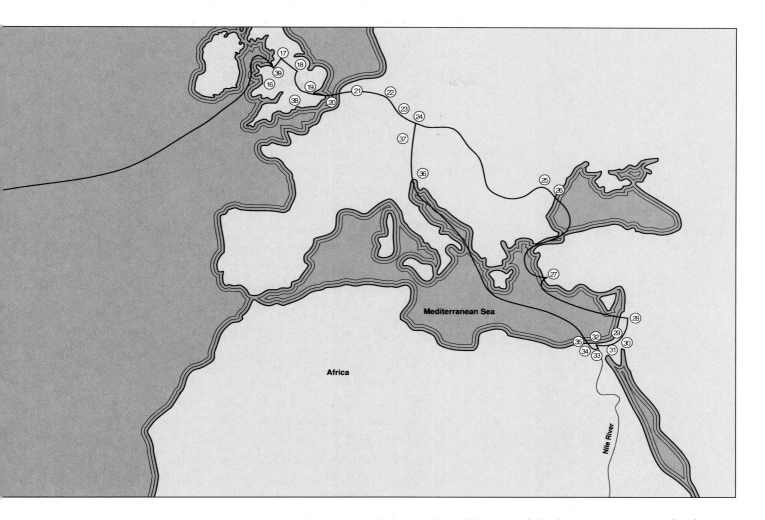

looked upon the holy city, his objective of the last nineteen months, he was moved to tears. He wrote to Parley P. Pratt that it looked "precisely according to the vision which I had."[21] Before daybreak on Sunday morning, 24 October, after several days of unsuccessful missionary work, Orson Hyde quietly passed through the open gates of Jerusalem, crossed the Kidron Valley, and climbed the Mount of Olives. As he looked below, he asked himself, "Is that city which I now look down upon really Jerusalem, whose sins and iniquities swelled the Savior's heart with grief, and drew so many tears from his pitying eye? Is that small enclosure in the valley of Kidron, where the boughs of those lonely olives are waving their green foliage so gracefully in the soft and gentle breeze, really the garden of Gethsemane, where powers infernal poured the flood of hell's dark gloom around the princely head of the immortal Redeemer?"[22]

While in this spiritual, reflective mood, "in solemn silence, with pen, ink, and paper, just as I saw in the vision," Orson Hyde wrote and offered up the prayer that officially dedicated the Holy Land for the return of the Jews and for the building of a future temple in Jerusalem. He pleaded with the Lord to "remove the barrenness and sterility of this land, and let springs of living water break forth to water its thirsty soil. Let the vine and olive produce in their strength, and the fig-tree bloom and flourish."[23] After this solemn experience, Orson erected a pile of stones as a witness of this occasion according to the ancient custom.

His mission accomplished, Elder Hyde toured some of the biblical sites and then sailed to Egypt, where he was forced to lay over at Alexandria. He met with many Jewish people there and sent a report of his mission to Parley P. Pratt, who published it in the *Millennial Star*. After arriving in Europe, he spent several months in Germany, where he published a 109-page treatise of the gospel in German entitled *A Cry Out of the Wilderness*. Orson traveled back to the United States with a company of British emigrants and arrived in Nauvoo on 7 December 1842. He had fulfilled one of the longest (twenty thousand miles), most perilous, and most significant missions in the history of the Church, one which rivals the travels of the Apostle Paul in its hardships.

MISSIONARIES TO THE PACIFIC

As soon as the Twelve returned to Nauvoo from Britain, the Prophet assigned them to direct the missionary work of the Church worldwide. The Apostles were now maturing in their ordained role. In the spring of 1843, four men were called to take the gospel to the islands of the Pacific Ocean. Two of them, Addison Pratt and Benjamin Grouard, had been sailors in the Pacific. They were joined by Noah Rogers and Knowlton Hanks. These missionaries, like the Twelve, left their wives and families behind. They sailed from New England in October 1843 and arrived in Tubuai, an island three hundred miles south of Tahiti, on 30 April 1844. Elder Hanks died of consumption (tuberculosis) during the voyage.

The missionaries intended to sail to the Sandwich Islands (Hawaii), but the islanders on Tubuai, who were already Christians and wanted a permanent minister, pleaded with Elder Pratt to remain with them. So he sent his two companions northward toward Tahiti. During his first year in Tubuai, he converted and baptized sixty people, a third of the island's population, including all but one of the few Caucasian shipbuilders on the island. Caring for the new members of the Church became a demanding responsibility as they sought him out for advice on temporal and spiritual matters.

Meanwhile, the progress in Tahiti and other islands was much slower. Representatives from the London Missionary Society carried on a campaign of misrepresentation and harassment that hindered the work. Hearing vague reports about violence against the Church in Illinois, and fearing for the safety of his family, Elder Rogers sailed for America and returned to Nauvoo in December 1845.

Elder Grouard enjoyed considerable success on the atoll of Anaa, a small part of the Tuamotus Islands east of Tahiti. He learned Tahitian and soon adapted himself to the culture of the island. Its friendly inhabitants

Addison Pratt (1802–72) was ordained a seventy in 1843 and sent with three other men to the islands of the Pacific. He arrived in Tahiti in the spring of 1844 and labored diligently until 1847. He spent a brief period in Utah and then returned to the Pacific area where he labored from 1849–52, when the French government banished the missionaries. He became disaffected from the Church upon his return and went to California, where he remained until his death.

were especially receptive to his message; within four months he baptized 35 people. At a conference of the Church on 24 September 1846, Elders Pratt and Grouard brought together members from ten branches totaling 866 people. In November, Elder Pratt left for America, hoping to return with more missionaries.

The mission of the Twelve to the British Isles, the journey of Orson Hyde to Palestine, and the opening of missionary work in the Pacific, began to fulfill the Lord's revelations to the Prophet Joseph Smith. In 1837, the Lord had promised, "Whosoever ye shall send in my name, by the voice of your brethren, the Twelve, duly recommended and authorized by you, shall have power to open the door of my kingdom unto any nation whithersoever ye shall send them" (D&C 112:21). Through the Twelve Apostles, the word of the Lord was now going out to the nations of the earth.

1. Elden Jay Watson, *Manuscript History of Brigham Young, 1801–1844* (Salt Lake City: Elden Jay Watson, 1968), p. 39.

2. Wilford Woodruff Journals, 2 July 1839, LDS Historical Department, Salt Lake City; spelling, punctuation, and capitalization standardized.

3. In Leonard J. Arrington, *Brigham Young: American Moses* (New York: Alfred A. Knopf, 1985), p. 74.

4. In Matthias F. Cowley, ed., *Wilford Woodruff* (Salt Lake City: Bookcraft, 1964), p. 109.

5. In Orson F. Whitney, *Life of Heber C. Kimball*, 3d ed. (Salt Lake City: Bookcraft, 1967), p. 266.

6. In Arrington, *Brigham Young: American Moses*, p. 77.

7. Parley P. Pratt, ed., *Autobiography of Parley P. Pratt*, Classics in Mormon Literature series (Salt Lake City: Deseret Book Co., 1985), p. 261.

8. See Wilford Woodruff Journals, "A synopsis of the travels and labours of W. Woodruff in A.D. 1840," entry following 30 Dec. 1840.

9. "Elder Woodruff's Letter," *Times and Seasons*, 1 Mar. 1841, p. 330.

10. In Cowley, *Wilford Woodruff*, p. 118.

11. In *Journal of Discourses*, 15:344.

12. In *History of the Church*, 4:222.

13. Arrington, *Brigham Young: American Moses*, p. 89.

14. In Arrington, *Brigham Young: American Moses*, p. 94; spelling standardized.

15. M. Hamlin Cannon, *Migration of English Mormons to America* (Reprint, The Church of Jesus Christ of Latter-day Saints), *American Historical Review*, Apr. 1947, pp. 436–55.

16. *History of the Church*, 4:390–91.

17. *Millennial Star*, 10 Dec. 1864, p. 792.

18. In *History of the Church*, 4:376; see also 4:106, 109.

19. *Times and Seasons*, 15 Jan. 1841, p. 287; see also *History of the Church*, 4:274.

20. *A Sketch of the Travels and Ministry of Elder Orson Hyde* (Salt Lake City: Deseret News Office, 1869), p. 24; spelling standardized.

21. *A Sketch of the Travels*, p. 20.

22. *A Sketch of the Travels*, p. 13; spelling standardized.

23. In *History of the Church*, 4:456–57; see also *A Sketch of the Travels*, pp. 20–21.

LIFE IN NAUVOO THE BEAUTIFUL

A S   T H E   Y E A R   1841 began, happiness and excitement prevailed in Nauvoo. Reports were arriving from England recounting the tremendous missionary success of the Twelve Apostles. Persecution, which the members of the Church had suffered since its founding in 1830, was at this point virtually non-existent. Furthermore, the Saints were ensured civil protection with the passage of the Nauvoo City Charter by the state legislature in December 1840.

THE LORD'S CALL TO BUILD A CITY

On 15 January 1841 the First Presidency published a proclamation to the Saints "scattered abroad" explaining and expressing appreciation for the Nauvoo Charter. The proclamation also expressed gratitude to the honorable citizens of Illinois, particularly those from the city of Quincy, who "like the good Samaritan, poured oil into our wounds, and contributed liberally to our necessities." The First Presidency also charged: "Let the brethren who love the prosperity of Zion, who are anxious that her stakes should be strengthened and her cords lengthened, and who prefer her prosperity to their chief joy, come and cast in their lots with us, and cheerfully engage in a work so glorious and sublime, and say with Nehemiah, 'We, His servants, will arise and build.' " They promised that "by a concentration of action, and a unity of effort" the Saints would see both their temporal and spiritual interests enhanced as the blessings of heaven would flow unto God's people.[1]

On 19 January the Prophet received a lengthy revelation outlining the development of Nauvoo as a "cornerstone of Zion, which shall be polished with the refinement which is after the similitude of a palace" (D&C 124:2). The Lord commanded Joseph Smith and the Saints to do many things in Nauvoo for the advancement of his kingdom. They were to publish a proclamation to the kings of the world, the president of the United States, and the governors of the several states; build a hotel to be called the Nauvoo House to accommodate strangers who would come to the city to learn about the Saints; build a temple where the Lord would reveal sacred ordinances to his people; ordain Hyrum Smith as the Patriarch to the Church to replace Joseph Smith, Sr., who had died; call William Law as second counselor in the First Presidency; organize the Nauvoo Stake with a presidency and a high council; and set in order each of the quorums of the priesthood.

Several attempts were made to write a proclamation in compliance with the Lord's commandment in Doctrine and Covenants 124, but other demands and difficulties hindered its completion. The instructions were fulfilled by the Quorum of the Twelve Apostles, and the proclamation was first published by Parley P. Pratt in April 1845.

The proclamation dealt with some of the preparations to be made for the second coming of the Lord. The Twelve testified that: (1) The kingdom of God has come with its accompanying revelation and priesthood authority. (2) The Lord has commanded the rulers and people of the nations to repent and accept baptism. (3) Many blessings come by having the gift of the Holy Ghost. (4) The American Indians, as a remnant of the tribes of Israel, were about to be gathered, civilized, and given the gospel. (5) The New Jerusalem was to be built in America. (6) The Jews were directed by the Lord to return to Jerusalem to rebuild the city and temple and create their own government. (7) The rulers of the Gentiles were to use their material means to assist in these objectives. (8) A great work lay ahead, which included an invitation to all to help, and a warning that as the work progressed no one could remain neutral toward the kingdom. And (9) the polarization would culminate in Armageddon.

The Twelve concluded with a plea to rulers and people of America to cease hindering the Saints in their work, promising that if they would help the Saints the great national blessings enjoyed heretofore would continue.

In October 1975, Elder Ezra Taft Benson, then President of the Quorum of the Twelve, reviewed and reconfirmed these invitations, predictions, and warnings in general conference.

Of all these projects, construction of the temple was the most important. This was one of the primary reasons for gathering. The Kirtland Temple, the first to be built in this dispensation, was inaccessible. Three more temples were planned in Missouri—Independence, Far West, and Adam-ondi-Ahman—but persecution and violence had prevented their construction. Therefore, the Lord excused them of this responsibility: "When I give a commandment to any of the sons of men to do a work unto my name, and those sons of men go with all their might and with all they have to perform that work, and cease not their diligence, and their enemies come upon them and hinder them from performing that work, behold, it behooveth me to require that work no more at the hands of those sons of men" (D&C 124:49).

In Nauvoo the Saints had to begin again. The First Presidency, in their proclamation to the Saints, also said that great exertions would be required of the Saints and that they would be "rejected as a church" by the Lord if they failed to accomplish the task (D&C 124:32). The Presidency wrote, "Therefore let those who can freely make a sacrifice of their time, their talents, and their property, for the prosperity of the kingdom, and for the love they have to the cause of truth, bid adieu to their homes and pleasant places of abode, and unite with us in the great work of the last days."[2]

In February the first elections were held in the city. John C. Bennett was elected mayor, and Joseph Smith and other Church leaders were elected aldermen and city councilors. Immediately the new government created the University of Nauvoo and the Nauvoo Legion, with Joseph Smith as the lieutenant general, according to the provisions of the Nauvoo Charter.

In March, Joseph Smith received another revelation: "Those who call themselves by my name and are essaying to be my saints, . . . let them gather themselves together unto the places which I shall appoint unto them by my servant Joseph, and build up cities unto my name, that they may be prepared for that which is in store for a time to come" (D&C 125:2). The first city other than Nauvoo to be built was on the Iowa side of the river. The stake there was to be called Zarahemla, after the famous city in the Book of Mormon. Several small stakes outside Nauvoo were formed during the early Nauvoo period.

BUILDING THE CITY BEAUTIFUL

The first homes in Nauvoo were huts, tents, and a few abandoned buildings. The first structures built by the Saints were frontier log cabins. As time and capital allowed, frame homes were erected and still later more substantial brick homes were built. Construction quickly became one of Nauvoo's principal industries and employed hundreds of craftsmen. Nauvoo had several brickyards to supply sufficient bricks for both homes and public buildings. To beautify their homes and surroundings, the Saints were encouraged to plant and cultivate fruit and shade trees, vines, and bushes on their large lots.

The Nauvoo Temple was the fifth temple contemplated by the early Church and the second one built. (The Independence, Far West, and Adam-ondi-Ahman, Missouri, temples were not built.) The plan and purpose were revealed to the Prophet Joseph Smith. William Weeks was the architect.

Construction took more than five years (January 1841 to May 1846) and required the efforts of many craftsmen who, because of the shortage of capital, either donated their labor as tithing or were paid with food, clothing, furniture, and other contributions of the Saints.

Here are some important dates in the history of the Nauvoo Temple:

19 Jan. 1841	Revelation commanding that the temple be built (D&C 124) was received.
6 Apr. 1841	Cornerstones were laid.
8 Nov. 1841	Basement rooms and baptismal font were dedicated.
21 Nov. 1841	First baptisms were performed.
5 Oct. 1845	General conference was held in the assembly room of the temple.
10 Dec. 1845– 7 Feb. 1846	Endowments were given.
8 Feb. 1846	Informal dedication was held by Brigham Young prior to leaving for the West.
30 Apr. 1846	Temple was privately dedicated; Joseph Young, Senior President of the Seventy offered the dedicatory prayer.
1 May 1846	Official prayer of dedication of the Nauvoo Temple was offered by Orson Hyde.
9 Oct. 1848	Interior of the temple was burned by an arsonist.
27 May 1850	Tornado demolished three of the exterior walls.
1856	Last remaining wall was leveled for safety reasons.

Of all the projects started under the Prophet's direction in Nauvoo, the one that most captured the enthusiasm of the Latter-day Saints was the temple. The hopes of the Saints centered around the temple. Its construction dominated the activities of Nauvoo for five years. At the October 1840 general conference Joseph Smith discussed the necessity of building a temple. Three brethren who had worked on the Kirtland Temple—Reynolds Cahoon, Alpheus Cutler, and Elias Higbee—were appointed as a committee to supervise the construction. The plans of architect William Weeks were approved by Joseph Smith, who thereafter gave strict attention to construction and architectural details.

Immediately workmen began the excavation for the temple's foundation. A stone quarry was opened on the outskirts of the city and was kept in nearly continuous operation. Solid blocks of limestone from four to six feet in diameter were roughly cut, to be polished later at the temple site. On 6 April 1841, Joseph Smith presided over the laying of the cornerstones for the temple.

The temple was built largely by donated labor. In February, Nauvoo was divided into *wards* for political purposes and also to better organize the work force. In nineteenth century America a *ward* was a term used for a political subdivision. Each ward was assigned a particular day for working on the temple. Most able-bodied men in Nauvoo contributed work either in the quarry or on the temple, often donating one day in ten as tithing labor. The women served by sewing clothing and preparing meals for the workmen.

In addition to the baptistery in the basement, the Nauvoo Temple had two main assembly rooms on the second and third floors with offices in the half stories on each side of the central arch. The assembly rooms had a series of pulpits at each end similar to those in the Kirtland Temple. Reversible benches allowed the worshipers to face either direction, according to the purpose of meeting. Meetings were often held here. The attic floor was devoted to offices and dressing and ordinance rooms.

The building was 128 feet long, 88 feet wide, and 60 feet from ground level to roof. The tower was another 98 1/2 feet above the eaves. It was constructed primarily of gray limestone from several quarries in the vicinity. Among its unique features were the sun, moon, and star stones decorating the thirty pilasters and the frieze.

Monetary donations were solicited from all the Latter-day Saints. Each member was expected to contribute one-tenth of all he possessed at the commencement of the construction and one-tenth of all increase from that time until its completion. Donors and the amount of their contributions were logged into a special book called the Book of the Law of the Lord.

Timber for the interior and the roof of the building, as well as for the Nauvoo House, was brought from the forests of Wisconsin via the Black River, a tributary of the Mississippi. A sizeable contingent of brethren led by Bishop George Miller went to the "pineries" and felled, cut, and rafted thousands of board feet of lumber down the river to Nauvoo.

The Prophet considered the construction of the Nauvoo House hotel nearly as urgent as construction of the temple. He envisioned it as a means for the Saints to entertain and teach the truth to "men of wealth, character and influence."[3] The cornerstone of the building was laid on 2 October 1841, and several valuable records, including the original Book of Mormon manuscript, were deposited in it. The brethren were constantly encouraged from the pulpit to work on the hotel; however, work progressed slowly because means and labor were meager. In March 1844 Joseph Smith postponed further construction on the hotel in order to press forward on the temple.

With the rapid growth of the city, the need for other public buildings increased. The Red Brick Store was constructed as an office for Joseph Smith and the First Presidency and as a business to help the Prophet support his family. The three-story Masonic hall, also called the cultural hall, was used for theatrical productions, concerts, Masonic ceremonies, political gatherings, art exhibits, funerals, banquets, and court sessions. Church, military, and police meetings were also held in this impressive building. The Seventies Hall was begun in the fall of 1843, and it was ready for dedication a year later. This two-story structure provided a place where the seventies, who were the missionary force of the Church, could meet and be trained. The first floor was filled with beautiful pews and a pulpit; the second floor contained an office, a small museum, and a library of 675 volumes.

Nauvoo City Government

The growth of Nauvoo was helped immeasurably by the liberal provisions of the Nauvoo Charter. The city council established a disciplined police force and passed ordinances for the efficient administration of the city. Laws were created guaranteeing the right of assembly and freedom of worship for individuals of all religious persuasions. The council implemented plans to drain the swamps and set up a public works program to provide employment and promote the construction of homes, hotels, stores, and other buildings. They also passed an ordinance prohibiting the sale of liquor in the city and established laws controlling public events in order to avoid any immoral or obscene exhibition.

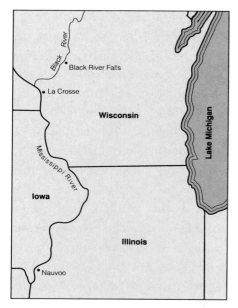

During the Nauvoo period Latter-day Saints brought lumber for the Mansion House, the interior of the temple, and other buildings from the Wisconsin "pineries" in the Black River Falls and vicinity. Operations began there in 1841. The small Mormon settlements of Mormon Coulee and St. Joseph were located just southeast of La Crosse. A sawmill in Melrose, between Black River Falls and La Crosse, and later another one fifteen miles closer to the logging operations, was purchased.

Logs were cut on the banks of the Black River and its tributaries and were floated to the sawmills. Some lumber was sold on the open market, but most of it was loaded onto rafts and floated more than five hundred miles down the Mississippi River to Nauvoo.

About 150 men worked in the forests in the spring and summer of 1842. The first raft with 50,000 board feet of pine arrived in May 1842. In 1843 more than 600,000 board feet, including hewed timbers, shingles, and barn boards, were cut. Operations in the summer of 1844 were hindered by financial problems, disputes with Indians over land claims, and the death of Joseph Smith. Nevertheless, two rafts totalling 155,000 board feet were sent to Nauvoo that year.

Establishment of the Nauvoo Legion and the city militia was of great importance. Because of their bitter experiences in Missouri, Latter-day Saints had an understandable mistrust of state militia forces. Although nominally part of the Illinois state militia and technically under the direction of the governor, the legion operated legally (according to the Charter) under local control. It enacted its own regulations and conducted its own internal and organizational affairs. The militia included able-bodied males between eighteen and forty-five years of age. It was organized into two cohorts, or brigades, one of infantry and the other of cavalry. Each cohort was commanded by a brigadier general, and the entire body was under the command of Lieutenant General Joseph Smith. At its peak the Nauvoo Legion numbered three thousand men.

Parades and military demonstrations staged by the legion drew considerable attention throughout western Illinois. One Latter-day Saint recalled, "Some of the most impressive moments of my life were, when I saw the 'Nauvoo Legion' on parade with the Prophet, then Gen. Joseph Smith, with his wife, Emma Hale Smith, on horseback at the head of the troops. It was indeed, an imposing sight, and one that I shall always remember. He so fair, and she so dark, in their beautiful riding-habits. . . . He also wore a sword at his side. His favorite riding-horse was named Charlie, a big black steed."[4]

ECONOMIC GROWTH IN NAUVOO

As in other American cities at that time, agriculture was the main economic enterprise in Nauvoo and surrounding Latter-day Saint communities. Most families with an acre of property in the city maintained a garden with fruit trees, grapevines, and vegetables. Poorer Saints farmed or gardened in the "big field," a community farm located on the outskirts of the city. The Big Field Association regulated the crops to be planted and the acreage to be cultivated. Other farmers outside the city or in outlying communities, such as Ramus, Lima, or Yelrome, sowed wheat, oats, rye, and potatoes and kept cattle, sheep, and hogs.

With the rapid influx of immigrants eager to build homes, cultivate the soil, set up businesses, or practice their trades, Nauvoo quickly became a bustling and productive community. This was in stark contrast to the rest of Illinois, which was suffering under an economic depression. In Nauvoo there were many small shops and factories: sawmills, several brickyards, a lime kiln, a tool factory, printing offices, flour mills, bakeries, tailor shops, blacksmith shops, shoe shops, a carpenter's and joiner's shop, and cabinetmaker's shops. These shops sprang up everywhere and anywhere in the city, since there were no zoning laws. Nauvoo craftsmen produced matches, leather goods, rope and cord, gloves, bonnets, pottery, jewelry, and watches.

Like the artisans of other American communities, Nauvoo's workers often banded together according to occupations to set prices, establish standards, and police their particular vocation. At least eighteen such

Construction of the Nauvoo House, a Church-owned hotel on the banks of the Mississippi in Nauvoo, was commanded by the Lord in Doctrine and Covenants 124. When the cornerstone was laid on 2 October 1841, Joseph Smith deposited the original manuscript of the Book of Mormon in it. Work proceeded vigorously for a while, but because of the tension aroused by anti-Mormon sentiment, building efforts were concentrated on the temple, and the Nauvoo House was never completed.

After the Martyrdom, the bodies of Joseph and Hyrum were temporarily buried in the basement of the Nauvoo House. Emma Smith's second husband, Louis Bidamon, completed a house on a portion of the foundation. In 1882 he found and opened the cornerstone. Much of the Book of Mormon manuscript was badly deteriorated. Throughout the years he gave portions of it to visitors who came to Nauvoo. The Church now has over 140 pages of the original manuscript.

associations came into being in Nauvoo, including the important Nauvoo House Association, the Botanic Association, the Nauvoo Coach and Carriage Manufacturing Association, the Tailors, Potters, Bricklayers, and finally the successful Nauvoo Agriculture and Manufacturing Association.

Since land and buildings were the chief assets in Nauvoo, buying, selling, and exchanging land became one of the city's major businesses. During his first two years in Nauvoo, the Prophet was heavily engaged in real estate transactions as the Church treasurer and later the trustee-in-trust. Since Church members had little or no money, they often obtained land in exchange for title to property they owned in Missouri or Ohio. Eventually private investors sold and traded land to new arrivals, especially on the bluffs in the eastern part of the city where the temple was being built. Since the Church owned most of the lowlands, leaders encouraged the Saints to buy lots and establish businesses there so the Church could divest itself of the land and pay its debts. Some landowners on the bluffs accused the Church of unfair competition and argued that it was healthier to live on the higher ground. Gradually seeds of jealousy over these and other problems led some members to apostatize from the Church.

EDUCATION AND SOCIETY IN NAUVOO

The interest in education that had been manifest in Kirtland was expanded in Nauvoo. Private schools preceded the more extensive public efforts that resulted from the passage of the Nauvoo Charter. At least eighty-one people—forty-eight men and thirty-three women—made part of their living teaching in Nauvoo. Over eighteen hundred students were enrolled in school. The school year was divided into terms that usually lasted three months. Eli B. Kelsey taught and directed the largest public school of well over one hundred students. The cost of attending school in

Orson Spencer (1802–55) was born in Massachusetts. He was highly educated for his time, graduating from Union College in Schenectady, New York, in 1824. After teaching briefly and studying law, he turned his attention to religion and in 1829 graduated from a theological college in Hamilton, New York. He was a minister for twelve years before accepting the restored gospel in 1841.

During the Nauvoo exodus, his wife died leaving him with six children under the age of thirteen. In the midst of these trials he was called to serve as mission president in England in 1847. He served there for two years and also edited the Millennial Star. *He was appointed chancellor of the newly founded University of Deseret in Utah in 1850. He served in the territorial legislature and later went on several missions, including one to Prussia, Germany, and another to the Cherokee Indians.*

Nauvoo ranged from $1.50 to $3.00 per term, and some of the scholars paid tuition with produce.[5]

The pinnacle of Nauvoo's education system was the University of the City of Nauvoo. Because of other building priorities, however, a campus was never constructed. University classes convened in private homes and public buildings. The faculty included Parley P. Pratt, professor of English, mathematics, and sciences; Orson Pratt, professor of English literature and mathematics; Orson Spencer, professor of foreign languages; Sidney Rigdon, professor of Church history; and Gustavus Hills, professor of music. Orson Pratt was the most popular professor. He offered courses in arithmetic, algebra, geometry, trigonometry, surveying, navigation, analytical geometry, calculus, philosophy, astronomy, and chemistry. Irregular schedules and the lack of a full-time faculty and a campus meant the university was only in its initial stages of development when the Saints were forced to leave Illinois. Nevertheless an important precedent was set for the involvement of the Church in higher education in the future.

Education for many of the Saints in Nauvoo came through public lectures and debates. Many traveling lecturers spoke in Nauvoo on such diverse topics as phrenology (the pseudo-science of character-reading from the shape of the cranium) and geology. The Nauvoo Lyceum conducted regular debates on current issues. The Saints also established a museum from the contributions of missionaries and other travelers. Addison Pratt made the first contribution. Some of the items he contributed were a whale's tooth, coral, and the jawbone of a porpoise.[6]

The chief source of news in Nauvoo was the newspaper. The Saints had published newspapers in Missouri and Ohio. During the siege in Missouri, Church leaders buried the printing press used for the *Elders' Journal.* It was recovered in 1839 and brought to Nauvoo where it was used to print the *Times and Seasons* starting in November of that year. As the official publication of the Church, the *Times and Seasons* was carefully controlled and supervised by the Prophet.

During its brief history, the *Times and Seasons* published significant doctrinal items and policy statements, including parts of Joseph Smith's official history, portions of the book of Moses, and the book of Abraham, which were all later included in the Pearl of Great Price. The paper also featured conference addresses, circular letters from the Council of the Twelve Apostles, minutes of important Church meetings, reprints from other newspapers, and the King Follett Discourse. There were dozens of articles on the Book of Mormon including items on archaeological evidence and discussion of geographical locations.

Nauvoo also had a weekly non-religious newspaper devoted to agriculture, business, science, art, and community events. When it first appeared in April 1842 it was known as the *Wasp,* but the name was later changed to the *Nauvoo Neighbor.* It was printed on the same press as the *Times and Seasons*

The Saints were kept informed of local, state, and national news through the columns of three newspapers during the Nauvoo period. The Times and Seasons was devoted primarily to Church matters, while the Prophet's brother William served as editor of the Wasp, a more secular newspaper that advocated the cause of the Saints. Later the Nauvoo Neighbor replaced the Wasp.

The cultural hall was dedicated in April 1844. Something of a public building, it housed musical and theatrical productions and other cultural activities as well as city council and other meetings. It also served as the Nauvoo Masonic lodge. Originally it was a three-story building, but the third story was taken off sometime after 1880. Since acquiring it in 1962 the Church has restored the building, including the third story.

and was edited by William Smith, brother of the Prophet. Later John Taylor was assigned the editorial responsibility.

Nauvoo's residents, like other Americans, had some time for and enjoyed participating in recreational activities. They attended the theater (in the cultural hall), lectures, balls, or dancing schools, sang in one of three choirs, performed in one of three brass bands, bowled, played ball, pulled sticks, wrestled, and watched prairie fires. Joseph Smith especially liked to pull sticks and wrestle and was widely hailed as one of the best at both. Wood cutting and quilting bees, cooperative barn and house building, fishing, picking wild berries, braiding, and weaving were practical as well as recreational pastimes that were also popular.

Death and disease continued to plague Nauvoo even after the swamps were drained and the fever and ague diminished. Almost half of the reported deaths in Nauvoo were among children under the age of ten. Death often hit a family more than once, sometimes taking both parents. Diseases that attacked and often killed the Saints were diarrhea, canker, measles, mumps, whooping cough, the bloody flux, consumption, and diphtheria. Letters to loved ones frequently spoke of sickness, death, and suffering.

Writing to her husband, John Taylor, while he was still serving his mission in England, Leonora Taylor reported, "This has been a distressed place since you left, with sickness. Almost every individual in every family [is] sick; George [John Taylor's son] got well of his fever but has a little sore on the edge of the sight in his eye that has given me great anxiety."[7] Bathsheba Smith wrote the following in 1842 to her missionary husband, George A. Smith, concerning their son: "George Albert was sick last Saturday and Sunday. He had quite a fever. I was very uneasy about him. I was afraid he was going to have the fever. I took him to the font and had him baptized and since then he has not had any fever. He is about well now."[8]

Nauvoo letters did not dwell exclusively on sickness, death, and suffering. Public events, progress with gardening, and current events in the Church were just a few of the other topics. Bathsheba Smith's confession of loneliness for her beloved George A. is a good example of the frequent expressions of affection that were part of nearly every letter: "I should be pleased to spend this afternoon with you. It seems to me I could not wish to enjoy my self better than to sit under the sound of your rich and lovely voice and hear you unfold the rich treasure of your mind. Even the sound of your footstep would be music in my ear."[9]

CHURCH ORGANIZATION EXPANDS

As thousands of Saints gathered to Nauvoo and surrounding communities, new organizational needs emerged. The three major stakes in the area, Nauvoo, Iowa (Zarahemla), and Ramus (Illinois), were provided with an organization consisting of a presidency and high council. In addition, the

Iowa and the Ramus stakes had a bishop to oversee the care of the poor and see to other essential welfare needs. In Nauvoo three bishops were originally assigned to serve the needy within the three municipal wards of the community. By August of 1842 the rapid influx of immigrants led to the restructuring of the city into ten wards with three additional wards on the outskirts. With the needs of the incoming Saints in mind, bishops were appointed for each ward. There was no ward ecclesiastical organization nor was there any idea of a ward congregation. Sunday services and priesthood quorums functioned at a stake or a general Church level.

Priesthood quorums were reconstituted in Nauvoo. There was one elders quorum, with John A. Hicks serving as president. The high priests quorum was presided over by Don Carlos Smith. Three seventies quorums, organized prior to Nauvoo, were primarily designed to provide a pool of missionaries. Thus the seventies were the largest of the Melchizedek Priesthood groups during the Nauvoo period. As such they constructed their own building, the impressive Seventies Hall on Parley Street, and were active in missionary and educational pursuits. Several more seventies quorums were organized following the Prophet's death.

When the Apostles returned from their mission to Great Britain, Joseph Smith gave them additional responsibility in the Church organizational structure. At a special conference on 16 August 1841, the Prophet announced that the Twelve were to remain at home where they could support their families, relieve the First Presidency of some financial duties, and attend to the needs of the many immigrants. Joseph said that while they would continue to direct missionary work, "the time had come when the Twelve should be called upon to stand in their place next to the First Presidency."[10] Previously the Twelve had operated as a traveling high council and had no jurisdiction where there were organized stakes with their own high councils. As a result, in the minds of many, the high councils sometimes rivaled the Twelve in authority. But now the Twelve became General Authorities over the stakes as well as over the missions. By the time the Prophet was martyred, he had trained the Twelve Apostles and blessed them with the keys of the kingdom, so that they were fully able to take over the leadership of the Church.

Latter-day Saint women were blessed with a new Church organization during the Nauvoo era. It had its inception when several women, led by Sarah M. Kimball, organized to make shirts for the men working on the temple. They drafted a plan of government typical of women's groups at that time, but when Joseph Smith was consulted, he offered to organize the women after the same pattern as the priesthood. Under his direction and at a gathering of eighteen women, the Female Relief Society of Nauvoo was organized on 17 March 1842. Emma Smith was selected as its president, thus, according to Joseph, fulfilling an earlier revelation identifying her as an

Plate depicting the organization meeting of the Relief Society. Beginning in Kirtland when the women of the Church united to make the veils of the Kirtland Temple, they drew the praises of Joseph Smith for being foremost in good works.

On Thursday afternoon, 17 March 1842 in Nauvoo the Prophet, in company with John Taylor and Willard Richards, formally organized the eighteen women present into a society. Joseph Smith stated, "The Church was never perfectly organized until the women were thus organized."[11] Emma Smith was called to be the first president with Sarah M. Cleveland and Elizabeth Ann Whitney as counselors and Eliza R. Snow as secretary.

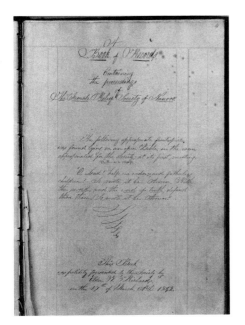

Title page of the minute book of the first Relief Society, entitled A Book of Records Containing the proceedings of the Female Relief Society of Nauvoo, *and containing a note "appropriate for the Society" taken from a scrap found in an old Bible in the room.*

The note reads "O, Lord! help our widows, and fatherless children! So mote it be. Amen. With the sword, *and the* word of truth, *defend thou them. So mote it be. Amen."*

"elect lady" (D&C 25:3). The organization's objective was "the relief of the poor, the destitute, the widow and the orphan, and for the exercise of all benevolent purposes."[12]

On 28 April the Prophet gave the sisters additional counsel and promises. He advised the women to treat their husbands "with mildness and affection" and to meet them with a "smile instead of an argument or a murmur," reminding them that when a mind is in despair it needs the "solace of affection and kindness." After promising that they would receive appropriate instruction through the order of the priesthood, he said, "I now turn the key in your behalf in the name of the Lord, and this Society shall rejoice, and knowledge and intelligence shall flow down from this time henceforth; this is the beginning of better days to the poor and needy, who shall be made to rejoice and pour forth blessings on your heads."[13]

Although at that time Latter-day Saint women had to apply to become members, the Relief Society was very popular and grew rapidly. Membership had grown to over thirteen hundred women at the time of Joseph Smith's death. Because of the crisis created by the Martyrdom and the exodus to and settlement in the West, there were few Relief Society meetings until the organization was revived in 1867.

Since worship was not conducted on a ward basis, it centered around the public ministry of the Prophet and private family devotions. When weather permitted, Sunday meetings were held in a grove west of the temple where several thousand people could be accommodated. Church authorities sat on a portable platform, while the audience rested on bricks, split logs, or on the grass. Sabbath worship usually included a spiritual meeting in the morning and an afternoon business meeting. The Saints loved to hear their Prophet speak and were faithful in attending these public services, but it was a strenuous exercise for him to speak for several hours to the vast audience in the open air. At times his voice gave out temporarily and he called others to take his place. Many of his sermons were recorded and provide an important source of doctrine and guidance for the Church today.

Families often met in their homes and enjoyed hot bread or other refreshments while listening to testimonies, counsel from the family head, and missionary reports. Private religious life in Nauvoo also included fasting and prayer, singing hymns, and administering to the sick. Even social events had a religious aspect and played a great role in uniting the Saints and fostering their way of life.

Life in Nauvoo was generally typical of life in American cities of the nineteenth century. But there were some unique aspects. Perhaps its greatest difference was that most of its citizens' fondest hopes centered on gathering together according to the principles of Zion, building their holy temple, learning the doctrines of salvation, and seeking the blessings of the Almighty.

ENDNOTES

1. Joseph Smith, Hyrum Smith, and Sidney Rigdon, in *History of the Church*, 4:267, 271–72.

2. Smith, Smith, and Rigdon, in *History of the Church*, 4:273.

3. *History of the Church*, 5:328; see also 5:137.

4. "A Sketch of the Life of Eunice Billings Snow," *Woman's Exponent*, Sept. 1910, p. 22.

5. See Paul Thomas Smith, "A Historical Study of the Nauvoo, Illinois, Public School System, 1841–1845," Master's thesis, Brigham Young University, 1969, pp. 82–98.

6. See *History of the Church*, 5:406.

7. In Ronald K. Esplin, "Sickness and Faith, Nauvoo Letters," *Brigham Young University Studies*, Summer 1975, p. 427; spelling and capitalization standardized.

8. In Kenneth W. Godfrey, Audrey M. Godfrey, and Jill Mulvay Derr, *Women's Voices* (Salt Lake City: Deseret Book Co., 1982), pp. 122–23; spelling and capitalization standardized.

9. In Godfrey, Godfrey, and Derr, *Women's Voices*, p. 125.

10. Brigham Young, in *History of the Church*, 4:403.

11. "Story of the Organization of the Relief Society," *Relief Society Magazine*, Mar. 1919, p. 129.

12. *History of the Church*, 4:567.

13. In *History of the Church*, 4:606–7.

DOCTRINAL DEVELOPMENTS IN NAUVOO

NAUVOO EXPANDED AND FLOURISHED, but the most important thing that happened in this period was the continuous flow of revelations through the Prophet Joseph Smith concerning gospel doctrines and ordinances. During the Nauvoo years, the Prophet exhibited an increasing spiritual maturity as he led the Saints to new and higher gospel insights. Many concepts that had been introduced were now given fuller attention and explanation. Joseph Smith promised in the October 1841 general conference that "the dispensation of the fullness of times will bring to light the things that have been revealed in all former dispensations; also other things that have not been before revealed."[1] In the earlier years of the Restoration the foundation of doctrine was laid; in the Nauvoo period the foundation was built upon.

BAPTISM FOR THE DEAD

On 10 August 1840, Seymour Brunson, one of the first settlers of Nauvoo, died. He had been one of the earliest missionaries in the Church and had served on the high council in Far West and Nauvoo. Joseph Smith's history states that Brunson "died in the triumph of faith, and in his dying moments bore testimony to the Gospel that he had embraced."[2] In a powerful funeral sermon delivered on 15 August, the Prophet read much of 1 Corinthians 15, including verse 29 which refers to the practice of baptism for the dead. Joseph announced to the congregation that the Lord would permit the Saints to be baptized in behalf of their friends and relatives who had departed this life. He told the Saints that "the plan of salvation was calculated to save all who were willing to obey the requirements of the law of God."[3]

Following the sermon, Jane Neyman asked Harvey Olmstead to baptize her in the Mississippi River in behalf of her deceased son, Cyrus. Joseph Smith asked what words were used in performing the ordinance, and then he approved what had taken place. In the ensuing weeks, several more baptisms for the dead were performed in the river or in nearby streams. On 19 January 1841, the Lord commanded the Saints to build a temple with a baptismal font for these vicarious ordinances. The Lord stated that baptism for the dead "belongeth to my house, and cannot be acceptable to me, only in the days of your poverty, wherein ye are not able to build a house unto me" (D&C 124:30).

This revelation generated considerable enthusiasm, and work on the

The Old Testament describes a large basin resting on twelve oxen used in conjunction with the temple in the days of Solomon (see 1 Kings 7:23–25). When the Nauvoo Temple was built, the Prophet Joseph Smith directed that the baptismal font be built in the basement on the backs of twelve oxen, which represented the twelve tribes of Israel.

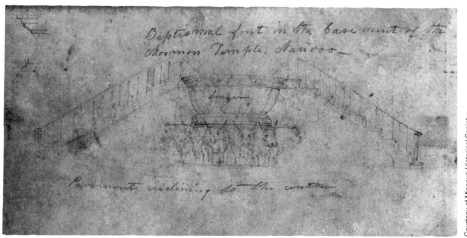

temple progressed quickly. On 3 October 1841, as the basement neared completion, Joseph Smith declared, "There shall be no more baptisms for the dead, until the ordinance can be attended to in the Lord's House."[4] The basement housed a temporary baptismal font built by Elijah Fordham. It was made from Wisconsin pine and mounted on twelve carefully crafted oxen. On 8 November the font was dedicated by Brigham Young. It was first used two weeks later when Elders Brigham Young, Heber C. Kimball, and John Taylor performed forty baptisms for the dead; Elders Willard Richards, Wilford Woodruff, and George A. Smith performed the confirmations.

In 1842, while forced into temporary exile by old Missouri enemies, the Prophet wrote two general epistles to the Saints on the doctrine of baptism for the dead. Both emphasized the importance of having a recorder present for the baptisms to be valid. The recorder was to see that each ordinance was performed correctly and to make an accurate record. The first letter stated, "Let all the records be had in order, that they may be put in the archives of my holy temple, to be held in remembrance from generation to generation, saith the Lord of Hosts" (D&C 127:9).

In the second and longer of the two letters the Prophet explained that the living and the dead are dependent upon each other for salvation. "They [the dead] without us cannot be made perfect—neither can we without our dead be made perfect" (D&C 128:15). The ordinances to help accomplish this mutual perfection, he later explained, include not only baptism for the dead, but also the endowment of the holy priesthood and marriage for time and eternity.

THE ENDOWMENT

Earlier as the Saints in Ohio were preparing to build the Kirtland Temple, the Lord had promised that in his house he would "endow those whom I have chosen with power from on high" (D&C 95:8). As that temple was completed and dedicated in early 1836, there was a great spiritual outpouring upon the Saints. The Savior appeared and accepted the temple. The ancient prophets Moses, Elias, and Elijah then appeared to Joseph Smith and Oliver Cowdery and restored keys of the priesthood for the gathering of Israel and the introduction of additional sacred ordinances (see D&C 110).

Temples were planned in Missouri but never constructed because persecution drove the faithful from the state. After Nauvoo was established as the new gathering place, the Lord revealed that a temple was needed because there was no place on earth where he could come and restore "the fulness of the priesthood" (D&C 124:28). The Saints were also instructed that their washings and anointings, like their baptisms for the dead, should be performed in a sacred place, hence the command to build the Nauvoo Temple. The revelation continued: "Let this house be built unto my name, that I may reveal mine ordinances therein unto my people;

"For I deign to reveal unto my church things which have been kept hid from before the foundation of the world, things that pertain to the dispensation of the fulness of times" (vv. 40–41).

As work on the temple progressed, Joseph Smith sought and received additional instructions from the Lord regarding the sacred endowment. However, it is not known exactly when he received all the instructions pertaining to the temple ordinances. He introduced these ordinances to a

Joseph Smith's red brick store was perhaps the most important building in the Church throughout the Nauvoo period because in addition to being a general store it served as the center of social, economic, political, and religious activity. Completed in December 1841, it was opened for business on 5 January 1842.

On the second floor Joseph Smith maintained an office, which became the headquarters for the Church. Prior to the completion of the temple, the upper floor of the store was used as an ordinance room, and the first endowments were given there. Church and civic meetings of various kinds were held at the store, including a public school and some youth meetings.

On 17 March 1842 the Relief Society was organized there with Emma Smith as the first president. The store was torn down in 1890, and for many years visitors could see only the foundation. In 1978–79 the building was rebuilt by the Reorganized Church of Jesus Christ of Latter Day Saints.

few trusted Latter-day Saints in the upper room of his red brick store on 4 May 1842. At that time it was virtually the only large place in Nauvoo where a group could assemble in privacy. The building was near the Mississippi River about a block west of the Mansion House and the Homestead. It was constructed in 1841 and opened for business in January 1842. Most of the second floor was an assembly room used for priesthood councils, the organization and meetings of the Female Relief Society of Nauvoo, municipal and Masonic meetings, school classes, theatrical presentations, debates, lectures, and staff meetings of the Nauvoo Legion.

The sign that hung on Joseph Smith's office in Nauvoo. The sign is painted tin and measures four-by-fourteen inches. It reads "Joseph Smith's Office. President of the church of JESUS Christ of LATTER day Saints."[5]

Development of doctrine relating to the temple as revealed to the Prophet Joseph Smith

21 Sept. 1823   Moroni reiterated Malachi's promise about the coming of Elijah and said he was to "reveal" the priesthood (see D&C 2; Joseph Smith— History 1:38–39).

Dec. 1830   First reference was made to temples in modern revelation (see D&C 36:8).

2 Jan. 1831   The Lord directed the Church to move to Ohio where they were to be "endowed with power from on high" (D&C 38:32).

20 July 1831   The Lord designated Jackson County, Missouri, as the site for his temple (see D&C 57:2–3).

16 Feb. 1832   The vision of the degrees of glory was received (see D&C 76).

Dec. 1832   The commandment to build the Kirtland Temple was given (see D&C 88:119).

21 Jan. 1836   Joseph saw his brother Alvin, who had died without baptism, in the celestial kingdom and was told that those who would have received the gospel here will inherit the celestial kingdom hereafter (see D&C 137).

27 Mar. 1836   The Kirtland Temple was dedicated (see D&C 109; History of the Church, 2:410–28).

3 Apr. 1836   The Savior, Moses, Elias, and Elijah came to the Kirtland Temple to accept the temple and restore the keys of the priesthood (see D&C 110).

15 Aug. 1840   The doctrine of baptism for the dead was first taught at the funeral of Seymour Brunson, who died 10 August 1840 (see History of the Church, 4:179, 231).

On 3 May, with the help of others, the Prophet arranged his office and Assembly Room to represent "the interior of a temple as much as the circumstances would permit."[6] On the afternoon of the following day the Prophet administered the first endowments to a select group, which included Hyrum Smith, Church patriarch; Brigham Young, Heber C. Kimball, and Willard Richards of the Twelve Apostles; Newel K. Whitney, general bishop; George Miller, president of the Nauvoo high priest's quorum and a general bishop; and James Adams, president of the Springfield Branch.[7]

Joseph Smith reported this significant event: "I spent the day in the upper part of the store . . . instructing them in the principles and order of the Priesthood, attending to washings, anointings, endowments and the communication of keys pertaining to the Aaronic Priesthood, and so on to the highest order of the Melchizedek Priesthood, setting forth the order pertaining to the Ancient of Days, and all those plans and principles by which any one is enabled to secure the fullness of those blessings which have been prepared for the Church of the First Born, and come up and abide in the presence of the Elohim in the eternal worlds."[8]

The Lord had pronounced these ordinances necessary to open the gate to eternal life and exaltation. Thus they were sought after by faithful Latter-day Saints. Gradually over the next two years, Joseph Smith introduced the endowment to approximately ninety men and women. He also gave particular instructions to the Twelve Apostles concerning the keys of these ordinances, instructing them to give the endowment to the worthy Saints in the temple when it was completed. By December 1845 the temple was sufficiently complete to perform the ordinance.

Many years later in Salt Lake City, President Brigham Young instructed the Saints on the significance of the endowment in the latter days. He reminded them that the first elders received only a portion of their endowments in the Kirtland Temple, terming them "introductory, or initiatory ordinances, preparatory to an endowment." He then defined the meaning of *endowment:* "Your *endowment* is, to receive all those ordinances in the House of the Lord, which are necessary for you, after you have departed this life, to enable you to walk back to the presence of the Father, passing the angels who stand as sentinels, being enabled to give them the key words, the signs and tokens, pertaining to the Holy Priesthood, and gain your eternal exaltation in spite of earth and hell."[9]

REVELATIONS ON MARRIAGE

The endowment of the holy priesthood is closely associated with the principle of eternal marriage. From the beginning of the Restoration, Latter-day Saints have been taught that "marriage is ordained of God unto man" (D&C 49:15). The marriage covenant has always been understood to be of great importance. Men in the Church are directed, "Thou shalt love thy wife with all thy heart, and shalt cleave unto her and none else" (D&C 42:22). Church members are not only charged to marry in righteousness, but to have children and to rear them according to the precepts of the gospel of Jesus Christ.

Shortly after the introduction of the endowment the Prophet revealed that a married couple could be sealed together by the power of the priesthood for time and all eternity. Many of the men and women who were endowed were also sealed by Joseph Smith to their spouses in the marriage covenant. Joseph taught that the marriage sealing, the endowment, and baptisms for the dead were to be performed in the house of the Lord and that these ordinances would be made available to all faithful Saints as soon as the temple was completed.

In the spring of 1843, Joseph Smith taught the eternal importance of the marriage covenant. While visiting the Mormon village of Ramus, twenty miles southeast of Nauvoo, the Prophet explained to a few members of the Church:

"In the celestial glory there are three heavens or degrees;

"And in order to obtain the highest, a man must enter into this order of the priesthood [meaning the new and everlasting covenant of marriage];

"And if he does not, he cannot obtain it" (D&C 131:1–3).

Later that summer Joseph recorded a revelation on marriage that incorporated principles that had been revealed to him as early as 1831 in Kirtland. In it the Lord declared, "If a man marry a wife by my word, which is my law, and by the new and everlasting covenant, and it is sealed unto them by the Holy Spirit of promise, by him who is anointed, unto whom I have appointed this power and the keys of this priesthood . . . [it] shall be of full force when they are out of the world; and they shall pass by the angels, and the gods, which are set there, to their exaltation and glory in all things, as hath been sealed upon their heads, which glory shall be a fulness and a continuation of the seeds forever and ever" (D&C 132:19).

The law of celestial marriage, as outlined in this revelation, also included the principle of the plurality of wives. In 1831 as Joseph Smith labored on the inspired translation of the holy scriptures, he asked the Lord how he justified the practice of plural marriage among the Old Testament patriarchs. This question resulted in the revelation on celestial marriage, which included an answer to his question about the plural marriages of the patriarchs.[10]

First the Lord explained that for any covenant, including marriage, to be valid in eternity it must meet three requirements (see D&C 132:7): (1) It must be "made and entered into and sealed by the Holy Spirit of promise." (2) It must be performed by the proper priesthood authority. (3) It must be by "revelation and commandment" through the Lord's anointed prophet (see also vv. 18–19). Using Abraham as an example, the Lord said he "received all things, whatsoever he received, by revelation and commandment, by my word" (v. 29). Consequently, the Lord asked, "Was Abraham, therefore, under condemnation? Verily I say unto you, Nay; for I, the Lord, commanded it" (v. 35).

Moreover, Joseph Smith and the Church were to accept the principle of plural marriage as part of the restoration of all things (see v. 45). Accustomed to conventional marriage patterns, the Prophet was at first understandably reluctant to engage in this new practice. Due to a lack of historical documentation, we do not know what his early attempts were to comply with the commandment in Ohio. His first recorded plural marriage in Nauvoo was to Louisa Beaman; it was performed by Bishop Joseph B. Noble on 5 April 1841.[11] During the next three years Joseph took additional plural wives in accordance with the Lord's commands.

As members of the Council of the Twelve Apostles returned from their missions to the British Isles in 1841, Joseph Smith taught them one by one the doctrine of plurality of wives, and each experienced some difficulty in understanding and accepting this doctrine. Brigham Young, for example, recounted his struggle: "I was not desirous of shrinking from any duty, nor of failing in the least to do as I was commanded, but it was the first time in my life that I had desired the grave, and I could hardly get over it for a long time. And when I saw a funeral, I felt to envy the corpse its situation, and to regret that I was not in the coffin."[12]

After their initial hesitancy and frustration, Brigham Young and others of the Twelve received individual confirmations from the Holy Spirit and accepted the new doctrine of plural marriage. They knew that Joseph Smith was a prophet of God in all things. At first the practice was kept secret and was very limited. Rumors began to circulate about authorities of the Church having additional wives, which greatly distorted the truth and contributed to increased persecution from apostates and outsiders. Part of the difficulty, of course, was the natural aversion Americans held against "polygamy." This new system appeared to threaten the strongly entrenched tradition of monogamy and the solidarity of the family structure. Later, in Utah, the Saints openly practiced "the principle," but never without persecution.

WENTWORTH LETTER

The Prophet was occasionally called on to explain the teachings and practices of Mormonism to outsiders. A significant example was the Wentworth Letter. In the spring of 1842, John Wentworth, editor of the *Chicago Democrat*, asked Joseph Smith to provide him with a sketch of "the rise, progress, persecution, and faith of the Latter-Day Saints."[13] Wentworth

John Wentworth was editor of the Chicago Democrat *and recipient of the famous Wentworth Letter from Joseph Smith. After graduating from Dartmouth College in 1836, young Wentworth went to Chicago, a city of less than five thousand people at the time. He bought the struggling* Chicago Democrat, *the city's first newspaper. He eventually became one of Illinois' leading citizens, being elected to the U.S. House of Representatives in 1843 at age twenty-eight. He served three terms in Congress. In 1857 he was elected mayor of Chicago.*

was originally from New Hampshire and desired this information to help in the compilation of a history of his native state, which was being written by his friend George Barstow. Joseph complied with this request and sent Wentworth a multi-page document containing an account of many of the early events in the history of the Restoration, including the First Vision and the coming forth of the Book of Mormon. The document also contained thirteen statements outlining Latter-day Saint beliefs, which have come to be known as the Articles of Faith. Barstow did publish his history, but the Wentworth Letter was not included, nor was anything about the Mormons.

Wentworth did not publish this document in the *Chicago Democrat*, nor did it ever appear in any history of New Hampshire. But the Church's newspaper, *Times and Seasons*, published it in March 1842, and it has become one of the most important statements of inspiration, history, and doctrine for the Church. The Articles of Faith were written for non-Mormons and were never intended to be a complete summary of gospel principles and practices. They do, however, provide a clear statement about the unique beliefs of the Latter-day Saints. Each article is a positive statement of the differences between Mormonism and the sectarian beliefs of other denominations.

In 1851 the Articles of Faith were included in the first edition of the Pearl of Great Price published in the British Mission. After the Pearl of Great Price was revised in 1878 and canonized in 1880, the Articles of Faith became official doctrine of the Church.

BOOK OF ABRAHAM

In early 1842, about the same time Joseph Smith wrote his letter to John Wentworth, he was also busily engaged in "translating from the Records of Abraham."[14] These records had been acquired in 1835 when the Church purchased several rolls of ancient Egyptian papyrus from Michael Chandler. Joseph and his scribes did some preliminary investigation of them, but labor on the Kirtland Temple and the subsequent apostasy and persecution precluded any opportunity for him to continue this work in Ohio or Missouri. Finally in the spring of 1842 he was able to dedicate himself to the task for several weeks with few interruptions.

Elder Wilford Woodruff, who learned in leadership councils of the Prophet's translation and some of its contents, recorded in his journal his feelings about the Prophet's work: "Truly the Lord has raised up Joseph the Seer . . . and is now clothing him with mighty power and wisdom and knowledge. . . . The Lord is blessing Joseph with power to reveal the mysteries of the kingdom of God; to translate through the Urim and Thummim ancient records and Hieroglyphics as old as Abraham or Adam, which causes our hearts to burn within us while we behold their glorious truths opened unto us."[15]

Extracts from the book of Abraham appeared first in the *Times and Seasons* and in the *Millennial Star* in the summer of 1842. Joseph Smith

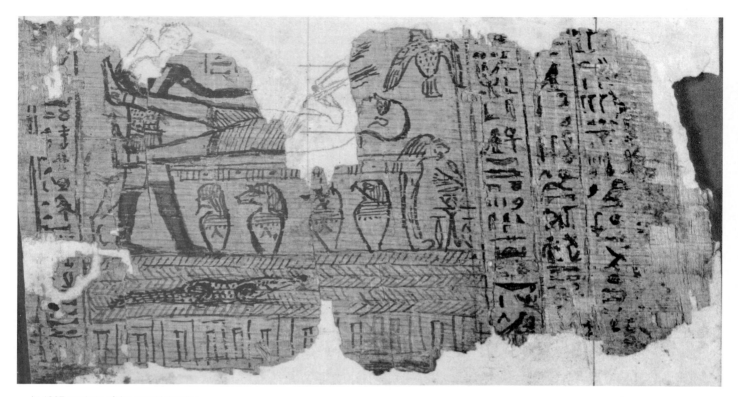

In 1967 portions of the papyri that the Church had purchased in 1835 were discovered and presented to the Church. Among the most important and interesting was the original of what became Facsimile 1 in the Pearl of Great Price.

indicated that more would be forthcoming, but he was unable to continue the translation after 1842. What the Church received—five chapters of the book of Abraham in the Pearl of Great Price—is only a portion of the original record.

In 1967 eleven fragments of the Joseph Smith papyri were rediscovered by Doctor Aziz S. Atiya, in the New York Metropolitan Museum of Art. Studies of them have confirmed that they are mainly ancient Egyptian funerary texts of the sort commonly buried with royalty and nobility and designed to guide them through their eternal journeyings.[16] This has renewed the question about the connection between the records and the book of Abraham. Joseph Smith did not explain the method of translating the book of Abraham, just as he did not explain fully how the Book of Mormon was translated. Nevertheless, like the Book of Mormon, the book of Abraham is its own evidence that it came about through the gift and power of God.

DISCOURSES OF JOSEPH SMITH

The Saints in Nauvoo frequently listened to the Prophet Joseph Smith preach, and many of them wrote of how moved they were by the experience. They thrilled to his words and were strengthened in their testimonies. Brigham Young said, "Such moments were more precious to me than all the wealth of the world. No matter how great my poverty—if I had to borrow meal to feed my wife and children, I never let an opportunity pass of learning what the Prophet had to impart."[17] Wandle Mace, a new convert, said that listening to the Prophet in public or private, in sunshine or shower, he became convinced that Joseph Smith had been taught by God. He never missed a chance to hear Joseph preach because, he said, Joseph "had been feeding us deliciously with spiritual food."[18] James Palmer, a British convert, said the Prophet "*looked* and *had*, the appearance of *one* that was heaven born while *preaching*, or as *tho* he had been *sent* from the heavenly worlds on a divine *mission*."[19]

There was no meetinghouse in Nauvoo large enough for all the Saints to gather to hear their Prophet, so in good weather they met outdoors under the trees. A typical place was in a grove that formed an amphitheater-like area on the hillside west of the temple. This was one of Joseph's favorite places to speak to the Saints. During the Nauvoo period he became accustomed to giving public discourses. In the early days of the Restoration he had left most of the preaching to others who he felt were better orators. Now, however, he preached with great power and authority in Nauvoo and surrounding communities. His nearly two hundred discourses during these years shaped Latter-day Saint understanding of gospel doctrines and immeasurably influenced the Church.

On Sunday, 20 March 1842, at the funeral of the deceased child of Windsor P. Lyon, Joseph chose to speak in the grove about the salvation of little children. He said that he had "asked the question, why it is that infants, innocent children, are taken away from us, especially those that seem to be the most intelligent and interesting." He said that they were taken to be spared the wickedness that was increasing in the world. He then stated one of the most comforting doctrines revealed in the latter days: "All children are redeemed by the blood of Jesus Christ, and the moment that children leave this world, they are taken to the bosom of Abraham. The only difference between the old and young dying is, one lives longer in heaven and eternal light and glory than the other, and is freed a little sooner from this miserable, wicked world."[20]

In the spring of 1843, Joseph frequently visited the outlying settlements of the Saints to teach and guide them. When in Ramus he stayed at the home of his friend Benjamin F. Johnson. The teachings of the Prophet in Ramus, Illinois, on Sunday, 2 April 1843, were so important that they were incorporated into the official history of the Church and later into the Doctrine and Covenants as section 130. In a morning meeting, Elder Orson Hyde had spoken about the Father and the Son dwelling in the hearts of the Saints and said that the Savior at his second coming would "appear on a white horse as a warrior." At lunch, Joseph Smith told Orson that he was going to offer some corrections to his sermon in the afternoon meeting. Elder Hyde replied, "They shall be thankfully received."[21]

The Prophet explained to the Saints, "When the Savior shall appear we shall see him as he is. We shall see that he is a man like ourselves" (D&C 130:1). In further correction he added that "The idea that the Father and the

Son dwell in a man's heart is an old sectarian notion, and is false" (v. 3). Later in his sermon he boldly declared that "The Father has a body of flesh and bones as tangible as man's; the Son also; but the Holy Ghost has not a body of flesh and bones, but is a personage of Spirit" (v. 22).

In that monumental discourse, Joseph Smith also taught other eternal truths that have since inspired Latter-day Saints to diligently search for truth and seek good works. He explained that "Whatever principle of intelligence we attain unto in this life, it will rise with us in the resurrection.

"And if a person gains more knowledge and intelligence in this life through his diligence and obedience than another, he will have so much the advantage in the world to come" (vv. 18–19). He also explained that "There is a law, irrevocably decreed in heaven before the foundations of this world, upon which all blessings are predicated—

"And when we obtain any blessing from God, it is by obedience to that law upon which it is predicated" (vv. 20–21).

A month and a half later the Prophet visited Ramus again. In an evening meeting, a Methodist preacher, Samuel Prior, who was visiting the town to find out more about the Church, was asked to speak to the congregation. Following his remarks, Joseph Smith arose and differed with Reverend Prior's remarks. Prior wrote: "This he did mildly, politely, and affectingly; like one who was more desirous to disseminate truth and expose error, than to love the malicious triumph of debate over me. I was truly edified with his remarks, and felt less prejudiced against the Mormons than ever."[22] Joseph Smith's teachings on this occasion reflect his prophetic calling and are now recorded as scripture:

"There is no such thing as immaterial matter. All spirit is matter, but it is more fine or pure, and can only be discerned by purer eyes;

"We cannot see it; but when our bodies are purified we shall see that it is all matter" (D&C 131:7–8).

As construction on the temple progressed, the Prophet Joseph gave some of his greatest sermons to special gatherings in the unfinished building. One such occasion was the April 1843 general conference. At that time William Miller's widely publicized prophecies that Christ would come on 3 April 1843 had caused quite a stir throughout America and among the Latter-day Saints. (Miller was a religious zealot who founded Millerism.) In the conference session on 6 April, Joseph said that as the Lord's prophet he had been praying and learned that "the coming of the Son of Man never will be—never can be till the judgments spoken of for this hour are poured out: which judgments are commenced." The Prophet also listed some events that had not occurred yet, but which would take place prior to the Second Coming: "Judah must return, Jerusalem must be rebuilt, and the temple, and water come out from under the temple, and the waters of the Dead Sea be healed. It will take some time to rebuild the walls of the city and the temple."[23]

The most renowned of all the Prophet's sermons was given at general conference in April 1844 as a funeral address in honor of his friend King Follett who had died in a construction accident. Joseph Smith spoke for over two hours mentioning at least thirty-four doctrinal subjects, including the importance of knowing the true God, the way to become as God is, the plurality of gods, eternal progression, the importance of the Holy Ghost, the nature of intelligence, the unpardonable sin, and little children and the Resurrection.

One of his most profound messages concerned God and man's destiny in relationship to him. He declared, "God himself was once as we are now, and is an exalted man, and sits enthroned in yonder heavens! . . .

". . . you have got to learn how to be gods yourselves . . . by going from one small degree to another, and from a small capacity to a great one; from grace to grace, from exaltation to exaltation, until you attain to the resurrection of the dead, and are able to dwell in everlasting burnings." Man, then, is to become like God now is. Joseph also explained the "first principles of consolation" for those mourning for the righteous dead: "although the earthly tabernacle is laid down and dissolved, they shall rise again to dwell in everlasting burnings in immortal glory, not to sorrow, suffer, or die any more, but they shall be heirs of God and joint heirs with Jesus Christ."[24]

How did the Saints respond to this lengthy, yet eloquent and inspiring sermon? Most were profoundly moved by it. Joseph Fielding wrote in his journal, "I never felt more delighted with his Discourse than at this time, It put me in Mind of Herod when they said at his Oration It is the Voice of a God and not of a Man" (see Acts 12:20–23).[25]

While the Saints sojourned in Nauvoo they witnessed a flowering of theology. They listened to their prophet leader elaborate upon doctrinal themes that had been only touched upon earlier. As they read the *Times and Seasons*, they tasted of a more fully developed theology than they had known in Ohio or Missouri. As they built the temple and participated in its sacred ordinances, they received power, knowledge, and blessings unknown in earlier years. The doctrinal developments in Nauvoo created an enduring legacy for the Church in the future.

ENDNOTES

1. In *History of the Church*, 4:426.

2. *History of the Church*, 4:179.

3. Journal History of The Church of Jesus Christ of Latter-day Saints, 15 Aug. 1840, Historical Department, Salt Lake City; Andrew F. Ehat and Lyndon W. Cook, comps., *The Words of Joseph Smith*, Religious Studies Monograph series (Provo: Religious Studies Center, 1980), p. 49.

4. In *History of the Church*, 4:426.

5. In possession of Museum of Church History and Fine Art.

6. *Deseret News, Semi-Weekly*, 15 Feb. 1884, p. 2.

7. See *History of the Church*, 5:1–2.

8. *History of the Church*, 5:1–2; spelling standardized.

9. In *Journal of Discourses*, 2:31.

10. See *History of the Church*, 5:xxix–xxx; Doctrine and Covenants 132 heading.

11. See Andrew Jenson, *The Historical Record*, Feb. 1887, p. 233.

12. In *Journal of Discourses*, 3:266.

13. "Church History," *Times and Seasons*, 1 Mar. 1842, p. 706.

14. *History of the Church*, 4:548.

15. Wilford Woodruff Journals, 19 Feb. 1842, LDS Historical Department, Salt Lake City; spelling and capitalization standardized.

16. See Hugh Nibley, *The Message of the Joseph Smith Papyri: An Egyptian Endowment* (Salt Lake City: Deseret Book Co., 1975), pp. 1–14, 48–55.

17. In *Journal of Discourses*, 12:270.

18. Biography of Wandle Mace as told to Rebecca E. H. Mace, his second wife (published under direction of his grandson William M. Mace), Brigham Young University Special Collections, Provo, pp. 13, 18.

19. James Palmer, Reminiscences, LDS Historical Department, Salt Lake City, p. 69; spelling standardized.

20. In *History of the Church*, 4:553–54.

21. In *History of the Church*, 5:323.

22. Samuel A. Prior, "A Visit to Nauvoo," *Times and Seasons*, 15 May 1843, p. 198.

23. In *History of the Church*, 5:336–37.

24. In *History of the Church*, 6:305–6.

25. Andrew F. Ehat, ed., " 'They Might Have Known That He Was Not a Fallen Prophet,'—The Nauvoo Journal of Joseph Fielding," *Brigham Young University Studies*, Winter 1979, p. 148.

GROWING CONFLICT IN ILLINOIS

FOR THREE YEARS Joseph Smith and the Latter-day Saints lived in relative peace in Illinois. Then, as had occurred in Ohio and Missouri, dissenters within and opponents without combined to create conflict for the Church. Again the Prophet Joseph Smith was harassed, persecuted, and threatened. As problems began to escalate in 1842, he wrote to the Saints. He assured his brothers and sisters in the gospel that "the envy and wrath of man have been my common lot all the days of my life; and for what cause it seems mysterious, unless I was ordained from before the foundation of the world for some good end. . . . I feel, like Paul, to glory in tribulation; for to this day has the God of my fathers delivered me out of them all" (D&C 127:2). The Prophet had tremendous confidence that despite all the emerging conflicts the Lord would help him triumph over all his enemies.

APOSTASY OF JOHN C. BENNETT

John C. Bennett arrived in Nauvoo in August 1840 and quickly rose to prominence. Only a year and a half older than the Prophet, Bennett had varied experience as a physician, Methodist preacher, founder of a college, university president, military leader, and, most recently, as the quartermaster general of Illinois. In April 1841 general conference he was presented before the Church "as Assistant President until President [Sidney] Rigdon's health should be restored."[1] For a time he was the Prophet's companion, confidant, and adviser.

On 15 June 1841, just two and a half months after Bennett had been sustained as Assistant President, Joseph Smith received a letter from Hyrum Smith and William Law, then in Pittsburgh, confirming a rumor that Bennett had an estranged wife and child in Ohio. When he first went to Nauvoo, Bennett had claimed that he was not married. The Prophet confronted him with these facts, and in feigned remorse, Bennett took poison in an apparent suicide attempt.

About this same time Bennett, by perverting the doctrine of plural marriage and misusing the prestige of his high Church position, was able to lure some women into immoral conduct. His "spiritual wifery," as he termed it, was adultery.

Before the true character of John C. Bennett was made apparent, he also engineered a clever plot to assassinate the Prophet and take over the Church.

John C. Bennett (1804–67) joined the Church in Illinois in 1840. Being flamboyant and energetic, he lobbied for the passage of the Nauvoo Charter in Springfield, was an officer in the Nauvoo Legion, was elected Nauvoo's first mayor, and counseled Joseph Smith as a temporary member of the First Presidency while Sidney Rigdon was ill. It soon came to the attention of the Prophet, however, that Bennett was seducing women under the guise of "spiritual wifery," and he was excommunicated in the spring of 1842. Embittered, he lectured against the Church throughout the United States, encouraged Missouri's attempts to extradite Joseph Smith, and wrote one of the first anti-Mormon books.

Albert P. Rockwood (1805–79) held several positions of trust in the Nauvoo Legion, was called to be a General Authority serving as one of the Presidents of the Seventy in 1845, and was a member of the original Pioneer Company in 1847.

On Saturday, 7 May 1842, a mock battle between the two cohorts, or brigade, of the Nauvoo Legion was arranged. Major General Bennett asked Lieutenant General Joseph Smith to take charge of the first cohort during the contest. When the Prophet declined, Bennett urged him then to take up a station in the rear of the cavalry without his staff during the engagement. This Joseph also declined to do. Instead he chose his own position with his lifeguard, Albert P. Rockwood, by his side. Joseph noted that he sensed through "the gentle breathings of that Spirit" that there was a plot afoot to have him exposed to being slain and that no one would know who the perpetrator was.[2]

When Bennett's personal immorality and sinister designs were discovered, he was excommunicated from the Church. He was also cashiered from the Legion, forced to resign as mayor, and expelled from the Masonic fraternity. With his reputation in Nauvoo ruined, he bitterly left the city and took up lecturing against the Prophet and the other leaders of the Church. His serialized expose, appearing in the *Sangamo Journal* newspaper in Springfield, Illinois, during the summer of 1842, was collected and published a few months later as part of *The History of the Saints; or, an Expose of Joe Smith and Mormonism.* Bennett claimed that he only became a Mormon to bring to light the alleged illicit conduct of the Prophet.

Bennett also stimulated anti-Mormon feelings among the Masons in Illinois. As early as October 1841 some Masons who were members of the Church obtained permission to initiate a Masonic lodge in Nauvoo. Joseph Smith could see advantages in belonging to this fraternal order. Presumably it was felt that other Masons in the state and nation, many of whom held prominent positions, would look more kindly upon the Church. Joseph Smith and many others in Nauvoo were formally introduced into the order in March 1842. Unaware that John C. Bennett had been expelled from an Ohio Masonic order for misconduct, Masons in Nauvoo elected him secretary of their lodge.

When he left Nauvoo, Bennett visited Masons in Hannibal, Missouri, who were also unaware that he had been expelled from the fraternity. He accused the leadership of the predominantly Mormon lodges in and around Nauvoo of violating Masonic procedure, keeping a false set of books, and doing other improper things. These accusations were passed on to the Illinois grand lodge, which launched a two-year investigation. Consequently many Illinois Masons believed Bennett's false charges.

POLITICAL COMPLICATIONS

During John C. Bennett's mercurial rise and fall in Nauvoo, political rivalries were developing between the Latter-day Saints and their neighbors in western Illinois. These difficulties stemmed from volatile frontier politics, where inter-party opposition was intense and feelings were easily enflamed. The problem was intensified because Democrats and Whigs were nearly

Thomas Sharp became one of the chief opponents of the Church in Illinois and rallied the opposition through the columns of his newspaper, the Warsaw Signal.

equal in Illinois. The Democrats took control of the state government in 1838, but the Whigs had retained a narrow edge in western Illinois when the Saints began to arrive in 1839. Both political parties hoped that the new citizens might help their cause.

In Hancock County, however, feelings soon polarized over the rapid growth of Nauvoo and other Mormon communities. The citizens of Warsaw, seventeen miles south of Nauvoo, became anxious and jealous over the growing economic, political, and religious dominance of the Mormon city. It was in Warsaw and in Carthage, the Hancock County seat seventeen miles east of Nauvoo, that the anti-Mormon feelings first began to coalesce in Illinois.

In an attempt to promote goodwill, Church leaders invited Thomas Sharp, a former lawyer, and the editor of the *Warsaw Signal* to the celebration at the laying of the temple cornerstone on 6 April 1841. As Thomas Sharp witnessed the day's events, including a parade and sumptuous banquet, and listened to Joseph Smith and other Church leaders speak about the prospects for the growth of Nauvoo and the kingdom of God, he became convinced that Mormonism was more than a religion. To him it appeared to be a dangerous, un-American political movement aimed at domination of a vast empire. Returning to Warsaw he launched a vigorous campaign against the Church in the columns of his newspaper, claiming that it was Joseph Smith's intent to unite church and state; he insisted that the Saints possessed too much power and autonomy in their Nauvoo Charter.

In June 1841, Sharp helped form an anti-Mormon political party in Hancock County which held conventions in Warsaw and Carthage and public meetings in other smaller communities. Thus, individuals from both national political parties united against the Church. In the county elections in July, an anti-Mormon slate was elected, which thwarted the political influence of the Saints, even when they voted as a bloc. But as Latter-day Saints continued to stream into Hancock County, including many British members who quickly became United States citizens, the political power of the Saints grew and further alienated their new enemies in Hancock County.

Meanwhile, the Saints found a friend in a leader of the Democratic party in Illinois—Judge Stephen A. Douglas of the state supreme court. While serving as secretary of state, Douglas had helped assure the passage of the Nauvoo Charter by the Illinois legislature.

When Joseph visited Church members in Adams County early in June 1841, he was arrested as a fugitive from the state of Missouri. In Quincy, however, Joseph obtained a writ of *habeas corpus*, which enabled him to appeal to Judge Douglas, who consented to give the matter a hearing a few days later at the circuit court in Monmouth, seventy-five miles northeast of Nauvoo.

When the trial opened on 9 June, the courtroom overflowed with spectators excited about a possible lynching of Joseph Smith. Judge Douglas fined

Stephen A. Douglas (1813–61) held many political offices during his illustrious career. He was judge of the Illinois Supreme Court from 1841–43, was elected to the United States House of Representatives in 1843, and was elected to the Senate in 1847. In 1860 he was defeated for the presidency by Abraham Lincoln. He died in Chicago while campaigning for the preservation of the union.

the sheriff twice for failing to keep the crowd under control. The defense arguments concerning atrocities against the Saints in Missouri moved many people in the courtroom, including Judge Douglas, to tears. The next day he dismissed the case on procedural grounds.

Judge Douglas's decision won him the gratitude of the Church, but it aroused strong suspicion in western Illinois that he had a political agreement with Joseph Smith. Whig newspapers statewide accused him of openly courting the Mormon vote by dismissing the case. The Whigs, therefore, stopped wooing the Latter-day Saints and stepped up their attacks on them as the gubernatorial election year of 1842 approached. Stephen A. Douglas became the target of many partisan blasts as he continued to befriend the Church. His appointment of several Church members to court positions in Hancock County aroused intense anti-Mormon feelings in Warsaw and Carthage.

The full measure of Mormon gratitude toward Judge Douglas appeared in a letter by Joseph Smith in the *Times and Seasons*: "We care not a fig for *Whig* or *Democrat*: they are both alike to us; but we shall go for our *friends*, our TRIED FRIENDS. . . . DOUGLAS is a *Master Spirit*, and *his friends are our friends*—we are willing to cast our banners on the air, and fight by his side in the cause of humanity, and equal rights—the cause of liberty and the law."[3] Later in 1842, with the undeniable aid of the Mormon vote, the Democratic candidate for governor, Thomas L. Ford, won the election over Joseph Duncan, the Whig candidate and an avowed opponent of the Saints.

In the same election campaign, William Smith, the Prophet's brother and one of the Twelve Apostles, ran on the Democratic ticket for the state house of representatives against Whig candidate Thomas Sharp. To counter Sharp's anti-Mormon comments, the *Wasp* was established under the editorship of William Smith. Later the *Nauvoo Neighbor,* under the editorship of John Taylor, replaced the *Wasp* and continued to proclaim the Latter-day Saint cause. With the support of the growing numbers of Latter-day Saints, the Apostle easily won the election and went to Springfield to fight for the continuation of the Nauvoo Charter. Sharp's defeat intensified his antagonism, and he broadened his attack over a ten-county area and cried for extermination or expulsion of the Mormons.

RENEWED THREATS FROM MISSOURI

In May 1842, Lilburn W. Boggs, former governor of Missouri, was wounded by a would-be assasin. Missouri authorities accused Joseph Smith of the attempted murder and again tried to extradite him back to Missouri.

John C. Bennett, filled with hatred and revenge after leaving Nauvoo, claimed that Joseph Smith had sent Porter Rockwell to Missouri for the express purpose of killing the ex-governor. Rockwell angrily confronted Bennett at Carthage and accused him of lying. Bennett then contacted the rapidly recovering Boggs in Missouri and persuaded him to swear to an affidavit that Porter Rockwell, acting on orders of Joseph Smith, had tried to murder him. In July, Boggs appeared before a justice of the peace in Independence, Missouri, to charge Orrin Porter Rockwell, one of Joseph Smith's bodyguards, with attempted murder. Governor Thomas Reynolds of Missouri then convinced Governor Thomas Carlin of Illinois to send officers to arrest Porter Rockwell and Joseph Smith. The Prophet, using the power of *habeas corpus* granted in the Nauvoo Charter, was temporarily freed. Knowing that if he returned to Missouri he would be killed, the Prophet sought seclusion on a Mississippi River island. Rockwell fled to Pennsylvania under a fictitious name.

Letters from Emma Smith, the Nauvoo Female Relief Society, and prominent Nauvoo citizens failed to persuade Governor Carlin of the impropriety of the extradition order. Carlin continued to offer a reward for the arrest of the Prophet and Porter Rockwell. At this time Church leaders prepared documents answering John C. Bennett's accusations and sent 380 elders to distribute the documents to public officials and Church members in various states. Meanwhile, United States district attorney Justin Butterfield offered the opinion that Joseph could obtain dismissal of the charges from the state supreme court. With protection provided by newly elected Governor Thomas Ford, Joseph Smith went to Springfield in December 1842 and was eventually released because the charges went beyond the evidence in Boggs's original affidavit and therefore lacked foundation. The Saints in Nauvoo rejoiced that their Prophet could come out of hiding and be with them once more. Unfortunately, Porter Rockwell was arrested in St. Louis in March on his way home to Nauvoo and languished in Missouri jails for ten months before being acquitted.

A third attempt by Missouri officials to return Joseph Smith to Independence for trial was made in June 1843 during the congressional race. John C. Bennett was in Daviess County, Missouri, and revived the old charge of treason against the Prophet. Governor Ford of Illinois agreed to a warrant of extradition. At this time Joseph and his family had left for a much-needed vacation at the home of Emma's sister, Elizabeth Wasson, near Dixon, Illinois, two hundred miles north of Nauvoo. Stephen Markham and William Clayton were sent from Nauvoo to warn the Prophet. While they were in the house, Sheriff Joseph Reynolds of Jackson County, Missouri, and Constable Harmon Wilson of Hancock County, Illinois, arrived and rudely arrested the Prophet in the yard. Cyrus H. Walker, Whig candidate for Congress and also a leading attorney, happened to be in Dixon and promised Joseph that he would defend him if Joseph would vote for him in the upcoming election, to which the Prophet agreed.

Stephen Markham and William Clayton then arrested Sheriff Reynolds and Constable Wilson for false imprisonment and for threatening Joseph Smith's life. En route, they were met by a mounted posse of the Nauvoo Legion and were ushered safely into Nauvoo before cheering citizens. The

Dixon, Illinois, was the home of Emma's sister Elizabeth Hale Wasson. While visiting here Joseph was arrested by Missouri officials. When the brethren in Nauvoo learned of his plight, they sent large groups of men in search of their leader. His subsequent release under the habeas corpus *laws, generated considerable controversy over the powers of the Nauvoo municipal government.*

Nauvoo municipal court released Joseph Smith on a writ of *habeas corpus*.

Reynolds and Wilson were treated to a sumptuous dinner and released. They then dashed to Carthage and incited further anti-Mormon feelings among the people. They swore out new writs for Joseph Smith's arrest, and a posse was organized to retake the Prophet. Governor Ford, however, honored the Nauvoo court's decision. While the matter was in litigation, public opinion in the state became increasingly anti-Mormon.

Before the congressional election in August, Church leaders decided that Joseph P. Hoge, the Democratic candidate, would best represent the Saints' interests. Joseph Smith kept his pledge to vote for Cyrus Walker. Hyrum Smith and John Taylor, however, urged other members of the Church to vote for Hoge. Both candidates, uncertain of Mormon leanings, spent four days campaigning in Nauvoo. The Nauvoo vote helped swing the election in favor of Hoge. The Whigs then charged the Mormons with misuse of corporate political power. Many Democrats joined the chorus of anti-Mormon feeling because they feared the power that had worked for them might one day be used against them. Thus Joseph Smith's sincere attempts to keep the Church aloof from partisan politics were unsuccessful.

DISSENSION WITHIN THE CHURCH

While forces from without threatened the Prophet, dissension within Nauvoo aided their hostile aims. During the Bennett scandal in 1842, three other members of the Church—Robert Foster, Francis Higbee, and Chauncey Higbee—were also severely reproved by Joseph Smith for immorality. Following the scandal, Francis Higbee went to Cincinnati for a year, but he returned following the death of his faithful father, Elias Higbee. In September, Francis was offended again when the Prophet publicly accused him and others of collusion with the Missourians in their third attempt to extradite him. Francis Higbee became the Prophet's bitter enemy.

The number of dissenters in Nauvoo grew with the addition of Church members who opposed plural marriage and other new doctrines taught by Joseph Smith. William Law, second counselor in the First Presidency, his brother Wilson Law, major general in the Nauvoo Legion, and high council members Austin Cowles and Leonard Soby all believed that Joseph Smith was a fallen prophet.

By late December 1843, Joseph Smith became aware of some of the evil designs of the dissidents. He told the Nauvoo police that he was much more worried about traitors within the Church than about any enemies in Missouri: "All the enemies upon the face of the earth may roar and exert all their power to bring about my death, but they can accomplish nothing, unless some who are among us and enjoy our society, have been with us in our councils, participated in our confidence, taken us by the hand, called us brother, saluted us with a kiss, join with our enemies, turn our virtues into faults, and, by falsehood and deceit, stir up their wrath and indignation

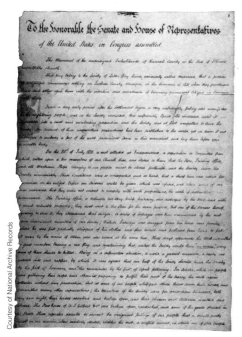

During the Nauvoo period the Saints formally petitioned the United States government on three occasions for redress of grievances related to the Missouri persecutions. The first effort was made in 1839–40 when Joseph Smith and others went to Washington, D.C., and petitioned the Senate Judiciary Committee. The Prophet said 491 individuals gave their claims; over two hundred of these documents have been located in the national archives.

A second petition was made to the House of Representatives Judiciary Committee in May 1842, and the third petition was a fifty-foot petition with 3,419 signatures dated 28 November 1843 and presented to the Senate Judiciary Committee on 5 April 1844. All three attempts failed to gain action from the government.

against us, and bring their united vengeance upon our heads. . . . *We have a Judas in our midst.*"[4]

The apostates' uneasiness grew as the police watched their activities carefully. Accusations were exchanged between the apostates and the Nauvoo city council. In April, Robert Foster and William and Wilson Law were excommunicated for un-Christian conduct. On 28 April these men and their sympathizers met and declared Joseph Smith a fallen prophet and inaugurated a reformed church with William Law as president. They appointed a committee to visit families and try to convert them to the new church. A printing press was ordered and plans were made to launch an opposition newspaper to be named the *Nauvoo Expositor*.

JOSEPH SMITH, CANDIDATE FOR UNITED STATES PRESIDENCY

While apostasy festered in Nauvoo in late 1843, the Prophet Joseph Smith was busy politically. Realizing that 1844 was a national election year, he wrote letters to John C. Calhoun, Lewis Cass, Richard M. Johnson, Henry Clay, and Martin Van Buren, the men most frequently mentioned as candidates for president of the United States. He asked each man what his course would be toward the Latter-day Saints if he were elected, especially in helping them obtain redress for property lost in Missouri. Of the five, Cass, Clay, and Calhoun responded by letter, but none proposed the kind of federal intervention that the Prophet and the Church members desired.

It seemed obvious that there was no one the Saints could endorse for the presidency. Therefore, Joseph Smith met with the Twelve on 29 January 1844 to consider their course for the coming elections. The brethren unanimously sustained a motion to propose their own ticket with Joseph Smith as their candidate for president. He told them that they would have to send every man in Nauvoo who could speak in public to campaign and preach the gospel and that he would be among them. "After the April Conference we will have General Conferences all over the nation, and I will attend as many as convenient. Tell the people we have had Whig and Democratic Presidents long enough: we want a President of the United States. If I ever get into the presidential chair, I will protect the people in their rights and liberties."[5]

With the help of William W. Phelps, John M. Bernhisel, and Thomas Bullock, Joseph synthesized his ideas for a platform into a pamphlet entitled *General Smith's Views of the Powers and Policy of the Government of the United States*. It was published on 7 February and mailed to about two hundred leaders in the country. Joseph's proposals were designed to appeal to voters in both major parties. He advocated revoking imprisonment for debt, turning prisons into seminaries of learning, abolishing slavery by 1850 and reimbursing slaveholders out of revenue from the sale of public lands, establishing a national bank with branches in each state, and annexing Texas and Oregon. Joseph Smith's first choice as his vice-presidential running mate was

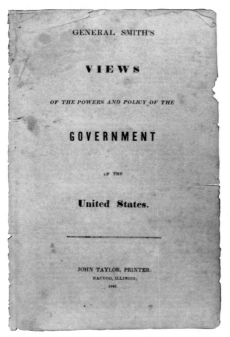

GENERAL SMITH'S

VIEWS

OF THE POWERS AND POLICY OF THE

GOVERNMENT

OF THE

United States.

JOHN TAYLOR, PRINTER:
NAUVOO, ILLINOIS;
1844.

When it was decided that Joseph Smith would be a candidate for the president of the United States, he issued a pamphlet expressing his views on some important issues. This is its title page. Among the pamphlet's most important points were the following:

1. *Review of noble sentiments on the purpose of the United States government expressed by Benjamin Franklin and in the inaugural addresses of several United States presidents. This included the point that President Van Buren had begun to lead the country away from the basic concepts of the founding fathers and that William Henry Harrison would have returned to them had he lived.*
2. *Reduce the size of Congress by two thirds, with one representative per million population. Also reduce congressional pay and power.*
3. *Pardon many people then in prison, establish public service sentences for lesser crimes, and turn penitentiaries into "seminaries of learning" because "rigor and seclusion will never do as much to reform the propensities of man, as reason and friendship."6*
4. *Abolish slavery by 1850 by having the federal government purchase the slaves and set them free.*
5. *Abolish military court martial for desertion and make honor the standard.*
6. *Practice greater economy in national and state governments.*
7. *Create a national bank with branches in each state and territory and circulate a standard medium of exchange.*

the prominent New York journalist and friend of the Saints, James Arlington Bennet. Bennet declined, however, and Joseph finally settled on Sidney Rigdon.

On 11 March 1844 a council meeting was held in Nauvoo to organize the political kingdom of God in preparation for the second coming of Christ. Now that the Prophet was a candidate for high political office, the time seemed right to inaugurate this body which would also serve as a committee to direct his campaign. The council consisted of about fifty members, including most of the Church leaders. It therefore came to be known as the Council of Fifty.

By the end of April, a list of elders and their campaign assignments was published in the *Nauvoo Neighbor*. It was also decided, in an early May convention held in Nauvoo, to secure the appointment of delegates from several states to a national convention to be held in Baltimore, Maryland, in July to nominate Joseph Smith for president of the United States.

OPPOSITION INTENSIFIES

In spite of the public relations efforts of the Church, opposition intensified in the early months of 1844. Thomas Sharp repeatedly attacked the Church and accused its leaders of every crime imaginable. He also promoted the anti-Mormon party's day of fasting and prayer on Saturday, 9 March, in an effort to speedily bring down the "false prophet" Joseph Smith. The anti-Mormon party in Carthage appointed a grand "wolf hunt" in Hancock County for the same day. These hunts were a common sport in the area, but in this and future cases the wolf hunt was merely a pretext for a mob to gather to harass, pillage, and burn the farms of the Saints in outlying areas.

In contrast to the lawless actions of the anti-Mormon party and the *Warsaw Signal*, Joseph Smith joined with Governor Ford that spring in an effort to establish more cordial relations among the citizens of western Illinois. An editorial in the *Nauvoo Neighbor* called upon all honest men to join with the governor "in his laudable endeavors to cultivate peace and honor the laws." The editorial urged the Saints to treat kindly those who did them wrong and reminded them of the wise man's proverb, "A soft answer turneth away wrath" (Proverbs 15:1). The *Neighbor* editorial declared that their motto was "Peace with all."7 In spite of these overtures, Thomas Sharp continued his attack through the *Warsaw Signal* and hinted that trouble was brewing between Joseph Smith and some Church members and that a breach was imminent.8

By May 1844 the Latter-day Saints were once again embroiled in an apparently irreconcilable conflict with their neighbors. There were many reasons for this: politically the Saints were alienated from nearly everyone else in Illinois, other communities were jealous of Nauvoo's economic growth and political autonomy, many people in Illinois feared the power of the Nauvoo Legion, the Masons were disturbed by alleged irregularities of

8. Repeal Article IV, Section 4 of the
Constitution, which required the
governor of a state to request
federal intervention to suppress
domestic violence because governors may themselves be mobbers.
9. Avoid "tangling alliances" with
foreign powers.
10. Accept Oregon, Texas, and others
who might apply for membership in
the union of states.
11. Have a president who is not a party
man, but president of the United
States and responsive to the wishes
of the majority of the people who
hold the sovereign power of
government.

the order in Nauvoo, and there was a general distaste among the people for peculiar Mormon doctrines and practices which had been misrepresented by John C. Bennett and others. Despite these factors, the Saints still might have been able to maintain peace if it had not been for the apostasy developing within the Church. Unhappily, all signs pointed toward eventual violence. On 29 May 1844, Thomas Sharp told his readers he "would not be surprised to hear of his [Joseph Smith's] death by violent means in a short time."[9]

ENDNOTES

1. *History of the Church*, 4:341.

2. *History of the Church*, 5:4.

3. "State Gubernatorial Convention," *Times and Seasons*, 1 Jan. 1842, p. 651.

4. *History of the Church*, 6:152.

5. *History of the Church*, 6:188.

6. *General Smith's Views of the Powers and Policy of the Government of the United States* (Nauvoo, Ill.: John Taylor, 1844), LDS Historical Department, Salt Lake City, p. 6.

7. In B. H. Roberts, *A Comprehensive History of The Church of Jesus Christ of Latter-day Saints, Century One*, 6 vols. (Salt Lake City: The Church of Jesus Christ of Latter-day Saints, 1930), 2:218.

8. See *Warsaw Signal*, 8 May 1844, p. 2.

9. *Warsaw Signal*, 29 May 1844, p. 2.

CHAPTER TWENTY-TWO

THE MARTYRDOM

◄ Forces of Evil *by Gary Smith*

EVEN WHEN HE BEGAN his ministry, the Prophet Joseph Smith knew he might have to die for his religion. While Joseph was translating the Book of Mormon the Lord promised him eternal life if he was "firm in keeping the commandments . . . even if you should be slain" (D&C 5:22). A month later the Lord again spoke of possible violent death. "And even if they do unto you even as they have done unto me, blessed are ye, for you shall dwell with me in glory" (D&C 6:30). The Prophet also received some important assurances, however, regarding his earthly mission. Several years later in Liberty Jail the Lord promised him: "Thy days are known, and thy years shall not be numbered less; therefore, fear not what man can do, for God shall be with you forever and ever" (D&C 122:9).

In 1840 his father's dying blessing promised him, " 'You shall even live to finish your work.' At this Joseph cried out, weeping, 'Oh! my father, shall I?' 'Yes,' said his father, 'you shall live to lay out the plan of all the work which God has given you to do.' "[1] Joseph Smith, heeding the Spirit's promptings, valiantly completed his mission, suffered martyrdom, and qualified for a glorious reward; thus these prophecies were fulfilled.

FOREBODINGS OF DEATH

As the Prophet continued his ministry during the Nauvoo period, he increasingly felt the forebodings of the Spirit that his ministry on earth was nearing its end. He expressed these feelings to those closest to him and occasionally spoke of them to the Saints in general. To a large congregation in the uncompleted Nauvoo Temple on 22 January 1843, Joseph spoke of the power of the priesthood being used to establish the kingdom of God in the latter days. He explained that the temple endowment would "prepare the disciples for their mission into the world." Referring to his own role, Joseph declared, "I understand my mission and business. God Almighty is my shield, and what can man do if God is my friend. I shall not be sacrificed until my time comes. Then I shall be offered freely."[2]

One of the most pointed and poignant of Joseph Smith's martyrdom prophecies was made to the Quorum of the Twelve Apostles in the spring of 1844. Orson Hyde remembered the account: "We were in council with Brother Joseph almost every day for weeks. Says Brother Joseph in one of those councils, there is something going to happen; I don't know what it is, but the Lord bids me to hasten and give you your endowment before the temple is finished. He conducted us through every ordinance of the holy priesthood, and when he had gone through with all the ordinances he rejoiced very much, and said, now if they kill me you have got all the keys and all the ordinances and you can confer them upon others, and the hosts of Satan will not be able to tear down the kingdom as fast as you will be able to build it up."[3]

Like everyone, the Prophet wanted to live. He wanted to enjoy the company of his wife, play with his children, speak to the Saints, and enjoy the fellowship of good people. Despite knowing that he would probably soon die, he was a man who loved life. He met often with the Saints, and some of his greatest sermons were delivered within weeks of his martyrdom.

CONSPIRACY AGAINST THE PROPHET

In stark contrast to the righteousness of most of the Saints who lived in prospering Nauvoo was the spreading apostasy in their midst. William Law, second counselor to Joseph Smith, and his brother Wilson led the conspiracy against the Prophet. Throughout the early months of 1844 their followers gradually grew to approximately two hundred people. Other leaders included the brothers Robert and Charles Foster, Chauncey and Francis Higbee, and two influential non-Mormons—Sylvester Emmons, a member of the Nauvoo city council, and Joseph H. Jackson, a notorious criminal.

On Sunday, 24 March 1844, Joseph Smith spoke at the temple about the conspiracy, having just learned of it from an informant. He revealed who some of his enemies were and added that, "The lies that Higbee has hatched up as a foundation to work upon is, he says that I had men's heads cut off in Missouri and that I had a sword run through the hearts of the people that I wanted to kill and put out of the way. I won't swear out a warrant against them for I don't fear any of them. They would not scare off an old setting hen."[4]

At the April general conference, the conspirators sought the downfall of the Prophet. Confident that the majority of the Saints would oppose the principle of plural marriage, they planned to bring up the subject at the business session of the conference. They were also prepared to argue that Joseph Smith was a fallen prophet because few if any revelations had been published and circulated among Church members in the previous months. In an effort to thwart the conspirators, the Prophet testified at the beginning of the conference that he was not a fallen prophet, that he had never felt nearer to God than at that time, and that he would show the people before the conference closed that God was with him.[5] The next day he addressed the conference for two hours in what became known as the King Follett Discourse. On that occasion, the faithful witnessed the majesty of their Prophet.

THE *EXPOSITOR* AFFAIR

The Nauvoo Expositor, *published on 7 June 1844, attempted to rally anti-Mormons against the Church in Nauvoo. The suppression of the paper, the destruction of the press, and the accidental razing of the building brought legal charges against Nauvoo mayor Joseph Smith, which resulted in his going to Carthage.*

Leaders of the conspiracy were exposed in the *Times and Seasons* and were excommunicated from the Church. Thwarted in their plans, the dissenters decided to publish an opposition newspaper. The first and only issue of their paper, which was called the *Nauvoo Expositor*, appeared on 7 June 1844. Throughout the paper they accused Joseph Smith of teaching vicious principles, practicing whoredoms, advocating so-called spiritual wifery, grasping for political power, preaching that there were many gods, speaking blasphemously of God, and promoting an inquisition.

The city council met in long sessions on Saturday, 8 June and again the following Monday. They suspended one of their members, the non-Mormon Sylvester Emmons, who was the editor of the *Expositor,* and discussed the identity of the publishers and their intent. Using the famous English jurist William Blackstone as their legal authority and having examined various municipal codes, the council ruled that the newspaper was a public nuisance in that it slandered individuals in the city. Moreover, they reasoned that if nothing were done to stop the libelous paper, the anti-Mormons would be aroused to mob action.

Joseph Smith, as mayor, ordered the city marshal, John Greene, to destroy the press, scatter the type, and burn any remaining newspapers. The order was carried out within hours. The city council acted legally to abate a public nuisance, although the legal opinion of the time allowed only the destruction of the published issues of the offending paper. The demolition of the press was a violation of property rights.[6]

After the destruction of the press, the publishers rushed to Carthage and obtained a warrant against the Nauvoo city council on charge of riot for the action. On 13 and 14 June, however, Joseph Smith and the other council members were released following a *habeas corpus* hearing before the Nauvoo municipal court. This further aroused the public. Also, even though Illinois had experienced twenty similar destructions of printing presses over the previous two decades without such a reaction, the enemies of the Church proclaimed the *Expositor* incident a violation of freedom of the press.

These actions prompted citizens' groups in Hancock County to call for the removal of the Saints from Illinois. Thomas Sharp vehemently expressed the feelings of many of the enemies of the Church when he editorialized in the *Warsaw Signal*: "War and extermination is inevitable! *Citizens* ARISE, ONE and ALL!!!—Can you *stand* by, and suffer such INFERNAL DEVILS! to ROB men of their property and RIGHTS, without avenging them. We have no time for comment, every man will make his own. LET IT BE MADE WITH POWDER AND BALL!!!"[7]

The situation was so dangerous that Joseph Smith wrote Governor Ford apprising him of the circumstances and including many affidavits to explain the threats against the Saints. Hyrum Smith wrote Brigham Young that the

Twelve and all other elders on political missions should return at once to Nauvoo. Hyrum stated, "You know we are not frightened, but think it best to be well prepared and be ready for the onset."[8] Joseph mobilized his guards and the Nauvoo Legion, and on 18 June placed the city under martial law. Meanwhile Hancock County citizens asked Governor Ford to mobilize the state militia and bring the Nauvoo offenders to justice.

The excitement was so intense that Ford published an open letter urging calmness and then went to Carthage to neutralize a situation that threatened civil war. He also wrote to Joseph Smith insisting that only a trial of the city council members before a non-Mormon jury in Carthage would satisfy the people. He promised complete protection for the defendants if they would give themselves up. The Prophet did not believe that the governor could fulfill his pledge. He wrote back, "Writs, we are assured, are issued against us in various parts of the country. For what? To drag us from place to place, from court to court, across the creeks and prairies, till some bloodthirsty villain could find his opportunity to shoot us. We dare not come."[9]

In counsel with his brethren, Joseph Smith read a letter from the governor that seemed to show no mercy toward them, and they considered what should be done next. In the course of the deliberations, Joseph's face brightened, and he declared, "The way is open. It is clear to my mind what to do. All they want is Hyrum and myself; then tell everybody to go about their business, and not to collect in groups, but to scatter about. . . . We will cross the river tonight, and go away to the West."[10] Stephen Markham, a close friend of the Prophet Joseph Smith, was present in the all-night council and heard Joseph Smith say that "it was the voice of the Spirit for him to go to the West among the Natives and take Hyrum and several others along with him and look out a place for the Church."[11]

Late in the evening of 22 June 1844, Joseph and Hyrum tearfully bade farewell to their families and, together with Willard Richards and Orrin Porter Rockwell, crossed the Mississippi River in a skiff. The boat was so leaky and the river so high that it took most of the night to get to the other side. Early in the morning a posse arrived in Nauvoo to arrest Joseph and Hyrum, but did not find them. The posse returned to Carthage after threatening the citizens with an invasion of troops if Joseph and Hyrum did not give themselves up. That same morning some of the brethren who had gone to see Joseph argued that mobs would drive the Saints from their homes despite his departure. Joseph replied, "If my life is of no value to my friends it is of none to myself."[12] Joseph and Hyrum then made plans to return to Nauvoo and to submit to arrest the next day.

JOSEPH AND HYRUM GO TO CARTHAGE

Upon returning to Nauvoo, Hyrum performed the marriage ceremony of his daughter Lovina to Lorin Walker. This small measure of joy preceded the sorrow that would soon come. Joseph wanted to speak to the Saints once

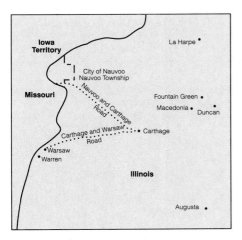

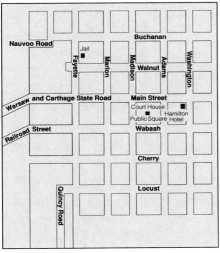

Carthage was the county seat of Hancock County and the location of the county jail. Many of the mob were state militia who had been released from duty and came to Carthage on the road from Warsaw.

more, but there was not enough time. He went home to his family, fully aware that it would probably be his last evening with them.

At 6:30 A.M. on Monday, 24 June, Joseph, Hyrum, John Taylor, and fifteen other members of the Nauvoo city council set out on horseback for Carthage, accompanied by Willard Richards and a number of other friends. It had rained for weeks, but this morning was sunny and beautiful. Pausing at the temple site, the Prophet looked on the sacred edifice, then on the city, and remarked, "This is the loveliest place and the best people under the heavens; little do they know the trials that await them."[13] To the assembled Saints, he said, "If I do not go there [to Carthage], the result will be the destruction of this city and its inhabitants; and I cannot think of my dear brothers and sisters and their children suffering the scenes of Missouri again in Nauvoo; no, it is better for your brother, Joseph, to die for his brothers and sisters, for I am willing to die for them. My work is finished."[14]

At about ten o'clock the group arrived at a farm four miles west of Carthage, where they met a company of sixty mounted Illinois militia. Captain Dunn presented an order from Governor Ford for all the state arms in the possession of the Nauvoo Legion to be surrendered. At Dunn's request, Joseph Smith agreed to return to Nauvoo to forestall any resistance. Joseph then sent a note explaining his delay to the governor in Carthage. Before returning to Nauvoo, Joseph prophesied, "I am going like a lamb to the slaughter, but I am calm as a summer's morning. I have a conscience void of offense toward God and toward all men. If they take my life I shall die an innocent man, and my blood shall cry from the ground for vengeance, and it shall be said of me 'He was murdered in cold blood!' "[15]

Upon returning to Nauvoo, Joseph directed that three small cannons and about two hundred firearms be turned over to the militia. This action revived agonizing memories of the Mormon disarmament that had preceded the Missouri massacre. The Prophet also had another opportunity to bid farewell to his family. He left for Carthage at 6:00 P.M.

Five minutes before midnight on 24 June, Captain Dunn and his company of sixty mounted men of the Augusta militia rode into Carthage with Joseph and Hyrum Smith and the members of the Nauvoo city council as voluntary captives. Joseph and Hyrum were weary from flight, hiding out, and the threat of assassination. Nevertheless the brothers were imposing figures as they rode into town—the Prophet, age thirty-eight, and Hyrum, forty-four—both tall men who towered over most of the others.

Carthage was in a riotous state. Mobs of irate townsmen and farmers from throughout western Illinois had been clamoring for the arrest of the Mormon prophet. They were now eager to see the captives. Among the mob were more than fourteen hundred unruly militia, including the local Carthage Greys. Crowds had been roaming the town all day, drinking and brawling. They wanted to get their hands on the Smith brothers. Through Captain Dunn's efforts, the prisoners were safely placed in the Hamilton

The Hamilton House was an inn where Joseph and Hyrum stayed when they first went to Carthage and where their bodies were taken after the Martyrdom.

House hotel. The Greys still clamored to see Joseph Smith. Finally Governor Ford put his head out the window and calmed the crowd by announcing that Mr. Smith would be paraded before the troops the next day.

Early the next morning Joseph and his brethren surrendered to constable David Bettisworth on the original charge of riot. Almost immediately Joseph and Hyrum were charged with treason against the state of Illinois for declaring martial law in Nauvoo. At 8:30 that morning the governor ordered the troops to the public ground where he addressed them. He told them that the prisoners were dangerous men and perhaps guilty, but that they were now in the hands of the law, and the law must take its course. These remarks only incited the soldiers to greater rage. Joseph and Hyrum were then paraded before the troops where they endured many vulgar insults and death threats.

At four o'clock that afternoon a preliminary hearing was held before Robert F. Smith, a justice of the peace who was also captain of the Carthage Greys and active in the anti-Mormon party. Each member of the Nauvoo city council was released on five hundred dollar bonds and ordered to appear at the next term of the circuit court. Most of the accused men then left for Nauvoo, but Joseph and Hyrum remained for an interview with Governor Ford. That evening a constable appeared with a mittimus (a commitment to prison) signed by Judge Smith to hold Joseph and Hyrum in jail until they could be tried for treason, a capital offense. Joseph and his lawyers protested that the mittimus was illegal, since there had been no mention of that charge at their hearing. Their complaints were taken to the governor, but he said he could not interrupt a civil officer in the discharge of his duty.

Judge Smith, as captain of the Greys, sent his soldiers to carry out the mittimus he had issued as justice of the peace. Joseph and Hyrum were hustled to Carthage Jail amidst a great rabble in the streets. Eight of their friends went with them, including John Taylor and Willard Richards. Dan Jones with his walking stick and Stephen Markham with his hickory cane,

The jail was begun in 1839 and completed two years later at a cost of $4,105. It was used for about twenty-five years. Later it was used as a private residence and became one of the nicest homes in Carthage. Under the direction of President Joseph F. Smith, the Church purchased the building and property in 1903 for $4,000. In 1938 the Church restored the building.

1. *This is where Hyrum Smith lay after the bullet penetrating the door hit him in the face. This room was also the jailer's bedroom.*
2. *Willard Richards stood behind the door and tried to ward off the attackers with a cane.*
3. *John Taylor crawled under the bed after being wounded.*
4. *The Prophet fell from the second story window and landed by the well—having received four bullets, which took his life.*
5. *There was a cell for prisoners located in this room; this area was called the dungeon, or criminal cell.*
6. *This was a summer kitchen and porch used by the jailer and his family.*
7. *The living room was located on the main floor.*
8. *The dining room was located on the main floor.*
9. *The debtor's cell is located on the northwest side of the main floor. This room was used to hold prisoners accused of a less severe offense.*

which he called the "rascal beater," walked on either side of the Prophet and his brother warding off the drunken crowd. As it turned out, the stone jail was the safest place in town. Several of Joseph and Hyrum's friends were permitted to stay with them.

The next day, 26 June, a hearing was held on the charge of treason. The defendants had no witnesses present; since treason was a non-bailable charge, they were required to remain in custody until another hearing could be held on 29 June. Some of the brethren met with Governor Ford and told him that if he went to Nauvoo, Joseph and Hyrum would not be safe in Carthage. Ford promised that he would take Joseph and Hyrum with him. Joseph spent the afternoon dictating to his scribe, Willard Richards, while Dan Jones and Stephen Markham whittled at the warped door to their room in the jail with a penknife so it could be latched securely to prepare against possible attack.

That night Willard Richards, John Taylor, and Dan Jones remained with Joseph and Hyrum in jail. They prayed together and read from the Book of Mormon. Joseph bore his testimony to the guards. Much later, Joseph was lying on the floor next to riverboat captain Dan Jones. "Joseph whispered to Dan Jones, 'are you afraid to die?' Dan said, 'Has that time come, think you? Engaged in such a cause I do not think that death would have many terrors.' Joseph replied, 'You will yet see Wales [Jones's native land], and fulfill the mission appointed you before you die.' "[16] Elder Jones later fulfilled the prophecy, serving a great mission in Wales.

About midnight several men surrounded the jail and started up the stairs to the prisoners' room. One of the brethren grabbed a weapon that had been smuggled into their room during the day. Members of the mob, standing near the door, heard them moving and hesitated. "The Prophet with a 'Prophet's voice' called out 'Come on ye assassins we are ready for you, and would as willingly die now as at daylight.' "[17] The mob retreated.

THE TRAGEDY AT CARTHAGE

The next morning, Thursday, 27 June, "Joseph requested Dan Jones to descend and inquire of the guard the cause of the disturbance in the night. Frank Worrell, the officer of the guard, who was one of the Carthage Greys, in a very bitter spirit said, 'We have had too much trouble to bring Old Joe here to let him ever escape alive, and unless you want to die with him you had better leave before sundown; . . . and you'll see that I can prophesy better than Old Joe. . . .'

"Joseph directed Jones to go to Governor Ford and inform him what he had been told by the officer of the guard. While Jones was going to Governor Ford's quarters, he saw an assemblage of men, and heard one of them, who was apparently a leader, making a speech, saying that, 'Our troops will be discharged this morning in obedience to orders, and for a sham we will leave the town; but when the Governor and the McDonough troops have left for Nauvoo this afternoon, we will return and kill those men, if we have to tear the jail down.' This sentiment was applauded by three cheers from the crowd.

"Captain Jones went to the Governor, told him what had occurred in the night, what the officer of the guard had said, and what he had heard while coming to see him, and earnestly solicited him to avert the danger.

"His Excellency replied, 'You are unnecessarily alarmed for the safety of your friends, sir, the people are not that cruel.'

"Irritated by such a remark, Jones urged the necessity of placing better men to guard them than professed assassins. . . .

". . . Jones remarked, 'If you do not do this, I have but one more desire, . . .

". . . 'that the Almighty will preserve my life to a proper time and place, that I may testify that you have been timely warned of their danger.'. . .

". . . Jones' life was threatened, and Chauncey L. Higbee said to him in the street, 'We are determined to kill Joe and Hyrum, and you had better go away to save yourself.' "[18]

That morning Joseph wrote to Emma, "I am very much resigned to my lot, knowing I am justified, and have done the best that could be done. Give my love to the children and all my friends. . . . May God bless you all."[19] The Prophet also sent a letter to the well-known lawyer Orville H. Browning asking him to come and defend him. Soon afterward, Joseph's friends, with the exception of Willard Richards and John Taylor, were forced to leave the jail.

Dan Jones (1811–62) was born in Flintshire, Wales, and later emigrated to America, where he joined the Church. In fulfillment of a prophetic promise given him by the Prophet in the Carthage Jail, Dan served a mission in Wales from 1845 to 1849. He wrote and translated Church publications for the Welsh, and assisted in bringing over two thousand converts into the Church.

He was called a second time to Wales in 1852 and became mission president in 1854, where he again performed a great work among the people of his native land.

The Prophet used this six-shooter, called a "pepper-box," to defend himself and his fellow prisoners.
John S. Fullmer took this single-barrel pistol into the jail, but it was never used by the prisoners.

Contrary to his promise, Governor Ford left that morning for Nauvoo without Joseph and Hyrum, taking instead Captain Dunn's Dragoons from McDonough County, the only troops that had demonstrated neutrality in the affair. En route, he sent an order to all other troops at Carthage and Warsaw to disband, except for a company of the Carthage Greys to guard the jail. The Greys were Joseph's most hostile enemies and could not be depended upon to protect him. They were part of a conspiracy to feign defense of the prisoners when enemies of the Prophet would later storm the jail.

In Nauvoo, Ford delivered an insulting speech. He said, "A great crime has been done by destroying the *Expositor* press and placing the city under martial law, and a severe atonement must be made, so prepare your minds for the emergency. Another cause of excitement is the fact of your having so many firearms. The public are afraid that you are going to use them against government. I know there is a great prejudice against you on account of your peculiar religion, but you ought to be praying Saints, not military Saints."[20]

Meanwhile, Colonel Levi Williams of the Warsaw militia read to his men the governor's orders to disband. Thomas Sharp then addressed the men and called for them to march east to Carthage. Shouts followed for volunteers to kill the Smiths. Some of the men disguised themselves by smearing their faces with mud mixed with gunpowder and started for Carthage.

At the jail, the four brethren sweltered in the sultry afternoon heat. Joseph gave Hyrum a single-shot pistol and prepared to defend himself with the six-shooter smuggled in that morning by Cyrus Wheelock. Gravely depressed, the brethren asked John Taylor to sing a popular song entitled "A Poor Wayfaring Man of Grief," about a suffering stranger who revealed himself at last as the Savior. Joseph asked John to sing it again, which he did. In view of their circumstances, one of the verses seems especially poignant:

In pris'n I saw him next—condemned
To meet a traitor's doom at morn;
The tide of lying tongues I stemmed,
And honored him 'mid shame and scorn.

My friendship's utmost zeal to try,
He asked, if I for him would die;
The flesh was weak, my blood ran chill,
But my free spirit cried, "I will!"[21]

At 4:00 P.M. the guard at the jail was changed. Frank Worrell, who had threatened Joseph Smith earlier that morning, was then in charge. A few minutes after five, a mob of about one hundred men with blackened faces arrived in town and headed for the jail. The prisoners heard a scuffle downstairs followed by a shout for surrender and three or four shots. The Prophet and the others rushed to the door to fight off the assailants who had ascended the stairs and poked their guns through the half-closed door. John Taylor and Willard Richards attempted to deflect the muskets with their

The Martyrdom of Joseph and Hyrum
by Gary Smith

Death of the Prophet *by Gary Smith*

John Taylor's watch and cane

canes. A bullet fired through the panel of the door struck Hyrum in the left side of his face, and he fell, saying, "I am a dead man!" Joseph, leaning over Hyrum exclaimed, "Oh dear, brother Hyrum!" John Taylor said the look of sorrow he saw on Joseph's face was forever imprinted on his mind. Joseph then stepped to the door, reached around the door casing, and discharged his six-shooter into the crowded hall. Only three of the six chambers fired, wounding three assailants.

The shots delayed the assassins only a moment. John Taylor attempted to jump out of the window, but was hit by gunfire. A shot through the window

Willard Richards (1804–54) was ordained an Apostle in 1840 and served as one of the personal secretaries to Joseph Smith. He was also appointed as historian in 1842 and general Church recorder in 1845. From his experiences in Carthage he wrote the moving account "Two Minutes in Jail." He became second counselor to President Brigham Young in 1847 and served in that position until his death.

John Taylor (1808–87), a member of the Quorum of the Twelve since 19 December 1838, was severely wounded at Carthage. He and Willard Richards became the apostolic witnesses to the shedding of the innocent blood of Joseph and Hyrum Smith. John Taylor presided over the Church from the death of Brigham Young on 29 August 1877 until his own death on 25 July 1887.

from below hit the watch in his vest pocket, stopping it at 5:16 and knocking him back into the room. He fell to the floor and was shot again in his left wrist and below his left knee. Rolling to get under the bed, he was hit again from the stairway, the bullet tearing away his flesh at the left hip. His blood was splattered on the floor and the wall. "Joseph, seeing there was no safety in the room," tried the same escape. Instantly the mob fired on him, and he fell mortally wounded through the open window exclaiming, "Oh Lord, my God!" The mob on the stairs rushed outside to assure themselves that Joseph Smith was dead.[22]

Willard Richards alone remained unscathed, having only had a bullet graze his ear. Earlier Joseph had prophesied in Willard's presence that one day he would stand while bullets whizzed around him and would escape unharmed. Only then did Willard fully understand what Joseph had meant. He dragged the terribly wounded John Taylor into the next room, deposited him on straw, and covered him with an old filthy mattress. The straw, Elder Taylor believed, saved his life by helping stop his bleeding. Meanwhile Willard, expecting to be killed at any moment, was surprised when the mob fled and left him alone with his dead and wounded comrades.

Samuel Smith, brother to the Prophet, heard about death threats to his brothers and hurried to Carthage. He arrived in Carthage that evening physically exhausted, having been chased by the mobbers. Through the exertion and fatigue of a life and death chase, Samuel contracted a fever that led to his death on 30 July. At Carthage, Samuel helped Elder Richards move the bodies of his martyred brothers to the Hamilton House. After a coroner's inquiry, Willard Richards wrote to the Saints at Nauvoo, "Joseph and Hyrum are dead."[23]

Mobbers fled to Warsaw, their hometown, and then, fearing retaliation from the Mormons, continued across the river into Missouri. Governor Ford heard about the assassinations shortly after he left Nauvoo to return to Carthage. When he arrived he urged the few remaining citizens to evacuate the town and had county records moved to Quincy for safety. None of this was necessary. When the Saints heard of the deaths of their beloved leaders, they were overwhelmed with grief rather than desire for revenge.

On the morning of 28 June 1844 the bodies of the slain leaders were gently placed on two different wagons, covered with branches to shade them from the hot summer sun, and driven to Nauvoo by Willard Richards, Samuel Smith, and Artois Hamilton. The wagons left Carthage about 8 A.M. and arrived in Nauvoo about 3 P.M. and were met by a great assemblage. The bodies lay in state the following day in the Mansion House while thousands of people silently filed past the coffins. The shock of the deaths was devastating to the families of the martyrs. Joseph and Hyrum were buried in secret in the basement of the Nauvoo House so that those who wanted to collect a reward offered for Joseph's head could not find the remains. A public funeral was held and caskets filled with sand were buried in the Nauvoo

Joseph Smith and his family moved into the Mansion House in August 1843. Later a wing was added to the east side of the main structure, making it L-shaped in appearance with a total of twenty-two rooms. Beginning in January 1844, Ebenezer Robinson managed the Mansion House as a hotel. The Prophet maintained six rooms for himself and his family.

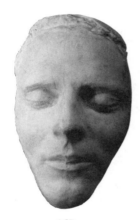

Death masks of Joseph and Hyrum Smith

Cemetery. For weeks the Saints sorrowed deeply over the tragedy at Carthage.

GREATNESS OF JOSEPH SMITH

Elder John Taylor, who miraculously survived Carthage, wrote an account of the event and a eulogy to the Prophet, which are found in Doctrine and Covenants 135. "Joseph Smith, the Prophet and Seer of the Lord, has done more, save Jesus only, for the salvation of men in this world, than any other man that ever lived in it" (v. 3). He added that the names of Joseph and Hyrum Smith "will be classed among the martyrs of religion; and the reader in every nation will be reminded that the Book of Mormon, and this book of Doctrine and Covenants of the church, cost the best blood of the nineteenth century to bring them forth for the salvation of a ruined world" (v. 6). The martyrdom, he said, fulfilled an important spiritual purpose: Joseph "lived great, and he died great in the eyes of God and his people; and like most of the Lord's anointed in ancient times, has sealed his mission and his works with his own blood; and so has his brother Hyrum. In life they were not divided, and in death they were not separated!" (v. 3).

While Joseph Smith lived only thirty-eight and a half years, his accomplishments in the service of mankind are incalculable. In addition to translating the Book of Mormon, he received hundreds of revelations, many of which are published in the Doctrine and Covenants and the Pearl of Great Price. He unfolded eternal principles in a legacy of letters, sermons, poetry, and other inspired writings that fills volumes. He established the restored Church of Jesus Christ on the earth, founded a city, and superintended the building of two temples. He introduced vicarious ordinance work for the dead and restored temple ordinances by which worthy families could be sealed by the priesthood for eternity. He ran for the presidency of the United States, served as a judge, mayor of Nauvoo, and lieutenant general of the Nauvoo Legion.

Josiah Quincy, a prominent New England citizen who later became the mayor of Boston, visited Joseph Smith two months before the Martyrdom. Many years later he wrote about the people who had most impressed him during his life. Regarding Joseph Smith, he wrote, "It is by no means improbable that some future text-book, for the use of generations yet unborn, will contain a question something like this: What historical American of the nineteenth century has exerted the most powerful influence upon the destinies of his countrymen? And it is by no means impossible that the answer to that interrogatory may be thus written *Joseph Smith, the Mormon prophet.*"[24]

ENDNOTES

1. Lucy Mack Smith, *History of Joseph Smith*, ed. Preston Nibley (Salt Lake City: Bookcraft, 1958), pp. 309–10.

2. Wilford Woodruff Journals, 22 Jan. 1843, LDS Historical Department, Salt Lake City; spelling, punctuation, and capitalization standardized; see also Richard Lloyd Anderson, "Joseph Smith's Prophecies of Martyrdom," in *Sidney B. Sperry Symposium,* 1980 (Provo: Brigham Young University, 1980), pp. 1–14.

3. In "Trial of Elder Rigdon," *Times and Seasons,* 15 Sept. 1844, p. 651; spelling, punctuation, and capitalization standardized.

4. Wilford Woodruff Journals, 24 Mar. 1844; spelling, punctuation, and capitalization standardized.

5. See Wilford Woodruff Journals, 6 Apr. 1844.

6. See Dallin H. Oaks, "The Suppression of the Nauvoo Expositor," *Utah Law Review,* Winter 1965, pp. 890–91.

7. *Warsaw Signal,* 12 June 1844, p. 2.

8. *History of the Church,* 6:487.

9. *History of the Church,* 6:540.

10. *History of the Church,* 6:545–46.

11. Letter from Stephen Markham to Wilford Woodruff at Fort Supply, Wyoming, 20 June 1856, LDS Historical Department, Salt Lake City, p. 1; spelling standardized.

12. *History of the Church,* 6:549.

13. *History of the Church,* 6:554.

14. Dan Jones, in "The Martyrdom of Joseph Smith and His Brother, Hyrum," Ronald D. Dennis, trans., in *Brigham Young University Studies,* Winter 1984, p. 85.

15. *History of the Church,* 6:555; see also Doctrine and Covenants 135:4.

16. *History of the Church,* 6:601.

17. Letter from Dan Jones to Thomas Bullock, 20 Jan. 1855, in "The Martyrdom of Joseph and Hyrum Smith," cited in *Brigham Young University Studies,* Winter 1984, p. 101.

18. *History of the Church,* 6:602–4.

19. *History of the Church,* 6:605.

20. In *History of the Church,* 6:623.

21. *History of the Church,* 6:615; or *Hymns,* 1985, no. 29.

22. *History of the Church,* 6:617–18.

23. In *History of the Church,* 6:621–22; see also Dean Jarman, "The Life and Contributions of Samuel Harrison Smith," Master's thesis, Brigham Young University, 1961, pp. 103–5.

24. Josiah Quincy, *Figures of the Past from the Leaves of Old Journals,* 5th ed. (Boston: Roberts Brothers, 1883), p. 376.

CHAPTER TWENTY-THREE

THE TWELVE TO BEAR OFF THE KINGDOM

Time Line

Date	Significant Event
3 Aug. 1844	Sidney Rigdon arrived in Nauvoo from Pittsburgh claiming to be "guardian" of the Church
6 Aug. 1844	Members of the Twelve arrived in Nauvoo from the East
8 Aug. 1844	Brigham Young was transfigured before the people, and the Twelve were sustained as the presiding quorum in the Church

WITH THE DEATH of the Prophet Joseph Smith, the First Presidency of the Church was dissolved. Mourning their slain leader, the Saints wondered who would now lead the Church. Sidney Rigdon, who had left Nauvoo earlier in 1844, reappeared in the city on 3 August and asserted that he should be appointed "guardian" of the Church. In the absence of most of the Twelve, who were still en route back to Nauvoo from their Eastern missions, Sidney made some inroads with his claim. A meeting was called for 8 August to consider his guardianship.

A MONTH OF GLOOM

When Joseph Smith was murdered, a deep gloom fell over the city of Nauvoo. As Saints in other branches of the Church learned of the Martyrdom, they grieved also. Only the arrival of the Quorum of the Twelve and the firm direction they gave the Church gradually turned away this depressive spirit. The Twelve, except for John Taylor and Willard Richards, were in the East serving missions at the time of the Martyrdom. Although Joseph wrote them in June calling them home during the *Expositor* crisis, they did not receive these instructions until after the Martyrdom. Within three weeks, however, everyone had learned the tragic news and hurried back to Nauvoo.

The greatest achievement in Nauvoo between the Martyrdom and the return of the Apostles was the maintenance of peace. Although citizens in western Illinois feared reprisals, the Saints obeyed John Taylor and Willard Richards who instructed them to stay calm and allow government officials to find the murderers. Three days after the Carthage tragedy, Elder Richards wrote to Brigham Young, "The saints have borne this trial with great fortitude and forbearance. They must keep cool at present. We have pledged our faith not to prosecute the murderers at present, but leave it to Governor Ford; . . . vengeance is in the heavens."[1] The city council also instructed the residents: "Be peaceable, quiet citizens, doing the works of righteousness, and as soon as the Twelve and other authorities can assemble, or a majority of them, the onward course to the great gathering of Israel, and the final consummation of the dispensation of the fulness of times will be pointed out."[2]

Elder John Taylor, seriously wounded in the Carthage Jail, returned to Nauvoo on 2 July. Throughout the month he improved steadily, but

Thomas Ford (1800–50) was born in Pennsylvania and raised in Illinois, where he studied law. He served as Illinois state attorney, then as a circuit judge, and as a justice of the Illinois Supreme Court. He was governor of Illinois from 1842 to 1846.

remained bedfast. Notwithstanding his disability, he helped Elder Richards direct the Church until the rest of the Twelve returned. Together Elder Richards and Elder Taylor wrote to the many Saints in Great Britain and explained:

"The action of the saints has been of the most pacific kind, remembering that God has said, 'Vengeance is mine, I will repay.'. . .

"These servants of God have gone to heaven by fire—the fire of an ungodly mob. Like the Prophets of ancient days they lived as long as the world would receive them; and this is one furnace in which the saints were to be tried, to have their leaders cut off from their midst, and not be permitted to avenge their blood."[3]

William W. Phelps—Church publisher, city councilman, and scribe to the Prophet—helped immeasurably in keeping order in the city. Since his return to the Church in 1842, Elder Phelps had indefatigably sought to build up the kingdom and had helped the Prophet with a number of important projects, such as the publishing of the book of Abraham and the campaign for the presidency. He was the principal speaker at the funeral services of Joseph and Hyrum. Now he helped Elders Taylor and Richards during this critical interim period. As a poet, he memorialized the Prophet in lines which later became a favorite Church hymn:

Praise to the man who communed with Jehovah!
Jesus anointed that Prophet and Seer.
Blessed to open the last dispensation,
Kings shall extol him, and nations revere.
Hail to the Prophet, ascended to heaven!
Traitors and tyrants now fight him in vain.
Mingling with Gods, he can plan for his brethren;
Death cannot conquer the hero again.[4]

Within a month the Saints suffered another tragedy: the death of Samuel H. Smith, brother to Joseph and Hyrum. Samuel was one of the first Saints on the scene at Carthage following the Martyrdom. He had fled from the enemies of the Church to reach his brothers in Carthage only to find them slain. The stress weakened him physically. He contracted a serious fever; his health gradually failed, and he died on 30 July 1844. He was lauded in the *Times and Seasons* as one of the great men of this dispensation. His grief-stricken mother, Lucy Mack Smith, had seen within four years the death of her husband and of four sons: Don Carlos, Hyrum, Joseph, and Samuel.

The Twelve Return

On the day of the Martyrdom, members of the Twelve were depressed and melancholic without knowing why. Elders Heber C. Kimball and Lyman Wight were traveling between Philadelphia and New York City when Elder

At the time of the death of Joseph and Hyrum Smith, the Apostles were located in various parts of the country.
Brigham Young, Orson Hyde, and Wilford Woodruff were in Boston.
Heber C. Kimball and Lyman Wight had left Philadelphia and were traveling to New York. William Smith at some point joined them, and they continued to Boston for an appointed conference that was held on 29 June. Seven members of the Twelve were present at the conference—Brigham Young, Heber C. Kimball, Orson Hyde, William Smith, Orson Pratt, Wilford Woodruff, and Lyman Wight.
Parley P. Pratt was returning to Nauvoo and was on a canal boat between Utica and Buffalo, New York.
George A. Smith was staying with members of the Church near Jacksonburg, Michigan.
Amasa Lyman was in Cincinnati.
The location of Orson Pratt on 27 June is not known, but on 29 June he attended the conference in Boston, so he must have been fairly close to Boston on the day of the Martyrdom.
John E. Page had been in Pittsburgh, where he edited and published the Gospel Light from June 1843 to May 1844. His exact location is not known, but in all probability he was in Pittsburgh or the surrounding area.
John Taylor and Willard Richards were in Carthage.

Kimball felt mournful, as if he had just lost a friend. In Boston, Orson Hyde was examining maps in the hall rented by the Church when he felt a heavy and sorrowful spirit come upon him. Tears ran down his cheeks as he turned from the maps and paced the floor. In Michigan, George A. Smith was plagued with a depressed spirit and foreboding thoughts all day long. When he retired to bed he could not sleep. He said that "Once it seemed to him that some fiend whispered in his ear, 'Joseph and Hyrum are dead; ain't you glad of it?' "5

Two days before the Martyrdom, Parley P. Pratt was moved upon by the Spirit to start home from New York State and coincidentally met his brother William on a canal boat on the day of the tragedy. Parley wrote that as they talked, "a strange and solemn awe came over me, as if the powers of hell were let loose. I was so overwhelmed with sorrow I could hardly speak. . . . 'Let us observe an entire and solemn silence, for this is a dark day, and the hour of triumph for the powers of darkness. O, how sensible I am of the spirit of murder which seems to prevade the whole land.' "6

Parley P. Pratt was the first Apostle outside of Nauvoo to learn of the Martyrdom. He was on a steamboat headed across the Great Lakes toward Chicago. At a landing in Wisconsin, boarding passengers brought news of the Carthage murders. There was great excitement on board, and many passengers taunted him, asking what the Mormons would do now. He replied that "they would continue their mission and spread the work he [Joseph Smith] had restored, in all the world. Observing that nearly all the prophets and Apostles who were before him had been killed, and also the Saviour of the world, and yet their death did not alter the truth nor hinder its final triumph."7

In sorrow Elder Pratt walked 105 miles across the plains of Illinois, hardly able to eat or sleep, wondering how he should meet the entire community bowed down with grief and unutterable sorrow. He prayed for assistance. "On a sudden the Spirit of God came upon me, and filled my heart with joy and gladness indescribable; and while the spirit of revelation glowed in my bosom with as visible a warmth and gladness as if it were fire. The Spirit said unto me: . . . 'Go and say unto my people in Nauvoo, that they shall continue to pursue their daily duties and take care of themselves, and make no movement in Church government to reorganize or alter anything until the return of the remainder of the Quorum of the Twelve. But exhort them that they continue to build the House of the Lord which I have commanded them to build in Nauvoo.' "8 Arriving in Nauvoo on 8 July, Parley helped Elders Richards and Taylor keep order in the stricken community.

George A. Smith learned of the Martyrdom from a newspaper account in Michigan on 13 July. At first he thought it a hoax, but when the report was confirmed, he hastened home with his three missionary companions. Worn out with anxiety and loss of sleep, he came down with hives. His whole body was swollen, and he was unable to eat, but he continued his journey, arriving in Nauvoo on 27 July. Soon he was meeting in council with the three Apostles already there.[9]

In Boston rumors of Joseph Smith's death began on 9 July. During the week before confirmation came from family letters and more complete newspaper accounts, Brigham Young, Wilford Woodruff, and Orson Pratt struggled within themselves about what the terrible news meant. Brigham recorded in his journal, "The first thing which I thought of was, whether Joseph had taken the keys of the kingdom with him from the earth; brother Orson Pratt sat on my left; we were both leaning back on our chairs. Bringing my hand down on my knee, I said the keys of the kingdom are right here with the Church."[10]

Brigham Young, Heber C. Kimball, Orson Pratt, Wilford Woodruff, and Lyman Wight contacted each other, joined together, and hastened home by railway, stagecoach, boat, and buggy. Subsequent events proved the wisdom of their haste. They arrived in Nauvoo the evening of 6 August. Wilford Woodruff recorded his feelings:

"When we landed in the city there was a deep gloom seemed to rest over the City of Nauvoo which we never experienced before.

". . . We were received with gladness by the Saints throughout the city. They felt like sheep without a shepherd, as being without a father, as their head had been taken away."[11]

THE SUCCESSION CRISIS

The arrival of most of the Apostles on 6 August was none too soon. A crisis had arisen as to who should lead the Church, and Willard Richards had nearly worn himself out trying to keep the Saints united. On Saturday, 3 August, Sidney Rigdon had returned from his self-imposed exile in Pittsburgh, Pennsylvania, where he had moved contrary to revelation (see D&C 124:108–9). Sidney returned with the expectation of taking over the Church. Not all of the Saints in Nauvoo realized that the Prophet had lost confidence in his first counselor quite a while before the Martyrdom.

Sidney avoided meeting with the four Apostles who were already in Nauvoo, choosing instead to speak to the assembled Saints at the grove on Sunday, 4 August. He asserted that he had received a vision:

"He related a vision which he said the Lord had shown him concerning the situation of the church, and said there must be a guardian appointed to build the church up to Joseph, as he had begun it.

"He said he was the identical man that the ancient prophets had sung about, wrote and rejoiced over, and that he was sent to do the identical work that had been the theme of all the prophets in every preceding generation."[12] Elder Parley P. Pratt later remarked that Sidney Rigdon was "the identical

Sidney Rigdon (1793–1876) was called to serve as a counselor to Joseph Smith in the First Presidency. He was a gifted orator and a spokesman for the Prophet on many occasions. Several of the revelations in the Doctrine and Covenants deal with Sidney Rigdon.

man the prophets *never* sang nor wrote a word about."[13] At the meeting, Sidney asked William Marks, Nauvoo stake president, who sympathized with Sidney's claims, to call a meeting of the Church on 6 August to sustain a new leader. President Marks changed the meeting to Thursday, 8 August, which proved providential since the remainder of the Twelve did not arrive until the evening of 6 August.

Sidney also met with William Marks and Emma Smith in Joseph Smith's home in order to appoint a trustee-in-trust for the Church. Emma wanted this done quickly to prevent loss of personal and Church property that was in Joseph Smith's name. Parley P. Pratt came into the meeting and immediately protested the move. He explained that appointing a trustee-in-trust was the business of the entire Church through its General Authorities, not the business of the local authorities of any one stake. Parley insisted that "dollars and cents were no consideration with me, when principle was at stake, and if thousands or even millions were lost, let them go. We could not and would not suffer the authorities and principles of the Church to be trampled under foot, for the sake of pecuniary interest."[14] The meeting broke up without any decision being made.

On Monday, 5 August, Sidney Rigdon finally met with the Apostles who were in Nauvoo. He declared, " 'Gentlemen, you're used up; gentlemen, you are all divided; the anti-Mormons have got you; the brethren are voting every way . . . everything is in confusion, you can do nothing, you lack a great leader, you want a head, and unless you unite upon that head you are blown to the four winds, the anti-Mormons will carry the election—a guardian must be appointed.'

"Elder George A. Smith said, 'Brethren, Elder Rigdon is entirely mistaken, there is no division; the brethren are united; the election will be unanimous, and the friends of law and order will be elected by a thousand majority. There is no occasion to be alarmed. President Rigdon is inspiring fears there are no grounds for.' "[15]

Under such circumstances the arrival of the Twelve from the East on the evening of 6 August was timely. They met the next morning in the home of John Taylor and rejoiced to be together again "and to be welcomed by the saints who considered it very providential for the Twelve to arrive at this particular juncture, when their minds were agitated, their hearts sorrowful, and darkness seemed to cloud their path."[16] Brigham Young took firm control of the meeting. After a discussion of all that had transpired, he announced there would be another meeting at 4:00 P.M., to be attended by the Apostles, the Nauvoo high council, and high priests, to discuss Sidney's claims made to the Saints the previous Sunday.

At the meeting Sidney Rigdon was invited to make a statement about his vision and revelations. He said, "The object of my mission is to visit the saints and offer myself to them as a guardian. I had a vision at Pittsburgh, June 27th [the day of the Martyrdom]. This was presented to my mind not as an open vision, but rather a continuation of the vision mentioned in the *Book of Doctrine and Covenants* [referring to the vision he and Joseph Smith had experienced that is recorded in D&C 76]."[17] He went on to say that no one could take the place of Joseph as the head of the Church and that he, as the designated spokesman for the Prophet, should assume the role of guardian of the Church. Wilford Woodruff recorded in his journal that Sidney's statement was a "long story. It was a kind of second class vision."[18]

Following Sidney's remarks, Brigham Young spoke:

"I do not care who leads the church . . . but one thing I must know, and that is what God says about it. I have the keys and the means of obtaining the mind of God on the subject. . . .

"Joseph conferred upon our heads all the keys and powers belonging to the Apostleship which he himself held before he was taken away, and no man or set of men can get between Joseph and the Twelve in this world or in the world to come.

"How often has Joseph said to the Twelve, 'I have laid the foundation and you must build thereon, for upon your shoulders the kingdom rests.'"[19]

President Young then designated Tuesday, 13 August as a special conference in which the people would be organized in a solemn assembly to vote on the matter. The next morning, however, the Apostles met privately and, "in consequence of some excitement among the People and a dispositions by some spirits to try to divide the Church," decided to hold the solemn assembly that afternoon rather than wait until the following Tuesday.[20]

THE MANTLE FALLS ON BRIGHAM YOUNG

Thursday, 8 August 1844, stands as one of the most important days in the history of the Restoration. On that day a miracle occurred before the body of the Church—Brigham Young was magnified before the people, and the succession crisis of the Church was resolved. A prayer meeting was held that morning at ten o'clock in the grove, according to the arrangements of William Marks. Sidney Rigdon spoke for an hour and a half about his desires to be the guardian of the Church, but he awakened no emotion and said nothing that marked him as the true leader. Brigham Young, who arrived after the meeting started, also spoke; his remarks were short. He told the audience that he would rather have spent a month mourning the dead Prophet than so quickly attend to the business of appointing a new shepherd.[21] While he was speaking, he was miraculously transfigured before the people.

People of all ages were present, and they later recorded their experiences. Benjamin F. Johnson, twenty-six at that time, remembered, "As soon as he [Brigham Young] spoke I jumped upon my feet, for in every possible degree it was Joseph's voice, and his person, in look, attitude, dress and appearance was Joseph himself, personified; and I knew in a moment the spirit and mantle of Joseph was upon him."[22] Zina Huntington, who was a young

Benjamin F. Johnson (1818–1905) was a close friend of the Prophet Joseph Smith. He served for a time as the Prophet's private secretary. He was one of the original pioneers who entered the Salt Lake Valley on 22 October 1848.[23] *He later served as a patriarch.*

Zina Diantha Huntington Young (1821–1901) was General President of the Relief Society from 1888 to 1901. Zina, a plural wife of Brigham Young, became known in Utah for her medical skills.

Amasa Lyman (1813–77) was a member of the Quorum of the Twelve from 1842 to 1867. He was replaced in the Quorum on 20 January 1843 due to the reinstatement of Orson Pratt. He was appointed a counselor in the First Presidency about 4 February 1843 and at the death of Joseph Smith was returned to the Quorum of the Twelve on 12 August 1844.

woman twenty-one years old at that time, said "President Young was speaking. It was the voice of Joseph Smith—not that of Brigham Young. His very person was changed. . . . I closed my eyes. I could have exclaimed, I know that is Joseph Smith's voice! Yet I knew he had gone. But the same spirit was with the people." [24]

George Q. Cannon, then a boy of fifteen, declared that "it was the voice of Joseph himself; and not only was it the voice of Joseph which was heard; but it seemed in the eyes of the people as though it was the very person of Joseph which stood before them. . . . They both saw and heard with their natural eyes and ears, and then the words which were uttered came, accompanied by the convincing power of God, to their hearts, and they were filled with the Spirit and with great joy." [25] Wilford Woodruff testified, "If I had not seen him with my own eyes, there is no one that could have convinced me that it was not Joseph Smith speaking." [26]

In view of these statements, Brigham Young's own record of the events that day is especially meaningful: "My heart was swollen with compassion towards them and by the power of the Holy Ghost, even the spirit of the Prophets, I was enabled to comfort the hearts of the Saints." [27] The meeting was then dismissed until 2 o'clock in the afternoon.

At 2 P.M. thousands of Saints gathered for what they knew would be a significant meeting. With the quorums of the priesthood seated in order, Brigham Young spoke frankly about the proposed guardianship of Sidney Rigdon and his alienation from Joseph Smith during the previous two years. He boldly prophesied, "All that want to draw away a party from the church after them, let them do it if they can, but they will not prosper." [28]

President Young continued, and then turning to his main point declared,

"If the people want President Rigdon to lead them they may have him; but I say unto you that the Quorum of the Twelve have the keys of the kingdom of God in all the world.

"The Twelve are appointed by the finger of God. Here is Brigham, have his knees ever faltered? Have his lips ever quivered? Here is Heber and the rest of the Twelve, an independent body who have the keys of the priesthood—the keys of the kingdom of God to deliver to all the world: this is true, so help me God. They stand next to Joseph, and are as the First Presidency of the Church." [29]

He pointed out that Sidney could not be above the Twelve because they would have to ordain him to be President of the Church. Brigham urged everybody to see Brother Rigdon as a friend and stated that if he were to sit in cooperation and counsel with the Twelve, they would be able to act as one. Following President Young's two-hour speech, talks were delivered by Amasa Lyman, William W. Phelps, and Parley P. Pratt; each eloquently contended for the authority of the Twelve.

Brigham Young then arose and asked the basic question: "Do you want Brother Rigdon to stand forward as your leader, your guide, your spokesman. President Rigdon wants me to bring up the other question first, and that is, Does the church want, and is it their only desire to sustain the Twelve as the First Presidency of this people?" The vote was then taken, and all hands went up. Brigham then asked, "If there are any of the contrary mind, every man and every woman who does not want the Twelve to preside, lift up your hands in like manner." No hands went up.[30]

Before concluding the conference, President Young called for the members' approval on the following issues: tithing the members to complete the temple, allowing the Twelve to preach to all the world, financing of the Church, teaching bishops in handling the business affairs of the Church, appointing a patriarch to the Church to replace Hyrum Smith, and sustaining Sidney Rigdon with faith and prayers. The conference was then adjourned. Once more the Church had a presidency—the Quorum of the Twelve Apostles—with Brigham Young as their president.

PREPARATION OF THE TWELVE FOR THEIR RESPONSIBILITIES

For several years the Lord had carefully prepared the Quorum of the Twelve to assume the leadership of the Church. When the Twelve were first called in 1835, their duties were restricted to areas outside the organized stakes, but in time their responsibilities were broadened to include authority over all the members of the Church. Thomas B. Marsh, David W. Patten, and Brigham Young were called to lead the stake in Far West in 1838. And while Joseph and Hyrum were in Liberty Jail in Missouri, Brigham Young, Heber C. Kimball, and John Taylor of the Twelve directed the exodus of the Saints from Missouri to Illinois.

The mission of the Twelve to Great Britain welded them into a united quorum under the direction of Brigham Young. When they returned to America, the Prophet Joseph increased their responsibilities in both temporal and ecclesiastical affairs. They were involved in raising funds for the Nauvoo House and the temple as well as constructing them, helping the poor, managing land, and directing the settlement of new immigrants into Illinois. They participated in decisions affecting Nauvoo business and economic development. The Twelve were among the first to receive instruction from Joseph Smith on plural marriage and the temple ordinances. Members of the Twelve were given responsibility over Church publishing, they directed the calling, assigning, and instructing of missionaries, they presided over conferences both in the field and in Nauvoo, and they regulated the branches abroad.

Most importantly, Joseph Smith, feeling that he might soon die, took great care during the last seven months of his life to carefully prepare the Twelve. He met with the quorum almost every day to instruct them and give them additional responsibilities. In an extraordinary council meeting in late March 1844, he solemnly told the Twelve that he could now leave them because his work was done and the foundation was laid so the kingdom of God could be reared.

Wilford Woodruff later recalled those days of 1844:

"I am a living witness to the testimony that he [Joseph Smith] gave to the Twelve Apostles when all of us received our endowments from under his hands. I remember the last speech that he ever gave us before his death. It was before we started upon our mission to the East. He stood upon his feet some three hours. The room was filled as with consuming fire, his face was as clear as amber, and he was clothed upon by the power of God. He laid before us our duty. He laid before us the fullness of this great work of God; and in his remarks to us he said: 'I have had sealed upon my head every key, every power, every principle of life and salvation that God has ever given to any man who ever lived upon the face of the earth. And these principles and this Priesthood and power belong to this great and last dispensation which the God of Heaven has set His hand to establish in the earth. 'Now,' said he addressing the Twelve, 'I have sealed upon your heads every key, every power, and every principle which the Lord has sealed upon my head.' . . .

"After addressing us in this manner he said: 'I tell you, the burden of this kingdom now rests upon your shoulders; you have got to bear it off in all the world, and if you don't do it you will be damned.' " [31]

On this same occasion, Joseph conferred the keys of the sealing power on Brigham Young, President of the Twelve. Brigham later explained that "this last key of the priesthood is the most sacred of all, and pertains exclusively to the first presidency of the Church." [32]

FORMATION OF SPLINTER GROUPS

Even as the Twelve began to firmly exercise their authority, Sidney Rigdon and James J. Strang, a new convert to the Church, worked behind the scenes to try and wrest the leadership away. Rigdon claimed his authority was superior to that of the Twelve and, being unwilling to submit to their counsel, was excommunicated on 8 September 1844. He returned to Pittsburgh and the following spring organized a "Church of Christ" with Apostles, prophets, priests, and kings. This attracted a few people, those who opposed the Twelve and felt that Joseph Smith had been a fallen prophet. He published the *Latter Day Saints' Messenger and Advocate* to promulgate his views. By 1847 this small organization disintegrated. Rigdon, however, hung on to a handful of followers for another thirty years as the self-appointed "President of the Kingdom and the Church." He finally died in obscurity in the state of New York in 1876.

James J. Strang was a more imaginative and charismatic leader. Following his baptism by Joseph Smith, four months before the Martyrdom, he returned to his home in Wisconsin. In August 1844 he presented a letter that he claimed had been written by Joseph Smith, appointing himself as the Prophet's successor and designating Voree, Wisconsin, as the new gathering

James J. Strang (1813–56)

William Smith (1811–93), younger brother of the Prophet Joseph Smith, was a member of the Quorum of the Twelve from 1835 to 1845.

place. Brigham Young and the Twelve correctly branded the letter a forgery and excommunicated Strang. He nevertheless convinced some to follow him to Voree, eventually winning over three former members of the Twelve who had lost their standing in the Church—William E. McLellin, John E. Page, and William Smith. For a time he also had the support of William Marks and Martin Harris. His church had some missionary success in the East. In 1849 he located his colony on Beaver Island in Lake Michigan and had himself crowned "king of the kingdom." The group eventually ran into numerous economic difficulties, and in 1856 Strang was murdered by disaffected followers and the movement virtually collapsed.

Some of Joseph Smith's own family did not follow the Twelve. The Prophet's widow, Emma, could not be reconciled with the Twelve on economic and theological matters. She became embittered and influenced her children against following the direction of the Twelve. When the Saints made their exodus to the West, Emma and her family stayed in Nauvoo. When William Smith belatedly returned to Nauvoo from the East, he was ordained Church Patriarch to replace Hyrum. After a few months, he advanced his own claims to be Church leader. He was consequently excommunicated. Following a short association with Strang, William taught that Joseph Smith's eldest son should, by right of lineage, inherit the presidency and that he, William, was to be guardian and president pro tem until Joseph III was of age.

There were others who refused to follow the leadership of Brigham Young and the Twelve. A few members were disaffected over plural marriage; some isolated branches did not go west and became confused as to what course they should take. During the 1850s a "new organization" gradually emerged. In 1860 leaders of the new organization (among them William Marks) formed the Reorganized Church of Jesus Christ of Latter Day Saints and succeeded in naming Joseph Smith III to be its president. Eventually it established its headquarters in Independence, Missouri.

THE TWELVE AND THE PROCESS OF SUCCESSION

The apostolic succession in 1844 established the principles and set the pattern for future reorganizations of the Presidency of the Church. Following the death of each President, the keys of the kingdom, which have been conferred upon each Apostle at his ordination, reside with the Quorum of the Twelve as a body (see D&C 107:23–24; 112:15).

Elder Spencer W. Kimball, in a general conference address in 1970, explained the process: "The moment life passes from a President of the Church, a body of men become the composite leader—these men already seasoned with experience and training. The appointments have long been made, the authority given, the keys delivered. . . . the kingdom moves forward under this already authorized council. No 'running' for position, no electioneering, no stump speeches. What a divine plan! How wise our Lord, to organize so perfectly beyond the weakness of frail, grasping humans."[33]

The Lord controls succession in his church. President Ezra Taft Benson explained, "God knows all things, the end from the beginning, and no man becomes President of the church of Jesus Christ by accident, nor remains there by chance, nor is called home by happenstance."[34]

ENDNOTES

1. In *History of the Church,* 7:148.

2. W. W. Phelps, Willard Richards, and John Taylor, in *History of the Church,* 7:152.

3. In *History of the Church,* 7:173.

4. "Praise to the Man," *Hymns,* 1985, no. 27.

5. *History of the Church,* 7:133.

6. Parley P. Pratt, *Autobiography of Parley P. Pratt,* Classics in Mormon Literature series (Salt Lake City: Deseret Book Co., 1985), p. 292.

7. Pratt, *Autobiography of Parley P. Pratt,* p. 292.

8. Pratt, *Autobiography of Parley P. Pratt,* pp. 293–94.

9. See Merlo J. Pusey, *Builders of the Kingdom* (Provo: Brigham Young University Press, 1981), p. 52.

10. Elden Jay Watson, *Manuscript History of Brigham Young, 1801–1844* (Salt Lake City: Elden Jay Watson, 1968), p. 171.

11. Wilford Woodruff Journals, 6–7 Aug. 1844, LDS Historical Department, Salt Lake City; spelling, punctuation, and capitalization standardized.

12. *History of the Church,* 7:224.

13. In *History of the Church,* 7:225.

14. Pratt, *Autobiography of Parley P. Pratt,* p. 295.

15. *History of the Church,* 7:226.

16. *History of the Church,* 7:229.

17. In *History of the Church,* 7:229.

18. Wilford Woodruff Journals, 7 Aug. 1844; punctuation and capitalization standardized.

19. In *History of the Church,* 7:230.

20. Wilford Woodruff Journals, 8 Aug. 1844.

21. Brigham Young's Journal 1837–45, 8 Aug. 1844, LDS Historical Department, Salt Lake City, pp. 47–49.

22. Benjamin F. Johnson, *My Life's Review* (Independence, Mo.: Zion's Printing and Publishing Co., 1947), p. 104.

23. Johnson, *My Life's Review,* p. 123.

24. In Edward W. Tullidge, *The Women of Mormondom* (New York: Tullidge and Crandall, 1877), pp. 326–27.

25. "Joseph Smith, the Prophet," *Juvenile Instructor,* 29 Oct. 1870, pp. 174–75.

26. *Deseret Weekly News,* 15 Mar. 1892, p. 3; see also Truman G. Madsen, "Notes on the Succession of Brigham Young," in *Seminar on Brigham Young,* 12 May 1962, Brigham Young University Department of Extension Publications Adult Education and Extension Services, Provo, 1963, p. 9.

27. Brigham Young's Journal 1837–45, 8 Aug. 1844, p. 48; spelling and punctuation standardized.

28. In *History of the Church,* 7:232.

29. In *History of the Church,* 7:233.

30. In *History of the Church,* 7:240.

31. *Deseret Weekly News,* 15 Mar. 1892, p. 406.

32. "P. P. Pratt's Proclamation," *Millennial Star,* Mar. 1845, p. 151.

33. In Conference Report, Apr. 1970, p. 118.

34. Ezra Taft Benson, in Korea Area Conference 1975, p. 52.

NAUVOO UNDER APOSTOLIC LEADERSHIP

WITH THE ISSUE of succession settled, the Quorum of the Twelve Apostles began immediately to exercise its authority in leading the Church. In the *Times and Seasons* of 15 August 1844, they assured the Saints that as a body they were prepared to preside over the Church and promote its growth. They also reaffirmed the importance of gathering to Nauvoo and finishing the temple. They were equally eager to continue in the footsteps of the Prophet Joseph Smith in sending the gospel "forth through every neighborhood of this wide-spread country, and to all the world."[1] Despite their optimism, new challenges and difficulties lay ahead which would threaten the existence of Nauvoo and test their ability as religious leaders.

SETTING THE CHURCH IN ORDER

The Twelve met in council the day after they were sustained as the presiding authority of the Church. In that meeting and in several others in succeeding weeks, they began to set in order the organization and affairs of the Church. They first freed themselves from many financial duties by appointing Bishops Newel K. Whitney and George Miller to the office of trustee-in-trust. Amasa Lyman was called to the Quorum of the Twelve, and William Smith, as the oldest living son of Joseph Smith, Sr., was appointed Church Patriarch. Wilford Woodruff was sent to England to preside over the Church in Europe, and Parley P. Pratt was called to New York as president, publisher, and immigration agent in the Eastern states and provinces. Lyman Wight went to Texas, in accordance with a previous assignment from Joseph Smith, to locate potential sites for settlements. John Taylor was reassigned to edit the *Times and Seasons,* while Willard Richards continued as Church historian and recorder.

Church organization in the United States and Canada was expanded. Both countries were organized into districts, each presided over by a high priest. This provided needed administration for hundreds of scattered branches. Brigham Young, Heber C. Kimball, and Willard Richards supervised this organization, and by October eighty-five presiding high priests had been called and charged to build up stakes as large as Nauvoo.[2] In Nauvoo and surrounding settlements, teachers in the Aaronic Priesthood were urged to visit the homes of the Saints regularly, and deacons were assigned to assist the bishops in the care of the poor. (Until the 1850s these

Aaronic Priesthood offices were held primarily by adults.)

One additional far-reaching change involved the expansion of the seventies quorums in the Church. On 18 August, President Young declared, "a presidency of seven men will be chosen out of the first quorum to preside over the first ten quorums."[3] At the following October general conference, the number of quorums increased to twelve, and 430 seventies were ordained and assigned to their ranks. Speaking at the conference, Brigham Young said that if a person desired to preach the gospel, he would be called to be a seventy. By January 1846 there were more than thirty quorums of seventy functioning. The Seventies Hall, an elegant two-story brick meeting-house, was pushed to completion and used as a preparatory school for the many new missionaries.

An important building during the late Nauvoo period was the Seventies Hall. Intended primarily as a meeting place for various quorums of the seventy, it was constructed by cooperative effort and was completed and dedicated in December 1844.

The Seventies Hall housed a training school for missionaries, a small library, and a museum of artifacts that missionaries had brought back from various parts of the world. It was also used for a variety of important Church meetings. It was completely razed before 1900, but archaeological excavations located the original foundations, and it was reconstructed in 1971–72.

The Twelve also continued to weed apostate elements out of the Church. Brigham Young recounted a dream where he saw a fruit tree with dead branches at the top, which had to be pruned away so the tree could flourish. He urged, "Let us cut off the dead branches of the church that good fruit may grow and a voice will soon be heard, go and build up Zion and the Temple of the Lord."[4]

THE CITY OF JOSEPH

In 1844 Nauvoo was one of the most flourishing cities in Illinois. By perseverance, industry, and unity, the Saints had replaced the swamps with a thriving community in only five years. Advantageously situated on the Mississippi River, it promised to become a great commercial center. Many citizens in the surrounding communities, however, feared the Latter-day Saints and their religion and were determined to thwart the growth and development of Nauvoo.

In this 1846 daguerreotype of Nauvoo, frame and brick buildings dominate. Nauvoo grew and changed rapidly in the few years the Saints were there. When they first arrived they lived in tents, wagons, dugouts, lean-tos, or simple log structures. As they struggled to improve their economic, social, and cultural conditions, these were gradually replaced by traditional frame homes. In the late Nauvoo period, brick homes became popular. Meanwhile, many public buildings and businesses were also constructed.

They were particularly unhappy with what they considered to be special privileges given Nauvoo by its charter, and they called for its repeal and for the disbandment of the Nauvoo Legion. When the legislature convened in January 1845, these demands were accepted, and the Nauvoo Charter was revoked. This action seemed justified in part because many people believed that Nauvoo harbored renegades, rogues, counterfeiters, and other fugitives. At this time some areas of frontier Illinois were infested with gangsters powerful enough to control the courts and avoid punishment. Some lawless people claimed Church membership and said that crimes committed against gentiles were sanctioned by the Church. In reality the Church consistently excommunicated those who were guilty of serious crimes.

In the wake of numerous newspaper reports in western Illinois concerning the presence of lawless Mormons, Nauvoo citizens held a public meeting. They noted:

"Thieves and counterfeiters have in some instances fled to our city, either under the mistaken apprehension that we would screen them, or from a malignant design to palm upon us their own crimes, and thereby draw us under the lash of persecution; and *whereas* it can be proved that individuals, in order to swell the list of Mormon depredations, have reported property to be stolen, which at another time they have acknowledged, they sold the same property and received pay. . . .

"*Therefore,* be it resolved, unanimously, that we will use all lawful means in our power to assist the public to prevent stealing and bogusmaking, and bring the offenders to justice."[5]

The damage to the reputation of the Mormons, however, was already done, and with the repeal of the Nauvoo Charter, the Saints were without a legal government or the protection of their own militia. The brethren

The example of Heber C. Kimball was probably typical of the way Latter-day Saints changed and improved their dwellings. In 1839 he built a lean-to out of stable logs on the back of another house for his family's first home. Two months later he erected a larger log house, and after his return from England in 1841 he built another log house. In 1843 he added a brick addition.

It was not until the fall of 1845 that this two-story brick home was finished. It is a modified Federalist style with a picturesque stepped fire-gable on each end, which was typical of English architecture in this period. The Kimballs lived in this home less than five months before leaving with the vanguard pioneers in February 1846 to face six more years of tents, wagon boxes, and log cabins.

decided to continue the legion on an extralegal basis as an instrument of internal control and as a means of defense. Guards were posted to prevent people from going into or out of the city without permission of the authorities. Brigham Young renamed Nauvoo "The City of Joseph," a name approved by the Saints at the April general conference. Although part of Nauvoo was reincorporated as an official town by the legislature, there was still a need for additional protective measures. The city was kept relatively free of unwanted characters by an organized group of young men and boys known as the "whistling and whittling brigade." They followed unwanted visitors whistling and whittling until the irritated and frightened persons left town.

In spite of the challenges, Nauvoo continued to grow. The building industry particularly flourished and outdistanced all other trades in Nauvoo. New frame and brick homes, gardens, and farms were established. Many earlier settlers to Nauvoo built new homes, since their original shelter was often a hastily constructed log or frame hut. Heber C. Kimball and Willard Richards replaced their log homes with handsome two-story brick houses in 1845. The Church also constructed a home for Lucy Mack Smith during this period. Public construction projects, such as the Seventies Hall and Concert Hall, complemented the residential building boom. A stone dike, or wing dam, in the Mississippi River, intended as a source of water power for workshops and machinery, was also begun. The largest project, however, continued to be the completion of the Nauvoo Temple.

In June of 1845, Brigham Young sent a letter to Wilford Woodruff, then serving as president of the British Mission, about the growth of Nauvoo. He wrote that the city "looks like a paradise. All the lots and land, which have heretofore been vacant and unoccupied, were enclosed in the spring, and planted with grain and vegetables, which makes it look more like a garden of gardens than a city. . . . Hundreds of acres of prairie land have also been enclosed, and are now under good cultivation, blooming with corn, wheat, potatoes, and other necessaries of life. Many strangers are pouring in to view the Temple and the city. They express their astonishment and surprise to see the rapid progress."[6] Indeed it was prospering, for by the end of 1845 Nauvoo had about eleven thousand residents. It was a showcase, and numerous visitors from the East and England wrote complimentary articles about the Mormon metropolis.

ANTAGONISM IN HANCOCK COUNTY

Nauvoo's spectacular growth only increased the antagonism of the Church's enemies. It was evident that the death of Joseph Smith had not diminished the strength and vigor of the Saints. The enemies of the Church supposed that it would not endure without its charismatic leader, and when they saw that the Church was not only surviving but was flourishing, their attempts to drive the Saints from the state were renewed and intensified.

As early as September 1844, Colonel Levi Williams of Warsaw, who had been involved in the murders at Carthage, organized a major military campaign to drive the Latter-day Saints from Illinois. It was advertised as "a great wolf hunt in Hancock County." When word of it reached Governor Ford, he ordered General John Hardin of the state militia to Hancock County to thwart the effort. General Hardin remained in Hancock County throughout the winter to keep the peace.

There was heightened tension in Hancock County in May 1845 when nine men were finally brought to trial in Carthage for the murder of Joseph Smith. Five of them were prominent citizens: Mark Aldrich, land promoter; Jacob C. Davis, state senator; William A. Grover, captain of the Warsaw militia; Thomas C. Sharp, newspaper editor; and Levi Williams, colonel in the fifty-ninth regiment of the state militia. The trial lasted for two weeks, an unusually long time for that era. Prosecution witnesses gave contradictory evidence, while defense attorneys argued persuasively before a non-Mormon jury that Joseph Smith was killed in response to the popular will of the people. Therefore, they asserted that no specific person or group could be held responsible. The defendants were acquitted. A separate trial scheduled for 24 June for the murder of Hyrum Smith was not held because the prosecutors did not appear.

Apparently free from any legal reprisals, Thomas Sharp unleashed a new anti-Mormon volley in the *Warsaw Signal* in the summer of 1845. He opposed Latter-day Saint officeholders in the county and reopened the debate over Mormon political activity. These actions provided a smoke screen for a barrage of vandalism against the Saints. Early in September, a mob of three hundred men led by Levi Williams systematically burned outlying Mormon farms and homes. They first raided Morley's settlement and torched many unprotected homes, farm buildings, mills, and grain stacks. In mid-September Brigham Young asked for volunteers to rescue the besieged Saints. One hundred thirty-four teams were secured and immediately sent to bring the families of the outlying settlements in south Hancock County and north Adams County safely to Nauvoo.

The sheriff of Hancock County, Jacob Backenstos, a friend of the Latter-day Saints, endeavored to preserve order, but citizens in Warsaw refused to join a posse he tried to organize. After he drove off the mob with a posse made up of ex-members of the Nauvoo Legion, his life was threatened by the non-Mormons of Hancock County, and he fled. Frank Worrell, who had supervised the guard at Carthage the day of the Martyrdom, led the chase after Backenstos. Near the railroad shanties north of Warsaw, Backenstos overtook several members of the Church and immediately deputized them. When Worrell raised his gun to fire at the sheriff, deputy Porter Rockwell took aim with his rifle and mortally wounded Worrell. This intensified hostilities in Hancock County, and with civil war imminent, citizens in Quincy, Illinois, and Lee County, Iowa, asked Church members to move

Jacob Backenstos was a friendly non-Mormon. He was the clerk of the circuit court in Hancock County, and in 1844 he was elected to the state legislature. In 1845 he was elected sheriff and became embroiled in controversy over the accused assassins of Joseph and Hyrum. Backenstos became an army officer in 1846 and served with distinction in the war with Mexico.

from Illinois. On 24 September 1845 the Quorum of the Twelve Apostles promised that the Church would leave the following spring.

Governor Ford dispatched four hundred militia troops under the direction of General Hardin and three other prominent citizens, including Congressman Stephen A. Douglas, to act as an independent police force during this period of civil unrest. The depredations ended, and peace was restored temporarily. Acting as the governor's on-the-spot advisory committee, the four leaders investigated the circumstances and learned that the anti-Mormons had initiated the conflict with their raids. They also recognized that there would be no peace in Hancock County until the Mormons left Illinois.

Congressman Douglas was an advocate of manifest destiny—a philosophy advocating the growth of the United States completely across the continent. He counseled Church leaders to find a place to settle in the West and promised to use his influence in assisting their move. For some time Church leaders had planned a move to the Rocky Mountains, so these negotiations proceeded smoothly. Finally the Saints agreed to leave Nauvoo the following spring as soon as the grass on the prairies was high enough to sustain their livestock. Trustees of the Church would remain in Nauvoo to sell the property of those who could not dispose of it by springtime.

COMPLETING THE TEMPLE

Throughout this period, Brigham Young and members of the Twelve kept work on the temple moving. They met frequently with the architect and temple committee and repeatedly invited the members to "gather to Nauvoo with their means" to help build the house of the Lord.[7] In the October 1844 general conference, Brigham Young said, "I believe this people is the best people of their age that ever lived on the earth, the church of Enoch not excepted. We want you to come on with your tithes and offerings to build this Temple."[8] In response the Relief Society sisters pledged to each contribute a penny per week for glass and nails, while those of means contributed large sums without which the project would not have progressed. Joseph Toronto handed Brigham Young twenty-five hundred dollars in gold, saying "he wanted to give himself and all he had" to build the kingdom of God.[9] Numerous craftsmen were called to help with the project. By the spring of 1845 the capstone was in position. The workers then assembled the roof and finished the interior. Plans were set for a formal dedication in April 1846.

Rooms in the temple were dedicated as they were completed so that ordinance work could begin as early as possible. General conference convened in the partially finished edifice in October 1845. Brigham Young "opened the services of the day by a dedicatory prayer, presenting the Temple, thus far completed, as a monument of the saints' liberality, fidelity, and faith, concluding: 'Lord, we dedicate this house and ourselves, to thee.'

The day was occupied most agreeably in hearing instructions and teachings, and offering up the gratitude of honest hearts, for so great a privilege, as worshiping God within instead of without an edifice, whose beauty and workmanship will compare with any house of worship in America, and whose motto is: 'HOLINESS TO THE LORD.' "[10]

The attic story of the temple was dedicated for ordinance work 30 November 1845. President Young prayed that the Lord would sustain and deliver his servants until they accomplished his will in the temple. The rooms were soon prepared for ordinances, and Brigham Young and Heber C. Kimball began giving endowments to faithful Latter-day Saints on the evening of 10 December. On 11 December endowment sessions were continued until 3 A.M.

When enemies of the Church observed this increased temple activity, they renewed their oppression. A new threat against the Church leadership soon came in the form of an indictment issued by the United States District Court in Springfield against Brigham Young and eight other Apostles on charges of instigating and harboring a counterfeiting operation in Nauvoo. On 23 December, government officials approached the temple, hoping to find and arrest Brigham Young. Knowing they were there, Brigham Young knelt down and asked for guidance and protection so that he could "live to prove advantageous to the Saints."[11] He noticed William Miller in the hall, who agreed to act as a decoy. Brother Miller, who was the same height as Brigham, left the temple dressed as Brigham Young and stepped into the president's carriage. Waiting marshals arrested him and took him to the Mansion House where friends and relatives of Brigham joined in on the charade. Miller was then taken to Carthage. Only after someone there identified him did his captors learn that they had a "bogus Brigham." Meanwhile Brigham Young and his brethren had gone into safe hiding.

The Brethren redoubled their efforts to endow as many Saints as possible before the evacuation of Nauvoo began. By the end of 1845, over a thousand members had received these ordinances. In January, Brigham Young recorded, "Such has been the anxiety manifested by the saints to receive the ordinances [of the Temple], and such the anxiety on our part to administer to them, that I have given myself up entirely to the work of the Lord in the Temple night and day, not taking more than four hours sleep, upon an average, per day, and going home but once a week."[12] There were many others among the brethren and sisters who gave freely of their time by washing the temple clothing each night so the work could continue unimpeded the next morning.[13]

On 3 February the Brethren planned to stop the ordinance work, and Brigham Young left the temple to make final preparation to leave the next day for the West. But seeing a large crowd gathered to receive their endowments, he compassionately returned to serve them. This delayed his departure for another two weeks. According to temple records, 5,615 Saints

William Miller (1814–75) was baptized in 1834 in Kirtland and moved there with his family for a short time before going on to Missouri. In 1839 they moved to Illinois with the rest of the Church. Following the "bogus Brigham" incident, the Millers left Nauvoo with the Saints. Because of sickness William was unable to build a log house at Winter Quarters, and the family lived in a dugout during the winter of 1846–47.

In Utah he played an important role in the settlement of Provo and Springville. In 1856 he served a mission to England and was later called to preside over the Utah Stake and at the same time serve as a bishop in Provo.

were endowed before going west, thus fulfilling one of Joseph Smith's fondest desires.

THE CHURCH IN OTHER AREAS

Following the Martyrdom, many important events occurred in other areas of the Church, particularly in Britain and the eastern United States. Arriving in England early in 1845, Wilford Woodruff traveled throughout Britain holding conferences, transacting mission affairs, and opening new areas for missionary activities. In Manchester, at a large manufacturing center, he met a crowded conference of eager Latter-day Saints. He recorded the incident in his journal: "The spirit of the Lord was with us. Love and union pervaded the congregation. I was made glad with the scene of beholding so many saints united in the New and Everlasting Covenant. I often thought I would like to see President Joseph Smith meet with a conference of Saints in England but he has gone. We can go to him but it is not expected he will come to us."[14]

At the end of 1845, Elder Woodruff was released from his short but effective mission. Even though there was some emigration from England to Nauvoo in 1845, the Church continued to prosper and grow rapidly in England, reaching a membership of over eleven thousand. By the end of 1845, the faithful Saints there had contributed over three hundred pounds worth of sterling for the Nauvoo Temple. As he again left this land where he performed so many great works during his two missions, Elder Woodruff noted how peaceful and happy the British Saints were.

Elder Parley P. Pratt's mission to the eastern states was not unlike Wilford Woodruff's to Britain. He was to put in order the affairs of the Church in the East before the Saints began their long-awaited exodus to the West. But Elder Pratt found more serious problems there than Wilford Woodruff did in England.

As he surveyed the situation, Parley and his two companions discovered that William Smith, George Adams, Samuel Brannan, and others were teaching "all manner of false doctrine and immoral practices, by which many of them had stumbled and been seduced from virtue and truth. While many others, seeing their iniquity, had turned away from the Church and joined various dissenting parties."[15] In accordance with instructions previously received from Brigham Young, the Brethren sent the guilty parties to Nauvoo for discipline by the Twelve. Parley also assumed editorship of the *Prophet*, the Church's newspaper in New York. His writings instructed and inspired many. One important item he published was a proclamation to the heads of government worldwide, thus fulfilling an assignment given by revelation to the Church in 1841 (see D&C 124:2–7).

Elder Jedediah M. Grant was one of those who ably assisted Elder Pratt "in setting in order the churches and reestablishing pure gospel principles."[16] For several years Elder Grant had made significant contributions as a

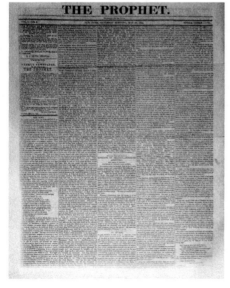

The newspaper Prophet, in which the important "proclamation" to heads of government appeared, was edited by Samuel Brannan, William Smith, and Parley P. Pratt in New York. It ran a little less than two years, beginning on 18 May 1844 and ending on 15 December 1845.

missionary, and in December 1845 he was called as one of the seven presidents of the First Quorum of the Seventy.

Elder Pratt returned to Nauvoo in August 1845. There he stood with his brethren as the Church faced the anti-Mormon outrages in Hancock County. He also contributed to the building of the temple and labored in it night and day during December and January administering the endowment to faithful Latter-day Saints.

PREPARING FOR THE MOVE WEST

Long before he died, the Prophet Joseph had discussed moving the Church to the West. In 1842 he had prophesied that the Saints would continue to suffer much affliction and "some of you will live to go and assist in making settlements and build cities and see the Saints become a mighty people in the midst of the Rocky Mountains."[17] In the spring of 1844 plans for colonizing in the West were initiated. An exploring party was organized to "investigate the locations of California and Oregon, and hunt out a good location, where we can remove to after the temple is completed, and where we can build a city in a day, and have a government of our own, get up into the mountains, where the devil cannot dig us out, and live in a healthful climate, where we can live as old as we have a mind to."[18] After the Prophet's death, further preparations for such an exodus were made.

The planned move west gave some people an excuse to lead away groups from the Church. Joseph Smith had authorized Lyman Wight and Bishop George Miller to establish a colony in Texas; President Young encouraged this effort until it became obvious that Wight and Miller wanted the whole Church to settle there. In late August 1844, Elder Wight was counseled to limit his company to those working with him at the Wisconsin pineries. These he led to Texas. Rather than exploring for a colony, however, he established a permanent settlement. In November 1845 the Saints in Texas were asked to return to Nauvoo, but the independent-minded leader and his followers refused. In 1848, after several more reconciliation attempts, Elder Wight was excommunicated from the Church.

Brigham Young and his colleagues wanted to stay in Illinois until the temple was completed and adequate preparations were made for the departure. During the winter of 1844–45 they read the journals of fur trappers, the reports of government exploring parties, and newspaper articles by western travelers to accumulate as much information about the region as possible. Resettlement committees considered three great western territories as potential sites: Texas, an independent nation; Upper California, a large ill-defined and loosely governed Mexican province (of which the later state of Utah was a part); and Oregon, encompassing the entire Northwest and jointly claimed and administered by the United States and England. Gradually their attention centered on the eastern rim of the Great Basin because this area provided the desired isolation and thousands of acres of fertile land.

Lyman Wight (1796–1858) was baptized in November 1830 and was one of the first to be ordained a high priest. He completed several assignments of trust in Ohio and Missouri and shared the Liberty Jail cell with Joseph Smith in Missouri. After moving to Illinois he was ordained an Apostle on 8 April 1841.

In the summer of 1843 he went to cut lumber in the forests of the Black River, Wisconsin country, and while there conceived of the idea of going to Texas to establish a gathering place. After the death of Joseph Smith he was determined to carry out his Texas proposal, which at first had the approval of Church leaders. He later rejected the leadership of the Twelve and was excommunicated 3 December 1848.

George Miller (1794–1856) was baptized into the Church in 1839 by John Taylor in Illinois. In 1841 he was called to serve as a bishop (see D&C 124:20–21). In 1842–44 he took several loads of wood down the Mississippi River from the Wisconsin pineries. Following the Martyrdom he was appointed trustee-in-trust for the Church.

In 1847, however, Miller refused to be governed by Brigham Young, so he joined Lyman Wight in Texas. In 1850 he joined the Strangites at Beaver Island in Michigan. After James J. Strang's death in 1856, Miller started for California but died in Illinois.

Exodus from Nauvoo by Lynn Faucett. The first Saints left Nauvoo on 4 February 1846. The first challenge they encountered was transporting themselves and their possessions across the Mississippi River. The river froze over for a brief period allowing some to cross on the ice, but most people went by ferry or small skiff; both methods were hazardous.

Although they did not realize it at the time, the hardest part of the journey west would be the three hundred miles across Iowa in the wet spring of 1846. It was sufficiently difficult to forestall plans to get to the Rocky Mountains that season and force the Saints to set up winter quarters.

Leaders of the Church assured the Saints, some of whom were surprised at the announcement, that the exodus was a well-planned transplanting necessary to give the Church the room it needed to grow. October general conference was largely devoted to preparing for an orderly and unified withdrawal. After the conference the Twelve issued a general epistle explaining that "a crisis of extraordinary and thrilling interests has arrived. The exodus . . . to a far distant region of the west, where bigotry, intolerance and insatiable oppression lose their power over them—forms a new epoch." It went on to counsel the Saints everywhere to sell their property and prepare for the gathering.[19] Despite the onset of winter, Nauvoo was a hive of activity as the Saints began to prepare for the exodus.

The evacuation from western Illinois was originally planned for April 1846, but two new threats prompted an early, hasty exit. The first was the indictment against Brigham Young and eight other Apostles, accusing them of counterfeiting. The second was a warning by Governor Thomas Ford and others that federal troops in St. Louis planned to intercept the Mormons and destroy them. Years later it was learned that this was only a rumor started to induce the Saints to leave sooner than they had planned.

In January 1846 the Brethren decided to prepare several companies to leave at a moment's notice. A committee was appointed to dispose of all property and effects left behind, including the temple and the Nauvoo House. The decision to leave was made on 2 February, and the first group, led by Charles Shumway, crossed the Mississippi River on 4 February. Soon there were several hundred Saints assembled in temporary camps in Iowa. Brigham Young and others who remained behind to administer endowments to the Saints did not leave Nauvoo until mid-February. Unfortunately too many left who were inadequately outfitted and chose to depart earlier than was wise.

If the Saints had left Nauvoo beginning in April, as originally planned, undoubtedly there would have been a more orderly exodus. The original blueprint called for twenty-five companies of one hundred families each with adequate provisions and presided over by a company captain. The companies were to have left at prearranged intervals to ensure order. But these plans were shattered by the Saints who panicked and did not want to be left behind after the Twelve had left. Many of the previously appointed captains abandoned their assignments to align themselves with the vanguard companies and be with the Twelve. But in spite of the confusion, there was optimism among the Saints in eastern Iowa. One of the most remarkable migrations in the history of Western civilization had begun.

ENDNOTES

1. "An Epistle of the Twelve," *Times and Seasons*, 15 Aug. 1844, p. 619.

2. See *History of the Church*, 7:305–7.

3. *History of the Church*, 7:260.

4. *History of the Church*, 7:260.

5. In *History of the Church*, 7:355–56.

6. In *History of the Church*, 7:431.

7. In *History of the Church*, 7:267.

8. *History of the Church*, 7:302.

9. In *History of the Church*, 7:433.

10. In *History of the Church*, 7:456–57.

11. In *Journal of Discourses*, 14:218.

12. *History of the Church*, 7:567.

13. See *History of the Church*, 7:547–48.

14. Wilford Woodruff Journals, 16 Feb. 1845, LDS Historical Department, Salt Lake City; spelling, punctuation, and capitalization standardized.

15. Parley P. Pratt, ed., *Autobiography of Parley P. Pratt*, Classics in Mormon Literature series (Salt Lake City: Deseret Book Co., 1985), p. 299.

16. Pratt, *Autobiography of Parley P. Pratt*, p. 300.

17. *History of the Church*, 5:85.

18. *History of the Church*, 6:222.

19. Brigham Young and Willard Richards, in *History of the Church*, 7:478; see also pp. 479–80.

THE TREK ACROSS IOWA

◄ The Winter Quarters monument, located in Omaha, Nebraska, was dedicated 20 September 1936. The monument depicts the agony of pioneer parents burying a child. On the monument is the following inscription:

"That the struggles, the sacrifices and the sufferings of the faithful pioneers and the cause they represented shall never be forgotten. This monument is gratefully erected and dedicated by The Church of Jesus Christ of Latter-day Saints.

"First Presidency: Heber J. Grant, J. Reuben Clark, Jr., David O. McKay.

"Sculptor, Avard Fairbanks, a descendant of pioneers buried here."

WHEN THE SAINTS crossed the Mississippi River into Iowa, they began a new quest for a home where they could build the kingdom of God without oppression. The way to this new refuge was not easy; it exacted toil, sacrifice, and death, and the first leg of the journey—the trek across Iowa territory—proved to be the hardest. The main "Camp of Israel" took 131 days to cover the 300 miles they traveled across Iowa. The Pioneer Company a year later took only 111 days to cover 1,050 miles from Winter Quarters to the Great Salt Lake Valley. Inadequate preparation, lack of knowledgeable guides, delays, miserable weather, and difficult terrain made the Iowa journey one of the most trying in the Church's history. Nevertheless, these hardy folk knew no such word as fail. The Iowa journey simply hardened their resolve and provided valuable experience for the future.

THE TREK BEGAN IN SORROW

The first wagons rolled out of Nauvoo to the ferry on 4 February 1846. Once across the Mississippi they broke a nine-mile trail to Sugar Creek, set up camp, and awaited the arrival of Brigham Young. During February over three thousand people crossed the river under the direction of Hosea Stout, captain of the Nauvoo police, and gathered at Sugar Creek.

Leaving Nauvoo was an act of faith for the Saints. They departed without knowing exactly where they were going or when they would arrive at a place to settle. They only knew that they were on the verge of being driven out of Illinois by their enemies and that their leaders had received revelation to locate a refuge somewhere in the Rocky Mountains.

Although springlike weather facilitated an early departure from Nauvoo, severe weather arose soon thereafter, which both hampered and blessed the already harried exodus. On 14 February it snowed and on 19 February a northwest wind brought eight inches of snow, a very cold night, and "much suffering in the camp, for there were many who had no tents or any comfortable place to lodge: many tents were blown down, some of them were unfinished and had no ends."[1] After Brigham Young had left Nauvoo and crossed the river to the Iowa side, the mud became so deep his teams had to be yoked double to pull the wagons up the hill to Sugar Creek camp.[2] A week later the temperatures plummeted and the Mississippi froze over, hastening the abandonment of Nauvoo by allowing numerous Saints to cross on the

The Nauvoo brass band (also known as William Pitt's brass band) was organized in 1842 to accompany the drills of the Nauvoo Legion. The band frequently played for social and religious gatherings, at patriotic and other celebrations, at arrivals and departures of important people, and as background to steamboat excursions. They even raised funds and built the Nauvoo Concert Hall in 1843.

During the first half of the Iowa trek the band not only provided entertainment for the weary Saints after a long day's march, but they also obtained money, provisions, and equipment through concerts for the settlers in towns and villages along the route.

After arriving in Garden Grove, the band dispersed as some of its members returned to Nauvoo, some went on to Winter Quarters, and others stayed in Garden Grove. In Utah the band was revived for a time and performed functions similar to those it had provided in Nauvoo.

William Pitt, a British convert and all-around musician, was the leader of the Nauvoo brass band, both because he was well versed in music and because when he left England he took with him a large collection of music arranged for brass instruments. Pitt had a reputation as an excellent flutist, but he preferred the violin and other instruments. He was one of three members of the band to travel to the Salt Lake Valley with the original Pioneer Company.

ice. Because of the extreme cold, however, many people, including Brigham Young and Willard Richards, fell ill at Sugar Creek. Also several women gave birth in the cold, makeshift camp; they and their new babies suffered most from exposure to the cold, wind, and snow.

Lack of food also plagued the departing Saints. Wishing to be with their leaders, many of them had failed to follow the counsel to be prepared before leaving. Brigham Young, Heber C. Kimball, and a few others had begun the journey from Nauvoo with a year's supply of provisions, but most others left with hardly any food. Their unpreparedness caused some, who had brought provisions and were willing to share, to deplete their supply within a few weeks. President Young had the overwhelming responsibility of being a father to all. One journal entry manifests his discouragement: "Unless this people are more united in spirit and cease to pray against Counsel, It will bring me down to my grave. I am reduced in flesh so that my coat that would scarcely meet around me last Winter now laps over twelve inches. It is with much ado that I can keep from lying down and sleeping to wait the resurrection."[3]

In spite of the harsh conditions, there was some merriment in camp. Almost every night William Pitt's brass band played the popular grand marches, quick-steps, and gallops of the time. Around the campfires the people danced to fiddle music and sang favorite songs as well as new ones that they composed for the occasion. One such was "The Upper California":

The Upper California—Oh that's the land for me!
It lies between the mountains and the great Pacific sea;
The Saints can be supported there,
And taste the sweets of liberty.
In Upper California—Oh that's the land for me![4]

Upper California referred to a largely undefined area administered by Mexico comprising most of the present states of Utah, Colorado, Nevada, and California.

Brigham Young noted that the Saints "were patient, and endured all their privations without murmuring." A month later he added, "I did not think there had ever been a body of people since the days of Enoch, placed under the same unpleasant circumstances that this people have been, where there was so little grumbling, and I was satisfied that the Lord was pleased with the majority of the Camp of Israel."[5]

THE CAMP OF ISRAEL MOVES WEST

The Saints did not begin leaving the encampment at Sugar Creek until 1 March 1846. The last week to ten days were largely dominated by discussion of travel plans and organization of the line of march. From the start the main body of Saints was known as the "Camp of Israel," with Brigham Young as its president. As with ancient Israel, there were companies and captains of hundreds, fifties, and tens. In the next two years more Old Testament parallels were made, as illustrated by terms such as, *Zion being in the tops of the mountains, chosen people, exodus, Mount Pisgah, Jordan River, Dead Sea, making the desert blossom as a rose,* and *a modern Moses* in the person of Brigham Young.

Part of the Saints' delay in leaving resulted from concern for the best route across Iowa. Eastern Iowa had been open to settlement since the Black Hawk Indian War of 1830–32, but beyond a hundred miles west of the Mississippi River the population was sparse, the roads few and bad. Furthermore there were numerous rivers and streams to traverse. The camp also faced the decision of where to cross the Missouri River. The Saints wanted to avoid crossings in the state of Missouri where there was still anti-Mormon sentiment.

When the Saints renewed their march, they planned to reach the Missouri by mid-April, plant small acreages along the way for those following, establish a portion of the camp somewhere west of the Missouri as a farm or way station for future travelers, and dispatch a swift company to the mountains with seeds to plant a spring crop. A Pioneer Company headed by Stephen Markham was sent ahead to scout the best routes, find trading settlements, build bridges, and make other preparations.

Three fundamental problems, however, inhibited the progress of the Saints across Iowa. The first was the lack of adequate food supplies. Each company had two commissary agents assigned to contact settlers and negotiate for food and provender. Because of the lack of provisions in general, many men found work in eastern Iowa towns to pay for needed supplies. William Pitt's brass band presented formal concerts in many Iowa communities to raise more funds. With large numbers of men on the job instead of in the wagons, progress was painfully slow. This explains why most of the camp tarried almost three weeks at Richardson's Point, only fifty-six miles from Nauvoo. Brigham Young was only halfway across Iowa when, because of his generosity, his family's own provisions were depleted. The other Apostles were in the same situation.[6] On 24 March, Hosea Stout reported that half of his men were out of provisions. And the problem grew worse before they arrived at the Missouri River.

The second problem was the disorganization of the camp, which was spread for miles across eastern Iowa. Several riders were kept busy just carrying dispatches between the leaders of the separated companies. Driven to exasperation by the disorder and by the adventurous, independent, and competitive spirit of Bishop George Miller and others, Brigham Young saw the necessity of establishing firmer control over the camp. He demanded stricter obedience and cooperation and dispatched a letter of rebuke to those who were far ahead of the rest of the camp, telling them to return for a council.

Stephen Markham (1800–78) accepted the gospel in Ohio in 1837. A prosperous farmer and faithful Saint, he sold his possessions at the counsel of Joseph Smith to help sixty people move from Kirtland to Far West, Missouri. During the Nauvoo era he served as a bodyguard for Joseph Smith and again sacrificed a new home (moving into a tent) to help the Prophet pay legal fees.

He was with the Brethren in Carthage, but was refused entrance to the jail a few hours before the Martyrdom. In addition to his pioneering role in Iowa, he was also a member of the first Pioneer Company to the Salt Lake Valley and subsequently was active in the colonization efforts in Utah.

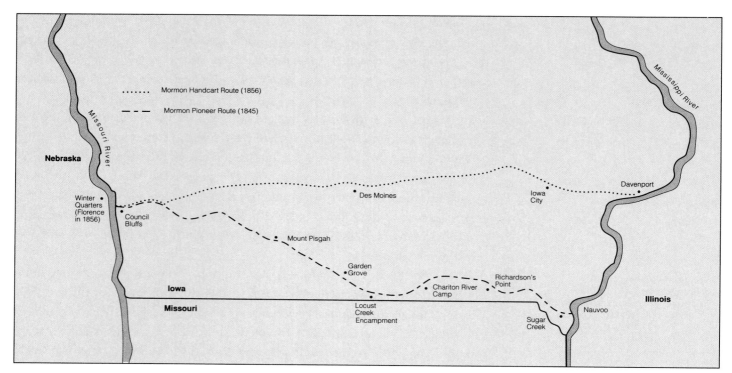

Two important Mormon trails crossed Iowa. The northern trail was the route of the handcart companies in 1856. The pioneers of 1846 traversed the southern route. Most of the camp remained at Richardson's Point for nearly two weeks to improve their organization during a spell of bad weather. Nevertheless, by the time they reached Chariton River, about one hundred miles west of Nauvoo, they had only averaged two to three miles per day, many people were widely scattered, and some had even returned to Nauvoo. A major reorganization was required.

The 1846 route hugged the Missouri border because of the proximity to civilization. Church leaders intended to cross northwestern Missouri to Banks Ferry, an important staging place for points west on the Missouri River. Hostile reaction from the Missourians led them to turn north again.

Further west, at Locust Creek, William Clayton composed the hymn "Come, Come, Ye Saints." Garden Grove, one of two "permanent" settlements, was just about halfway across Iowa, being 144 miles west of Nauvoo and 120 miles east of the Missouri River. The Saints reached Garden Grove on 24 April, and on 18 May, Mount Pisgah was designated by Parley P. Pratt as the second permanent camp. Brigham Young celebrated his forty-fifth birthday there on 1 June 1846.

Parley P. Pratt, who was with Miller, was severely reproved along with the others. What followed demonstrated that the Spirit was prompting Brigham Young. Parley P. Pratt said, "For Bishop Miller, who was a leading and active member of our camp, has since left us and gone his own way, having refused to be led by the counsels of the Presidency; and removed to Texas. And here I would observe that, although my own motives were pure, so far as I could know my own heart, yet I thank God for this timely chastisement; I profited by it, and it caused me to be more watchful and careful ever after."[7]

On 26 March on the banks of the Chariton River, Brigham Young and Heber C. Kimball regrouped the camp into three companies of one hundred families each. Although travel thereafter was more orderly, improved organization could not overcome the final and perhaps most challenging factor of all—wet spring weather. Sudden melting snows, almost constant rain, swollen creeks, interminable mud, and violent wind retarded progress. Brigham Young's comment late in March, that they had passed through only one mud hole that day "which was about six miles in length," illustrates the effects of spring thaws and rains that left the roads and campsites a bog.[8] Diaries and journals show that it rained or snowed for at least eleven days in March, beginning on the tenth. The weather continued to deteriorate in April, and it rained or snowed half of the month, including every day of the last week. So many wagons mired in the mud that travel was reduced to less than half a mile per day.

They had a particularly bad day on 6 April. Hosea Stout said it "was of all mornings the most dismal dark and rainy after such a fine day as yesterday was. . . . This day capped the climax of all days for travelling. The road was the worst that I had yet witnessed up hill and down through sloughs on spouty oak ridges and deep marshes, raining hard, the creek rising. The horses would sometimes sink to their bellies on the ridges, teams stall going down hill. We worked and toiled more than half the day and had at last to leave some of our wagons and double teams before we could get through." That evening after most in the camp had retired, the wind began to blow. Hosea had not secured his tent with stay ropes and "had to get out of my bed and hold it a long time in the wind and rain which beat upon me until I was wet thoroughly nor could I leave to secure it because it would blow down." He stood there until some of the brethren came to his assistance.[9]

Eliza R. Snow recorded that the wind was a "perfect gale attended with a heavy shower of rain—and several of our habitations were leveled and the roofs of our wagons barely escaped the wreck of elements."[10] The weary travelers awoke the next morning to a little snow, a slight freeze, and a rising creek. With clothes and bedding often drenched and with the cold temperatures, frequent illnesses and occasional deaths further hindered travel.

By 15 April the camp found itself on Locust Creek near the present-day Iowa-Missouri state line. William Clayton, frustrated with the slow progress of the camp and the burdens of caring for a large family, gratefully received news that his plural wife, Diantha, left behind for care and safety in Nauvoo, had given birth to a healthy boy. He thereupon composed a new song of praise to the Lord entitled "All Is Well" (today called "Come, Come, Ye Saints"), which became an anthem for many Mormon pioneers who subsequently crossed the plains to the Great Basin.

William Clayton (1814–79) was born in England and was among the first to accept the gospel there in 1837. He emigrated to Nauvoo in 1840, and his skills in writing and accounting were quickly recognized. In 1842 he became Joseph's clerk and private secretary, and he served in similar capacities throughout his life.

He was the Nauvoo Temple recorder. In Utah he was treasurer of ZCMI, territorial recorder of marks and brands, and territorial auditor of public accounts. He is perhaps most noted for recording the revelation on plural marriage on 12 July 1843 and for writing "Come, Come, Ye Saints" near Corydon, Iowa.

Come, come, ye Saints, no toil nor labor fear;
But with joy wend your way.
Though hard to you this journey may appear,
Grace shall be as your day.
'Tis better far for us to strive
Our useless cares from us to drive;
Do this, and joy your hearts will swell—
All is well! All is well!
. . . .
We'll find the place which God for us prepared,
Far away in the West,
Where none shall come to hurt or make afraid;
There the Saints will be blessed.
We'll make the air with music ring,
Shout praises to our God and King;
Above the rest these words we'll tell—
All is well! All is well![11]

As rain continued to pour into the swollen Locust Creek, Church leaders began to revise their plans. The agonizing delays, the sufferings of the travelers, the weakened condition of their draft animals, the unaffordable high prices for feed grain, the disrepair of the wagons and equipment, their rapidly depleting food supplies, and no prospects for better weather all contributed to a reevaluation of the Saints' course. The dream of reaching the Rocky Mountains later that season was fading.

ESTABLISHMENT OF WAY STATIONS AND MOVING ON TO MISSOURI

At Locust Creek the Brethren prayerfully forged a new plan to establish farms or way stations along the route west. By 24 April the pioneers reached a place they named Garden Grove, sixty miles northwest of Locust Creek and about halfway across Iowa. Within three weeks they had broken 715 acres of tough prairie sod, built cabins, and established a small community. A high council was called to regulate both Church and civic affairs, and two hundred people were assigned to improve this first way station.

Garden Grove did not have enough timber to accommodate all the companies soon to arrive from Nauvoo, so the brethren sent scouts to explore the region. Parley P. Pratt located some grassy hills crowned with beautiful groves twenty-five miles northwest of Garden Grove. He was overjoyed. Referring to the mountain Moses saw the promised land from, Parley cried out, "This is *Mount Pisgah.*"[12]

A few days later Brigham Young arrived and immediately organized a second way station at Mount Pisgah. Another high council was appointed, and several thousand acres were cooperatively enclosed, planted, and farmed. One of the new leaders, Ezra T. Benson (great-grandfather of the thirteenth President of the Church), declared, "This was the first place where I felt willing in my heart to stay at, since I left Nauvoo."[13] Soon Mount Pisgah outstripped Garden Grove in size and significance. Both, however, were important pioneer way stations from 1846 to 1852.

During the first of June 1846 an advance company, including members of the Twelve, left Mount Pisgah and headed for the Missouri River. Although they were two months behind the original schedule, the Brethren still hoped that an express company would be able to make it to the Rocky Mountains by fall. It took only fourteen days to cover the final one hundred miles to the Council Bluffs area on the Missouri River, partly because they enjoyed the unfamiliar luxury of dry trails and abundant grass. Temporary headquarters were established at Mosquito Creek on Pottawattomie Indian land. They found that their first task was to prepare landings and a boat to ferry the emigrant wagons across the Missouri. This was accomplished in just two weeks.

Nevertheless, two issues remained unresolved. Where would the Saints winter on the Missouri, since they were still on Indian lands? And was there still time for some of the Apostles and others to press on to the West before the onset of winter storms? The latter issue was decided after consultations

The first permanent camp established for the benefit of those to follow was Garden Grove. Samuel Bent, Aaron Johnson, and David Fullmer were called to preside over the settlement at Garden Grove.

John R. Young remembered, "They were instructed to divide the lands among the poor without charge; but to give to no man more than he could thoroughly cultivate. There must be no waste and no speculation."[14]

Samuel Bent died in Garden Grove on 16 August 1846.

Mount Pisgah, the second permanent camp in Iowa, was established 18 May 1846 and presided over by William Huntington, Ezra T. Benson, and Charles C. Rich. Many of the Saints who left Nauvoo after Brigham Young caught up with the camp here, and part of the Mormon Battalion was recruited here.

Pisgah was maintained as a camp until at least 1852 and at its height had a population of over three thousand Saints. Noah Rogers, who had recently returned from a mission to the South Sea Islands, was the first to die and be buried here. Many others also died and were buried here. In 1886 the Church purchased the one-acre plot where the cemetery lay and in 1888 erected a monument to mark the site.

with Captain James Allen of the United States army, who arrived on 1 July to raise a battalion of Mormon soldiers. With the loss of so many men to the battalion, the westward migration was delayed for a season.

CALL OF THE MORMON BATTALION

In 1845 the United States annexed Texas, thereby angering Mexico, which still claimed much of Texas territory. Mexican troops and United States dragoons had a skirmish on 24 April 1846, but Congress did not declare war until 12 May 1846. American expansionists were excited about the war because it offered an opportunity to acquire territory extending to the Pacific Ocean. President James K. Polk, himself an expansionist, included in his war aims the acquisition of New Mexico and Upper California. The U.S. army of the West was charged with conquering this vast territory.

The war with Mexico came precisely when the Latter-day Saints were petitioning in Washington, D.C., for assistance in their move west. Before leaving Nauvoo, Brigham Young called Elder Jesse C. Little to preside over the Church in the East and to go to the nation's capital with a request for help. Elder Little was assisted by his friend, twenty-four-year-old Thomas L. Kane, son of John Kane, a prominent federal judge and political associate of President Polk. Thomas had worked with his father as a law clerk and was therefore well-known in Washington, D.C. Together Little and Kane negotiated with officials for government contracts to build blockhouses and forts along the Oregon Trail, but the war with Mexico provided a better opportunity for the Saints and the government to help each other.

With Kane's urging, Elder Little suggested in a letter to President Polk that although the Saints were loyal Americans, the government's refusal to assist them could "compel us to be foreigners."[15] Polk did not want the Saints to join the British interests in the Oregon territory nor to antagonize the Missouri volunteers in the army of the West, so, following conversations with Elder Little, he authorized the recruiting of five hundred Mormon volunteers *after* they reached California. This way he could retain the loyalty of the Saints without antagonizing any anti-Mormons. But when Secretary of War, William Marcy, wrote to Colonel Stephen W. Kearny at Fort Leavenworth, Polk had apparently changed his mind because Kearny was authorized to immediately enlist a Mormon battalion. In late June, Kearny sent Captain James Allen to Mormon encampments in southern Iowa to recruit the volunteers.

Captain Allen went first to the new Mormon settlement of Mount Pisgah. There he encountered stiff opposition to the plan. Elder Wilford Woodruff, en route to join his fellow Apostles at the Missouri River, was suspicious. He recorded, "I had some reasons to believe them to be spies and that the President had no hand in it. We however treated them with civility and directed them on to Council Bluffs to lay the case before the President."[16]

Jesse C. Little (1815–93) was serving in 1846 as president of the mission in the New England middle states. He left his family temporarily in the East and traveled to Nebraska, where he joined Brigham Young and the original Pioneer Company seventy miles west of Winter Quarters.

After entering the Salt Lake Valley, he returned to the East where he continued serving as a mission president until 1852, when he and his family went to Utah. In 1856 he was called to serve as second counselor to Edward Hunter in the Presiding Bishopric, a position he held until 1874.

Messengers dispatched by Elder Woodruff warned Brigham Young of Captain Allen's mission two days before he arrived in Council Bluffs. Before greeting him, Brigham Young, Heber C. Kimball, and Willard Richards hurriedly met in Orson Pratt's tent, where they "decided it was best to meet Captain Allen in the morning and raise the men wanted."[17] President Young realized that Allen's request was probably the result of Elder Little's negotiations. The Brethren also recognized that the request for Mormon men provided an opportunity to earn desperately needed capital for the exodus and provided a rationale for establishing temporary settlements on Indian lands. During negotiations Captain Allen assured the Church that they could remain on Indian lands during the winter.

After Allen recruited the men at Council Bluffs, President Young spoke to the Saints and tried to clear their minds of prejudice against the federal government. He said, "Suppose we were admitted into the Union as a State and the government did not call on us, we would feel ourselves neglected. Let the Mormons be the first men to set their feet on the soil of California. . . . This is the first offer we have ever had from the government to benefit us."[18] On 3 July, Brigham Young, Heber C. Kimball, and Willard Richards went east to recruit more men. Before they arrived in Mount Pisgah, every Latter-day Saint had opposed the venture, but after their several recruiting speeches, many able-bodied men signed up.

Recruiting continued until 20 July, the day before the battalion's departure to Fort Leavenworth. Within three weeks five companies of one hundred men were organized. Both Thomas L. Kane and Jesse C. Little had arrived at the Missouri River and assured the Saints that there was no adverse plot behind the government's request. Church leaders promised that the families of the volunteers would be carefully provided for. Brigham Young selected the officers over each company and counseled them to be fathers to the rest of the men. He also counseled the volunteers to be faithful soldiers, keep the commandments, and abide by the counsel of their leaders. He promised that if they conducted themselves properly, they would not have to fight. A farewell ball was held in honor of the battalion on a cleared square along the Missouri River on the evening of Saturday, 18 July. At noon on Tuesday, 21 July, they began their historic march.

ESTABLISHING WINTER QUARTERS

With the battalion gone, energies were directed toward finding a suitable winter way station. Even prior to the call of the battalion, Brigham Young had concluded that most Saints would settle at Grand Island on the Platte River. It was the longest fresh water river island in America, with rich soil and abundant timber. One drawback, however, was the existence of unfriendly Pawnee Indians in the area. The arrival in camp of Thomas L. Kane and Wilford Woodruff in mid-July modified the Grand Island plan. Kane suggested that the federal Office of Indian Affairs would interfere less

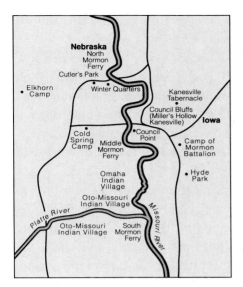

This map shows the main Mormon settlements along the Missouri River in 1846–47. Grand Island was west along the Platte River. There were about twelve thousand Church members scattered throughout the country in 1846; approximately four thousand were in Winter Quarters.

with Mormon settlements on the Missouri than at locations further west.

Elder Woodruff came with sad news that Reuben Hedlock, temporary presiding authority of the Church in England, was channeling money originally earmarked for emigration purposes into schemes for his own enrichment. Furthermore, apostate James J. Strang had deployed Martin Harris to England to work with Latter-day Saint congregations. Unless something was done immediately, the Church stood to lose a great deal in the British Isles. Elder Woodruff also reported on the condition of the Saints in Nauvoo who were too poor to leave for the West. By late July 1846 the Brethren concluded that a main encampment would be established on the west bank of the Missouri River and other camps scattered throughout western Iowa. Also, Orson Hyde, Parley P. Pratt, and John Taylor were dispatched to England to solve the problems of the Church there.

In August, explorers located a temporary site, known as Cutler's Park, three miles west of the river. But after negotiations with both Otoe and Omaha Indian tribal leaders, Church leaders decided to establish the camp closer to the river itself. A good area near a proposed ferry site was selected in early September and surveying was begun. By the end of the month a town of 820 lots had been laid out and some lots spoken for. Winter Quarters, as the Brethren called the community, came into being.

RESCUING THE NAUVOO "POOR SAINTS"

Over two thousand Saints left Nauvoo by mid-March 1846, and additional hundreds left in both April and May. But many still remained in the city. Before leaving, President Young had appointed three men—Joseph L. Heywood, John S. Fullmer, and Almon W. Babbitt—to act as legal trustees to sell Church and private properties, pay the most pressing debts and obligations, and provide for the safe departure of those unavoidably left behind. He also assigned Orson Hyde to supervise the completion and dedication of the Nauvoo Temple.

Temple workmen completed their assignment by the end of April, and the sacred edifice was prepared for dedication. Wilford Woodruff arrived from his mission to Great Britain in time for the ceremonies. On 30 April, Orson Hyde, Wilford Woodruff, and about twenty others dressed in their temple robes dedicated the house of the Lord.

Wilford Woodruff recorded, "Notwithstanding the many false prophesies of Sidney Rigdon and others that the roof should not go on nor the house be finished and the threats of the mob that we should not dedicate it, yet we have done both."[19]

The next day, 1 May 1846, Church leaders in Nauvoo conducted a public dedication. Elders Hyde and Woodruff then left for Iowa to join the rest of the Twelve.

When opponents of the Church realized that not all the Saints were going to leave Nauvoo by summer, persecution began anew. Men and women harvesting grain were attacked and some were severely beaten. This type of harassment lasted all summer and into the fall of 1846.

Meanwhile the Quorum of the Twelve decided to sell the Nauvoo Temple to raise funds for outfitting the remaining Nauvoo Saints. All attempts to sell the edifice failed. By mid-August less than fifteen hundred Saints remained in Nauvoo, some of them new converts from the East who had arrived too late to join the earlier companies. Most of them had exhausted their savings just to reach Nauvoo and now looked to Church leaders as their only hope to proceed West.

By the second week in September the anti-Mormons were determined to drive the Saints out of Nauvoo. Approximately eight hundred men equipped with six cannons prepared to lay siege to the city. The Saints and some new citizens, numbering only about 150 fighting men, prepared to defend the city. The Battle of Nauvoo began on 10 September, with sporadic firing. During the following two days there were minor skirmishes. On 13 September an anti-Mormon column advanced in an attempt to rout the defenders. A spirited counterattack led by Daniel H. Wells saved the day, but there were casualties on both sides. The battle continued the next day, which was the Sabbath.

On 16 September, the "Quincy committee," which had helped keep the peace in previous months, interceded once again. The Saints were forced to surrender unconditionally in order to save their lives and gain a chance of escaping across the river. Only five men and their families were allowed to stay in Nauvoo to dispose of property. Those who could quickly crossed the river without provisions or additional clothing. Finally, the mob entered the city, looted homes, and desecrated the temple. Some Saints who were not able to escape fast enough were beaten or thrown into the river by the mob.

Refugee camps of five to six hundred dispossessed men, women, and children, including those who had been left as too sick to travel, were scattered along two miles of riverbank above Montrose, Iowa. Most people had only blankets or bowers made of brush for shelter and little more than boiled or parched corn to eat. Some died. Bishop Newel K. Whitney purchased some flour and distributed it among the poor camps. The Church trustees went to river towns, including St. Louis, pleading for money and supplies for the refugees, but because of religious prejudices they only raised one hundred dollars.

On 9 October, when food was in especially short supply, several large flocks of quail flew into camp and landed on the ground and even on tables. Many of them were caught, cooked, and eaten by the hungry Saints. To the faithful it was a sign of God's mercy to modern Israel as a similar incident had been to ancient Israel (see Exodus 16:13).

Even before they realized the terrible plight of the Nauvoo Saints, Church leaders in Iowa had sent a rescue mission, and when word of the Battle of Nauvoo reached Winter Quarters, a second mission was mobilized. Brigham Young declared,

"Let the fire of the covenant which you made in the House of the Lord, burn in your hearts, like flame unquenchable, till you, by yourselves or delegates . . . [can] rise up with his team and go straightway, and bring a load of the poor from Nauvoo. . . .

". . . This is a day of action and not of argument."[20] Rescue teams arrived in time to save the Saints from starvation and winter exposure. The poor Saints were dispersed throughout various camps in western Iowa. A handful made it all the way to Winter Quarters.

ISRAEL IN THE WILDERNESS

Throughout the fall of 1846, the nearly twelve thousand Latter-day Saints in various parts of the Midwest prepared for winter the best ways they could. The headquarters of the Church was at Winter Quarters in Indian territory, where almost four thousand Saints resided by the end of the year. Another twenty-five hundred were camped on Pottawattomie Indian lands on the east side of the Missouri River. An estimated seven hundred people were at Mount Pisgah, six hundred at Garden Grove, at least a thousand were spread throughout other parts of Iowa, and five hundred were in the Mormon Battalion on their way to California. Many Saints gathered for the winter in Mississippi River towns; the Mormon population in St. Louis swelled to fifteen hundred.[21] Never had the Church's membership been so scattered and so poorly housed. The phrase "Zion in the wilderness" aptly depicts the Church's difficult situation during the winter of 1846–47.

Even in these conditions, the presiding Brethren tried to provide adequate church and civil government for the Saints. High councils were organized in the main camps to superintend ecclesiastical and municipal affairs. At Winter Quarters this council was called the "municipal high council." In early October, Brigham Young divided Winter Quarters into thirteen wards, but he soon increased the number to twenty-two to facilitate the care of the members of the Church. In November the high council voted that even smaller wards be created and "that every laboring man be tithed each tenth day to be applied for the benefit of the poor, or pay an equivalent to his Bishop."[22] Although under this arrangement bishops cared primarily for the temporal needs of the people, it was another step in the development toward the ward organization that exists in the Church today.

To enhance their economic well-being, many wintering Saints traded with settlements in northern Missouri and in Iowa for hogs, grain, vegetables, and emigrant supplies. Some young men sought employment to earn money to pay for these goods. The Saints were expected to pool their resources for the good of all.

Sickness and death stalked the camps of the Saints. The hasty, wintry exodus from Nauvoo earlier in the year, the exhausting trek across Iowa, the endless spring storms, insufficient provisions, inadequate and improvised shelter, the forced exodus of the poor from Nauvoo, and unhealthy

Jane Richards (1823–1913) made the trek across Iowa late in 1846 without her husband, Franklin D. Richards, who was on his way to England. Franklin D. Richards was a high priest who would be called into the Quorum of the Twelve three years later. Jane's little daughter, Wealthy, was ill and died at Cutler Park after weeks of incredible suffering. Sister Richards wrote one incident of the story:

"A few days previously she had asked for some potato soup, the first thing she had shown any desire for for weeks, and as we were then travelling, we came in sight of a potato-field. One of the sisters eagerly asked for a single potato. A rough woman impatiently heard her story through, and putting her hands on her shoulders, marched her out of the house, saying, 'I won't give or sell a thing to one of you damned Mormons.' I turned on my bed and wept, as I heard them trying to comfort my little one in her disappointment. When she was taken from me I only lived because I could not die."[23]

Once the location for "winter quarters" was decided upon, the first necessity was to survey the site. The plat was laid out in forty-one blocks with 820 lots. Streets and spacing of buildings were properly supervised.

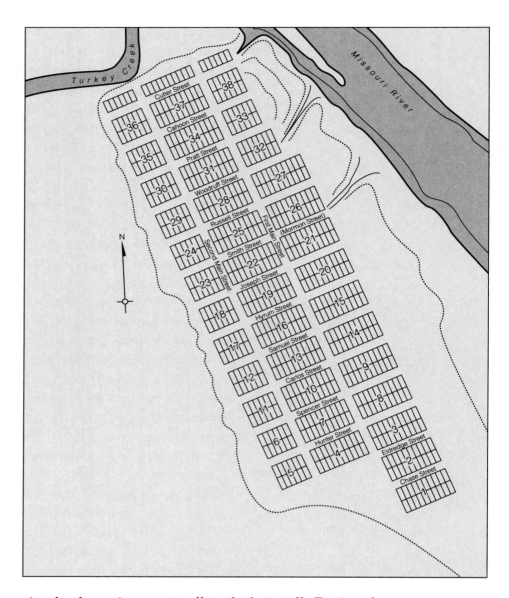

riverbank environments all took their toll. During the summer many travelers suffered from the exposure-related diseases of malaria, pneumonia, and tuberculosis. In Missouri that fall, lack of fresh vegetables brought on a plague of scurvy, which the Saints called "black canker." Serious sickness was no respecter of persons or position, and many of the leaders, including Brigham Young and Willard Richards, became seriously ill. Wilford Woodruff wrote, "I have never seen the Latter Day Saints in any situation where they seemed to be passing through greater tribulations or wearing out faster than at the present time."[24] Over seven hundred people died in the camps by the end of the first winter.[25]

But all was not sorrow, especially in Winter Quarters. Life there could still be generally pleasant, rewarding, and meaningful. Church meetings were held twice a week, and the sermons from the leaders raised the morale of the entire settlement. Many family meetings were held as well. After much of the hard labor of establishing the community was complete, Brigham Young encouraged the wards to celebrate with feasts and dancing. Women often came together in neighborhood groups to gather food, quilt, braid straw, comb each other's hair, knit, wash clothes, and read letters.

Throughout the winter of 1846–47, additional preparations were made for continuing the westward exodus. Though the Church and its members had suffered almost beyond measure during the previous year, the Saints still harbored fond hopes for the future. Much was learned in 1846 that would pay tremendous dividends in the future.

ENDNOTES

1. Willard Richards, in *History of the Church*, 7:593.

2. See Juanita Brooks, ed., *On the Mormon Frontier: The Diary of Hosea Stout*, 1844–1861 (Salt Lake City: University of Utah Press, 1964), p. 123.

3. Elden J. Watson, *Manuscript History of Brigham Young*, 1846–1847 (Salt Lake City: Elden Jay Watson, 1971), pp. 150–51.

4. Thomas E. Cheney, ed., *Mormon Songs from the Rocky Mountains*, reprint ed. (Salt Lake City: University of Utah Press, 1981), p. 68.

5. Watson, *Manuscript History of Brigham Young*, pp. 44, 131.

6. See "History of the Church," *Juvenile Instructor*, 1 Oct. 1882, p. 293.

7. Parley P. Pratt, ed., *Autobiography of Parley P. Pratt*, Classics in Mormon Literature series (Salt Lake City: Deseret Book Co., 1985), p. 307.

8. Watson, *Manuscript History of Brigham Young*, p. 106.

9. Brooks, *On the Mormon Frontier*, p. 149; spelling and punctuation standardized.

10. Eliza R. Snow, "Pioneer Diary of Eliza R. Snow," *Improvement Era*, Apr. 1943, p. 208; spelling standardized.

11. "Come, Come, Ye Saints," *Hymns*, 1985, no. 30.

12. Pratt, *Autobiography of Parley P. Pratt*, p. 308.

13. Journal History of The Church of Jesus Christ of Latter-day Saints, 16 July 1846, Historical Department, Salt Lake City, p. 21.

14. John R. Young, *Memoirs of John R. Young,*

Utah Pioneer, 1847 (Salt Lake City: Deseret News, 1920), p. 19.

15. In Watson, *Manuscript History of Brigham Young*, p. 217; see also B. H. Roberts, *A Comprehensive History of The Church of Jesus Christ of Latter-day Saints, Century One*, 6 vols. (Salt Lake City: The Church of Jesus Christ of Latter-day Saints, 1930), 3:72.

16. Wilford Woodruff Journals, 26 June 1846, LDS Historical Department, Salt Lake City; punctuation and capitalization standardized.

17. Watson, *Manuscript History of Brigham Young*, p. 202.

18. Watson, *Manuscript History of Brigham Young*, p. 205.

19. Wilford Woodruff Journals, 30 Apr. 1846; spelling, punctuation, and capitalization standardized.

20. Journal History of the Church, 28 Sept. 1846, pp. 5–6.

21. See Richard Edmond Bennett, "Mormons at the Missouri: A History of the Latter-day Saints at Winter Quarters and at Kanesville, 1846–52—A Study in American Overland Trail Migration," Ph.D. diss., Wayne State University, 1984, pp. 173–75.

22. Watson, *Manuscript History of Brigham Young*, p. 464.

23. In Hubert Howe Bancroft, *History of Utah* (Salt Lake City: Bookcraft, 1964), p. 246.

24. Wilford Woodruff Journals, 17–21 Nov. 1846.

25. Bennett, "Mormons at the Missouri," pp. 280–92.

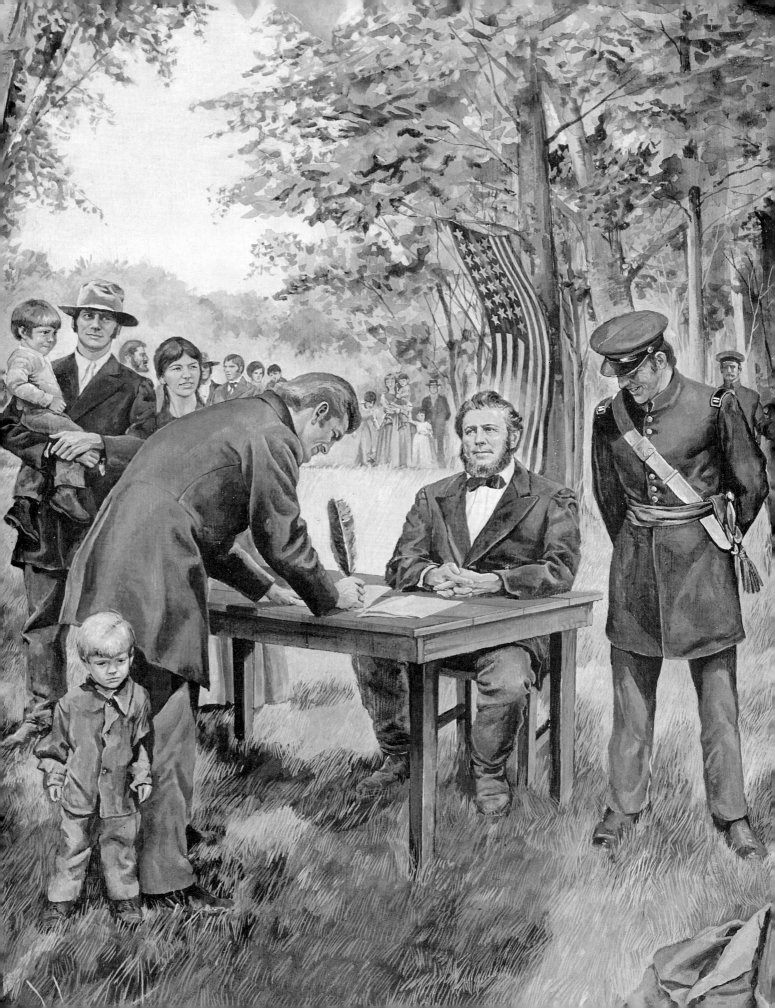

PIONEERS TO THE WEST

◄ *Brigham Young recruiting the Mormon Battalion*

WHILE THE LATTER-DAY SAINTS in Winter Quarters and in the wilderness of Iowa waited out the winter of 1846–47 and planned for the momentous trek the following spring, three other groups of Saints were already on the move to the West: the Mormon Battalion, members from the eastern United States who sailed on the ship *Brooklyn*, and a small party known as the Mississippi Saints.

THE MARCH OF THE MORMON BATTALION

Captain James Allen of the United States army was promoted to Lieutenant Colonel after enlisting five companies of Mormon men. Under his direction 541 soldiers, 35 women (20 of whom were designated as laundresses), and 42 children began their march to Fort Leavenworth on 21 July 1846. Before they left, the officers, all of whom had been selected by Church leaders, met privately with members of the Twelve. The Brethren promised them that their lives would be spared if they were faithful. Sergeant William Hyde reported that they were charged "to remember their prayers, to see that the name of the Deity was revered, and that virtue and cleanliness were strictly observed. [The troops were instructed] to treat all men with kindness . . . and never take life when it could be avoided."[1]

Nevertheless the departure of the Mormon Battalion worried many. Sergeant William Hyde, who left a wife and two small children with aged relatives said, "When we were to meet with them again, God only knew. Nevertheless, we did not feel to murmur."[2] Drusilla Hendricks, whose husband had been wounded in the Battle of Crooked River in Missouri, would not let her oldest son, William, join until the voice of the Spirit convinced her otherwise. On the morning the battalion left, she was still heartsick and could not follow her husband to where the drum was beating for the troops to assemble. Instead she went to milk the cows and pray for William's safety. She wrote, "Then the voice . . . answered me saying, It shall be done unto you as it was unto Abraham when he offered Isaac on the altar. I don't know whether I milked or not for I felt the Lord had spoken to me."[3]

The new soldiers marched two hundred miles down the east side of the Missouri River, then crossed over to Fort Leavenworth, arriving on 1 August 1846. There they were outfitted with supplies, guns, and forty-two dollars per man as clothing money for the year. The paymaster at the fort was surprised when every man was able to sign his name on the payroll. Only a

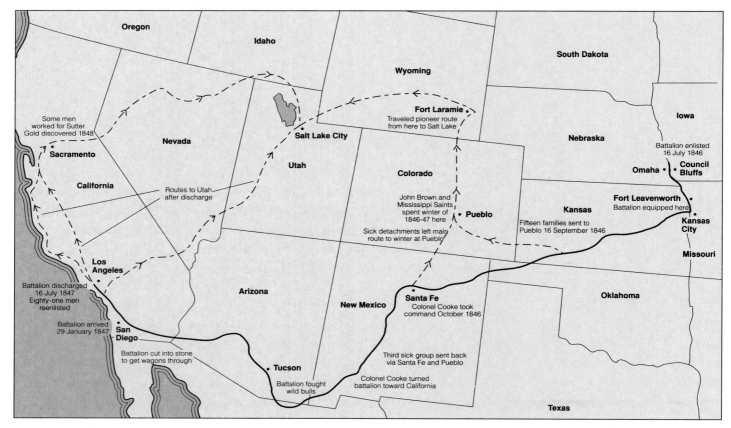

The route of the Mormon Battalion from Iowa to California. Note that three separate sick detachments were sent to Pueblo, Colorado. They later joined the pioneers on the main trail in Wyoming.

Jefferson Hunt (1803–79) and his wife accepted the gospel in 1834. Brother Hunt became commander of Company A in the Mormon Battalion. Two of his sons also enlisted in the battalion. Later he assisted the colonization effort in Provo, Utah, and San Bernardino, California. Huntsville, Utah, was named in his honor.

third of the volunteers he had previously paid could write. A portion of the money was collected by Parley P. Pratt and others sent by the Church. This was used to support the battalion members' families in Iowa and in unorganized territory, to assist in evacuating the poor from Nauvoo, and to help Parley P. Pratt, John Taylor, and Orson Hyde on their mission to England.

General Stephen W. Kearny's regiment had already embarked in June toward Santa Fe to conquer New Mexico for the United States. The Mormon Battalion was to follow him and aid his operations if necessary. For two weeks the battalion remained at Fort Leavenworth. The weather was very hot, and many men suffered, particularly with fevers. Their commanding officer, Colonel Allen, became severely ill and was not able to leave with them when they took up their march. Captain Jefferson Hunt, the ranking Mormon officer, took temporary command of the battalion. About two weeks after leaving the Missouri River, the men learned that Colonel Allen had died. This saddened them because they had grown to admire this benevolent officer.

The Mormon officers felt that Captain Hunt should continue as their leader and requested by letter that President Polk appoint him to the position. But First Lieutenant A. J. Smith of the regular army was already en route to assume command. "The appointment of Smith, even before his character was known, caused a greater gloom throughout the command than the death of Colonel Allen had," wrote battalion historian, Daniel Tyler.[4]

Lieutenant Smith set a rapid pace for Santa Fe, hoping to overtake General Kearny before the latter left for California. This wore heavily on the soldiers, and more especially on the wives and children who were allowed to travel with the battalion. With the relentless push, the men had little rest, and often the weary fell behind, trudging into camp hours after the others. Worse than the fast travel were the ministrations of the military doctor, George B. Sanderson of Missouri. He clearly disliked the Mormons and forced the men to swallow calomel and arsenic for their ills from the same rusty spoon. The men justifiably referred to him as "mineral quack" and "Doctor Death." William L. McIntire, a good botanic physician, had been appointed assistant surgeon to the battalion but was unable to administer to his afflicted friends in any way unless ordered to by Dr. Sanderson, the battalion surgeon.

On 16 September at the last crossing of the Arkansas River (in present-day Kansas), Smith sent Captain Nelson Higgins and ten men to convey most of the soldiers' families up the river to the Mexican village of Pueblo (in present-day Colorado) for the winter. The men strongly protested this "division" of the battalion because they had been promised that their families could accompany the army to California. The decision proved to be wise, however, in light of the difficult trek that lay ahead. A month later at Santa Fe, a detachment of sick men and all but five of the remaining women were sent under the direction of Captain James Brown to join the earlier group at Pueblo. There the battalion members met John Brown and his company of Mississippi Saints who were wintering in Pueblo.

On 9 October 1846 the weary soldiers dragged themselves into Santa Fe, the provincial capital of New Mexico, which had some six thousand inhabitants. General Kearny had already left for California, leaving the city under the command of Colonel Alexander Doniphan, a friend of the Saints from the Missouri days. Doniphan ordered a one hundred gun salute in honor of the arrival of the Mormon Battalion. In Santa Fe, Lieutenant Smith relinquished command to Lieutenant Colonel Philip St. George Cooke, whom the men came to respect as a fair but firm leader. The new commander had orders to blaze a wagon trail from Santa Fe to California. Veering south along the Rio Grande, the soldiers sometimes followed Spanish or Mexican trails but generally cut new roads. Once again the march took its toll in sickness; on 10 November a third detachment of fifty-five worn and weakened men turned back toward Pueblo.

Not only did lack of water and food plague the remaining 350 officers and men, but the sandy trails were a constant challenge. The soldiers were either pulling long ropes to help the teams get through the deep sand, or they were walking double file in front of the wagons to make firm trails for the wheels. After they turned northwest toward Tucson they encountered a herd of wild bulls. These were bulls abandoned by Spanish and Mexican ranchers. The bulls stampeded the line of march, sending the soldiers rushing

Philip St. George Cooke (1809–95) entered the United States Military Academy at age fourteen. Most of his service in the military was on the frontier, and he crossed the plains several times. When he assumed command of the Mormon Battalion at Santa Fe, he was welcomed by the men, who were happy to be relieved of Lieutenant Smith.

Under Cooke's direction the women and sick were sent to Pueblo to enable the healthy men to resume their march toward California. Upon arriving in San Diego, he praised the efforts of his men saying they "exhibited some high and essential qualities of veterans."5

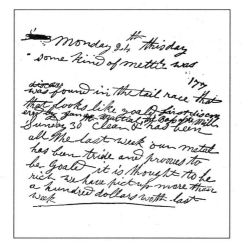

The officially recognized discovery of gold at Coloma in Northern California occurred on 24 January 1848 at John Sutter's lumber mill. Of the eleven white men and one woman present, at least six were Church members from the Mormon Battalion. The most widely accepted record of this famous discovery comes from the journal of battalion member Henry Bigler: "Monday 24th this day some kind of mettle was found in the tail race that looks like goald first discovered by James Martial [Marshall], the Boss of the Mill."[6]

Mormon Battalion veterans.
In 1898, at the fiftieth anniversary celebration of the discovery of gold in California, four men who had been at the initial find were present. All four were Latter-day Saints. They are from left to right: Henry W. Bigler, William J. Johnston, Azariah Smith, and James S. Brown.

for safety. The "battle" lasted only a few minutes, but ten to fifteen animals were killed, two of the battalion's mules were gored to death, and three soldiers were wounded. The event was immortalized as the Battle of the Bulls, and was the only fight during the battalion's long journey.

The battalion passed without incident through Tucson, where a small Mexican garrison was stationed. They then rejoined Kearny's route along the Gila River. Beyond the Colorado River lay over a hundred miles of trackless desert, where water was obtained only by digging deep wells. There the battalion encountered the heaviest sands, the hottest days, and the coldest nights. Weakened animals were butchered for food and all parts were eaten, including the hide, which was boiled until it was tender enough to eat. By this time many of the men were nearly barefoot, and some of them wrapped rawhide and old clothing around their feet to protect them from the hot sands. Beyond the desert they transported wagons through the narrow mountain passes of the coastal range with ropes and pulleys. Finally on 29 January 1847 they reached Mission San Diego at the end of their 2,030-mile march and reported to General Kearny. Kearny was named governor of California by President Polk in February.

Since California was already in the hands of the United States, the battalion men served as occupation troops with garrison duty in San Diego, San Luis Rey, and Los Angeles. While in southern California, the Saints gained the respect of the local citizens. Those in San Diego built a courthouse and houses, burned brick, and dug wells, thus contributing significantly to the building of the community. On 16 July, at the end of their year's enlistment, the battalion members were discharged, although eighty-one men chose to reenlist for an additional six months.

Most of the discharged men left for northern California, intending to travel east to join the Saints in the Salt Lake Valley. They were met by Captain James Brown, pioneer, founder of Ogden, and counseler in Ogden's stake presidency for many years. He conveyed a message from Brigham Young asking those without families to stay in California to work during the winter of 1847–48. Most of them did. Many spent the winter at Sutter's Fort on the Sacramento River and assisted in the discovery of gold in January 1848 that began the California gold rush. The following summer they honorably completed their contracts with Sutter, abandoned the gold fields, and joined their families in Salt Lake City or at the Missouri River.

THE BROOKLYN SAINTS

The Mormon Battalion was not the first group of Saints to reach the West. That honor belongs to a company of Saints who sailed out of New York harbor aboard the ship *Brooklyn* on 4 February 1846, coincidentally the same day the first Saints left Nauvoo. In August 1845 Church leaders had decided that a way station on the California coast would be needed for immigrating Saints from the South Pacific or England who came around the tip of South

The Brooklyn *was built in Newcastle, Maine, in 1834 and was a 445 ton fullrigger, 125 feet long, 28 feet wide, and 13 feet deep. She was piloted by Captain Abel W. Richardson, a part owner.*

In addition to the 238 Latter-day Saints led by Samuel Brannan, the company also took with them tools for eight hundred people, the printing press of the Prophet, *a large quantity of school books, and provisions for six or seven months. Coincidentally, the* Brooklyn *set sail on 4 February 1846, the same day the exodus from Nauvoo began.*

Samuel Brannan (1819–89) went east to the Salt Lake Valley from California but was unable to convince Brigham Young to continue on to California. He became disaffected and returned to the coast, where he was prominent in California as a politician, land speculator, and publisher. Before his death he lost the wealth he had gained during California's boom days.

America. Apparently Brigham Young envisioned the young, energetic Samuel Brannan as a Church agent in the San Francisco bay region. The publisher of the *Prophet*, the Church newspaper in New York, he was appointed in September 1845 to charter a ship and direct the company.

During the last three months of 1845, Samuel Brannan and Parley P. Pratt visited various branches in the East and recruited seventy men, sixty-eight women, and one hundred children to sail for the West about the middle of January. They were chiefly farmers and mechanics who carried with them all the tools necessary to build a new colony on the west coast. They also took a large quantity of school books and the printing press on which the *Prophet* had been printed. In December, Brannan chartered a ship at seventy-five dollars per adult, including provisions, and half fare for children. Known as the *Brooklyn* Saints they left for California expecting to help choose and establish the final destination for the Church.

The voyage of the *Brooklyn* was relatively pleasant except for two severe storms—one encountered in the Atlantic and the other in the Pacific Ocean. Twenty-one specific rules governed the conduct of the Saints during their journey. Reveille was at six o'clock, and the Saints were not permitted to leave their staterooms "without being completely dressed (i e) without their coats, &c." The rooms were to be cleaned by seven and to be inspected and aired daily. Breakfast was at eight-thirty (children first) and dinner from

The route of the Brooklyn. After rounding Cape Horn, a storm drove the Saints five hundred miles east, where they put in at the island of Juan Fernandez (Robinson Crusoe's island) on 4 May 1846. There they loaded fresh water, fruit, and vegetables. After five days they set sail for the Sandwich (Hawaiian) Islands, arriving there on 20 June. The Brooklyn entered Yerba Buena (San Francisco) Harbor late in July 1846 after over five months at sea.

After leading the Mississippi Saints to Pueblo, Colorado, John Brown (1820–97) was active in assisting emigration until about 1870. He also served as bishop of the Pleasant Grove Ward in Utah for twenty-nine years. He held numerous civil offices and was mayor of Pleasant Grove for twenty years.

three to five o'clock, with a "cold lunch" served at eight in the evening. Provisions were made for attending to the sick and for cooking for the group, and Sabbath morning services were held at which "all that are able must attend, shaved, and washed clean, so as to appear in a manner becoming the solemn, and holy occasion."[7] Rounding Cape Horn, the ship stopped at Juan Fernandez, the island made famous by Daniel Defoe's *Robinson Crusoe*. They also spent ten days in the Sandwich Islands (now the Hawaiian Islands). There were two births during the voyage, and the children were named Atlantic and Pacific, after the oceans where they first saw life. Ten of the passengers died on the voyage.

When the *Brooklyn* arrived at San Francisco Bay on 31 July 1846, Brannan, who had hoped to be the first American to fly the United States flag in California, was disappointed to see it atop the Mexican customhouse. Some of the company sought employment along the coast, but others founded a colony further inland, which they called New Hope. Brannan dreamed that New Hope would become the center for the Saints in the West. By January 1847 he was publishing the *California Star*, the second English newspaper in California. Most of the *Brooklyn* Saints were unaware the Church was settling in the Great Basin and willingly followed Brannan's direction.

In April 1847, Samuel Brannan headed east to meet the body of the Church and offer to guide them to California. He met Brigham Young and the Pioneer Company in June at the Green River (in present-day Wyoming). Thomas S. Williams and Samuel Brannan were sent to guide the members of the battalion and also members of the Mississippi Company into the Salt Lake Valley. These two groups had wintered at Pueblo and were at the time en route toward Salt Lake City. After spending a few days in the Salt Lake Valley with Brigham Young and the Saints, Brannan returned to California with Captain James Brown of the Mormon Battalion to conduct Church business. Disenchanted with Brigham Young's decision not to establish Church headquarters on the coast, Brannan soon apostatized. Some of the *Brooklyn* Saints followed him. Brannan publicized the California gold rush and became the region's first millionaire, but eventually lost his fortune through unwise investments and died a pauper.

THE PUEBLO SAINTS

As we have seen, during the winter of 1846–47 about 275 Latter-day Saints formed a substantial community at Pueblo, hundreds of miles west of the main body of the Saints at the Missouri River. This group consisted of the three sick detachments from the Mormon Battalion and approximately sixty "Mississippi Saints" who had come to Pueblo in August.

These southern members of the Church were led by John Brown, who had come from Mississippi to Nauvoo in 1845. He was appointed by Brigham Young in January 1846 to return to his fellow Saints in the South and urge them to join in the westward migration. Brown led forty-three people 640 miles to Independence, Missouri, where they were joined by fourteen others. They continued west along the Oregon Trail expecting to find the main body of the Saints led by Brigham Young. In July, however, when they reached Chimney Rock in western Nebraska, there were still no Saints. Trappers returning from California told them there were no Mormons ahead of them. Unaware that Brigham Young had decided to establish Winter Quarters on the Missouri, they decided to move to Fort Laramie. There they met John Richard, a trapper who invited them to winter near his trading post at Pueblo. Word finally reached them in Pueblo that Brigham Young had stopped at Winter Quarters.

Life was somewhat settled in Pueblo. In addition to hunting for venison, the Mississippi Saints planted turnips, pumpkins, beans, and melons and worked for fur trappers who paid them with corn. With the incoming battalion men, they built a school which doubled as a church. The battalion kept up regular military drills, and dances were frequent. Seven babies were born during the winter, but there were also nine deaths.

In the spring, Brigham Young wrote to the Pueblo Saints and told them of the plans of the main Pioneer Company to go to the Great Basin in the vicinity of the Great Salt Lake. An advance party from Pueblo went north to Fort Laramie where they met Brigham Young and the pioneers. President Young then dispatched Elder Amasa Lyman and others to guide the rest of the Pueblo Saints to the Salt Lake Valley, where they arrived just five days after the Pioneer Company.

WINTER QUARTERS: A STAGING GROUND FOR THE PIONEER COMPANY

The winter of 1846–47 saw the Mormon Battalion en route across a trackless desert—the *Brooklyn* Saints on the sea and then arriving at San Francisco Bay, and the Pueblo Saints waiting out the winter. Meanwhile, Winter Quarters, Nebraska, was bustling with activity in preparation for a Pioneer Company to make the trek west to the Rocky Mountains.

During the fall of 1846 plans were laid for the westward trek. It was decided that a relatively small party should make the initial crossing of the plains to blaze a trail for the larger companies to follow. But even this smaller undertaking required extensive preparation. Wagons were built and outfitted, horses and oxen sturdy enough to withstand the rigorous thousand-mile trip were procured, foodstuffs and other supplies were gathered, and sustenance and protection were arranged for those who remained behind.

Equally important was the need for more information about the largely-uncharted regions of the West. Besides conferring in November and December with local traders and trappers, such as Peter Sarpy, about the trail west of Winter Quarters, council leaders consulted with four men who had recently been in the Rocky Mountain region. Father Pierre Jean DeSmet, a Catholic priest and missionary among the Indians of the Oregon country, arrived in camp en route to St. Louis after five years in the mountains. He was one of the few white men who had visited the Great Salt Lake. Taking advantage of this good fortune, the Brethren questioned him carefully. Five days later two American Fur Company traders gave detailed accounts of the regions west of the Rockies and drew a map of the best areas to settle. Later, Logan Fontenelle, an interpreter for the Omaha Indians, described in detail the westward trail and the best locations for settlement in the mountains.

George Miller, a headstrong leader, argued with Brigham Young over prospective travel and settlement plans. Miller did not agree that the Twelve Apostles held supreme authority in the Church, therefore, he took a small group of Saints to live among the Ponca Indians on the Niobrara River in northern Nebraska. President Young, realizing that dissension in Church leadership was dangerous, sought the will of the Lord on how to deal with Miller and his followers. On 11 January 1847 he related a dream he had the night before where he discussed with Joseph Smith the best method of organizing the companies. Three days later he presented to the Church "the Word and Will of the Lord concerning the Camp of Israel in their journeyings to the West" (D&C 136:1).

Accepted by the assembled priesthood quorums as a revelation to the Church, this document became a constitution governing the westward migration. It said that the trek was "under the direction of the Twelve Apostles" (v. 3) and required the Saints to enter into a "covenant and promise to keep all the commandments and statutes of the Lord our God" (v. 2). It contained much practical direction about preparing for the pioneer journey and caring for the poor, widows, orphans, and Mormon Battalion families. Each man was to "use all his influence and property to remove this people to the place where the Lord shall locate a stake of Zion" (v. 10). The Saints were also to cease contending with each other and were directed to eliminate other vices that were among them.

Delegations went to each encampment to read the revelation and to announce the names of men Brigham Young desired to go in the Pioneer Company and in the companies to follow during the first year. Throughout the spring Church leaders held many meetings with various emigrating companies, providing information relative to their tentative location, the construction of boats for fording rivers, methods of pioneer travel, planting seeds, and irrigation.

The original idea was to handpick 144 men for the Pioneer Company—twelve for each of the twelve tribes of Israel—but as it turned out the original group consisted of 143 men (including three slaves of southern members), three women (wives of Brigham Young, Heber C. Kimball, and Lorenzo Dow Young), and two children. Collectively they had a variety of pioneering talents and skills. They included mechanics, teamsters, hunters, frontiersmen, carpenters, sailors, soldiers, accountants, bricklayers,

The three women of the Pioneer Company: Harriet Wheeler Young, wife of Lorenzo D. Young; Clara Decker Young, wife of President Brigham Young; and Ellen Sanders Kimball, wife of Heber C. Kimball.

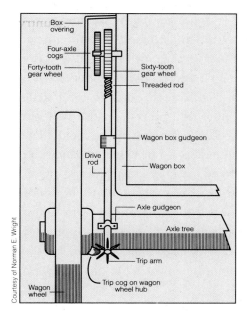

On 16 May 1847, midway between Council Bluffs and Fort Laramie, the famous "odometer" was installed to relieve the camp historian, William Clayton, from the tedium of counting the revolutions of a wagon wheel to calculate the distances traveled. It could tally ten miles before starting over. (The picture commonly labeled as the "odometer" in many books was built in 1876.)

On the return trip to Winter Quarters a new odometer that could count up to one thousand miles was built, and William Clayton successfully measured the complete distance from the Salt Lake Valley to Winter Quarters.

The Pioneer Company of 1847 traversed eleven hundred miles from Winter Quarters, near present-day Omaha, Nebraska, to the Salt Lake Valley. Their route followed the broad and gentle Platte River valley for six hundred miles to Fort Laramie in Wyoming, where they arrived on 1 June. They crossed to the south side of the Platte and followed the Oregon Trail for almost four hundred more miles to Fort Bridger.

West of Independence Rock in Wyoming, their trail crossed the Continental Divide at South Pass. Somewhere southwest of there the Pioneers met Jim Bridger. On 7 July the pioneers reached Fort Bridger. Continuing south, they picked up the Reed-Donner trail into the Salt Lake Valley.

During this final phase of the trek, which was the roughest section of the trip, Brigham Young contracted mountain fever, and the company split into three groups—the vanguard, the main company, and the rear guard with Brigham Young.

blacksmiths, wagon makers, lumbermen, joiners, dairymen, stockmen, millers, and engineers. Eight of the party were Apostles, and several had been with Zion's Camp. The company's equipment included a boat, a cannon, seventy wagons and carriages, ninety-three horses, fifty-two mules, sixty-six oxen, nineteen cows, seventeen dogs, and some chickens.

JOURNEY OF THE PIONEER COMPANY

Some of the vanguard company left Winter Quarters on 5 April 1847, but because of delays caused by general conference and the arrival of Parley P. Pratt and John Taylor from England, little progress was made during the first several days. The arrival of the two Apostles was a blessing because they brought money contributed by the English Saints and scientific instruments for calculating latitude, elevation, temperature, and barometric pressure. Orson Hyde, who had accompanied the two to England, arrived during the middle of May. Since these three were not yet outfitted, they remained in Winter Quarters. Elders Pratt and Taylor traveled with other companies later in the season, and Elder Hyde superintended the Saints who remained at the Missouri River.

Finally on 16 April the camp began its one thousand-mile trek. After two days on the trail, Brigham Young organized the camp in military fashion in case they encountered hostile Indians. William Clayton, the official camp historian, recorded accurate mileage for later emigrants. For the first few days this meticulous record keeper counted the monotonous revolutions of the wagon wheel to calculate the daily mileage. He soon proposed using a mechanical odometer for the job. Scientific-minded Orson Pratt designed the device, and Appleton Harmon, an experienced woodworker, constructed it.

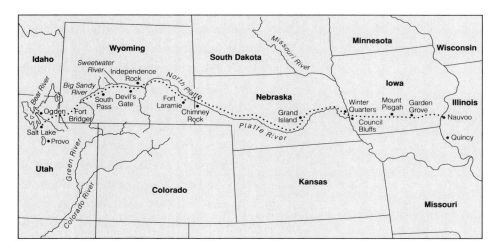

Wherever possible the pioneers followed existing roads and trails. They did very little trailblazing between Winter Quarters and the Salt Lake Valley. Across Nebraska the Oregon Trail ran along the south side of the Platte River. The first part of the Mormon Trail paralleled the Oregon Trail to Fort Laramie, Wyoming, but was on the north side of the river because the

Chimney Rock, one of the most famous landmarks for the western emigrants, could be seen for days as the companies crossed western Nebraska. Near here the pioneers met a band of Sioux, their first meeting with Great Plains Indians.

pioneers hoped to find better grazing and to avoid conflict with immigrants on their way to Oregon. The next section of the trail crossed Wyoming from Fort Laramie to Fort Bridger. Forbidding bluffs on the north side of the Platte forced the Saints to cross over at Fort Laramie and follow the Oregon Trail for 397 miles. At Fort Bridger the Oregon Trail turned north to the Pacific Coast, and the final segment of the Mormon Trail picked up the year-old track of the Reed-Donner party through the Rockies into the Salt Lake Valley.

On 26 May the company passed Chimney Rock—a principal landmark in Wyoming—which was considered the halfway mark by emigrating Saints. It was near Chimney Rock that Brigham Young and Heber C. Kimball expressed concern over the lightmindedness and profanity of some camp members who were holding mock trials and elections, gambling, and playing cards. Late one evening the two senior Apostles, moved by the Spirit, discussed calling the camp to repentance. The next day Brigham Young spoke to the men plainly.

William Clayton recalled Brigham saying, "Give me the man of prayers, give me the man of faith, give me the man of meditation, a sober-minded man, and I would far rather go amongst the savages with six or eight such men than to trust myself with the whole of this camp with the spirit they now possess. . . . Do we suppose that we are going to look out a home for the Saints, a resting place, a place of peace where they can build up the kingdom and bid the nations welcome, with a low, mean, dirty, trifling, covetous, wicked spirit dwelling in our bosoms? It is vain!" He concluded with a call to repentance: "If they [the brethren] will not enter into a covenant to put away their iniquity and turn to the Lord and serve Him and acknowledge and honor His name, I want them to take their wagons and retreat back, for I shall go no farther under such a state of things. If we don't repent and quit our wickedness we will have more hinderances than we have had, and worse storms to encounter."[8]

The following day, Sunday, Brigham Young convened a special meeting of the leaders. They went out on the bluffs, clothed themselves in their temple robes, and held a prayer circle. William Clayton said they "offered up prayer to God for ourselves, this camp and all pertaining to it, the brethren in the army, our families and all the Saints."[9] Thereafter a more saintly atmosphere prevailed in the camp.

At Fort Laramie the pioneers halted for repairs, Brigham Young celebrated his forty-sixth birthday, and the camp was joined by some of the Pueblo Saints. At the last crossing of the Platte (in present-day Casper, Wyoming), the pioneers used their boat, the *Revenue Cutter*, to ferry their goods and belongings across. They built rafts to ferry their wagons. Several Oregon-bound people paid $1.50 per wagon to be ferried across as well. Recognizing an opportunity to earn needed funds, Brigham Young left nine men behind to continue the lucrative ferry. The rest pushed on through South Pass, rafted across the Green River, and arrived at Fort Bridger early in July.

Independence Rock, another famous site, marked the beginning of the ninety-six mile route along Wyoming's Sweetwater River. Today, the graffiti of emigrants from pioneer days to the present can still be seen carved in the rock.

The pioneers encountered a number of mountain men as they traveled west, such as Moses Harris, Jim Bridger, and Miles Goodyear. Harris and Bridger were not optimistic about planting crops in the Salt Lake Valley. Goodyear was the most enthusiastic about agricultural success and encouraged the Saints to settle in Weber Valley, where he lived.

Beyond Fort Bridger travel through the mountain passes became more difficult. By the time they reached the Salt Lake Valley, the company was separated into three groups. Brigham Young, ill from mountain fever, lagged behind the main group. After 13 July, a third division, under the direction of Orson Pratt, moved ahead to chart the route and prepare a wagon road through what became known as Emigration Canyon. On 21 July, Orson Pratt and Erastus Snow caught the first glimpse of the Salt Lake Valley and shouted for joy at the sight. After a twelve-mile circuit into the valley, the two men returned to camp.

The advance company of pioneers entered the Salt Lake Valley on 22 July 1847 and immediately set up a crude irrigation system to flood the land and prepare for planting. On 24 July, Brigham Young and the rear company arrived at the mouth of what is now called Emigration Canyon. Wilford Woodruff drove President Young in his carriage. They looked to the future as they gazed over the valley. Wilford Woodruff wrote, "Thoughts of pleasing meditations ran in rapid succession through our minds while we contemplated that not many years that the House of GOD would stand upon the top of the mountains while the valleys would be converted into orchard, vineyard, gardens and fields by the inhabitants of Zion and the standard be unfurled for the nations to gather there to." Brigham Young said he was satisfied with the appearance of the valley as a "resting place for the Saints and was amply repaid for his journey."[10]

On a later occasion, Wilford Woodruff explained that when they came out of the canyon he turned the carriage so that President Young could see the whole valley. "While gazing upon the scene before us, he was enwrapped in vision for several minutes. He had seen the valley before in vision, and upon this occasion he saw the future glory of Zion and of Israel, as they would be, planted in the valleys of these mountains. When the vision had passed, he said, 'It is enough. This is the right place. Drive on.' "[11]

ESTABLISHING A SETTLEMENT IN THE VALLEY

Sunday, 25 July was a day of worship and thanksgiving. Members of the Twelve spoke at morning and afternoon meetings on the importance of industry and upright behavior. For the first few days in the valley, there was some exploring to the north and south to determine the best place to settle. By 28 July, Brigham Young's decision about the location of a city was firm. Between two forks of City Creek, he designated the lot where the temple would stand. The city would be laid out evenly and perfectly square from that point.

The first weeks were filled with activity. Within a week, a survey of the area had begun and men not engaged in farming were making adobes for a temporary fort, as protection from Indians and wild animals. The Mississippi Saints and some of the "battalion boys" who arrived in the valley in October built a bowery for public meetings on the temple block. The first child born in the valley was Elizabeth Steel, who was born to a Mormon Battalion family on 9 August. Two days later the Saints mourned the death of the son of a Mississippi couple, three-year old Milton Threlkill who had wandered from camp and drowned in City Creek.

Exploration of the surrounding country was also undertaken. Brigham Young and the Twelve climbed a mount-like promontory to the north where they prophesied of Zion and which they named Ensign Peak after the prophecy of Isaiah which reads: "He shall set up an ensign for the nations, and shall assemble the outcasts of Israel" (Isaiah 11:12). Expeditions were sent to investigate adjacent valleys. The Saints also discovered the enjoyment of bathing in the Great Salt Lake to the west and in some warm sulphur springs north of the city.

Brigham Young, the Twelve, and most of the original Pioneer Company spent only thirty-three days in the valley in 1847. On 16 August they commenced their return to Winter Quarters to prepare their families to come to the valley the next year. En route they met with 1,553 Saints who were already on their way to the Salt Lake Valley. More familiar with the terrain this time, and with fewer wagons and light loads, men and teams found the traveling considerably faster. Their major excitement consisted of losing many valuable horses to the Indians and seeing Brigham Young and Heber C. Kimball chased by a grizzly bear.

Meanwhile the arriving Saints settled in at the "Old Fort," now the site of Pioneer Park in Salt Lake City, and prepared for winter. Before leaving the valley, Brigham Young designated John Smith, who he knew was in a later company, to preside over the newly created Salt Lake Stake. After he arrived in September, President Smith selected Charles C. Rich and John Young as counselors and organized a high council. This organization, like the high council established in Winter Quarters a year earlier, acted as both spiritual and civic leaders of the community. It was the only government in Utah until January 1849.

REORGANIZATION OF THE FIRST PRESIDENCY

Brigham Young and his company arrived in Winter Quarters just before sunset on 31 October 1847, rejoicing to be with their families again. While en route Brigham Young discussed the possibilities of reorganizing the First Presidency of the Church with members of the Quorum of the Twelve. Although he emphasized that the Spirit was prompting him, not all of the Brethren were immediately in favor. In the absence of a precedent for such action they were uncertain if it was appropriate to reorganize the First Presidency at that time.

John Smith (1781–1854), brother of Joseph Smith, Sr., was ordained Presiding Patriarch of the Church on 1 January 1849 by Brigham Young.

During the three years the Quorum of the Twelve presided over the Church, a great deal of significant work was accomplished. They completed and dedicated the Nauvoo Temple, administered the temple endowment to a host of faithful Saints, evacuated Nauvoo, expanded missionary work and Church administration in Great Britain, organized the Mormon Battalion, founded several settlements in Iowa, presided over the settling of Winter Quarters, and blazed the way to a new home in the West. Nearly all of these tasks were revealed to Joseph Smith prior to his death, and the Twelve completed them in a wonderful manner. Next was the question of whether the Twelve was to remain the presiding quorum of the Church or whether there should be another First Presidency; and this question needed to be resolved.

After arriving at Winter Quarters, Brigham Young continued to meet and discuss the matter with his colleagues. On 30 November he raised "the subject of appointing three of the Twelve as the Presidency of the Church," suggesting that such a course would liberate the remainder so they could "go to the nations of the earth to preach the gospel."[12] This was consistent with previous revelations which identified this as the Twelve's chief calling (see D&C 107:23; 112:1, 16, 19, 28).

While the pioneers journeyed westward in 1847, a more permanent and larger settlement was built in Iowa and named Kanesville in honor of Thomas L. Kane, who had befriended the Saints. The west side of the Missouri River was abandoned for health reasons and because the Saints had promised they would leave Indian land with all improvements after two years. By the time the pioneers returned, most of the Saints had already moved or were moving to Kanesville or other Iowa settlements that Orson Hyde presided over. On 5 December 1847, President Young convened another meeting of the Quorum of the Twelve in Hyde's home in Kanesville. He said the subject of the First Presidency had been weighing heavily upon his mind and that the Spirit of the Lord had been stirring him on this matter. He asked the nine members of the Quorum present (Parley P. Pratt and John Taylor were in the Salt Lake Valley, and Lyman Wight was in Texas) to freely express their views on the subject, beginning with the oldest.[13]

Following the discussion, Orson Hyde moved that Brigham Young be sustained as President of The Church of Jesus Christ of Latter-day Saints, that he nominate his two counselors, and that they form the new First Presidency. The motion was seconded by Wilford Woodruff and carried unanimously. President Young then nominated Heber C. Kimball and Willard Richards as his counselors. They were also unanimously approved.

Three weeks later the Brethren held a general conference in a commodious log tabernacle that had been rushed to completion in Kanesville. During the joyful sessions of 24–26 December, suspense grew that a new First Presidency was about to be announced. On Monday, 27 December 1847, one thousand members crowded into the tabernacle and heard Brigham

Young explain the need for a full organization of the Church, including a First Presidency, the Quorum of the Twelve, the Seventies, and the Patriarch to the Church. Then Orson Pratt presented Brigham Young as the new President, and the Saints readily sustained him. President Young then presented his counselors who were likewise sustained. Finally "Uncle" John Smith, president of the new Salt Lake Stake, was sustained as the new Patriarch to the Church. Each of these officers was again sustained in the Salt Lake Valley in October 1848.[14]

As important as the first arrival of Latter-day Saints in the Salt Lake Valley was, no event in 1847 was more significant than the smooth transference of leadership from the Quorum of the Twelve to a new First Presidency, thus setting the precedent for future transitions up to the present day.

ENDNOTES

1. In Daniel Tyler, *A Concise History of the Mormon Battalion in the Mexican War, 1846–1847*, reprinted, 1881 (Glorieta, N. Mex.: Rio Grande Press, 1964), pp. 128–29.

2. In Tyler, *A Concise History*, p. 128.

3. Marguerite H. Allen, comp., *Henry Hendricks Genealogy* (Salt Lake City: Hendricks Family Organization, 1963), pp. 26–27.

4. Tyler, *A Concise History*, p. 144.

5. A. R. Mortensen, ed., "The Command and Staff of the Mormon Battalion in the Mexican War," in *Utah Historical Quarterly*, Oct. 1952, p. 343.

6. Henry Bigler's journal entry; spelling standardized.

7. "Rules and Regulations," *Times and Seasons*, 15 Feb. 1846, pp. 1127–28.

8. William Clayton, *William Clayton's Journal* (Salt Lake City: Deseret News, 1921), pp. 191, 194, 197; spelling standardized.

9. Clayton, *William Clayton's Journal*, pp. 202–3.

10. Wilford Woodruff Journals, 24 July 1847, LDS Historical Department, Salt Lake City; spelling and capitalization standardized.

11. In "Pioneers' Day," *Deseret Evening News*, 26 July 1880, p. 2.

12. Wilford Woodruff Journals, 30 Nov. 1847; capitalization standardized.

13. See Wilford Woodruff Journals, 5 Dec. 1847.

14. See *History of the Church*, 7:623–24.

ESTABLISHING A REFUGE IN DESERET

Pioneer companies of 1847

Company	Number of People
Brigham Young	148
Mississippi	47
Mormon Battalion	210
Daniel Spencer	204
Parley P. Pratt	198
Abraham O. Smoot	139
Charles C. Rich	130
George B. Wallace	198
Edward Hunter	155
Joseph Horne	197
Joseph B. Noble	171
Willard Snow	148
Jedediah M. Grant	150
Total	**2,095**

ONLY FOUR DAYS after arriving in the Salt Lake Valley, Brigham Young told the pioneers that "he intended to have every hole and corner from the Bay of [San] Francisco to Hudson bay known to us and that our people would be connected with every tribe of Indians throughout America."[1] President Young named the region *Deseret*, which is a word from the Book of Mormon meaning honeybee (see Ether 2:3). The prophet intended the new settlements to be a hive of activity. The Saints were virtually the only white settlers in the vast Great Basin, the name for an area approximately the size of Texas between the Rocky Mountains on the east, the Sierra Nevada Mountains on the west, the Columbia River watershed on the north, and the Colorado River to the south. The area was relatively isolated and arid and short on timber and game. The Saints realized that settling here would require considerable faith and their best efforts, but they believed that with God's help they could succeed.

FIRST YEAR IN THE SALT LAKE VALLEY

In August 1847, Brigham Young, the Apostles, and about one hundred others left the Salt Lake Valley for Winter Quarters, Nebraska. At the same time approximately fifteen hundred Saints in ten companies were on the plains en route to the valley. There was great rejoicing when Church leaders met these companies in present-day western Wyoming. After feasting together, President Young's company continued their journey east while the other companies continued west, arriving in the Salt Lake Valley during the months of September and October.

Crossing the plains was difficult for these Saints who came as entire families. Many were not able to bear the arduous journey and died on the plains. Jedediah M. Grant, member of the First Council of the Seventy and captain of the third company, lost his wife, Caroline, and their infant daughter, Margaret, who, like many others, contracted cholera on the Sweetwater River. Caroline died four days after her daughter. Before her death, she requested that their bodies be buried in the valley, but Jedediah was forced to inter the baby in a shallow grave and continue on to the Salt Lake Valley where he buried his wife. Then he and his friend Joseph Bates Noble returned to the Wyoming plains to exhume Margaret's body, only to find that wolves had found the grave first.

But before they reached the grave, the Spirit of God had already

Jedediah Morgan Grant (1816–56), one of the great missionaries of the Church, served in Zion's Camp, labored on the Kirtland Temple, and during the Nauvoo period was called as one of the Seven Presidents of Seventy.

He helped bring the Saints across the plains into the Salt Lake Valley, where he became Salt Lake City's first mayor. The last two years of his life he served in the First Presidency of the Church as second counselor to Brigham Young.

comforted him. Elder Grant confided to his friend, "Bates, God has made it plain. The joy of Paradise where my wife and baby are together, seems to be upon me tonight. For some wise purpose they have been released from the earth struggles into which you and I are plunged. They are many, many times happier than we can possibly be here." Sad that they could not fulfill his promise, they returned to Salt Lake.[2]

Several years later Jedediah was permitted to see his wife and daughter in the world of spirits. Not long before Elder Grant died, President Heber C. Kimball gave him a blessing. On that occasion Elder Grant related a vision he had received. "He saw the righteous gathered together in the spirit world, and there were no wicked spirits among them. He saw his wife; she was the first person that came to him. He saw many that he knew, but did not have conversation with any except his wife Caroline. She came to him, and he said that she looked beautiful and had their little child, that died on the Plains, in her arms, and said, 'Mr. Grant, here is little Margaret; you know that the wolves ate her up, but it did not hurt her; here she is all right.' "[3]

Charles C. Rich and John Young organized a municipal high council in the Salt Lake Valley similar to the one formed a year previously at Winter Quarters. Under the council's direction, two ten-acre blocks were added to the fort, 450 log cabins were built, an adobe wall around the fort was completed, a fence was constructed around the city to control the livestock, and a number of roads and bridges were built. The "big field," an area of 5,133 acres, was cultivated, with 872 acres being planted in winter wheat. When Captain James Brown arrived from California with approximately $5,000 in Mormon Battalion pay, the council appointed a group to take some of the money to southern California to buy cows, mules, wheat, and a variety of seeds. The council also approved the use of $1,950 to purchase the Miles Goodyear ranch and trading post on the Ogden River thirty-five miles north of Salt Lake, eliminating a possible obstacle in settling that large and promising area.[4]

The Saints were not alone in the valley. A few of the approximately twelve thousand American Indians who inhabited the Great Basin in 1847 lived in the Salt Lake Valley. In the fall a group of Ute Indians came to the fort. One of them offered to sell two young Indians who had been captured in a raid. When the Saints recoiled at the suggestion, the Indian threatened to kill the children. After another refusal, one was killed. Then Charles Decker, Brigham Young's brother-in-law, purchased the other and gave her to Lucy Decker Young to raise. Sally, as she was named, later became chief cook in the Beehive House and eventually married the Pauvant Ute chief Kanosh.[5]

The first winter in the valley was mild, but there were many discomforts in the Old Fort. Wolves, foxes, and other predators annoyed the people with their incessant howling and depredations. One night Lorenzo Dow Young spread some strychnine around the area and in the morning found fourteen dead white wolves. Swarms of mice were also a nuisance. One contrivance

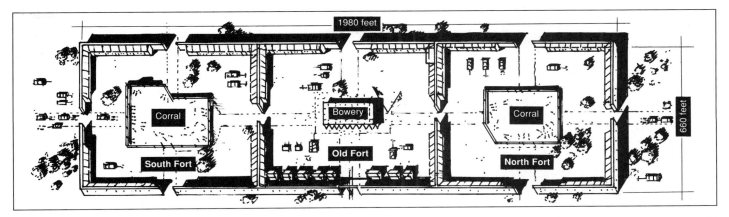

1980 feet			
Corral	Bowery	Corral	660 feet
South Fort	Old Fort	North Fort	

The Old Fort was erected in August 1847 and was located three blocks south and three blocks west of the temple block. Two additions to the fort were later added to accommodate expected arrivals. These were called the North Fort and the South Fort.

for catching them was a bucket partially filled with water and a board sloping at each end, greased and balanced on the bucket edge, so that the mice would run onto the board to lick the grease, fall in, and drown. One of the most valuable possessions in the fort was a cat.

During March and April heavy spring snow and rain descended upon the valley. Unfortunately, the Saints had not realized this would happen. Their homes had flat sod roofs, which leaked profusely. Food was gathered into the center of the rooms and protected with buffalo skins obtained from the Indians. "It was no uncommon thing to see a woman holding an umbrella over her while attending to her household duties. The Fort presented quite a ludicrous appearance when the weather cleared up. In whatever direction one looked, bedding and clothing of all descriptions were hanging out to dry."[6]

In the spring of 1848, provisions became scarce. Many of the Saints were without shoes and adequate clothing, so they made moccasins and other clothing out of animal skins. The people were placed on rations. Each person was limited to about one-half pound of flour per day. They also ate crows, thistle tops, bark, roots, and sego lily bulbs.

Priddy Meeks graphically described his attempts to find food while his "family went several months without a satisfying meal of victuals. I went sometimes a mile up Jordan to a patch of wild roses to get the berries to eat which I would eat as rapidly as a hog, stems and all. I shot hawks and crows and they ate well. I would go and search the mire holes and find cattle dead and fleece off what meat I could and eat it. We used wolf meat, which I thought was good. I made some wooden spades to dig seagoes [sego lilies] with, but we could not supply our wants." He worked particularly hard for thistle roots: "I would take a grubbing-hoe and a sack and start by sunrise in the morning and go, I thought six miles before coming to where the thistle roots grew, and in time to get home I would have a bushel and sometimes more thistle roots. And we would eat them raw. I would dig until I grew weak and faint and sit down and eat a root, and then begin again."[7]

Because of these difficult conditions, the settlers naturally looked forward to the harvest of new crops, but late spring frosts injured much of

Sego lily, which is now Utah's state flower

The Sea Gull Monument, located on Temple Square in Salt Lake City, was designed and executed by Mahonri M. Young, a grandson of Brigham Young. The monument was dedicated 1 October 1913 by President Joseph F. Smith. Today the sea gull is Utah's state bird.

the wheat and garden vegetables. Then a May and June drought injured more of the crops. Worse yet, hordes of crickets descended from the foothills and began devouring what remained. Men, women, and children turned out with sticks, shovels, brooms, and gunny sacks to combat the pests. They used fire and even dug trenches to drown the crickets, but these measures failed to stop the onslaught. For about two weeks they battled and prayed for relief. Crop failure meant disaster for the present colony and no food for the more than two thousand Saints planning to immigrate that year.

Finally on a Sabbath day, while Charles C. Rich was preaching, sea gulls from the Great Salt Lake flew in and began to devour the insects. "They would eat crickets and throw them up again and fill themselves again and right away throw them up again," reported Priddy Meeks. The gulls continued their attacks for over two weeks until the crickets were effectively eliminated. Meeks said, "I guess this circumstance changed our feeling considerable for the better."[8] Many of the crops were preserved. Today the sea gull is Utah's state bird, and a monument to the sea gulls stands on Temple Square.

The Saints nurtured the remaining crops throughout the summer and on 10 August held a harvest feast. Parley P. Pratt described it: "Large sheaves of wheat, rye, barley, oats and other productions were hoisted on poles for public exhibition, and there was prayer and thanksgiving, congratulations, songs, speeches, music, dancing, smiling faces and merry hearts. In short, it was a great day with the people of these valleys, and long to be remembered by those who had suffered and waited anxiously for the results of a first effort to redeem the interior deserts of America, and to make her hitherto unknown solitudes 'blossom as the rose.' "[9]

The settlers also anxiously awaited the return of a number of their fellow Saints, including Brigham Young and other Church leaders, who arrived in September. Before the end of 1848, nearly three thousand Saints, including members of the Mormon Battalion, had arrived in the valley. About one-fourth of the exiles from Nauvoo were now in their new refuge in the West. In Deseret for the second time, Brigham Young enthusiastically wrote to those in Iowa that the Saints had surely found "a haven of rest, a place for our souls, a place where we may dwell in safety." This was happy news to refugees who had been driven from their homes more than once. He also affirmed that they would "once more rear a temple to his [God's] names' honor and glory."[10]

THE PROVISIONAL STATE OF DESERET

During the first year in the valley, the high council drafted laws, levied taxes, apportioned land, issued water and timber rights, established a cemetery, and imposed fines and punishments for criminal offenses. When the First Presidency arrived in the fall of 1848, civic responsibilities for the growing community passed to a general council of about fifty leading priesthood holders, presided over by the First Presidency, which met weekly at the house of Heber C. Kimball. There was no separation of church and state because the Latter-day Saints considered all affairs of the kingdom of God to be one, whether spiritual, economic, or political.

This provisional government continued to lay out the expanding city. Throughout the fall and winter of 1848, under the direction of Brigham Young and Heber C. Kimball, lots were apportioned to applicants who could adequately care for their property. The city was then divided into nineteen wards, each nine blocks in size. Bishops were placed in charge of each ward, and, under their supervision, fences were built, a network of irrigation ditches was constructed, and trees were planted along the ditch banks.

A plan for distribution of farming lands worked out in the fall of 1848 was consistent with President Young's philosophy that the land should not be monopolized by the earliest settlers, but should be put to its most productive use for the good of the community. There was to be no private ownership of water and timber—natural resources important to the entire community. Under the direction of bishops, workers turned out to build irrigation systems and roads to the canyons. Families received the right to use water and timber in proportion to the work they put into building and maintaining these systems. Disputes over land and resource use were mediated by priesthood leaders. Even though there was considerable cooperation among the Saints in the use of land, water, and timber, private business enterprises gradually developed to regulate these same resources.

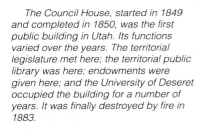

The Council House, started in 1849 and completed in 1850, was the first public building in Utah. Its functions varied over the years. The territorial legislature met here; the territorial public library was here; endowments were given here; and the University of Deseret occupied the building for a number of years. It was finally destroyed by fire in 1883.

The first gold coins in Utah were minted in September 1849. Later the crucibles were broken, making it impossible to make more coinage until materials could be ordered from the East. It was then decided to issue paper currency.

Cooperation also characterized the erection of public works. Daniel H. Wells was placed in charge of this department, which began building a wall around the temple block, a tithing house, the Council House (used for public and political meetings), a small adobe Church office building, a public bathhouse at the warm springs just north of the city, an armory, and a bowery on Temple Square to be used for a central meeting place. A tannery and leather manufacturing establishment, gristmills, sawmills, and a foundry were built with a combination of public and private effort.

The first means of economic exchange in the valley was the thousands of dollars worth of gold dust brought from California by members of the Mormon Battalion who had participated in the discovery of gold near Sacramento. Later the First Presidency sent a few men to California on a "gold mission" for more of the precious metal to help with Deseret's economy. The gold dust was minted into coins. Paper currency based on the Church's gold supply was also used.[11]

With the culmination of the Mexican War and the signing of the Treaty of Guadalupe Hidalgo on 2 February 1848, the fledgling colony of the Saints became part of the Union. The treaty granted the United States all of the territory comprising the present states of California, Nevada, Utah, most of New Mexico and Arizona, and parts of Wyoming and Colorado. When Church leaders realized that their colony was part of America, they began planning to become a state. Early in 1849 the general council formally established a provisional State of Deseret with Brigham Young as governor, Willard Richards as secretary of state, Heber C. Kimball as chief justice, Newel K. Whitney and John Taylor as associate justices, and Daniel H. Wells as attorney general.

The provisional State of Deseret was the civil government in the Great Basin for two years. It organized counties, granted rights to natural resources, regulated trade and commerce, established the Nauvoo Legion as an official state militia, and fulfilled all functions of a regular government. The "state legislature" consisted of men selected by Brigham Young and ratified by the voters. This government performed admirably and smoothly until the United States Congress formally established the Territory of Utah in September 1850.

"HERE WE WILL STAY"

Even though the Saints were efficiently governed, there were several challenges in establishing a strong refuge in Deseret. In contrast to the previous winter, the winter of 1848–49 was very severe and created serious needs among the people. It snowed frequently, and the snow remained on the ground throughout the entire winter, making it difficult for the cattle to feed. Heavy snowfall in the mountains made it difficult to gather wood. Excessive cold and violent winds often made life miserable for the settlers.[12]

Food was again so scarce that the people ate wolves, hawks, crows, dogs, and animals that had been dead for some time. The council sponsored a contest to eliminate the "wasters and destroyers" that were diminishing what little food supply there was. Numerous predatory animals were killed in this hunt. The brethren also instituted a voluntary rationing and community storehouse system. Those with surplus food were asked to give it to their bishop to be divided among the needy.

The harshness of the winter, constant hunger, a meager harvest the previous year, and the pull of what was called "California fever" created some discontent, and a few settlers loaded their wagons and prepared to leave in the spring. During those trying times, President Heber C. Kimball was moved upon to prophesy, "Never mind, boys, in less than one year there will be plenty of clothes and everything that we shall want sold at less than St. Louis prices."[13]

President Brigham Young also encouraged the Saints: "God has appointed this place for the gathering of His Saints, and you will do better right here than you will by going to the gold mines. . . . We have been kicked out of the frying-pan into the fire, out of the fire into the middle of the floor, and here we are and here we will stay. . . . As the Saints gather here and get strong enough to possess the land, God will temper the climate, and we shall build a city and a temple to the Most High God in this place. We will extend our settlements to the east and west, to the north and to the south, and we will build towns and cities by the hundreds, and thousands of the Saints will gather in from the nations of the earth. . . . We have the finest climate, the best water, and the purest air that can be found on the earth; there is no healthier climate anywhere. As for gold and silver, and the rich minerals of the earth, there is no other country that equals this; but let them alone; let others seek them, and we will cultivate the soil."[14]

Most Saints remained loyal to the cause and planted their seeds. As summer came, the prophets of God were vindicated. The Lord did temper the elements, and there was a bounteous harvest, enough to feed the nearly five thousand Saints who were already in the valley and the fourteen hundred who immigrated during the summer. Moreover, an estimated ten to fifteen thousand gold seekers passing through Salt Lake City in both 1849 and 1850 provided an economic windfall for the Saints. Merchant companies, organized to haul goods to California, learned upon reaching Salt Lake City that food, clothing, implements, and tools sent by ship had already reached the marketplace. They sold their goods to the Saints at devalued prices rather than take an even heavier loss in California. The overland immigrants' wagons needed servicing and re-outfitting, thus providing employment to Mormon blacksmiths, wagonsmiths, teamsters, laundresses, and millers. The Saints established ferries on the upper crossing of the North Platte, and on the Green and Bear rivers, which were used by the California-bound trains.

Parties with empty wagons were sent out from Salt Lake to collect valuable items discarded along the route by those who had attempted to lighten their loads so they could hurry faster to the gold fields of California. John D. Lee spent several days looking for a suitable stove for his family. He finally "found one to his liking, a fine large Premium Range No. 3 which would have cost more than fifty dollars to purchase. On the way back he started loading up with powder and lead, cooking utensils, tobacco, nails, tools, bacon, coffee, sugar, trunks of clothing, axes, and harness."[15] Thus the famous 1849 gold rush directly enabled the Saints to survive in the Salt Lake Valley.

EARLY EXPLORATION AND COLONIZATION

Although the major effort of the Saints during their first two years in Deseret was to establish a base of operations, Church leaders also sought other locations for settlement. Exploring parties determined the natural resources of the different areas, including water supply, soil fertility, availability of timber and other building materials, altitude of surrounding mountains, and mineral deposits.

In July and August of 1847, men from the Pioneer Company were sent to explore southward in the Salt Lake Valley, northward along the Bear River, and eastward into Cache Valley. During the fall of 1847, two routes to California were traversed by Mormon companies. Captain James Brown accompanied Samuel Brannan along the northern trail back to his colony at San Francisco. Jefferson Hunt, senior Latter-day Saint captain of the Mormon Battalion, led a group of eighteen men to southern California to secure cattle and other needed supplies. Hunt was successful in reaching the Chino Rancho by way of the Old Spanish Trail, although members of his party were forced to eat some of their horses to survive.

In December 1847, Parley P. Pratt led an exploring party southward toward the large, fresh-water Utah Lake. They launched a boat, caught fish with a net, and explored the lake and Utah Valley for two days before returning home by way of the Oquirrh mountain range on the west of the Salt Lake Valley. They explored both Cedar and Tooele valleys and the southern end of the Great Salt Lake before finishing their week-long expedition.

Within a year of the pioneers' arrival, small towns were settled in the southern part of the Salt Lake Valley and also in what became Davis and Weber counties to the north. One of these, Brownsville, named in honor of James Brown, grew into Utah's second largest city (later called Ogden in honor of Peter Skeen Ogden, a fur trapper). Other colonists joined the Brown family to establish Brownsville, and they successfully raised wheat, corn, cabbage, turnips, potatoes, and watermelons with seed brought from California. They also milked about twenty-five cows and were the first Mormons to produce cheese in the area. This produce helped fellow Saints in the Salt Lake Valley survive the starvation period in 1848–49. In 1849 Brigham Young visited the rapidly growing colony and sent Lorin Farr to

Lorin Farr (1820–1909) joined the Church at age eleven along with his family, being baptized by Lyman E. Johnson and confirmed by Orson Pratt. He served as president of the Weber Stake and as mayor of Ogden for many years.

Fort Utah was also called Fort Provo in honor of Etienne Provot, an early French trapper.

take charge of all Church and political affairs there. President Farr became Ogden's first mayor and the president of the Weber Stake, serving in both capacities for the next twenty years.

The attractive and fertile Utah Valley—named after the Ute Indians who lived there—to the south of Salt Lake Valley was another logical place for settlement. Church leaders first proposed using this valley as a stock range and as a source to supply fish for the Saints in Salt Lake City, but potential Indian problems led them to establish a permanent fortified settlement instead. Thirty-three families, numbering about 150 people, with John S. Higbee as the president of the company, arrived at the Provo River on 1 April 1849. They built Fort Utah about a mile and a half east of Utah Lake and began farming the rich river bottom lands. In September, Brigham Young visited the fort and recommended that the city be moved to higher ground farther east.

This new location became the nucleus of the city of Provo. During the winter of 1849–50, the Utes threatened war against the new settlers, and the Nauvoo Legion was called upon to protect the people of Provo. In a two-day encounter called the Battle at Fort Utah, forty Indians and one settler were killed and several others were wounded.[16] This confrontation effectively ended Indian resistance in Utah Valley and made it possible for other settlements to be developed in 1850 and 1851, including Lehi, Alpine, American

Courtesy of Utah State Historical Society

Fork, Pleasant Grove, Springville, Spanish Fork, Salem, Santaquin, and Payson. This line of settlements utilized every mountain stream and was spaced so that the outlying farms and pasture lands of each community bordered the next, and all settlers could rally together in case of danger. Provo became the stake center and county seat.

Tooele Valley, west of Salt Lake Valley, was colonized in 1849. In November of that same year, one of the first Ohio converts to the Church, Isaac Morley, led 225 colonists to Sanpete Valley, about a hundred miles south of Salt Lake City. They spent a cold and difficult winter in dugouts on the hill where the Manti Temple was later constructed. The next year Elder Morley and his associates established friendly relations with Ute chief Wakara and his people, who had invited the settlers to locate near them.

A fifty-man exploration company, headed by Parley P. Pratt, was formed on 23 November 1849 for the purpose of choosing locations for additional colonies south of the Salt Lake Valley. Four days later they visited the thriving settlement of Provo, which boasted fifty-seven log houses. The company made detailed observations throughout their exploration. They continued south through Juab and Sanpete valleys, arriving at Manti just twelve days after the colonists began that settlement. On 10 December, while on the Sevier River, over two hundred miles south of Salt Lake City, their thermometer registered twenty degrees below zero Fahrenheit. After another hundred miles, part of the company crossed the rim of the Great Basin into what would become known as Utah's Dixie, and they noticed a marked change in the climate and topography. By New Year's Day they had reached the present-day site of St. George.

Indian guides and villagers informed them that the country to the south was desolate and forbidding, so they decided to return north. Returning through Mountain Meadows and Pahvant Valley, they were forced to stop at Chalk Creek (now Fillmore) because of heavy snow. It was decided that half of the company would push on to Provo, while the other half would remain at Chalk Creek until spring. This decision was based on the fact that there were only enough supplies to see half of the company through the winter. One morning the brethren of the forward-moving camp were completely buried by the night's snow. Elder Pratt arose and shouted at his sleeping brethren: "I raised my voice like a trumpet, and commanded them to arise; when all at once there was a shaking among the snow piles, the graves were opened, and all came forth! We called this Resurrection Camp."[17]

GATHERING TO ZION

During this early exploration and settlement, the First Presidency developed plans to gather the remaining Saints, most of whom were quite poor, from the Iowa camps near the Missouri River.

In 1848 the First Presidency left Orson Hyde in Kanesville, Iowa, to direct the fortunes of the Saints. Approximately thirty communities had developed in Pottawattomie County. Agriculture flourished, craftsmen pursued their trades, and schools were held. Elder Hyde established a newspaper, the *Frontier Guardian*, in 1849 and edited about one hundred issues before being called to Utah in 1852. This newspaper served to keep the Iowa and eastern Saints informed regarding the progress of the kingdom of God.

Kanesville, the largest of the Mormon communities in Iowa, served Church migration as the staging ground for crossing the plains. Close by were three Church-operated ferries on the Missouri River, which were also utilized by one hundred forty thousand emigrants on their way to Oregon and California. One of the happiest events that occurred in Kanesville was the return of Oliver Cowdery in October 1848. On 12 November 1848, Oliver was rebaptized. Unfortunately, before he could gather to the Salt Lake Valley,

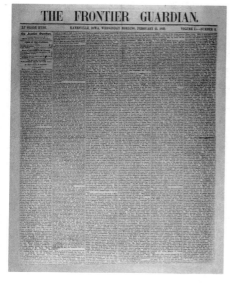

Orson Hyde commenced publication of the Frontier Guardian *on 7 February 1849 in Kanesville, Iowa. In 1852 the paper was sold to Jacob Dawson, who changed the name to the* Iowa Sentinel.

Documents signed by Church members going to Utah through the Perpetual Emigrating Fund Company

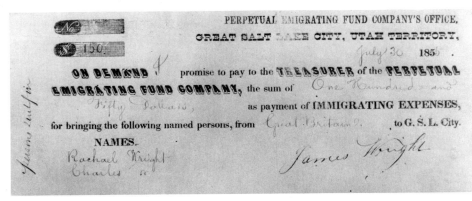

Oliver became ill and died on a visit to his wife's family in Richmond, Missouri. He died on 3 March 1850 in the home of his father-in-law, Peter Whitmer, Sr.

The rich harvest of 1849 and the economic boost of the gold rush pioneers generated confidence for the Church to gather the ten thousand

Edward Hunter (1793–1883) was baptized 8 October 1840 by Orson Hyde, who was on his way to Palestine at the time. Edward Hunter was a wealthy man who gave liberally to the Church and its leaders. Brigham Young called him to be the Presiding Bishop of the Church in 1851.

Saints still in the Missouri Valley, the hundreds still in branches scattered throughout the eastern states, and the thirty thousand members of the Church in England. In the fall of 1849 the Brethren launched the Perpetual Emigrating Fund, or the PEF. Its purpose was to solicit contributions in Deseret and use these funds to outfit the poor Saints who had gathered to the camps in Iowa. Then when the immigrants arrived in the valley, they would be expected to labor on the public works or pay back their debt, thus keeping the PEF a "perpetual" fund. PEF assistance to the Saints in Europe began as soon as possible after the removal of the Nauvoo exiles to the West.

Some six thousand dollars was raised that first fall, and Bishop Edward Hunter was appointed as agent to go to Iowa and purchase wagons, livestock, and provisions to outfit numerous Saints to gather to Zion. Approximately twenty-five hundred people immigrated to Deseret in 1850 and another twenty-five hundred were aided in 1851, leaving approximately eight thousand Saints still in Iowa, including those gathered from the eastern branches under the direction of Elder Wilford Woodruff and thousands of British Saints who had come that far.

Elders Ezra T. Benson and Jedediah M. Grant were appointed in the fall of 1851 to help Orson Hyde in evacuating the camps of the Saints in 1852. To those remaining, the First Presidency implored:

"What are you waiting for? Have you any good excuse for not coming? No! you have all of you, unitedly, a far better chance than we had when we started as Pioneers to find this place: you have better teams and more of them. You have as good food and more of it; you have as much natural strength. . . .

". . . Therefore we wish you to evacuate Pottawatamie, and the States, and next fall be with us all ye Saints of the Most High."[18]

Accordingly, most of the Saints sold their land and improvements in Iowa to other American frontiersmen. Twenty-one companies, averaging over sixty wagons each, migrated to the Great Basin in 1852. Only a skeleton force was left on the Missouri River to aid future emigrants.

INTERNATIONAL EXPANSION

Coincident with their interest in the gathering was the renewed attention given by the First Presidency to the spreading of the gospel of Jesus Christ to the nations of the earth. The responsibility for this vast undertaking resided with the Quorum of the Twelve Apostles. Four vacancies in the Quorum (due to the formation of the First Presidency and the apostasy of Lyman Wight) were filled in February 1849 by the call of Charles C. Rich, Lorenzo Snow, Erastus Snow, and Franklin D. Richards. Many of the Twelve and several elders under their direction were assigned to take the gospel message to the nations of the earth. John Taylor was sent to France and Germany; Lorenzo Snow went to Italy; and Erastus Snow was sent to the Scandinavian countries; each of them was accompanied by several missionaries.

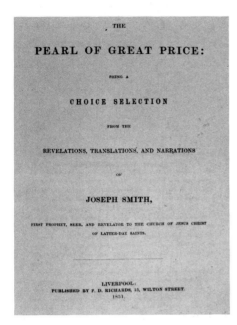

THE

PEARL OF GREAT PRICE:

BEING A

CHOICE SELECTION

FROM THE

REVELATIONS, TRANSLATIONS, AND NARRATIONS

OF

JOSEPH SMITH,

FIRST PROPHET, SEER, AND REVELATOR TO THE CHURCH OF JESUS CHRIST
OF LATTER-DAY SAINTS.

LIVERPOOL:
PUBLISHED BY F. D. RICHARDS, 15, WILTON STREET.
1851.

*Title page of the 1851 edition of the
Pearl of Great Price*

In the general conference of October 1849, Franklin D. Richards was called, along with others, to a mission in England. Elder Richards was to succeed Orson Pratt as mission president. Missionary work in Great Britain had continued with great success following the short mission of Parley P. Pratt, Orson Hyde, and John Taylor in 1846–47. Thereafter, Orson Spencer and then Orson Pratt directed the mission. Thousands of converts entered the Church between 1847 and 1850. Elder Pratt also supervised the emigration of over three thousand people to Kanesville, Iowa, in the first use of the PEF in England.

Elder Franklin D. Richards officially replaced Orson Pratt as mission president in England on 1 January 1851. Under his able leadership for the next seventeen months, thousands more joined the Church, and arrangements continued unabated for the gathering of these Saints to Zion. Both Orson Pratt and Franklin D. Richards published numerous tracts, which helped the missionary effort. The most important publication, however, was a compilation of several revelations and books of scripture translated by the Prophet Joseph Smith, which the English Saints had not previously seen. Elder Richards aptly named this compilation the *Pearl of Great Price*. This small volume, first published in 1851, became the foundation for the scriptural book by the same name that would be accepted as a standard work of the Church in 1880. Clearly the British Saints contributed greatly to the strength of the Church. Of the thousands who gathered to Zion in the Rocky Mountains in the nineteenth century, over half came from Great Britain.

Other members of the Twelve introduced the gospel to the continent of Europe. John Taylor directed the first missionary activity in France and Germany in 1849 and 1850. The revolutions that racked Europe in 1848 so stirred society there that Elder Taylor and his companions found little success in either nation, but the Book of Mormon was published in both French and German, and a branch of the Church was established in Hamburg, Germany. Sporadic missionary work continued in Germany for several more years.

Elder Lorenzo Snow, assigned to take the gospel to Italy, arrived in the Piedmont region in June 1850 with two companions, Joseph Toronto, a native of Italy, and T.B.H. Stenhouse, a convert from Britain. The missionaries enjoyed some success among a Protestant group known as the Waldenses, but were unsuccessful with the larger Catholic population. Lorenzo Snow arranged for the translation of the Book of Mormon into Italian and sent the first missionaries to Malta and India. In December 1850, Elder Stenhouse introduced the gospel to Switzerland. In February 1851, Elder Snow dedicated this land for the spreading of the gospel. The work there progressed slowly but steadily throughout the 1850s, and Switzerland became the third most productive mission of the Church in Europe after England and Denmark.

The task of taking the gospel to Denmark was given to Elder Erastus

Snow of the Twelve. He arrived in 1850 and enjoyed almost immediate success under Denmark's strong constitutional guarantee of religious freedom. From among the many converts, Elder Snow set apart 150 native missionaries, who in turn helped speed the dissemination of the gospel message. From Denmark the work quickly spread to Norway, Sweden, and Iceland. Although not as many converts joined the Church in these other countries as in Denmark, all of Scandinavia contributed thousands of Saints to the great gathering to Zion during the next fifty years.

During this time of renewed international missionary zeal, many courageous attempts were made to take the gospel to other nations of the earth. These were usually only marginally successful. Parley P. Pratt was assigned the responsibility of heading the Pacific Mission and sent missionaries to China, Hawaii, Australia, and New Zealand. In 1851 he went to Chile but a revolution paralyzed his efforts. The T'ai-ping Rebellion in China thwarted Hosea Stout's work there. Labors in Australia and New Zealand bore some fruit, and a few immigrants came to Salt Lake City in the 1850s.

The greatest success in the Pacific was in the Hawaiian Mission, which was opened in 1850. George Q. Cannon felt impressed to take the gospel to the native islanders instead of only to the Europeans and Americans. Learning Hawaiian, Elder Cannon and the brethren who followed him found thousands of people ready to accept the gospel.

In the first years following the 1847 founding of a refuge in the West, The Church of Jesus Christ of Latter-day Saints, under inspired leadership, achieved a remarkable work. It began to conquer a desert, establish a core of settlements, gather thousands of refugees to Deseret, and courageously take the gospel to many nations of the earth.

ENDNOTES

1. In Wilford Woodruff Journals, 28 July 1847, LDS Historical Department, Salt Lake City; spelling standardized.

2. In Carter E. Grant, "Robbed by Wolves: A True Story," *Relief Society Magazine,* July 1928, pp. 363–64.

3. Heber C. Kimball, in *Journal of Discourses,* 4:136.

4. See B. H. Roberts, *A Comprehensive History of The Church of Jesus Christ of Latter-day Saints, Century One,* 6 vols. (Salt Lake City: The Church of Jesus Christ of Latter-day Saints, 1930), 3:476–77.

5. See John R. Young, *Memoirs of John R. Young, Utah Pioneer,* 1847 (Salt Lake City: Deseret News, 1920), p. 62; Solomon F. Kimball, "Our Pioneer Boys," *Improvement Era,* Aug. 1908, pp. 734–35.

6. M. Isabella Horne, "Pioneer Reminiscences," *Young Woman's Journal,* July 1902, p. 294.

7. Priddy Meeks, "Journal of Priddy

Meeks," in *Utah Historical Quarterly,* 1942, p. 163.

8. "Journal of Priddy Meeks," p. 164; see also William Hartley, "Mormons, Crickets, and Gulls: A New Look at an Old Story," *Utah Historical Quarterly,* Summer 1970, pp. 224–39.

9. Parley P. Pratt, ed., *Autobiography of Parley P. Pratt,* Classics in Mormon Literature series (Salt Lake City: Deseret Book Co., 1985), p. 335.

10. In James R. Clark, comp., *Messages of the First Presidency of The Church of Jesus Christ of Latter-day Saints,* 6 vols. (Salt Lake City: Bookcraft, 1965–75), 1:341.

11. See Eugene Edward Campbell, "The Mormon Gold Mining Mission of 1849," *Brigham Young University Studies,* Autumn 1959–Winter 1960, pp. 23–24; Leonard J. Arrington, *Great Basin Kingdom: An Economic History of the Latter-day Saints, 1830–1900* (Cambridge: Harvard University Press, 1958), pp. 71–74.

12. See Brigham Young, Heber C. Kimball, and Willard Richards, in Clark, *Messages of the First Presidency*, 1:352.

13. In *Journal of Discourses*, 10:247.

14. In James S. Brown, *Giant of the Lord: Life of a Pioneer* (Salt Lake City: Bookcraft, 1960), pp. 132–33.

15. Juanita Brooks, *John Doyle Lee: Zealot-Pioneer Builder-Scapegoat*, new ed.

(Glendale, Ca.: Arthur H. Clark Co., 1972), pp. 48–49.

16. See Peter Gottfredson, *Indian Depredations in Utah*, 2d ed. (Salt Lake City: Merlin G. Christensen, 1969), pp. 28–35.

17. Pratt, *Autobiography of Parley P. Pratt*, p. 340.

18. In Clark, *Messages of the First Presidency*, 2:75–76.

UTAH IN ISOLATION

John M. Bernhisel (1799–1881) was born and raised in Pennsylvania. He studied medicine at the University of Pennsylvania. After joining the Church he was called to serve as a bishop in New York in 1841.

After the Saints had established a home in the Rocky Mountains, Bernhisel was chosen to represent them as a delegate to Congress. He served in this office for four consecutive terms (1851–59). He was reelected in 1861 and served until 1863, when he retired from public office.

W HEN THE SAINTS first arrived in the Salt Lake Valley, they were satisfied that they were isolated from their enemies and could build the kingdom of God in peace and safety. Brigham Young declared to members of the Pioneer Company on 24 July 1847, "If the people of the United States will let us alone for ten years, we will ask no odds of them."[1] With the sustaining help of the Lord and by their own industry, the Saints established a strong refuge within the ten years. Success, however, did not come easily. Conflicts developed with government appointees, and great sacrifice was required to gather Church members to Zion and to colonize.

ORGANIZATION OF UTAH TERRITORY

Church leaders laid plans in 1848 to negotiate with the United States government for either statehood or territorial status. In March of 1849 an election was held to ratify officers for the proposed territory, and by early May a twenty-two-foot long petition containing 2,270 signatures was on its way to Washington, D.C., proposing the creation of an immense territory including all of what is now Utah and Nevada, portions of Arizona, New Mexico, Colorado, Wyoming, and Oregon, and a third of California, including a narrow strip on the Pacific coast taking in the port city of San Diego.

John M. Bernhisel, a medical doctor with political acumen, was chosen to take Deseret's petition to the nation's capital. En route to Washington from Deseret he met with several key politicians in the East and succeeded in soliciting considerable support for his project. In November 1849, Dr. Bernhisel met in Philadelphia with Wilford Woodruff and Colonel Thomas L. Kane, a close friend of the Church. A year earlier at the request of Brigham Young, Kane had been in Washington and had spoken with President James K. Polk and other leading officials about a territorial government for Deseret. He had found little sympathy for the Mormons in Washington and therefore recommended that Deseret apply for statehood. Under territorial status officials would be appointed by the president.

Kane told Wilford Woodruff, "You are better without any Government from the hands of Congress than a Territorial Government. The political intrigues of government officers will be against you. You can govern yourselves better than they can govern you. . . . You do not want corrupt political men from Washington strutting around you with military epaulets

Thomas Leiper Kane (1822–83) was one of the great philanthropists of his time, helping those in prison, the Quakers, and also the Saints for almost forty years. From 1861 to 1863 he fought in the Civil War on the side of the Union, and he was wounded several times.

Four months after Thomas L. Kane died of pneumonia , Elder George Q. Cannon performed his temple work for him in the St. George Temple.

and dress who will speculate out of you all they can." Kane also recommended that Brigham Young be the governor because "His head is not filled with law books and lawyers tactics but he has power to see through men and things."[2]

By the time Bernhisel met with Kane, Church officials in Salt Lake City had also concluded that they should direct their lobbying efforts toward becoming a state rather than a territory. They drew up a formal constitution for the State of Deseret, complete with the necessary elected officials, including First Presidency members Brigham Young as governor, Heber C. Kimball as lieutenant governor, and Willard Richards as secretary of state. Almon W. Babbitt was selected as a delegate to Congress, and he left in July with a draft of the constitution. Babbitt printed the document in Kanesville, Iowa, and then in December met Dr. Bernhisel in Washington.

Unfortunately, Deseret's application for statehood was not given any real consideration. As Colonel Kane and Dr. Bernhisel quickly perceived, Washington officials were preoccupied with the conflict between the northern and southern states over the extension of slavery into the territory obtained in the war with Mexico. From December 1849 through September 1850 Congress vehemently debated slavery-related issues and showed little concern for the Mormon colony in the Great Basin.

The Church's best friend in Congress proved to be Senator Stephen A. Douglas of Illinois, who had befriended Joseph Smith and the Saints during the Nauvoo period. Douglas, the chairman of the Senate committee on territories, graciously met with Dr. Bernhisel and promised to help take the petition through the legislative process. Although Congress willingly agreed to rapidly growing California's petition for statehood, the slavery controversy prohibited serious consideration of the statehood petitions for sparsely populated Deseret and New Mexico. Senator Douglas decided to call for territorial status instead, to appease the South, which could not accept more senators from "free" states. He also changed Deseret's name to Utah (after the Ute Indians) to avoid offending his colleagues, particularly Senator Thomas Benton of Missouri, who thought Deseret sounded too much like desert.[3]

After lengthy debate, Congress completed a legislative package known as the Compromise of 1850, which, among other things, admitted California into the Union as a free state and designated Utah and New Mexico as territories with the right to decide by popular sovereignty whether they would eventually become slave or free states. On 9 September 1850 President Millard Fillmore signed the bill creating the Utah Territory. Neither the Latter-day Saints nor the federal officials knew then that this action would begin forty-six years of mistrust and conflict before statehood was finally granted.

Bernhisel's skill as a lobbyist became particularly important as President Fillmore considered appointment of officers for the new territory. Meeting

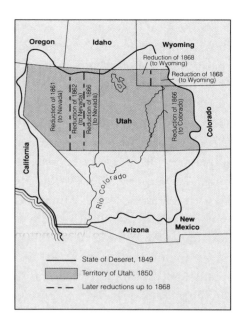

The proposed state of Deseret

with the president, Bernhisel stated, "The people of Utah cannot but consider it their right, as American citizens to be governed by men of their own choice, entitled to their confidence, and united with them in opinion and feeling."[4] Fillmore, fearing that the Senate would not approve an all-Mormon slate, compromised and selected four Mormons (Young, Snow, Blair, and Heywood) and four others to the federally appointed slots. The appointees for the new territory of Utah were Brigham Young, governor and superintendent of Indian affairs; Broughton D. Harris of Vermont, secretary; Joseph Buffington of Pennsylvania, chief justice; Zerubbabel Snow of Ohio and Perry E. Brocchus of Alabama, associate justices; Seth M. Blair of Utah, U.S. attorney; Joseph L. Heywood of Utah, U.S. marshal; and Henry R. Day, Indian agent.

CONFLICT WITH THE NON-MORMONS

Throughout the fall and winter of 1850–51, fragments of information about the federal government's action reached the Salt Lake Valley. Upon learning that he was appointed governor and assigned to take a census and establish legislative districts, Brigham Young got to work immediately after taking the oath of office on 3 February 1851. An election for other officials was held in August, the most important official elected being John M. Bernhisel, as territorial delegate to Congress.

The non-Mormon appointees arrived during the following summer. The first to come was Chief Justice Lemuel D. Brandebury, who had replaced Joseph Buffington after he had refused his appointment. The Saints charitably greeted Brandebury and entertained him with a banquet and several dances. Each of the other officials was accorded similar treatment. The last to come was Associate Judge Perry E. Brocchus, who told his traveling companion, Orson Hyde, that he would like to be considered for the position of congressional delegate from Utah Territory. When he arrived on 17 August, he was disappointed to learn of Bernhisel's election.

Conflict between the Saints and the "gentile" officials began almost immediately. The territorial secretary, Broughton Harris, accused Brigham Young of irregularities in handling the census and election, which technically could not be certified without the secretary. Mrs. Harris condescendingly referred to the Mormon men and their plural wives as hardly better than animals. Because of his alienation, Harris refused to turn over to Governor Young the territorial seal and the twenty-four thousand dollars appropriated for running the government.

In September, Judge Perry Brocchus asked Brigham Young for permission to speak in the Church's general conference. After expressing gratitude for the kindness and hospitality of the Saints, he launched into a diatribe against the Mormons for their lack of patriotism and the immorality of their women (because of plural marriage). The audience was infuriated with Brocchus's speech. President Young took the stand and rebuked Brocchus for his imprudent remarks. The two men later exchanged letters, which, instead of achieving accord, revealed an irreconcilable difference. From the non-member point of view, the Mormons were guilty of sedition for speaking harshly against the United States and its officials, they were a peculiar and immoral people because of their unusual marriage practices, and they were under the "un-American" political domination of their church leaders. The Latter-day Saints, on the other hand, felt justified in criticizing the United States for not redressing their grievances against Missouri and not bringing the murderers of Joseph and Hyrum Smith to justice. Furthermore, they pointed out that despite these injustices, they were loyal to the Constitution.

Brocchus, Harris, Brandebury, and Day left Utah on 28 September 1851. These "runaway officials" as the Saints called them, went to Washington, D.C., with highly colored stories about the Mormons, including the practice of plural marriage. They claimed they had been compelled to leave Utah because of the lawless acts and seditious tendencies of Brigham Young and the majority of the residents. Anticipating these charges, Governor Young wrote to President Fillmore setting forth his own view of affairs in the territory. He also sent Jedediah M. Grant to join John M. Bernhisel and Thomas L. Kane in Washington to represent the Church's interest. After reading Governor Young's letter and conducting a preliminary investigation, U.S. Secretary of State Daniel Webster ordered the "runaway officials" to return to their posts or to resign; they resigned.

Back in Utah territorial business proceeded unhindered, and the laws previously enacted by the provisional State of Deseret were officially incorporated into territorial law. In honor of the president of the United States, the legislature created Millard County, christened its county seat Fillmore,

Initially the leaders of the Church preferred a geographically centralized location for the territorial capital. Thus, Fillmore was chosen in October 1851. The capital building, designed by Truman O. Angell, was started in December 1851 with only the south wing being completed by March 1857.

The territorial legislature first met here in December 1855. Only the one session was held in Fillmore. It was decided to hold the legislative sessions in Salt Lake City until the federal government provided enough funds to complete the building.

If the money had been appropriated and President Young's plans followed, the building would have included wings to the east, west, and north. These would have then been connected by a central rotunda with a dome. The south wing has been used as a place for religious meetings, a school house, a city and county civic center, a theater, a jail, a dance hall, and finally as a museum.

Courtesy of Utah State Historical Society

and designated it as the future territorial capital. The most important legislative act, passed on 4 February 1852, gave original jurisdiction in both civil and criminal cases to local probate courts, which were presided over by Church officials. This, in effect, made it possible in most instances for these local courts to displace the federal courts, which were presided over by judges appointed by the president of the United States. This situation prevailed in Utah until Congress repealed the territorial statute in 1874. Meanwhile President Fillmore appointed officials who, because they did not criticize the Saints, were more to the citizens' liking.

In the fall of 1853, a tragedy brought sorrow to both Saints and gentiles alike. Captain John W. Gunnison led a party of army topographical engineers to survey in the Utah Territory for the proposed transcontinental railroad. In October, a band of vengeful Indians, angered because members of a California emigrant train had killed one of their tribe and wounded two others, attacked Gunnison's party, killing the commander and seven others. The tragedy cast gloom over the Latter-day Saint settlements because Gunnison was respected for his kindness and friendliness. Even though Church members had no part in the killing, the image of the Church suffered from rumors that the Mormons had planned and ordered the awful deed.

In 1854 at the conclusion of Brigham Young's term of four years as governor, President Franklin Pierce refused the entreaties of the Utah citizens to reappoint him. Instead, he selected Colonel E. J. Steptoe as governor. Steptoe was in Utah on assignment to study the feasibility of a military road through the territory and to assist in capturing the murderers of the Gunnison party. Instead of accepting the governorship, Steptoe signed a petition that Brigham Young be reappointed; he then left for California. Pierce offered the position to others, but when they also declined he reappointed Brigham Young as governor.

GATHERING TO ZION ACCELERATED

In spite of the seemingly all-consuming task of building a model city in their new Zion, Church leaders took on additional challenges. Few things were more urgent than spreading the gospel of Jesus Christ and preparing for the arrival of converted Saints. It was the goal of the Church to gather all members to the West. Missionary work was so successful first in Britain and then in various parts of the European continent, that in the early 1850s Church members there outnumbered those in Utah. For example, there were 30,747 Latter-day Saints in the British Isles in 1850 and 11,380 in Utah. As missionary success continued, it became a Herculean task to arrange for the emigration of so many people, particularly since most converts were poor.

Despite these challenges, with the organization of the Perpetual Emigrating Fund (PEF) in 1849, the remaining Saints at the camps in Iowa were brought into the valley by 1852. Attention could then be given to gathering the many thousands of Church members in Europe. Friends and relatives in Utah played an important part in gathering the European Saints. Church leaders encouraged friends and family members to contribute cash, or items that could be converted to cash, to the PEF office in Salt Lake City, which in turn directed the agents abroad to send the persons named under the care of the company. Most immigrants, however, did not come totally by way of PEF funds. Many European Saints paid all or part of their own way.

The PEF employed various agents along the route to the Great Basin to assist the immigrating Saints. The agent in Liverpool, England, chartered ships and assembled and instructed prospective emigrants. During the first few years, the emigrants sailed to New Orleans, where another representative met them and booked passage up the Mississippi River to St. Louis. A third agent arranged transit up the Missouri River about five hundred miles to an outfitting post, where a final agent prepared them for the overland journey to Utah. In 1855 the New Orleans-Mississippi River route was abandoned for health reasons in favor of entry into the United States at Philadelphia, New York, or Boston, where immigrants traveled by rail either to St. Louis or another railhead farther west. The entire journey usually required eight or nine months.

Sea routes of Mormon emigration

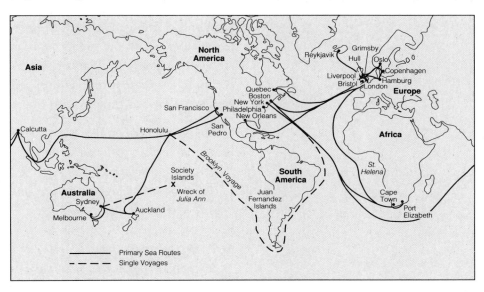

In over half a century of sea travel, the Saints "experienced only one sea disaster, the wreck of the American bark *Julia Ann*."[5] Twenty-eight members of the Church were aboard the *Julia Ann,* which set sail from Australia bound for San Francisco. Five people lost their lives when the ship encountered strong winds that swept them into a coral reef. "The Saints and some masters attributed this remarkable safety record to the hand of Providence and the fact that ships were often dedicated and blessed before embarking on an emigrant voyage. Many of these vessels were eventually lost at sea, but not while carrying Mormon passengers."[6]

A grasshopper plague during the summer of 1855 seriously jolted the economy in Utah, and even with the donations from the Saints, the PEF was in financial difficulty. Church leaders therefore sought a way to cut the costs of immigration. Brigham Young wrote to Franklin D. Richards, the European mission president, in September 1855: "We cannot afford to purchase wagons and teams as in times past, I am consequently thrown back upon my old plan—to make hand-carts, and let the emigration foot it, and draw upon them the necessary supplies, having a cow or two for every ten. They can come just as quick, if not quicker, and much cheaper—can start earlier and escape the prevailing sickness which annually lays so many of our brethren in the dust."[7] A general epistle by the First Presidency giving detailed instructions on handcart travel was read at the October 1855 general conference but was not acted upon until 1856. It was estimated that using handcarts would reduce emigration costs by a third to a half for each person. Consequently many more people could come to Zion through the available PEF funds.

Immigration during 1856 was unusually large with many of the Saints crossing the plains for the first time by handcart. Arriving at eastern United States seaports, they made their way by rail to the terminus at Iowa City, Iowa. There agents arranged for the preparation of handcarts designed for either pushing or pulling a load of one hundred to five hundred pounds of food and clothing. The first three companies, led by returning missionaries, heroically walked the plains, arriving safely in the Salt Lake Valley between 26 September and 2 October. Elder J.D.T. McAllister, who helped the first company get outfitted, composed a merry song, which the handcart emigrants sang as they crossed the plains:

Ye Saints that dwell on Europe's shores,
Prepare yourselves with many more
To leave behind your native land
*   For sure God's Judgments are at hand.*
Prepare to cross the stormy main
Before you do the valley gain
And with the faithful make a start
*   To cross the plains with your hand cart.*

Chorus
Some must push and some must pull
*   As we go marching up the hill,*
As merrily on the way we go
*   Until we reach the valley, oh.*[8]

Like those who preceded them, the handcart companies had their share of adventure and trial. A rescue of six-year-old Arthur Parker occurred as the first handcart company was en route on a forest trail between Iowa City and Florence, Nebraska. One day Arthur, who had been ill, sat down unnoticed to rest along the trail. The company traveled on until a sudden storm came up, and they hurriedly made camp. Finding that Arthur was not with the children, they began an organized search. After two days of searching, the company was forced by dwindling supplies to move on. Brother Parker went back on the trail alone to search for his son. As he left, his wife gave him a bright red shawl. If the son were found dead, the father was to wrap him in the shawl; if alive, he was to wave the shawl as a signal to the watchful family.

For hours Brother Parker retraced their route, calling, searching, and praying for his helpless little son. At a mail and trading station he learned that a farmer and his wife had found Arthur and helped him. For three days Ann Parker and her children watched and waited, and the entire company prayed for little Arthur. On the third day as she looked back along the trail she saw her husband in the distance. He was waving the shawl. Ann sank to the sand. She slept that night for the first time in six days.[9]

Twiss Birmingham, also a member of the first handcart company, recorded that the company averaged about twenty-five miles a day pulling the handcarts. On 3 August 1856, Twiss recorded in his journal: "Started at 5 o'clock without any breakfast and had to pull the carts through 6 miles of heavy sand. Some places the wheels were up to the boxes and I was so weak from thirst and hunger and being exhausted with the pain of the boils that I was obliged to lie down several times, and many others had to do the same. Some fell down. I was very much grieved today, so much so that I thought my heart would burst—sick—and poor Kate—at the same time—crawling on her hands and knees, and the children crying with hunger and fatigue. I was obliged to take the children and put them on the hand cart and urge them along the road in order to make them keep up."[10]

As the Saints prepared for general conference in Salt Lake City in October 1856, everyone assumed that the arrival of the third handcart company ended the immigration that year. But Franklin D. Richards, who had come into the valley two days prior to the conference, announced that two more handcart companies and two ox-cart supply trains were still on the plains and desperately needed food and clothing to finish the journey. The Willie and Martin companies had started late from Liverpool and were further delayed in Iowa City awaiting the construction of new handcarts. Because the wood for these carts was not properly seasoned, extensive repairs were necessary in Florence, Nebraska, which further slowed them down.

One of their leaders, Levi Savage, had urged the Saints to remain at Winter Quarters until spring, but he was voted down by the enthusiastic but naive immigrants. Brother Savage then declared, "Brethren and sisters, what I have said I know to be true; but seeing you are to go forward, I will go with you, will help you all I can, will work with you, will rest with you, will suffer with you, and, if necessary I will die with you. May God in his mercy bless and preserve us."[11] In early October the immigrants were toiling through the middle of Wyoming, where each member's scant allotment of clothing gave little comfort in the frosty mornings.

When Brigham Young learned that these companies were still on the plains, he spoke to the Saints who had gathered for general conference. The meeting was actually held on 5 October, one day before the conference officially convened. Brigham Young said:

"The text will be, 'to get them here.'. . .

"I shall call upon the Bishops this day, I shall not wait until to-morrow, nor until next day, for 60 good mule teams and 12 or 15 wagons. . . .

"I will tell you all that your faith, religion, and profession of religion, will never save one soul of you in the celestial kingdom of our God, unless you carry out just such principles as I am now teaching you. Go and bring in those people now on the plains."[12] The response was impressive. Sixteen wagon loads of food and supplies were quickly assembled; and on the morning of 7 October, sixteen good four-mule teams and twenty-seven hardy young men (known as Brigham Young's "Minute Men") headed eastward with the first provisions. More help was solicited and obtained from all parts of the territory. By the end of October, two hundred and fifty teams were on the road to give relief.

Meanwhile early snows trapped the Willie Company a few miles east of South Pass and the Martin Company further back near the last crossing of the North Platte River. Relief parties finally found the Willie Company on 19 October and the Martin Company nine days later. Some rescuers looking for the Martin Company had even turned back thinking that the immigrants must have found some kind of winter quarters. The Saints in both companies were freezing, listless, and near starvation. Scores of them were already dead, and even after help arrived, nearly a hundred more died.

One of the first to find the desperate Martin Company was the hardy Ephraim Hanks, who had killed and butchered a buffalo on his way. Ephraim recalled, "I reached the ill-fated train just as the immigrants were camping for the night. The sight that met my gaze as I entered their camp can never be erased from my memory. The starved forms and haggard countenances of the poor sufferers, as they moved about slowly, shivering with cold, to prepare their scanty evening meal was enough to touch the stoutest heart. When they saw me coming, they hailed me with joy inexpressible, and when they further beheld the supply of fresh meat I brought into camp, their gratitude knew no bounds."[13]

Bringing the suffering immigrants into the valley was difficult. Many of the women were widowed and the children orphaned. Several could not walk because of frozen feet and legs. When shoes and stockings were removed from the feet of fourteen-year-old Maggie Pucell and her ten-year-old sister Ellen, the skin came off. The dead flesh was scraped off Maggie's feet, but Ellen's were frozen so badly that amputation just below the knees was necessary. The Willie Company arrived in Salt Lake City on 9 November, and the Martin Company dragged into the city before cheering Saints on 30 November. In December, members of the independent wagon

Ephraim Knowlton Hanks (1826–96) was ordained a seventy while living in Nauvoo, where he labored on the Nauvoo Temple. He served in the Mormon Battalion. After going to Utah he carried the United States mail between Salt Lake and the Missouri River, a distance of over twelve hundred miles. Ephraim crossed the plains over fifty times in seven years. Three years prior to his death he was ordained a patriarch by Brigham Young, Jr.

Handcart companies

Leader	Crossed Plains
1. Edmund L. Ellsworth	1856
2. Daniel D. McArthur	1856
3. Edward Bunker	1856
4. James G. Willie	1856
5. Edward Martin	1856
6. Israel Evans	1857
7. Christian Christiansen	1857
8. George Rowley	1859
9. Daniel Robinson	1860
10. Oscar O. Stoddard	1860

trains, who had rested at Fort Bridger, reached the valley.

Over two hundred members of the two ill-fated handcart companies were buried in frozen graves before they could reach Zion. More people died in these two companies than in any other immigrant group in the United States. The fault was not in the method of travel, but was the result of a combination of many unusual and largely unforseen circumstances. In subsequent years the Church sponsored five more handcart companies, and each of them arrived in the valley without undue hardship.

COLONIZATION EXPANDS

When immigrants arrived in Salt Lake City, they were usually met as they emerged from Emigration Canyon and escorted to a city block named Emigration Square. Brigham Young or some other Church leader welcomed them, and wards in the city treated them to a well-deserved celebration feast. After a few days of being cared for by the local Saints, these new arrivals were sent to other communities or were given land and work in the Salt Lake City area. Especially in the early years, the immigrants were usually assigned a location, often based on a correlation between their skills and the needs of the various communities. Between 1847 and 1857, over one hundred towns were founded and colonized.

Following the work of Parley P. Pratt's Southern Exploring Company in 1849–50, Church leaders began establishing communities along the "Mormon Corridor" on the line of mountains leading southwestwardly toward southern California. The first of these were Parowan, an agriculture center, and Cedar City, the headquarters of the "iron mission," both founded in 1851. By 1853 nearly all the sites recommended by the Southern Exploring Company had been settled.

San Bernardino, in southern California, was also founded in 1851. It was designed to serve as a base of supplies and a receiving station near a Pacific port. Elders Amasa Lyman and Charles C. Rich of the Quorum of the Twelve presided over the colony, which grew to some seven thousand people by 1857. Plans to bring the European Saints around South America's Cape Horn and through San Bernardino up the Mormon Corridor to Salt Lake City never materialized because ships could not be chartered. Some of the Saints from Australia, New Zealand, and the South Pacific islands, however, did come via San Bernardino. Brigham Young eventually came to doubt the wisdom of having such a large center in California. In 1857 members of the colony were called home, partly because federal troops were approaching Utah and partly because the colony was experiencing internal dissension and problems with non-Mormon neighbors. Some residents of San Bernardino did not respond to the prophet's direction and remained in California.

The expansion of the settlements was also influenced by missionary work among the Indians. Soon after the founding of Cedar City, groups were

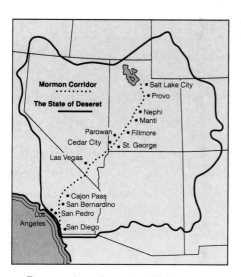

The route through southern Utah across Nevada and into southern California was known as the Mormon Corridor. A string of settlements or forts along this route provided shelter and protection for the traveler all the way to the Pacific Ocean.

sent to explore the Virgin and Santa Clara rivers, and in 1854 men were sent to work among the Indians of that region. The missionaries not only taught the gospel, but also tried to help the Indians build homes and learn better agricultural methods. Missionaries were also assigned to establish Indian missions in Las Vegas, Nevada, at Elk Mountain on the Colorado River near present-day Moab, Utah, and at Fort Lemhi on the Salmon River in central Idaho. The Elk Mountain mission, while experiencing some success among the Utes, was abandoned in 1855 because fighting erupted between the Utes and Navajos, and some Indians attacked the missionaries. The settlers in Las Vegas and Fort Lemhi were recalled by Brigham Young in 1858. A primary reason for closing the fort was an attack by the Shoshone Indians upon Fort Lemhi, which resulted in the death of several of the missionaries.

The Church set up two outposts near the point where the Oregon and Mormon trails divided. The purposes of the outposts were to supervise access to Utah from the east and to serve as supply stations for immigrants. Brigham Young wanted to purchase Fort Bridger from mountain man Jim Bridger, but when Orson Hyde led a group of colonists to the fort in 1853, Bridger and his companions refused to sell. Disappointed, but not discouraged, the brethren set up a new colony, Fort Supply, approximately twelve miles to the south. Here they did missionary work among the Indians. In 1855 the Church was finally able to buy Fort Bridger from owners James Bridger and Louis Vasquez. The two outposts provided supplies for both Mormon and non-Mormon travelers.

The final outlying settlement formed during these first ten years was Carson Valley in present-day western Nevada (still part of Utah Territory in the 1850s). Brigham Young sent Elder Orson Hyde there in 1855 to act as probate judge and to organize a county government. In 1856 some 250 people were called to colonize the beautiful valley and to proselyte and civilize the Indians. Difficulties soon arose, however, with non-Mormons who fretted at the political control and cultural influence of the Church. Discovery of gold in the area added to the problems, and in 1857 the colony was disbanded.

Despite problems with outlying settlements, several factors assured the general success of the Church's colonization efforts. It was rare for individuals or groups to start their own settlements. Most of the sites were preselected and settled under Church auspices. Sites were carefully chosen to ensure adequate water, fertile soil, access to other important resources, and safety from Indian attack. Furthermore, large numbers of capable men headed up the colonies. Hundreds of bishops, presiding elders, and stake presidents directed the building of individual towns and villages and acted as civil officials as well as spiritual advisers. Many men served one, two, three, or more decades in these assignments. The lifeblood of the colonies was the thousands of immigrants who arrived each year. In Utah's first decade, almost forty thousand Saints emigrated to Zion.

Cove Fort was begun in 1867. Ira Nathaniel Hinckley was called by Brigham Young to leave his home in Coalville in 1867 and build the fort along Cove Creek between the settlements of Fillmore on the north and Beaver on the south. A day's journey from either town, the fort provided protection for travelers.

Each wall of the fort was one hundred feet long, with the walls being four feet wide at the base and narrowing to two feet at the top. The walls were eighteen feet high.

On 13 August 1988 the deed to the historic fort was presented to the Church. The fort is now used as a visitors' center.

Thomas Bullock (1816–85) served many years in the Church as a clerk in one capacity or another. He was a clerk to Joseph Smith and then to Brigham Young. He was also the clerk of the pioneer camp that entered the Salt Lake Valley on 24 July 1847. An ordained seventy, he served two missions to England—in 1842 and again in 1856.

There were different methods of obtaining personnel for the colonies. Brigham Young selected families whose names were then presented during general conference when new colonies were announced. Occasionally idle brethren who gathered on streets were assigned to serve missions or colonize. In the winter of 1855–56 for example, while court was in session, scores of men filled the council house to watch the proceedings or simply milled around. After several weeks of this, Brigham Young sent his clerk Thomas Bullock "to take their names, for the purpose of giving them missions, if they had not anything to do of any more importance."[14] From the names, President Heber C. Kimball selected thirty men to go to Las Vegas, forty-eight to Fort Bridger and Fort Supply, and thirty-five to go to Fort Lemhi. Others were assigned to the lead business near Las Vegas, and some were called to the East Indies. At other times Church officials designated the leaders and authorized them to select or recruit families. Not everyone was enthusiastic about the assignments, but in most instances these calls were accepted and viewed as a test of religious commitment.

The leadership for each new settlement was carefully selected, and persons were chosen to supply the wide variety of useful talents and skills required to build a new town. Farmers were the mainstay of most settlements, but carpenters, millwrights, mechanics, cabinetmakers, plasterers, painters, brick makers, masons, dam builders, weavers, tailors, tanners, surveyors, butchers, bakers, schoolteachers, musicians, wagon makers, wheelwrights, and others were also needed. The typical settlement was carefully designed to encourage close-knit social life and religious activity. The center square was set apart for a meetinghouse, which served as both church and school. Typically, communities were laid out in square blocks separated by wide streets. Each family had acreage in town for a garden, a small orchard, and sheds for poultry and livestock, but the main planting and the herding of cattle took place outside the village.

Many of the unsung heroines of the colonization effort were the women who went to the new outposts. In most Latter-day Saint communities there was an almost equal balance of men and women. Women colonists did nearly as many traditionally male jobs as they did domestic chores. The sisters labored next to their husbands building homes, laying chimneys, chinking cracks, mudding the outside of log houses, and plastering and painting the inside. Women dug irrigation ditches, plowed, planted, harvested, chopped wood, stacked hay, and herded and milked cows.

Often Mormon women carried a heavier load than other western pioneer women because their husbands, fathers, and brothers were frequently away on missions or other Church assignments, and the managing of the family resources fell to the women and the older children. All of this was in addition to their normal duties of cooking and canning, drying fruit, grinding wheat, washing, ironing, quilting, sewing, darning, spinning, weaving, making soap and sugar, preparing for weddings, attending funerals, maintaining and beautifying homes, raising children, and attending to Church duties. Some women had additional home-based employment to help the family survive economically. They sewed, took in laundry, and made and sold butter, cheese, dried fruit, rag carpets, shoes, hats, yarn, cloth, candlewick, and candles. Others taught school or were midwives. The sisters cooperated with each other in the settlements, since few homes were totally self-sufficient.

GROWTH OF THE CHURCH IN EARLY UTAH

Throughout the Saints' first decade in Utah, when approximately one hundred smaller communities were being colonized, Salt Lake City was developing into a major center. It was a planned community purposely designed to be the hub of a widespread religious commonwealth in the Great Basin. It was unique in the West because of its equitable distribution of land, community farms and herds, public work projects, organized immigration, and controlled use of natural resources. Emphasis on public convenience rather than the profitable sale of prime public lots also permitted the building of unusually wide streets.

General conferences were held semiannually in Salt Lake City, and the Saints often traveled hundreds of miles to attend. Conferences were a time of reunion and socializing and became one of the important symbols of Latter-day Saint unity. These conferences were held in the Old Tabernacle, which was dedicated on 6 April 1852 by President Willard Richards. The Old Tabernacle was also used for regular Sunday services attended by Brigham Young and other Church leaders. Most of the sermons delivered at the conferences and the Sunday meetings were recorded in the Church's official newspaper, the *Deseret News*, founded in 1850; many of them, beginning in 1854, were compiled annually in England in the *Journal of Discourses*.

As part of his aim for economic self-sufficiency for the Saints, Brigham Young directed the building of tithing houses or bishops' storehouses in every community. These served as supply sources for most goods needed by the Saints. Many people donated one day of labor in every ten toward various Church projects. Most common, however, was the payment of tithing "in kind." Farmers brought chickens, eggs, cattle, vegetables, and home manufactured goods to the tithing houses. About two-thirds of the tithing donated at local offices went to the general tithing office in Salt Lake City for general Church needs.

From the beginning of their settlement in the Great Basin, the Saints exhibited interest in education and cultural life. During the first winter in Salt Lake City, a single school class for children was taught in a tent. Later Church leaders directed every ward to establish a school. The University of Deseret was created by the legislature of the provisional State of Deseret in 1850. That same year the Deseret Dramatic Association was organized,

The *Deseret News* was first published 15 June 1850 in Salt Lake City, Utah. It was published as a weekly paper until 10 December 1898. The Deseret Semi Weekly News was published 8 October 1865 until 12 June 1922. The Deseret Evening News, a daily newspaper, began publishing 2 November 1867. On 15 June 1920, Evening was dropped from the masthead, and it has been called the Deseret News since that time.

The Brigham Young schoolhouse, located east of the Beehive House, was where President Young's children and a few of the neighbor children attended school.

which performed several plays annually. Lorenzo Snow organized the Polysophical Society in 1852 to encourage people of all ages to study and develop themselves in all fields of thought and endeavor. He created the word *polysophical* when he could not think of an appropriate title for the organization.

"The society met weekly in Lorenzo's home, where the members were treated to wide-ranging intellectual fare that included commentaries on scientific and philosophical subjects interspersed with instrumental and vocal music selections, readings, poems, and essays. Nor was it unusual for parts of the programs to be presented in languages other than English."[15] In general, social life centered around the ward. Ward socials, dances, and dramas, and even some music clubs, contributed to the feeling of community among the Saints. Other associations that developed in the 1850s were the Deseret Agricultural and Manufacturing Society, the Deseret Theological Association, and the Horticultural Society.

The Church organization also adapted to the expanding community of Saints in Utah. Each settlement had at least one ward, which was presided over by a bishop. The bishop supervised both temporal and spiritual activities in the community. Preaching meetings were held each Sunday, and fast meetings were held one Thursday each month with members asked to contribute money saved by fasting. Block teaching was inaugurated. Block teachers were either adults from the Aaronic Priesthood or acting teachers from the Melchizedek Priesthood who visited the families in the ward and exhorted them to good works. Boys had not usually been ordained to the Aaronic Priesthood, but by January 1854 Wilford Woodruff recorded, "We are now beginning to ordain our young sons to the lesser priesthood here in Zion."[16]

The most dramatic religious event of the 1850s was the reformation of 1856–57. While the new communities were being settled, many members of the Church had drifted into spiritual lethargy as they struggled to survive on the frontier. During their first decade in the West, most Saints had concentrated on temporal affairs and had often neglected individual spiritual matters. The need for a reformation became especially apparent in 1856 when the effects of rapid immigration into Utah and the severe drought and grasshopper plague of 1855 combined to threaten the economic stability of Utah. Many Saints wore threadbare clothing and were on the verge of starvation. Church leaders taught that these conditions had come about partly because of the Saints' laxity in keeping the commandments.

In 1856 the First Presidency commenced a reform movement. Leaders traveled throughout the territory preaching repentance with unprecedented fervor. Second Counselor Jedediah M. Grant in particular stirred many congregations with his enthusiastic sermons. Special reformation missionaries preached and called upon congregations to repent. Block teachers took

Questions that block teachers asked the Latter-day Saint families they visited

QUESTIONS

TO BE ASKED THE

LATTER DAY SAINTS.

Have you committed murder, by shedding innocent blood, or consenting thereto?

Have you betrayed your brethren or sisters in anything?

Have you committed adultery, by having any connection with a woman that was not your wife, or a man that was not your husband?

Have you taken and made use of property not your own, without the consent of the owner?

Have you cut hay where you had no right to, or turned your animals into another person's grain or field, without his knowledge and consent?

Have you lied about or maliciously misrepresented any person or thing?

Have you borrowed anything that you have not returned, or paid for?

Have you borne false witness against your neighbor?

Have you taken the name of the Deity in vain?

Have you coveted anything not your own?

Have you been intoxicated with strong drink?

Have you found lost property and not returned it to the owner, or used all diligence to do so?

Have you branded an animal that you did not know to be your own?

Have you taken another's horse or mule from the range and rode it, without the owner's consent?

Have you fulfilled your promises in paying your debts, or run into debt without prospect of paying?

Have you taken water to irrigate with, when it belonged to another person at the time you used it?

Do you pay your tithing promptly?

Do you teach your family the gospel of salvation?

Do you speak against your brethren, or against any principle taught us in the Bible, Book of Mormon, Book of Doctrine and Covenants, Revelations given through Joseph Smith the Prophet and the Presidency of the Church as now organized?

Do you pray in your family night and morning and attend to secret prayer?

Do you wash your body and have your family do so, as often as health and cleanliness require and circumstances will permit?

Do you labor six days and rest, or go to the house of worship, on the seventh?

Do you and your family attend Ward meetings?

Do you preside over your household as a servant of God, and is your family subject to you?

Have you labored diligently and earned faithfully the wages paid you by your employers?

Do you oppress the hireling in his wages?

Have you taken up and converted any stray animal to your own use, or in any manner appropriated one to your benefit, without accounting therefor to the proper authorities?

In answer to the above questions, let all men and women confess to the persons they have injured and make restitution, or satisfaction. And when catechising the people, the Bishops, Teachers, Missionaries and other officers in the Church are not at liberty to pry into sins that are between a person and his or her God, but let such persons confess to the proper authority, that the adversary may not have an opportunity to take advantage of human weaknesses, and thereby destroy souls.

a list of questions about moral behavior into the homes. Saints everywhere were called upon to rededicate themselves to the Lord and his commandments through rebaptism. Church leaders led the way. Elder Wilford Woodruff characterized the reformation: "The spirit of God is like a flame among the Leaders of this people and they are throwing the arrows of the Almighty among the people. JM Grant is pruning with a sharp two edged sword and calling loudly upon the people to wake up and repent of their sins. The Elders who have returned are full of the Holy Ghost and power of God."[17]

The reformation had a positive effect upon the Saints. Religion and moral practices once again took prominence in their lives. They demonstrated by rescuing the stricken handcart companies that they truly cared for each other and could successfully organize to meet emergencies. By the summer of 1857, ten years after first entering the Great Basin, the Church was on a strong footing and was accomplishing the things it was restored to the earth to do.

ENDNOTES

1. In *Journal of Discourses*, 5:226.

2. In Wilford Woodruff Journals, following 31 Dec. 1849 entry, LDS Historical Department, Salt Lake City; spelling and capitalization standardized.

3. See Journal History of The Church of Jesus Christ of Latter-day Saints, 5, 21, 27 Mar. 1850, Historical Department, Salt Lake City.

4. In Journal History of the Church, 16 Sept. 1850.

5. Conway B. Sonne, *Saints on the Seas: A Maritime History of Mormon Migration, 1830–1890* (Salt Lake City, University of Utah Press, 1983), p. 78.

6. Sonne, *Saints on the Seas*, p. 58.

7. "Foreign Correspondence," *Millennial Star*, 22 Dec. 1855, p. 813.

8. In LeRoy R. and Ann W. Hafen, *Handcarts to Zion* (Glendale, Calif.: Arthur H. Clark Co., 1960), p. 272.

9. See *Treasures of Pioneer History*, 6 vols.

(Salt Lake City: Daughters of Utah Pioneers, 1952–57), 5: 240–41.

10. "To Utah—By Hand," *American Legion Magazine*, in Eliza M. Wakefield, *The Handcart Trail* (Sun Valley Shopper, 1949), p. 13.

11. In Hafen and Hafen, *Handcarts to Zion*, pp. 96–97.

12. "Remarks," *Deseret News*, 15 Oct. 1856, p. 252.

13. Hafen and Hafen, *Handcarts to Zion*, p. 135.

14. Letter from Heber C. Kimball to his son William, in "Foreign Correspondence," *Millennial Star*, 21 June 1856, p. 397.

15. Francis M. Gibbons, *Lorenzo Snow: Spiritual Giant, Prophet of God* (Salt Lake City: Deseret Book Co., 1982), p. 73.

16. Wilford Woodruff Journals, 31 Jan. 1854; spelling and capitalization standardized.

17. Wilford Woodruff Journals, 9 Oct. 1856; spelling standardized.

THE UTAH WAR

THE LATTER-DAY SAINTS considered themselves loyal American citizens and were indignant when they heard a large army was on its way west to put down a "Mormon rebellion." Recalling the persecutions of earlier years, the settlers feared being driven once again from their homes. For the next few months the Saints prepared to defend themselves. Church leaders and members alike were unwilling to suffer oppression again.

Two issues were at the center of the Church's conflict with the federal government: the Saints' practice of plural marriage and the Church's control of the Utah territorial government. When Utah reapplied for statehood in 1856 and ran into stiff opposition, the "Mormon question" entered national politics.

The national Republican party was founded in 1854 as a staunchly anti-slavery party and fielded its first presidential candidate in 1856. In its platform it urged Congress to prohibit in the territories the twin relics of barbarism—polygamy and slavery. The Democrats, not wishing to imply support of polygamy by their support of slavery, denounced the Mormons as vehemently as the Republicans did. Successful Democratic candidate James Buchanan vowed during his presidential campaign that if elected he would replace Brigham Young as governor of Utah.

About this same time new troubles developed in Utah between the Saints and some disgruntled territorial officials who took it upon themselves to try to change the Latter-day Saints' way of life. Letters and verbal reports from the surveyor general, three Indian agents, two supreme court justices, and the former United States mail contractor reached Washington, D.C., further poisoning the minds of eastern politicians against the Church. The worst damage was caused by Associate Judge William W. Drummond, who came into conflict with the Saints as soon as he arrived in Utah in 1854. He attacked the jurisdiction of the probate courts, which Utahns considered their most important legal defense against enemy assaults. He was also an unprincipled man who brought a Washington, D.C., prostitute to Utah as his mistress. At times he had her sit on the bench with him while he harangued the Saints about their lack of morals. It was later learned that he had abandoned his wife and children in the East.

When Levi Abrahams, a Jewish convert to Mormonism, made a truthful comment regarding the judge's character, Drummond sent his body servant to Abrahams's home in Fillmore to horsewhip him. Both the judge and his servant were later arrested for assault and battery with intent to commit murder. When freed on bail, Drummond quietly fled to California and then to New Orleans, where he made public a letter of resignation he had written to the Buchanan administration. He alleged that the Mormons had destroyed the territorial supreme court records, their leaders were disrespectful of federal officials, a secret oath-bound band operated in Utah that knew no law save Brigham Young's, the Mormons and not the Indians had massacred John W. Gunnison's surveying party in 1854, and a state of rebellion existed in Utah.

Unfortunately Drummond's charges were believed and used to form a major part of the Buchanan administration's image of the Church. Shortly after receiving the letter, President Buchanan, without investigating the situation in Utah or communicating his intentions to Governor Young, appointed Alfred Cumming of Georgia to be governor and directed a military force of twenty-five hundred men to escort him to Salt Lake City. The military orders of 18 May 1857 came from Secretary of War John B. Floyd, who was bitterly anti-Mormon and who advocated the need for military force. Secretary of State Lewis Cass, however, urged Cumming to uphold the law but not to interfere with the Mormons' way of living.

Throughout the summer of 1857 many politicians of both major parties spoke out against the Latter-day Saints and their alleged wrongdoing. Among them was Senator Stephen A. Douglas, who was trying to mend some political fences in his home state of Illinois, where rabid anti-Mormon feelings still existed. The Saints were especially stung by Douglas's denunciation, since they had considered him a loyal friend. They remembered a prophecy by Joseph Smith to Douglas in 1843 and printed it in the *Deseret News*. The Prophet had declared that Douglas would one day aspire to the presidency of the United States, but that if he ever lifted his hand against the Latter-day Saints, he would "feel the weight of the hand of the Almighty upon you."[1] Douglas became the Democratic candidate for President in 1860, but he was defeated by Abraham Lincoln.

THE CHURCH RESPONDS

On 1 July 1857, officials of Brigham Young's mail delivery and express company, the Y. X. Company, stopped at the federal post office in Independence, Missouri, to pick up the mail. En route they had become curious when they saw several supply trains heading west on the overland route. In Independence they learned that the government had simultaneously canceled the mail contract with the Y. X. Company and sent a large consignment of federal troops to Utah. The supply trains they had observed were for the army. Abraham O. Smoot, mayor of Salt Lake City and leader of this group of trusted Latter-day Saints, and his companions Porter Rockwell and Judson Stoddard, sped as quickly as possible to Salt Lake City with the

Alfred Cumming (1802–73) served as governor of the Utah Territory from 1858 to 1861. Prior to this appointment, he had served as mayor of Augusta, Georgia, in 1836.

news, arriving on 23 July. On 24 July they found Brigham Young and many of the Saints in Big Cottonwood Canyon celebrating the Saints' first ten years in the Great Basin. Not wanting to dampen the merry event, Brigham Young waited until nightfall to announce the government's designs.

After pondering how to meet this "invasion," Church leaders in early August issued a broadside proclamation to the citizens of Utah:

"We are invaded by a hostile force, who are evidently assailing us to accomplish our overthrow and destruction. . . .

". . . The government has not condescended to cause an investigating committee, or other persons to be sent, to inquire into and ascertain the truth, as is customary in such cases. . . .

"The issue which has thus been forced upon us, compels us to resort to the great first law of self-preservation, and stand in our own defense and right, guarantied unto us by the genius of the institutions of our country, and on which the government is based. Our duties to ourselves and families requires us not to tamely submit to be driven and slain, without an attempt to preserve ourselves. Our duty to our country, our holy religion, our God, to freedom and liberty, requires that we shall not quietly stand still."[2]

The broadside proclaimed three intentions: to forbid all armed forces from coming into Utah Territory on whatever pretense, to hold all forces in Utah in readiness to repel any invasion, and to declare martial law in the territory.[3]

Brigham Young then mustered the territorial militia and ordered that no grain or other staple be sold to passing immigrants or speculators. He ordered the building of fortifications and also selected raiding parties to harass the army and supply trains. He also sent a group known as the White Mountain Expedition to find another suitable location for settlement, should the Saints have to abandon their homes. Missionaries and settlers in distant colonies were called home to aid the defense. Companies of immigrants on the plains were safely guided into the valley, and all emigration plans for the next season were cancelled.

Governor Young sent Samuel W. Richards with a letter to President Buchanan informing him that his army could not enter Utah until satisfactory arrangements were made by a peace commission. Elder Richards also carried a letter to the Saints' long-time friend Thomas L. Kane asking him to intervene with the government on the Church's behalf. Richards also went to New York, where he was interviewed by the *New York Times*, which published the Saints' point of view "without prejudice."[4]

On 7 September, Captain Stewart Van Vliet of the Quartermaster Corps arrived in Salt Lake City to arrange for food and forage for the incoming army. He tried to assure Church leaders of the army's peaceful intentions. Van Vliet was the first official contact the Saints had with either the military or the government since the problems had arisen. Treated kindly, Van Vliet interviewed Church leaders, inspected their resistance measures, and attended a public meeting in the Old Tabernacle where he heard many recountings of the persecutions in Missouri and Illinois. Speakers insisted that the people would burn their homes, destroy their crops, and harass the troops before they would allow them to enter the valley. The Saints pledged unanimous support of Brigham Young's resistance policy.

Van Vliet became convinced that the Mormons were not in rebellion against the authority of the United States, but that they felt justified in preparing to defend themselves against an unwarranted military invasion. Unsuccessful in making arrangements for the troops, he returned to the army and then to Washington, D.C., where he became a strong advocate of peaceful reconciliation. He was accompanied by the Utah congressional delegate, John M. Bernhisel, who carried more letters to Thomas L. Kane.

Meanwhile, Brigham Young went forward with his plans. In mid-September 1857 he proclaimed martial law in the territory and forbade the entry of armed forces. He ordered the Nauvoo Legion to prepare for the invasion. In nearly every Utah community, preparations for defense were accelerated. He also instructed bishops in the villages to prepare to burn everything should hostilities actually break out.

MOUNTAIN MEADOWS MASSACRE

The same week that Captain Van Vliet appeared in Salt Lake City, a tragic event took place nearly three hundred miles to the south; it can best be understood in the context of the war hysteria surrounding the approach of federal troops to Utah. As soon as it was known that an army was coming, George A. Smith, who was responsible for the southern settlements, went to southern Utah to mobilize troops and put that region on war alert.

About this same time the Fancher Train—an emigrant company composed of several families from Arkansas and a group of horsemen who called themselves the Missouri Wildcats—made its way through central Utah. They were taking the southern route to California because of the lateness of the season. Since Utah was under martial law, the party was unable to buy grain and supplies. Some of the travelers, however, pilfered from local farmers. Some also boasted about participating in the Haun's Mill Massacre, the murder of Joseph Smith, and other mob actions against the Mormons. A few local settlers connected the group from Arkansas with the recent brutal murder of Elder Parley P. Pratt in that state. Some of the Saints thought this party was a scouting or reconnoitering party in advance of the federal army.

The Indian problem in southern Utah complicated these circumstances. The Saints had endeavored to cultivate good relationships with the Indians, but there was still danger. The Indians distinguished between the "Mericats" (any Americans traveling through Utah), whom they entirely distrusted, and the "Mormonee," whom they generally liked. The possibility existed, however, that the Indians would turn on the Mormon settlers.

George A. Smith (1817–75) was a participant in Zion's Camp, a missionary, an Apostle, a counselor in the First Presidency of the Church, Church historian, and a member of the Utah legislature. He was a cousin of the Prophet Joseph Smith.

James Holt Haslam (1825–1913) was born in Bolton, England. He came to Utah in 1851 and settled in Cedar City. He later moved to Wellsville in northern Utah, where he lived the rest of his life.

On Tuesday, 7 September 1857, a band of Indians attacked the Fancher Train, which was camped thirty-five miles from Cedar City. The emigrants were well armed, and the Indians were forced to retreat.

Meanwhile, the citizens in Cedar City had met and discussed what course to pursue relative to the Fancher Train. Some of those with quicker tempers argued that the emigrants should be destroyed. They were afraid the emigrants might join a California-based army and fight against the Saints as they had publicly threatened to do. It was decided to dispatch a messenger, James Haslam, to seek the advice of Brigham Young. With little rest or sleep, Haslam reached Salt Lake City in only three days and obtained a letter from President Young urging the Saints to let the emigrants go in peace. As Haslam left Salt Lake City, Brigham urged, "Go with all speed, spare no horse flesh. The emigrants must not be meddled with, if it takes all Iron county to prevent it. They must go free and unmolested."[5] Haslam hastened to Cedar City, arriving on Sunday, 13 September, two days too late.

John D. Lee, who had been appointed "Indian Farmer" by Brigham Young in the absence of Jacob Hamblin, the Indian agent, had been sent to quiet the Indians. He arrived at the Indian camp shortly after the first skirmish between them and the emigrants had occurred. Finding the Indians highly excited, Lee was in the dangerous situation of being the only white man present. He finally convinced the Indians that they would get their revenge, and he was allowed to leave.

Later that night, more Indians arrived at the camp together with a few white men from Cedar City. Sometime during the night, a diabolical plan was concocted, partly to placate the angry Indians. The next day, the morning of 11 September, the whites promised the emigrants protection if they would give up their weapons. The men of the Iron County militia, acting under orders from their local commanders, killed the men, while Indians slew the women and older children, approximately 120 in all. Only eighteen very young children were spared. They were later returned, with government help, to relatives in the East.

The dead were buried in shallow graves, and commitments were made to blame the massacre entirely upon the Indians. More than two weeks after the tragedy, John D. Lee was sent to Salt Lake City to report the incident to Brigham Young. Lee placed all the blame on the Indians as had previously been agreed. Later Brigham Young learned that members of the Iron County militia had been full participants in the affair. He offered Governor Alfred Cumming full support in an investigation, but none was undertaken at the time because the Mormons had been pardoned for all alleged crimes in connection with the Utah War.

For the next two decades, rumors and allegations continued to circulate, and finally the case came to trial in the 1870s. John D. Lee, a key participant, but certainly not the only officer responsible for the deed, was the only Latter-day Saint indicted. Lee was tried twice. The first trial resulted in a hung jury. Lee was finally convicted in September 1876 and a year later was taken by federal officials to the area of Mountain Meadows and executed.

WARFARE AVERTED

At the time of the Mountain Meadows massacre the United States army was approaching the area called South Pass in what is now Wyoming. They were under the temporary command of Lieutenant Colonel Edmund B. Alexander. Two Utah militiamen claiming to be California immigrants mingled with the troops. They heard firsthand the anti-Mormon threats that did not represent the official instructions of the expedition, but made Church leaders in Utah nervous about a possible confrontation. Mormon scouts watched the movements of the troops throughout their entire march.

Following Governor Young's declaration of martial law in September, General Daniel H. Wells of the Nauvoo Legion sent about eleven hundred men east to Echo Canyon, which lay on the route through the mountains to Salt Lake City. These soldiers built walls and dug trenches from which they could act as snipers. They also loosened huge boulders that could easily be sent crashing down on the moving columns, and they constructed ditches and dams that could be opened to flood the enemy's path.

Forty-four "Mormon raiders," a unit of the Nauvoo Legion under the direction of Major Lot Smith, were sent to eastern Utah (now western Wyoming) to harass the oncoming troops. They were instructed, among other things, "on ascertaining the locality or route of the troops, proceed at once to annoy them in every possible way. Use every exertion to stampede their animals, and set fire to their trains. Burn the whole country before them and on their flanks. Keep them from sleeping by night surprises. . . . Take no life, but destroy their trains, and stampede or drive away their animals, at every opportunity."[6]

On the night of 4 October, Major Smith and twenty others rode up to a lead wagon train carrying freight for the army. To the wagon masters it appeared that Smith commanded a large body of troops, and they were sufficiently impressed to evacuate their wagons when ordered to do so. James Terry recorded in his journal, "I never saw a scareder lot in my life until they found that they was not going to be hurt. They laughed and said they was glad the wagons was going to be burnt as they would not have to bull whack any more, as they called it. The teamsters were permitted to take their private clothing and guns out of the wagons and then they were burnt."[7]

The next morning Lot Smith and his men met another train loaded with supplies moving toward the valley. After disarming the teamsters, Lot rode out and met the captain who was securing cattle, and demanded his pistols. The captain replied, " 'No man ever took them yet, and if you think you can, without killing me, try it.' We were all the time riding towards the train, with our noses about as close together as two Scotch terriers would have held theirs—his eyes flashing fire; I couldn't see mine—I told him that I admired a

Lot Smith (1830–92) served in the Mormon Battalion when he was sixteen years old. In 1869 he was called on a mission to England. He later served as president of the Little Colorado Stake for ten years.

brave man, but that I did not like blood—you insist on my killing you, which will only take a minute, but I don't want to do it. We had by this time reached the train. He, seeing that his men were under guard, surrendered, saying: 'I see you have me at a disadvantage, my men being disarmed.' I replied that I didn't need the advantage and asked him what he would do if we should give them their arms. 'I'll fight you!' 'Then,' said I, 'We know something about that too—take up your arms!' His men exclaimed, 'Not by a d—n sight! We came out here to whack bulls, not to fight.' 'What do you say to that, Simpson?' I asked. 'Damnation,' he replied, grinding his teeth in the most violent manner, 'If I had been here before and they had refused to fight, I would have killed every man of them.' "8

In this and succeeding engagements, the raiders torched a total of seventy-four wagons, containing enough supplies to outfit the large army for three months. They also captured fourteen hundred of the two thousand head of cattle accompanying the expedition. Major Smith's militia assisted in burning the two key Mormon outposts, Fort Bridger and Fort Supply, which government forces had expected to occupy.

These tactics succeeded so well in delaying the army that when its commanding officer, Colonel (soon to become General) Albert Sidney Johnston, finally joined his troops in early November, it was clearly too late in the season to reach Salt Lake City. It took the army fifteen days to push thirty-five miles through storms and sub-zero weather to burned-out Fort Bridger. Approximately twenty-five hundred American soldiers and several hundred civilian officials (including Governor Cumming and his wife), freighters, and camp followers spent a miserable winter in western Wyoming in a city of tents and improvised shelters called Camp Scott and in a newly created community named " 'Eckelsville,' after the new chief justice of the territory."9 Meanwhile, the eastern press expressed second thoughts about the whole enterprise, and President James Buchanan in Washington and Brigham Young in Utah weighed their options for 1858.

PEACE ESTABLISHED

In the early winter three influential men—Captain Stewart Van Vliet, Utah Congressional delegate John M. Bernhisel, and Colonel Thomas L. Kane—visited President Buchanan in Washington and urged him to send an investigation commission to Utah. Not yet willing to take that step, Buchanan gave his unofficial blessing to Kane to go to Salt Lake City to try to achieve a peaceful solution. Leaving on a steamer from New York in January 1858 at his own expense, Kane sailed to California via Panama. He traveled under the name of Dr. Osborne to avoid having his movements known.

Colonel Kane arrived in Salt Lake City on 25 February and was most cordially received. Except for telling the leading authorities of the Church, he kept his true identity secret for some time to ascertain whether the Saints

Albert Sidney Johnston (1803–62) was from Kentucky. He graduated from West Point in 1826, fought in the Black Hawk War, and fought with the army of the Republic of Texas. He served as a Confederate general during the Civil War and was killed at the Battle of Shiloh.

would be as friendly to a stranger in 1858 as they had been to him a decade earlier in Winter Quarters. Brigham Young and other Church leaders were certain that God had sent him. After several meetings with the leaders of the Church, Kane convinced them to allow the new governor, Alfred Cumming, to enter Utah Territory unmolested. Brigham Young insisted, however, that the army not come in with Cumming.

In early March, accompanied by an escort of Mormon militiamen, Kane, who was in poor health, traveled to Camp Scott in bitterly cold weather. As he neared the camps he dismissed the escorts and rode in alone. A shot from one of the guards nearly hit him. Courageously he identified himself and after much wrangling was successful in meeting with Governor Cumming. He persuaded Cumming that he would be recognized by the people in Utah as their new governor and that they were not in a state of rebellion against the government. He also explained that the Mormons would not allow the army to remain in the Salt Lake Valley.

In April, Colonel Kane and Governor Cumming left Camp Scott without a U.S. military escort. When Cumming arrived in Salt Lake City he found that Kane was right. Governor Cumming was treated with dignity and respect. Brigham Young delivered the territorial records and seal to the new governor, and after several meetings, good feelings were engendered. For the next three years Cumming administered his office with tact and diplomacy, and he won the respect and confidence of the people. For his part in the negotiations, Colonel Thomas L. Kane won the undying gratitude of the Latter-day Saints.

Before Kane and Cumming arrived in Salt Lake City, Church leaders had decided in a "council of war" that the Saints in northern Utah would evacuate their homes and move south to avoid conflict with the United States army when it arrived later in the season. Brigham Young vowed, "Rather than see my wives and daughters ravished and polluted, and the seeds of corruption sown in the hearts of my sons by a brutal soldiery, I would leave my home in ashes, my gardens and orchards a waste, and subsist upon roots and herbs, a wanderer through these mountains for the remainder of my natural life."[10]

For this "move south," the Church was divided into three groups, each with a specific mission: (1) Those living in southern Utah were not to move, but were instructed to send wagons, teams, and teamsters to northern Utah to assist in the move. (2) The young and vigorous Saints living in northern Utah would remain behind to irrigate crops and gardens, guard property, and set fire to the straw-filled homes if need be. And (3) some thirty-five thousand Saints living north of Utah Valley were to actually make the move. Each ward was allotted a strip of land in one of four counties south of Salt Lake County. Provisions were to be moved first and then families.

The move was carried out in strict military order, each ward being organized into tens, fifties, and hundreds, with a captain over each. Families were expected to transport their own furniture, in addition to food and clothing. One pioneer teenager recorded, "We packed all we had into father's one wagon and waited for the command to leave. At night we lay down to sleep, not knowing when word would come of the army which we thought was coming to destroy us. . . .

". . . One morning father told us that we should leave with a large company in the evening. . . .

"Along in the middle of the day father scattered leaves and straw in all the rooms and I heard him say: 'Never mind, little daughter, this house has sheltered us, it shall never shelter them.' "[11]

Hulda Cordelia Thurston, a young girl living in Centerville, Utah, recalled the difficulty of the move: "In the spring of 1858 we moved at the time of the great Mormon exodus. We went as far south as Spanish Fork, and on the Spanish Fork bottoms there was good feed for our stock and plenty of fish in the river. At that time all the people living north of Utah Valley moved south leaving their homes with furniture, farming implements, in fact their all, not knowing where they were going nor what their destiny. . . .

"During that exodus I shall never forget the distress and poverty of the people. I have seen men wearing trousers made of carpet, their feet wrapped in burlap or rags. Women sewed cloth together and made moccasins for their feet. Many women and children were barefoot. One good sister, a neighbor who had a family of seven, told my mother that aside from the clothing on their bodies, she could tie up in a common bandanna handkerchief every article of clothing they possessed. She would put the children to bed early Saturday night and repair and wash and iron their clothing preparatory for Sunday. The people were practically all poor for we had, had several years of great scarcity of crops because of the grasshoppers."[12] Upon arriving at their destination, families lived either in the boxes of their heavy covered wagons, canvas tents, dugouts, or in temporary board shanties and cabins.

Church records and assets were removed or buried by the public works department. One group hid all the stone that had been cut for the Salt Lake Temple, and leveled and covered over its foundation so that the plot would resemble a plowed field and remain unmolested. Another group boxed all of the tithing grain in bins and transported twenty thousand bushels to specially erected granaries in Provo. Additional wagon trains carried machinery and equipment to be housed in hastily constructed warehouses and sheds.

The move south occupied almost two months. It was completed by mid-May. A daily average of six hundred wagons passed through Salt Lake City during the first two weeks of the month. An estimated thirty thousand Saints left their homes in Salt Lake and the northern settlements.[13] Governor Cumming and his wife pleaded with Church members not to leave their homes, but the Saints chose to heed their prophet. The exodus of such a large body of people drew national and international attention to the Church. The

London Times reported: "We are told that they have embarked for a voyage over five hundred miles of untracked desert." The *New York Times* declared: "We think it would be unwise to treat Mormonism as a nuisance to be abated by a posse comitatus."[14]

The move placed the United States government in an unfavorable light as a persecutor of an innocent people, and demonstrated the leadership ability of Brigham Young.

Fortunately, negotiations between the government and the Church kept the army from invading. Some time early in 1858, President Buchanan decided to send a peace commission to Utah; in early June two commissioners, Ben McCulloch and Lazarus W. Powell, arrived in Salt Lake City, carrying an offer of pardon for the Saints if they would reaffirm their loyalty to the government. Church leaders were indignant at the idea of a pardon, for they had never been disloyal. Nevertheless, after several negotiation sessions, it was accepted. Church leaders felt they could accept the pardon because of the raiding activities of the Nauvoo Legion. One of the agreements between the peace commission and Church leaders was that the army would quietly enter the capital city and then establish a federal military post at least forty miles away from both Salt Lake City and Provo.

On 26 June 1858 the army entered the quiet and mostly deserted capital city. As they marched they sang, "One Eyed Riley," a coarse, yet long treasured, barracks ditty reported to have had a thousand verses, most of which are unprintable.[15] The band had to be commanded to stop and serenade Governor Cumming at his new home. Because they believed him to be sympathetic to the Latter-day Saints, they were less than enthusiastic in their performance. Only a few Latter-day Saints had been left behind to set the torch to the city if the army did not respect its pledge to leave the property alone. Those Saints who were left behind saw Lieutenant Colonel Philip St. George Cooke take off his hat and place it over his heart as a gesture of respect for the soldiers he had led in the long march of the Mormon Battalion. In the next few days General Johnston led his troops to Cedar Valley, west of Utah Lake, and established Camp Floyd, named after the Secretary of War. On 1 July, Brigham Young authorized the return of the bedraggled Saints to their homes.

ARMY OCCUPATION

Tension between the soldiers and the Saints existed throughout the army's deployment, but fortunately no serious long-term conflicts developed. This was largely due to the restraint exercised by General Johnston, who, while he did not have much fondness for the Saints, recognized the need to keep order among his troops.

The negative effect of the army in Utah was the introduction of various vices into the territory. Frequently street fights broke out in Salt Lake City and in nearby towns between gamblers, teamsters, and other camp

Masthead of the Valley Tan

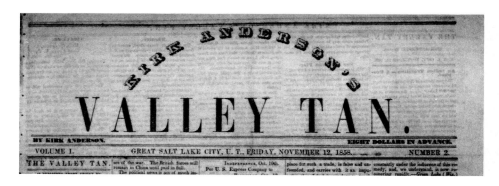

followers. Saloons and houses of prostitution were also established in Utah. Main Street in Salt Lake City for a short time was nicknamed "Whiskey Street." The prevailing social fabric was damaged. A bitterly anti-Mormon newspaper, the *Valley Tan*, began publication in November 1858 and ran for sixteen months. This newspaper charged the people of the Utah Territory as being murderers and traitors; it was circulated chiefly at Camp Floyd. The Saints' isolation from so-called "civilization" had clearly ended. The presence of the army symbolized the growing number of gentiles who would come to live among them.

Three new United States judges came to Utah with the army. Each enthusiastically tried to undermine the Latter-day Saint way of life. One of these, Judge John Cradlebaugh, with General Johnston's consent took one thousand soldiers with him to Provo to back up his work in court. This excited the townspeople to the point of hysteria, which could have easily escalated into a major confrontation. Through the efforts of Governor Cumming and others, the Buchanan administration in Washington ordered the troops withdrawn to Camp Floyd, and the crisis ended.

The army's stay in Utah, however, also proved an economic windfall to the Saints. A small community named Fairfield, settled in 1855 by John Carson and located adjacent to Camp Floyd, grew to a population of seven thousand. Many citizens found a market for agricultural and other goods. When the army finally abandoned the fort in the summer of 1861, approximately four million dollars worth of surplus goods were sold for a fraction of their value. The government conducted a war surplus sale, which greatly enriched the Utah economy.[16] Colonel Cooke presented the camp flagpole as a gift to Brigham Young on 27 July 1861. President Young had the flagpole placed on the hillside east of the Lion House, and the United States flag flew from it for many years. In addition, a few soldiers investigated the religion of the Latter-day Saints and joined the Church.

From 1859 to 1861 Church leaders quietly and cautiously resumed sending missionaries to preach the glad message to the inhabitants of the earth and encouraged the Saints to gather to Zion. Missionaries again proselyted in the United States, Canada, Great Britain, and western Europe. Emigration, both by wagon train and handcart, resumed slowly in 1859 and more vigorously in 1860. Once more President Young initiated a new period of geographical expansion. He did not reinstitute the far-flung settlements, such as San Bernardino and Fort Lemhi, but instead gradually stretched the boundaries of the agriculturally based colonies in the valleys of the mountains. Thirty new settlements were founded in 1859 and another sixteen in 1860. This pattern continued throughout the 1860s. Most of the new communities were in Cache and Bear Lake valleys in northern Utah and southern Idaho, as well as in the Wasatch, Sevier, and Sanpete valleys of Utah.

ENDNOTES

1. "History of Joseph Smith," *Deseret News*, 24 Sept. 1856, p. 225.

2. In "Citizens of Utah," *Pioneer and Democrat*, 1 Jan. 1858, p. 2.

3. See "Citizens of Utah," p. 2.

4. B. H. Roberts, *A Comprehensive History of The Church of Jesus Christ of Latter-day Saints, Century One*, 6 vols. (Salt Lake City: The Church of Jesus Christ of Latter-day Saints, 1930), 4:242.

5. In Roberts, *Comprehensive History of the Church*, 4:150.

6. In Leonard J. Arrington, *Brigham Young: American Moses* (New York: Alfred A. Knopf, 1985), p. 255.

7. James Parshall Terry, "Utah War Incidents," in *Voices from the Past: Diaries, Journals, and Autobiographies*, Campus Education Week Program (Provo: Brigham Young University Press, 1980), p. 66.

8. In Roberts, *Comprehensive History of the Church*, 4:284.

9. Roberts, *Comprehensive History of the Church*, 4:314.

10. Letter from Brigham Young to Elder W. I. Appleby, 6 Jan. 1858, in Brigham Young Letterpress copybooks, typescript, LDS Historical Department, Salt Lake City.

11. In E. Cecil McGavin, *U.S. Soldiers Invade Utah* (Boston: Meador Publishing Co., 1937), p. 216.

12. Hulda Cordelia Thurston Smith, "Sketch of the life of Jefferson Thurston," July 1921, typescript, Daughters of the Utah Pioneers Museum, Salt Lake City, pp. 17–18.

13. See Hubert Howe Bancroft, *History of Utah* (Salt Lake City: Bookcraft, 1964), p. 535.

14. In Bancroft, *History of Utah*, p. 536; *posse comitatus* is a group organized to keep the public peace, usually in emergencies.

15. See James M. Merrill, *Spurs to Glory: The Story of the United States Cavalry* (Chicago: Rand McNally and Co., 1966), p. 102.

16. See Roberts, *Comprehensive History of the Church*, 4:540–41.

THE CIVIL WAR PERIOD

T HE UNITED STATES had experienced a decade of intense sectional division between the North and the South. In 1861 after Abraham Lincoln was elected president of the United States several southern states seceded from the Union. On 12 April 1861 the first shots of the Civil War were fired on Fort Sumter, South Carolina. This fratricidal conflict lasted four years, destroying the Old South and costing 602,000 lives. In Utah during this period the Latter-day Saints enjoyed relative peace and progress.

THE SAINTS AND THE CIVIL WAR

When the Civil War broke out, many Saints remembered the "revelation and prophecy on war" received by the Prophet Joseph Smith 25 December 1832:

"Verily, thus saith the Lord concerning the wars that will shortly come to pass, beginning at the rebellion of South Carolina, which will eventually terminate in the death and misery of many souls. . . .

"For behold, the Southern States shall be divided against the Northern States" (D&C 87:1, 3). In 1843 the Prophet had declared that the bloodshed that would begin in South Carolina "may probably arise through the slave question" (D&C 130:13). Many missionaries had often referred to this prophecy and felt some satisfaction in seeing the word of the Lord so literally fulfilled.

As the conflict deepened, the Saints viewed the Civil War with mixed emotions. They considered the bloodshed and devastation in the "states" a judgment upon the nation for the murders of Joseph and Hyrum Smith, for not keeping the commandments of God, and for the injustices inflicted upon the Saints in Missouri and Illinois. Members of the Church followed Joseph Smith's lead in firmly supporting the American Constitution. John Taylor expressed the feelings of many Latter-day Saints when he addressed them:

"We have been driven from city to city, from state to state for no just cause of complaint. We have been banished from the pale of what is termed civilization, and forced to make a home in the desert wastes. . . .

"Shall we join the North to fight against the South? No! . . . Why? They have both, as before shown, brought it upon themselves, and we have had no hand in the matter. . . . We know no North, no South, no East, no West; we abide strictly and positively by the Constitution."[1]

◄ Fort Sumter

After war had raged for nearly a year, President Young acknowledged that the Saints were much better off in the West: "Had we not been persecuted, we would now be in the midst of the wars and bloodshed that are desolating the nation, instead of where we are, comfortable located in our peaceful dwellings in these silent, far off mountains and valleys. Instead of seeing my brethren comfortably seated around me to-day, many of them would be found in the front ranks on the battle field. I realize the blessings of God in our present safety. We are greatly blessed, greatly favored and greatly exalted, while our enemies, who sought to destroy us, are being humbled."[2]

Church leaders never seriously considered supporting the Confederacy, and when President Abraham Lincoln asked them for soldiers to guard the transcontinental telegraph lines and transportation routes, the Church responded enthusiastically. The Saints also willingly paid an annual war tax of $26,982 imposed on the Utah Territory by the United States Congress. The Brethren repeatedly reaffirmed their loyalty to the Union. Indeed, just as some states were trying to get out of the Union, Utah was trying to get in.

Utah and the Church immediately felt the effects of the Southern States seceding. Governor Alfred Cumming, whose native state was Georgia, felt it his duty to resign from his federally appointed position. He quietly left Utah for his home. General Albert Sidney Johnston, from Virginia, resigned his post and joined the Confederate army. After a few months the army of Utah was withdrawn altogether. In March 1861 the Union, now minus several southern states, created the Territory of Nevada out of the western portion of Utah, and in 1862 and 1866 more territory was added to Nevada, which became a state in 1864.

With the federal troops gone from Utah, the overland mail and telegraph needed protection from Indians who were reportedly becoming more hostile and had destroyed several mail stations between Fort Bridger and Fort Laramie in Wyoming. In the spring of 1862 war officials contacted Brigham Young (though he was no longer governor) with a request that he organize a cavalry to give ninety days' service on the trail until other U.S. troops could arrive. Soon a company of 120 men was raised and ready to travel. Ironically their commander was Captain Lot Smith of the Utah Militia, who had been instrumental just four years earlier in delaying federal troops. He was charged by Brigham Young to prevent the use of profanity and disorderly conduct among the men and to cultivate friendly and peaceful relations with the Indians. The men performed their work admirably, encountered no real fighting, pursued only a few Indians, and received compliments from the United States government for their service.[3] This service was the only direct military participation by an organized unit of the Latter-day Saints in the Civil War.

Also in 1862 the citizens of Utah made their third attempt to gain statehood. The Saints drafted a constitution for the proposed State of Deseret and elected a full slate of officers with Brigham Young as governor. But their petition was denied, mostly because of polygamy, which the ruling Republican Party was determined to oppose.

Republican President Abraham Lincoln, although he signed the Morrill Anti-Bigamy Act of 1862, which was directed against the Latter-day Saints, did not press for its enforcement. He was fair-minded regarding the Mormon question and was more concerned about dealing with the southern rebellion. When Brigham Young sent *Deseret News* assistant editor T.B.H. Stenhouse to Washington, D.C., to ascertain Lincoln's plans for the Mormons, the president told him, "Stenhouse, when I was a boy on the farm in Illinois there was a great deal of timber on the farms which we had to clear away. Occasionally we would come to a log which had fallen down. It was too hard to split, too wet to burn and too heavy to move, so we plowed around it. That's what I intend to do with the Mormons. You go back and tell Brigham Young that if he will let me alone, I will let him alone."[4] Throughout the remainder of the war, President Lincoln's tolerant attitude won him the respect of the Saints.

IMPROVED COMMUNICATION

Although disgruntled politicians had biased many people against the Mormons, other noteworthy visitors to Utah were favorably impressed with what they saw and published their observations. In 1855 Jules Remy, a French botanist, arrived in Salt Lake City to stay a month. Remy published his observations in Europe in 1860, describing the Saints as an industrious and worshipful people, which helped change some of the negative perceptions many Europeans had of the Church. *New York Tribune* editor Horace Greeley, one of the most prominent journalists in America, visited Utah in 1859 and relayed his more balanced impressions of Brigham Young and the Mormons to the nation. One of the most instructive pieces of contemporary observation came from the famous world traveler Richard Burton, who arrived in Utah in 1860 and later published an insightful book about the Mormons entitled *The City of the Saints*, which was widely read.

Communication with the outside world was further enhanced starting in April 1860 with the pony express. Eighty daring, lightweight riders relayed the mail from St. Joseph, Missouri, to Sacramento, California, nearly two thousand miles, in just ten days. The riders changed horses approximately every ten miles, at 320 stations, to accomplish this legendary feat. The pony express route crossed Utah, and numerous Mormon men participated in this dangerous but romantic venture during its eighteen months of existence.

The transcontinental telegraph line, completed through Salt Lake City in October 1861, was the main reason for the discontinuation of the pony express. From then on, messages could be sent to key centers in the United States without delay. This put a stop to problems like the false information disseminated by the "runaway officials" in 1851 and President Buchanan's

Transcontinental telegraph

deployment of the Utah Expedition in 1857.

President Brigham Young was given the privilege of sending the first message over the new telegraph line. The prophet wired his congratulations to the Honorable J. H. Wade, president of the Pacific Telegraph Company in Cleveland, Ohio, saying also, "Utah has not seceded, but is firm for the Constitution and laws of our once happy country; and is warmly interested in such useful enterprises as the one so far completed."[5]

Immediately after the transcontinental telegraph reached Salt Lake City, Brigham Young began laying plans for a local telegraph line to connect all the settlements. He established a telegraphy school in Salt Lake City. Wire, batteries, insulators, sending and receiving sets, and other equipment was ordered but, due to the Civil War, could not be obtained until 1866. In 1867 some five hundred miles of line were completed. Over a series of years the line was extended to nearly all Mormon settlements, including southern Idaho and northern Arizona. By 1880 over one thousand miles of line had been installed.

ANOTHER ARMY OCCUPATION

Some of President Lincoln's first political appointments to Utah proved unfortunate. John W. Dawson of Indiana, the territorial governor, remained only a month in Utah. Upon arriving, he unwisely spoke to the legislature about imposing a tax upon the Mormon people to vindicate the community of the charge of disloyalty. Within a few days he had made an indecent proposal to a woman in Salt Lake City, was exposed, and left the city in disgrace. He was discovered at the Mountain Dell mail station, where he was beaten by a number of drunken, lawless men, who were later brought to justice.

About two months later President Lincoln appointed Stephen A. Harding, also of Indiana, to replace Dawson. Harding had known the Joseph Smith family in Manchester, New York, and when he arrived in Utah, he pretended friendship with the Saints. Soon, however, he showed his contempt for the Church and its institutions and accused the Saints of disloyalty.

Harding's accusations provided justification to the war department in Washington, D.C., for not renewing the enlistment of the Mormon military company and for sending to the area instead the "California volunteers" under the direction of Colonel Patrick Edward Connor. Church leaders and members were naturally distressed at the arrival of an outside military force, especially since they had been so willing to assume responsibility for maintaining the safety of the mail routes and telegraph lines and for keeping the Indians under control. What made matters worse was that Connor clearly felt that the Mormons were disloyal to the Union and that his most important task was to keep them under surveillance. The Saints expected Connor to take his seven hundred men to the military post recently vacated

Patrick Edward Connor (1820–91). After leaving the military, Connor stayed in Utah and continued in mining ventures until his death. He was never really successful in mining. His assets at his death were only about five thousand dollars.

by Johnston's Army, but instead he chose a site in the foothills directly east of Salt Lake City and named it Camp Douglas after the late Stephen A. Douglas.

The troops came in October 1862 and remained until the end of the Civil War. They proved an irritant to the community life of Utah. The California soldiers were not happy to be in Utah because they wanted to be in the actual war. Charges and counter-charges went back and forth between the members of the Church and the army. The Saints considered the army a nuisance and a contributor to the lowering of the morals in their beloved mountain home. As a military officer, Connor, who became a general during his stay in Utah, led his troops well. He protected the trade routes, and in the famous Battle of Bear River in January 1863, rid northern Utah and southern Idaho of the threat of marauding Indians. This meant the Saints could safely colonize these inviting regions. Connor also kept his men busy prospecting for precious metals in the mountains. Because of his efforts, he became known as the "father of Utah mining."[6]

Meanwhile, Governor Harding became such an irritant to the Saints that they petitioned President Lincoln to remove him from office. Lincoln agreed, but to satisfy the "gentiles" in Utah, he also released Judge John F. Kinney, who had shown respect and friendship toward the Mormons. Under Brigham Young's direction, the Saints turned around and elected Kinney to be their delegate to Congress between 1863 and 1865. He thus became the only non-Mormon delegate in Utah Territory's history. Lincoln appointed James Duane Doty, the Indian agent in Utah, to be the new governor. He assumed office in June 1863 and governed diplomatically throughout the duration of the Civil War.

THE MORRISITE AFFAIR

During the summer of 1862 Utah experienced the unfortunate Morrisite War. The Morrisites were an apostate faction led by former English convert Joseph Morris. They established a settlement at South Weber known as Kington Fort, thirty-five miles north of Salt Lake City. Morris had claimed as early as 1857 that he was the prophet, seer, and revelator of the Lord; by 1860 he had attracted a few followers, including the bishop of South Weber and some of his congregation. In February 1861, President Young sent Apostles John Taylor and Wilford Woodruff to South Weber to investigate. They excommunicated sixteen members of the ward, including the bishop who refused to support Brigham Young and who maintained that Joseph Morris was the prophet. The Morrisites consecrated all their belongings to a common fund and awaited the imminent coming of Christ as described in Morris's "revelations."

In early 1862, after successive incorrect prophecies about the Second Coming, some of Morris's followers became disenchanted and wanted to leave with the property they had consecrated. Three dissenters who

Robert Taylor Burton (1821–1907) played in the Nauvoo brass band, served as a missionary, and was a member of the Nauvoo Legion in Utah, a deputy to the territorial marshal, a member of the board of regents for the University of Deseret, and a member of the legislative body of Utah. He was bishop of the Fifteenth Ward in Salt Lake. In 1875 he was called to serve as a counselor in the Presiding Bishopric of the Church.

attempted to escape were imprisoned by Morris, causing their wives to appeal to legal authorities for assistance. Chief Justice Kinney issued a writ on 22 May for the release of the prisoners and the arrest of Morris and his main lieutenants. When Morris refused to obey and continued instead to announce his revelations, Kinney urged acting governor Frank Fuller to call out the militia as a posse to enforce the writs.

Robert T. Burton, chief deputy for the territorial marshal, led approximately 250 men to the bluffs south of Kington Fort early in the morning of 13 June. They sent a message to Morris demanding his surrender and compliance with the writ. Morris and his group assembled in an open bowery while Morris awaited a revelation. Impatient with the delay, Burton ordered two warning shots from a cannon to be fired over the fort. The second shot fell short, struck the plowed ground in front of the fort, and ricocheted into the bowery where the Morrisites were assembled. Two women were killed, and a young girl was seriously wounded. The fighting that erupted resulted in a three-day siege.

On the third day a white flag of truce appeared from inside the fort, and the fighting ceased. After demanding unconditional surrender, Burton and thirty militiamen entered the fort. Morris then asked the privilege of speaking to his people one more time. But instead of delivering a farewell address, he shouted, "All who are for me and my God, in life or in death follow me!" Whereupon a rush was made for the stacked rifles that had been surrendered.[7] Shots rang out, and Joseph Morris and John Banks, second in command, were killed. Ten Morrisites and two members of the Utah posse were killed during the three days of fighting. Ninety Morrisite men were taken to Salt Lake City for trial on charges of murdering the two posse members and resisting due process of law. Seven of them were convicted, but they were pardoned by Governor Harding. Most of the remaining Morrisites who wished to go were escorted by Connor's army to Soda Springs in Idaho Territory. Although the Church was not directly involved in this unfortunate affair, the reputation of the Church suffered in the East as a result.

DIFFICULTIES IN HAWAII

Another person to concern Church officials during this period was soldier of fortune Walter Murray Gibson. Gibson had advocated the Church's cause in Washington, D.C., during the Utah War and came to Salt Lake City to learn more about the Saints. He became acquainted with numerous Church leaders, spoke to large crowds in the Old Tabernacle about his travels, and was baptized by Heber C. Kimball on 15 January 1860 along with his daughter Talula. He was confirmed by Brigham Young. President Young rejected Gibson's proposal that the Saints move to the islands of the East Indies, but called Gibson on a mission to the eastern

United States. He served only six months and then convinced the Saints in New York that he was needed in Salt Lake City immediately. They responded generously to his request for funds to make the return trip.

In November 1860 he was called by President Brigham Young to do missionary work in the Pacific. President Young told Gibson that he would do more good than he ever anticipated if he would magnify his calling.

Arriving in Hawaii in the summer of 1861, Gibson exceeded the bounds of his authority, mixed native traditions with gospel teachings, and won support of the Hawaiian Saints. Because the missionaries had been called home during the Utah War, Gibson was able to take over the leadership of the Saints. He proclaimed himself "Chief President of the Islands of the Sea, and of the Hawaiian Islands, for the Church of Latter-day Saints." Gibson persuaded the Hawaiian members to turn over to him all of their property. He ordained twelve apostles, charging them $150 each for that office. For other offices, such as high priest, seventy, and elder, he charged proportionate fees. He also installed archbishops and minor bishops.[8] He conducted church services with extraordinary pomp and ceremony and even wore robes and required members to bow and crawl in his presence. Gibson's design was to build an army, unite all the Hawaiian Islands into one empire, and proclaim himself king.

Finally in 1864, concerned native Saints wrote to Salt Lake City about the situation. President Young sent Ezra T. Benson and Lorenzo Snow of the Quorum of the Twelve and Joseph F. Smith, Alma Smith, and William Cluff, who all had labored in Hawaii as missionaries, to take care of the problems.

Arriving at the island of Lanai, where Gibson had his headquarters, the Brethren encountered stiff winds and turbulent seas in the harbor. While going ashore in a smaller craft, they were capsized. Except for Lorenzo Snow, everyone was safely rescued by natives who witnessed the accident from the shore. Lorenzo's lifeless body was finally found under the capsized boat. There was little doubt in the minds of any of those present that he was dead. His devoted brethren laid his body across their knees and with faith prayed over him and administered to him, although the natives declared there was no use. The Brethren endeavored to stimulate breathing by rolling him over a barrel and then by compressing his chest and breathing into his mouth and drawing the air out again. It was one hour or more after the accident before the first signs of life returned.[9]

After locating Gibson, the elders found that conditions were even worse than they had been told. They confronted Gibson and ordered him to turn over to them all the property and money he had acquired in the name of the Church. He refused. The Brethren then excommunicated him. After a few weeks, most of the Hawaiian Saints were reconciled to the leaders of the Church who had been sent to them. One incident that helped the brethren regain the confidence of the Hawaiian Saints occurred when two of them

William Wallace Cluff (1832–1915) was called to serve as Presiding Bishop over Morgan, Summit, and Wasatch counties. He was released in 1877 when President Brigham Young, as part of the priesthood reorganization of the Church, announced that there would only be one Presiding Bishop of the Church—Edward Hunter. William was called to preside over the Scandinavia mission and also served as president of the Summit Stake.

walked on a rock that Gibson had identified as a sacred shrine and had warned that anyone who walked on it would be struck dead. After setting the Church in order the Apostles returned home and left Joseph F. Smith and his two companions in charge of the mission. Elder Smith obtained and began to develop a plantation at Laie, which became mission headquarters and the home of many Hawaiian Saints. In the twentieth century this site would become the location of the Hawaii Temple, Brigham Young University—Hawaii, and the Polynesian Cultural Center.

MISSIONARY WORK AND IMMIGRATION

Despite the Civil War that was raging in the United States, Connor's army, the Morrisites, and Walter Murray Gibson, the greatest interest of Church leaders was still the expansion of Zion—converting more people to the Church and gathering as many members as possible to Utah.

Approximately fifty more colonies were started during this time when most of the nation was experiencing its greatest turmoil. New settlements included St. George in southern Utah, which was part of the "cotton mission" begun when supplies could not be obtained from the American South. Pipe Springs was founded in northern Arizona; Monroe, Salina, and Richfield in central Utah; and Laketown, Paris, and Montpelier in the Bear Lake country of Utah and Idaho. Older colonies, most of them agriculturally based, became stronger. When mining in Colorado, Montana, Idaho, and Nevada became big business during the early 1860s, hundreds of Utah wagons were filled with flour, grain, and other farm produce and freighted to the mining camps for sale, thus greatly increasing the Saints' well-being. This was a tremendous boon to the people who had recently suffered during the Utah War and the move south.

Missionary work was also strengthened again during the Civil War. While virtually no missionary activity occurred in North America during this time, the Church grew throughout Europe. The development of the transatlantic telegraph greatly aided communication with the European Saints. In 1860 the First Presidency sent three members of the Council of the Twelve—Amasa M. Lyman, Charles C. Rich, and George Q. Cannon—to preside over both the British and European missions, headquartered in Liverpool. These three Apostles presided over the European mission until 14 May 1862 when Elders Lyman and Rich returned home. Elder Cannon went to Washington, D.C., to work briefly on obtaining statehood for Utah, then he returned to England to preside until his return to Utah in 1864.

Using native British and Scandinavian missionaries where American elders were not available, these Apostles rejuvenated the gathering of Israel both in the British Isles and on the European continent. The number of conversions surged again following a decline that had occurred during and after the Utah War. England and the Scandinavian countries were the most

George Quayle Cannon (1827–1901) was a gifted and talented man whose contributions were legion. He labored as a missionary, European mission president, writer, publisher, and Apostle. He was a counselor to John Taylor, Wilford Woodruff, and Lorenzo Snow.

Elder Cannon was the first to translate the Book of Mormon into the Hawaiian language, having helped open the Hawaiian Islands to missionaries in 1850.

Much of his biography on the life of Joseph Smith was written while Elder Cannon was incarcerated in the Utah State Penitentiary for the practice of plural marriage.

fertile fields of labor. To save costs to the Church, Brigham Young directed the missionaries to travel "without purse or scrip" and to obtain their board and bed from willing members of the Church. Most missionaries also had wives and families at home and depended upon local priesthood quorums to help care for them if the families could not provide for themselves.

Church leaders were constantly on the lookout for new and better ways to bring the European Saints to Zion. In the fall of 1860, John W. Young brought immigrants by ox teams from the Missouri River after having taken an ox train of produce to the East to sell to provide for immigrants. His venture was so successful that he was allowed to speak in October general conference about it.

Thereafter ox teams were sent from Utah in April with provisions for the yearly immigration, and they returned with immigrants in the summer and early fall. Young men were called as missionaries to be teamsters for these "Church trains." Between 1861 and 1868 the Church brought more than sixteen thousand Europeans to Utah at a reduced cost because of the voluntary donation of labor, teams, and supplies from the Saints. Furthermore, fewer supplies needed to be purchased from outsiders.

GROWTH IN SALT LAKE CITY

By 1860 there were 8,200 people in Salt Lake City; by 1870 there were 12,800. According to the 1870 census, 65 percent of the population was foreign born. Most were from the British Isles, but there were also many from Scandinavia. Salt Lake City served as the hub of colonization for the rest of the Church.

Utilizing the labor of recently arrived immigrants, the department of public works constructed numerous important buildings. During the 1850s

Salt Lake Theatre. Feeling that the people needed amusement as well as religion, Brigham Young instructed his son-in-law Hiram Clawson to commence work on a theatre to meet the needs of the Saints. Social Hall, built in 1852–53, which had been the city's major entertainment center, was no longer adequate.

The Salt Lake Theatre, completed in 1862, had a seating capacity of three thousand. The building was 80 feet wide, 144 feet long, and 40 feet high. No liquor could be served there, all performances were to be opened and closed with prayer, and the actors and actresses were expected to set a good example for the community. Many first-class actors and performers went to Utah and performed on the stage of this theatre. The Salt Lake Theatre was torn down in 1929.

Daniel H. Wells (1814–91) lived in Commerce, Illinois, when the exiled Saints went there from Missouri. Throughout the Church's stay in Nauvoo he was a friendly and sympathetic nonmember. He was baptized in the summer of 1846 and joined the pioneers, being one of the last to leave Nauvoo.

In 1857 he was called to be Second Counselor to President Brigham Young, where he served for twenty years. He was elected mayor of Salt Lake City in 1866 and occupied that position for a decade. In 1884 he was sent to preside over the European mission, and upon his return he was appointed the first president of the Manti Temple.

William H. Folsom was the architect for City Hall, which was completed in 1866 at a cost of seventy thousand dollars. At first the building served as the meeting place for the territorial legislature. It later became the headquarters for the city police. In 1960 the building was numbered, dismantled, and reconstructed just south of the Utah State Capitol Building.

the Council House, the Social Hall, the Endowment House, and a tithing store had been constructed in the growing community. Then in the 1860s the Salt Lake Theatre, the city hall, an arsenal, the Beehive House, the Lion House, and the Salt Lake Tabernacle were constructed. The Salt Lake Theatre, completed in 1862, became the center of much of the recreational and cultural activity in the valley.

From 1850 to 1870, Daniel H. Wells served as Superintendent of Public Works in Salt Lake City. He also served as commanding officer of the Nauvoo Legion, as Second Counselor in the First Presidency from 1857, and as mayor of Salt Lake City from 1866.

Believing that the Saints would be strengthened spiritually if they had an adequate building where they could gather to receive instruction from their leaders, President Brigham Young laid plans for a new tabernacle. He envisioned a large, dome-shaped house of worship. President Young, with the help of Henry Grow, a bridge builder, William H. Folsom, Church architect at the time, and Truman O. Angell, largely responsible for the interior, directed the construction of the unique building. It was 150 feet wide, 250 feet long, and 80 feet high. The tabernacle was completed in time for the October 1867 general conference. At the same time, a gigantic organ for the tabernacle was constructed by the superb craftsman Joseph H. Ridges, a convert from Australia. The right kind of wood for the organ was finally located in Pine Valley three hundred miles away in southern Utah and was carefully transported by as many as twenty wagon teams to Salt Lake City. Acoustics were at first a problem in the tabernacle, but with the addition of a balcony by 1870, the famed structure, seating eight thousand people, became an ideal place for large meetings.

Work on the Salt Lake Temple was reinstituted in 1860, but in 1861 Church leaders concluded that the foundation was defective. Brigham Young decided that a new foundation made entirely of granite quarried from nearby mountains was required to carry the massive weight of the proposed temple. The new footings were to be sixteen feet thick. President Young declared, "I want this Temple to stand through the Millennium and I want it so built that it will be acceptable to the Lord."[10] The work of rebuilding the foundation moved slowly, and the walls did not reach ground level until 1867.

Despite the problems with apostates and military troops, improvements in communication and transportation, growth in missionary work, increased colonization, and better economic opportunities all brought joy to the Church. While most of the nation suffered a bloody conflict, the circumstances of the Latter-day Saints during the Civil War period formed a stark contrast to those of the rest of the United States. Citizens of Utah enjoyed peace and prosperity. After the difficult years associated with the Utah War, the Church was once again moving forward in its divinely designed course.

ENDNOTES

1. "Ceremonies at the Bowery," *Deseret News*, 10 July 1861, p. 152; spelling standardized.

2. In *Journal of Discourses*, 10:38–39.

3. See "Requisition for Troops," *Deseret News*, 30 Apr. 1862, p. 348.

4. In Preston Nibley, *Brigham Young: The Man and His Work* (Salt Lake City: Deseret News Press, 1936), p. 369.

5. Brigham Young, "The Completion of the Telegraph," *Deseret News*, 23 Oct. 1861, p. 189.

6. See Gustive O. Larson, *Outline History of Utah and the Mormons* (Salt Lake City: Deseret Book Co., 1958), p. 195; Richard D. Poll, ed., *Utah's History* (Provo: Brigham Young University Press, 1978), p. 204.

7. In B. H. Roberts, *A Comprehensive History of The Church of Jesus Christ of Latter-day Saints, Century One*, 6 vols. (Salt Lake City: The Church of Jesus Christ of Latter-day Saints, 1930), 5:47.

8. In Andrew Jenson, "Walter Murray Gibson," *Improvement Era*, Dec. 1900, p. 87.

9. See Joseph Fielding Smith, comp., *Life of Joseph F. Smith*, 2d ed. (Salt Lake City: Deseret Book Co., 1969), pp. 215–16.

10. Wilford Woodruff, Historian's Private Journal 1858, entry for 22 Aug. 1862, LDS Historical Department, Salt Lake City; spelling and capitalization standardized.

CHAPTER THIRTY-ONE

THE QUEST FOR SELF-SUFFICIENCY

◄ Engines from the two companies, the Union Pacific (right) and the Central Pacific (left), met at Promontory Summit, Utah, on 10 May 1869 to commemorate the completion of the transcontinental railroad with the driving of the golden spike.

Shaking hands in the center are Samuel S. Montague (left), chief engineer of the Central Pacific, and Grenville M. Dodge (right), chief engineer of the Union Pacific. Estimates of the number of people in attendance vary from five hundred to three thousand, but photographs suggest five to six hundred.

Lorin Farr, mayor of Ogden, Utah, represented Brigham Young, who was in southern Utah at the time.

AFTER THE CIVIL WAR, Church leaders recognized more than ever before the wisdom of being self-sufficient and the strength this would give the Saints both economically and spiritually. This was especially true with the arrival of the transcontinental railroad, which eliminated Utah's isolation. Several measures were taken at this time to establish the Church's independence from contaminating worldly influences.

EARLY MEASURES

Because he saw it as a great aid in making it easier for immigrants to reach the Great Basin, Brigham Young had encouraged a railroad as early as the 1850s. Leading public officials outside the Church also wanted the "iron horse" running through the Utah Territory, not only because of the wealth that they could accrue from this but also because they were confident that when the transcontinental railway reached Utah, the Church would collapse. Their confidence was based on an erroneous belief that Brigham Young was an evil dictator who held his people in captive subjection. Therefore, they reasoned that when the railroad came it would allow the oppressed Latter-day Saints a convenient means of fleeing to the freedom of the East—even though one of them acknowledged that President Young, upon learning of this idea, remarked that his religion "must, indeed, be a poor religion, if it cannot stand one railroad."[1]

Little did the nation's leaders know that Brigham Young and his followers waited with anticipation and enthusiasm as workers laid track at a frantic pace. Church members, however, were not unaware, because of their experiences in the East, that potential problems were not just shadows lurking in the rails and ties being laid from both ends of the continent to rendezvous at Promontory Summit, Utah.

Realizing that the railroad would bring more non-Mormons to the territory, Brigham Young reorganized the School of the Prophets, promoted cooperatives, and revitalized the Church's auxiliaries. To help strengthen the brethren in doctrine and policies of the Church, the School of the Prophets was instituted as early as 1867. President Young wanted the brethren to help him make economic decisions that would promote home industry and cooperative enterprises so that the Saints could maintain a degree of financial independence. The school was also intended to purify Church meetings and minimize the promulgation of false doctrines.[2]

In addition to Salt Lake City the School of the Prophets was also organized in Logan, Ogden, Brigham City, Provo, Parowan, and other principal settlements. Brigham Young sought a self-sufficient economy and encouraged Church members through this organization to purchase goods from their fellow Saints. Home industry was also stressed, which meant that Church members manufactured their own clothes, produced their own food, and constructed their own iron works. They also produced their own silk, cotton, and flax. They dug their own coal and even manufactured their own paper, some of which was made from rags.

Other activities of the School of the Prophets included raising funds for the Perpetual Emigrating Fund, instituting a mercantile boycott of merchants who opposed the Church, establishing the Provo Woolen Mills, reducing wages for Utah workers to make the prices of Utah manufactured goods more competitive with goods that would now be shipped from the East, and finally promoting the construction of the railroad from Salt Lake City to Ogden.

The School of the Prophets also motivated Church members to clean up their homes, yards, and public thoroughfares. Honesty, personal cleanliness, and neatness were stressed so that Zion's people would indeed be a light to the world. While the Saints made their economy more secure, their personal property more tidy, and their lives more Christlike, the railroad began to penetrate the mountains that surrounded them.

In 1868 Brigham Young, on behalf of the School of the Prophets, signed a contract with Union Pacific officials to build the railroad from the head of Echo Canyon to Salt Lake City if the route came that way, or from the canyon to Ogden if that was the route chosen. The School of the Prophets considered such a contract advantageous for several reasons. First, it would avoid the troubles that always followed the railroad camps. The morality of the community was threatened by gamblers, prostitutes, and ruffians who followed the railroad to take advantage of the laborers and their earnings. Second, "it would insure that the income earned under the contract would go to the church and its members." Third, it would "minimize an influx of undesirable 'outsiders' by deflating the reports on Utah's mineral wealth, thus diminishing the prospect of a rush of miners to Utah." And fourth, it would supply much needed employment for Latter-day Saints.[3]

Prominent Church members, including Ezra T. Benson, Bishop Chauncy West, and Ogden Stake president Lorin Farr, also signed contracts to build two hundred miles of track east from Humboldt Wells, Nevada, to Ogden, Utah. Thus hundreds of the territory's residents secured jobs. When the Union Pacific reached Ogden on 8 March 1869, the citizens celebrated and greeted the workmen with many banners, one of which read, "HAIL TO THE HIGHWAY OF NATIONS! UTAH BIDS YOU WELCOME!"[4]

It was 10 May 1869 when the two rail lines met at Promontory Summit, fifty-three miles northwest of Ogden, Utah. The last tie laid was made of

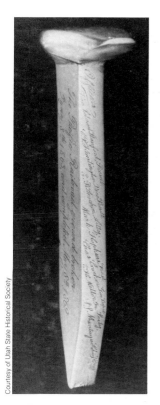

The famous ceremonial gold spike that was to be used to join the two sections of the railroad was donated by David Hewes of San Francisco. It is inscribed on all four sides with the names of railroad officials, the donor, and a salutation. After the ceremony the spike was returned to Mr. Hewes, who gave it to Stanford University in 1892.

A significant economic institution among Latter-day Saints during the nineteenth century was the tithing office. Since tithing was paid for the most part either in kind or labor, tithing offices served as something of a general store where local produce and manufactured items could be obtained. This is the Deseret Store and Tithing Office of Salt Lake City in the 1860s. It occupied the site of the Hotel Utah building east of Temple Square.

California laurel wood with an inscription on a silver plate celebrating this great event in the nation's history. At 12:47 P.M., using sledge hammers, both Leland Stanford, president of the Central Pacific, and Thomas C. Durant, vice-president of the Union Pacific, swung and missed hitting an iron spike. Still, the telegraph wires sent the message to U.S. President Ulysses S. Grant that the last spike had been driven. Guns were fired in San Francisco, and the rest of the nation joined in the rejoicing of this historic event.[5] Brigham Young was on an extended visit to the Saints in the southern part of the territory and missed the celebration.

In an effort to further improve transportation within the territory and to provide employment for Church members, the First Presidency, with the help of ward bishops and territorial surveyor Jesse W. Fox, began plans for the Utah Central Railroad that would connect Salt Lake City with the transcontinental line at Ogden. On 17 May 1869 the first ground was broken, not with a miner's pick but with a farmer's shovel to represent the Saints' commitment to agriculture. The laying of the track was completed 10 January 1870. Thousands of spectators gathered to watch President Brigham Young drive home the last spike, which was made of Utah iron.

The construction of this line was followed with Church support by the laying of track for the Utah Southern Railroad, which ran through Provo and other southern settlements, and the Utah Northern lines, which were laid as far north as Butte, Montana.

For years the federal government had withheld giving land titles to the people of Utah; therefore, as the railroad approached, the citizens grew concerned about their holdings. Should the "iron horse" significantly increase the number of non-Latter-day Saints in the territory, there was a distinct possibility that without clear property title many residents would be denied both their land and the improvements they had made. That the Saints had lived in peace for so many years without clear title to their land is a tribute to their ability to cooperate with one another. Even the coming of some gentiles had elicited very few land disputes in contrast to the many conflicts between ranchers and squatters in California, for example.

The Saints' concern grew to such an extent that in 1869 the School of the Prophets appointed a committee to inform themselves "upon the land question and report to the people what steps were necessary to take to preserve their homesteads being claimed by the railway companies."[6] (This would also apply to others who might want to settle in the Great Basin.) "This committee made periodic reports to the school, and sent individuals on missions to assist local settlers throughout the territory with their land title applications."[7] Because of their efforts a minimum of injustice was done to the people.

By congressional decree the railroad had been given land along their right-of-way, except where property rights were already vested in private citizens. The committee visited the territory's communities and assisted residents with their land title applications.

In the October 1865 general conference, Brigham Young announced that the Latter-day Saints had to help one another economically. He declared, "Let every one of the Latter-day Saints, male and female, decree in their hearts that they will buy of nobody else but their own faithful brethren, who will do good with the money they will thus obtain. I know it is the will of God that we should sustain ourselves, for, if we do not, we must perish, so far as receiving aid from any quarter, except God and ourselves. . . . We have to preserve ourselves, for our enemies are determined to destroy us."[8]

Again in 1868, President Young carefully explained that our policy "must be to let this trade [with outside merchants] alone, and save our means for other purposes than to enrich outsiders. We must use it to spread the Gospel, to gather the poor, build temples, sustain our poor, build houses for ourselves, and convert this means to a better use than to give it to those who will use it against us."[9] Church leaders then began to promote locally-owned and Church-supervised cooperatives to avert the threat to the economic stability of the Saints.

The first Latter-day Saint cooperative institution was founded in 1864 in Brigham City under the direction of Elder Lorenzo Snow of the Quorum of the Twelve, and proved so successful that it served as a model to the Church's cooperative movement later that decade. Elder Snow had been sent in 1854 by Brigham Young to supervise the Saints in Box Elder, which was renamed Brigham City in 1864. That same fall President Young and Elder Snow had a lengthy conversation about instituting principles of the united order in Brigham City. President Young had long been anxious to apply principles of the law of consecration from the Doctrine and Covenants, and now that self-sufficiency was being stressed, Brigham City appeared to be the ideal place to start.

Elder Snow explained in an 1875 letter to President Young that his main objective for the cooperative was "to unite together the feelings of the people by cooperating their interests with their means and make them self-sustaining according to the spirit of your teachings and to make them independent of Gentile stores."[10]

First, Lorenzo Snow supervised the organization of a cooperative general store. It was his intention to use this mercantile cooperative as the basis for the organization of the entire economic life of the community and the development of the industries needed to make Brigham City self-sufficient. A joint-stock enterprise was formed to which all members of the community were invited to subscribe. As the only store in town, the enterprise soon was producing dividends to the subscribers. But most of the profits were reinvested in home industries. The first was a tannery, which was built with cooperative labor and supervised by an English convert who had much experience in the business. This, in turn, was followed by a shoe manufacturing plant and a leather industry. Over the next several years other industries were added until the entire community became self-sustaining.

Zion's Cooperative Mercantile Institution (ZCMI) in Salt Lake City was the parent outlet of what eventually became a territory-wide operation. In recent years the corporation has restored the cast-iron storefront of the original building.

The fame and success of this cooperative spread throughout the nation, and the famous writer, Edward Bellamy, who was studying cooperative movements in America, came to Brigham City and spent several days with Lorenzo Snow observing how the association worked.

In 1868 President Young established an economic system known as Zion's Cooperative Mercantile Institution. The purpose of ZCMI, as it was popularly known, was to bring goods to the territory, sell them as inexpensively as they could possibly be sold, and "let the profits be divided with the people at large."[11] Furthermore, the directors were empowered to set standard retail prices, and these were to be charged to all cooperating concerns. Such prices were to be "reasonable" and "such as would tend to the satisfaction and benefit of both the merchants and the whole people."[12] The purposes of uniform retail prices was not to prevent price competition but to stifle exorbitant prices. The first such list of prices was adopted in the winter of 1869 "with the understanding that the Superintendent of Zion's Co-operative Mercantile Institution be permitted to vary them according to circumstances."[13] ZCMI eventually had its own factories for boots, shoes, overalls, coats, vests, overshirts, undershirts, and men's underwear.[14]

Within six weeks of the opening of the parent institution in Salt Lake City, 81 cooperative stores throughout the territory were in operation. The Saints in individual communities were urged to buy one or more shares in the joint-stock endeavor. Eventually over 150 stores were in operation in Utah and Southern Idaho. These stores managed nearly all the business of the Latter-day Saints.

Eliza R. Snow (1804–87) accepted the gospel in 1835. Throughout her life she was known as "Zion's poetess" because of the comfort, solace, and enlightenment she conveyed to her fellow Saints as she articulated her own unswerving fidelity to the gospel.

Eliza was the first secretary of the Relief Society organized in Nauvoo. In Utah she presided over the sister's work in the Endowment House. Sister Snow served as the second general president of the Relief Society for twenty years, beginning in 1867.

The cover of a second grade reader book published in the Deseret alphabet and examples of the alphabet. The Deseret alphabet was begun in October 1853 by a committee composed of Heber C. Kimball, Parley P. Pratt, and George D. Watt. The alphabet was primarily the work of George D. Watt. This reader and a few other books, including the Book of Mormon, were published before 1870.

In metropolitan Salt Lake City nearly every ward organized its own co-op, and many established individual manufacturing enterprises. Most of these provided dividends to their subscribers. Stockmen also managed their cattle, horses, and sheep on a cooperative basis and improved the quality of these herds by importing breeding stock.[15] This cooperative system proved imminently successful in fulfilling the self-sufficiency goals of Church leaders until the Saints began feeling the effects of the nationwide panic of 1873. Some of the co-ops even survived into the twentieth century.

REVITALIZING THE RELIEF SOCIETY

At the same time that the School of the Prophets was reorganized in 1867, President Brigham Young reorganized the Church's Relief Society. He sought to involve the sisters in promoting home industry and self-sufficiency and encouraged them to teach each other how to withstand life's temptations and how to fashion their own clothing and styles so that the community's capital would remain within the territory and help stimulate economic growth. The importance of the Relief Society was emphasized when Brigham Young called Eliza R. Snow, probably the most respected woman in the Church, as its president. He wanted the sisters "to visit the sick and the helpless and the needy, and learn their wants, and, under their Bishops, collect the means necessary to relieve them."[16] They were, furthermore, to prevent or diminish female extravagance, inform themselves on political matters, and lobby against anti-Mormon legislation.

STRENGTHENING ZION FURTHER

Conscious that the variety of languages converts brought with them to their new mountain homes made communication difficult and reading English periodicals a problem, President Young promoted for a time a new phonetic alphabet. He believed that this new alphabet would stimulate unity among the Saints. The president asked several of his associates to develop a new phonetic alphabet called Deseret. Drawing on Pitman shorthand as a source for the sounds and characters, these brethren soon accomplished their task. President Young then authorized the printing of the Book of Mormon and several school books using the new symbols. Orson Pratt transcribed the Book of Mormon into the new alphabet in 1869, and a small sized edition was produced.

President Young explained the merits of this new alphabet, stating that it would make it easier for children to learn to read and minimize the amount of time they would have to spend in school. In addition, he said it would reduce the time foreign converts would need to learn English. After the primers were printed, classes were held and other attempts were made to convert the Saints to implementing this alphabet. Soon it was discovered that using a new alphabet created more difficulties than it solved, and the experiment was abandoned.

Prior to the construction of the domed Tabernacle known to most Latter-day Saints today, Church members gathered in the "Old" Tabernacle shown here. To the right of it was the North Bowery, which accommodated larger crowds in good weather. Construction on the first Tabernacle began 21 May 1851. The building was completed and dedicated 6 April 1852 by President Willard Richards. It was torn down in 1870 and replaced by the Assembly Hall.

Henry Grow (1817–91), a millwright and bridge builder, joined the Church in 1842. He was responsible for constructing the trusses of the dome of the Tabernacle.

Joseph Harris Ridges (1827–1914), builder of the Tabernacle organ, was born and reared near an organ factory in England. His family left England for Australia in November 1851. His curiosity about how organs were built proved a blessing to the Church. Brother Ridges was baptized in Australia on 15 November 1853 and then came to Utah.

When the Tabernacle opened, the organ was only one third complete. Through the years the organ has been rebuilt, electrified, and enlarged.

Believing that the Saints could be strengthened spiritually if they had an adequate building where they could be called together and instructed by their leaders, President Young began planning for such a structure. Following several council meetings, a pattern for a great dome-shaped house of worship stamped itself vividly upon the mind of President Young. To make this vision a reality, he called to his office Henry Grow, who was a master mechanic as well as an experienced millwright. Brigham Young had recently watched Elder Grow complete a wooden arch bridge over the Jordan River—a rather unusual structure having no center supports, sustained wholly by fitting together wooden triangles and arches. President Young felt that it was just such a continuous bridge, or set of wooden bridges, that he needed to support the roof of the spacious, dome-shaped edifice that he had in mind.

With the assistance of architect William H. Folsom, President Young and Henry Grow worked out tentative architectural plans for the proposed pioneer Tabernacle, one of the largest buildings of its kind in the world—150 feet wide, 250 feet long, and 80 feet high, on the outside. The most novel part was that the massive ceiling was to be "bridged over," without supporting pillars. Since some Saints doubted and others questioned the feasibility of such a high dome-shaped roof, President Young supervised the construction of a model tabernacle, which answered the Saints' questions. Construction of the Tabernacle commenced during the spring of 1863.

By the fall of 1867 the Tabernacle and its famed organ were completed sufficiently to be used at the October conference. The organ and other inside

The Tabernacle as it looked while under construction and when finished. The unique "eggshell" construction of the Tabernacle was a result of the large bridgelike trusses used to span the 150-foot width of the building, which was 80 feet high and 250 feet long.

William Harrison Folsom (1815–1901) was converted to the gospel in New York in 1842. After his arrival with the Saints in Nauvoo, he worked as a joiner on the Nauvoo Temple. At the general conference held at Salt Lake City in October 1861 he was sustained as Church architect. He held this position until April 1867 when he was released at his own request. He remained as an assistant Church architect, however.

William Folsom was the architect for such buildings as the Salt Lake Theatre, City Hall, the Tabernacle, and the Manti Temple. William was a seventy, member of the high council of the Salt Lake Stake, counselor in the Salt Lake Stake presidency, missionary, and patriarch.

fixtures were not entirely finished until after 1870. The gallery—30 feet wide and 480 feet long, extending entirely around three sides of the structure and resting upon seventy-two columns—was started in 1870, which improved the acoustics and added many seats to the Tabernacle. Finally, John Taylor, President of the Quorum of the Twelve Apostles, dedicated the completed Tabernacle at the October conference of 1875.

Joseph H. Ridges, a convert to the Church from Australia, brought with him to Utah a small pipe organ he had built. President Young, upon learning of Elder Ridges and his organ building capabilities, appointed him to construct the first Tabernacle organ. Finding the proper wood to build an organ was a major problem. Finally the desired timber was located in the Parowan and Pine Valley Mountains of Utah three hundred miles south of Salt Lake City.

Chipping and hauling heavy logs for this project was no small task in the 1800s; roads had to be constructed and canyon creeks bridged. Moreover, almost all the labor had to be done by volunteers. Sometimes as many as twenty teamsters with three yoke of oxen on each wagon journeyed to these distant mountains to chop and haul logs. In less than twenty months Elder Ridges had completed the organ sufficiently for it to be played at the October conference of 1867. Combined choirs from Payson, Springville, and Spanish Fork, Utah, provided music for part of this conference, and the newly organized Tabernacle Choir, under the direction of Robert Sands, provided the music for the Sunday services. The Tabernacle Choir grew in quality from this beginning and has today become world famous.

THE GOSPEL CONTINUES TO SPREAD

Even as President Young and the Saints were busily engaged in establishing Zion in the tops of the mountains, the Church continued to grow in other parts of the world as well, but not without opposition.

In New Zealand, Elder Robert Beauchamp, a missionary from Melbourne, Australia, was peppered with rotten eggs in Wellington. On another occasion he escaped injury through the intervention of his Heavenly Father, who hid Elder Beauchamp from the eyes of the wicked men who were going to tar and feather him. In spite of mobs and a bitter attack by the newspaper, the Wellington *Advertiser*, a conference was held and the Saints "enjoyed a goodly portion of the Holy Spirit."[17]

In Scandinavia, Elder Knud Peterson reported that during the year 1871, 1,021 souls were baptized into the Church. He continued, "A good many of the native Elders have been appointed to missions during the winter." Crowded meetings were reported in Sweden, although in that country and Norway, Church elders "are still subjected to fines and imprisonment for administering the ordinances of the Gospel. In Norway exists religious liberty for all Christian denominations, but the supreme court has passed the strange sentence that the church of Jesus Christ of Latter-day Saints is not a Christian religion," and therefore Church members were denied religious freedom. The Saints in Norway were also very poor, but 630 of them had raised sufficient means to emigrate to Zion that year.[18]

Missionaries in Switzerland were described by Edward Schoenfeld as being as "united as a clover leaf," and were sacrificing to publish a pamphlet that would plainly set forth the principles of the gospel to combat the distortions about the Church in the popular press.[19]

Near the end of 1872, one elder in Switzerland reported that the Saints there were striving to live their religion and were doing their best to sustain the missionaries. He added that in just a short time he had baptized twenty-seven persons and blessed ten children.

While laboring in Hawaii, Elder George Nebeker reported that over one hundred converts had been baptized and that the meetinghouse was too small; hence, the Saints were busily engaged in constructing a new one. In the Hawaiian Islands as a whole, during the last six months of 1872 there were more than six hundred souls added to the Church. The spring conference of 1872 reported an attendance of more than seven hundred Saints. There were healings of the sick, and emphasis was placed on obeying the Word of Wisdom.[20]

Meanwhile, beginning in 1869, the Church required emigrating Saints to pay in advance for their entire journey to Zion. Previously most had been allowed credit for the portion of the trip covered by the Church trains (ox teams that met the emigrants at Winter Quarters and took them on to Salt Lake City). In order to help their friends and relatives emigrate, the Saints in the Great Basin established a Welsh Fund, a Scottish Fund, and similar area

William S. Godbe (1833–1902) was converted to the gospel in his youth in England. He became a prominent merchant in Utah and one of the territory's richest men. He served as a city councilman, a president of a local seventies quorum, and as a counselor in the Thirteenth Ward bishopric.

funds, which they then gave to Church officials to help those gathering to Zion from those areas of the British Isles. Ward Primaries contributed to the emigration of children, but perhaps the most popular kind of assistance was that sent by friends and relatives who deposited cash at the Church offices and had a "Church draft" sent to the prospective emigrants along with a notification that the funds were now available for their journey.

DEALING WITH APOSTASY

Unfortunately, not all members of the Church supported the leaders and their philosophy of economic self-sufficiency. Some people fell into apostasy. Just as Brigham Young was promoting the cooperative system, certain Mormon businessmen and intellectuals who called themselves "liberals" publicly questioned his policies. This faction, known as the Godbeites, because they were led by William S. Godbe, called for cooperation with gentile merchants nationwide and argued that Utah should focus upon mining as its natural source of wealth rather than upon agriculture and stock raising. The outlet for their opinions was the *Utah Magazine*, which they founded in 1868.

Church leaders sought diligently to reclaim these men and tried calling some of them on missions. The calls were rejected, and their public outcries became even more strident. The men were summoned to the School of the Prophets to discuss the issues, but only an unpleasant confrontation took place. After further attempts at reconciliation, the Salt Lake Stake high council brought charges against the leaders of the New Movement, as they were also called, and the men were excommunicated from the Church. In 1870 they started their own church, named the Church of Zion, and made their periodical into a daily anti-Mormon newspaper, the *Salt Lake Tribune*. Together with leading non-Mormons in Salt Lake City, they formed the Liberal Party to oppose the Church's political activities.

By 1870 the New Movement had taken into its ranks former Apostle and colonizer Amasa M. Lyman, who had been dropped from the Twelve in 1867 for teaching false doctrine regarding the Atonement and for espousing spiritualist ideas. Lyman joined with others in the Church of Zion in conducting seances. By 1873, the Church of Zion had collapsed from lack of support, while the Liberal Party lived on and was a disruptive force in Utah politics until 1893.

THE UNITED ORDER

With the success of the cooperative movement, Brigham Young and other Church leaders desired a still better economic system. In the October 1872 general conference, Elder George Q. Cannon indicated that the three and one-half years of success of the cooperative institutions pointed to even more valuable results to be expected from the "order of Enoch." This new order was needed, he insisted, to bring a time "when there shall be no rich and no poor among the Latter-day Saints; when wealth will not be a temptation; when every man will love his neighbor as he does himself; when every man and woman will labor for the good of all as much as for self." The cooperative system was merely "a stepping stone to something beyond that is more perfect," and the higher order "which exists in heaven will be practiced and enjoyed by men on the earth."[21]

Brigham Young took up the same theme the next day in his conference address, and for the next several months the General Authorities delivered messages to the Saints preparing them for the establishment of the united order system.

Several factors contributed to the forming of the united order in 1874. Brigham Young and other Brethren who had been closely associated with the Prophet Joseph Smith sought for a reformation among the Saints and the reestablishment of the principles and practices of the law of consecration. When the United States was hit by the depression of 1873, the Saints found that despite their efforts for independence, their economy was clearly affected by the economic rhythms of the nation. Thus, Church leaders began to establish orders of Enoch to soften the effects of future economic cycles upon the Latter-day Saints.

Also, village life in southern Utah had been disrupted for a few years by the mining industry headquartered in nearby Pioche, Nevada. Building materials and foodstuffs among the Saints had been drawn away by the miners, causing a shortage in the Mormon communities. Several young men had also left their homes for the mining camps to obtain cash wages, where they were subject to influences of the world. This also caused labor shortages at home.

St. George was particularly in need of an economic boost, and it was there that Brigham Young organized the first united order. Its management board was composed primarily of the ecclesiastical officers of the stake and the various ward bishops. One of the order's earliest acts was to direct the transportation of goods to and from the northern settlements. Soon thereafter they established community-owned flocks of poultry and herds of pigs, and helped construct the St. George Temple. The members agreed to follow a list of fourteen spiritual rules, such as not taking the name of Deity in vain, observing the Word of Wisdom more fully, treating family members with kindness and affection, living the law of chastity, keeping the Sabbath day holy, and wearing non-extravagant clothing. Each member of the order signified his intent to comply with the rules by being rebaptized.

Convinced that conditions were right for establishing united orders throughout Zion, Brigham Young dispatched Church leaders to organize all the southern settlements according to the St. George model. Because of severe weather and bad roads, President Young was unable to arrive in Salt Lake City in time for the scheduled April general conference, where he had planned to introduce the united order to all the Church. Conference was therefore postponed to the first week of May. When the Prophet arrived in Salt Lake City, he immediately went to work to implement the united order in the Salt Lake City wards. During the four-day general conference, more than a dozen sermons were preached explaining all the favorable ramifications of the united order.

By the end of 1874, over two hundred united orders were established in Latter-day Saint settlements, including settlements in Idaho, Nevada, and Arizona. In the larger communities of Ogden, Provo, and Logan, more than one order was set up, with each one specializing in different production projects. Salt Lake City had a separate order for each of its twenty wards. Brigham City and other communities, following the same model, maintained their cooperative network of industries. Under this pattern each person retained his own private property in addition to the stock he held in the cooperative business.

Another variation of the united order was the type established in small communities of no more than 750 people. In this variation each person shared equally in the community's production, and everyone lived and ate together as a well-regulated family. The most famous of these was Orderville, Kane County, located in southern Utah, which was founded by twenty-four families in 1875. Within five years the town had grown to 700 people. By cooperative labor the citizens "built apartment house units or 'shanties' in a semi-fort arrangement around the town square and constructed a large common dining hall in the center."[22] They also built shops, bakeries, and barns, and established farms, orchards, dairies, livestock projects, and various manufacturing enterprises, such as the building of furniture. The people all wore the same style of clothes, manufactured at Orderville, and no one could improve his or her situation unless all were likewise improved. For ten years this community was a model of cooperation and love, and the system only ended due to the accelerated anti-polygamy persecution of 1885. Those who labored to build Orderville continued to look back with genuine nostalgia for the happy feelings they had living in a well-ordered Christian community.

Generally speaking, most of the orders did not fare as well. Because of some selfishness and some mismanagement, as well as difficult economic pressures from the nation at large, most orders were abandoned by 1877. Some continued until the political problems of the 1880s forced their demise.

Nevertheless, there were several noteworthy accomplishments from the decade-long system of cooperatives and united orders in Zion. The Saints became less dependent upon imports, which consequently decreased drastically. Home production and local investment in manufacturing and retailing all increased considerably. Economic inequality diminished among the Saints. Noble qualities of thrift and industry were developed, which would benefit several generations in the Church. And finally, the economic self-sufficiency programs helped significantly in the building of the temples at St. George, Logan, Manti, and Salt Lake City by providing both labor and material.

ENDNOTES

1. In Samuel Bowles, *Our New West* (Hartford, Conn.: Hartford Publishing Co., 1869), p. 260.

2. See Leonard J. Arrington, *Great Basin Kingdom: An Economic History of the Latter-day Saints*, 1830–1900 (Cambridge: Harvard University Press, 1958), pp. 245–51.

3. Arrington, *Great Basin Kingdom*, pp. 246–47.

4. Joseph Hall, "Railway Celebration at Ogden," *Deseret Evening News*, 9 Mar. 1869, p. 2.

5. See John J. Stewart, *The Iron Trail to the Golden Spike* (Salt Lake City: Deseret Book Co., 1969), pp. 225–27; LeRoy R. Hafen, W. Eugene Hollon, and Carl Coke Rester, *Western America*, 3d ed. (Englewood Cliffs: Prentice Hall, 1970), pp. 405–6.

6. Journal History of The Church of Jesus Christ of Latter-day Saints, 20 Mar. 1869, Historical Department, Salt Lake City.

7. Arrington, *Great Basin Kingdom*, p. 249.

8. In *Journal of Discourses*, 11:139.

9. In *Journal of Discourses*, 12:301.

10. In Thomas C. Romney, *The Life of Lorenzo Snow* (Salt Lake City: Deseret News Press, 1955), p. 317.

11. Brigham Young, in ZCMI *First Record Book*, Minute Book A, p. 17, cited in Arden Beal Olsen, "The History of Mormon Mercantile Cooperation in Utah," Ph.D. diss., University of California, 1935, p. 80.

12. *First Record Book*, p. 19, in Olsen, "History of Mormon Mercantile Cooperation," p. 81.

13. Olsen, "History of Mormon Mercantile Cooperation," p. 93.

14. See Arrington, *Great Basin Kingdom*, pp. 308–9.

15. See Leonard J. Arrington, Feramorz Y. Fox, and Dean L. May, *Building the City of God* (Salt Lake City: Deseret Book Co., 1976), pp. 108–9.

16. "Female Relief Societies," *Deseret Evening News*, 6 Dec. 1867, p. 2.

17. "The Church in New Zealand," *Millennial Star*, 9 Jan. 1872, p. 25.

18. *Millennial Star*, 30 Jan. 1872, pp. 75–76.

19. *Millennial Star*, 20 Feb. 1872, p. 125.

20. See *Millennial Star*, 5 Nov. 1872, p. 714.

21. In *Journal of Discourses*, 15:207, 209.

22. Arrington, *Great Basin Kingdom*, p. 334.

BRIGHAM YOUNG'S PRESIDENCY: THE FINAL DECADE

SINCE ARRIVING IN the Great Basin in 1847, the Saints had organized sundry, often short-lived, groups for theological, scientific, and literary study. During the last decade of Brigham Young's life, under the inspiration of God, he established religious auxiliaries that would help meet the needs of Church members for the next century. He also worked to expand Zion and to increase the spirituality of Church members, as exemplified by the colonization of northern Arizona, the reorganization of the priesthood leadership of the Church, the building and dedication of the St. George Temple, and the establishment of the Brigham Young Academy.

DEVELOPMENT OF THE AUXILIARIES

As mentioned, the first of the Church auxiliaries to receive renewed impetus and consolidation from general Church leadership was the Relief Society. Since arriving in Deseret, Latter-day Saint sisters had exemplified the ideals of work and compassionate service they had learned from the Prophet Joseph Smith in their Relief Society meetings in Nauvoo. By 1858 there were organizations of the society functioning in ten Salt Lake City wards and in Ogden, Provo, Spanish Fork, and Nephi. But the move south that same year, as a result of the coming of Johnston's Army, interrupted Relief Society work.

In December 1867, President Brigham Young authorized Eliza R. Snow to reestablish Relief Societies in Salt Lake City. During the next two years the prophet gave official endorsement to the program and directed every bishop to cooperate with Sister Snow and her counselors, Zina Diantha Huntington Young and Elizabeth Ann Whitney, as they travelled throughout the territory setting up branch organizations of the society. Women in each settlement would travel miles—sometimes in carriages and wagons or sometimes on a horse or mule or simply on foot—to attend the semi-monthly Relief Society meetings. One meeting each month was devoted to sewing and caring for the needs of the poor. The second meeting featured discussions on elevating educational and spiritual themes and the bearing of testimonies.

Brigham Young gave the Relief Society several special "missions" during the last years of his life. In 1873 he instructed every Relief Society president to appoint three young women to study hygiene and nursing. In 1875 he called Zina Young to establish sericulture (the cultivation of silkworms and the production of silk) among the women of all the settlements. The "gospel

Portrait of Brigham Young by Seal Van Sickle. Painting portrays Brigham with his right hand on a book entitled Law of the Lord. *On the table are the Book of Mormon and the Bible.*

Weber Stake Relief Society building, located in Ogden, Utah. The building was erected in 1902. In 1926 the building was deeded to the Daughters of the Utah Pioneers and became known as the Weber County Pioneer Hall. It is now used as a museum to house pioneer artifacts.

Jane Snyder Richards was called to be the first Weber Stake Relief Society president in 1877 by Brigham Young, and she served in this position for thirty-one years. When the Weber Stake Relief Society building was dedicated on 19 July 1902, Sister Richards conducted the dedicatory services.

of silk" was a major activity of sisters in the Church for many years as they were striving to produce enough silk for their own clothing and for temples and meetinghouses of the Church. In 1876 the prophet called Emmeline B. Wells to head a grain-saving movement among women. They were to store and save wheat against a time of need. President Young also constantly encouraged that the sisters support and participate in all the home industries spawned by the Church's cooperative and United Order movements.

A group of sisters closely associated with the Relief Society also promoted a women's newspaper. The enterprising semi-monthly newspaper, the *Woman's Exponent*, started in 1872 with Louisa Lula Greene Richards as its first editor. "The aim of this journal will be to discuss every subject interesting and valuable to women. It will contain a brief and graphic summary of current news local and general, household hints, educational matters, articles on health and dress, correspondence, editorials on leading topics of interest suitable to its columns and miscellaneous reading."[1] The *Woman's Exponent* helped unite the sisters throughout all the settlements in numerous causes.

As a final organizational development, just one month before his death in July 1877, President Young, accompanied by Eliza R. Snow, traveled to Ogden and organized the first stake Relief Society. He called Jane S. Richards, wife of Elder Franklin D. Richards, to serve as its president. The Saints, both men and women, were pleasantly surprised on this occasion at the unexpected creation of a stake Relief Society organization. The *Woman's Exponent* described the day as one of rejoicing.[2]

The initial Relief Society meetings were often held in private homes, but with the help of the brethren in the settlements, the sisters had Relief Society

Richard Ballantyne (1817–98) was born and reared in Scotland, where as a young man he was a Sunday School teacher in the Presbyterian Church. At age twenty-five he was baptized a member of the Church. He went to Nauvoo with his mother in 1843.

When asked why he was so involved in the Sunday School he replied: "I was early called to this work by the voice of the spirit, and I have felt many times that I have been ordained to this work before I was born, for even before I joined the Church, I was moved upon to work for the young."[3] In 1852 he was called on a mission to India, which lasted about three years.

halls of their own constructed. Relief Society cooperative stores often occupied the ground floor of these halls.

The second auxiliary to take more permanent shape was the Sunday School. The Sunday School concept began with Protestants in the British Isles in 1780 and came to the United States as early as 1790. In 1824 an American Sunday School Union was formed. Sunday Schools generally preceded or accompanied public education and taught reading and Bible subjects to youthful "scholars." Latter-day Saints had sporadically introduced Sunday Schools, like the Protestant ones that many members of the Church had participated in, at Kirtland, Nauvoo, Winter Quarters, and in Britain before arriving in the Great Basin.

With permission from his bishop, Richard Ballantyne organized the first Sunday School in the Salt Lake Valley during the winter of 1849. Fifty children ranging from eight to fourteen years of age met in an especially built addition to the Ballantyne home. Later they met in the Fourteenth Ward meetinghouse. Sunday Schools were set up in a few other wards, but the approach of Johnston's Army in 1857 and the move south the following year caused their disbandment.

In 1864, when Elder George Q. Cannon returned from serving in the presidency of the European Mission, he saw the need for teaching the gospel in Zion. He later said, "When I reflected upon the numbers of our children at home, I felt a burning desire to spend all the time I could in trying to teach them the principles of the Gospel."[4] He reorganized a Sunday School program in the Fourteenth Ward, and soon his example was followed in other Salt Lake City wards.

In early 1866 Elder Cannon launched the *Juvenile Instructor* as a personal project. On its pages, children's conferences, weekly Sunday meetings, scriptural reading, and religious instructions were highlighted. Elder Cannon realized that a journal devoted to the needs of the Sunday Schools would be of great value, particularly since there was so little curriculum available. The *Juvenile Instructor* "was a means of strengthening the hands of those who had the Sunday School cause at heart."[5] This biweekly periodical, though dedicated entirely to the Sunday School cause, remained under the private direction of Elder Cannon until 1900, when it came under direct auspices of the Church.

In November 1867 steps were taken toward establishing a permanent Sunday School organization. President Brigham Young spoke to numerous local leaders concerning his desires for the education of the youth of Zion.

As the Church and its auxiliary organization grew, so did the need for communication. In 1866 the Juvenile Instructor was edited and published privately by George Q. Cannon for the Sunday School. Later the magazine was published by the Deseret Sunday School Union. The magazine was called the Juvenile Instructor from 1866 to 1929 and the Instructor from 1930 to 1970.

THE JUVENILE INSTRUCTOR. of Latter-day Saints.

NO. 1   GREAT SALT LAKE CITY, JANUARY 1, 1866.   VOL. I.

Mary Isabella Horne (1818–1906), who was converted by Parley P. Pratt in Canada in July 1836, experienced many of the trials and tribulations of the Saints. She was driven from her home in Far West, Missouri, and later gave up her home in Nauvoo to cross the plains into the Salt Lake Valley.

Mary was an original member of the Relief Society which was organized in 1842. She was the stake Relief Society president in Salt Lake Stake for thirty years. In 1880 she was called to the Central Board of the Relief Society, which later became the General Board. Here she served until her death. Sister Horne was the mother of fifteen children.

Junius F. Wells (1854–1930) was born in Salt Lake City. Besides being involved with the organization of the YMMIA and being the editor of the Contributor *for thirteen years, he also served two missions for the Church—one from 1872–74 to Great Britain and one in 1875–76 to the eastern United States. In 1921 he was sustained as an assistant Church historian.*

Elder George Q. Cannon was selected as president of the fledgling general organization to unite the already existing local Sunday Schools and to promote the establishment of new ones throughout the Church. In 1872, the name Deseret Sunday School Union was formally adopted and "union meetings" of Sunday School workers were held the first Monday in each month. Year by year the union increased in numbers of youthful students. (There were no adult courses at that time.) Uniformity was reached in the methods of teaching and the mode of conducting the schools. Punctuality, memorization of gospel facts, and robust singing of hymns were highly prized in these early years of the Sunday School in the Church.

In the summer of 1874, the Deseret Sunday School Union organized and promoted a great jubilee throughout the territory. In Provo, on 15 June, five thousand persons, three-fourths children, assembled for a day of instruction from President Young and his counselors. There was also singing, recitations, and comic speeches, all by area children. The jubilee held in Salt Lake City netted twelve hundred dollars, which was used to purchase song books and other materials for Sunday Schools.

An organization for the young women of the Church came into being as part of the plans of President Young to protect the Saints against the gentile world at the coming of the railroad. On 28 November 1869, Brigham Young called his daughters together and addressed them on the responsibilities of the women of Zion and organized them into a "Retrenchment Society." The girls pledged themselves to avoid all extravagant practices, to retrench (cut back their excesses) in regard to dress, eating, and speech. The society was also to receive instruction in the principles of the gospel like that which the young men were receiving in their priesthood activities.

By the end of 1870 the Retrenchment Association was operating on a firm basis in nearly every ward in Salt Lake City. Eliza R. Snow and Mary Isabella Horne then went from settlement to settlement establishing groups that soon were participating in all kinds of practical economic and cultural activities. After the Young Men's Mutual Improvement Associations were organized, President Young expressed the desire that the name of the Retrenchment Association should be the Young Ladies Mutual Improvement Association (or YLMIA), but the name was not permanently changed until 1878.

Although a few literary and debating societies for young men had existed in Utah, Brigham Young expressed a desire in 1875 that a unified organization for young men be established in the Church. The prophet wanted the boys to develop intellectually and spiritually and to have needed recreation under proper supervision. Accordingly he called twenty-one-year-old Junius F. Wells, son of his counselor Daniel H. Wells, to establish Young Men's Mutual Improvement Associations, first in Salt Lake City and then throughout the territory. The first meeting was held in the Thirteenth Ward meetinghouse, where Henry A. Woolley, son of Bishop Edwin D. Woolley, was chosen as president. He selected B. Morris Young, son of President

Young, as first counselor and Heber J. Grant, son of Jedediah M. Grant, as the second counselor. Within the following months more than a hundred young men's organizations were functioning.

A general board for the YMMIA was formed in 1876 and directed a unified recreational program and course of study. The YMMIA had a powerful impact on the lives of thousands of the Church's young men. The association began its own periodical, the *Contributor*, in 1879. As the name suggests, several articles in each issue came from the young men themselves.

In 1877, Bishop John W. Hess of the Farmington Ward called the mothers in his ward together and discussed the responsibility of their children being trained properly. He felt that "the responsibility of guiding their young minds" rested "almost entirely upon the mothers."[6]

Aurelia Spencer Rogers, a devout, thoughtful Latter-day Saint, took the bishop's charge seriously. After much prayer, she heard a voice say "that there was an auxiliary organization for all ages except the children, where members learned to do things and use their time wisely." Bishop Hess, when approached by Sister Rogers, was excited by the idea of an organization for the children. He explained that he would carry Sister Rogers's thoughts and inspiration to the First Presidency to see what should be done. The First Presidency directed Eliza R. Snow to discuss the matter with Sister Rogers when she attended auxiliary conferences in Farmington.[7]

This mural depicting the first Primary was painted by Lynn Faussett and dedicated by Charles A. Callis of the Quorum of the Twelve on 24 November 1941. The mural is located in the Rock Chapel in Farmington, Utah.

During the summer of 1878, Aurelia spoke with Eliza R. Snow, who had been charged by President Brigham Young with the responsibility of overseeing the Church's women's auxiliaries and had come to Farmington for Relief Society and Young Women conferences. Sister Rogers "expressed a desire that something more could be effectuated for the cultivation and improvement of the children morally and spiritually."[8]

After returning to Salt Lake City, Eliza R. Snow met with President John Taylor and secured his blessing for a children's organization to be held one day a week other than Sunday. Sister Snow then wrote to Bishop Hess and indicated President Taylor's approval for Sister Rogers to organize and preside over a Primary in Farmington, Utah.

Aurelia Spencer Rogers (1834–1922). When Aurelia was twelve years old her mother, Catherine, died at Sugar Creek Camp in Iowa. A few months later at Winter Quarters where they had established a temporary home, her father, Orson, was called to serve as the European Mission president. Along with her five brothers and sisters, she crossed the plains two years later and settled in Salt Lake City, where her father joined them in September 1849.

At the age of seventeen Aurelia married Thomas Rogers and moved to Farmington, Utah. There she raised ten children and led an active life. She was the founder of the Primary, and she served on the General Board of the Primary Association from 1893 until her death. She was a delegate to the Woman's Suffrage Convention in Georgia and the National Council of Women in Washington, D.C., both in 1895.

Sister Rogers organized the first Primary. On 11 August 1878, she gathered the parents together to explain the importance of the new organization. On Sunday, 25 August, Sister Rogers commenced Primary work in her Farmington Ward. She organized the children into their age groups, with the oldest child in each group serving as a monitor. Sister Rogers then told the children to be obedient to their parents and teachers and to be kind to one another.

As the primary movement spread into the various settlements, Eliza R. Snow attended the organizational meetings and spoke to the young children in the area impressing upon them the vital part that each of them played in the great movement begun by the Prophet Joseph Smith. She displayed the Prophet's watch and then let each child hold it, subsequently admonishing them never to forget that they had held the Prophet's watch.[9]

MEETING EDUCATIONAL NEEDS

The conflict between the gentiles and the Saints in Utah contributed to a crisis in education that led to a reevaluation of the Church's role in educating its youth. In the early days of settlement the Saints had made every effort to establish elementary schools in each ward. These were private schools in which teachers' salaries were generally paid for by tuition. As the influx of gentiles increased in the state as a result of the railroad reaching Utah, conflicts developed between Church and government officials over the administration of the "district schools." The gentiles objected to the teaching of Mormon values in the schools and demanded that all schools become tax-supported and freed from Church domination.

Another aspect of this debate climaxed in the 1870s. Like schools in many other areas of the country, Utah schools used the Bible as a reader. Federal office holders insisted that neither the Bible nor any other religious subjects be taught in public schools. President Young emphatically stated that the Mormons would not remove the Bible from their schools, even if the rest of the Christian world did so. The Church position received support when other religious leaders in Utah also opposed the elimination of the Bible, which they considered the cornerstone of all character building, in the schools.

Recognizing that secular forces were at work in the nation, Church leaders rejuvenated the University of Deseret and considered establishing branches in other communities. The Dusenberry brothers, Warren and Wilson, operated a school in Provo which they organized in 1869. In 1870 Church and territorial educational officials recommended to them that the Provo school be made a branch of the university. In April the Dusenberry school was established as the Timpanogos Branch of the Deseret University, and students began receiving both secular and religious training.

Because of his devotion to education, Salt Lake Mayor Abraham O. Smoot was assigned by Brigham Young to move to Provo, where he served

When Brigham Young established the academies he required that each one have at least one woman on its board of trustees. Martha Jane Knowlton Coray (1821-81) was the first woman to serve on the board of trustees of the Brigham Young Academy, which is now called Brigham Young University.

Martha Coray was a mother of twelve children, assayer, herbalist, church worker, prolific writer, and school-teacher. Her scholarly interests included geology, geography, politics, chemistry, and biblical studies.

as stake president, community leader, and supporter of the Provo branch of the university. In spite of President Smoot's support, the school failed financially. Subsequently, in 1875, President Young appointed President Smoot and five other prominent Utah County men and one woman, Martha Jane Knowlton Coray—an author and teacher—as trustees of the school. A deed was drawn up and put into force. The new school was called the Brigham Young Academy. To ensure that there would be religious instruction at the school, "Brigham Young specifically stipulated that the 'Old and New Testaments, the Book of Mormon and the Book of Doctrine and Covenants shall be read and their doctrines inculcated in the Academy.' " A few weeks later Warren N. Dusenberry was appointed the school's first principal.[10]

In 1876 skilled German educator Karl G. Maeser took over the principalship of the Brigham Young Academy and began a stellar career in Church education, which later included serving as Superintendent of Church Schools. By the twentieth century this small institution had grown to become Brigham Young University.

In 1877 a second academy, Brigham Young College, was opened in Logan and continued until 1926. The buildings of the college were then turned over to the city of Logan. Plans also went forward to establish a third academy, called Salt Lake Stake Academy, in Salt Lake City. This academy did not begin actual operations until 1886. It went by several names and eventually came to be known as Latter-day Saints' College. The college officially closed in 1931 during the depression. Faculty members then organized a business college on their own, which was later acquired by the Church and named LDS Business College.

These three academies exemplified Brigham Young's educational ideals, emphasizing a broad, liberal arts education, high moral principles, and religious training from the scriptures. Teacher training (normal) schools were also established at these institutions. These academies were forerunners of over twenty academies in various communities that would characterize Church education during the rest of the century and the early part of the twentieth.

LOOKING OUTWARD

During the last decade of his life, Brigham Young continued to extend the borders of the Latter-day Saint commonwealth by colonization and to oversee further expansion in missionary work and immigration. By the end of his life, Mormon colonies had been established in Arizona, and missionary work extended into the Republic of Mexico.

Because missionaries continued to bring in converts who then immigrated to Utah Territory, Church leaders regularly sought new areas to colonize. As early as the 1850s, Church explorers had penetrated Arizona, but the aridity of the deserts, the lack of information on the territory south of the massive Colorado River, and the raiding Indians made it difficult to attempt any colonizing during the 1850s and 1860s. In 1870 the government

Karl G. Maeser (1828–1901), one of the leading educators of the Church, was born, reared, and educated in Germany. While teaching there he met the missionaries and was baptized in 1855 in the Elbe River by Franklin D. Richards. Following the baptism the two men engaged in a conversation through the gifts of tongues and interpretation of tongues.

Brother Maeser came to America in 1857, but did not arrive in Utah until 1860. He became the private tutor of Brigham Young's family in 1864. In 1888 he was called by the First Presidency to be the first superintendent of all Church schools.

pacified the Navajos, who had been raiding settlements in southern Utah since 1865. This led the way for a string of settlements to be established from Kanab, Utah, to Lee's Ferry on the Colorado River in Arizona as a springboard for further colonization.

As the winter of 1872–73 began, Brigham Young invited long-time friend of the Saints Thomas L. Kane and his wife, Elizabeth, to accompany him to St. George. During this trip President Young laid plans for a gathering place for the Saints in Sonora Valley, Mexico. Proposed settlements in Arizona were to form a connecting link between Utah and Mexico.

Establishing colonies in Arizona continued to be exceedingly difficult. In the early spring of 1873, President Young dispatched another set of explorers, the Arizona Exploring Company, which consisted of fourteen men, to visit the Little Colorado River area, the Rio Verde country, and the San Francisco mountain region, all south of the Colorado River. These explorers also became discouraged because the arid, broken countryside was difficult to traverse. Nevertheless, the determination of Brigham Young to colonize Arizona was not to be denied, and in 1874–75 he sent additional scouting parties to study the area.

Early in 1876 the First Presidency called two hundred "missionaries" to be part of four companies under Lot Smith, Jessie O. Ballenger, George Lake, and William C. Allen. By year's end four struggling colonies were established in the lower valley of the Little Colorado. For many years these citizens in Arizona struggled to harness the water of the river through dams. By 1880 other colonizing parties settled along Silver Creek, a major tributary of the Little Colorado, further upstream, and near Mesa, in central Arizona. One successful village was Snowflake, named after Elder Erastus Snow of the Quorum of the Twelve, who encouraged the colony, and their leader, William J. Flake.

Because Arizona settlements were struggling to survive, there was not an immediate push further south into Mexico. Brigham Young, however, desired that missionaries be sent to Mexico. In 1875 the prophet called Daniel Webster Jones, who had served in Mexico during the Mexican-American War, to head a mission and translate the Book of Mormon into Spanish. Elder Jones was soon unexpectedly joined in this project by Meliton G. Trejo, a native of Spain, who had recently joined the Church, stating that he had been inspired to seek out the Lord's people in the Rocky Mountains. By the end of the year Elders Jones and Trejo and four others departed for Mexico. They crossed the border in January 1876. Although they encountered much opposition from the various clergy, the missionaries held some public meetings and also mailed out five hundred copies of "Selected Passages of the Book of Mormon" to leaders of more than one hundred communities throughout Mexico.

The missionaries also located an area in the state of Chihuahua that they felt would be suitable for a future Church colonization. In the fall of 1876,

This map shows the route of the first Mormon exploration and proselyting party to northern Mexico in 1875–76. Eight colonies were established in Mexico during the nineteenth century.

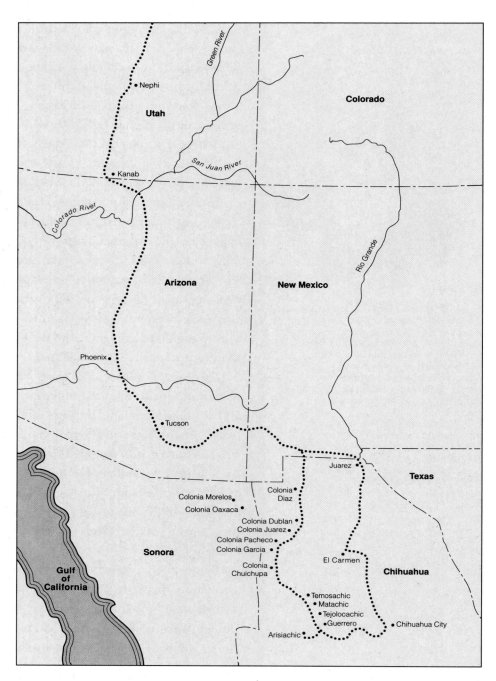

This map shows the route of the first Mormon exploration and proselyting party to northern Mexico in 1875–76. Eight colonies were established in Mexico during the nineteenth century.

Elder Trejo and Elder Helaman Pratt proselyted in the state of Sonora. In 1879, Elder Moses Thatcher of the Quorum of the Twelve headed a delegation of missionaries into Mexico City and succeeded in laying a solid foundation for the Church in that land.

Throughout the 1870s the greatest number of converts to the Church continued to come from the British Isles and Scandinavia. Each year this long-established pattern was followed: the Perpetual Emigrating Fund Company chartered transportation to gather the European Saints to Zion. In 1869 the Church began using steamships rather than sailing ships to cross the ocean. At about the same time, completion of the transcontinental railroad enabled the Saints to quickly cross the United States to Utah. Instead of approximately five months, the emigrating Saints now took less than three weeks to make the long trip. The cost of passage remained approximately the same.

In 1872–73, George A. Smith, first counselor in the First Presidency, led a delegation of Church leaders to Europe and Palestine to see what opportunities there might be for preaching the gospel and to rededicate the Holy Land preparatory to the return of the Jews. Orson Hyde had conducted a similar mission in 1840–41 but had been forced to go alone. Now the Brethren felt it was time to reassert the great interest the Church had in a regathering of the Jews to Palestine while the Saints were gathering to a new Zion in the West. The party visited several locations in Europe, and on 2 March 1873 both President Smith and Elder Lorenzo Snow of the Twelve offered prayers of dedication on the Mount of Olives.[11]

THE ST. GEORGE TEMPLE

Throughout the last years of his life, President Brigham Young persisted in working toward his desire to erect temples in the Saints' "mountain home." The Endowment House on Temple Square in Salt Lake City had served as a temporary holy place since 1855, and many Latter-day Saints had received their temple ordinances there, but still there was no permanent structure. Although Brigham Young had identified the site of the Salt Lake Temple in 1847, actual construction did not begin until 1853. The project was seriously delayed by the approach of the United States army and the move south in 1857–58. Progress was gradual on the construction of the Salt Lake Temple in the 1860s and 1870s. On Temple Square, over a hundred stonecutters were cutting blocks from granite, which was being delivered from Little Cottonwood Canyon.

The first temple to be completed in the West, however, was in St. George, which became a second headquarters of the Church as President Young spent most of his last several winters there. He dedicated the location for the sacred structure in November 1871. With the encouragement of the prophet, local Saints, helped by workmen called from the north, hastened the construction. Sandstone quarries were opened, and some timber was hauled from Pine Valley in southern Utah and the Kaibab Forest in northern Arizona, but most of the lumber came from Mount Trumbull in Arizona, eighty miles away. Many Saints donated food and clothing for the workers, and others donated one day in ten as "tithing labor."

The temple and its interior were constructed almost entirely from native materials, reflecting President Young's concern for the development of local industry. For example, the Provo Woolen Factory made carpet for the temple, and the fringe for the altars and pulpits was made from silk produced by the Relief Society organizations. The structure was completed in 1877, and individual rooms of the temple were dedicated in January. It was decided to

The St. George Temple holds a special place in Church history because it was here on 11 January 1877 that the first endowments for the dead were performed. Prior to this time, endowments for the living had been performed in the Endowment House in Salt Lake City, but President Young had explained that work for the dead required a temple. Therefore, in his advanced age and failing health he was most anxious for the Saints to complete the St. George Temple.

Brigham Young personally directed the work for his own kindred dead and the development of a "perfect form of the endowments," which was taught to the temple workers. By the end of March 1877, 3,208 endowments for the dead had been given. This view of the temple prior to completion shows the lower half of the sandstone being prepared for a whitewash coating, symbolizing purity and light. The main tower was later damaged by lightening and replaced with a taller one.

hold the annual general conference in St. George; as part of the proceedings, the whole of the temple was dedicated on 6 April 1877. Daniel H. Wells read the dedicatory prayer.

President Young was involved with other important aspects in connection with temple work in 1877. Together with other Church leaders, the prophet supervised the writing down of the endowment of the holy priesthood in correct form so that the work for the dead could be carried out more effectively. In a dramatic address given in the temple, President Young exclaimed, "What do you suppose the fathers would say if they could speak from the dead? Would they not say, 'We have lain here thousands of years, here in this prison house, waiting for this dispensation to come? Here we are, bound and fettered, in the association of those who are filthy?' What would they whisper in our ears? Why, if they had the power the very thunders of heaven would be in our ears."[12]

President Young called Wilford Woodruff of the Quorum of the Twelve Apostles to be the temple president in St. George and directed him to begin in earnest the ordinance work for the dead. It was in this temple that the first endowments for the dead were performed. Furthermore, that same year President Young dedicated sites for two more temples to be built in Utah—Logan and Manti.

Elder Woodruff went immediately to his task. "His whole soul was wrapped up in the temple work for both the living and the dead."[13] He conducted several people through the ordinances for deceased persons, many of whom were his own relatives. In Salt Lake City, in September 1877,

One of the precious documents of the Church is this record from the St. George Temple detailing the work for the deceased presidents of the United States and the signers of the Declaration of Independence, as well as for several other noted figures in history.

when he reported on his labors, Elder Woodruff said, "For the last eighteen hundred years, the people that have lived and passed away never heard the voice of an inspired man, never heard a Gospel sermon, until they entered the spirit-world. Somebody has got to redeem them, by performing such ordinances for them in the flesh as they cannot attend to themselves in the spirit." He declared, "The Lord has stirred up our minds, and many things have been revealed to us concerning the dead. . . . The dead will be after you, they will seek after you as they have after us in St. George. They called upon us, knowing that we held the keys and power to redeem them."

Wilford Woodruff then announced that the signers of the Declaration of Independence had appeared to him for two days and nights, inquiring why no ordinance work had been done for them, even though they had established the United States government and remained true to God. Elder Woodruff immediately was baptized by J.D.T. McAllister for these men and for fifty other prominent individuals, including John Wesley and Christopher Columbus. He then baptized Brother McAllister "for every President of the United States, except three [Martin Van Buren, James Buchanan, and Ulysses S. Grant]; and when their cause is just, somebody will do the work for them."[14] Under the administration of President Heber J. Grant the work for these three men was finally done.

PRIESTHOOD REORGANIZATION

Realizing that his advancing age was cutting back on his ability to labor and knowing that he would not live much longer, Brigham Young made a number of important priesthood leadership and organizational changes during his last years. In 1873 he resigned from several Church business posts, including Trustee-in-Trust, and appointed a dozen others under the direction of his first counselor, President George A. Smith, to handle these affairs. He also called five additional counselors—Lorenzo Snow, Brigham Young, Jr., Albert Carrington, John W. Young, and George Q. Cannon—to labor with him in the First Presidency.

Senority in the Quorum of the Twelve was also corrected by President Young. Wilford Woodruff, who had been sustained for a number of years ahead of John Taylor because he was older, was sustained after John Taylor at the October general conference of 1861. President Young determined that senority among the Twelve was based on date of ordination; thus, John Taylor who was ordained first was senior to Wilford Woodruff in the Quorum. Further refinement came at the April 1875 general conference when John Taylor and Wilford Woodruff were placed before Orson Hyde and Orson Pratt. Both Orson Hyde and Orson Pratt had been dropped from the Quorum of the Twelve at one time because of disobedience. During the time of their disaffection from the Church, John Taylor, Wilford Woodruff, and George Albert Smith (who was serving in the First Presidency in 1875 and thus not sustained as a member of the Twelve at the time) were ordained to the apostleship. When Orson Hyde and Orson Pratt were reinstated they were given their original place in the Quorum. President Young corrected this explaining that continuous service also determined senority.[15]

In 1876 President Young clarified the interrelationship of the stakes of Zion. He announced that the Salt Lake Stake held no primacy over the others as a "center stake," that all stakes were equal and autonomous in relation to each other. In 1877, over half of the Apostles had been serving as stake presidents. They were relieved of these responsibilities so they could reassume more general leadership roles.[16]

Brigham Young directed a major priesthood reorganization and reform throughout the stakes in 1877. New stake presidencies were called in nearly every stake, and the number of stakes was increased from thirteen to twenty.[17] To clarify leadership responsibilities on the local level, the "Circular of the First Presidency, July 11, 1877" and later messages instructed that all bishoprics were to be composed of three high priests, and that the bishops were to be the presiding high priests in their respective wards in addition to being responsible for taking care of temporal needs. Bishops were to begin handling temple donations, and their responsibility to preside over the Aaronic Priesthood quorums was reemphasized.

More young men were to be called into Aaronic Priesthood quorums and trained. Elders quorums were to be organized with ninety-six elders in each, even if it meant that the men came from several wards to form a quorum. Seventies were to meet only for missionary purposes. High priests were a stake quorum and were not to meet on a ward basis. Stake presidents were to hold quarterly conferences and monthly priesthood meetings. The priesthood leaders were to see that Sabbath meetings, Sunday Schools, YMMIA, and YWMIA were held in each ward.[18] The priesthood reorganization movement is a monument to Brigham Young. This action has been viewed as his last major achievement as the Lord's prophet on this earth.

LASTING CONTRIBUTIONS OF BRIGHAM YOUNG

Brigham Young kept in close contact with Church affairs to the end. As always, he met with a steady stream of visitors. On 23 August 1877, the seventy-seven-year-old prophet instructed a group of bishops gathered in the Council House. Following the meeting, he fell ill with violent cramps and vomiting. Despite the efforts of four physicians and the fasting and prayers of the Saints throughout the Church, he died on 29 August 1877. According to his daughter Zina, his final words were " 'Joseph! Joseph! Joseph!' and the divine look in his face seemed to indicate that he was communicating with his beloved friend, Joseph Smith, the Prophet."[19]

Brigham Young's body was placed in state in the Tabernacle, where an estimated twenty-five thousand people passed by. Speakers at his funeral included John Taylor, Wilford Woodruff, Daniel H. Wells, and George Q. Cannon. These words, offered by President Cannon, aptly summarize the contributions of this mighty prophet of the Lord:

"He has been the brain, the eye, the ear, the mouth and hand for the entire people of the Church of Jesus Christ of Latter Day Saints. From the greatest problems connected with the organization of this Church down to the smallest minutiae connected with the work, he has left upon it the impress of his great mind. From the organization of the Church and the construction of Temples, the building of Tabernacles; from the creation of a Provisional State government and a Territorial government, down to the small matter of directing the shape of these seats upon which we sit this day; upon all these things, as well as upon all the settlements of the Territory, the impress of his genius is apparent. Nothing was too small for his mind; nothing was too large."[20]

Brigham Young served longer as the President of The Church of Jesus Christ of Latter-day Saints than has any other President of the Church. His contributions were numerous and many-faceted. So much of what is cherished, revered, or even taken for granted in the Church today has roots in the contributions and leadership of President Young. Brigham Young felt he was only following the lead of his mentor and friend, the Prophet Joseph Smith. He exclaimed, "I feel like shouting hallelujah, all the time, when I think that I ever knew Joseph Smith, the Prophet whom the Lord raised up and ordained, and to whom He gave keys and power to build up the kingdom of God on earth and sustain it."[21] On another occasion he stated, "What I have received from the Lord, I have received by Joseph Smith: he was the instrument made use of. If I drop him, I must drop these principles:

The United States government invited each state to furnish statues of one or two of its most illustrious citizens to be displayed in the National Statuary Hall in Washington, D.C. In 1950 Utah donated this statue of Brigham Young sculpted by Mahonri M. Young. President George Albert Smith was present and offered a dedicatory prayer. It now resides in the nation's capitol.

they have not been revealed, declared, or explained by any other man since the days of the Apostles."[22]

One of Brigham Young's greatest legacies was his leadership in keeping the Church relatively self-sufficient from the gentile world—in recreation, business, government, and education. Historians recognize the massive kingdom of the Saints built up in the Rocky Mountains as a tribute to this man. This was achieved against great odds—the interference of federal troops and government officers, a desert climate and rough terrain, "outside" businessmen, the fashions of "Babylon," the coming of the transcontinental railroad, and the discovery of precious metals in Utah.

Brigham Young led his people in one cooperative venture after another. As a leading member of the Twelve in 1838–39, he organized the persecuted Saints in their exodus from Missouri and in their establishment of a refuge in Illinois. Later, Brigham led the Saints from Nauvoo, across the Iowa plains to Winter Quarters, and on to the Great Salt Lake. Between 1848 and 1852, he directed the gathering of thousands from the camps in Iowa to the emerging stronghold in the West. Then, directing his attention to the tens of thousands of new converts in Britain and Europe, he founded the Perpetual Emigrating Fund Company, which established the best system of regulated immigration in American history. He organized colonization parties to lay out agricultural villages in some three hundred and fifty locations in Utah and in parts of Idaho, Wyoming, Nevada, Arizona, and Colorado.

President Young taught the people the importance of cooperation in conquering the difficult frontier. That same spirit continues in abundance in the Church throughout the world today. He directed the disseminating of the gospel to many nations of the earth and the erecting of temples unto the Most High God. He was inspired to set up cooperative economic enterprises and institute the united order among his people. Brigham Young gave the Latter-day Saints all manner of doctrinal and practical instruction. His more than eight hundred recorded sermons ranged widely in diverse subjects. He spoke on the nature of God, the power of evil, the necessity of "working" out one's salvation, the principles of the priesthood, behavior in the family and marriage, women's fashions, and keeping one's earthly possessions clean and orderly. In the twentieth century John A. Widtsoe compiled some of Brigham Young's teachings into the classic volume, *Discourses of Brigham Young*. Brigham Young urged the secular and spiritual education of the members of the Church and left an educational legacy that continues to bless the Saints.

Brigham Young left an enduring stamp on all members of the Church since his time. He was both kind-hearted to the meek and humble and fierce with the haughty, bigoted, and proud. He cried when he saw the suffering of helpless people and took many downtrodden people under his wing. He was patient with violators of Church standards, was a good listener, had a sense of humor, and enjoyed theatrical performances and dances. As a political leader, he was astute. He was a person of strong determination, resolute and unwavering. His spirituality was exhibited by his prayers, temple work, and healing of the sick. Over his long and colorful career, he exercised all manner of leadership to do what the Lord had sent him to do.

ENDNOTES

1. "Woman's Exponent: A Utah Ladies' Journal," *Woman's Exponent*, 1 June 1872, p. 8.

2. "Home Affairs," *Woman's Exponent*, 1 Aug. 1877, pp. 36–37.

3. In Andrew Jenson, *Latter-day Saint Biographical Encyclopedia*, 4 vols. (Salt Lake City: Publishers Press, 1901–36), 1:705.

4. In Conference Report, Oct. 1899, p. 88.

5. *Jubilee History of Latter-day Saints Sunday Schools, 1849–1899* (Salt Lake City: Deseret Sunday School Union, 1900), p. 14.

6. Aurelia Spencer Rogers, *Life Sketches of Orson Spencer and Others, and History of Primary Work* (Salt Lake City: George Q. Cannon and Sons Co., 1898), pp. 206–7.

7. Clara Richards, *Insights of Early Farmington History* (Bountiful, Utah: Horizon Publishers, n.d.), p. 15.

8. *Eliza R. Snow, an Immortal* (Salt Lake City: Nicholas G. Morgan, Sr., Foundation, 1957), p. 40.

9. See Aurelia S. Rogers, *Life Sketches* (Salt Lake City: George Q. Cannon and Sons, 1898), pp. 205–17, 221–22; Farmington Ward, Davis Stake, Primary Minute Book, 1878–88, 11 Aug. 1878, pp. 1–4; 25 Aug. 1878, p. 5, LDS Historical Department, Salt Lake City; Eliza R. Snow Smith, "Sketch of My Life," microfilm of holograph, LDS Historical Department, Salt Lake City, pp. 38-39; Carol Cornwall Madsen and Susan Staker Oman, *Sisters and Little Saints* (Salt Lake City: Deseret Book Co., 1979), pp. 1–13.

10. Ernest L. Wilkinson and W. Cleon Skousen, *Brigham Young University: A School* of Destiny (Provo: Brigham Young University Press, 1976), pp. 48–49.

11. See B. H. Roberts, *A Comprehensive History of The Church of Jesus Christ of Latter-day Saints, Century One*, 6 vols. (Salt Lake City: The Church of Jesus Christ of Latter-day Saints, 1930), 5:474-75.

12. In *Journal of Discourses*, 18:304.

13. Matthias F. Cowley, *Wilford Woodruff: History of His Life and Labors* (Salt Lake City: Bookcraft, 1964), p. 495.

14. In *Journal of Discourses*, 19:228–29; see also Conference Report, Apr. 1898, pp. 89–90.

15. John Taylor, *Succession in the Priesthood*, Priesthood meeting, 7 Oct. 1881, LDS Historical Department, Salt Lake City, pp. 16–17; *Deseret News*, 14 Apr. 1875, p. 168.

16. See William G. Hartley, "The Priesthood Reorganization of 1877: Brigham Young's Last Achievement," *Brigham Young University Studies*, Fall 1979, p. 5.

17. See Hartley, "Priesthood Reorganization of 1877," pp. 3, 34–35.

18. See Hartley, "Priesthood Reorganization of 1877," pp. 20–21.

19. In Susa Young Gates with Leah D. Widtsoe, *The Life Story of Brigham Young* (New York: Macmillan Co., 1930), p. 362.

20. In Gates and Widtsoe, *Life Story of Brigham Young*, p. 364; spelling standardized.

21. In *Journal of Discourses*, 3:51; spelling standardized.

22. In *Journal of Discourses*, 6:279.

A DECADE OF PERSECUTION, 1877–87

THE CHURCH FACED one of its most difficult, as well as one of its most exciting, decades immediately following the death of Brigham Young. The United States government, with the encouragement and support of many reform groups, passed laws, saw that they were enforced, and launched a media campaign against the practice of plural marriage. In spite of intense persecution, the Church under John Taylor's able leadership continued to grow in numbers, expand its colonies, and unfold its programs.

EVENTS DURING APOSTOLIC PRESIDENCY

Following the death of President Young, the Quorum of the Twelve Apostles once more led the Church. In a meeting of this body on 4 September 1877, three important decisions were made. First, that the Twelve should take their place as the presiding quorum of the Church; second, that Elder John Taylor should be appointed as president of that quorum; and third, that Elders John W. Young and Daniel H. Wells were "to stand as counselors to the Twelve as they did to Brigham Young."[1]

A month later, on 6 October 1877, following a pattern that dated back to the dedication of the Kirtland Temple but had not been practiced for many years, Elder George Q. Cannon announced to those assembled at the general conference that the afternoon session would be a priesthood solemn assembly. Elder Cannon then gave directions for the seating of the various priesthood quorums. The solemn assembly that afternoon voted unanimously by quorums to accept President John Taylor as the President of the Quorum of the Twelve Apostles and "the Twelve Apostles as the presiding quorum and authority of the Church."[2]

Born in England and trained there as a cooper, or barrel maker, John Taylor went to Canada as a young man. There he met and married Leonora Cannon, who was ten years his senior. Although he was a devout Methodist, when he encountered the Church he began an earnest investigation and for a period of three weeks did not miss a single sermon delivered by Elder Parley P. Pratt. He wrote them down, compared them with the scriptures, prayed about the Church, and was converted. Ordained an Apostle in 1839, he served as editor of many of the Church's periodicals, almost lost his life with the Prophet Joseph in Carthage Jail, and served many Church missions. He was known as a fearless defender of the faith; his personal motto was

President John Taylor (1808–87)

"The kingdom of God or nothing." He responded faithfully to all of the calls given him during his almost thirty years in the Quorum of the Twelve and was thus prepared in every way to lead the Church through a tumultuous sea of persecution.

After Brigham Young's funeral, John Taylor and the Twelve turned to the difficult problem of sorting through President Young's estate to determine how much of it belonged to the Church and how much to his heirs. The Morrill Anti-Bigamy Act of 1862 had made it illegal for the Church to own property valued at more than fifty thousand dollars, other than that which was used exclusively for religious purposes. As a result of the law, properties that were acquired by the Church were placed in the hands of President Brigham Young. President Taylor continued the policy of secretly holding certain Church business properties in the names of individual trustees. President Taylor assigned George Q. Cannon, Albert Carrington, and Brigham Young, Jr. (the latter to represent the family's interests) as executors of the estate. Their task was made more difficult by the tremendous publicity and speculation that appeared in the nation's newspapers. Rumors were rampant that the estate was worth millions of dollars, raising the expectations of some of his large family.

After several months of dedicated work, the three executors determined that the estate was worth approximately $1,626,000. Over a million dollars of this actually belonged to the Church, however. When the monetary amount did not meet their high expectations, seven of Brigham's heirs filed a complaint in the third district court, and the case went into litigation, causing even more national publicity. Siding with the heirs, the clearly anti-Mormon judge, Jacob S. Boreman, ruled that the executors were in contempt of court. Elders Cannon, Young, and Carrington spent three weeks of August 1879 in the Utah Territorial Penitentiary before the Territorial Supreme Court reversed Judge Boreman's decision. Church leaders then agreed to give the heirs an additional $75,000 to settle the case.

In the April 1880 general conference, the Church celebrated its fiftieth anniversary, and President Taylor, drawing from the Old Testament, declared the year one of jubilee. He announced on behalf of the Church that he was striking $802,000 (half the total deficit) from the amount still owed by certain Saints to the Perpetual Emigrating Fund Company. Then he asked that cattle and sheep be given to the poor and encouraged the Relief Society to lend wheat, which they had stored, without interest to less fortunate farmers. He called on everyone to give a helping hand to the destitute so that poverty in the territory might be eliminated.[3]

During the years of the apostolic presidency, the Twelve continued to expand the kingdom's perimeters. Over one hundred new settlements were founded in such areas as Star Valley in western Wyoming, Castle Valley in eastern Utah, the rugged San Juan River country in southeastern Utah, the Virgin River territory in southern Nevada, and more in northern Arizona.

In October 1880, over three years after the death of President Young, a new First Presidency was created and sustained by the membership of the Church. Once again priesthood holders were asked to sit in a solemn assembly and vote by quorums. When the names of John Taylor, George Q. Cannon, and Joseph F. Smith were presented to the Saints, there was unanimous approval. Elders Cannon and Smith were men of great capabilities who served as counselors to President Taylor and to two subsequent presidents as well.

THE PRACTICE OF PLURAL MARRIAGE

A large part of the persecution experienced by the Latter-day Saints centered around the practice of plural marriage, which was instituted under the direction of the Prophet Joseph Smith. The law of plural marriage was revealed to the Prophet as early as 1831, but he mentioned it only to a few trusted friends. Under strict commandment from God to obey the law, the Prophet began in 1841 to instruct leading priesthood brethren of the Church concerning plural marriage and their responsibility to live the law. The Prophet Joseph Smith dictated the revelation to William Clayton in 1843, when it was first written. Nine years passed, however, before the revelation was read in general conference and published.[4]

On 28–29 August 1852 a special conference was held in the Old Tabernacle on Temple Square in Salt Lake City. On the first day of the conference over one hundred missionaries were called to labor throughout the United States, Australia, India, China, and the islands of the sea. By holding the conference in August the missionaries were able to get an early start in crossing the plains before the cold weather set in.

On the second day of the conference, under the direction of President Brigham Young, Orson Pratt made the public announcement that the Church was practicing plural marriage under commandment of God. Speaking of the United States, he declared that "the constitution gives the privilege to all the inhabitants of this country, of the free exercise of their religious notions, and the freedom of their faith, and the practice of it. Then, if it can be proven to a demonstration, that the Latter-day Saints have actually embraced, as a part and portion of their religion, the doctrine of a plurality of wives, it is constitutional. And should there ever be laws enacted by this government to restrict them from the free exercise of this part of their religion, such laws must be unconstitutional."[5]

Brother Pratt then delivered a lengthy discourse from a scriptural standpoint concerning plural marriage. He explained that marriage was ordained of God as the channel for spirits to acquire mortal bodies and that through plural marriage worthy priesthood holders could raise up a numerous righteous posterity unto the Lord. Brigham Young then spoke giving a brief history concerning the revelation on celestial marriage. Thomas Bullock, a clerk in the historian's office, then read the revelation to the congregation for their sustaining vote.

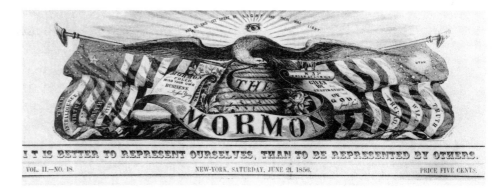

Expecting a great public outcry and a flood of negative publicity, Church leaders promptly sent four of its most faithful and articulate leaders to key population centers to launch newspapers that would both explain and justify "celestial marriage" and other restored gospel principles. Orson Pratt edited the *Seer* in the nation's capital; John Taylor, the *Mormon* in New York City; Erastus Snow, the *Saint Louis Luminary* in St. Louis; and George Q. Cannon, the *Western Standard* in San Francisco. In each of these publications the righteous motives of the Saints in entering plural marriage were portrayed, which contrasted sharply with the view put forth in the nation's newspapers, pulp magazines, and cheap novels. Soon, in spite of the articles published by the Church's best writers and the talks given by its most articulate speakers, groups formed and began to pressure the government to pass laws that would completely eradicate such a marriage system.

ANTI-POLYGAMY CRUSADE

In spite of all the attempts by the Latter-day Saints to convince their fellow citizens that the practice of plural marriage was their religious and moral right, the nation united against the Church. Missionaries in England and on the continent of Europe were often mobbed, and some elders in America lost their lives. Many people believed polygamy was immoral, barbaric, and deplorable. A mass of anti-polygamy literature claiming to expose the true story of the degradation of women under polygamy was written, primarily by people who never came to Utah or who were only superficial observers.

In 1862, President Lincoln signed into law the anti-bigamy bill known as the Morrill Law, but because of the Civil War its enforcement was overlooked. This legislation struck at both polygamy and Church power by prohibiting plural marriage in the territories, disincorporating the Church, and restricting the Church's ownership of property to fifty thousand dollars. The Saints, believing that the law unconstitutionally deprived them of their First Amendment right to freely practice their religion, chose to ignore this law at this time until it was constitutionally defined.

In the ensuing years, several bills aimed at strengthening the anti-bigamy law failed to pass the United States Congress. These included the Wade,

Courtesy of Daughters of Utah Pioneers, Salt Lake City

Dr. Ellis R. Shipp (1847–1939) was born in Iowa and went to Utah in 1853 with her parents.

Dr. Ellis Shipp, herself a plural wife, believed that without polygamy she would never have had the time nor been able to leave her children in the careful care of loved sister-wives to pursue her medical degree. She graduated from medical school in Philadelphia in 1878, becoming the second Utah woman doctor. She also did graduate work at the University of Michigan Medical School.

While mothering her own ten children, Dr. Shipp delivered over six thousand babies in her sixty years of practice. Sister Shipp served as a member of the general board of the Relief Society from 1898 to 1907.

Cragin, and Cullom bills which had their origin in the territory of Utah and were initiated by men who were bitterly opposed to the Church. The Wade Bill initiated in 1866 would have destroyed local government if it had passed. Three years later the Cragin Bill was proposed, but within a few days it was substituted by the Cullom Bill, which was more radical than the Wade or Cragin bills. Members of the Church rose en masse to work for the defeat of the bill. Women of the Church held mass meetings throughout the territory in January 1870 in opposition to the bill.

"While they opposed all the features of the anti-'Mormon' legislation, their action was principally in protest against the measures, and the remarks of would-be reformers, in which the women of the Church were spoken of as being 'down-trodden' and 'degraded' by their husband-oppressors."[6] Opposition by Latter-day Saint women was a great surprise to politicians and suffragettes who saw them as the epitome of suffering and bondage. Newspapers in the East also opposed the bill because of its military features. The president of the United States would have power to send an army to Utah to execute the provisions of the bill. The *New York World* said: "Its execution will assuredly be followed by war."[7] The Cullom Bill was defeated.

In June 1874, however, the Poland Law was passed. This act dismantled Utah's judicial system by giving the United States district courts (controlled by non-Mormon federal appointees) exclusive civil and criminal jurisdiction. Individuals could now be brought to trial for breaking the Morrill Law. Under the Poland Act, jury lists were to be drawn by the district court clerk (a non-Mormon) and the probate judge (a Mormon) in order to give equal representation of members and nonmembers of the Church on juries. Immediately the United States attorney tried to bring leading Church officials to trial but experienced problems. Many of the Brethren had married before the law was passed in 1862 and could not be tried *ex post facto*. Furthermore, the wives could not be required to testify against their husbands, and the records for plural marriage that were kept privately in the Endowment House were not public record.

Church leaders became anxious to have a "test case" brought before the Supreme Court to determine the constitutionality of the anti-bigamy law. So when the U.S. attorney, William Carey, promised to stop his attempts to indict General Authorities during the test case, the First Presidency chose thirty-two-year-old George Reynolds, a secretary in the office of the President, who had recently married a second wife, to stand in for the Church in the courts. Reynolds provided the attorney numerous witnesses who could testify of his being married to two wives. When Carey did not keep his promise and arrested President George Q. Cannon, Church leaders decided that they would no longer cooperate with him.

In 1875 Reynolds was finally convicted and sentenced to two years hard labor in prison and a fine of five hundred dollars (later changed by the United States Supreme Court to imprisonment only). In 1876 the Utah

George Reynolds (1842–1909) was converted to the gospel as a young boy but was unable to be baptized for several years because of the opposition of his parents. He was finally baptized on 4 May 1856 at the age of fourteen.

George held many Church positions in England before coming to America in 1865. Soon thereafter he became secretary to the First Presidency, a calling he fulfilled until the end of his life. He was also called as a President of the First Quorum of the Seventy in 1890. His famous concordance of the Book of Mormon⁹ required twenty-one years of labor to produce.

Territorial Supreme Court upheld the sentence. In 1878 his appeal reached the United States Supreme Court, and in January 1879 that body ruled the anti-polygamy legislation constitutional and upheld Reynold's sentence. George Reynolds was released from prison in January 1881, having served eighteen months of his original sentence. During his incarceration he taught reading, writing, arithmetic, grammar, and geography to other prisoners. Brother Reynolds also worked on a book which he completed and later published. It was called *A Complete Concordance of the Book of Mormon*. At the time of his release he had completed twenty-five thousand entries of this concordance.[8]

In 1882 Congress passed the Edmunds Act, which defined "unlawful cohabitation" as supporting and caring for more than one woman. Proof of a second marriage was no longer needed. The law also disenfranchised polygamists and declared them ineligible for public office. Not only those who practiced but also those who believed in plural marriage were disqualified from jury service. All registration and election officers in Utah Territory were dismissed, and a board of five commissioners was appointed by the president of the United States to administer elections.

Shortly after the passage of the Edmunds Act, the April 1882 general conference convened. As the Saints gathered on the second day, the gusting wind pelted them with sleet. Referring to both the weather and the recent legislation, President Taylor mentioned the nation's bitter prejudice against the Saints and "warned them that a storm was coming, and that it would break in its fury upon them. 'Let us treat it,' said he, half humorously, 'the same as we did this morning in coming through the snow-storm—put up our coat collars (suiting the action to the word) and wait till the storm subsides. After the storm comes sunshine. While the storm lasts it is useless to reason with the world; when it subsides we can talk to them.' " On the next day he said that the Saints would "contend inch by inch" for their liberties and rights as American citizens.[10]

Many Latter-day Saint men, and even some women, had to go "underground" to avoid arrest. Thus began one of the most difficult times in Latter-day Saint history. To avoid incarceration, codes were made up to warn polygamist fathers of the approach of federal officers. St. George's stake president, J.D.T. McAllister, had the code name of *Dan*; Henry F. Eyring's was *Look*. Communities had code names also. St. George was *White*, Beaver was *Black*, and Toquerville was *Cloudy*. United States marshals were coded *Ring*, and Judge Boreman was *Herod*. The warnings could be sent by telegraph and would have no meaning if confiscated by federal authorities.

At times officials became obsessed in their harassment of the Latter-day Saints. United States Marshal Fred T. Dubois, in an attempt to use anti-Mormonism for his own political ends in Idaho, crawled into hidden holes under houses, commandeered trains to make trips to Mormon centers, slipped into Latter-day Saint towns, and raided homes during the night in an attempt to capture polygamous men. In order to avoid arrest, the bishop of the Oxford, Idaho, ward, left town at "night stowed away in a box marked pork, Ogden freight." He remained twenty-four hours in the box before being set free by a Brother Nesbitt. Then in the night he made his way to a brother-in-law's home in Ogden, Utah, where he remained safe.

James Morgan went deep into the hills with his fifth wife, Anna, where he cut logs, which his boys hauled to town.

Hyrum Poole was a young man who lived in Menan, Idaho. "In the winter of 1883 he was having a late supper with his brother, William. . . . As they were eating there was a loud knock on the door, and as Hyrum opened it a gun barrel was rammed through and the intruder shouted, 'Let us in or we'll break the door down.' Hyrum grabbed the gun barrel and threw his weight against the door as his brother and two hired men came to his assistance.

"Finally the persons forcing admittance condescended to explain that they were deputies with a warrant to search the premises for N. A. Stevens. They were permitted to enter at once, but Hyrum Poole reprimanded them for attempting to force their way in 'like a band of cutthroats.' Whereupon the leader, one William Hobson, an Eagle Rock saloonkeeper, partly intoxicated at the time, swiped him across the face with his rifle and said, 'Consider yourselves under arrest for resisting an officer.'

"The search proved futile, and as the men withdrew they ordered Poole to come along. As he stepped outside into the dark, Hobson mashed him over the head with the end of his rifle, which cut him badly and knocked him down." Poole and another prisoner "were taken to Blackfoot and thrown in jail, where they remained two days without food, medical attention, a hearing, or bonds."[11]

Some Latter-day Saints were convicted and sent as far east as Detroit, where they served out their sentences in loneliness and fear.

Most of the Saints who were convicted were sent to Utah's territorial penitentiary, where they were model prisoners. They were often found studying the gospel, writing books, or teaching the other prisoners reading, writing, and other neglected skills. When someone was released, community

During the anti-polygamy crusade, Latter-day Saints from the intermountain west were arrested, tried, and, if convicted, they were often given prison sentences. One little-known aspect of the crusade is that many Idaho Mormons convicted of "unlawful cohabitation" served their sentences in the Detroit House of Corrections. This is a picture of the Detroit, Michigan, prison about the time of their incarceration.

The United States Congress, on 3 March 1853, approved an appropriation for a penitentiary in Utah. Several months later a prison site was selected by Almon W. Babbitt, who was serving as territorial secretary of Utah. The prison, located in the Salt Lake City area, was completed in 1854 and enclosed an area of about seven acres. The exterior walls were made of adobe and were twelve feet high and four feet thick.

Courtesy of Utah State Historical Society

parties were held and tributes given to those who had preferred the laws of God to those of man. Perhaps it was more difficult for the families left behind. Some suffered from poverty, hunger, and sickness, without a husband and father to help. Thus, the crusade against the Church disrupted economic, social, ecclesiastical, and family life, and as the late 1880s drew near, darker clouds loomed on the horizon.

THE KINGDOM MOVES FORWARD

Despite the "storm" of the anti-polygamy crusade, President Taylor guided the Church in the early 1880s through continuing progress. He regularly toured the stakes of Zion, setting them in order, teaching, counseling, and encouraging the Saints with great energy. He urged the people to upgrade their behavior in all the relations of life—as husbands, wives, parents, children, neighbors, and citizens—and to observe unity, honor, integrity, honesty, and purity in thought and act.

In 1881, President Taylor published a pamphlet he had written entitled *Items on Priesthood*; it instructed the various priesthood holders, especially young men then being ordained into the Aaronic Priesthood, in their respective offices. The following year he issued his book *Mediation and Atonement*, bringing together a collection of scriptural passages with commentary, illustrating the necessity and the glory and power of the Savior's atonement for the sins of the world.

His instructions to the Saints were founded upon the revelations he received. Following a pattern set by the Prophet Joseph Smith, President Taylor often wrote and published the inspiration given to him. One such revelation was dictated on 13 October 1882, just a few days after general conference. For two years the Quorum of the Twelve Apostles had only ten members, and the vacancies had weighed heavily on the prophet's mind. The revelation called George Teasdale and Heber J. Grant to the apostleship and physician Seymour B. Young to the First Council of the Seventy. It also called for increasing missionary work among various Indian tribes and for an increase in righteousness among priesthood bearers and all the Saints.[12]

An experience of Elder Heber J. Grant a few months later gives some

Wood carving and autograph book of James Paxton. During this period many Latter-day Saints were imprisoned for their religious beliefs. While in prison they carved wooden objects, compiled autograph books, and kept journals of their thoughts and actions.

background to this revelation. Heber reported that for the first few months of his apostleship he felt that he was not qualified to be a special witness of the Savior. While traveling on the Navajo reservation in northern Arizona in February 1883, helping establish the Church among the Indians, Elder Grant told his companions he wanted some time by himself and took a different route to their destination. He later recounted what happened as he rode:

"I seemed to see, and I seemed to hear, what to me is one of the most real things in all my life, I seemed to see a Council in heaven. I seemed to hear the words that were spoken. . . . The First Presidency and the Council of the Twelve Apostles had not been able to agree on two men to fill the vacancies in the Quorum of the Twelve. . . . In this Council the Savior was present, my father [Jedediah M. Grant] was there, and the Prophet Joseph Smith was there. They discussed the question that a mistake had been made in not filling those two vacancies and that in all probability it would be another six months before the Quorum would be completed, and they discussed as to whom they wanted to occupy those positions, and decided that the way to remedy the mistake that had been made in not filling these vacancies was to send a revelation. It was given to me that the Prophet Joseph Smith and my father mentioned me and requested that I be called to that position. I sat there and wept for joy. . . .

". . . From that day I have never been bothered, night or day, with the idea that I was not worthy to stand as an Apostle."[13]

On 17 May 1884, President Taylor dedicated the Logan Temple. It was the fourth temple in the Church and the second to be completed in Utah. The evening before, President Taylor asked the Lord if the building was acceptable. His prayer was answered and a revelation given to him, in which the Lord told him that "in these houses which have been built unto me, and which shall be built, I will reveal the abundance of those things pertaining to the past, the present, and the future, to the life that now is, and the life that is to come, pertaining to law, order, rule, dominion and government, to things affecting this nation and other nations; the laws of the heavenly bodies in their times and seasons, and the principles or laws by which they are governed."[14] The Saints the next day witnessed a rich outpouring of the Spirit at the temple's dedication.

During President Taylor's administration several Church publications were republished or published for the first time. Of greatest importance were the Book of Mormon and the Doctrine and Covenants, which were reissued in 1879 with extensive cross-references and explanatory notes. The Pearl of Great Price, published in 1878, had previously been a missionary tract. The work on these publications was performed by Elder Orson Pratt. These new editions of the Doctrine and Covenants and the Pearl of Great Price were formally canonized in the October 1880 general conference. Beginning in 1879, Junius F. Wells produced the first edition of the monthly periodical the *Contributor*, which became the official publication of the Mutual

A native of Switzerland, Jacob Spori (1847–1903) became the first Church missionary in Palestine.

Upon migrating to Utah he devoted himself to education. Later locating in Rexburg, Idaho, he was appointed principal of the new Bannock Stake Academy, which eventually became Ricks College. He made great sacrifices to achieve this success. At one point he even went to work at the railroad to pay the salaries of two other teachers so he could keep the school operating.

John Morgan (1842–94) fought as a Union soldier in the Civil War and then moved to Utah in 1866 where he was an educator. He was converted to the gospel and baptized on 26 November 1867. Brother Morgan was then called to serve a mission to the southern states between 1875 and 1877. In 1878 he returned to preside over that mission. He was called as a member of the First Quorum of the Seventy in 1884, and he served in this capacity until his death.

Joseph Standing (1854–79) is one of the martyrs of the Church. Between 1875 and 1876 he fulfilled a mission to the southern states. He returned for a second mission there in 1878, and because of his kind, mild, and wise manner, President John Morgan assigned him to the hostile district of Georgia. Elder Rudger Clawson joined him early in 1879.

News of Joseph Standing's murder in Georgia greatly affected the Church in Utah, and nearly ten thousand people attended his funeral in the Salt Lake Tabernacle.

Improvement Association. Andrew Jenson, assistant Church historian, published the *Historical Record*, which contained numerous accounts and chronologies that have become invaluable to the study and writing of Church history. The Church also continued to emphasize economic unity. Zion's Central Board of Trade was organized to replace united orders. Boards of trade were created in each stake to function under the coordination of the central organization. They promoted business activities, sought new markets, disseminated information to farmers and manufacturers, prevented competition harmful to home industry, and sometimes regulated wages and prices for community benefit.

MISSIONARY WORK CONTINUES

Missionary work continued to expand. Elder Moses Thatcher dedicated Mexico for the preaching of the gospel in 1881, though there had been some successful efforts in that land since 1876. Work also began among the Maori people in New Zealand in 1881. In 1884 Jacob Spori opened the Turkish Mission, which was later extended to include Palestine. Led by a vision he had received in Constantinople, Elder Spori found converts among the German-speaking people in Haifa who had come to the Holy Land to await the second coming of Christ. Missionary work also continued successfully in the British Isles, Scandinavia, Switzerland, Holland, and Germany.

In the United States missionary work was also growing. For example, John Morgan, remembering a dream he had even before he joined the Church, was led to a small community in Georgia, where he taught the gospel and baptized almost everyone who lived there. Missionary work, however, was not without dangers, especially in the American south. As the Church continued to grow in the South, opposition increased rapidly.

On 21 July 1879, Elders Joseph Standing and Rudger Clawson were planning to leave for a conference of the Church in Rome, Georgia. While traveling in the area of Varnell's Station, they were surrounded by a dozen armed ruffians who threatened them and led them into a forest. While three of the men rode off to search for a more secluded area, the elders were verbally abused. When the three returned, Elder Standing, who had somehow gotten a gun, suddenly stood, aimed it at them, and yelled, "Surrender!" Quickly a man seated next to him fired at the young elder, hitting him in the face. Faced with a dozen rifles, Elder Clawson folded his arms and calmly awaited death. The rifles were lowered, and he was allowed to go for help for his companion. Returning with others Elder Clawson found his companion dead, having been shot several times in the head and neck at point-blank range. Elder Standing's body, attended by Elder Clawson, was taken to Salt Lake City where he was reverently honored by the Saints as yet another martyr to the divine cause they shared.[15]

At the time of the murder, Joseph Standing had served sixteen months of a second mission to the southern states and was expecting his release at any

B. H. Roberts (1857–1933) here posed for the camera in the disguise he used to enable him to retrieve the bodies of Elders Gibbs and Berry. Brother Roberts spent his childhood in England. When he came to America, he walked nearly all the way across the plains to Utah.

To his formal education at the University of Deseret he added considerable self education and became one of the most articulate and eloquent orators and writers in the Church's history. He edited and published the seven-volume History of the Church *(History of Joseph Smith) and later published a six-volume history of the first century of the Church, known as* A Comprehensive History of the Church.

He became a member of the First Quorum of the Seventy in 1888 at the age of thirty-one. He was elected to the United States House of Representatives in 1898 but was not allowed to take his seat because of controversy over his involvement in polygamy.

Beyond the age of sixty he was a chaplain in America and France for Utah soldiers serving in World War I during 1917–18.

time. President John Morgan and Elder Clawson later returned to Georgia to testify against the murderers, who were nevertheless acquitted.

Five years later, on 10 August 1884, the Cane Creek Massacre took place. This incident was directly attributable to the wide dissemination, following its publication by the *Salt Lake Tribune,* of the "Bishop West address," a spurious sermon purportedly delivered by a Mormon bishop in Juab, Utah, in March 1884. Although it was quickly ascertained that no Bishop West existed in Juab and that the vile sermon against the gentiles was concocted, nevertheless the supposed address was circulated widely in the eastern and southern United States. A copy found its way to Lewis County, Tennessee, and its contents were spread among anti-Mormon elements.

Mobsters approached a Sabbath meeting of the Saints at the residence of James Condor and began shooting. Two missionaries—John H. Gibbs and William S. Berry—two members of the Condor family, and the leader of the mob were killed. The mission president was temporarily absent, and a young B. H. Roberts, who had been left in charge of the mission, disguised himself and risked his life to go to Cane Creek, exhume the bodies of the elders, and return them to Utah for burial.[16] He later bore witness that he was given divine help. As in the case of Elder Standing, the murderers were tried and acquitted.

AGAIN THE STORM INCREASED

Before the end of the 1880s every community of the Saints was increasingly subject to harassment by deputy marshals. More than a thousand men, and even a few women, went to prison on charges of polygamy. President Taylor went into hiding, as did Wilford Woodruff and other Church officials.

By the end of 1885 because of persecution, hundreds of colonists, chiefly from Arizona and New Mexico, poured into hastily established settlements in Mexico. Elder George Teasdale presided over these exiled Saints. In 1886 Charles Ora Card, president of the Cache Stake in northern Utah, was asked to find a place of asylum in Canada. He succeeded in securing land in what is now known as the Cardston, Alberta, area, and Mormon settlements were soon established in that region.

As the judicial crusade against polygamy continued, a new way of life was created for many Saints. Otherwise law-abiding men escaped to the underground and frequently moved from place to place to avoid the marshals who were hunting them. Fleeing "cohabs" (as they were called) went into canyons, barns, fields, and cellars to avoid their pursuers. Federal officers countered by disguising themselves as peddlers or census takers in order to gain entry into homes. Some marshals raided houses, invading privacy and even mistreating wives and children to catch their prey. Ten- and twenty-dollar bounties were offered for every Latter-day Saint captured, and much larger amounts were available if a General Authority was apprehended. One tragedy occurred on 16 December 1886.

Edward M. Dalton of Parowan was shot and killed by Deputy Marshal William Thompson, Jr., as Dalton was riding on horseback down a street in Parowan. Dalton had been indicted in 1885 for unlawful cohabitation and had evaded trial by going to Arizona. He had returned to Parowan when the incident took place.[17]

In 1886, President John Taylor, still in hiding, moved into the comfortable farm home of Thomas F. Rouche, mayor of Kaysville, Utah. There he continued his practice of communicating with the Saints by means of general epistles. Messages were conveyed between him and other Church leaders by horse and buggy under guard and cover of darkness. During this period President Taylor's health continued to deteriorate, and President George Q. Cannon handled much of the Church's business, even though he was also in hiding. Second Counselor Joseph F. Smith was so sought after that he went on a mission to Hawaii.

Because of the severe nature of the anti-polygamy raids, President John Taylor went "underground" on 1 February 1885 and moved about periodically. On 22 November 1886 he was moved to the Thomas F. Rouche home in Kaysville, Utah. Surrounded by shade trees and with a pleasant view to the east across a mile of farm land to the village of Kaysville, and the mountains behind it, the Rouche home was the last dwelling of John Taylor. Diarists attending him noted that he was ill intermittently from April to June of 1887.

Meanwhile, his counselor George Q. Cannon secretly traveled between Kaysville and Salt Lake City to conduct much of the Church's business. Late in June, President Taylor began to fail. He ate little, lapsed into unconsciousness for periods of time, and on the evening of 25 July he quietly passed away.

On 25 July 1887, President Taylor died while still in exile. Marshals were present at his funeral, but no arrests were made. Wilford Woodruff, who now presided over the Church, was in hiding. It was a time that tested the Saints' loyalty to their God, who had commanded them to live plural marriage amidst a nation who opposed and legislated against it.

With the passage of the Edmunds-Tucker Act in March 1887, wives were required to testify against their husbands, and all marriages were to be publicly recorded. The law also provided that county probate judges be appointed by the president of the United States. Women's suffrage was abolished in Utah, the Perpetual Emigrating Fund was dissolved, as was the Nauvoo Legion, and a public education system was established. The Church was disincorporated, and authority was given to the United States attorney general to escheat (turn back to the United States) all Church property and holdings valued over fifty thousand dollars. Federally sponsored persecution of the Church thus continued into the new administration of President Wilford Woodruff.

The Gardo house was the official Salt Lake residence of President John Taylor. Upon his death, his body was returned there and prepared for burial. On 29 July 1887 his body was taken to the Tabernacle to lie in state.

Construction on the Gardo house began under the direction of Brigham Young and was completed during John Taylor's administration. It was dedicated by Franklin D. Richards on 22 February 1883. Following the death of John Taylor, the Gardo house was used by Wilford Woodruff as a Church office. The Gardo house was purchased from the Church by the Federal Reserve Bank of San Francisco, and they had it razed in November 1921.

ENDNOTES

1. Wilford Woodruff Journals, 4 Sept. 1877, LDS Historical Department, Salt Lake City; spelling standardized.

2. "General Conference," *Deseret News Semi-Weekly*, 9 Oct. 1877, p. 2.

3. See B. H. Roberts, *The Life of John Taylor* (Salt Lake City: Bookcraft, 1963), pp. 334–37.

4. See Journal History of The Church of Jesus Christ of Latter-day Saints, 4 Mar. 1883, Historical Department, Salt Lake City, pp. 8–10; *Territorial Enquirer*, 6 Mar. 1883; "Celestial Marriage: How and When the Revelation Was Given," *Deseret Evening News*, 20 May 1886, p. 2.

5. *Millennial Star*, Supplement, 1853, p. 18.

6. Joseph Fielding Smith, *Essentials in Church History*, Classics in Mormon Literature series (Salt Lake City: Deseret Book Co., 1979), p. 444.

7. B. H. Roberts, *A Comprehensive History of The Church of Jesus Christ of Latter-day Saints, Century One*, 6 vols. (Salt Lake City: The Church of Jesus Christ of Latter-day Saints, 1930), 5:314.

8. See Bruce A. Van Orden, "George Reynolds: Secretary, Sacrificial Lamb, and Seventy," Ph.D. diss., Brigham Young University, 1986, pp. 53, 57–62, 71, 76–77, 80–86, 103, 108.

9. George Reynolds, *A Complete Concordance of the Book of Mormon*, 2 vols. (Salt Lake City, Deseret Book Co., 1957).

10. Roberts, *Life of John Taylor*, pp. 360, 362.

11. M. D. Beal, *A History of Southeastern Idaho* (Caldwell, Idaho: Caxton Printers, 1942), pp. 86, 312–13.

12. See Roberts, *Life of John Taylor*, pp. 349–51.

13. In Conference Report, 4 Apr. 1941, pp. 4–5.

14. Paul Thomas Smith, "John Taylor," in Leonard J. Arrington, ed., *The Presidents of the Church* (Salt Lake City: Deseret Book Co., 1986), pp. 110–11.

15. See "The Murder of Joseph Standing," *Deseret News*, 6 Aug. 1879, pp. 428–29; "The Funeral Services of Elder Joseph Standing," *Deseret News*, 6 Aug. 1879, p. 429.

16. See B. H. Roberts, *A Comprehensive History of The Church of Jesus Christ of Latter-day Saints, Century One*, 6 vols. (Salt Lake City: The Church of Jesus Christ of Latter-day Saints, 1930), 6:86–93; "Death of James Condor," *Improvement Era*, Oct. 1911, pp. 1107–8.

17. See B. H. Roberts, *A Comprehensive History of The Church of Jesus Christ of Latter-day Saints, Century One*, 6 vols. (Salt Lake City: The Church of Jesus Christ of Latter-day Saints, 1930), 6:116–21; "Homicide at Parowan," *Deseret News*, 22 Dec. 1886, p. 777.

AN ERA OF RECONCILIATION

Wilford Woodruff (1807–98)

THE DECADE BEFORE the death of President John Taylor in 1887 was turbulent and marked with persecution. The following decade became an era of reconciliation. Wilford Woodruff became President of the Church, the anti-polygamy crusade ended, Utah became a state, the Salt Lake Temple was finally completed and dedicated, and the Latter-day Saints looked to the new century with greater hope and optimism.

WILFORD WOODRUFF LEADS THE CHURCH

During the "underground" era, Wilford Woodruff, President of the Quorum of the Twelve Apostles, lived in exile in St. George and surrounding areas. Friends there protected him from searching marshals. When Elder Woodruff learned from President George Q. Cannon that President Taylor's condition afforded no hope of recovery, Elder Woodruff set out for Salt Lake City. Informed en route of President Taylor's death, Wilford Woodruff recorded the following in his journal:

"Thus another President of the Church of Jesus Christ of Latter Day Saints has passed away. President John Taylor is twice a martyr. At the death of the Prophet Joseph and Hyrum Smith in Carthage Jail he was shot with four balls and mingled his blood with the martyred Prophet. This was in 1844. Now in 1887 . . . he is driven into exile by the United States officers for his religion until through his confinement and suffering he lays down his life and suffers death. . . .

"President John Taylor died to day at 5 minutes to 8 o'clock which lays the responsibility and the care of the Church of Jesus Christ of Latter Day Saints upon my shoulders. As President of the Church or President of the Twelve Apostles, which is the presiding authority of the Church in the absence of the First Presidency, this places me in a very peculiar situation, a position I have never looked for during my life, but in the providence of God it is laid upon me."[1]

Wilford Woodruff was then eighty years old. He had joined the Church in 1833 in his native Connecticut. He accompanied Joseph Smith on Zion's Camp in 1834 and spent the next five years in dedicated and fruitful missionary service. Following his ordination to the Quorum of the Twelve Apostles in 1839, Elder Woodruff and his fellow Apostles experienced remarkable success in England. For over sixty years he meticulously kept a daily journal, which has become a source of much of the history of the Church. He ceaselessly labored all his days for the salvation of both the living and the dead.

President Woodruff was in Salt Lake City during the funeral of John Taylor but did not attend for fear of being arrested. Immediately after the services he met with the Twelve and began leading the Church, but continued to avoid any public appearances. On 9 October 1887, however, President Woodruff entered the Tabernacle for the afternoon session of general conference in company with Lorenzo Snow and Franklin D. Richards. As the Saints recognized their leader, they greeted him with applause. President Woodruff addressed them and then left before the singing, again to avoid arrest.

The government's crusade was by no means ended. During the next several months President Woodruff quietly conducted Church business at his home, consulting often with the other Apostles, particularly George Q. Cannon, who had been so closely associated with President Taylor. These were difficult days for President Woodruff. Church property was confiscated by the government, and some private individuals were enriching themselves at the expense of the Church.

A major event in 1888 was the dedication of the Manti Temple. In 1877 President Brigham Young had dedicated the site and broken the ground for the Manti Temple. The construction of the beautiful edifice of cream-colored limestone was delayed somewhat by the government's crusade, but the building was completed in the spring of 1888. President Woodruff noted that it "is the finest temple, best finished, and most costly of any building the Latter Day Saints have ever built since the organization of the Church."[2]

Church leaders gathered in the new temple on 17 May 1888 for a private dedication, at which Wilford Woodruff offered the dedicatory prayer. Later that day he recorded in his journal: "I felt to thank God that I had lived on the earth to once more have the privilege of dedicating another temple in the Rocky Mountains unto the Most High God and I pray God, my Eternal Father, that He will protect the Manti Temple and all other temples we have built . . . unto His holy name that they may never go into the hands of the Gentiles, our enemies, to be defiled by them."[3] Elder Lorenzo Snow conducted public dedicatory services on 21–23 May, reading the prayer originally offered by President Woodruff. Daniel H. Wells was set apart as the first president of the Manti Temple.

Two years after the death of John Taylor, the First Presidency was again reorganized. At a solemn assembly held during the April general conference of 1889, President Woodruff was sustained as the fourth President of the Church. George Q. Cannon and Joseph F. Smith, who had served as counselors to President Taylor, were once again sustained as counselors in the First Presidency.

EDMUNDS-TUCKER LAW AND NATIONAL POLITICS

From 1887 to 1890 the relationship between the Latter-day Saints and the United States government and its citizens continued to deteriorate. President Wilford Woodruff wrote concerning this on New Year's Eve 1889: "Thus ends the year 1889 and the word of the Prophet Joseph Smith is beginning to be fulfilled that the whole nation would turn against Zion and make war upon the Saints. The nation has never been filled so full of lies against the Saints as to day."[4]

Buildings on Temple Square

1. *Old bowery. This was 28 feet by 40 feet. The bowery was constructed in the summer of 1847 from upright poles with horizontal poles fastened at the top. Boughs were then criss-crossed over the horizontal poles to provide shade.*
2. *Bowery. This was a larger facility constructed in 1848. It had boards and planks for seats and a stage at one end.*
3. *Old Tabernacle. This structure, begun in 1851, was 62 feet by 100 feet and made out of adobe. The building ran north and south and seated twenty-five hundred people. It was torn down in 1870 to make way for the Assembly Hall.*
4. *Endowment House. Heber C. Kimball dedicated this building in May 1855. It was torn down in 1889.*
5. *Huge bowery. Built at the same time the Endowment House was under construction, this bowery was used for general conferences and later became a workshop for construction of the Tabernacle.*
6. *Tabernacle. Started in 1863, the Tabernacle was dedicated in October 1875 by John Taylor.*
7. *Assembly Hall. It was started in 1877 and completed in 1880. Joseph F. Smith dedicated the Assembly Hall in 1882.*
8. *First bureau of information. This was a small octagonal building measuring 20 feet across. It opened 4 August 1902.*
9. *Salt Lake Temple. Started in 1853 by Brigham Young, the temple was dedicated 6 April 1893 by Wilford Woodruff.*
10. *North Visitors' Center. This building was dedicated by President David O. McKay on 7 March 1963.*
11. *Temple annex. The annex to the temple was completed 21 March 1966.*
12. *South Visitors' Center. This center was dedicated 1 June 1978 by President Spencer W. Kimball.*

The Edmunds-Tucker Act of 1887 included provisions aimed at destroying the Church as a political and economic entity. The law officially dissolved The Church of Jesus Christ of Latter-day Saints as a legal corporation and required the Church to forfeit to the government all property in excess of fifty thousand dollars. Government officials set out immediately to confiscate Church holdings. For example, the buildings on Temple Square and other Church offices were placed in receivership and then rented back to the Church. In an attempt to stop the flow of European converts, the government dissolved the Perpetual Emigrating Fund Company, the chief agency for immigration. More and more Saints were stripped of their voting rights. Schools were placed under the direction of the federally appointed territorial supreme court. U.S. marshals arrested more men who were then nearly automatically sentenced to prison. Among them was President George Q. Cannon.

Although arrests and imprisonments caused families to suffer, the greatest problem for the Church was its inability to acquire and hold the funds necessary to build temples, do missionary work, publish material, and provide for the welfare of the Saints. Church leaders succeeded in getting their case before the United States Supreme Court, arguing that the confiscation of Church property under the Edmunds-Tucker Act was unconstitutional. But in May 1890 the Court upheld, in a five to four decision, the constitutionality of all the government had done under the Edmunds-Tucker Law. Though disappointed by the decision, there was little the Saints could do to ward off the impending economic destruction of the Church.

The gradual loss of voting rights added to the distress of the Church. The Edmunds-Tucker Act provided for the disfranchisement of anyone convicted of polygamy or unwilling to pledge obedience to anti-polygamy laws. By 1890 some twelve thousand Utah citizens had been deprived of their right to vote. In Idaho, where there were several communities of Saints in the south-east portion of the state, the legislature disfranchised all believing members of the Church by requiring voters to swear that they did not belong to a church that believed in plural marriage. In February 1890 the United States Supreme Court upheld the constitutionality of this Idaho test oath. This decision encouraged the Saints' opponents in Utah, who sent representatives to Washington to lobby for a similar oath for Utah citizens. The Cullom-Strubble bill was thus introduced, and by the spring of 1890 it appeared likely to pass. This bill would have deprived all members of the Church anywhere in the nation of the basic rights of citizenship.

Throughout this difficult period, the Church had several influential advocates in the nation's capital. These included John T. Caine, Utah's delegate to Congress; John W. Young, former member of the First Presidency and now a railroad promoter; Franklin S. Richards, the Church's chief attorney and son of Elder Franklin D. Richards; and George Ticknor Curtis, a non-Mormon. On occasion George Q. Cannon and Joseph F. Smith of the First Presidency and other Church authorities also labored with politicians in Washington. Among other things, these men struggled to obtain statehood for Utah. President Grover Cleveland and his fellow Democrats were somewhat agreeable to the proposition, but their efforts were not enough to give Utah statehood before they lost power to the Republican Party in the national election of 1888.

In Utah the Liberal Party was gaining influence as many members of the Church lost their voting rights. The Liberal Party's political crusade matched the severity of the crusade of the federal officials. Using some illegal voting tactics, the Liberal Party succeeded in gaining control of the Ogden city government in 1889. Then they turned their attention to campaigning in Salt Lake City, where an election was scheduled for February 1890. The non-members were helped by the decision of a United States judge that no Latter-day Saint immigrants were worthy of becoming U.S. citizens or of having the right to vote. Many gentile (nonmember) registrars also unfairly prevented members of the Church from registering to vote.

Church leaders sought in vain to convince government officials that the charge of Mormons being disloyal to the United States was false. Church members were asked to fast on Sunday, 23 December 1889, the anniversary of the birth of Joseph Smith, to implore the help of Almighty God during this crisis. In January 1890 the People's Party, the Church's political organization, held a rousing rally to gain support for its candidates. Nevertheless, the non-Mormons gained control over the government in Salt Lake City in the February balloting.

After this disappointing loss and the rulings of the U.S. Supreme Court against them, Church leaders in the spring of 1890 searched harder than ever to find influential friends in Washington, D.C. For the previous forty years the Democratic Party had been more lenient toward the Church than had the Republicans, but the Republicans were now in power, and the Church needed friends in that party to achieve a change in government policy and avoid disaster in Utah. Through Isaac Trumbo, a prominent businessman and lobbyist from California who had been a long-time friend to the Church, the First Presidency cultivated close ties with several Republicans—Leland Stanford, senator of California; Morris M. Estee, the chairman of the Republican national convention in 1888; and James S. Clarkson, chairman of the Republican national committee. All four of these men helped the lobbying effort of the Saints in 1890.[5]

President George Q. Cannon made two trips to Washington, D.C., in the spring and summer of 1890. There he found several leading Republicans who were willing to cooperate with the Saints. Among these was the powerful Secretary of State James G. Blaine, who had befriended Elder Cannon years before when Cannon was Utah's delegate to Congress. When President Cannon returned from his second trip in June, he confided that prospects were brighter for Utah than they had been for many years.

The Manifesto

Because so many Latter-day Saints were barred from voting, the anti-Mormon party won the Salt Lake City school election in July 1890, and with it control of secular education in the territorial capital. Before July ended, the Supreme Court ruled that children from polygamist marriages could not inherit their father's estate. In the first week in August the anti-Mormon party won most of the elected offices in Salt Lake and Weber counties. Finally, Church leaders learned that the U.S. attorney for Utah was conducting an investigation as to whether or not Church property, especially the

Isaac Trumbo (1858–1912) was born in Nevada but grew up in Salt Lake City. Isaac's mother was a member of the Church, but he never joined.

Isaac moved to California where he became a wealthy businessman. He also became a colonel in the California national guard. For over a decade he labored to help the people of Utah gain statehood. This dream was finally realized in large part because of his efforts in the political arena.

temples in St. George, Logan, Manti, and Salt Lake City, were being properly escheated as had been directed by the United States Congress. It was the end of August when President Woodruff received confirmation that the U.S. government, in spite of an 1888 agreement promising that temples would not be disturbed, was going to confiscate them.

President Woodruff, learning that he and his counselors were to be subpoenaed to testify in court regarding plural marriage, went to California to avoid confrontation. There he met with political leaders and found that, although the politicians were willing to exert what influence they could, they were ineffective when faced with the forces determined to eradicate plural marriage among the Saints.

President Woodruff wrote in his journal, within a week of his return to Salt Lake City, that after much anguish, prayer, and discussion with his counselors, he was prepared to act "for the temporal salvation of the Church."[6]

President Woodruff said later that the Lord had shown him by revelation exactly what would take place if plural marriage did not cease. He was shown that the Church would suffer the "confiscation and loss of all the Temples, and the stopping of all the ordinances therein, both for the living and the dead, and the imprisonment of the First Presidency and Twelve and the heads of families in the Church, and the confiscation of personal property of the people (all of which of themselves would stop the practice); or, after doing and suffering what we have through our adherence to this principle to cease the practice and submit to the law, and through doing so leave the Prophets, Apostles and fathers at home, so that they can instruct the people and attend to the duties of the Church, and also leave the Temples in the hands of the Saints, so that they can attend to the ordinances of the Gospel, both for the living and the dead" (Official Declaration—1, Excerpts from Three Addresses by President Wilford Woodruff Regarding the Manifesto).

As the Church president entered his office the morning of 24 September 1890, he told Bishop John R. Winder and President George Q. Cannon that he had not slept much the night before. He had been "struggling all night with the Lord about what should be done under the existing circumstances of the Church. And, he said, laying some papers upon the table, 'here is the result.' Upon these was written what, with the exception of some slight changes, is known as the manifesto."[7] He then showed the Brethren assembled before him the document he had written. After they had approved it and prepared it for publication, President Woodruff declared that the Lord had made it plain to him what he was to do and that it was the right thing. In the *Manifesto,* as it was called, he stated that the Church was no longer teaching plural marriage nor permitting any person to enter into it. He expressed his intent to obey the laws of the land, which forbade plural marriage, and to use his influence with Church members to do likewise. In closing he wrote, "I now publicly declare that my advice to the Latter-day Saints is to refrain from contracting any marriage forbidden by the law of the land" (Official Declaration—1).

The Manifesto was released to the nation's newspapers the next day. It even appeared in the *Washington Post*, having been given to that newspaper by Utah's territorial delegate, John T. Caine.

In the first week of October, delegate Caine informed the First Presidency in a telegram that the Secretary of the Interior had told him the government would not recognize the official declaration unless it was formally accepted by the Church's general conference.

General conference convened Saturday morning, 4 October 1890, and lasted three days. It was on the third day of the conference that President George Q. Cannon mentioned the Manifesto and then asked Orson F. Whitney, then bishop of the Salt Lake City 18th Ward, to read the document. President Lorenzo Snow then proposed that because the Saints recognized Wilford Woodruff as the President of The Church of Jesus Christ of Latter-day Saints and as the one who held the sealing keys, that they support the Manifesto as it had been issued by him. The vote was unanimous.

President Cannon then gave a lengthy discourse laying before the Saints the position of the Church concerning the doctrine of plural marriage. He explained that the Church had accepted plural marriage as a revelation from God binding upon them as a people and that they had endeavored to show that the law of 1862, which stopped the practice, was unconstitutional and in conflict with the First Amendment of the United States Constitution guaranteeing freedom of religion. He further testified that in this view they had been sustained by some of the best legal minds in the country. President Cannon reminded the Saints of the persecution they had endured, with upwards of thirteen hundred men in the Church having gone to prison as a result of their obedience to the commandment. Even with all the pressure from government leaders, as well as some members of the Church, they had obeyed the law of God until he sent the revelation directing that the practice of plural marriage be stopped.

President Cannon concluded his remarks by testifying that the Manifesto was from God and was supported by the General Authorities. He challenged the Saints that if their faith was tried because of the Manifesto, they must do as their leaders had done, which was to go to their Heavenly Father in prayer so they might have a testimony for themselves.[8]

President Wilford Woodruff then closed the conference bearing testimony of the revelation that had come to him: "I want to say to all Israel that the step which I have taken in issuing this manifesto has not been done without earnest prayer before the Lord. I am about to go into the spirit world, like other men of my age. I expect to meet the face of my heavenly Father—the Father of my spirit; I expect to meet the face of Joseph Smith, of Brigham Young, of John Taylor, and of the apostles, and for me to have taken a stand in anything which is not pleasing in the sight of God, or before the heavens, I would rather have gone out and been shot. My life is no better than other men's. I am not ignorant of the feelings that have been engendered through the course I have pursued. But I have done my duty, and the nation of which we form a part must be responsible for that which has been done in relation to this principle."[9] As President Woodruff closed his remarks, he made the following promise: "I say to Israel, the Lord will never permit me or any other man who stands as president of this Church to lead you astray. It is not in the programme. It is not in the mind of God. If I were to attempt that the Lord would remove me out of my place, and so He will any other man who attempts to lead the children of men astray from the oracles of God and from their duty."[10]

QUEST FOR STATEHOOD CONTINUES

Issuing the Manifesto was the important first step toward achieving reconciliation between the Latter-day Saints and the United States government. A new era of understanding began. Chief Justice Charles Zane, heretofore a harsh opponent of polygamy, adopted a more lenient attitude toward those brought before his court. Hence the raids against men with more than one wife came to an end. It was also generally understood that husbands would not be required to reject their wives or their children. After much petitioning, U.S. President Benjamin Harrison granted a limited pardon to all Mormon men who had lived in compliance with the anti-polygamy laws since 1890, and in September 1894, President Grover Cleveland issued a more general amnesty. In 1893 Congress passed a law allowing the escheated property to return to the Church. The quest for Utah statehood was also renewed. Before Congress would allow this to happen, however, it required the Church to relinquish participation in politics. The Church's party—the People's Party—would have to be disbanded, and Utah's citizens would have to align themselves with national political parties. The First Presidency publicly supported all these actions. Accordingly, in June 1891 the People's Party was formally dissolved and, after some contention, the anti-Mormon Liberal Party disbanded two years later.

Establishing the national Democratic and Republican parties in Utah proved exceedingly difficult. Traditionally the Saints had leaned toward the Democratic Party because the Republicans, who had been in power most of the time since 1861, had promoted and enforced the anti-polygamy legislation. Furthermore, the Democratic-appointed officials of 1885–89 had been more lenient with the Saints. Considering the political tendency of Church members and the fact that most nonmembers in Utah were Republican oriented, the First Presidency wanted to avoid the Democrats becoming another Church party.

Meetings were held with stake presidents and bishops where they were instructed to encourage more Latter-day Saints to vote Republican. This would demonstrate to national party leaders that a viable two-party system

Heber M. Wells (1859–1938) was elected the first governor of the state of Utah at the age of thirty-six in the general election of November 1895. He successfully served as governor for two terms.

President Grover Cleveland proclaimed on Saturday, 4 January 1896 that Utah had been granted admission into the Union as a state. Monday, 6 January was declared a general holiday. Inaugural ceremonies were held in the Salt Lake Tabernacle, which was filled to capacity.

A huge flag covered the dome of the Tabernacle. A new star was displayed at the front of the building with an electric light inserted behind it, which shone throughout the ceremonies.

could exist in Utah. Local leaders, however, were also urged to use good sense and caution in their encouragement. Church members who were known to have strong Democratic convictions were not asked to switch parties, but those whose commitment was not particularly strong were encouraged to change. This method was effective, and by 1892 the Republican Party was strong in Utah politics.

Delicate negotiations continued for Utah statehood in both houses of Congress. Of importance to most congressmen was an assurance that the Church was sincere about stopping the practice of plural marriage and staying out of the political process. By means of astute political moves by lobbyists, primarily non-Mormon Isaac Trumbo and Bishop Hiram B. Clawson, the Utah Enabling Act was finally passed in July 1894. Throughout the rest of 1894 and in 1895, Utahns, both in and out of the Church, cooperated to produce a state constitution that achieved Congress's acceptance. The constitution specifically prohibited plural marriage and ensured the complete separation of church and state.

On 4 January 1896, Utah finally became a state, with Heber M. Wells, son of Daniel H. Wells, as its first governor.

Throughout this arduous process of reconciliation, disagreements and misunderstandings over political matters continued between Church members. Even some General Authorities were affected as some campaigned for Democratic candidates and policies and others for the Republicans. The political issue came to a head in 1895 when Elder Moses Thatcher of the Quorum of the Twelve accepted the nomination of the Democratic Party for senator from Utah and Elder B. H. Roberts of the First Council of the Seventy ran for Congress from the same party. They were disciplined for accepting nominations without first consulting their Church leaders. Neither man was elected.

In April 1896 the General Authorities issued a formal statement, known as the political rule of the Church or the Political Manifesto. It emphasized

Moses Thatcher (1842–1909) was ordained an elder at the age of fourteen and called to serve as a missionary in California. Ten years later he was again called to serve a mission to Europe.

In 1879 Moses was called into the Quorum of the Twelve, a position he held until 1896. A few months after his call to the apostleship, President John Taylor assigned Elder Thatcher to open Mexico for the preaching of the gospel.

the separation of church and state and the Church's intention not to encroach upon the political rights of any citizens. The statement also added that for peace and goodwill to continue in Utah, it was inadvisable for high Church leaders "to accept political office or enter into any vocation that would distract or remove them from the religious duties resting upon them, without first consulting and obtaining the approval of their associates and those who preside over them."[11]

At first B. H. Roberts, who felt that the document abridged his political rights, refused to sign. After being reasoned with, prayed with, and worked with by his Brethren among the General Authorities, he finally signed. Elder Moses Thatcher, in spite of similar efforts in his behalf, still refused to add his signature to the document. Therefore, he was released from the Quorum of the Twelve Apostles, although he retained his membership in the Church. The Political Manifesto has continued to be the standard that governs the actions of the General Authorities with respect to politics.

Another important development during this period of reconciliation was the change of some of the Church's economic policies. Most Church-owned concerns were sold to private interests or were operated under the competitive policies of private enterprise as income producing ventures, thus fitting into the national economic pattern. Throughout the 1890s the Church continued to suffer severe economic distress owing both to temporary divestiture of Church property to the government and to the nationwide financial panic of 1893.

SALT LAKE TEMPLE AND WORK FOR THE DEAD

President Young laid the cornerstones of the Salt Lake Temple in a solemn ceremony on 6 April 1853, not quite six years after seeing the temple in vision.[12] He sensed that he would not live long enough to attend its dedication. President Young had insisted on only the best materials and craftsmanship in the temple's construction. Forty years later, after the hard work and dedication of thousands of Latter-day Saints, President Wilford Woodruff prepared himself and the Church for the dedication ceremonies.

Construction of the Salt Lake Temple had been delayed many times, but since the late 1880s the full resources of the Church were consecrated to its completion. In April 1892, President Woodruff directed the laying of the capstone in connection with general conference. The audience of fifty thousand Saints (the largest assembly to that time) filled Temple Square and adjoining streets. A march was played, after which a special temple anthem was sung by the Tabernacle Choir. A prayer was offered by President Joseph F. Smith, and the choir then sang, "Grant Us Peace." As noon approached, President Woodruff stepped to the platform, pressed an electric button, and the capstone was lowered into position. The congregation then shouted, "Hosanna, hosanna, hosanna to God and the Lamb.

The development of the Salt Lake Temple, 1873, 1882, and 1892

Amen, amen, amen." This was repeated three times, accompanied by the waving of white handkerchiefs. Then everyone sang "The Spirit of God Like a Fire Is Burning."

The next month the Saints held a special fast, and the money saved was sent to the First Presidency to help finish the temple by 6 April 1893, the fortieth anniversary of the laying of the cornerstone. Church leaders urged the members to discipline their thoughts and lives, to disregard partisan political feelings, and to make themselves pure in all things so they would be ready to participate in the temple dedication.

As the temple with its striking architecture neared completion, it engendered considerable curiosity in Utah and throughout the nation. Prior to the dedication more than a thousand government officials and prominent businessmen and their wives were taken on a tour of the temple. Such courtesy on the part of Church leaders helped continue the good feelings that had prevailed since the issuance of the Manifesto.

On 6 April 1893, dedicatory ceremonies commenced. President Woodruff saw in the events of the day the fulfillment of a prophetic dream. He told the Saints that many years before in a nocturnal visitation Brigham Young had given him the keys of the temple and had told him to dedicate it to the Lord. In his opening remarks President Woodruff prophesied that from that time the power of Satan would be broken and his power over the Saints diminished, and there would be an increased greater interest in the gospel message.[13]

Workmen had labored day and night for weeks to prepare the edifice in time. It had been decided that dedicatory sessions would be held twice daily until every worthy member of the Church who wished to could attend. Andrew Jenson, who attended all the sessions as a recommend examiner, wrote that on the first day of the dedication "the prince of the air, as if displeased with what was going on, opened a terrible wind storm, accompanied with hail and sleet; and while the glorious services were going on inside the building, the elements outside roared with such violence and force that the like was not remembered by the oldest inhabitants of Utah. Several buildings were blown down in the vicinity of the city and much damage done throughout the valley."[14] In spite of the stormy weather, a spirit of love and harmony was felt at the first dedicatory session and at subsequent sessions held for twenty-two days and attended by more than seventy-five thousand people. Even Sunday School children were invited to a special session.

The prophet noted in his journal, "The spirit and power of God rested upon us. The spirit of prophecy and revelation was upon us and the hearts of the people were melted and many things were unfolded to us."[15] Some saw angels, while others viewed past Presidents of the Church and deceased Apostles.[16] One unusual event occurred when Emma Bennett from Provo gave birth to a baby boy in the temple. A week later the child was blessed in the temple by President Joseph F. Smith and given the name Joseph Temple Bennett.[17]

If the dedicatory services had a theme, it was unity. Over and over speakers stressed the value of being one in the fold of the Master. Having lived through decades of bitter attacks upon the Church, anti-Mormon legislation, and partisan political conflicts, the Saints looked with anticipation toward an era of peace and harmony. Members and leaders alike had worked hard and had fasted and prayed to be able to attend the dedicatory ceremonies with bitter feelings resolved. They were successful, and said often in their sermons that the Church was now more unified than it had ever been.

The Salt Lake Temple became the symbol of the Church in many ways. Forty years of sacrifice and work, some of it the finest workmanship the Church could produce, went into the structure. Earlier Church leaders had sent Latter-day Saint artists on art missions to France where they studied under the world's best artists so that the inside walls of the temple could be properly adorned. The Saints were now firmly convinced that their efforts had not been in vain and that the "mountain of the Lord's house" was now raised in the tops of the mountains.

Much of the rest of President Woodruff's life was dedicated to one of his greatest ambitions: promoting the salvation of the dead. A visionary man, he had numerous dreams about this work. In March 1894 he saw Benjamin Franklin, who he had been baptized and confirmed for in 1877 in the St. George Temple. This distinguished patriot sought further ordinances through President Woodruff, which the prophet promptly saw to in the temple. This appearance of Benjamin Franklin satisfied President Woodruff that Franklin at least had joyfully received the blessings that had come to him earlier.[18]

President Woodruff also prayerfully considered the ordinance of "adoption," which had been performed for many years in the Church. It had been the custom for many members to have themselves and their families sealed to prominent Church leaders, such as Joseph Smith or Brigham Young, with the thought of being attached to these righteous families in the hereafter. In April 1894 general conference, President Woodruff announced that he had received a revelation on the subject. He was careful to point out that the revelation was consistent with principles taught by Joseph Smith. He began his talk by having President George Q. Cannon read Doctrine and Covenants 128:9–21, in which the Prophet wrote of the need for a welding link between the generations of the human family.

President Woodruff announced that it was the will of the Lord for the Saints "from this time to trace their genealogies as far as they can, and to be sealed to their fathers and mothers" thus uniting the generations through temple ordinances. Reassuringly, he then referred to Joseph Smith's teaching that all who would have received the gospel in this life, had they heard it, would go to the celestial kingdom. He added, "So it will be with your fathers. There will be very few, if any, who will not accept the Gospel."[19]

The results of this new revelation were impressive. Previously the Saints had done little genealogical work and had performed relatively few sealing ordinances. With the prophet's urging, the Saints began tracing their genealogies as far as they could. That same year the Church established the Genealogical Society of Utah. Thus was launched one of the Church's most enduring and productive enterprises.

NEW DIRECTIONS

During times of both stress and reconciliation, the Church continued to move forward. Missionary work continued to expand, areas of settlement were widened, many new stakes and wards were organized, auxiliary programs were augmented and refined, some doctrines were clarified, increasing attention was paid to education, and anniversary celebrations were held to commemorate significant events.

Ever interested in the dissemination of the gospel, President Woodruff expanded missionary work by opening eleven new missions, some of them in the United States. Nearly three times as many missionaries were called in the 1890s as had been during the previous decade. Much of the new activity centered in the South Pacific. The Samoan Mission was formally organized in 1888, and missionaries entered Tonga in 1891. At the same time elders were finding success among the Maori people of New Zealand, and by 1898 the New Zealand Mission was separated from the Australian Mission. Numerous South Sea islanders began emigrating to Zion. The colony of Iosepa (Hawaiian for *Joseph*), in western Utah's Skull Valley, was opened in 1889 for Hawaiian members of the Church who had migrated to Utah to be near the Salt Lake Temple.

The Church also continued its missionary labors in its organized European missions, and there was some emigration, although much less than before due to the dissolution of the Perpetual Emigrating Fund Company in 1887. Another telling factor in the decline of immigration to Utah was the lessening of economic opportunities in the Mormon colonies.

The original purpose of immigration, to fill the region with Latter-day Saints so the kingdom could not be shaken loose again, had been fulfilled. Even with fewer immigrants, new colonies were added in western Wyoming, Arizona, New Mexico, Colorado, and Alberta, Canada.

The auxiliaries of the Church continued to assess their programs and improve their efficiency as the Church expanded. In 1889 annual conferences were begun in Salt Lake City for Relief Society and Primary workers, which significantly reduced the amount of travel required of general board members. Stake representatives could now carry instructions back directly from the conferences. The Deseret Sunday School Union also convened its own annual conference, and in 1893 added Sunday School conferences in each stake. Sunday School leaders also promoted teacher training classes held at Brigham Young Academy in Provo and LDS College in Salt Lake City.

The growth of cities and the subsequent increase in the number of Saints employed outside of agriculture necessitated a reexamination of the long-standing practice of having fast day and testimony meeting the first Thursday of the month. In 1896 the First Presidency issued instructions that henceforth the Saints would observe fast day on the first Sunday of each month, following the pattern already established by the Saints in Great Britain.

Church leaders also discontinued the long-standing practice of rebaptism. Oftentimes Latter-day Saints had been rebaptized in conjunction with important milestones, such as marriage or entering the United Order or sometimes for improvement of health. These rebaptisms were recorded on Church membership records. The First Presidency grew concerned that some members were substituting rebaptism for true repentance. In 1893, stake presidents were instructed not to require rebaptism of Saints wishing to attend the dedication of the Salt Lake Temple, and in 1897 the practice of rebaptism was discontinued altogether. As President George Q. Cannon explained, "It is repentance from sin that will save you, not rebaptism."[20]

As the Church lost its influence over Utah's public schools during this period, it established a program of religion classes in various ward meetinghouses after school, where religious training could take place without violating the laws governing separation of church and state. In 1888 President Woodruff directed the formation of the Church Board of Education to oversee all educational enterprises of the Church. Between 1888 and 1891 over thirty academies were started in the larger settlements of Utah, Idaho, Arizona, Canada, and Mexico. These academies provided secondary education, which emphasized classical and vocational training as well as religious instruction. One of the largest academies was Brigham Young Academy, started in 1875, which became Brigham Young University.

The year 1897 saw two significant anniversary celebrations. The first was for the ninetieth birthday of the Church's greatly respected prophet,

President Wilford Woodruff. On Sunday, 28 February 1897, the day before President Woodruff's birthday, over ten thousand Sunday School children crowded into the beautifully decorated Tabernacle, filling even the aisles, to honor the prophet. This experience deeply touched President Woodruff. As he spoke, he told the children about when he was ten years old and attended Sunday School and read in the New Testament of Apostles and prophets. He said he remembered praying that he might live to see prophets and Apostles like those in the New Testament. Then he testified to the children—"sons and daughters of prophets, patriarchs and men of Israel"—that he had seen many times over the fulfillment of his humble youthful prayer.[21] The next day, on the prophet's actual birthday, celebrations were once again held in his honor, this time for the general public. Seldom had members of the Church seen such an overpowering expression of love for a leader.

The week of 24 July 1897 was set aside as a special jubilee celebration, the fiftieth anniversary of the Saints' arrival in the Salt Lake Valley. This was an opportunity for the new state of Utah to display herself to the world, and enthusiasm and patriotism marked every feature of the celebration. The festivities opened with the unveiling of the Brigham Young monument before an estimated crowd of fifty thousand people. Sculptured by Cyrus E. Dallin and cast in bronze, the monument weighed over twenty tons. It still stands in the center of Salt Lake City.

The surviving twenty-four members of the original pioneer company, including Wilford Woodruff, were honored in the Tabernacle, and each of them received an inscribed gold medallion. Several parades with gorgeous

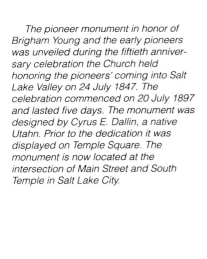

The pioneer monument in honor of Brigham Young and the early pioneers was unveiled during the fiftieth anniversary celebration the Church held honoring the pioneers' coming into Salt Lake Valley on 24 July 1847. The celebration commenced on 20 July 1897 and lasted five days. The monument was designed by Cyrus E. Dallin, a native Utahn. Prior to the dedication it was displayed on Temple Square. The monument is now located at the intersection of Main Street and South Temple in Salt Lake City.

The Isaac Trumbo home, located on the corner of Octavia and Sutter Streets in San Francisco. Here President Woodruff died on 2 September 1898.

floats and thousands of excited children marked the occasion, while the finest products of Utah agriculture, mining, and industry were also displayed.

In 1898, following what had become a yearly tradition, President Woodruff, accompanied by President Cannon and others, escaped the summer heat of Utah for a vacation in California. The prophet's health, however, totally failed him, and on 2 September he passed away in his sleep in the home of Isaac Trumbo in San Francisco, California. At his funeral in Salt Lake City a few days later, President George Q. Cannon declared, "President Woodruff was a man of God. He had finished the fight and had been called hence to mingle with his brethren, and to receive his well-earned reward. He was a heavenly being. It was heaven to be in his company, and his departure from this sphere of action, robs the community of a great and good man, and one who fully merited all the blessings promised to those who remain true and steadfast unto the end."[22]

ENDNOTES

1. Wilford Woodruff Journals, 25 July 1887, LDS Historical Department, Salt Lake City; spelling, punctuation, and capitalization standardized; see also Matthias F. Cowley, *Wilford Woodruff: History of His Life and Labors* (Salt Lake City: Bookcraft, 1964), p. 560.

2. Wilford Woodruff Journals, 15 May 1888; spelling, punctuation, and capitalization standardized.

3. Wilford Woodruff Journals, 17 May 1888; spelling, punctuation, and capitalization standardized.

4. Wilford Woodruff Journals, 31 Dec. 1889; spelling, punctuation, and capitalization standardized.

5. See Edward Leo Lyman, *Political Deliverance: The Mormon Quest for Utah Statehood* (Urbana, Ill.: University of Illinois Press, 1986), pp. 130–31.

6. Wilford Woodruff Journals, 25 Sept. 1890; spelling and capitalization standardized.

7. In Salt Lake Temple Historical Record, 1893–1922, LDS Historical Department, Salt Lake City, p. 71.

8. See *Millennial Star*, 17 Nov. 1890, pp. 723–25; 24 Nov., pp. 737–38.

9. *Millennial Star*, 24 Nov. 1890, p. 739.

10. *Millennial Star*, 24 Nov. 1890, p. 741.

11. "To the Saints," *The Deseret Weekly*, 11 Apr. 1896, p. 533.

12. See Brigham Young, in *Journal of Discourses*, 1:133.

13. See Cowley, *Wilford Woodruff*, pp. 582–83.

14. *Autobiography of Andrew Jenson* (Salt Lake City: Deseret News Press, 1938), p. 205.

15. Wilford Woodruff Journals, 6 Apr. 1893; spelling, punctuation, and capitalization standardized.

16. See John Nicholson, "Temple Manifestations," *The Contributor*, Dec. 1894, pp. 116–18.

17. See James H. Anderson, "The Salt Lake Temple," *The Contributor*, Apr. 1893, p. 301.

18. See Wilford Woodruff Journals, 19 Mar. 1894; Cowley, *Wilford Woodruff*, pp. 586–87.

19. "The Law of Adoption," *The Deseret Weekly*, 21 Apr. 1894, pp. 541–43.

20. In Conference Report, Oct. 1897, p. 68.

21. Cowley, *Wilford Woodruff*, p. 602; see also Wilford Woodruff Journals, 28 Feb. 1897.

22. In Cowley, *Wilford Woodruff*, p. 633.

THE CHURCH AT THE TURN OF THE CENTURY

CHURCH MEMBERS, now secure in the Great Basin, anticipated the twentieth century with confidence that the restored Church would be more than equal to any challenges. With the death of their respected leader, Wilford Woodruff, the prophetic mantle fell on the equally seasoned eighty-five-year-old Lorenzo Snow. No previous Church president had entered this office at such an advanced age.

PREPARATION OF A PROPHET

Only five feet six inches tall, and weighing barely 130 pounds at the time he became President of the Church, Lorenzo Snow was the last of the General Authorities to have been personally acquainted with the Prophet Joseph Smith. In a November 1900 discourse delivered in the Salt Lake Tabernacle, President Snow told the Saints that he had often visited the Prophet Joseph and his family, dined at his table, had private interviews with him, and knew that he was an honorable, moral man who was greatly respected. He feelingly declared that "the Lord has shown me most clearly and completely that he was a Prophet of God."[1]

President Snow had many experiences that prepared him for his prophetic calling. As a youth in Ohio, Lorenzo had obtained some academic training at Oberlin College and had gone on to teach school. Having become acquainted with the Prophet Joseph Smith and motivated by his sister Eliza, Lorenzo was baptized in 1836. Always a great missionary, he first served in Ohio in 1837 and in subsequent years also preached the gospel in Missouri, Kentucky, and Illinois. In 1840 he was called on a mission to Great Britain, where he labored under the direction of the Twelve Apostles. As a member of the Quorum of the Twelve he directed the first preaching of the gospel in Italy and Switzerland in 1849–51. In 1853 he was called to preside over the settlements in Box Elder County of northern Utah, where he named the principal settlement Brigham City in honor of President Young. For the next forty years his main residence was in that region, and he was greatly beloved of the Saints there. Under his direction the community developed a series of cooperative enterprises that brought prosperity to the area and acclaim to the Church.

One of Lorenzo Snow's great contributions was his elucidation of the doctrine that man might one day become like God. As President of the Church he gave a discourse entitled "The Grand Destiny of Man." He related how as a young man he had been inspired by one of the Prophet Joseph

Lorenzo Snow (1814–1901), fifth President of the Church

Smith's sermons about the manifestations of God and Jesus Christ to him. Two and one-half years later, after a patriarchal blessing meeting, Joseph Smith, Sr., had promised Lorenzo that he could become as great as God himself. Two and one-half years after that, while Lorenzo listened to an explanation of the scriptures, the Lord inspired him to compose this couplet: "As man now is, God once was; As God now is, man may be." President Snow stated, "Nothing was ever revealed more distinctly than that was to me."[2] Shortly before Joseph Smith's death, Lorenzo heard him teach the same doctrine. Thereafter Elder Snow made this doctrine one of the subjects of his own discourses.

SUCCESSION IN THE PRESIDENCY

Almost six years before his death Wilford Woodruff asked Lorenzo Snow, President of the Quorum of the Twelve Apostles, to speak with him privately after a meeting with other Church leaders. With much feeling and energy, President Woodruff told President Snow that if he should die before President Snow, he was not to delay but was to organize the First Presidency immediately and take George Q. Cannon and Joseph F. Smith as his counselors. He wished Lorenzo to regard this as a revelation.[3]

In 1898, as President Woodruff's health deteriorated, Lorenzo visited him at his home nearly every evening. One night, shortly after the leader had been taken to California in an attempt to improve his physical condition, President Snow went into the Salt Lake Temple, of which he was president, and implored the Lord to extend the prophet's life beyond his so that he would not have the burden of Church leadership. "Yet he promised the Lord that he would devotedly perform any duty required at his hands."

Traveling to Brigham City, President Snow took care of some personal obligations. On 2 September 1898, President Snow was informed in Brigham City that Wilford Woodruff had passed away. Reaching Salt Lake City that evening, he again retired to the Salt Lake Temple and "poured out his heart to the Lord. He reminded the Lord how he had plead for President Woodruff's life. . . . 'Nevertheless, . . . Thy will be done. . . . I now present myself before Thee for Thy guidance and instruction. I ask that Thou show me what Thou wouldst have me do.'

"After finishing his prayer he expected a reply, some special manifestation from the Lord. So he waited—and waited—and waited. There was no reply, no voice, no visitation, no manifestation." President Snow left the room greatly disappointed. As he was walking through one of the temple hallways, he saw before him, standing above the floor, the Savior of the world. He was told that he was to be President Woodruff's successor. He was again instructed "to go right ahead and reorganize the First Presidency of the Church at once and not wait as had been done after the death of the previous presidents."[4]

The day following President Woodruff's funeral, the Apostles met in the Salt Lake Temple. President Snow, in apparent deference to the principles of agency and common consent, without disclosing to his brethren his conversation with the Savior, volunteered to step down from the leadership of the Quorum and yield to anyone his fellow Apostles might designate. His long service as a member of the Quorum of the Twelve and his brilliant leadership of that body for almost a decade had given his brethren a great love and admiration for him. The Twelve therefore, acting under inspiration, quickly sustained Lorenzo Snow as President of their Quorum.[5] Later they met again in the President's office. There Elder Francis M. Lyman reminded them that President Woodruff had left instructions that when he died, the First Presidency should be reorganized without delay. Only a little discussion followed before Lorenzo Snow was unanimously sustained as President of the Church.

President Snow then told his brethren that the Lord had revealed to him several days previously that this step should be taken and that George Q. Cannon and Joseph F. Smith should be his counselors. "I have not mentioned this matter to any person, either man or woman. I, wanted to see what the feelings of the brethren were. I wanted to see if the same spirit which the Lord manifested to me was in you. I had confidence in you that the Lord would indicate to you that this was proper and according to his mind and will." George Q. Cannon and Joseph F. Smith were then sustained as his counselors (both men had served as counselors to Brigham Young, John Taylor, and Wilford Woodruff), and Franklin D. Richards became the President of the Quorum of the Twelve Apostles.[6] Rudger Clawson, Brigham City stake president, was called a month later to fill the vacancy in the Quorum.

APOSTOLIC SENIORITY CLARIFIED

When Elder Franklin D. Richards, President of the Twelve, died in 1899, the First Presidency did not replace him with a quorum president, since George Q. Cannon, who was next in line, was serving in the First Presidency. There also arose a question whether Brigham Young, Jr., or Joseph F. Smith was next in line after President Cannon. Both men had been ordained Apostles by Brigham Young for an extended period of time before they had been called to the Quorum of the Twelve.[7] Brigham Young, Jr., was the first to be ordained to the apostleship, but Joseph F. Smith had been the first to enter the Quorum of the Twelve.

On 5 April 1900, at a meeting held in the Salt Lake Temple, the First Presidency and the Twelve unanimously decided that the time an Apostle entered the Quorum of the Twelve established his position in the quorum. Furthermore, it was ruled that when the First Presidency was dissolved upon the death of the President, the counselors who were ordained Apostles in the Quorum of the Twelve would resume their places in the Quorum according to seniority.[8] Hence Joseph F. Smith ranked ahead of Brigham Young, Jr. This turned out to be a crucial factor in 1901 when the next president was selected.

	Ordained Apostle	Entered Quorum
Joseph F. Smith	1 July 1866	8 Oct. 1867
Brigham Young, Jr.	4 Feb. 1864	9 Oct. 1868

Brigham Young, Jr., was first ordained to the apostleship, but Joseph F. Smith first entered the Quorum of the Twelve.

SOLVING THE CHURCH'S FINANCIAL PROBLEMS

Only four days after his ordination, President Snow called a special meeting of the First Presidency and Quorum of the Twelve to discuss the serious financial difficulties facing the Church. The Church went about $300,000 in debt as a direct result of the Edmunds-Tucker Act. It had also undertaken the care of the families of men incarcerated for plural marriage, as well as their legal fees and court costs and its own legal expenses. The building of the Salt Lake Temple, the increased needs of Church education and welfare expenditures, and start-up costs of various industries added to the large debt.

While the Church's financial obligations had increased, tithing revenues had declined in the 1880s because members had been reluctant to contribute when the federal government was confiscating the money. Furthermore, hostile writers and speech makers so effectively spread the idea that tithing was compulsory that the words *voluntary offering* were printed on tithing certificates. Thus, Latter-day Saint leaders were forced to borrow large sums of money from various financial institutions during the 1890s, until the interest payments alone totaled $100,000 annually. "By July 1898 the church owed $935,000 to banks (about half was owed to banks outside Utah), more than $100,000 to business houses in Salt Lake City, and more than $200,000 to individual Latter-day Saints."[9]

Frank J. Cannon, who had negotiated with financiers in the East for a $1,500,000 loan before President Woodruff's death, was invited by the First Presidency to explain the status of his negotiations. Troubled by what he heard in this meeting, President Snow continued to study, ponder, and pray about the Church's financial troubles. He was seriously concerned at the financial involvement of the Church in so many purely business ventures. He concluded that if half the means used for business enterprises had been devoted to spreading the gospel, a great work could have been accomplished. Therefore, he quietly announced to his fellow General Authorities that the Church would no longer borrow money from eastern financial institutions; it would, for the time being at least, follow a definite policy of financial retrenchment and free itself from debt as quickly as possible. The Church then proceeded to divest itself of such holdings as the Deseret Telegraph System, the Utah Sugar Company, the Utah Light and Railway Company, its Saltair holdings, and some of its mining property.

President Snow authorized the issuance of short-term 6 percent bonds in the amount of $1,000,000 instead of the $1,500,000 for which Frank J. Cannon had been negotiating. In spite of these measures, by the spring of 1899 no completely satisfactory answer to the complex problems of church finances had been found.

Following the April 1899 sessions of general conference, President Snow felt impelled to again seek the Lord in earnest prayer for wisdom in solving the Church's financial problems. He received no immediate answer. He was nevertheless impressed that he and other General Authorities should visit St. George and other settlements in southern Utah. At least sixteen of the Brethren, including President Joseph F. Smith, and their wives accompanied him. At the time of their visit the settlements of southern Utah were experiencing a severe drought.

On Wednesday, 17 May 1899, at the opening session of the conference in the St. George Tabernacle, President Snow told the Saints that "we are in your midst because the Lord directed me to come; but the purpose of our coming is not clearly known at the present, but this will be made known to me during our sojourn among you."[10]

LeRoi C. Snow, son of the President, who was reporting the conference for the *Deseret News*, recalled what happened: "All at once father paused in his discourse. Complete stillness filled the room. I shall never forget the thrill as long as I live. When he commenced to speak again his voice strengthened and the inspiration of God seemed to come over him, as well as over the entire assembly. His eyes seemed to brighten and his countenance to shine. He was filled with unusual power. Then he revealed to the Latter-day Saints the vision that was before him."[11]

President Snow told the Saints that he could see that the people had neglected the law of tithing and that the Church would be relieved of debt if members would pay a full and honest tithing. He then said that the Lord was displeased with the Saints for failing to pay their tithing and promised them that if they would pay their tithes the drought would be removed and they would have a bounteous harvest.

The St. George Tabernacle was the site of President Snow's revelation and sermon reemphasizing the payment of tithing as the way for the Church to achieve stability.

The tabernacle's foundation stones were laid June 1863, and the building was completed in 1875. On 7 May 1876, Brigham Young, Jr., offered the dedicatory prayer.

Following the conference session, President Snow was again impressed that the solution to the Church's financial problems lay in the payment of tithing. In meetings held at Leeds, Cedar City, Beaver, and Juab, other southern Utah communities, he delivered powerful discourses relative to this gospel principle. In Nephi, in central Utah, a remarkable meeting was held where President Snow mentioned the revelation he had received on the law of tithing and "commissioned every one present to be his special witness to the fact that the Lord had given this revelation to him."[12]

At Church headquarters, President Snow again spoke powerfully about tithing at the Mutual Improvement Association conference in June. Elder B. H. Roberts then made a motion, which was unanimously adopted, that the Saints accept the doctrine of tithing now presented. Visibly moved, President Snow stood up and declared, "Every man who is here, who has made this promise, will be saved in the Celestial Kingdom."[13]

Tithing was preached in all the stake conferences, and a year later President Snow reported that the Saints had contributed twice as much tithing during the past year as they had paid the previous two years. Under inspiration, he had set in motion the program that would, by 1907, completely free the Church from debt. Many Saints testified that not only were the windows of heaven opened to save the Church, but those who followed this divine law were spiritually and temporally blessed as well.

The life of Charles W. Penrose (1832–1925) is remarkable, although not well known. He was converted to the Church at age eighteen in England and seven months later was called on a mission in that country which lasted ten years. At age twenty-two he wrote the popular hymn "Oh, Ye Mountains High."

After immigrating to Utah from England with his family, he was twice called to serve missions to England. In Utah he was active in politics, wrote for and edited newspapers, served as assistant Church historian, and wrote many articles for the Church, including a popular series of missionary tracts entitled "Rays of Living Light."

In 1904, Charles W. Penrose was called to the Quorum of the Twelve at age seventy-two. Two years later he returned to England as president of the European mission. In 1911 he was called to be second counselor to President Joseph F. Smith and then became first counselor to President Heber J. Grant in 1921.

President Snow also took measures to control more tightly the disbursements of Church funds. He created a comprehensive plan for the expenditure of those monies. Some financial experts recommended that there be a diffusion of authority relative to the spending of tithing. President Snow notified those involved that he did not intend to carry out such a plan, but rather would keep such power vested in the First Presidency as the Lord intended (see D&C 120).

Three months after being sustained as the Church's president, President Snow brought the *Deseret News* back under Church control. Since 1892 the newspaper had been leased to George Q. Cannon and his sons. President Snow called Charles W. Penrose as editor, and the newspaper again became the official organ of the Church. Brother Penrose, a seasoned newspaperman with years of missionary service, was a few years later called to the Quorum of the Twelve and, still later, became a member of the First Presidency.

CALLING THE FIRST WOMEN MISSIONARIES

An innovative development in missionary work was announced at a reception the general board of the Young Ladies' Mutual Improvement Association held for the general board of the Young Men's Mutual Improvement Association in 1898. In the course of his talk to the two groups, President Cannon announced, "It has been decided to call some of our wise and prudent women into the missionary field."[14] In the past a few sisters, such as Louisa Barnes Pratt and Caroline Crosby, had accompanied their husbands who were serving as missionaries, but never before had the Church officially called and set apart sisters as ambassadors of the Lord Jesus Christ.

Elizabeth Claridge McCune laid the foundation for the First Presidency's decision. In the winter of 1897–98, before leaving for a tour of Europe with her family, Sister McCune went to Lorenzo Snow for a blessing. Among other things, he blessed her that "thy mind shall be as clear as an angel's when explaining the principles of the Gospel." This blessing was remarkably fulfilled in many gospel conversations abroad, and one day she told her daughter of her belief that it would not be very long before young women would be called to serve missions.[15] Upon returning home, she told President Snow of her experiences in explaining gospel principles to nonmembers all over Europe. She told him, further, that her teachings were instrumental in bringing some members of her English family into the Church. It was shortly after this that President Cannon made his announcement in behalf of the First Presidency.

"The very first sister to be set apart and formally commissioned as a missionary of the Church of Jesus Christ of Latter-day Saints was Harriet Maria Horsepool Nye, wife of President E. H. Nye of the California mission. She was set apart at San Francisco, March 27, 1898, by Apostle Brigham Young.

"Shortly after this Bishop Joseph B. Keeler of the Fourth Ward, Provo,

Elizabeth McCune (1852–1924), mother of nine children, was a member of the Relief Society and the YWMIA general boards for many years. She chaired the Genealogical Society of Utah, was a temple ordinance worker, and was a missionary on Temple Square. She was also active in the women's rights movement and attended international women's conferences in London and Rome.

conferred with the stake presidency in regard to calling two young women of that ward on a mission to Europe." As a result, Lucy Jane Brimhall and Inez Knight were called as full-time missionaries to the British mission.[16] Both sisters were well educated, gifted teachers and well versed in the principles of the gospel.

After the sisters' arrival in the mission field, several issues of the *Young Woman's Journal* carried articles or letters regarding their proselyting activities. President George Q. Cannon even published an article in the *Juvenile Instructor* entitled "Women as Missionaries," later printed in the *Millennial Star*, in which he quoted a letter praising their performance.[17] These sisters energetically involved themselves in missionary work tracting door-to-door, taking part in street meetings, and even drawing large crowds. In the face of the degrading images painted on the pages of the English anti-Mormon press, it was a novelty for the British people to see two Mormon women who were not only attractive but intelligent, forceful speakers as well.

In a published letter, they reported, "We take part frequently in street meetings and have thus far been listened to attentively, with no interruptions. Having accepted many invitations to call upon people at their homes to talk upon Utah and her people, also the Gospel, as a result we already have some dear friends in Bristol."[18] The sisters' presence in the mission was publicly acknowledged when their first mission priesthood meeting was renamed a "missionary meeting" for their sake.[19]

Gaining experience, they wrote that sometimes unkind things were said to them; in general their letters reflect the same kind of successes and disappointments that are characteristic of the elder's epistles. By January 1899 an anti-Mormon league had been founded in Bristol and was attempting to hinder the work of the missionaries.[20] Other parts of Great Britain also saw opposition to the efforts of the young men and women proclaiming the restored gospel. Sister Knight, in a letter, reported: "Although we do not always have clear sailing and have even been forced to seek protection from

Lucy Jane Brimhall and Amanda Inez Knight were the first single sister missionaries called in the Church. They were called 1 April 1898 to serve in Great Britain.

Sister Brimhall had graduated from Brigham Young Academy in 1895 and had taught school afterward. She was an intimate friend of Inez Knight, daughter of Jesse Knight and granddaughter of Newel and Lydia Knight who were prominent in early Church history. The two had planned a European tour, but these plans were interrupted by their mission call.

mob violence in a police station, receiving the slurs of the mob and even spat upon by the enemy, together with rocks and sticks from their hands, yet we rejoice in the work."[21] Inez Knight and Lucy Brimhall were only the first of thousands of women to valiantly proclaim the gospel in missions all over the world.

The Church's emphasis upon missionary work during the decade of 1890 to 1900 is reflected in the fact that the number of missionaries doubled. The number of missions and the number of missionaries would consistently rise throughout the decades to come.

THE CHURCH MOVES INTO THE TWENTIETH CENTURY

As the world looked forward to a new century, Church members were also filled with anticipation. President Snow prepared a proclamation entitled *Greeting to the World*, in which he clearly described the kind of world that the Church was trying to build. He hoped the twentieth century would be an "age of peace, of greater progress, of the universal adoption of the golden rule. . . . War with its horrors should be but a memory. The aim of nations should be fraternity and mutual greatness. The welfare of humanity should be studied instead of the enrichment of a race of the extension of an empire. Awake, ye monarchs of the earth and rulers among nations, and gaze upon the scene which the early rays of the rising Millennial day gild the morn of the twentieth century! . . . Disband your armies; turn your weapons of strife into implements of industry; take the yoke from the necks of the people." He bore his testimony that God, his Son, and holy angels had spoken to men and that God called upon all people to repent and come unto him. President Snow, then in his eighty-seventh year, concluded by invoking the blessing of heaven upon the earth's inhabitants, and wished them peace.[22]

To usher in the new year and the new century, special services were held in the Tabernacle on 31 December 1900 commencing at 11:00 P.M. Five thousand Saints gathered and saw the famed organ pipes illuminated with a cluster of electric lights fashioned into the words, "Welcome, 1901, Utah." A devotional spirit pervaded the meeting, which was conducted by Salt Lake Stake President Angus Cannon. No doubt many in the audience contemplated the growth and accomplishments of the Church as it now boldly faced a new century. There were, at the end of 1900, forty-three stakes, twenty missions, and 967 wards and branches in the stakes and missions. The Church had 283,765 members, most of whom lived in the intermountain West. Four temples were in operation—St. George, Manti, Logan, and Salt Lake City. In 1900, 796 new missionaries had been set apart to preach the gospel among the nations of the earth.[23]

With the increase in the number of missionaries being called, Church leaders recognized the need of training the missionaries more completely for their service. The First Council of the Seventy, in conjunction with the

Area Missionary Training Centers of
the Church

Location	Date of Opening
Sao Paulo, Brazil	Nov. 1977
Provo, Utah	Oct. 1978
Hamilton, New Zealand	Nov. 1978
Mexico City, Mexico	Jan. 1979
Tokyo, Japan	May 1979
Santiago, Chile	July 1981
Manila, Philippines	Oct. 1983
London, England	Feb. 1985
Seoul, Korea	Apr. 1985
Buenos Aires, Argentina	Feb. 1986
Guatemala City, Guatemala	May 1986
Lima, Peru	July 1986
Tonga	Apr. 1987
Samoa	Sept. 1987

General Church Board of Education, agreed in 1900 to open missionary training courses at Brigham Young Academy in Provo, the Latter-day Saints University in Salt Lake City, Brigham Young College in Logan, and the Latter-day Saints Academy in Thatcher, Arizona. Prospective missionaries were taught theology, religious history, and teaching methods from the scriptures in a six-month curriculum. The Church schools charged no tuition for the class, and stake presidents were expected to provide for board and lodging for their students.

Church members participated each Sunday in a two-hour afternoon sacrament meeting. Once a month a fast and testimony meeting was held, usually following the Sabbath morning Sunday School. During the winter months, young men and young women meetings were held during the week, often on Thursday nights. The Relief Society met during the day each Tuesday, and Primary for the children was held each Wednesday after school. Priesthood quorum meetings were conducted either on Monday evening or on Sunday morning and were discontinued during the summer months because most Church members were busy farming.

Ward conferences presided over by stake officials were convened once a year, beginning in 1892, where members had the privilege of sustaining their leaders and receiving instruction and motivation from their presiding officials. Many wards sponsored social outings under the direction of the Sunday School, where members presented programs in the morning, held children's parties in the afternoon, and danced away the evening. Each spring, wards sponsored old people's parties that were usually climaxed by a "grand" evening dinner in a splendidly decorated hall.

At the turn of the century, the Church's young women, in their official periodical, *Young Woman's Journal*, read articles about Longfellow's home, how to obtain a testimony of the truth, and ethics for young girls. They were also introduced to the Apostle Paul and the reminiscences of Elder Heber J. Grant. Women leaders wrote material that would not only deepen the young ladies' understanding of the gospel but would also acquaint them with the world's best literature. In addition they were instructed in quilting, basting, hemming, and buttonholing.

In January 1900 the *Juvenile Instructor*, which was designed to be read by all Church members, began a series entitled "Lives of Our Leaders—The Apostles." In each subsequent issue there was a biographical essay on one of the General Authorities of the Church. Latter-day Saints also read short stories and became acquainted with such places as Alaska, Belgium, and Ireland through the series of articles entitled "History of the Nations." Sunday School conferences were held in the stakes of the Church each year, at which reports were made and instructions given by general board members and General Authorities. Songs were sung by children's choruses, and in-service training was conducted to improve the quality of teaching. Stakes were large. The Utah Stake, for example, had forty-nine Sunday Schools organized with a total enrollment of eleven thousand Saints.

The *Improvement Era*, which replaced the *Contributor* as the organ of the Young Men's Mutual Improvement Association, published articles regarding the translation of the Book of Mormon, sermons of General Authorities, and responses to attacks by ministers and anti-Mormon writers. The Young Men and the Young Women organizations held annual general conferences that were attended by thousands of youth. In these gatherings the General Authorities gave instruction, and the people held dances, presented plays, and highlighted programs for the new year.

As the twentieth century began, Utah was a state, the Church was on a secure financial basis, and the Saints, for the most part, no longer feared being driven from their homes by mobs. They had made the desert blossom and were looking forward with anticipation to the fulfillment of the prophecies about the latter days.

RESPONSIBILITY OF THE TWELVE FURTHER CLARIFIED

As the twentieth century dawned and it became obvious that the pioneering period in the Intermountain West was over, President Lorenzo Snow became most concerned with the necessity of taking the gospel to all the world. The duty of such an undertaking rested with the Quorum of the Twelve Apostles. Under President Snow's direction the Apostles laid plans to open new areas of the world for missionary work.

In 1901, President George Q. Cannon, speaking for the First Presidency, announced that a mission would be opened in Japan. As he said these words, Elder Heber J. Grant received a very strong impression, as plainly as though a voice had spoken to him, informing him that he would be called to preside there. Twenty-five minutes later, President Cannon announced that Elder Grant had been selected to go to Japan. Although he was greatly in debt, he decided that he would not use that as an excuse but would go as called. The First Presidency gave him a year to put his affairs in order and prepare for his mission.

Elder John W. Taylor, who knew Heber's true financial condition and sacrifice, prophesied privately: "You shall be blessed of the Lord and make enough money to go to Japan a free man financially." Elder Grant went home immediately and prayed to the Lord for help in dealing with his financial challenges. By a series of resourceful moves, all of which Elder Grant testified were inspired by God, and through other blessings, he was out of debt within four months.[24] Elder Heber J. Grant called three others—Louis A. Kelsch, former president of the Northern States Mission, twenty-nine-year-old Horace S. Ensign, and eighteen-year-old Alma O. Taylor—to assist him in Japan. They left Salt Lake City on Pioneer Day, 24 July 1901, and arrived in Yokohama Harbor, after a turbulent ocean crossing, on 12 August.

Upon arriving in the city of Yokohama, the missionaries began making contacts. They made tentative arrangements for translation and publication of some Church literature and began to seek permanent lodgings. They

Heber J. Grant (1856–1945) at age twenty-three was called to be the president of the Tooele Stake. Two years later, just before his twenty-sixth birthday, he was called as a member of the Quorum of the Twelve Apostles. Nineteen years later he was sent to open Japan to missionary work.

This photograph was taken at the dedication of Japan. Left to right: Horace Ensign, Louis A. Kelsch, Heber J. Grant.

experienced much opposition, inspired largely by the ministers of other Christian sects who had learned of their coming and, being misled by false reports about the Church, were determined that it would not get a foothold.

The missionaries, however, were equally determined that the gospel would go forth. On 21 September 1901 they found a secluded spot in the woods outside Yokohama where they knelt, and Elder Grant offered up the dedicatory prayer. His tongue was loosed, and the Spirit rested mightily upon him—so much so that he recounted feeling that angels of God were near.

Elder Grant also prepared an " 'Address to the Great and Progressive Nation of Japan,' which tells in plain and positive terms the reason why the 'Mormon' missionaries are there. . . .

" '. . . We do not come to you for the purpose of trying to deprive you of any truth in which you believe, or any light that you have been privileged to enjoy. We bring to you greater light, more truth and advanced knowledge, which we offer you freely. . . .

" 'By His authority we turn the divine key which opens the kingdom of heaven to the inhabitants of Japan.' " He signed his letter, "Your servant for Christ's sake."[25]

After touring Japan, Elder Grant began a series of articles in the pages of the *Japan Mail*, one of the most influential newspapers in Tokyo, trying to counter the libelous attacks on the Church made by other Christian denominations.

Elder Grant returned to Utah after two years, but the other missionaries remained. Elder Taylor stayed for nine years, during which time he translated the Book of Mormon into Japanese. Due to the policy called "Japan for the Japanese," which the Japanese government began during the 1890s to minimize the westernization that had crept into their country, the Latter-day Saints and other Christian religions met with little success at this time. The Japanese Mission was finally closed in 1924. The great success that later attended missionary work in Japan came after 1945 and the end of World War II.

After Elder Grant left for Japan in 1901, the First Presidency and Council of the Twelve discussed taking the gospel to South America, the Austrian Empire, and Russia. The mission to Mexico was reopened in 1901 as a first step into Latin America. Elder Ammon M. Tenney was able to reestablish several former branches in Mexico. But due to insurmountable political problems, no further action was taken during this period.

Throughout the summer and early fall of 1901, which proved to be the last months of President Snow's life, the Spirit brooded upon the venerable prophet. Often in council meetings of the First Presidency and the Quorum of the Twelve, President Snow referred to the duty of the Apostles and Seventies to preach to the nations of the earth before the second coming of the Lord Jesus Christ. He bemoaned the fact that the Apostles and the Seven Presidents of Seventy were spending so much of their time on matters that

First Japanese missionary tract, "An Announcement Concerning the Church of Jesus Christ of Latter-day Saints" by Heber J. Grant, published in 1901. This same pamphlet was published in Japanese in 1903.

Heber J. Grant's missionary calling card. The inscription in the upper left corner is the name of the Church in Japanese.

should be attended to by local priesthood leaders. Even though he had been afflicted for weeks with a severe cold and hacking cough, President Snow was anxious to deliver an important address on this subject in the October general conference.

The prophet was excused from all the early sessions of conference because of his health, but he appeared in the Tabernacle to speak in the concluding Sunday session on 6 October 1901. These were his last public words to the Saints. President Joseph F. Smith noted a month later, "While it was plain to be seen then that he was feeble, yet it was generally remarked how clear he was in his mind and with what emphasis and freedom his words flowed from him."[26]

As he proceeded into this monumental address, President Snow explained, "This Church is now nearly seventy-two years of age, and we are not expected to do the work of the days of our youth, but to do greater, larger and more extensive work." The prophet then urged the stake presidents to regard the Saints in their charge as their own family and to look after their interests as they would those of their own sons and daughters. He continued, "Do not lay this duty upon the shoulders of the Apostles. . . . There is a certain channel by and through which the Lord intends to exalt His sons and daughters, to remove wickedness from the earth and to establish righteousness, and that channel is the Priesthood. . . . The Apostles and the Seventies, it is their business by the appointment of the Almighty, to look after the interests of the world. The Seventies and the Twelve Apostles are special witnesses unto the nations of the earth."[27] To channel the work of the Twelve in this direction, the First Presidency released them from all their administrative duties in the stakes.

Regarding President Snow's last charge to the General Authorities and the Saints, President Joseph F. Smith stated: "We accept what is contained therein on the duties of the Twelve, and presiding Priesthood, as the word of the Lord to us all. It is so plain and so convincing as to leave no room for doubt; and there remains but one thing for us to do, and that is to zealously and arduously labor to successfully accomplish all that is required at our hands."[28]

END OF AN ERA

During the three years that President Snow presided over the Church, several important Church leaders passed away. In some respects their passing was indicative that an era was coming to an end and a new leadership would guide the expanding kingdom. The periodicals of the Church noted with pictures and bold headlines the death of Karl G. Maeser, who at the time was serving in the superintendency of the General Sunday School of the Church and was one of the Church's most illustrious educators. Elder Franklin D. Richards, President of the Quorum of the Twelve Apostles, died in Salt Lake City on 9 December 1899. His loss was deeply felt in all parts of Zion, and the *Millennial Star* especially noted his passing.[29]

On 12 April 1901, Church members learned of the death of Elder George Q. Cannon. At the time of his death he was serving as the first counselor in the First Presidency and as President of the Quorum of the Twelve Apostles. He had served four Church presidents as a counselor and left his imprint upon the Church through the pages of the *Juvenile Instructor*, a magazine he had founded and had edited for more than three decades. His public discourses were masterpieces and filled volumes. He was an astute politician who had represented the Utah Territory in Congress for more than a decade and was very influential in obtaining statehood for Utah.

Zina Huntington Young, who had succeeded Eliza R. Snow as the Church's General Relief Society President, died at her Salt Lake home on 28 August 1901. She was a wife of President Brigham Young and had been a delegate to the National Women's Conference in Buffalo, New York. She had also served as president of the Deseret Hospital for more than a decade.

President Snow had heeded his family's and physician's advice and attended only the last session of general conference because of a severe chest cold. But the strain of projecting his voice so he could be heard by the vast audience in the Tabernacle returned him to his sickbed. On 10 October 1901, he quietly passed away. After a large funeral, his body was interred in the Brigham City Cemetery.

President Lorenzo Snow placed his apostolic calling above all else. He taught the Latter-day Saints how to live a life of culture and refinement, despite their poverty and desert environment. He also taught them how to convert the commonplace into something of uncommon beauty. He lived with poise and dignity and gave God the credit for his power. He clearly taught the Saints what they could become if they followed the teachings they had received through their prophets.

Franklin D. Richards (1821–99) was a devout student and avid reader as a youth. He welcomed the opportunity to read the Book of Mormon and was converted at age fifteen but was not baptized until 1838. Four months later his brother George S. was killed by the mob at Haun's Mill.

Franklin was on his way to a mission in England when he heard the news of the martyrdom of Joseph and Hyrum Smith in 1844. He completed the mission in 1846 while his wife Jane and infant daughter went West with the pioneers. His daughter died along the way. Meanwhile, another brother, Joseph W., died of illness during the march with the Mormon Battalion.

In 1849, Franklin was ordained an Apostle at the age of twenty-seven. He served as a General Authority for fifty years.

The three years Lorenzo Snow presided over the Church were significant ones. He made sound decisions that placed the Church once more on the road to financial solvency. He died as he lived, firm in the faith he had embraced when just a young man in Mantua, Ohio.

Endnotes

1. "The Redemption of Zion," *Millennial Star*, 29 Nov. 1900, p. 754.

2. "The Grand Destiny of Man," *Millennial Star*, 22 Aug. 1901, p. 547; see also "The Grand Destiny of Man," 15 Aug. 1901, pp. 541–42; LeRoi C. Snow, "Devotion to a Divine Inspiration," *Improvement Era*, June 1919, p. 656.

3. See "Memorandum in the Handwriting of President Lorenzo Snow," *Elder's Journal*, 1 Dec. 1906, pp. 110–11; Reed C. Durham, Jr., and Steven H. Heath, *Succession in the Church* (Salt Lake City: Bookcraft, 1970), pp. 103–4.

4. LeRoi C. Snow, "Remarkable Manifestation to Lorenzo Snow," *Church News*, 2 Apr. 1938, pp. 3, 8; see also N. B. Lundwall, comp., *Temples of the Most High* (Salt Lake City: N. B. Lundwall, 1968), pp. 139–41; Thomas C. Romney, *The Life of Lorenzo Snow* (Salt Lake City: Deseret News Press, 1955), pp. 441–42.

5. See Romney, *Life of Lorenzo Snow*, pp. 443–44.

6. Journal History of The Church of Jesus Christ of Latter-day Saints, 13 Sept. 1898, Historical Department, Salt Lake City, pp. 2–6.

7. An Apostle at large is a special witness of Christ ordained to bear witness to the world of the divine mission of the Savior. Unless placed in the Quorum of the Twelve, however, he is not part of the governing body of the Church.

8. See Joseph Fielding Smith, comp., *Life of Joseph F. Smith*, 2d ed. (Salt Lake City: Deseret Book Co., 1969), pp. 310–11.

9. Leonard J. Arrington, *Great Basin Kingdom: An Economic History of the Latter-day Saints, 1830–1900* (Cambridge: Harvard University Press, 1958), p. 402.

10. In Romney, *Life of Lorenzo Snow*, p. 456.

11. LeRoi C. Snow, "The Lord's Way out of Bondage Was Not the Way of Men," *Improvement Era*, July 1938, p. 439.

12. Snow, "The Lord's Way out of Bondage," p. 440.

13. In Snow, "The Lord's Way out of Bondage," p. 442.

14. J. [Susa Young Gates], "Biographical Sketches: Jennie Brimhall and Inez Knight," *Young Woman's Journal*, June 1898, p. 245.

15. In Susa Young Gates, "Biographical Sketches: Elizabeth Claridge McCune," *Young Woman's Journal*, Aug. 1898, pp. 339–40.

16. J. [Gates], "Jennie Brimhall and Inez Knight," pp. 245–46.

17. See "Women as Missionaries," *Millennial Star*, 23 June 1898, p. 398.

18. "A Letter from Bristol," *Millennial Star*, 28 July 1898, p. 477.

19. See Inez Knight, in "Our Girls," *Young Woman's Journal*, Sept. 1898, p. 416.

20. See "Bristol Conference," *Millennial Star*, 26 Jan. 1899, p. 58.

21. In "Our Girls," *Young Woman's Journal*, Apr. 1899, p. 187.

22. Lorenzo Snow, *Greeting to the World* (pamphlet, 1900), p. 1.

23. See *Deseret News 1987 Church Almanac* (Salt Lake City: Deseret News, 1986), pp. 239, 253.

24. Heber J. Grant, "Ram in the Thicket," *Improvement Era*, Dec. 1941, pp. 713, 765, 767.

25. "Address to the Japanese," *Millennial Star*, 26 Sept. 1901, pp. 625–27.

26. Joseph F. Smith, "The Last Days of President Snow," *Juvenile Instructor*, 15 Nov. 1901, p. 689.

27. In Conference Report, Oct. 1901, p. 61.

28. Smith, "Last Days of President Snow," p. 690.

29. "Biographical Sketch of President F. D. Richards," *Millennial Star*, 4 Jan. 1900, pp. 1-8.

THE CHURCH IN THE EARLY TWENTIETH CENTURY

B. H. Roberts (1857–1933), distinguished looking in his mature years, was a fearless defender of the faith. (Additional biographical information accompanies his photograph on page 433 in chapter 33.)

AFTER THE BRIEF period of comparative goodwill, which followed the issuance of the Manifesto and the admission of the state of Utah into the union, the Church again faced serious internal and external problems. As the twentieth century began, the progressive movement was calling the nation's attention to the wrongs, both alleged and real, in all aspects of American society. During this time, the media focused on the B. H. Roberts' case directing the attention of the progressive and national leaders in the country once again upon the Church and its members.

THE CASE OF BRIGHAM H. ROBERTS OF UTAH

In the summer of 1896, the First Presidency sent Elder Brigham Henry Roberts, a member of the First Quorum of the Seventy and one of the finest orators in the Church, and a quartet selected from members of the Tabernacle Choir, on a goodwill mission to the eastern United States. George D. Pyper, an outstanding vocalist, led the quartet as tenor soloist. Elder Roberts visited such eastern cities as St. Louis, Cincinnati, Pittsburgh, Philadelphia, and New York. At St. Louis he delivered a series of forty-two lectures, each averaging an hour and a quarter in length and "when the lectures were over, sixty persons had been baptized, forming the nucleus of a flourishing and vital branch of the Church in St. Louis."[1] Because of his love for the gospel of Jesus Christ and his defense of it throughout his lifetime, B. H. Roberts became known as "Defender of the Faith."

When he returned to Utah, Elder Roberts was asked by some of the state Democratic leaders to run for a seat in the United States House of Representatives. After obtaining the approval of the First Presidency, he consented to run. He received his party's nomination in September 1898. After a vigorous campaign, Roberts was elected with nearly a six thousand vote plurality. Almost immediately after his victory, however, a group of sectarian ministers joined forces with attorney A. Theodore Schroeder, who was also the editor of the Utah based anti-Mormon periodical *Lucifer's Lantern*, in an attempt to keep Roberts from being seated.

Schroeder, born and educated in Wisconsin, had come to Utah to practice law so he could "see and study a new religious establishment in the making." While in Salt Lake City he "helped revamp the *Salt Lake Herald* as the official organ of the Democratic Party of which he was also one of forty charter organizers in Utah." He also befriended people in Utah who opposed the Church, and he prosecuted "the case against B. H. Roberts resulting in the exclusion of Roberts from the Congress of the United States."[2]

Because Elder Roberts was a polygamist, his opponents were able to collect from throughout the nation over seven million signatures on a petition proposing that he not be allowed to take his congressional seat. This was the largest number ever to sign a petition up to that time in American history. However, President Lorenzo Snow said, "As Roberts later put it, 'the storm was the equivalent of a mosquito lighting on the moon.' "[3]

After arriving in Washington, D.C., Representative Roberts found that he would not be allowed to take his seat in Congress until after the petition issue was decided. Meanwhile he prepared to defend himself and his right as a polygamist to be a member of Congress. The debate raged on for fifteen months. The opposition, motivated by a variety of religious, moral, and political reasons, united in their efforts to deny Roberts his congressional seat. Some attacked the Church with the charge that many of its polygamous men were still supporting more than one family, while others charged that Mormons were not supporting their wives and children. They attacked those members who believed plural marriage to be God-given and condemned others for abandoning its practice. Yet another charge they made was that the Church had given up the practice of plural marriage but had not relinquished the belief in it. And finally, Latter-day Saints were accused of both loving and failing to love the children of former polygamous unions.[4]

The controversy frequently made the front pages of the country's major newspapers. The women of the nation who believed that plural marriage was demeaning to females also opposed Roberts; some politicians concluded that the pressure exerted by these suffragettes led to his exclusion. Meanwhile, the nation's cartoonists and satirists featured his caricature so often that he was recognized everywhere he went.

Just before the final balloting, a tired, yet determined Elder Roberts was allowed one last defense. Known in some circles as "the Blacksmith Orator," because he had been a blacksmith as a youth, he concluded his defense with this declaration:

"Some of the papers in discussing the Roberts case have said, 'Brand this man with shame and send him back to his people.' Mr. Speaker, I thank God that the power to brand me with shame is something quite beyond the powers of this House, great as this power is. The power to brand with shame rests with each man and nowhere else. The Almighty God has conferred it upon none else. I have lived up to this day in all good conscience in harmony with the moral teachings of the community in which I was reared, and am sensible of no act of shame in my life. Brand me or expel me, I shall leave this august chamber with head erect and brow undaunted and walk God's earth as the angels walk the clouds, with no sense of shame upon me.'

"(Applause from the floor, and hisses from the gallery)

"And, if in response to the sectarian clamor that has been invoked against the member from Utah, you violate the Constitution of your country, either in excluding or expelling me, the shame that there is in this case will be left behind me and rest with this House.

"(Applause)."[5]

In spite of the magnificence of his final speech, two hundred and sixty-eight voted for his exclusion, fifty were against it, and thirty-six abstained from voting. Though Elder Roberts fought valiantly and conducted himself with dignity so that he was a credit to his Church and his country, the House was of the opinion that no man with more than one wife could serve in its chambers. B. H. Roberts never ran for public office again.

PRESIDENT JOSEPH F. SMITH

Just one month before his sixty-third birthday, Joseph F. Smith, who had been a counselor to four Church presidents, was ordained to succeed Lorenzo Snow, who died 10 October 1901. He was a son of the martyred Hyrum Smith and a nephew of Joseph Smith, for whom he was named. His widowed mother, Mary Fielding Smith, was a woman of great faith, who taught him the gospel by example as well as by precept. When only fifteen years old, Joseph F. commenced a successful mission to Hawaii. Ten years later, in 1864, he accompanied Lorenzo Snow to the islands to put a stop to the heresy in the Church caused by Walter Murray Gibson. While they were on the island of Maui, it was revealed to Elder Snow that Joseph F. Smith would some day preside over the Church.[6] He was only twenty-eight years old when he was called by Brigham Young to be an Apostle.

Joseph F. Smith studied the gospel assiduously and was known for his scriptural understanding, his love of doctrine, and his powerful sermons. He was also a devoted father whose letters to his children are filled with love and sound instruction. At a special solemn assembly held 10 November 1901, he was sustained as Church president. He chose as his counselors John R. Winder, who had served in the Presiding Bishopric of the Church, and Anthon H. Lund of the Quorum of the Twelve Apostles.

Early in his administration, President Smith gave Reed Smoot, who had been called to the apostleship in the spring of 1900 at the age of thirty-eight, permission to campaign for the United States Senate. Prominent in Utah politics and one of the founders of the state's Republican Party, he was elected to the United States Senate in 1903. His successful quest embroiled the Church and the nation in hearings that lasted almost five years. The news coverage of these hearings once again cast the Church into a glaring spotlight of publicity throughout the nation.

THE REED SMOOT HEARINGS

Upon becoming "dean" of the United States Senate in 1930, Apostle Reed Smoot was, according to the editor of the *Salt Lake Telegram*, "Utah's Most Distinguished Native Citizen." This followed the newspaper's poll, which

Joseph F. Smith (1838–1918) became the sixth President of the Church in October 1901. He had distinguished himself in Church service for forty-five years since becoming an Apostle as a young man in 1866.

He was an authority on Church doctrine. Selections from his sermons and writings were collected in 1919 in a volume entitled Gospel Doctrine. *This has been a standard reference work for Latter-day Saints in the twentieth century.*

Reed Smoot (1862–1941) showed considerable energy and ambition as a young man in Provo's Cooperative and Woolen Mills. He eventually became a successful businessman who held important positions in a number of Utah businesses. He was also a member of the board of trustees of Brigham Young Academy for years.

In 1900, Lorenzo Snow ordained Reed Smoot an Apostle. For thirty of his forty-one years in the Council of the Twelve, he served as United States Senator from Utah.

found that Senator Smoot was overwhelmingly number one.[7] During the thirty years he served in the Senate, he became one of its most influential and powerful members and had the opportunity of associating with the world's presidents, prime ministers, kings, and queens. His beginning as a member of that august body, however, did not foretell this success.

In 1906, soon after the Smoot hearings, one friend of Joseph F. Smith concluded that Elder Smoot should not be reelected; while traveling from Europe with President Smith, he broached the subject "as cautiously and as adroitly" as he could. President Smith heard him out, then pounded the railing between them, and emphatically said, "If I have ever had the inspiration of the spirit of the Lord given to me forcefully and clearly it has been on this one point concerning Reed Smoot, and that is, instead of his being retired, he should be continued in the United States Senate."[8]

Divine approval to seek a seat in the Senate, however, had not guaranteed victory. In 1902 senators were elected by state legislators, not by popular vote; therefore, Elder Smoot began to organize his supporters in the Utah legislature to secure his election. In January 1903 he received forty-six votes in the Republican controlled legislature; his opponents won a total of sixteen. An Apostle was now a United States senator.

Within days of his victory, a group of nineteen Salt Lake citizens protested to the president of the United States against the senator's election. They charged him with being "one of a self-perpetuating body of fifteen men who, constituting the ruling authorities of the Church of Jesus Christ of Latter-day Saints, or 'Mormon' Church, claim, and by their followers are accorded the right to claim, supreme authority, divinely sanctioned, to shape the belief and control the conduct of those under them in all matters whatsoever, civil and religious, temporal and spiritual."[9] Soon the same groups that had opposed the seating of B. H. Roberts in the House of Representatives four years earlier united again in popular opposition against Senator Smoot. One of the nation's more sensational newspapers printed the following verse on its front page. This was typical of the sentiment at the time.

"Can't you get wise to the fact, that you're not wanted?
Don't you understand that an apostle would be out of place in
a bunch of politicians?
Don't you see that you wouldn't fit?
Smoot,
Leave
Washington and the Gentile Roost,
Back, pack your old carpet sack,
And spank your feet on the homeward track,
Scoot—Smoot—Scoot."[10]

When Elder Smoot arrived in Washington, D.C., late in February 1903, Senator J. C. Burrows introduced the "Citizen's Protest" to the committee on privileges and elections. A few days later, John L. Leilich, superintendent of missions of the Utah district of the Methodist Church, brought additional charges against Smoot, including the accusation that he was a polygamist. This was untrue, and Elder Smoot was able to prove it. Unlike B. H. Roberts, Elder Smoot was allowed to take his seat while the investigation ran its course. In March 1903 he received the senatorial oath. As a senator, his administrative skills, wise judgment, and integrity soon became apparent. He also became adroit in parliamentary skills, which proved to be a valuable asset when it came time for the final vote to be taken on his case.

"'The Smoot Case,' as it was beginning to be called, stimulated the revival of old anti-Mormon stories and inspired the creation of new ones. The Danites reappeared, the Mountain Meadows Massacre was revived, Brigham Young's 'harem' again became a subject for popular discussion. The *New York Herald* devoted a full page to the horrors of polygamy." The *New York Commercial Advertizer* made the ridiculous charge that Mormon "missionaries were paid by head for their converts, a meager $4.00 for a male, but up to $60 for a girl over 16 whom they could and did place in polygamy."[11]

In January 1904, with the help of several non-Mormon lawyers, Senator Smoot filed a formal reply to the charges against him, but the actual hearings did not begin until March. President Joseph F. Smith, the first witness, was interrogated for three days. His honesty and forthrightness in answering the questions won him the grudging respect of many of the senators. Other Church witnesses included James E. Talmage, who clarified points regarding Mormon doctrine; Francis M. Lyman, President of the Quorum of the Twelve; Andrew Jenson, assistant Church historian; B. H. Roberts; and Moses Thatcher, who had been dropped from the Quorum of the Twelve in 1896. Thatcher's testimony was particularly helpful in countering the charge that the Church leaders "controlled" the lives of the Saints. The testimonies of these Church leaders made the front page news in the nation's newspapers.

After more than two years, the hearings finally ended. Those opposing the senator alleged that Church leaders were still practicing plural marriage, that the Church was exerting too much influence in Utah politics, that members were required to take oaths in the temple opposing constitutional principles, and that Church members believed revelation from God was higher than the laws of the land. Senator Fred T. Dubois of Idaho, fighting for his political life, ranted and raved so much against Smoot and other Church leaders that many of the Republicans who controlled the Senate believed that Senator Smoot was as powerful as Dubois declared him to be.

On 20 February 1907 the Republican Party defeated the proposal that Reed Smoot be removed from his seat. The victory was won in part because Republican leaders, including President Theodore Roosevelt, concluded that if Smoot remained in the Senate he would be a significant influence in keeping Utah a Republican state. With this victory finally behind him,

Senator Smoot spent the next twenty-six years in the nation's capital as one of its most influential figures.

THE AFTERMATH OF THE SMOOT HEARINGS

Through the observations of Senator Smoot and other prominent Latter-day Saints in the East, the First Presidency learned that the general populace of the United States perceived Church leaders as trying to circumvent the law. They were accused of not being serious in their efforts to end plural marriage. On 6 April 1904, after deliberation and prayer and in response to these allegations, President Joseph F. Smith issued a statement that has become known as the "second manifesto." In the pronouncement, President Smith declared that any officer of the Church who solemnized a plural marriage, as well as the participating couple, would be excommunicated. He stated clearly that this pronouncement applied everywhere in the world.

Unfortunately, two members of the Quorum of the Twelve, John W. Taylor and Matthias F. Cowley, were not in harmony with their fellow leaders regarding the scope and meaning of the original Manifesto, nor were they able to agree with the second pronouncement issued by President Smith. At the commencement of the Smoot hearings, Taylor and Cowley went into seclusion to avoid testifying in Washington, D.C.

Following the Smoot hearings, these two Apostles submitted their resignations from the Quorum of the Twelve. It was widely known that they had performed more than a few plural marriages after the Manifesto was issued. Their resignations from the Twelve did much to symbolize that plural marriage had indeed ended. Six years later John W. Taylor was excommunicated from the Church because he had married another plural wife after his resignation. Elder Cowley, although never reinstated as a member of the Quorum of the Twelve, remained faithful to the Church. In the 1930s he served a mission to England. One of his sons, Matthew Cowley, who had served as mission president in New Zealand, was later called as an Apostle.

THE MEDIA ATTACKS THE CHURCH

Serving simultaneously with Reed Smoot as the other senator from Utah was the non-Mormon mining tycoon, Thomas Kearns, who had secured his election to the Senate partly because of the support he had received from President Lorenzo Snow. During his first term in office, he was neither effective nor popular with his senatorial colleagues, with the people of Utah, or with the Utah state Senate, which had elected him. Furthermore, the new Church president, Joseph F. Smith, did not believe Kearns should retain his Senate seat. These factors cost him reelection. Bitter and angry, he placed full blame upon the Church. In his final senatorial speech, he delivered a blistering tirade condemning the Church leadership as a "monarchy" which monopolized the business, political, and social life of Utah. He further declared, "This monarchy permits its favorites to enter into polygamy."[12]

Thomas Kearns (1862–1918) was born in Canada. As a young boy he moved to Nebraska, where he grew up on a farm. Most of his life was spent mining in the Black Hills of Dakota, in Arizona, and finally in Utah. He made his fortune mining silver in Park City, Utah.

After returning to Utah, Kearns helped form the American political party, which was a revival of the old anti-Mormon Liberal party that had been disbanded in 1893. He also purchased the *Salt Lake Tribune* and hired Frank J. Cannon, the excommunicated son of President George Q. Cannon, as its editor.

Cannon's editorials in the *Tribune* raged against the Church and its leaders. As his editorials and anti-Mormon articles increased in hate, Cannon's credibility decreased. He finally moved to Denver, where he continued writing until his death in 1933. Nevertheless, for a time Cannon's virulent anti-Mormon books and articles greatly affected many people's perception of the Latter-day Saints. Likewise Kearns's actions and speeches stimulated other editors and led them to print vicious statements against the Church. Between 1907–11 with the *Salt Lake Tribune* leading the way, there was an increase in anti-Mormon propaganda that was much more sinister than that of the Roberts and Smoot episodes.

President Smith chose not to respond to such charges but rather declared: "I bear no malice toward any of the children of my Father. But there are enemies to the work of the Lord, as there were enemies to the Son of God. There are those who speak only evil of the Latter-day Saints. There are those—and they abound largely in our midst, who will shut their eyes to every virtue and to every good thing connected with this latter-day work, and will pour out floods of falsehood and misrepresentation against the people of God. I forgive them for this. I leave them in the hand of the just Judge."[13]

Four national magazines—*Pearson's, Everybody's, McClure's,* and *Cosmopolitan*—viciously attacked the Latter-day Saints. They demonstrated little understanding of the Church and its divine mission. Partly because of his friendship with Senator Smoot, President Theodore Roosevelt came to the defense of the Church and published a letter in *Collier's* that refuted many of the false charges being made against Church officials. The president also denied the rising allegations being circulated that he had made political deals with the Mormons. He also strongly proclaimed the virtues and high standards of the Latter-day Saints.[14] This letter helped temper the allegations being made against the Church in the United States. The letter was not published in Europe, however, where the Church was also under heavy attack. A dozen or more anti-Mormon books and articles from the American muckraking press had made there way to Europe and were being circulated there.

During the years 1910–14 there were scenes of unparalleled violence against the LDS missionaries in Great Britain. Britain was undergoing great social change during this period, and many people there came to believe that the Church represented a threat to their established ways and traditional moral values. Furthermore, they were convinced that plural marriage was still being practiced and that missionaries were luring away British girls.

British popular novelist Winifred Graham (Mrs. Theodore Cory) wrote several anti-Mormon novels; on one occasion she declared, "I found it thrilling to fight with voice and pen this mighty kingdom working for self-interest, a vampire in fact, sucking the blood of Europe with its wolf-like emissaries in sheep's clothing hot on the heels of British womanhood."[15]

As a result of all this propaganda, the British Parliament debated whether or not to expel all Latter-day Saints from English soil. Young Winston Churchill, displaying great courage, helped the Church's cause by invoking the right of religious freedom. No expulsions took place. Still, there were scenes of violence and mobocracy at Birkenhead, Boothe, Heywood, and eight other cities in England. In the course of these confrontations one elder was tarred and feathered, another was hit in the face, and still another had lime dust thrown into his face, causing temporary blindness. Other missionaries were roughly handled by the infuriated populace who gathered in the streets by the thousands.

In spite of the opposition, miracles did happen. A young, inexperienced elder from Canada named Hugh B. Brown was laboring in Cambridge in 1904. On his arrival in that city, he saw posters in the train station declaring "Beware of the vile deceivers; the Mormons are returning. Drive them out." For two days he went from house to house leaving tracts where he could and unsuccessfully attempting to engage Britons in gospel conversations.[16] One Saturday evening, as he later remembered, a knock came on the door.

"The lady of the house answered the door. I heard a voice say, 'Is there an Elder Brown lives here?' I thought, 'Oh, oh, here it is!'

"She said, 'Why, yes, he's in the front room. Come in, please.'

"He came in and said, 'Are you Elder Brown?'

"I was not surprised that he was surprised. I said, 'Yes, sir.'

"He said, 'Did you leave this tract at my door?'

"Well, my name and address were on it. Though I was attempting at that time to get ready to practice law, I didn't know how to answer it. I said, 'Yes, sir, I did.'

"He said, 'Last Sunday there were 17 of us heads of families left the Church of England. We went to my home where I have a rather large room. Each of us has a large family, and we filled the large room with men, women and children. We decided that we would pray all through the week that the Lord would send us a new pastor. When I came home tonight I was discouraged, I thought our prayer had not been answered. But when I found this tract under my door, I knew the Lord had answered our prayer. Will you come tomorrow night and be our new pastor?'

"Now, I hadn't been in the mission field three days. I didn't know anything about missionary work, and he wanted me to be their pastor. But I was reckless enough to say, 'Yes, I'll come.' And I repented from then till the time of the meeting.

"He left, and took my appetite with him! I called in the lady of the house and told her I didn't want any tea [supper]. I went up to my room and prepared for bed. I knelt at my bed. My young brothers and sisters, for the first time in my life I talked with God. I told Him of my predicament. I pleaded for His help. I asked Him to guide me. I pleaded that He would take it off my hands. I got up and went to bed and couldn't sleep and got out and prayed again, and kept that up all night—but I really talked with God."

He spent the next day without breakfast or lunch, walking and worrying that he had to be the religious leader for these people.

"Finally it came to the point where the clock said 6:45. I got up and put on my long Prince Albert coat, my stiff hat which I had acquired in Norwich, took my walking cane (which we always carried in those days), my kid gloves, put a Bible under my arm, and dragged myself down to that building, literally. I just made one track all the way.

"Just as I got to the gate the man came out, the man I had seen the night before. He bowed very politely and said, 'Come in, Reverend, sir.' I had never been called that before. I went in an saw the room filled with people, and they all stood up to honor their new pastor, and that scared me to death.

"Then I had come to the point where I began to think what I had to do, and I realized I had to say something about singing. I suggested that we sing 'O My Father.' I was met with a blank stare. We sang it—it was a terrible cowboy solo. Then I thought, if I could get these people to turn around and kneel by their chairs, they wouldn't be looking at me while I prayed. I asked them if they would and they responded readily. They all knelt down and I knelt down, and for the second time in my life I talked with God. All fear left me. I didn't worry any more. I was turning it over to Him.

"I said to Him, among other things, 'Father in Heaven, these folks have left the Church of England. They have come here tonight to hear the truth. You know that I am not prepared to give them what they want, but Thou art, O God, the one that can; and if I can be an instrument through whom You speak, very well, but please take over.'

"When we arose most of them were weeping, as was I. Wisely I dispensed with the second hymn, and I started to talk. I talked 45 minutes. I don't know what I said. I didn't talk—God spoke through me, as subsequent events proved. And He spoke so powerfully to that group that at the close of that meeting they came and put their arms around me, held my hands. They said, 'This is what we have been waiting for. Thank God you came.'

"I told you I dragged myself down to that meeting. On my way back home that night I only touched ground once, I was so elated that God had taken off my hands an insuperable task for man.

"Within three months every man, woman and child in that audience was baptized a member of the Church."[17]

THE TEMPLE SQUARE MISSION

In an effort to explain to non-Church members the true story of the Latter-day Saint people and to combat adverse publicity, the Church established the Temple Square Mission. As early as 1875, Charles J. Thomas, custodian of the Salt Lake Temple, then under construction, was assigned to meet tourists, show them around Temple Square, and answer their questions. He kept a book in which visitors to Temple Square could sign their names. In subsequent years, many famous people, including two presidents of the United States signed Brother Thomas's register.[18] Several attempts were made during the next twenty-five years to provide guides and information on a continual basis for the visitors.

During the 1880–90s, James Dwyer, a book merchant in Salt Lake City, went to Temple Square daily where he discussed the gospel with tourists and gave each one an Articles of Faith card, which he had had printed. On the reverse side was a picture of the temple and an imprint which stated: "Should you wish any further information concerning Church doctrines, please write James Dwyer, North Temple Street, Salt Lake City." Because of his efforts, James "was the father of the information movement in Salt Lake City."[19] In July 1901, President Snow's son LeRoi overheard a hack (cab) driver telling colorful falsehoods regarding the Church. As a result of LeRoi Snow's efforts, the First Presidency in 1901 requested the seventies of the Church to establish a bureau of information on Temple Square.[20]

In March of that year, a small pavilion, from which the Church could dispense correct information, was built for about five hundred dollars. One

This small building built on Temple Square for the 1897 jubilee celebration was the first bureau of information. The first mission on Temple Square was not established until 1902.

hundred men and women were called to serve as guides. They were assigned regular schedules to conduct tours of Temple Square and tell the true story of the Latter-day Saints. In addition, organ recitals in the Tabernacle were held twice a day in the summer. Over 150,000 people visited Temple Square that year.

The first visitors' center was built on Temple Square in 1903. A second story was added in 1915. The building served as both a museum and an information bureau until it was replaced by today's modern visitors' center, which was built north of the Tabernacle in the 1970s.

The mission was not without its opponents. Local non-LDS groups and the *Salt Lake Tribune* united their efforts to undermine the positive impact the guides and literature had on tourists. They occasionally posted anti-Mormon "guides" at the entrances to Temple Square in an attempt to give visitors misinformation regarding the Latter-day Saints. By 1904, because of the large number of tourists and the success of the mission, the Church constructed a much larger building of granite and brick. By 1905 the number of visitors swelled to a yearly total of 200,000. In 1915 a second story was added to the bureau building to house the Deseret Museum. Many other changes were made later, but the essential work of the Temple Square Mission has remained an important part of the Church's missionary program.[21]

HISTORIC SITES PURCHASED

Believing that the truths of the Restoration could be effectively told through visitors' centers at various historical sites, the Church, as its means allowed, began acquiring places of historical significance. President Joseph F. Smith's personal background heightened his interest in Church history, and it was during his administration that many of the sites of early Church history were purchased.

On 5 November 1903 the first site was acquired: Carthage Jail, where Joseph and Hyrum Smith were martyred. In June 1907 the Church purchased

Early in 1915 newlyweds Willard (1868–1949) and Rebecca (1891–1976) Bean attended a conference in Richfield, Utah, presided over by President Joseph F. Smith. President Smith was looking for the right man to represent the Church and run the Joseph Smith farm in Manchester, New York. President Smith later said that when Willard walked in, "The impression was so strong—it was just like a voice said to me, 'There's your man.'"[22]

Despite severe anti-Mormon prejudice, the Beans persevered and eventually won the respect of the people in the nearby village of Palmyra. Willard was instrumental in helping the Church purchase several other important historical sites in the area. What was expected to be "five years or more" of service in Palmyra turned out to be twenty-five. When the Beans returned to Salt Lake City, they were grandparents.

Efforts to erect a monument on the centennial date of the Prophet Joseph Smith's birth at his birthplace in Vermont were led by Junius F. Wells. The granite stones for the monument included a base stone, a shaft stone, and a capstone. The shaft stone was 38 1/2 feet long and was cut from a sixty ton block. To move the shaft stone the six miles from the railhead to the site took twenty days. Through the faith and energy of Brother Wells, the monument was ready for the dedicatory services on 23 December 1905.

This beautiful visitors' center was built in 1971 in Independence, Missouri, on property reacquired by the Church in 1904. President Joseph Fielding Smith, grandson of Hyrum Smith, presided at the dedication. President N. Eldon Tanner offered the dedicatory prayer.

the one-hundred-acre Smith homestead near Palmyra, New York, which included the Sacred Grove, where in 1820 the Prophet received the First Vision. Willard Bean, a former boxer from Utah, and Rebecca, his bride of less than a year, were sent in 1915 to take care of the farm after the former owner moved. They were challenged to preach the gospel and make friends for the Church in that area. They became the first Latter-day Saints to live in Manchester in eighty-four years.[23]

Between 1905 and 1907 the Church also obtained, through four separate purchases, title to the Mack family farm near the village of Sharon, Vermont, the site of the Prophet's birth. A memorial cottage, or small visitors' center, was constructed on the site, and nearby an imposing monument of polished Vermont granite was erected in honor of the Prophet Joseph Smith. It was dedicated by his nephew President Joseph F. Smith on 23 December 1905, the one-hundredth anniversary of the Prophet's birth. The monument stands 38 1/2 feet high—one foot for each year of his life.

Significant Missouri properties were also acquired during this era. The first was a tract of about twenty acres of land purchased in 1904 in Independence, Missouri. This was part of the original sixty-three acres bought by the Church in 1831. A chapel and a visitors' center have since been built on this property. The Church also later purchased the temple site at Far West in northern Missouri.

In addition to attracting large numbers of Latter-day Saints interested in the history of their faith, these sites also provided opportunities for the Church to share its message with the world. On several of these sites, bureaus of information, patterned after the successful program on Temple Square, were constructed to facilitate the missionary effort. At others, visitors learned the story of the Latter-day Saints as it pertained to the specific site they were visiting.

THE CHURCH PUBLISHED ITS OWN HISTORY

B. H. Roberts read an article in the *Salt Lake Tribune* reviving the false theory that Solomon Spaulding was the true author of the Book of Mormon. Elder Roberts contacted the editor and asked if he could write a reply. He was informed that the article was a reprint of one written by Theodore Schroeder that had appeared in the *New York Historical Magazine.*

Elder Roberts sent his rebuttal to the *New York Historical Magazine.* It was received so favorably that he was invited to write a history of the Church for them. By the time arrangements were completed, the name of the magazine had been changed to *Americana,* and monographs written by Elder Roberts appeared in it for the next six years. These articles became the basis for his six-volume *Comprehensive History of the Church,* which was presented as a memorial to the Latter-day Saints for the centennial celebration in 1930.

For years Elder Roberts had collected copies of materials by or about the Prophet Joseph Smith that appeared in various magazines, but largely from Church periodicals. On one occasion he showed his collection to Francis M. Lyman, who enthusiastically suggested to the Quorum of the Twelve, of which he was a member, that Elder Roberts be commissioned to publish his collection with extensive footnotes, to provide context and clarity to the early documents of Church history. The Twelve accepted Elder Lyman's suggestion, and B. H. Roberts was asked to submit a cost estimate for the project.

A few weeks later Elder Roberts turned in his estimate. President George Q. Cannon believed that Roberts's costs were too high and offered to do the same thing at his own expense. Lorenzo Snow accepted President Cannon's offer. At the outset of the project, however, President Cannon died, and Elder Roberts was asked to finish the work. After reading the documents President Cannon had intended to publish, Elder Roberts went to the First Presidency and told them he wanted to do much more with the material. He was given permission to do the work as he saw fit, and with their approval he started over.

Elder Roberts consulted diaries, printed sources, and remembrances of Church members to prepare a history of the Church that centered mainly on the life of Joseph Smith. Before it was published, Elder Anthon H. Lund and President Joseph F. Smith read and approved the work. The resulting seven volumes, over forty-five-hundred pages, known as the *History of the Church* has since become a great resource to Church members and historians alike. This multi-volume work, along with his six-volume *Comprehensive History of the Church,* made B. H. Roberts the foremost Latter-day Saint historian of the first century of the Church's existence.

Emmeline B. Wells (1828–1921) was converted to the gospel in 1842 and was married the next year at age fifteen and a half. After the martyrdom of the Prophet Joseph Smith, her husband went to sea and never returned. Staying faithful to the Church, she became a plural wife of Newel K. Whitney in 1845, and after his death she became a plural wife of Daniel H. Wells in 1852.

In 1877, Emmeline became editor of the Womans' Exponent. She remained at that post until the publication was suspended in 1914. In the late nineteenth century she was heavily involved in the woman's suffrage movement and attended numerous conferences on women's issues.

Throughout her life she maintained an interest in education and writing. She served for many years as general secretary to the Relief Society and was called as the fifth general president of the Relief Society in 1910.

LATTER-DAY SAINT WOMEN HELP IMPROVE THE CHURCH'S IMAGE

Acquiring historic sites, constructing visitors' centers, and publishing its own history helped improve the public image of the Church, but singular honors were coming to Latter-day Saint women as well. Many women in the Church, with the support of the General Authorities, were active in the suffrage movement. As a result they became national figures. The Relief Society had sent delegates to both the National and International Council of Women conventions. During the Chicago world's fair, Emmeline B. Wells, one of the Church's delegates to a special women's conference, was asked by the president of the National Council of Women to speak to the group. She delivered a forceful address entitled "Western Women in Journalism." She also received the honor of presiding over one of the conference sessions. In 1899, Sister Wells was privileged to speak as an official delegate from the United States at the International Council of Women's convention in London, where she again displayed her eloquent speaking gifts.

In 1910, as she neared the age of eighty-three, Emmeline B. Wells was called to preside over the Relief Society of the Church. Although she was surprised at the call, "no one was better qualified than Emmeline Wells to lead the Relief Society, nor more deserving" to hold this high position. In 1912 this remarkable woman received an honorary doctorate from Brigham Young University, the first woman in the Church's history to be so honored.[24]

ENDNOTES

1. Truman G. Madsen, *Defender of the Faith: The B. H. Roberts Story* (Salt Lake City: Bookcraft, 1980), p. 233.

2. Isley Boone, "He Became an Evolutionary Psychologist," *Evolutionary Psychology,* in A. Burt Horsley, "Theodore Schroeder, Mormon Antagonist—Content and Significance of the Theodore Schroeder Collection, New York Public Library," typescript, pp. 2–3.

3. In Madsen, *Defender of the Faith,* p. 247.

4. See Madsen, *Defender of the Faith,* pp. 248–49.

5. Brigham H. Roberts, *Defense before Congress and Defiers of the Law* (pamphlet of Congressional record and of 1886 *Contributor*), pp. 12–13.

6. See Joseph Fielding Smith, comp., *Life of Joseph F. Smith,* 2d ed. (Salt Lake City: Deseret Book Co., 1969), p. 216.

7. In Milton R. Merrill, "Reed Smoot, Apostle in Politics," Ph.D. diss., Columbia University, 1950, p. i.

8. Charles W. Nibley, *Reminiscences,* 1849–1931 (Salt Lake City: Charles W. Nibley family, 1934), p. 125.

9. In Merrill, "Reed Smoot, Apostle in Politics," pp. 27–28.

10. *San Francisco Call,* in Milton R. Merrill, "Reed Smoot, Apostle in Politics," Ph.D. diss., Columbia University, 1950, p. 32.

11. Merrill, "Reed Smoot, Apostle in Politics," p. 45.

12. In B. H. Roberts, *A Comprehensive History of The Church of Jesus Christ of Latter-day Saints, Century One,* 6 vols. (Salt Lake City: The Church of Jesus Christ of Latter-day Saints, 1930), 6:405.

13. In Conference Report, Oct. 1907, p. 5.

14. See "Mr. Roosevelt to the 'Mormons,' " *Improvement Era,* June 1911, pp. 712, 715, 718.

15. Winifred Graham, *That Reminds Me* (London: Skeffington and Son, n.d.), p. 59.

16. See Eugene E. Campbell and Richard D. Poll, *Hugh B. Brown: His Life and Thought* (Salt Lake City: Bookcraft, 1975), pp. 30–31.

17. "Father, Are You There?" Brigham Young University fireside address (Provo, 8 Oct. 1967), pp. 13–15.

18. See Preston Nibley, "Charles J. Thomas: Early Guide on Temple Square, "*Improvement Era*, Mar. 1963, pp. 167, 202–6.

19. Levi Edgar Young, "The Temple Block Mission," *Relief Society Magazine*, Nov. 1922, p. 560.

20. See Edward H. Anderson, "The Bureau of Information," *Improvement Era*, Dec. 1921, pp. 132–33.

21. See Nibley, "Charles J. Thomas," pp. 205–6; Young, "Temple Block Mission," pp. 561–63; Anderson, "Bureau of Information," pp. 137–39.

22. Vicki Bean Zimmerman, "Willard Bean: Palmyra's 'Fighting Parson,' "*Ensign*, June 1985, p. 27.

23. Zimmerman, "Willard Bean," p. 26.

24. Carol Cornwall Madsen, "Emmeline B. Wells: Romantic Rebel," in Donald Q. Cannon and David J. Whittaker, eds., *Supporting Saints: Life Stories of Nineteenth-Century Mormons* (Provo: Brigham Young University, 1985), pp. 332–34.

MOVING FORWARD INTO THE NEW CENTURY

◄ Church Administration Building, headquarters of The Church of Jesus Christ of Latter-day Saints since 1917

A NEW ERA was beginning for the Church. Many of the challenges of the former century were left behind, and the Church could now turn attention to the opportunities ahead. President Joseph F. Smith guided the Church during most of the twentieth century's first two decades. His administration moved the Church forward as it reached out to bless the lives of members worldwide.

PROGRESS DURING AN ERA OF PROSPERITY

President Smith continued his predecessor's emphasis on tithing, and the Saints' faithful response enabled the Church to pay off all its debts by the end of 1906. In the April 1907 general conference he gratefully announced, "Today the Church of Jesus Christ of Latter-day Saints owes not a dollar that it cannot pay at once. At last we are in a position that we can pay as we go. We do not have to borrow any more, and we won't have to if the Latter-day Saints continue to live their religion and observe this law of tithing."[1] Obedience to this law of revenue permitted the Church to begin purchasing historic sites, establish visitors' centers, and undertake other activities that were not possible under the burden of debt.

The Church's building program particularly benefited from this era of prosperity. New buildings included many local meetinghouses, as well as several key structures in Salt Lake City. In 1905 the Latter-day Saints Hospital opened, the first in a system of Church-operated hospitals built during the twentieth century.

To help finance its religious program, the Church continued to make selected investments. It maintained or acquired interest in such businesses as the *Deseret News*, the Beneficial Life Insurance Company, and Zion's Cooperative Mercantile Institution. One of the Church's largest investments was in the new Hotel Utah, which opened just east of Temple Square in 1911. President Smith defended the Church's interest in this venture by quoting from Doctrine and Covenants 124:22–24, 60 and pointing out that the Hotel Utah would fill a function similar to that which the Lord had specified for the Nauvoo House. The hotel would be a place where "the weary traveler" could find rest and "contemplate the glory of Zion."[2] In 1919 a book store operated by the Deseret Sunday School Union and one run by the Deseret News combined to form the Deseret Book Company.

Indications of the growth, prosperity, and stability of the Church at the beginning of the twentieth century can be seen with the construction of the Bishop's Building in 1910 (below) and the Hotel Utah in 1911 (right).

The Church badly needed adequate office space. For many years the work of the General Authorities, auxiliaries, and other Church organizations had been conducted from offices scattered throughout downtown Salt Lake City. The new Bishop's Building, dedicated in 1910 and located behind the Hotel Utah and directly across the street from the Salt Lake Temple, provided offices for the Presiding Bishopric and most of the auxiliary organizations. Seven years later the Church Administration Building was opened at 47 East South Temple Street. This five-story granite structure featured marble and fine woodwork. It symbolized the Church's strength and stability and provided dignified accommodations for the General Authorities. It also provided badly needed space on its upper three floors for the Church historian's office and the Genealogical Society.

AUXILIARY AND PRIESTHOOD EXPANSION

In the early years of the twentieth century a major expansion and reform took place in both priesthood and auxiliary programs. The Church's auxiliary organizations were greatly affected by these new developments. Although specific changes varied from one organization to another, they generally involved an improvement in teaching specific age groups, and a greater emphasis was placed upon scriptural rather than on secular study materials.

During the nineteenth century the Relief Society sponsored sewing or other projects directly related to assisting the needy. In 1902, however, the Society inaugurated "Mothers' Classes" Churchwide. At first, local Relief Societies provided their own study materials, but in 1914 the general board issued uniform lessons for these weekly classes. A pattern soon developed of studying theology the first week, followed by homemaking, literature, and social science respectively during the remaining weeks of the month.

David O. McKay, a young returned missionary, college graduate, and professional educator, had a profound impact on the development of the Sunday School during the first part of the twentieth century. He was called to be a member of the Weber Stake Sunday School superintendency in Ogden and was asked to give particular attention to the instruction being taught. After some observation, he introduced some refinements in the teaching methods being used, such as defining the lesson goals, outlining the materials, using teaching aids, and making practical application of the lessons to daily life. A specific course for each age group was developed to be used throughout the stake. In 1906, David O. McKay was called to the Quorum of the Twelve and was also called as a member of the general Sunday School superintendency. In this position he was able to promote similar improvements throughout the Church. Before 1906 the Sunday School had been essentially an organization for children and youth. In that year, however, the first class for adults, the "Parents' Class," was inaugurated Churchwide.

During the nineteenth century, meetings of the Young Men's and Young Women's Mutual Improvement Associations had consisted of both youth and adults. Together they would listen to lectures on theology, science, history, and literature. By 1903, however, the practice of conducting separate junior and senior groups was implemented throughout the Church. In 1911 the Young Men's organization adopted a Scouting program, which stressed wholesome virtues and physical skills. By 1913 the Church became officially affiliated with the Boy Scouts of America and lowered the age of entry into YMMIA to twelve. The Church eventually became one of the largest sponsors of the Boy Scout movement in the world. In 1915 the young ladies began the Beehive Girls program for the same age group. Later years saw the formation of still other age-group programs designed to better meet the needs of the youth of the Church. As more and more Latter-day Saints moved into cities, Church leaders emphasized such traditional values as modesty, chastity, and temple marriage. The First Presidency in 1916 organized the Social Advisory Committee, which was assigned to discourage the youth from improper dances, smoking, and immodest dress. Social advisory committees at the ward level sponsored various wholesome recreational activities. The Mutual Improvement Association also expanded recreational and social programs. Church leaders emphasized that efforts be

Louie B. Felt (1850–1928) was the first general president of the Primary Association. She was sustained in 1880 and held the position for forty-seven years. She initiated the Children's Friend magazine in January 1902, established a hospital fund in 1911, and oversaw the building of a hospital for children in 1922.

► For thirty years the Primary Children's Hospital was located on North Temple Street in downtown Salt Lake City in a home the Church had renovated.

made by the wards to prevent problems such as juvenile delinquency and immorality. Special summer school workshops in 1920 at Brigham Young University provided training for stake leaders in teacher development, social and recreational leadership, charity, and relief work.[3]

The Primary Association also enhanced its educational and activity programs for children. Class names and emblems were introduced to increase interest—boys became known as Trail Builders and girls as Home Builders. Like other auxiliaries, the Primary reached out to meet broader social needs and in 1922 opened its own children's hospital. Louie B. Felt, president of the Primary, and May Anderson, one of her counselors, had seen many crippled children and felt impressed that their organization should do something for such children. They studied the latest methods used in children's hospitals in the eastern United States before moving ahead with this project. The result was the Primary Children's Hospital, which is still helping children today.

During this rapid expansion of the auxiliaries, President Joseph F. Smith looked forward to a time when priesthood quorums would occupy a position of preeminence in the Church. At the April general conference in 1906 he declared: "We expect to see the day . . . when every council of the Priesthood in the Church of Jesus Christ of Latter-day Saints will understand its duty, will assume its own responsibility, will magnify its calling. . . . When that day shall come, there will not be so much necessity for work that is now being done by the auxiliary organizations, because it will be done by the regular quorums of the Priesthood. The Lord designed and comprehended it from the beginning, and He has made provision in the Church whereby every need may be met and satisfied through the regular organizations of the Priesthood."[4]

Toward the end of the nineteenth century, most priesthood quorums met only monthly, and not all the quorums within a given ward met at the same time. With infrequent and often irregular meetings, quorum effectiveness suffered. The increased emphasis on, or intensification of, priesthood activity started among the seventies under the direction of the First Council of the Seventy. In 1907, President Joseph F. Smith reminded the seventies of their responsibility to be prepared for missionary service. They were told that they should not depend on the auxiliaries or Church schools for a knowledge of the gospel, but should make the seventies quorums "schools of learning and instruction, wherein they may qualify themselves for every labor and duty that may be required at their hands."[5] The resulting lesson manual, entitled *The Seventy's Course in Theology*, written by Elder B. H. Roberts, did much to spark an enthusiasm for gospel study throughout the Church.

The First Presidency appointed a General Priesthood Committee, soon headed by Elder David O. McKay. By their recommendation, weekly ward priesthood meetings were inaugurated in 1909. At first these gatherings were held Monday evenings, but Sunday mornings gradually became the preferred time.

The General Priesthood Committee also systematized the ages for ordinations to offices in the Aaronic Priesthood. It recommended that deacons be ordained at age twelve, teachers at fifteen, priests at eighteen, and elders at twenty-one. This enabled the committee to more effectively plan a progressive course of study for each quorum. The concept of established ages for ordination of worthy young men has continued, although some of the ages for ordination have at times been modified.

These developments in Church meetings and programs created a need for printed instructions and lesson materials. In contrast to many of the nineteenth century publications, which had been sponsored by private individuals or groups, those dating from the early twentieth century were published mainly by the Church auxiliary organizations. In 1897 the Young Men's Mutual Improvement Association launched its own periodical, the *Improvement Era*. Upon being told that there was no capital for such a venture, Elder B. H. Roberts spearheaded a fund-raising drive. He became the magazine's first editor, and Elder Heber J. Grant of the Council of the Twelve became the business manager. The magazine became a powerful voice for good among the Saints and provided a forum for the works of Church writers and poets. In 1929 this periodical was merged with the *Young Woman's Journal* and became the Church's leading magazine for adults.

In 1900 the Sunday School purchased the *Juvenile Instructor* from the George Q. Cannon family and made it their official publication. The Primary

Susa Young Gates (1856–1933), daughter of Brigham Young, was well educated. She attended her father's private school, as well as the University of Deseret, Brigham Young University, and Harvard University.

She served on the general board of the YWMIA from 1899 to 1911 and the Relief Society from 1911 to 1922.

She was directed by Brigham Young to strengthen the youth through writing. She wrote extensively for local publications all of her life. She founded the Young Woman's Journal *and later edited the* Relief Society Magazine *from 1914 to 1922. Two years before her death she published* The Life Story of Brigham Young.

Sister Gates was also a trustee of Brigham Young University for forty years and was actively involved in the local and national women's movement. She was the mother of ten sons and three daughters.

Association launched its *Children's Friend* in 1902. Beginning in 1910, the *Utah Genealogical and Historical Magazine* carried helpful articles on research, pedigrees, and local history. In 1914 the Relief Society established its own magazine called the *Relief Society Bulletin.* In 1915 the name was changed to the *Relief Society Magazine.* Under the editorship of Susa Young Gates, daughter of Brigham Young, the magazine addressed the needs of Latter-day Saint women, carrying articles on such topics as current events, genealogy, home ethics, gardening, literature, art, and architecture.

While these programs and publications were developing, the First Presidency also emphasized the central role of the family in gospel teaching. In 1903, President Smith emphasized that the other programs of the Church should be "supplements to our teachings and training in the home. Not one child in a hundred would go astray, if the home environment, example, and training, were in harmony with the truth in the Gospel of Christ," he promised.[6] In 1909 the Granite Stake in Salt Lake City inaugurated a weekly home evening program for families, and President Joseph F. Smith declared that the stake presidency's action was inspired. Following the success of this stake program, the First Presidency recommended in 1915 that a similar activity be adopted monthly and used Churchwide:

"We advise and urge the inauguration of a 'Home Evening' throughout the Church, at which time fathers and mothers may gather their boys and girls about them in the home and teach them the word of the Lord. They may thus learn more fully the needs and requirements of their families. . . .

"If the Saints obey this counsel, we promise that great blessings will result. Love at home and obedience to parents will increase. Faith will be developed in the hearts of the youth of Israel, and they will gain power to combat the evil influence and temptations which beset them."[7]

UNDERSTANDING OF GOSPEL DOCTRINES CLARIFIED

The early twentieth century was a period of heated debate between religious fundamentalists and liberals or modernists. Many asked where the Mormons stood on the various theological controversies of the time. The Latter-day Saints were fortunate to have the leadership of President Joseph F. Smith, an unusually able and inspired exponent of gospel principles. President Smith and his counselors in the First Presidency issued several doctrinal treatises clarifying the Church's stand on the issues of the day.

Some Latter-day Saints wondered about the relative roles of God the Father, Jesus Christ, the Holy Ghost, and Michael, or Adam. The First Presidency's 1916 exposition entitled *The Father and the Son* explained, "The term 'Father' as applied to Deity occurs in sacred writ with plainly different meanings": God is the father, or literal parent, of our spirits. Jesus Christ is the father, or creator, of this earth. The Savior is also the father of those who receive spiritual rebirth through living the gospel. Jesus may be called father as he represents Elohim here on earth "in power and authority." Nevertheless, "Jesus Christ is not the Father of the spirits who have taken or yet shall take bodies upon this earth, for He is one of them."[8]

President Smith also answered a related question in connection with the Godhead. Although the terms "Holy Ghost" and "Spirit of the Lord" were often used interchangeably, he explained that "the Holy Ghost is a personage in the Godhead," while the light of Christ, or the spirit of the Lord, "is the Spirit of God which proceeds through Christ to the world, that enlightens every man that comes into the world, and that strives with the children of men, and will continue to strive with them, until it brings them to a knowledge of the truth and the possession of the greater light and testimony of the Holy Ghost."[9] Church members can also look to Joseph F. Smith's book, *Gospel Doctrine*, which is a compilation of his sermons and writings, for more helpful definitions and information about basic gospel concepts.

During these years, a further contribution to gospel understanding was made by a group of capable Latter-day Saint scholars. One of these was James E. Talmage, who had taught science at Brigham Young Academy and who had also served as president of the University of Utah.

As early as 1891 the First Presidency discussed the desirability of publishing a work on theology that could be used in the Church schools as well as religion classes generally. Dr. Talmage was asked by Church leaders to write this book. Before writing the requested work, Elder Talmage prepared and gave a series of lectures on the Articles of Faith. So many people attended the first meeting, and so many others had to be turned away, that the classes were moved to the Assembly Hall on Temple Square. Attendance reached almost thirteen hundred. These lectures were first published in the *Juvenile Instructor*. A reading committee, which included two members of the Twelve plus Karl G. Maeser and others, reviewed the manuscript and suggested a few changes. This material was published in book form under the direction of the First Presidency in 1899. Talmage's *The Articles of Faith* has since gone through more than fifty editions in English, and has been translated into more than a dozen other languages. This book, still used today by Church members, represents the first officially approved serious study of the theology of the Restoration.

Two other important works followed Elder Talmage's call to the Twelve in 1911: *The House of the Lord*, published in 1912, and *Jesus the Christ*, published in 1915. The first of these was prompted by unique circumstances. A non-Mormon using unethical practices secured interior photographs of the Salt Lake Temple and attempted to sell them to the Church for forty thousand dollars. Otherwise he threatened to peddle them to magazines in the East, who would be glad to print them to discredit the Church. Rather than succumbing to this attempted blackmail, President Joseph F. Smith accepted Elder Talmage's recommendation that a book be written discussing in general terms what took place in Latter-day Saint temples. It was to be

James E. Talmage (1862–1933) was born in England and immigrated to the United States with his family in May 1876. The family arrived in Salt Lake City on 14 June 1876. Brother Talmage completed a four-year course at Lehigh University in Bethlehem, Pennsylvania, in one year and went on to do advanced work at Johns Hopkins University in Baltimore, Maryland.

Upon his return to Utah, he taught chemistry and geology at Brigham Young Academy in Provo from 1884–88. Later he served as the president of the University of Utah from 1894–97.

In 1911, when Charles W. Penrose was called to be a counselor in the First Presidency, Brother Talmage was called to fill the resulting vacancy in the Quorum of the Twelve Apostles. He had an exceptional command of the English language and was a noted lecturer and author.

illustrated with photographs from the interior of the Salt Lake Temple. This volume, written by Elder Talmage, not only thwarted the blackmail but became a valuable resource for Latter-day Saints.

The First Presidency asked James E. Talmage to compile a series of lectures he had given a decade earlier on the life of the Savior into another book that could be used by the general membership of the Church. Elder Talmage began in earnest to work on the manuscript, but he still had to squeeze the actual writing between his other duties. He was spared many of his stake conference assignments, however, and wrote most of the book in the Salt Lake Temple. He seldom returned home before midnight, and the marvelous book *Jesus the Christ* was completed in just seven months.

On 19 April 1915, Elder Talmage wrote in his journal: "Finished the actual writing on the book 'Jesus the Christ,' to which I have devoted every spare hour since settling down to the work of composition on September 14th last [1914]. Had it not been that I was privileged to do this work in the Temple it would be at present far from completion. I have felt the inspiration of the place and have appreciated the privacy and quietness incident thereto. I hope to proceed with the work of revision without delay."[10]

During eighteen separate sessions over a two-month period, Elder Talmage read the chapters to the First Presidency and Quorum of the Twelve for their input and approval. This book is still widely read and is a monument to Elder Talmage's scholarship and inspiration.

RESPONDING TO THE AGE OF SCIENCE

For several decades, the world had seen a growing interest in the emerging discoveries and theories of modern science. As the twentieth century dawned, the pace of technological development was quickening, and important inventions, such as the gasoline-powered automobile and the Wright brothers' airplane flight, had a far-reaching impact on everyday life. These developments also further heightened the interest in science. This, in turn, increasingly led people to look to human intellect rather than to theology for an understanding of the nature of the universe and of society.

Scholars took a hard look at the Bible during this new age of science; they began questioning the meaning and even the authenticity of the scriptures. This so-called "higher criticism" was directed at the Latter-day Saint scriptures as well. In 1912, Reverend F. S. Spalding, Episcopal Bishop of Utah, published a pamphlet entitled *Joseph Smith, Jr., As a Translator*. The brochure contrasted the interpretations of eight Egyptologists with the explanations of Joseph Smith concerning the facsimiles in the book of Abraham in the Pearl of Great Price. Although most Latter-day Saints accepted the truthfulness of the scriptures as a matter of faith, the Church still recognized a need to respond to such criticism. From February through September 1913 a series of articles appeared almost every month in the *Improvement Era* providing possible answers.

Perhaps the most heated and prolonged discussions during the late nineteenth and early twentieth centuries centered on the creation of the earth and the theories of organic evolution. In the midst of these controversies the First Presidency asked Elder Orson F. Whitney of the Quorum of the Twelve to draft a statement that would convey the Church's official position on the origin of man. Elder Whitney's statement was subsequently approved and signed by the First Presidency and the Quorum of the Twelve and published in 1909 as an official declaration of the Church. This statement affirmed that:

"All men and women are in the similitude of the universal Father and Mother, and are literally the sons and daughters of Deity. . . .

". . . Man, as a spirit, was begotten and born of heavenly parents, and reared to maturity in the eternal mansions of the Father, prior to coming upon the earth in a temporal body to undergo an experience in mortality. . . .

"It is held by some that Adam was not the first man upon this earth, and that the original human being was a development from lower orders of the animal creation. These, however, are the theories of men. The word of the Lord declares that Adam was 'the first man of all men' (Moses 1:34), and we are therefore in duty bound to regard him as the primal parent of our race. . . . Man began life as a human being, in the likeness of our heavenly Father."[11]

President Joseph F. Smith was concerned that discussions of the theory of evolution only left the young people of the Church "in an unsettled frame of mind. They are not old enough and learned enough to discriminate, or put proper limitations upon a theory which we believe is more or less a fallacy. . . . In reaching the conclusion that evolution would be best left out of discussions in our Church schools we are deciding a question of propriety and are not undertaking to say how much of evolution is true, or how much is false. The Church itself has no philosophy about the *modus operandi* employed by the Lord in His creation of the world. . . . God has revealed to us a simple and effectual way of serving Him."[12]

THE SAINTS IN OTHER LANDS

Beginning in the 1890s Church leaders encouraged the Saints to remain in their homelands and build up the Church. As a result, Latter-day Saint missions and branches abroad expanded. This growth was reflected in Joseph F. Smith's becoming the first Church president to visit Europe. For about two months in 1906, he visited missions in the Netherlands, Germany, Switzerland, France, and England. His visit did much to strengthen the Church in these lands. Inspirational events strengthened the faith of the Saints. In Rotterdam, Holland, President Smith was the means for restoring full sight to a faithful eleven-year-old boy with severe eye problems who had told his mother that he believed "the Prophet has the most power of any missionary on earth. If you will take me with you to meeting and he will look into my eyes I believe they will be healed."[13]

During his visit to Europe, President Smith made an important prophetic statement. At a 1906 conference in Bern, Switzerland, he stretched out his hands and declared: "The time will come when this land will be dotted with temples, where you can go and redeem your dead."[14] He also explained that "Temples of God . . . will be reared in diverse countries of the world."[15] The first Latter-day Saint temple in Europe was dedicated nearly a half century later in a suburb of the city where President Smith had made his prophecy.

President Smith recognized the need for temples to bless Church members living outside of Utah: "They need the same privileges that we do, and that we enjoy, but these are out of their power. They are poor, and they can't gather means to come up here to be endowed, and sealed for time and eternity, for their living and their dead."[16] The first of these new temples was located in Cardston, Alberta, Canada. President Joseph F. Smith dedicated the site in 1913. In 1915 he dedicated a site for a temple in Hawaii, where he had served as a missionary many years before. Both temples were dedicated following his death.

During the same period, events in Mexico had a far-reaching impact on the future of the Church in that land and in adjoining sections of the United States. By 1901 conditions seemed right for reopening the mission in Mexico. The Latter-day Saint colonies in Chihuahua were prospering; the young people there who could speak Spanish fluently and were familiar with the Mexican culture were available for proselyting missions. During the next ten years the missionary force increased to twenty, and the local Latter-day Saint men and women were called and trained as leaders. They received great strength from Rey L. Pratt who became the mission president in 1907 and presided for nearly a quarter of a century. Many new converts were added to the Church, so that by 1911 membership in the mission exceeded one thousand people.

Nevertheless, by this time revolutions and counter-revolutions swept the country, and missionary work became increasingly difficult. These conditions were complicated by a growing nationalistic, anti-America sentiment. By August 1913 it was again necessary to evacuate the missionaries.

The Mexican Saints were left in a large part to care for themselves. In San Marcos, about fifty miles northwest of Mexico City, for example, Rafael Monroy, a comparatively recent convert, was given the responsibility of serving as branch president. In 1915, however, just two years after the departure of the missionaries, the brutal forces of revolutionary conflict and religious prejudice resulted in the execution of President Monroy and his cousin Vincente Morales. They were killed because they were accused of being members of a rival revolutionary group and because they would not deny their testimony of the gospel.

In 1912 the same forces that disrupted missionary work also brought trouble to the colonists in northern Mexico. When rebels confiscated some of the weapons belonging to the Saints, Mormon leaders responded by

Rafael Monroy was branch president of the San Marcos branch. He was killed for refusing to deny the faith.

Anson B. Owen Call (1863–1958) was born in Bountiful, Utah. In 1890 he moved to Mexico. He served as the bishop of the Dublan Ward in the Juarez Stake for twenty-nine years.

ordering an evacuation of the colonies by 26 July. Women and children, with a few men as escorts, journeyed 180 miles to El Paso on a crowded train. The majority of the men followed a few days later in a wagon and horse caravan that stretched for a mile. By the end of the month, more than thirteen hundred refugee Saints were in El Paso. Many of them had left beautiful homes and farms and were now forced to live in a deserted lumber yard with no more than a roof overhead and rough boards under their feet. Another group of refugees was housed in the upper floor of an old building. This structure was covered with corrugated iron and became stifling under the burning rays of the sun. Some observers confessed that they wept when they witnessed such living conditions. By February 1913 some of the Saints returned to Mexico even though the revolution raged for several more years. Others remained permanently in the United States.

The Mormon colonists, however, repeatedly experienced divine protection. Bishop Anson Call of Colonia Dublan was taken from his home by rebels who falsely accused him of giving information that had led to the death of one of their comrades. Two days after his arrest, Bishop Call stood before a firing squad with rifles ready to fire. The executioner stopped the execution at the last second in exchange for a promise of being paid two hundred pesos. Bishop Call, attended by his captors, was able to raise the money from the Saints at Colonia Juarez. The incident fulfilled a prophetic promise to him from Elder Anthony Ivins of the Quorum of the Twelve, "They may rob you of all you possess and put you to every test that the enemy of righteousness can imagine, but they shall not have power to take your life."[17]

During later years the colonists' superior schools and advanced agricultural methods attracted favorable attention for the Church in Mexico. Furthermore, when the Mexican government began enforcing laws prohibiting foreign clergy from serving in Mexico, most of the Latter-day Saint missionaries, almost all of the mission presidents, and the leaders in the Church's growing school system came from these colonists who had become Mexican citizens. In this way, the Mormon colonies provided the strength that eventually enabled the Church to grow throughout Mexico and elsewhere in Latin America.

The difficulties in Mexico also led to Church expansion in the southwestern United States. Many of the exiled families provided new vitality and leadership to Latter-day Saint congregations in Arizona, New Mexico, and Texas. In 1915 the First Presidency assigned Rey L. Pratt to direct the proselyting among the Spanish-speaking people in the United States. This later became an important missionary field.

Rey L. Pratt (1878–1931) went to Mexico with his family in 1887. In 1906 he was called on a mission, and late in 1907 he became president of the Mexican Mission. He served in this capacity until 1931. In 1925 he was chosen to become a member of the First Council of the Seventy.

THE SAINTS AND WORLD WAR I

World War I broke out in Europe in 1914. The Saints overseas responded patriotically to the calls of their own countries. In England, a local newspaper reported that Saints in the Pudsey Branch had "a record of patriotism which will be hard to beat, as every man of military age, with the exception of those engaged in government and munition work has enlisted. Whatever we may say about the so-called 'Mormons,' we must admit that they are certainly, 'very patriotic at Pudsey.' "[18] Also in Germany, Latter-day Saints fought for their fatherland; about seventy-five of these soldiers gave their lives in the conflict.

The United States did not officially enter the conflict until three years later. Woodrow Wilson, president of the United States, declared that it was a war for the purpose of preserving democracy, liberty, and peace. Since this agreed with long-expressed feelings of the Church, members found no religious conflict in responding quickly to the call to arms.

Since Utah was still the home of most Latter-day Saints, the response of its citizens reflected the attitude of the Saints in general toward the war. A total of 24,382 men enlisted, far exceeding the state's quota. Six of President Joseph F. Smith's own sons served in the military forces. The Red Cross asked for $350,000 for aid from Utah and received $520,000. When the government began to sell liberty bonds, the people of Utah were given the quota of $6,500,000; instead they purchased bonds worth $9,400,000. The Church, as an institution, participated officially by purchasing $850,000 in liberty bonds. In addition, auxiliary organizations purchased bonds from their own funds amounting to nearly $600,000; and women of the Relief Society actively participated with the Red Cross.

It was the custom for each state to raise a volunteer military unit. Utah provided the 145th Field Artillery Regiment. An overwhelming majority of its approximately fifteen hundred officers and men were members of the Church. The unit's chaplain was Elder B. H. Roberts of the First Council of the Seventy. Six hundred of this modern "Mormon Battalion" saw duty overseas.

The Church was uniquely prepared to help provide food for the starving peoples of war-torn Europe. For years the Relief Society had stored wheat in preparation for just such an emergency. They sold over two hundred thousand bushels to the United States government and put the proceeds into a special wheat fund for future charitable purposes. The prompt response of the Church and its members to the war emergency was effective evidence of the Saints' loyalty and patriotism. The American press praised their actions, reducing any negative impressions that may have lingered from the anti-Mormon magazine crusade of earlier years.

The Church's April general conference was in session when the United States officially entered the war in 1917. The attitude of the Church toward war was well expressed in President Joseph F. Smith's opening address. He reminded the Saints that even in the face of conflict, the spirit of the gospel must be maintained. He declared that even in war the people should maintain "the spirit of humanity, of love, and of peace-making." He instructed prospective soldiers to remember that they were "ministers of life and not of death; and when they go forth, they may go forth in the spirit of defending the liberties of mankind rather than for the purpose of destroying the enemy."[19]

VISION OF THE REDEMPTION OF THE DEAD

On 23 January 1918, Hyrum M. Smith, a member of the Quorum of the Twelve and the eldest son of President Joseph F. Smith, died. His death was a blow to his father, who was in poor health himself. "In his grief he cried: 'My soul is rent asunder. My heart is broken, and flutters for life! O my sweet son, my joy, my hope! . . . He was indeed a prince among men. Never in his life did he displease me or give me cause to doubt him. I loved him through and through. He has thrilled my soul by his power of speech, as no other man ever did. Perhaps this was because he was my son, and he was filled with the fire of the Holy Ghost. And now, what can I do! O what can I do! My soul is rent, my heart is broken! O God, help me!' "[20]

Eight months later a glorious revelation was given to President Joseph F. Smith concerning the labors of the righteous in the world of spirits. On 3 October 1918, while President Smith was pondering the atonement of Jesus Christ, he opened his Bible and read in 1 Peter 3:18–20 and 4:6 about the Savior's preaching to the spirits in prison. While he was meditating on these passages, the Spirit of the Lord rested upon him, and he saw in vision the "hosts of the dead" who were gathered in the spirit world. He saw the Savior appear among them and preach the gospel to the righteous. He was shown that the Lord had commissioned others to continue this work of preaching, and that the faithful elders in the present dispensation would also preach to the dead after leaving mortality. Thus all of the dead may be redeemed.

This "Vision of the Redemption of the Dead" was presented by President Smith to the First Presidency and the Twelve, who unanimously accepted it as revelation. In 1976 this revelation was officially added to the standard works of the Church and soon afterward designated as section 138 in the Doctrine and Covenants.

The opening decades of the twentieth century saw the Church move forward in several important ways. A period of prosperity enabled the Church to erect badly-needed chapels and temples and allowed the prophet to travel and bless the Saints in faraway lands. Priesthood and auxiliary classes, First Presidency doctrinal expositions, and President Smith's significant 1918 revelation all helped expand the Saints' understanding of certain gospel principles. Meanwhile, the Church met with characteristic vigor the challenges posed by radical scientific theories, revolutions in Mexico, and the horrors of a world war.

ENDNOTES

1. In Conference Report, Apr. 1907, p. 7; punctuation standardized.

2. In Conference Report, Oct. 1911, pp. 129–30.

3. See Thomas G. Alexander, "Between Revivalism and the Social Gospel: The Latter-day Saint Social Advisory Committee, 1916–1922," *Brigham Young University Studies*, Winter 1983, pp. 24–37.

4. In Conference Report, Apr. 1906, p. 3.

5. In Conference Report, Apr. 1907, pp. 5–6.

6. Joseph F. Smith, "Worship in the Home," *Improvement Era*, Dec. 1903, p. 138.

7. In James R. Clark, comp., *Messages of the First Presidency of The Church of Jesus Christ of Latter-day Saints*, 6 vols. (Salt Lake City: Bookcraft, 1965–75), 4:338–39.

8. In Clark, *Messages of the First Presidency*, 5:26, 32, 34.

9. Joseph F. Smith, *Gospel Doctrine*, 5th ed. (Salt Lake City: Deseret Book Co., 1939), pp. 67–68.

10. James E. Talmage Journals (typed copy), 19 Apr. 1915, Brigham Young University Archives, Provo, p. 19; spelling standardized.

11. "The Origin of Man," *Improvement Era*, Nov. 1909, pp. 78, 80; Clark, *Messages of the First Presidency*, 4:203, 205.

12. "Philosophy and the Church Schools," *Juvenile Instructor*, Apr. 1911, p. 209.

13. See Joseph Fielding Smith, comp., *Life of Joseph F. Smith*, 2d ed. (Salt Lake City: Deseret Book Co., 1969), p. 397.

14. Serge F. Ballif, in Conference Report, Oct. 1920, p. 90.

15. "Das Evangelium des Tuns" ["The Gospel of Deeds"], *Der Stern*, 1 Nov. 1906, p. 332; translated from German.

16. In Conference Report, Oct. 1915, p. 8.

17. In Thomas Cottam Romney, *The Mormon Colonies in Mexico* (Salt Lake City: Deseret Book Co., 1938), p. 227.

18. In "Messages from the Missions," *Improvement Era*, Feb. 1916, p. 369.

19. In Conference Report, Apr. 1917, p. 3.

20. Smith, *Life of Joseph F. Smith*, p. 474.

CHANGE AND CONSISTENCY

THE DECADE OF the 1920s was in many ways a comparatively peaceful era in the Church's history. Following World War I, many Latter-day Saints left Utah to find employment in California and other states. An increasing number of Church members remained in the lands of their births, as instructed, and helped strengthen the branches and districts in many areas of the world. In a dramatic symbol of their interest in all of the earth's peoples, the First Presidency sent Elder David O. McKay and Hugh J. Cannon on a world tour of the missions. Also during the twenties the Church established seminaries and inaugurated the first institute of religion program. Utah's first radio station, KZN, began transmitting gospel messages, and a new Church president was sustained who would lead the Church for almost three decades.

THE REORGANIZATION OF THE FIRST PRESIDENCY

Even as he lay dying, President Joseph F. Smith's thoughts turned to the man who would succeed him as prophet, seer, and revelator. Elder Heber J. Grant was told the stricken president wanted to see him. Taking President Smith's hand, Elder Grant felt his spiritual power and strength. He was then given a special blessing by his terminally ill leader. President Smith told him that the Lord makes no mistake in choosing someone to lead his Church. With tear-filled eyes and a heart full of love, Elder Grant left the room with the prophet's last words echoing in his ears, "The Lord bless you, my boy, the Lord bless you."[1]

On 23 November 1918, four days after the death of President Joseph F. Smith, the Twelve convened in the Salt Lake Temple. There they ordained and set apart Heber J. Grant as the seventh President of the Church. He was the first native Utahn to be president. President Grant, who had served as a member of the Quorum of the Twelve since 1882, was known for his determination. He loved to relate in his talks how he had overcome personal limitations and excelled despite them. His favorite saying came from Ralph Waldo Emerson: "That which we persist in doing becomes easier, not that the nature of the thing has changed but our ability to do it has increased."

President Grant was a very spiritual man. It was reported in several meetings, including one held in the temple, that President Grant's countenance when he spoke resembled that of the deceased Joseph F. Smith.[2]

Heber J. Grant (1856–1945) became the seventh President of the Church at age sixty-two, having served as an Apostle since 1882. He was set apart as President of the Quorum of the Twelve Apostles in 1916.

President Grant greatly influenced the Church in the twentieth century. He served as a General Authority longer than any other man except David O. McKay. His twenty-seven years of service as President of the Church marked the second longest administration, exceeded only by Brigham Young's.

Because of the worldwide flu epidemic, which eliminated all large public meetings, President Grant was not sustained as Church president until June 1919. He chose Elders Anthon H. Lund and Charles W. Penrose, respectively, as his first and second counselors.

The death of President Smith and the reorganization of the First Presidency had left a vacancy in the Quorum of the Twelve. Many of the Apostles thought President Grant would call his good friend and faithful Church member Richard W. Young to that position. President Grant intended, with the consent of his two counselors, to call Richard Young to the apostleship. He began to reflect and pray about the vacancy. When the First Presidency met with the Quorum of the Twelve, President Grant reached into his pocket and pulled out a slip of paper with Richard W. Young's name written on it, fully intending to present it for approval. Instead, he found himself saying that the Lord wanted Melvin J. Ballard, the Northwestern States mission president, to fill the vacancy in the Quorum of the Twelve. President Grant later testified that he learned from this experience that the Lord does indeed inspire the President of the Church.[3]

Prior to Elder Ballard's birth, his mother had learned in a remarkable way that the baby she was carrying would become an Apostle of the Lord Jesus Christ.[4] This spiritual experience was confirmed when Elder Ballard was told in his patriarchal blessing that he would be one of the Lord's special witnesses.

In 1921, President Anthon H. Lund died, and President Grant chose Anthony W. Ivins as a counselor in the First Presidency. John A. Widtsoe, president of the University of Utah, was called to fill the vacancy in the Council of the Twelve Apostles created by Elder Ivins's call. Four years later when Charles W. Penrose passed away, Presiding Bishop Charles W. Nibley became a member of the First Presidency. He and President Ivins served as President Grant's counselors for the remainder of the decade. Joseph Fielding Smith, son of Joseph F. Smith, replaced President Lund as Church historian and served in that position for more than half of a century.

Soon after being set apart as Church president, Heber J. Grant instituted several administrative changes and procedures that would have a lasting impact on the Church. First he announced that the First Presidency would no longer serve as presidents of the various auxiliary organizations as they had heretofore done with other General Authorities as their assistants. Second, early in 1922, the Corporation of the President was organized to hold and administer the ecclesiastical property of the Church. This corporation was designed to administer the Church's tax-free properties. At the same time, Zion's Securities Corporation was founded to manage property considered strictly investment and revenue producing. On these holdings the Church voluntarily paid taxes, although it could generally claim nonprofit status.

THE CHURCH AND THE LEAGUE OF NATIONS

With the end of the First World War, United States president Woodrow Wilson presented plans to establish permanent world peace. His goals included a league of nations that would, by discussion and parliamentary procedures, solve the conflicts that might arise among the world's countries. Since the farewell address of George Washington, the United States had refrained as much as possible from entanglements with foreign nations, especially those in Europe. Wilson's plans reflected a departure from traditional United States foreign policy. When the president sought to have his treaty ratified in the United States Senate, a partisan battle ensued. Many Republican senators, including Apostle Reed Smoot, only favored the league if certain amendments were added to the charter to preserve American sovereignty. Others vigorously opposed the league altogether.

In February 1919, in an effort to promote the treaty, the Mountain Congress of the League to Enforce Peace held its convention in Salt Lake City. Former U.S. President William Howard Taft attended, and President Heber J. Grant conducted some of the sessions. In July, President Ivins, representing the First Presidency, spoke out in favor of the league, and several more of the Brethren also spoke in support of it at stake conferences that summer.

In spite of the efforts of those who supported the Wilson treaty, it suffered a crushing defeat in the United States Congress. That some Church members had vigorously opposed the league, while others had favored it, caused some divisions within the Church. Therefore, in the October general conference following the Senate defeat, President Grant reminded the congregation of what had happened the year before and expressed regret at the bitterness the controversy had caused. He made a plea for the spirit of forgiveness to permeate among the Latter-day Saints. He then referred to the advice he had received from President John Taylor when President Grant was a young Apostle, "My boy, never forget that when you are in the line of your duty your heart will be full of love and forgiveness."

That no hard feelings were in President Grant's heart is evidenced by the fact that he remained a great friend and admirer of Reed Smoot, and that those of the Brethren who had opposed the League of Nations—Charles W. Nibley, J. Reuben Clark, and David O. McKay—subsequently became his counselors in the First Presidency of the Church.[5] Yet there was still another political problem, this one deemed a moral issue, that waited to be resolved.

THE WORD OF WISDOM AND THE REPEAL OF PROHIBITION

During this era some people in the United States joined in a movement to stamp out many of the nation's evils and injustices. An essential part of this movement, centered in evangelical Protestant groups, involved prohibiting the sale of alcoholic beverages. The Church and its leaders supported this great moral effort. Soon the Utah Prohibition League was organized and led by President Heber J. Grant. Some Church leaders, including Senator Reed Smoot, preferred a local option on Prohibition rather than a nationwide ban on the sale of liquor. Others saw the ban as an infringement upon their freedom and urged Church members to continue to be taught the evils and consequences of consuming liquor, but be left to choose what course they wanted to pursue. The forces favoring outlawing the sale of alcohol, however, were so strong that the Eighteenth Amendment passed, making Prohibition a national law.

During the 1920s bishops interviewing members who wanted to enter the temple were asked to encourage them to comply with the principles in the Word of Wisdom. The Church also used its publications, especially the *Improvement Era*, to campaign against the use of tobacco. Many articles appealed to both scientific authority and Church doctrine to promote abstinence from both liquor and tobacco. Church leaders also urged anti-tobacco legislation, including the banning of advertising cigarettes on billboards. President Grant frequently preached against smoking and the consumption of liquor and firmly supported strict enforcement of the law. He even insisted that the *Deseret News* officially support Prohibition enforcement. Moreover, the Church provided financial aid to the Prohibition League.

During those years when Prohibition was in effect, there were strong forces working for its repeal. In spite of the vigorous support of the Church and public knowledge that President Grant stood unalterably behind Prohibition, Utah became the thirty-sixth state to vote for the repeal of the Eighteenth Amendment. Ironically, it was this affirmative vote that ended Prohibition. President Grant publicly expressed his disappointment that Church members had not followed his lead nor his counsel. Had they done so, he insisted, much of the suffering, sorrow, spiritual degeneration, and deterioration of physical health that accompany the consumption of liquor and tobacco, could have been avoided. Elder George Albert Smith later spoke on the consequence that had resulted and would continue because of the foolishness of those who had not heeded the counsel of the living prophet:

"There are those among us today who have been blinded by the philosophies and foolishness of men. There are those who reject the advice and counsel of the man that God has placed at the head of this Church.

"I am grieved as I stand here and think of the way we rejected the counsel of President Grant. And I don't want to be counted among that 'we' for I was not—but there were those among us who rejected the advice of the President of this Church and voted to repeal the Eighteenth Amendment and approved of bringing intoxicating liquor back into our community and legalizing it. That action has increased our accidents and murders and thousands of the sons and daughters of America are losing themselves and are being debauched beyond the possibility of recovery.

"Had we listened to the man who stands at our head and done our duty we would not in this valley and other places be suffering from the distresses that have come upon us, at least, we would not be responsible for them.

"People who haven't very much information suddenly come along with a bright idea, and they suggest 'this is the way' or 'that is the way,' and although it is in conflict with the advice of the Lord some are persuaded to try it. The Lord has given safe advice and appointed the President of his Church to interpret that advice. If we ignore what he advises, as the President of the Church, we may discover that we have made a serious mistake."[6]

CONTINUAL EMPHASIS ON MISSIONARY WORK

Following World War I the Church had some difficulty securing permission for missionaries to reenter several European countries. However, European mission president George F. Richards, working closely with his successor Elder George Albert Smith and with Senator Reed Smoot, finally obtained permission for missionaries to proselyte in Holland, Norway, Sweden, and Denmark. It was the fall of 1920 when the gospel was again preached in Germany and the spring of 1921 when South Africa was reopened.

In an effort to obtain firsthand information regarding Latter-day Saints in all parts of the world and to dramatize the scriptural injunction that the gospel be proclaimed to every nation, kindred, tongue, and people, President Grant sent Elder David O. McKay and Hugh J. Cannon, editor of the *Improvement Era*, around the world. The *Deseret News* noted that Elder McKay would tour the missions under the title of Commissioner of Education so that he would be officially welcomed by the world's leaders. In his charge to Elder McKay, President Grant told him, "Make a general survey of the missions, study conditions there, gather data concerning them, and in short obtain general information in order that there may be some one in the deliberations of the First Presidency and the Council of the Twelve thoroughly familiar with actual conditions."[7]

The world tour of David O. McKay (right) and his companion, Hugh J. Cannon (left), fulfilled the directions of President Heber J. Grant to gather information so that during their deliberations, Church leaders would have someone familiar with the conditions Latter-day Saints were living under.

For the remainder of his life, Elder McKay had his finger on the pulse of the world and the Church. As an Apostle he traveled widely, and he continued to do so into the early years of his administration as President of the Church. Under his leadership the Church became a worldwide institution.

The two ambassadors departed on 4 December 1920, accompanied by the good wishes of Church leaders, family, and friends. Traveling to Japan on the *Empress of Japan*, President McKay was sick much of the time. In describing his seasickness he wrote: "Good-bye last night's dinner! Good-bye yesterday's Rotary luncheon! And during the next sixty hours, Good-bye everything I had ever eaten since I was a babe on Mother's knee. I am not sure I didn't even cross the threshold into the pre-existent state."[8]

After meeting with the missionaries in Japan, they traveled to China via Korea and Manchuria. In Peking, they wandered the streets searching for a suitable place to dedicate the land. At length they walked to the walls of the Forbidden City, the former home of emperors. There they entered the gate and moved to a grove of cypress trees, which symbolized for the Chinese sorrow and sadness. Elder McKay sensed that this was a peculiarly fitting place in which to invoke the blessing of heaven upon this oppressed and sorrowing people. With bowed head, the modern witness for Christ quietly prayed to turn the key that unlocked the door for authorized servants of God to enter into China to preach the restored gospel of Jesus Christ.

After traveling to Hawaii, Elders McKay and Cannon inspected the Church school at Laie and then visited the other islands. Elder Cannon particularly requested they visit Pulehu on Maui where his father, George Q. Cannon, had baptized the first Hawaiian in July 1851. Thirty-four years later, President McKay recalled the events of their visit to Maui.

"So we came up here, and this is where I was [pointing to a spot where a pepper tree had been], and as we looked at an old frame house that stood there then, he said, 'That is probably the old chapel.' It seemed to me it was over in the distance. Nothing else was here. We said 'Well, probably that is the place. We are probably standing on the spot upon which your father, George Q. Cannon, and Judge Napela addressed those people.' We became very much impressed with the surroundings, association, and spiritual significance of the occasion; as we had also been with the manifestations we had had on our trip to the Orient and thus far in Hawaii. I said, 'I think we should have a word of prayer.'. . .

"I offered the prayer. We all had our eyes closed, and it was a very inspirational gathering. As we started to walk away at the conclusion of the prayer, Brother Keola Kailimai took Brother E. Wesley Smith to the side and very earnestly began talking to him in Hawaiian. As we walked along, the rest of us dropped back. They continued walking, and Brother Kailimai very seriously told in Hawaiian what he had seen during the prayer. They stopped right over there [pointing a short distance away] and Brother E. Wesley Smith said, 'Brother McKay, do you know what Brother Kailimai has told me?' I answered, 'No.' 'Brother Kailimai said that while you were praying, and we all had our eyes closed, he saw two men who he thought were Hugh J. Cannon and E. Wesley Smith step out of line in front of us and shake hands with someone, and he wondered why Brother Cannon and Brother Smith were shaking hands while we were praying. He opened his eyes and there stood those two men still in line, with their eyes closed just as they had been. He quickly closed his eyes because he knew he had seen a vision.'

"Now Brother Hugh J. Cannon greatly resembled Brother George Q. Cannon, his father. I spoke during the trip of his resemblance. Of course, E. Wesley Smith has the Smith attribute just as President Joseph Fielding Smith has it. Naturally, Brother Keola Kailimai would think that these two men were there. I said, 'I think it was George Q. Cannon and Joseph F. Smith, two former missionaries to Hawaii, whom that spiritual-minded man saw.'

"We walked a few steps farther and I said, 'Brother Kailimai, I do not understand the significance of your vision, but I do know that the veil between us and those former missionaries was very thin.' Brother Hugh J.

Cannon who was by my side, with tears rolling down his cheeks, said *'Brother McKay, there was no veil.'* "[9]

From Hawaii the two men sailed to San Francisco in anticipation of making better connections for their journey to the South Pacific. There they were met by President Heber J. Grant and their wives. Hearing of the death of President Grant's counselor, Anthon H. Lund, they decided to return briefly to Salt Lake City. They were back in San Francisco by late March prepared to begin a twelve-day voyage to Tahiti. They arrived there on 12 April, but were unable to contact the mission president, who was touring the mission. From Tahiti they sailed to Raratonga and then on to Wellington, New Zealand, where they had their first scheduled appointment. They spent nine days visiting with the missionaries and the Saints of New Zealand. It was the first time an Apostle in this dispensation had been in New Zealand.

Leaving Auckland on 30 April 1921 they sailed for Samoa. Arriving aboard the *S. S. Tofua* they were greeted in Samoa with songs and shouts of glee by a huge throng of Church members. They spent more than a month traveling from island to island and holding meetings with the Saints and governmental officials. At each stop Elder McKay would speak to large congregations—at times as many as fifteen hundred natives, officials, and visitors. When speaking to these groups he used an interpreter. On one occasion, however, he stopped the interpreter and continued speaking, realizing that the members were able to understand him. The entire congregation had received the gift to interpret tongues.

By their demeanor and their testimonies Elder David O. McKay and Hugh J. Cannon won a place in the hearts of the Samoan people. When the time came to leave, there were tears and appeals for the men to stay. Under the promptings of the Spirit, Elder McKay turned back, slipped from his horse, made known what he was about to do, and then with hands raised aloft pronounced upon them blessings in the authority and power of the apostleship and priesthood. It was a splendid end to a perfect farewell, and quickly turning away, they left while the Saints waved good-bye with white handkerchiefs. The Samoan people later placed a monument to honor the spot where Elder McKay had prayed.

Because of an epidemic of measles in Tonga, anyone entering the country had to undergo a quarantine of twelve days. Elder McKay decided to visit the area anyway but sent Elder Cannon to New Zealand to avoid the quarantine.

From Tonga he returned to New Zealand for an additional two weeks, visiting Auckland and Hastings. On 2 August 1921 the two travelers sailed for Sydney, Australia. In contrast to the multitudes who had gathered at other places, the numbers of Saints in Sydney, Melbourne, Adelaide, and Brisbane were small. The brethren, however, detected deep spirituality among the people.

Joseph Wilford Booth (1866–1928) labored most of his life as a missionary in the Middle East. His first mission in the Middle East was to Turkey in 1898. He later served twice as president of the Turkish Mission in 1903–9 and 1921–24.

He dedicated Greece for the preaching of the gospel while on Mars Hill in Athens in 1905. The name of the Turkish Mission was changed to the Armenian Mission, and he presided over it from 1924 to 1928. He died and was buried at Aleppo, Syria, just before the news came of his release.

From Australia they moved through Southeast Asia into lands overflowing with hungry and haggard faces, exemplified by the beggar who died near where Elder McKay was standing on a street in India. The hot, sticky boat ride from India to Egypt provided time for the two missionaries to think of home and family. One evening Elder McKay sat on deck next to a lady who was exhausted from jostling her little boy to keep him from crying. Elder McKay smiled at her, then asked if he could hold the child while she rested. She gladly consented, and soon the boy was asleep in the Apostle's arms.

In Palestine they were to meet President J. Wilford Booth, the new president of the Armenian Mission, and travel with him among the small branches in the region. When they arrived in Jerusalem, however, they did not know where President Booth would be joining them. After several days of visiting the shrines and other historic locations, they determined to leave for Haifa, a seaport town north of Jerusalem along the Mediterranean coast, en route to Aleppo in the northwest corner of Syria. Originally they had planned to travel by car through Samaria, but Elder McKay was impressed to go by train instead.

They arrived in Haifa not knowing where they would stay, and while Elder McKay went to inquire regarding a suitable hotel, Brother Cannon took care of their luggage. Ten minutes later, Elder McKay returned with a runner for a prominent hotel. About to exit through the large door of the train station, Elder McKay felt a tap on his shoulder, and someone asked, "Isn't this Brother McKay?" Elder McKay whirled about and saw President Booth. Had the two elders gone by car, or had they remembered to seek advice on a hotel before leaving Jerusalem, or had they remained there longer, they would not have met President Booth. As it turned out, they held many spiritual meetings with the Saints and distributed the funds collected during a special fast in Utah, which greatly blessed Church members in that part of the world.

They concluded the world tour with a visit to the missions of Europe. After traveling sixty-two thousand miles in five months, the two elders arrived home on Christmas Eve, 1921. In the April 1922 general conference, Elder McKay reported their successful mission and bore a powerful testimony that "Christ is ever ready to give you help in time of need, and comfort and strength, [if] you would approach Him in purity, simplicity, and faith."[10]

Shortly after returning home, David O. McKay was called as the Church's European mission president. He was charged with improving the public's view of the Church, especially in Great Britain. Elder John A. Widtsoe and Senator Reed Smoot visited London at President McKay's instigation and held a meeting with the owners of the leading British newspapers and with Stanley Baldwin, a former prime minister. When the owners learned that much of the material their newspapers had printed about the Latter-day Saints was untrue, they agreed not to accept anti-Mormon material.

This is the exact spot where Elder Melvin J. Ballard (1873–1939), a member of the Quorum of the Twelve, dedicated South America for the preaching of the gospel on 25 December 1925 in Buenos Aires, Argentina. This photo was taken June 1926.
Left to right: President Reinholdt Stoof, president of the South American Mission; his wife, Sister Ella Stoof; Elder Melvin J. Ballard; President Rey L. Pratt; and James Vernon Sharp.

Soon relationships for the Church improved in other parts of the world as well, and missions were either opened or reopened in France, Czechoslovakia, and Bavaria. In 1925, Melvin J. Ballard reopened the South American Mission. His dedicatory prayer, given in Buenos Aires, Argentina, included the following prophecy: "The work of the Lord will grow slowly for a time here just as an oak grows from an acorn. It will not shoot up in a day as does the sunflower that grows quickly and then dies. But thousands will join the Church here. It will be divided into more than one mission and will be one of the strongest in the Church. . . . The day will come when the Lamanites in this land will be a power in the Church."[11]

Symbolic of the commitment by Church members to missionary work was the example of Percy D. McArthur. Percy, a gifted runner who observed the Word of Wisdom, was the California champion in the 440-yard race. He often prayed before he ran, not that he would win but that he would do his best. He represented the Los Angeles Athletic Club at the national track meet held in 1927 in Lincoln, Nebraska, and tied with two others in a dead heat. Speaking of the 1928 Olympic team, he said, "I was confident I could make the team—was all primed and in trim, when I received my call to fill a mission. That meant more to me than any race." Soon he was laboring in the Mexican Mission.[12] He was neither the first nor the last great athlete to put the Church first in life. He turned his back on fame, and perhaps fortune, to proclaim to a humble people that the gospel was once more on the earth.

In an effort to send better trained missionaries into the field, Church leaders established a missionary training center in Salt Lake City with LeRoi C. Snow as its first director. The missionaries received two weeks of intensive instruction regarding such things as manners, punctuality, and missionary methods. They also heard instruction from General Authorities on gospel principles. The Mission Home, as it was called, was dedicated on

For many years most newly called missionaries traveled to Salt Lake City to be given instruction, receive their temple endowment, and be set apart for their labors. In 1924 approval was given to establish a home for missionaries during their stay. A home was purchased and remodeled in 1925, and President Lorenzo Snow's son LeRoi was named director.

Gradually the training program initiated there increased to two weeks and came to include seventy-one classes in such subjects as gospel instruction, Church organization, English and language instruction, personal health and hygiene, physical fitness, table etiquette and manners, personal appearance, and punctuality.

3 February 1925 by President Heber J. Grant, and its first class numbered only five elders. By 1927, however, nearly three thousand young men and women had been instructed.[13] The increase in the number of missionaries trained was due in part to President Grant's announcement in the October 1925 general conference of the need for one thousand additional missionaries.

It was also during this time that several innovative methods were tried to better facilitate the preaching of the gospel. A young elder in the California Mission, Gustive O. Larson, produced a series of illustrated lectures, which he delivered with his mission president's approval, all over the state. The slides and the dialogue centered on three themes: ancient American civilization, the history of the Mormons, and Latter-day Saint temples and temple work. Thousands of nonmembers came to see the slides and hear Elder Larson. Meanwhile, President B. H. Roberts, newly called leader of the Eastern States Mission, trained his missionaries in the fundamentals of proselyting and encouraged them to organize and teach the gospel message in a sequential manner and to make better use of the Book of Mormon. He also frequently called them into mission headquarters where he delivered lectures on the principles of the gospel.

Missionary work in Japan suffered a temporary setback during the 1920s. After twenty-three years of effort and sacrifice on the part of missionaries, President Grant, who had opened the Japanese mission, closed proselyting work there. A number of factors were involved in making the painful decision to withdraw the missionaries. Difficulties with the language and culture and the failure of the Church to attract converts all played an important role in the decision. Additional reasons included the Tokyo earthquake of 1923 and the Japanese exclusion law of 1924.

The earthquake was so devastating that missionary work completely stopped as the few missionaries who were there helped in the reconstruction effort. The Japanese exclusion law, which was passed in the United States in July 1924, prevented the Japanese people from immigrating to the United States. This caused bitterness toward all Americans living in Japan. Because of these factors, the First Presidency, after prayer and careful consideration, announced the mission closure in August 1924. It was not until after the Second World War that the restored gospel would attract thousands of Japanese converts.[14]

NEW DIRECTIONS IN CHURCH EDUCATION

Prior to World War I, Latter-day Saints realized that they could not continue to support two systems of education. The Church could not build enough Church schools, then called academies, for all the children of member families. Members found it burdensome to support the legally required public schools and at the same time provide funds for the operation of local Church schools. So, beginning in 1920, most of the academies were transformed into public schools or converted into community junior colleges and normal schools.

To ensure that Latter-day Saint youth would have some means of receiving daily religious instruction, the Church established seminaries adjacent to public high schools, beginning in 1912 with Granite High School in Salt Lake City. Some local school districts granted released time, and buildings separate from the high schools were erected. Qualified teachers were hired, and the entire system was supervised by a general Church board of education and a Church-appointed commissioner. Thus, the Church's great seminary system was initiated.

With increasing numbers of Latter-day Saints attending colleges and universities in the 1920s, some Church members became concerned about how students would integrate secular learning with their religion. The early twenties were marked by the rising reputation of science and a decline in the influence and power of the churches. One popular work at the time was entitled *A History of the Warfare of Science with Theology in Christendom*, written by Andrew Dixon White, a distinguished professor of history and president of Cornell University. He vigorously attacked fundamental Christian doctrines, which he called "a menace to the whole normal evolution of society."[15] His book was considered a standard to help students of science understand the philosophical war between science and Christianity.

During this period of ferment and challenge, a group of Latter-day Saints at the University of Idaho sought help from the First Presidency because of the large number of Mormon students there without access to Church education to supplement their secular training. The First Presidency responded to their appeal and sent the recently released South African Mission president, J. Wyley Sessions and his wife Magdeline, to Moscow, Idaho, with authority

In the school year of 1912–13, the Granite Seminary in Salt Lake City housed the Church's first "released-time" seminary classes, with seventy students attending. The next year Guy C. Wilson was hired as a full-time teacher.

Although begun as an experimental program, the seminary idea spread rapidly because of its success. A decade later almost five thousand students were enrolled in seminary, and that figure more than doubled by the time the first institute of religion, located in Moscow, Idaho, was created in 1926–27. By the mid-1980s over 225,000 students were enrolled in

The Moscow institute building in Moscow, Idaho, was dedicated on 25 September 1928 by Charles W. Nibley, a member of the First Presidency.

to organize a program for those Latter-day Saint students. Working closely with university officials, Brother Sessions soon developed a social organization and taught scriptural and ethics classes in a Church environment for which the students received university credit.

The first classes were held in the fall of 1926 with fifty-seven students enrolled. A large building was constructed near the university. Soon institutes were organized and buildings constructed adjacent to Utah State Agricultural College in Logan, Idaho State University in Pocatello, and the University of Utah in Salt Lake City.

It was also during the early twenties that Brigham Young University administrators established the first adult-oriented Education Week. Originally these classes were designed to train stake and ward leaders and were taught by the First Presidency and other General Authorities. Because of demands upon their time, the General Authorities later instructed university officials to use university teachers as instructors and to open the classes to the public. Education Weeks now involve thousands of Latter-day Saints across the United States and Canada, with more than twenty-five thousand people attending the instruction held annually on Brigham Young University campus in Provo.

FURTHER CHURCH EXPANSION

During the twenties, many Latter-day Saints left Utah and settled in other areas, such as southern California. Missionary work brought in many converts and added to the large number of Church members residing in that part of the United States. In January 1923, President Heber J. Grant, his first counselor, Charles W. Penrose, and other General Authorities assembled with three thousand California members and organized the Los Angeles Stake, the Church's eighty-eighth stake, which covered all of southern California. Creation of this stake symbolized that the Church was no longer just a Utah organization but was beginning to expand into every corner of the nation. Because of early colonization efforts, there were also sufficient Church members to justify erection of temples in Canada in 1923 and in Arizona in 1927. Both of these sacred edifices were dedicated by President Grant.

On 6 May 1922 the prophet dedicated the new Deseret News radio station, KZN and, for the first time in the Church's history, delivered a message over the airways. In his talk, the Church president bore his testimony that Joseph Smith was a prophet of the true and living God. Two years later the station began broadcasting sessions of general conference. Thousands of Church members as well as nonmembers were able to hear the inspired messages of the General Authorities. During the summer of 1924 the station's call letters were changed to KSL.

On 15 July 1929 the Tabernacle Choir began its first broadcast. The "Spoken Word," a message of inspiration and hope, created by Richard L. Evans, also

President Heber J. Grant began the first radio broadcast over KZN (later KSL), the Deseret News sponsored radio station in Salt Lake City, on 6 May 1922. Pictured left to right are Nathan O. Fullmer, Anthony W. Ivins, George Albert Smith, not identified, not identified, Augusta Winters Grant, Heber J. Grant, C. Clarence Neslen, and George J. Cannon.

became a regular part of the program. Over the years thousands of people have come into the Church after hearing the choir's inspiring singing and the eloquent and spiritual Spoken Word. Thousands more have received additional comfort and hope from choir broadcasts.

CENTENNIAL CELEBRATION AND INCREASING INTEREST IN CHURCH HISTORY

Believing that the Church needed a one-volume, easy-to-read history that would tell the story of the Restoration, the First Presidency asked Joseph Fielding Smith to write such a book. The finished work, entitled *Essentials in Church History*, was first published in 1922. This volume, which was used in the early twenties as a manual for the Melchizedek Priesthood, subsequently went through more than twenty editions.

Andrew Jenson, assistant Church historian, spent much of the decade traveling the world in his assignment to gather historical records from the wards and branches. It is because of his interest, perseverance, and efforts that historians today have the material in which to research the history of the Church.

Also during the twenties, the Church marked the centennial of the appearance of the Father and the Son and of the Angel Moroni to Joseph Smith with special cantatas and ceremonies in Palmyra, New York. On Sunday morning, 6 April 1930, thousands of Church members packed the Salt Lake Tabernacle to participate in a solemn assembly where Church leaders were sustained by quorum vote, and the impressive hosanna shout was majestically rendered. B. H. Roberts wrote, "It seemed, as the mighty shout was given, to vibrate waves of emotion which were sustained by the choir's rendition, at this point, of Handel's ever glorious and joyous chorus, 'Hallelujah,' from 'The Messiah.' "[16]

It was also during this conference that the Salt Lake Temple was first illuminated by giant floodlights, and a centennial pageant, "The Message of the Ages," was presented on a special stage constructed in the Tabernacle. Newly written for this celebration, the pageant depicted the various dispensations of the gospel. Admission was free, and the pageant was so enthusiastically received that performances were continued for more than a month. Elder B. H. Roberts also presented his monumental six-volume *A Comprehensive History of The Church of Jesus Christ of Latter-day Saints* to the membership as a fitting climax to the centennial celebrations.

As a further evidence of the Church's interest in its history, leaders announced in April 1928 that they had completed the purchase of the Hill Cumorah. Soon this location became one of the sites most frequently visited by Latter-day Saints traveling in the eastern United States. Many non-Mormons also visited the hill, and a visitors' center was established at its base.

The twenties were a time in the Church's history when its roots became better established. It was a decade of comparative peace, a time when bitterness and attacks for the most part had subsided. In this relatively tranquil decade, the Church slowly yet steadily grew in numbers and strengthened programs, and its members increased in their faith.

ENDNOTES

1. Heber J. Grant, in Conference Report, Apr. 1941, p. 4.

2. See Journal of Anthon H. Lund, 25 May 1919, LDS Historical Department, Salt Lake City, pp. 49–50; Charles W. Penrose, Journal History of The Church of Jesus Christ of Latter-day Saints, 1 June 1919, LDS Historical Department, Salt Lake City.

3. See Francis M. Gibbons, *Heber J. Grant: Man of Steel, Prophet of God* (Salt Lake City: Deseret Book Co., 1979) pp. 174–76.

4. See Bryant S. Hinckley, *Sermons and Missionary Services of Melvin Joseph Ballard* (Salt Lake City: Deseret Book Co., 1949), p. 23.

5. In James B. Allen, "Personal Faith and Public Policy: Some Timely Observations on the League of Nations Controversy in Utah," *Brigham Young University Studies*, Autumn 1973, p. 97; see also James B. Allen, "J. Reuben Clark, Jr., on American Sovereignty and International Organization," *Brigham Young University Studies*, Spring 1973, pp. 347–72.

6. In Conference Report, Oct. 1936, p. 75.

7. "Two Church Workers Will Tour Missions of Pacific Islands," *Deseret News*, 15 Oct. 1920, p. 5.

8. Llewelyn R. McKay, comp., *Home Memories of President David O. McKay* (Salt Lake City: Deseret Book Co., 1956), p. 41.

9. David O. McKay, *Cherished Experiences*. Rev. and enl. Compiled by Clare Middlemiss (Salt Lake City: Deseret Book Co., 1976), pp. 115-16.

10. In Conference Report, Apr. 1922, p. 69; see also pp. 62–68.

11. In "Prophecies for Children of Lehi Are Being Fulfilled," *Church News*, 26 Feb. 1984, p. 10.

12. M. C. Morris, "Olympic Games or a Mission?" *Improvement Era*, Mar. 1929, p. 382; see also pp. 378–83.

13. See LeRoi C. Snow, "The Missionary Home," *Improvement Era*, May 1928, pp. 552–54.

14. See R. Lanier Britsch, "The Closing of the Early Japan Mission," *Brigham Young University Studies*, Winter 1975, pp. 171–90.

15. Andrew Dickson White, *A History of the Warfare of Science with Theology in Christendom*, 2 vols. (New York: D. Appleton and Co., 1897), 1:vi.

16. B. H. Roberts, *A Comprehensive History of The Church of Jesus Christ of Latter-day Saints, Century One*, 6 vols. (Salt Lake City: The Church of Jesus Christ of Latter-day Saints, 1930), 6:540.

THE CHURCH DURING THE GREAT DEPRESSION

FEW EXTERNAL EVENTS have influenced the course of Church history more than the Great Depression of the 1930s. On 29 October 1929, known as Black Tuesday, the bottom fell out of the New York stock market, ruining millions of investors. People stopped buying unnecessary goods, and many businesses soon failed. The impact of the Great Depression was quite severe in the Mountain West, where most Latter-day Saints lived. In 1932 unemployment in Utah reached 35.9 percent, and per capita income fell by 48.6 percent.[1] Heads of families had to swallow their pride and wait in long lines for handouts of bread or other foods. In rural areas, families lost their farms when they could not meet mortgage payments.

Along with its individual members, the Church organization felt the depression. Expenditures from tithes, the Church's major source of income, dropped from $4 million in 1927 to only $2.4 million in 1933, resulting in many activities being curtailed.[2]

EARLY EFFORTS TO RELIEVE SUFFERING

In 1933, in the midst of the depression, the United States government under President Franklin D. Roosevelt enacted a series of sweeping measures popularly known as the New Deal. Although these programs were supported by most Latter-day Saints, Church leaders were concerned that some Saints could succumb to a "dole mentality." President Grant sadly acknowledged:

"Many people have said, . . . 'Well, others are getting some [government relief], why should not I get some of it?'

"I believe that there is a growing disposition among the people to try to get something from the government of the United States with little hope of ever paying it back. I think this is all wrong."[3]

As Church leaders sought to counsel the Saints and meet their needs during the depression, they found guidance in the scriptures. From the beginning the Lord has commanded, "Thou shalt love thy neighbour as thyself," a principle which the Apostle James designated as "the royal law" (James 2:8). When the Lord gave this commandment to the children of Israel, he also instructed them to provide for the poor (see Leviticus 19:10). He has

Sylvester Quayle Cannon (1877–1943), son of George Q. Cannon, twice served as president of the Netherlands Belgium Mission. He also served as President of the Pioneer Stake.

In 1925 he was called to be the Presiding Bishop of the Church. At the October 1939 general conference he was sustained as a member of the Quorum of the Twelve.

vigorously condemned those who are able to but refuse to help their less fortunate brethren (see Mosiah 4:16–27; D&C 56:16; 104:14–18).

The Church had a welfare program even before the depression. During the 1920s the Presiding Bishopric and the Relief Society General Board were active in finding employment, maintaining a storehouse, and in other ways helping the needy. Therefore, as economic conditions grew worse following the stock market crash, the Church was able to build on existing foundations.

In 1930, Presiding Bishop Sylvester Q. Cannon insisted bishoprics were responsible "to see to it that none of the active members of the Church suffers for the necessities of life. . . . The effort of the Church . . . is to help people to help themselves. The policy is to aid them to become independent, . . . rather than to have to depend upon the Church for assistance."[4] Local leaders developed innovative solutions to the economic distress of members. The Granite Stake in Salt Lake County put the unemployed to work on various stake projects, operated a sewing shop where donated clothing was renovated, and secured food for the needy through cooperative arrangements with nearby farmers. The Pioneer Stake, in an even less prosperous area, was especially hard hit by the depression. Under the leadership of its young stake president, Harold B. Lee, a storehouse was stocked with goods produced on stake projects or donated by Church members. Through local Church units the General Authorities gave encouragement, counsel, and support to these efforts to help meet the emergency.

Particularly influential in the early development of Churchwide welfare activities was J. Reuben Clark, Jr., who became a counselor to President Grant in 1933. Before receiving this call, President Clark had a distinguished career in international law and diplomacy, having served as under secretary of state and as the United States' ambassador to Mexico. President Grant instructed his new counselor to formulate a plan for assisting the Saints.

In July 1933 the First Presidency set forth fundamental principles and for the first time outlined specific relief measures that could be carried out Churchwide. "Our able-bodied members must not, except as a last resort, be put under the embarrassment of accepting something for nothing. . . . Church officials administering relief must devise ways and means by which all able-bodied Church members who are in need, may make compensation for aid given them by rendering some sort of service." In compensation for help received, individual wards were asked to be prepared to meet the needs of their own members and then to give assistance to other units requiring help. The Presidency concluded its message by encouraging the Saints to teach the members the "paramount necessity of living righteously, of avoiding extravagance, of cultivating habits of thrift, economy, and industry, of living strictly within their incomes, and of laying aside something, however small the amount may be, for the times of greater stress that may come to us."[5]

Joshua Reuben Clark, Jr. (1871–1961) was born of pioneer heritage in Grantsville, Utah. He served for many years in the Department of State for the United States government, where he became recognized as a leading authority in international law. In 1930 he was named United States ambassador to Mexico.

In 1933, while still in Mexico, J. Reuben Clark was called by President Heber J. Grant to serve as a counselor in the First Presidency of the Church. President Clark served for twenty-eight years as a member of the First Presidency, laboring with Heber J. Grant, George Albert Smith, and David O. McKay.

He was a prolific writer and gifted speaker. His conference talks were often centered on unity, the Constitution, and care of the poor.

LAUNCHING THE WELFARE PROGRAM CHURCHWIDE

A significant step in developing the Church's welfare program took place in 1935. At this time the federal government was considering shifting to the states the burden of providing relief, a load which hard-hit Utah was not in a position to assume. On 20 April of that year the First Presidency assigned stake president Harold B. Lee to introduce the welfare program Churchwide. He later recalled, "I was astounded to learn that for years there had been before them [Church leaders], as a result of their thinking and planning and as the result of the inspiration of Almighty God, the genius of the very plan that is being carried out and was in waiting and in preparation for a time when in their judgment the faith of the Latter-day Saints was such that they were willing to follow the counsel of the men who lead and preside in this Church."[6]

At the conclusion of his meeting with the First Presidency, Harold B. Lee drove up to the head of nearby City Creek Canyon and walked into the trees where he could pray about the organization that might need to be set up. He later recounted, "My spiritual understanding was opened, and I was given a comprehension of the grandeur of the organization of the Church and the Kingdom of God, the likes of which I had never contemplated before. The significant truth which was impressed upon me was that there was no need for any new organization to do what the Presidency had counseled us to do. It was as though the Lord was saying: 'All in the world that you have to do is to put to work the organization which I have already given.' "[7]

For the next year Harold B. Lee and other Church leaders met repeatedly to formulate the program for the entire Church. President David O. McKay, who had become President Grant's second counselor in 1934, played a key administrative role in this planning phase. The committee felt assured that their deliberations were guided by inspiration and their decisions received divine approval.

On Monday, 6 April 1936, following the close of the final regular general conference session, a special meeting for stake presidencies and ward bishoprics convened in the Assembly Hall on Temple Square. The First Presidency reported the distressing fact that about one-sixth of all Church members were being supported by public relief and many of them were not being required to work for what they received. The Presidency appealed to local leaders "to build again within the ranks of Latter-day Saints a feeling of financial independence." Church leaders declared: "The Lord has given us, within our Church, the government, organization and leadership to accomplish this great purpose and if we fail we stand condemned." An immediate goal was to provide sufficient food and clothing for all the needy in the Church. Ward teachers (later known as home teachers) were to work closely with the Relief Society in discovering and appraising the wants of the needy of the ward. The Saints were challenged to increase their fast offerings in order to provide funds for relief efforts. The First Presidency concluded with the admonition that the program's success depended on the faithfulness of the Saints.[8]

The First Presidency appointed a Church Relief Committee to help the Presiding Bishopric with the details of administration. This committee included Elder Melvin J. Ballard of the Council of the Twelve and Harold B. Lee. Their assignment was to motivate and coordinate the welfare activities of local Church units. A new level of Church administration, the region, was created to coordinate the functioning of the welfare program. Each region, consisting of from four to sixteen stakes, was to have a storehouse where surpluses from its own stakes or from other regions could be exchanged.

In May 1936, Elder Ballard was invited to Washington, D.C., to explain the Church's "security" program (as the welfare plan was known at first) to President Franklin D. Roosevelt. The president knew of and was pleased with the Church's efforts. He and Elder Ballard each pledged full cooperation with the other's efforts to meet the continuing challenges of the depression. President Roosevelt said that he hoped the Church's success would inspire other groups to launch similar programs of their own.[9]

At the October 1936 general conference, the First Presidency reviewed basic principles underlining the welfare plan, stating, "Our primary purpose was to set up, in so far as it might be possible, a system under which the curse of idleness would be done away with, the evils of a dole abolished, and independence, industry, thrift and self respect be once more established amongst our people. The aim of the Church is to help the people help themselves. Work is to be re-enthroned as the ruling principle of the lives of our Church membership."[10]

Speaking for the First Presidency at the April 1937 general conference, President J. Reuben Clark, Jr., exhorted the Saints to live within their means:

"Let us avoid debt as we would avoid a plague. . . .

"Let every head of every household see to it that he has on hand enough food and clothing, and, where possible, fuel also, for at least a year ahead.

. . . Let every head of household aim to own his own home, free from mortgage.

"Let us again clothe ourselves with these proved and sterling virtues—honesty, truthfulness, chastity, sobriety, temperance, industry and thrift; let us discard all covetousness and greed."[11]

Statistics during the later 1930s reflect a quickened pace in providing relief for the economically distressed. Church expenditures for welfare increased by more than one-third between 1935 and 1936. The output of welfare projects in the latter year included 134,661 bottles of fruit, 175,621 cans of fruit or vegetables, 134,425 pounds of fresh vegetables, 105,000 pounds of flour, 1,393 quilts, and 363,640 items of clothing. Fast offerings, the major source of cash for the welfare program, also increased. The gains were substantial in both the number of people paying and in the size of the

Welfare Square, located in west Salt Lake City, covers an area of ten acres. It contains an administration building and a canning center, root storage facility, milk processing plant, grain elevator, maintenance shop, and visitors' center.

offerings. Wards and stakes continued to acquire farms, canneries, and other projects to produce food, clothing, and other items required to help those in need. The Co-operative Securities Corporation was created in 1937 to hold title to welfare program properties and to coordinate its finances. This corporation also made loans to individuals who could not borrow from banks or through other ordinary channels.

Deseret Industries opened its doors in September 1938 with Stuart B. Eccles as its first manager. The aim of Deseret Industries at the time was fourfold: "First, those who have will be given another type of opportunity to help those who have not. Second, waste will be reduced by keeping our possessions in use as long as possible. Third, the work of renovation will employ many now unemployed. Fourth, articles in common use, of good quality, will be available at a low cost."12

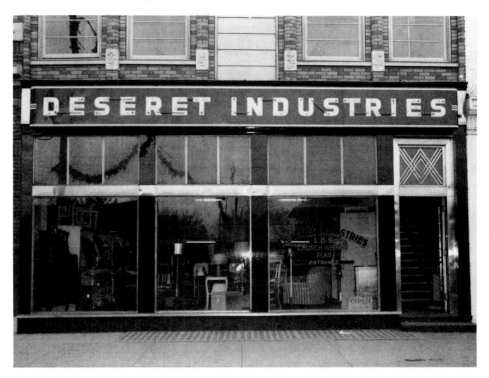

Although Latter-day Saints believed in the importance of self-reliance, many who wanted to work could not find jobs because of age or physical, mental, or emotional handicaps. Consequently, in 1938 Church leaders initiated the Deseret Industries program. Members donated clothing, furniture, appliances, newspapers, magazines, or other items they no longer needed. Employees sorted, cleaned, and repaired these materials. They were then sold at thrifty prices in the Deseret Industries' own retail stores. Proceeds paid the employees' wages and covered operating expenses. Modest salaries could be supplemented with help from the bishops' storehouse if necessary. The program was consistent with the Church's welfare philosophy. Members were off the dole, performed worthwhile work, and achieved a sense of self-reliance.

The Relief Society continued to play a vital role in helping families to help themselves. In 1937, with the encouragement of the First Presidency, the sisters sponsored courses in sewing, baking, and food preservation. Individual instruction was provided in the home, and group classes convened at welfare canning or sewing centers.

Elder Harold B. Lee regarded the welfare program as a fulfillment of prophecy. He reminded the Church that in 1894 President Wilford Woodruff had anticipated the time when "we shall see the necessity of making our own shoes and our own clothing, and providing our own foodstuffs, and uniting together to carry out the purposes of the Lord."[13]

President J. Reuben Clark, Jr., was convinced that the welfare plan had a purpose beyond providing help to the poor. He pointed out that although this program was not the same as the law of consecration, "when the Welfare Plan gets thoroughly into operation—it is not so yet—we shall not be so very far from carrying out the great fundamentals of the United Order."[14]

Elder Marion G. Romney, a key participant in directing the welfare program of the Church, also gave his testimony: "The welfare program was a direct revelation from the Lord to President Heber J. Grant. I heard President (J. Reuben) Clark tell that to a group of stake presidents at a meeting in Orem."[15]

ENRICHING LIVES THROUGH INCREASED CHURCH ACTIVITY

During the decade of the Great Depression, Church leaders were concerned not only with temporal needs but also with the importance of blessing the lives of both members and nonmembers in other ways. For example, they gave considerable thought to how Church programs could better work together in meeting the needs of young men and preparing them for missionary service. As a result the Aaronic Priesthood Correlation Plan was introduced at the April 1931 general conference. Quorums trained their members in priesthood responsibilities, encouraged worthiness and activity, and promoted feelings of brotherhood. The Sunday School provided instruction in gospel principles and ordinances, while the Young Men's Mutual Improvement Association taught proper application of these principles in the physical, social, cultural, and spiritual dimensions of life. The roles of these organizations were not redefined, but their work was correlated more closely than ever before. Under the direction of the bishop, officers and teachers came together monthly to consider the welfare of the young men.[16]

To involve the youth more completely in Church activity, the Presiding Bishopric announced the goal for 1935 of having one million "priesthood assignments" performed, emphasizing that every boy should fulfill at least one assignment. Certificates of achievement were provided for local quorums meeting specified standards. This was the beginning of group and individual awards programs that would be important in Church activity during the following decades.

Church leaders emphasized that the increasing number of inactive young men growing to maturity without receiving the Melchizedek Priesthood should not be neglected. Much of the credit for developing a successful means of reaching them belongs to A.P.A. Glad, bishop of the Salt Lake Twenty-eighth Ward. He realized that these inactive men needed a separate class where they could feel comfortable. In 1932 he called a group of enthusiastic and devoted leaders to give their full attention to these brethren. Group members helped plan their own activities. One of Bishop Glad's slogans was, "We learn to do by doing."[17]

After eight months of persistent effort, forty men were brought into activity. One member of the original group recalled how he had been rousted out of bed to attend the class. For him this began a pattern of regular Church activity, which led to his receiving the Melchizedek Priesthood and serving as a high priest group leader, bishop, and high councilor.[18] Bishop Glad's work became the basis of a similar Adult Aaronic program introduced throughout the Church during the fall of 1933.

MISSIONARY WORK DURING THE DEPRESSION

The Church continued to emphasize missionary work despite the problems caused by the depression. Because many families needed their sons to work at home and could not afford to send them on missions, the number of missionaries entering the field fell sharply as the effects of the depression spread. In 1932 only 399, or 5 percent of the potential missionaries were able to serve. Despite this missionary shortage, missionary work continued, with notable success in some places. Missionaries developed more innovative and systematic methods in order to maintain productivity. In 1937, LeGrand Richards, president of the Southern States Mission, issued "The Message of Mormonism," outlining twenty-four weekly presentations of gospel topics. This outline, published as *A Marvelous Work and a Wonder*, became the basis of many subsequent proselyting plans.

Missionaries employed various techniques to reach interested persons: A missionary chorus attracted favorable attention in England and Ireland. A missionary basketball team made friends in Czechoslovakia, and in Germany four elders were recruited as basketball judges for the 1936 Berlin Olympics. Lectures on ancient America featuring color slides were particularly productive in making contacts. The Church Radio, Publicity, and Mission Literature Committee was organized in 1935 to supply materials for these illustrated lectures. With Gordon B. Hinckley, who had recently returned from a mission to Britain, as executive secretary, the committee directed the preparation of tracts, other mission literature, and scripts for radio programs.

One beneficial by-product of the depression was a greater involvement of local members in missionary work. In California, missionaries lived in members' homes to reduce expenses. Alabama Saints traveled long distances in order to take investigators to district conferences. In many areas members provided referrals, enabling missionaries to reduce time spent in less productive door-to-door tracting. The missionary force around the world was expanded by local members who donated several hours weekly to work with the full-time missionaries or accepted special short-term mission calls.

LeGrand Richards (1886–1983) was one of the greatest missionaries this dispensation has produced. He served four missions and presided over two missions.

Elder Richards served as the Presiding Bishop of the Church from 1938–52 and as a member of the Quorum of the Twelve from 1952 until his death in 1983. His father, George F. Richards, and his grandfather, Franklin D. Richards, had also served in the Quorum of the Twelve.

In many areas congregations had been led by missionaries, but during the depression local Saints assumed more responsibility for their own affairs. This not only freed the missionaries' time for proselyting, it also fostered the Saints' pride in their own branches. President Grant concluded that the shortage of missionaries "has probably been a blessing in disguise, because it has forced us to make greater use of the local saints."[19]

Hundreds of people were converted as a result of the missionary efforts that were organized in the stakes of Zion.[20] At April general conference in 1936 all stakes were instructed to organize a mission, and supervision of these missions was assigned to the First Council of the Seventy.[21] As a result, hundreds of converts were baptized each year, and the spirituality of the Saints seemed to increase. One ward reported that there was a 50 percent increase in overall activity among its members as a result of local missionary work.[22]

During the depression the Church adopted a variety of other methods to supplement the work being done by its increasingly scarce proselyting missionaries. The continuing success of the weekly Tabernacle Choir broadcasts prompted the Church to expand its use of radio. Several wards and stakes as well as missionary groups produced programs for local stations. A portion of general conference was broadcast to Europe via international shortwave radio on 5 April 1936. Partly as a result of the Tabernacle Choir's increasing popularity, Temple Square continued to be an effective missionary tool. Many visitors went miles out of their way to attend choir broadcasts or noon organ recitals. Temple Square attracted even more visitors than popular national parks in the area.

Temple Square

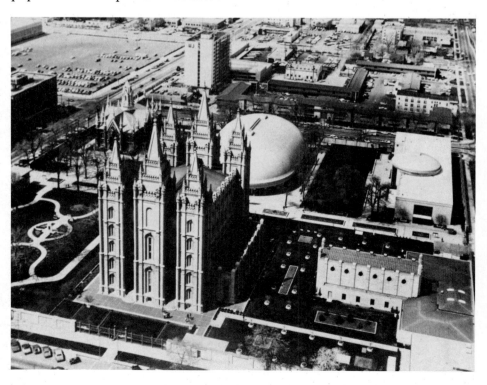

The Church also began more regular participation in national and international fairs and exhibitions. An estimated 2.3 million people visited the Church's booth at the Chicago Century of Progress exposition in 1933–34. The Church's new positive image was apparent as Elder B. H. Roberts, who had been denied the opportunity to speak at Chicago's 1893 Columbian Exposition, was well received as he spoke at the Congress of Religions held in conjunction with the 1933 Chicago exposition. At the California-Pacific International Exposition held in San Diego during 1935–36, the Church erected its first exhibit building. The Golden Gate International Exposition was held on Treasure Island in San Francisco Bay in 1939–40. Capitalizing on the Tabernacle Choir's popularity, the Church designed its exhibit building in the form of a miniature Tabernacle with a fifty-seat auditorium in which missionaries could present illustrated lectures on the history and beliefs of the Church.

Begun in 1937, the Hill Cumorah Pageant became one of the Church's most successful public relations ventures. Featuring a cast composed mostly of missionaries serving in the area, "America's Witness for Christ" was presented on three large stages constructed on the slopes of the hill. It depicted scenes from the Book of Mormon, culminating with the Savior's visit to the ancient inhabitants of America. Just a month before the first pageant was presented, Elder Harold I. Hansen, who had just received his bachelor's degree in drama, entered the Eastern States Mission. He was immediately assigned to help with the final preparations and rehearsals. Elder Hansen was convinced that his call to this particular mission at this time resulted from divine guidance. He would continue to be associated with the annual pageant for the next forty years, most of this time as its director. Over the years additional stages, lighting, and other technical effects were added.

GIVING DIRECTION TO CHURCH EDUCATION

As the depression's impact eased, the Church expanded its educational programs. During the later 1930s the number of campuses served by institutes of religion grew to seventeen, including all the major schools in the mountain west and in California. A companion program, the Deseret Club, began in 1933 when a group of southern California Latter-day Saints felt the need to bring students together for intellectual and social activities within the influence of Church ideals and standards. In 1936, while visiting in the Los Angeles area, Elder John A. Widtsoe recognized the value of Deseret Club activities in the lives of students and helped bring this program under the sponsorship of the Church Board of Education. Deseret Clubs were organized on campuses where there were not enough Church members to justify a full institute program. Eventually they were replaced by the organization of the Latter-day Saint Student Association.

Church educational leaders placed greater emphasis on adequate professional training for college-level faculty members, especially in religion. Noted scholars offered summer workshops at BYU, and promising graduate students were encouraged to attend various theological seminaries.

By the mid-1930s, however, an increasing number of Church members and leaders were concerned over religion teachers being trained by non-Latter-day Saint scholars. They felt that "higher criticism" of the scriptures (the scientific investigation into the origin and authenticity of biblical texts) and other humanistic ideas were creeping into the curriculum. These concerns led the General Authorities to give closer supervision to the Church's educational system, especially to religious instruction. By this time, David O. McKay, with his rich background in Church education, had become a counselor in the First Presidency. Both Presidents Clark and McKay exerted a powerful influence over the Church's educational program.

In 1938, President J. Reuben Clark, Jr., was assigned to set forth the mission of the Church's education program and to outline the qualifications and duties of those employed to teach in the Church's schools, institutes of religion, and seminaries. His address, *The Charted Course of the Church in Education*, was delivered on 8 August at a summer gathering of these teachers at Aspen Grove in Provo Canyon near the BYU campus and has become an oft-quoted classic. President Clark insisted that two fundamental truths must be proclaimed fearlessly and cannot be explained away:

"First: That Jesus Christ is the Son of God, the Only Begotten of the Father in the flesh, . . . that He was crucified; that His spirit left His body; that He died; that He was laid away in the tomb; that on the third day His spirit was reunited with His body, which again became a living being; that He was raised from the tomb a resurrected being, a perfect Being, the First Fruits of the Resurrection; that He later ascended to the Father; and that because of His death and by and through His resurrection every man born into the world since the beginning will be likewise literally resurrected. . . .

"The second of the two things to which we must all give full faith is: That the Father and the Son actually and in truth and very deed appeared to the Prophet Joseph in a vision in the woods; that other heavenly visions followed to Joseph and to others; that the Gospel and the holy Priesthood after the Order of the Son of God were in truth and fact restored to the earth from which they were lost by the apostasy of the Primitive Church; that the Lord again set up His Church, through the agency of Joseph Smith; that the Book of Mormon is just what it professes to be; that to the Prophet came numerous revelations for the guidance, upbuilding, organization, and encouragement of the Church and its members; that the Prophet's successors [are] likewise called of God."

President Clark then reminded teachers that the youth of the Church are hungry for these truths to be taught in a straightforward manner, and he warned teachers that doubt must never be sown in the hearts of trusting students. He concluded by charging his listeners to teach the gospel of Jesus

Christ from the standard works and from the words of latter-day prophets.[23]

Because of their interest in the spiritual growth of LDS youth, the General Authorities desired to be involved personally in the direction of Church schools. Brigham Young University, Ricks College, and the LDS Business College had each been under a separate board of trustees. To achieve a more centralized control, these local boards were released in 1938, and all units were brought under the direct supervision of the General Church Board of Education, which consisted of General Authorities and a few others.

Latter-day Saints understandably pointed with pride to their educational attainments in the decade of the depression. Census data in 1940 indicated that Utah, where the majority of the population were Church members, had the highest level of educational attainment of any state in the Union: young adults in Utah completed an average of 11.7 years of school compared to 11.3 in the next two highest states, and the national median was 10.3 years.[24] Church magazines proudly reported the results of studies conducted by E. L. Thorndike of Columbia University who found that Utah had the highest proportion of persons listed in *Who's Who* and *American Men of Science*. Thorndike concluded that "the production of superior men is surely not an accident, that it has only a slight affiliation with income, that it is closely related to the kind of persons."[25]

MEETING THE ADMINISTRATIVE CHALLENGE

The expansion of Church activities during the 1930s increased demands on the time and financial resources of the Saints. To lessen this load, the General Authorities undertook a new study of all Church programs with the goal of correlation and simplification where possible.

At the beginning of 1939, the First Presidency wanted the work of the auxiliary and other organizations to be "coordinated, unified, and standardized to avoid duplication and overlapping." They therefore appointed a Committee of Correlation and Coordination, headed by three members of the Twelve. The First Presidency affirmed that the real reason for all Church organizations "is to instruct the people in the Gospel, to lead them to a testimony of the Truth, to care for those in need, to carry on the work entrusted to us by the Lord."[26]

In 1940, President J. Reuben Clark, Jr., instructed a group of Church executives that "the home is the basis of a righteous life, that no other instrumentality can take its place nor fulfil its essential functions, and that the utmost the Auxiliaries can do is to aid the home in its problems, giving special aid and succor where such is necessary."[27]

A tangible step toward greater simplification was discontinuing weekly genealogy meetings in 1940 and incorporating genealogical instruction into the curriculum of the Sunday School. At the same time, the *Utah Genealogical and Historical Magazine*, published since 1910, was discontinued and its function assumed by the *Improvement Era*.

During the 1930s the Church continued to grow throughout North America and abroad. This expansion was reflected in two extended overseas trips by General Authorities. During three months of 1937, President Heber J. Grant and other Church leaders visited the missions of Europe. Everywhere he went President Grant encouraged the Saints to stay where they were and build up the Church. Large public meetings and extensive press coverage helped build goodwill for the Mormons in areas where they had been unknown or misunderstood. When President J. Reuben Clark, Jr., joined President Grant to commemorate the British Mission's centennial, this marked the first occasion when two members of the First Presidency were in Europe at the same time.

During the first one hundred years of this key mission's existence, over 125,000 converts had been baptized. Approximately half of these had emigrated, providing strength to the Church in the West. In 1938, Elder George Albert Smith of the Council of the Twelve spent six months visiting the Pacific missions, where he was warmly received by the Saints. A high point was his participation in the Maori Saints' annual "hui tau," or conference. As President Grant had done in Europe the year before, Elder Smith strengthened Church members in the Pacific and also encouraged more favorable attitudes toward the Church through giving interviews with the press, speaking on the radio, and meeting with government officials.

Continued Church growth and the multiplication of stakes and missions around the world placed a heavier administrative load on the shoulders of the General Authorities. Not only did this mean a greater number of conferences to conduct, but it also involved more travel, as during the 1930s the Saints increasingly moved to scattered areas, and stakes were organized in such distant cities as New York, Washington, D.C., Chicago, Seattle, and Honolulu.

This was the setting for the decision to create a new group of General Authorities to help shoulder the increased load. At the April 1941 general conference the First Presidency announced the appointment of "Assistants to the Twelve, who shall be High Priests, who shall be set apart to act under the direction of the Twelve in the performance of such work as the First Presidency and the Twelve may place upon them."[28] Initially, five men were called—Marion G. Romney, Thomas E. McKay, Clifford E. Young, Alma Sonne, and Nicholas G. Smith. As the administrative burden continued to increase, additional members were added.

The decade of the 1930s is best known for the formation of the welfare plan, but many other important and far-reaching strides were made in enlarging and refining Church programs. A stronger and more confident Church emerged from the depression years. Nevertheless, while the Church was successfully coping with problems caused by the depression, the threat of war began to pose new challenges.

ENDNOTES

1. University of Utah School of Business, "Measures of Economic Changes in Utah, 1847–1947," *Utah Economic and Business Review*, Dec. 1947, p. 23.

2. See Conference Report, Apr. 1928, pp. 3–4; Conference Report, Apr. 1934, pp. 4–5.

3. In Conference Report, Oct. 1933, p. 5.

4. In Conference Report, Oct. 1930, p. 103.

5. In James R. Clark, comp. *Messages of the First Presidency of The Church of Jesus Christ of Latter-day Saints*, 6 vols. (Salt Lake City: Bookcraft, 1965–75), 5:332–34.

6. In Conference Report, Apr. 1941, p. 121; see also Conference Report, Oct. 1972, p. 124; or *Ensign*, Jan. 1973, p. 104.

7. "An Enlarged Vision of Church Organization and Its Purposes," *Church News*, 26 Aug. 1961, p. 8.

8. In "Launching of a Greater Church Objective," *Church News*, 25 Apr. 1936, p. 1; see also Clark, *Messages of the First Presidency*, 6:10–13.

9. See "Church Security Program Indorsed by President Roosevelt," *Deseret News*, 9 June 1936, p. 1.

10. Heber J. Grant, in Conference Report, Oct. 1936, p. 3.

11. In Conference Report, Apr. 1937, p. 26.

12. John A. Widtsoe, "Deseret Industries," *Improvement Era*, Sept. 1938, p. 544.

13. In Conference Report, Apr. 1943, p. 126.

14. In Conference Report, Oct. 1942, p. 57.

15. In "New Storehouse Is Dedicated at Welfare Square Complex," *Church News*, 29 May 1976, p. 4.

16. Minutes of the Aaronic Priesthood Convention Held in the Assembly Hall, 4 Apr. 1931, Presiding Bishopric, LDS Historical Department, Salt Lake City, pp. 2–4, 10.

17. "An Opportunity for Adult Members," *Church News*, 6 June 1936, p. 4; see also *Instructor's Manual and Lesson Outline for Adult Aaronic Priesthood Classes*, 1936, pp. 7–8; "Adult Aaronic Priesthood Class Outstanding Success," *Improvement Era*, Nov. 1933, p. 812.

18. See "Fifty Years Ago, Adult Aaronic Program Started," *Church News*, 18 Sept. 1982, p. 10.

19. Letter from J. Reuben Clark, Jr., to Leah D. Widtsoe, 13 Oct. 1933, First Presidency Letterpress copybooks, 1877–1949, LDS Historical Department, Salt Lake City, p. 867.

20. See letter from J. Golden Kimball to the Seventies, 31 Jan. 1934, First Council of the Seventy, Circular letters, 1860–1985, LDS Historical Department, Salt Lake City, p. 1.

21. See letter from Rudger Clawson to stake presidents, 24 Apr. 1936, LDS Historical Department, Salt Lake City.

22. See "Stake Mission Program Accomplishments Reported," *Deseret News*, 17 July 1937, p. 7.

23. *The Charted Course of the Church in Education*, reprint ed., 1980, pp. 2–3; see also *Charge to Religious Educators*, 2d ed. (1982), p. 3.

24. See United States government 1940 census data, in *Utah Economic and Business Review*, Dec. 1947, p. 58.

25. E. L. Thorndike, "The Origin of Superior Men," *Scientific Monthly*, May 1943, p. 430; see also "Utah Holds High Rank as Birthplace of Scientists," *Improvement Era*, Oct. 1940, p. 606.

26. Letter from J. Reuben Clark, Jr., and David O. McKay to Elders Joseph Fielding Smith, Stephen L Richards, and Albert E. Bowen, 19 Jan. 1939, First Presidency Letterpress copybooks, 1877–1949, LDS Historical Department, Salt Lake City, pp. 635–36.

27. J. Reuben Clark, Jr., "Memorandum of Suggestions," 29 Mar. 1940, Papers, 1933–61, LDS Historical Department, Salt Lake City, p. 3.

28. J. Reuben Clark, Jr., in Conference Report, Apr. 1941, p. 95.

CHAPTER FORTY

THE SAINTS DURING WORLD WAR II

Time Line

Date	*Significant Event*
24 Aug. 1939	The First Presidency ordered evacuation of missionaries from Europe
1 Sept. 1939	Hitler's invasion of Poland marked the beginning of World War II in Europe
1940	Hugh B. Brown named as LDS servicemen's coordinator
1940	Missionaries evacuated from the Pacific and South Africa
7 Dec. 1941	Japanese attack on Pearl Harbor led United States to declare war
Apr. 1942	First Presidency declared Church's position on war
Oct. 1942	Servicemen's Committee was organized
14 Aug. 1945	World War II ended

THE WORLD WAS still recovering from the effects of the Great Depression when World War II broke out in Europe. Under Adolf Hitler and the Third Reich, Germany was enlarging its boundaries. At the same time Japan was also expanding its empire into the Pacific in quest of political domination, raw materials, and new markets for her industries. Before long most of the world was engulfed in the war. Just as the depression significantly affected the Latter-day Saints during the 1930s, World War II and its aftermath exerted a powerful impact on the Church and its members during the succeeding decade.

THE CHURCH AND THE THIRD REICH

During the 1920–30s the German missions of the Church experienced unprecedented success, particularly in the eastern provinces. When the National Socialists, or Nazis, gained control of Germany in 1933, Church members had to become increasingly circumspect. Gestapo agents frequently observed Church meetings, and most branch and mission leaders were thoroughly interrogated by the police about Mormon doctrines, beliefs, and practices, and were warned to stay out of political matters. By the mid-1930s, Latter-day Saint meetings were often canceled during Nazi rallies, and the Church was forced to drop its Scouting program because of the Hitler Youth Movement.

Gospel teachings about Israel were out of harmony with the Nazi's anti-Jewish policies, so copies of Elder James E. Talmage's popular doctrinal work *The Articles of Faith* with its references to Israel and Zion were confiscated. In one town, police ripped all hymns referring to these topics out of the hymnbooks. Uneasy and concerned because of these conditions, some Church members ceased attending Church to avoid trouble with the police. Other German Saints felt an intensified interest in emigrating from the country.

The Church was never officially banned in Germany as some other small religious groups were. In fact, the Church received favorable publicity when the Nazi government invited Mormon elders to help coach some of the German basketball teams and to assist them at the 1936 Berlin Olympics. Furthermore, because the Nazis emphasized racial purity, they promoted genealogical research. Government officials, who had earlier regarded the Mormons as an unpopular sect and thus denied them access to vital records, now respected them because of their interest in genealogy.[1] Nevertheless, the situation for the Church and its missionaries became much more difficult during the late 1930s.

The rise of the Nazis in Germany also affected Church activity in South America where there were large colonies of German immigrants. In Brazil the government, fearing a subversive threat from Nazi sympathizers, banned the speaking of German in public meetings and the distribution of literature in that language. During their first decade in Brazil, Latter-day Saint missionaries had worked almost exclusively among the German-speaking minority, so most branch meetings were conducted in their language. Under pressure from the government, the local police in one area even forced the Saints to turn over their German scriptures, which were then burned in a public bonfire. In the face of such conditions during the late 1930s, missionaries shifted their emphasis to the Portuguese-speaking majority, thus laying the foundation for the great growth of later decades.

THE EVACUATION OF MISSIONARIES

As early as autumn 1937, Adolf Hitler vowed to expand his domain by annexing the German-speaking peoples in Austria and Western Czechoslovakia.

In March 1938, Germany succeeded in annexing Austria, and by September, Hitler accused the Czechs of persecuting the German minority in their country, and he insisted on his right to intervene. As troops massed on both sides of the German-Czech border, war seemed inevitable. As tensions grew in Europe, the General Authorities became increasingly concerned about the safety of the missionaries serving there. On 14 September 1938 the First Presidency ordered the evacuation of all missionaries from these two countries. At a meeting in Munich, Germany, Great Britain and France agreed to Hitler's annexation of Western Czechoslovakia on the condition that he commit no further aggression. War was temporarily averted, and the First Presidency permitted the evacuated missionaries to return to their fields of labor.

The agreement at Munich, however, did not bring lasting peace. In 1939, Hitler turned his attention to Poland, demanding greater access through the Polish Corridor to German-populated East Prussia. Echoing the charges he had brought against Czechoslovakia a year earlier, Hitler now sought to justify military intervention by accusing Poland of mistreating its German minority. As tension increased, President J. Reuben Clark's diplomatic background proved valuable to the Church. Through his contacts at the State Department, he kept Church leaders apprised of the developments in Europe on an almost hourly basis. Finally, on Thursday, 24 August 1939 the First Presidency, for the second time, ordered the evacuation of all missionaries from Germany and Czechoslovakia. They instructed Elder Joseph Fielding Smith, who was in Europe conducting the annual tour of missions, to take charge.

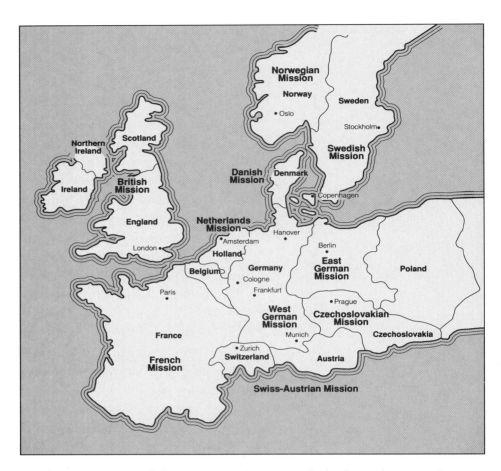

European missions, 1938

The evacuation of the missionaries, particularly from the West German Mission, posed great challenges and provided the setting for some remarkable examples of divine assistance.

The First Presidency's telegram arrived in Germany on Friday morning, 25 August. Elder Joseph Fielding Smith and M. Douglas Wood, mission president, were conducting conferences in Hanover, but President Wood and his wife immediately returned to mission headquarters in Frankfurt. By Friday afternoon they had telegraphed all missionaries, directing them to leave for Holland at once. On Saturday morning, a missionary called from the border to tell them that the Netherlands had closed its borders to almost all foreigners fearing that the influx of thousands of refugees would seriously deplete the already short food supply. Meanwhile, bulletins on German radio warned that by Sunday night all railroads would be under military control and no further guarantees could be made for civilian travel.

When the Dutch closed their border, the resulting crisis challenged the resourcefulness of President Wood and his missionaries. Knowing that they could not take German currency out of the country, almost all of the missionaries had used their excess funds to purchase cameras or other goods that they could take with them. Therefore, they did not have enough money to buy tickets to Copenhagen, Denmark, the alternate point of evacuation, leaving several groups of missionaries stranded at the Netherlands border.

Norman George Seibold was born 18 October 1915 and is currently (1989) living in Rupert, Idaho.

Wallace F. Toronto (1907–1968) was called to the German-Austrian Mission in 1928. In July of 1929, Elder John A. Widtsoe dedicated Czechoslovakia as a mission of the Church. He traveled there in company with six missionaries, one of whom was Wallace Toronto. Elder Toronto was then asked to labor in the new mission.

In 1936, Elder Toronto was called back to Europe as president of the Czechoslovakia Mission along with his wife, Martha. They labored there until World War II broke out. In 1946, President Toronto was asked to return to Czechoslovakia and resume duties as mission president.

In Frankfurt, President Wood gave one of his missionaries, Elder Norman George Seibold, a former football player from Idaho, a special assignment:

"I said: 'Elder, we have 31 missionaries lost somewhere between here and the Dutch border. It will be your mission to find them and see that they get out.' . . .

"After four hours on the train he arrived at Cologne, which is about half way to the Dutch border. We had told him to follow his impressions entirely as we had no idea what towns these 31 Elders would be in. Cologne was not his destination, but he felt impressed to get off the train there. It is a very large station, and was then filled with thousands of people. . . . This Elder stepped into this station and whistled our missionary whistle—'Do What is Right, Let the Consequence Follow.' " Thereby he located eight missionaries.[2]

In some towns Elder Seibold remained on board the train, but at others he was impressed to get off. In one small community he recalled, "I had a premonition to go outside the station and out into the town. It seemed silly to me at the time. But we had a short wait and so I went. I passed a Gasthaus, a restaurant there, and I went inside and there were two missionaries there. It was fantastic, in that they both knew me and of course they were quite happy to see me. . . . As surely as if someone had taken me by the hand, I was guided there." In Copenhagen on Monday, 28 August, President Wood learned that fourteen of the thirty-one missing missionaries had entered Holland safely. That afternoon he received a telegram from Elder Seibold stating that the remaining seventeen would arrive in Denmark that evening.[3]

While the West German missionaries struggled to reach Denmark, quite a different drama unfolded in Czechoslovakia. On 11 July four missionaries were arrested by the German Gestapo and thrown in Pankrac Prison where political prisoners were held. For the next six weeks their mission president, Wallace Toronto, worked persistently for their release. He did not succeed until 23 August 1939, the day before the Czech Mission received the directive to evacuate. Most of the missionaries, as well as Sister Toronto and the Toronto children, left promptly for Denmark. But President Toronto remained behind to help the elders who had been in prison recover their passports and other possessions.

As Hitler's armies massed for the invasion of Poland, communications with Czechoslovakia were cut off. Sister Toronto explained, "Seeing that I was very worried and getting more upset by the minute, President [Joseph Fielding] Smith came over to me, put his protecting arm around my shoulders and said, 'Sister Toronto, this war will not start until Brother Toronto and his missionaries arrive in this land of Denmark.' "

In Czechoslovakia, President Toronto and his missionaries concluded their business by Thursday, 31 August. Just before leaving, however, one of the missionaries was rearrested and again thrown into prison. Quick and inspired action on the part of President Toronto enabled him to show the

German authorities that it was a case of mistaken identity, and the elder was promptly released. That night the group boarded a special train sent to evacuate the British delegation; it was the last train to leave Czechoslovakia. They passed through Berlin early the next day and that afternoon boarded the last ferry to cross from Germany to Denmark.[4] Germany invaded Poland that same day, the event that is generally regarded as the beginning of World War II. Elder Joseph Fielding Smith's prophetic promise to Sister Toronto was fulfilled precisely.

In Salt Lake City the First Presidency closely monitored the mounting crisis and soon ordered the evacuation of all missionaries from Europe. Most missionaries crossed the Atlantic Ocean on cargo ships with makeshift accommodations for several hundred passengers each. Typically, these ships' holds were filled with bunks, with only a curtain separating the men's and women's areas. President J. Reuben Clark, Jr., regarded the successful evacuation of missionaries as truly miraculous:

"The entire group was evacuated from Europe in three months, at a time when tens of thousands of Americans were besieging the ticket offices of the great steamship companies for passage, and the Elders had no reservations. Every time a group was ready to embark there was available the necessary space, even though efforts to reserve space a few hours before had failed. . . .

"Truly the blessings of the Lord attended this great enterprise."[5]

In 1940 more countries were drawn into the rapidly expanding war. Belgium, Holland, and France quickly fell to the Germans, and Britain prepared to fight for its life. As a result the overseas colonies of these countries were vulnerable to attack. In September 1940 Japan signed a ten-year mutual assistance treaty with Germany and Italy and began occupying French Indochina.

These developments prompted the First Presidency to withdraw all Latter-day Saint missionaries from the South Pacific and South Africa the following month. Communications between these areas and Church headquarters in America were not cut off as they had been in Europe, and mission presidents were permitted to remain in their areas. Missionaries were not evacuated from South America, but after 1941 no new missionaries were sent to that continent, and by 1943 none remained there. By that time proselyting by the regular full-time missionaries was limited to North America and Hawaii. Even in these areas the number of missionaries was drastically reduced as more and more young men were drafted into military service.

EUROPEAN SAINTS CARRY ON

When the missionaries and their leaders were withdrawn, the European Saints were left on their own, often in isolated circumstances. Many of them personally witnessed destruction and death. Even outside the combat zone, preoccupation with war was demoralizing and tended to diminish interest in

Helmuth Hubener (1925–42) was a German Latter-day Saint who lost his life during Hitler's regime.

spiritual concerns. Another problem faced the Saints in the occupied countries and in Germany. While some felt that the wisest course was to cooperate with the Nazis, others were convinced that their patriotic duty was to resist. Helmuth Hubener, a teenaged member of the Church in Hamburg, for example, dared to distribute copies of news he had picked up by shortwave radio from the British Broadcasting Corporation presenting a view contrary to Nazi propaganda. For these actions, he was eventually beheaded in a Gestapo prison.[6]

The evacuated missionaries were encouraged to write letters of faith and hope to members where they had served, and the mission presidents were given special assignments to keep in touch through correspondence with the local leaders whom they had left in charge. Unfortunately, however, the war disrupted the mail, and even from neutral Switzerland no letters were received for two years. In these circumstances local leaders learned to depend on personal revelation for guidance.

Although there were some isolated exceptions, most European Saints' faithful adherence to Church doctrines and procedures grew during the war. In several areas, tithes, fast offerings, and attendance at Church meetings increased. In Switzerland local member missionaries spent two evenings per week proselyting and baptized more converts than the full-time missionaries had just before the outbreak of the war. During the prewar years mission presidents had actively prepared the Saints for the isolation they were to experience. Time and again during his 1937 visit to Europe, President Heber J. Grant, with prophetic insight, urged members to assume their own responsibilities and not to lean so much on the elders from America. Max Zimmer, who headed the Swiss Mission during the war, is a good example of one of these capable leaders. He conducted effective training programs for local priesthood and auxiliary leaders and distributed Church periodicals to the Saints.

Numerous German male members, both single and married, were drafted into the armed forces of their country. This depleted the priesthood strength of the branches, which in many areas had grown quite strong during the late 1930s. Many of the brethren left wives and children behind. In the early months of the war most of the German Saints felt they were fighting a just war, but as the war lengthened and atrocities heightened, more and more members of the Church began hoping and praying for an Allied victory. On the eastern front, the suffering and killing were especially bad as the Russian army marched ruthlessly into Germany. Several Latter-day Saint soldiers returned to their families only after many years of being in the prison camps, and some never returned to their families at all.

One notable Saint who died in the war was Herbert Klopfer, who had been called as the president of the East German Mission in 1940. That same year Brother Klopfer was also called into military service and stationed in Berlin. He was thus able to conduct mission business from his military office.

Three years later he was ordered to the Western front. He left the mission affairs in the hands of his two counselors, who also took care of his family. He then spent a short time in Denmark, where he visited some Danish Saints. The Danes feared him at first because of his German uniform, but they came to trust him as he bore witness to them of the truthfulness of the gospel. In July 1944, Herbert Klopfer was listed as missing in action on the Eastern front. Following the war, it was learned that he had died in March 1945 in a Russian hospital.

Another young Latter-day Saint soldier, Hermann Moessner from Stuttgart, had experiences of a different sort during the war. While fighting in Western Europe, he was taken captive by the British, transported to England, and placed in a prison camp. With little else to do, Brother Moessner began sharing the gospel with fellow prisoners. Four men accepted his message and requested baptism. Elder Moessner wrote to Church headquarters in London for advice on what to do. Soon Elder Hugh B. Brown visited young Moessner in the camp and authorized him to baptize the converts. Many years later Hermann Moessner was called to serve as the president of the Stuttgart Stake in Germany.

Even German Saints who were not in the military suffered, especially in areas being bombed. Local leaders felt they were often inspired as they carried out their responsibilities amid these trying conditions. For example, Hamburg was bombed 104 times during a ten-day period in 1943. During Church meetings it was necessary to monitor the radio for information about air raids. One Sunday the branch president had not heard anything about a raid, but he felt impressed to close the meeting abruptly and immediately send his congregation to the nearest shelter, a ten-minute walk. Branch members had just reached the shelter when bombs hit the area.[7]

When regular meeting places were destroyed, the Saints held religious services in their homes. In one mission, however, 95 percent of the members lost their homes. Local leaders initiated a variety of self-help programs to meet this emergency. They directed their members to bring food, clothing, and household supplies to branch meeting places to be stockpiled. The Saints willingly responded, agreeing that all people should share alike in whatever was available. Family after family brought their entire stores and shared them with their brothers and sisters who were destitute. Everyone contributed to a fund that the Relief Society used to purchase material to patch or remake old clothing or to sew new.[8] Members in Hamburg also participated "in *Loeffelspende* (spoon contributions), which meant they were each to bring one spoonful of sugar or flour to every meeting they attended. This small amount seemed almost ridiculous to members at first, but soon 'this one spoon multiplied by 200 was sufficient to bake a cake for a young couple for their wedding, or to give a mother who was expecting or nursing a baby.' "[9]

THE CHURCH RESPONDS TO WAR

Japan launched an attack against the United States naval base at Pearl Harbor, Hawaii, on 7 December 1941. When the United States responded the following day by declaring war on Japan and then on Germany, many Latter-day Saints became directly involved in the hostilities. Once again the Saints had to examine their feelings about war. They were guided by the Book of Mormon's teachings which denounced offensive war but condoned fighting "even to the shedding of blood if it were necessary" in defense of home, country, freedom, or religion (Alma 48:14; see also 43:45–47). In their annual Christmas message, issued less than a week after the attack on Pearl Harbor, the First Presidency stated that only through living the gospel of Jesus Christ would enduring peace come to the world. Echoing the counsel given by President Joseph F. Smith at the outbreak of World War I, the Presidency exhorted members in the armed forces to keep "all cruelty, hate, and murder" out of their hearts even during battle.[10]

These same principles were incorporated in the First Presidency's official statement read at the April 1942 general conference. This declaration was a comprehensive and authoritative review of the Church's attitude on war and was widely distributed in pamphlet form. The Saints were told that although "hate can have no place in the souls of the righteous," the Saints "are part of the body politic" and must loyally obey those in authority over them. The Presidency continued, "The members of the Church have always felt under obligation to come to the defense of their country when a call to arms was made." If in the course of combat servicemen "shall take the lives of those who fight against them, that will not make of them murderers, nor subject them to the penalty that God has prescribed for those who kill. . . . For it would be a cruel God that would punish His children as moral sinners for acts done by them as the innocent instrumentalities of a sovereign whom He had told them to obey and whose will they were powerless to resist. . . .

". . . This Church is a worldwide Church. Its devoted members are in both camps," the message affirmed. The Presidency also promised those servicemen who lived clean lives, kept the commandments, and prayed constantly that the Lord would be with them and nothing would happen to them that would not be to the honor and glory of God and to their salvation and exaltation.[11] Heeding the counsel of their Church leaders, Latter-day Saints responded when called into military service.

THE SAINTS IN UNIFORM

Even though LDS servicemen's groups had been organized during the Spanish-American War and Elder B. H. Roberts had served as a chaplain during World War I, the complete development of the Church's programs for LDS servicemen did not come into existence until World War II.

In April 1941, just nine months before the United States officially

During World War II, Hugh B. Brown (1883–1975) served as the servicemen's coordinator for the entire Church. He was an officer in the Canadian armed forces, a lawyer, an educator, an orator, and an ecclesiastical leader.

Elder Brown was called to be a General Authority in 1953. He served as an Assistant to the Quorum of the Twelve, as a member of the Quorum of the Twelve, and as a member of the First Presidency of the Church.

entered World War II, the First Presidency announced the appointment of Hugh B. Brown to serve as servicemen's coordinator. Having attained the rank of major in the Canadian army during World War I, he capitalized on this title in making contact with military authorities. Elder Brown traveled extensively during the war meeting with LDS servicemen and giving them encouragement. His warm personality and deep spirituality made him particularly well-suited for this assignment.

A Church Servicemen's Committee was organized in October 1942, with Elder Harold B. Lee, a new member of the Twelve, as chairman. The committee worked with United States military officials to secure the appointments of Latter-day Saint chaplains. This was a formidable challenge. Army and navy officials were reluctant to appoint chaplains who did not meet the usual requirements of being professional clergymen. Nevertheless, the Army Chief of Chaplains favorably remembered how a local Mormon bishop had cared for the spiritual well-being of the servicemen in his area. As a result, military officials gradually approved the appointment of LDS chaplains, and by the end of World War II forty-six had served or were serving as such.[12]

To supplement the work of these chaplains, the Servicemen's Committee appointed approximately one thousand "group leaders." Once set apart, these men officiated anywhere their services might be needed. Each received a certificate identifying him as "an Elder in the Church of Jesus Christ of Latter-day Saints, and that he is as an authorized Group Leader of the Mutual Improvement Association of said Church to serve among his fellow Latter-day Saint members in the armed services. He is empowered, after first obtaining permission of the proper military officials, to conduct study classes and other worshipping assemblies."[13]

The Church sponsored several other measures to benefit members in the service. Homes were opened in Salt Lake City and California where servicemen could stay in a wholesome environment while traveling to and from assignments. "Budget cards" became passports to wholesome Church-sponsored social and recreational activities for servicemen away from home. Members entering military service were given pocket-sized copies of the Book of Mormon and a Church publication entitled *Principles of the Gospel.* They also received a miniature version of the *Church News,* which carried messages of inspiration, reports of servicemen's activities, and other important announcements.

Many of the Latter-day Saint servicemen set outstanding examples of faith and devotion. Military officials were frequently astonished at the initiative and ability of the Mormon soldiers to conduct their own worship services without the need of a professional clergymen. On the island of Saipan, L. Tom Perry (later a member of the Quorum of the Twelve) and other LDS marines had no place to meet, so they set to work building a chapel. Latter-day Saint German soldiers during the occupation of Norway shared their rations with needy members in that land. Similarly, American soldiers helped their fellow Saints in Germany to rebuild as the war drew to a close. Always eager to share the gospel, Church members took advantage of opportunities even under wartime conditions. Elder Ezra Taft Benson lamented the drop in the number of full-time missionaries, but was convinced that Latter-day Saint servicemen were responsible for "more total missionary work today than we have ever done in the history of the Church. . . .

". . . One of [the servicemen] said, 'Brother Benson, it is just like being on another mission. Conditions are different, but we have opportunities to preach the gospel, and we are taking advantage of it.' "[14]

Numerous servicemen were influenced by the worthy examples of Mormon buddies. Private Paul H. Dunn's adherence to Church standards influenced his hardened U.S. army sergeant to eventually accept baptism. Paul H. Dunn later became a member of the First Quorum of the Seventy. Likewise, another serviceman was deeply impressed by a young Latter-day Saint named Neal A. Maxwell, with whom he shared a foxhole in Okinawa. Nineteen-year-old Neal A. Maxwell, later a member of the Quorum of the Twelve, did not have to preach Mormonism, because he lived his religion as he should. While in a German prison camp, a Dutch member shared the gospel with fellow prisoner of war Jay Paul Jongkees, who later became the first stake president in their native country.

Latter-day Saint servicemen were also responsible for introducing the gospel into new areas of the world. For example, they provided the Church's first contact with the Philippine Islands.[15]

By the war's end, the number of Latter-day Saints in military service approached one hundred thousand. This was about one out of every ten Church members. While some appeared to be miraculously protected, the lives of all were not spared. Elder Harold B. Lee sought to comfort those who lost a loved one in the war. He said, "It is my conviction that the present devastating scourge of war in which hundreds of thousands are being slain, many of whom are no more responsible for the causes of the war than are our own boys, is making necessary an increase of missionary activity in the spirit world and that many of our boys who bear the Holy Priesthood and are worthy to do so will be called to that missionary service after they have departed this life."[16]

IMPACT ON THE CHURCH IN NORTH AMERICA

While the Saints in North America did not suffer as their European counterparts did, the war had a substantial impact on Church members and programs there also. As World War II began, shipyards, aircraft plants, and other defense industries created many new jobs on the U.S. west coast. These economic opportunities drew many families from the intermountain area to the Pacific coast. The establishment of defense industries in Utah and surrounding areas, however, later led many Saints to return.

These war-stimulated population shifts created several challenges for the Church. Single Mormon youth were among those employed in the defense industry. Hence, by the end of the war an increasing number of young people were living away from the stabilizing influence of their home and family.[17] The General Authorities encouraged Church leaders in the areas where these young men and women were going to take a special interest in them. The coming of new industries to predominantly Mormon areas also resulted in a sudden influx of non-LDS residents into certain Utah communities. While some of the longtime residents of these communities were concerned about the introduction of such a large "outside element," Church leaders encouraged the Saints to fellowship the newcomers and to share the gospel with them whenever possible. This created a fertile field for the stake missions that had been established in the 1930s.

Wartime conditions affected programs sponsored by the Church in still other ways. In January 1942, just a month after the United States entered World War II, the First Presidency announced that all stake leadership meetings would be suspended immediately for the duration of the war. This cutback in leadership instruction came at the very time when Church activities had to become more effective than ever before to reach the growing numbers of members cut free from the guiding and sustaining influence of the family. The First Presidency stressed, "This action places increased responsibility upon the ward and branch auxiliary organizations to see that their work not only does not suffer, but is increased in intensity, improved in quality, and in general made more effective." Auxiliary general boards kept in touch with local workers and gave direction by mail, and the home was stressed more as the key to preserving the faith among the youth.[18]

The First Presidency also limited attendance at general conferences to specifically invited priesthood leaders. The Tabernacle was closed to the public since the weekly Tabernacle Choir programs were broadcast without live audiences. Observations of the Relief Society's 1942 centennial had to be postponed, and the annual Hill Cumorah pageant was canceled for the duration of the war.

On 27 April 1942, U.S. President Franklin D. Roosevelt spoke of the need for increased taxes, wage and price controls, gasoline rationing, and rationing of other strategic materials. Latter-day Saint leaders had already taken steps to adapt Church programs.

Elder Harold B. Lee was convinced that the timing of the Church's precautions was the result of revelation. Referring to the Church's January 1942 restrictions on auxiliary meetings and travel, he declared: "When you remember that all this happened from eight months to nearly a year before the tire and gas rationing took place, you may well understand if you will only take thought that here again was the voice of the Lord to this people, trying to prepare them for the conservation program that within a year was forced upon them. No one at that time could surely foresee that the countries that had been producing certain essential commodities were to be overrun and we thereby be forced into a shortage."

Furthermore, Elder Lee was convinced that Church leaders had been inspired when, beginning in 1937, they counseled the Saints to produce and store a year's supply of food. He believed that this helped prepare Church members for rationing and scarcity and anticipated the government's emphasis on victory gardens.[19]

Because of the war effort "Church activities were hampered in yet other ways. As building supplies were diverted to military use, construction of meetinghouses and even of the Idaho Falls Temple came to a halt. Perhaps no Church activity felt the impact of the war more than did the missionary program. In 1942 the Church agreed not to call young men of draft age on missions. Hence the number of missionaries serving plummeted. While 1,257 new full-time missionaries had been called in 1941, only 261 were called two years later. Before the war, five-sixths of all missionaries were young men holding the offices of elder or seventy; by 1945, most new missionaries were women or high priests. Members living in mission fields again assumed more responsibilities, just as they had done when the number of missionaries dropped during the Great Depression a decade earlier. Throughout North America these Saints accepted calls as local part-time missionaries and assumed greater roles in district or branch organizations.

"The Church sponsored special wartime programs and in other ways encouraged its members to patriotically support the war effort. The first Sunday in 1942 was designated as a special day of fasting and prayer. As they had done during World War I, the General Authorities again commended the Saints for their generous contributions to the Red Cross and other charitable funds. Women in the Relief Society put together first aid kits for home use and prepared bandages and other supplies for the Red Cross. During the winter of 1942–43 the Church's twelve- and thirteen-year-old Beehive Girls donated 228,000 hours, collecting scrap metal, fats, and other needed materials, making scrapbooks or baking cookies for soldiers, and tending children for mothers working in defense industries. A special 'Honor Bee' award was offered for such service. Then in 1943, Mutual Improvement Association youth in the United States and Canada raised more than three million dollars to purchase fifty-five badly needed rescue boats to save the lives of downed airmen."[20]

While Latter-day Saints, at home and in military service and on both sides of the conflict, labored patriotically to support the cause of their respective nations, all longed for a return to peace. Even though some activities advanced during the war, the major effort of the conflict hindered the

Church's work. Only with the longed-for cessation of hostilities in 1945 could the Church resume its progress.

ENDNOTES

1. See Gilbert W. Scharffs, *Mormonism in Germany* (Salt Lake City: Deseret Book Co., 1970), pp. 86–88.

2. M. Douglas Wood, in Conference Report, Apr. 1940, pp. 79–80.

3. David F. Boone, "The Worldwide Evacuation of Latter-day Saint Missionaries at the Beginning of World War II," Master's thesis, Brigham Young University, 1981, pp. 39–40; see also pp. 35–43.

4. Martha Toronto Anderson, *A Cherry Tree behind the Iron Curtain: The Autobiography of Martha Toronto Anderson* (Salt Lake City: Martha Toronto Anderson, 1977), pp. 31–32.

5. In Conference Report, Apr. 1940, p. 20.

6. See Scharffs, *Mormonism in Germany*, pp. 102–3.

7. See Scharffs, *Mormonism in Germany*, pp. 104–5.

8. See Frederick W. Babbel, *On Wings of Faith* (Salt Lake City: Bookcraft, 1972), pp. 110–11.

9. In Scharffs, *Mormonism in Germany*, p. 111.

10. In James R. Clark, comp. *Messages of the First Presidency of The Church of Jesus Christ of Latter-day Saints*, 6 vols. (Salt Lake City: Bookcraft, 1965–75), 6:141.

11. In Conference Report, Apr. 1942, pp. 90, 92–95.

12. See Joseph F. Boone, "The Roles of The Church of Jesus Christ of Latter-day Saints in Relation to the United States Military, 1900–1975," Ph.D. diss., Brigham Young University, 1975, pp. 548–52.

13. Boone, "Roles of the Church," pp. 698–99.

14. In Conference Report, Apr. 1945, pp. 108–9.

15. See Lowell E. Call, "Latter-day Saint Servicemen in the Philippine Islands," Master's thesis, Brigham Young University, 1955, pp. 98, 103.

16. In Conference Report, Oct. 1942, p. 73.

17. See report from Lee A. Palmer to the Presiding Bishopric, 21 Sept. 1944, Subject files of LeGrand Richards, 1937–47, LDS Historical Department, Salt Lake City.

18. See First Presidency notice to Church officers, 17 Jan. 1942, Circular letters, 1889–1985, LDS Historical Department, Salt Lake City.

19. In Conference Report, Apr. 1943, p. 128; see also p. 126.

20. Richard O. Cowan, *The Church in the Twentieth Century* (Salt Lake City: Bookcraft, 1985), pp. 186–87.

POSTWAR RECOVERY

George Albert Smith (1870–1951)

T H E H O R R O R S and devastation of World War II finally ended in 1945. President Heber J. Grant died on 14 May of that year, just one week after the fighting in Europe had ended and three months before the surrender of Japan. His successor, George Albert Smith, faced the challenge of leading the Church during an era when the world needed to rebuild and overcome the hate that existed following the war. Church leaders reminded the Saints and the world that the only hope for an enduring peace was adherence to the principles of the gospel of Jesus Christ.

A LOVING LEADER FOR THE POSTWAR YEARS

President George Albert Smith's experience and Christlike love for others suited him well for this task. President Smith affirmed, "I do not have an enemy that I know of. . . . All men and all women are my Father's children, and I have sought during my life to observe the wise direction of the Redeemer of mankind—to love my neighbor as myself."[1]

George Albert Smith was called to the Quorum of the Twelve in 1903. He represented the fourth generation of the Smith family to serve as a General Authority. At the time of his call, his father, John Henry Smith, was serving as an Apostle. This was the first and only time in Church history that a father and son have served simultaneously in the Quorum of the Twelve.

From 1919 to 1921, Elder George Albert Smith had presided over the European Mission. In the aftermath of World War I, several countries refused to readmit the missionaries. As Elder Smith negotiated with these governments to gain permission for missionaries to enter their borders, he gained vital experience that proved valuable when the Church faced similar circumstances following the close of World War II.

Upon his return home from the European Mission, Elder Smith was called to preside over the Young Men's Mutual Improvement Association. He served in this capacity for over a decade. For years he had been vitally interested in the youth. He was a prime booster of the Boy Scout movement from its earliest days. In 1932 he was elected to the national executive committee of the Boy Scouts of America. Two years later Elder Smith received the Silver Buffalo, the highest award presented by this national organization, in recognition of his outstanding service. His concern for young people assisted President Smith as he counseled returning servicemen about meeting their challenges following the end of World War II.

Beginning with the latter months of 1945, thousands of Latter-day Saints were discharged from military service. The return to civilian life was not without problems, and the Church took steps to help its members successfully make this transition. Bishops interviewed servicemen promptly and saw to it that they received Church callings. Priesthood quorums sponsored welcome home parties for the servicemen and assisted them in finding employment. The Mutual Improvement Association played a key role in fellowshipping veterans through athletic and social activities.

HELPING THE SAINTS IN WAR-TORN EUROPE

A high priority for Church leaders following the close of World War II was reestablishing contact with the Saints in war-devastated Europe where communication had been cut off for up to six years. Hundreds of Saints were left homeless when cities were destroyed, especially in Germany and Holland. An acute shortage of food after the war greatly compounded their suffering.

Latter-day Saint servicemen in the Allied armies brought the first help to these suffering members. Hugh B. Brown, president of the British Mission, was the first Church official to visit the European continent following the end of the war. Only two months after the hostilities in Europe had ended, President Brown flew to Paris. There, in the large ballroom of an exclusive hotel, he conducted a meeting attended by 350 servicemen and local Saints. He then continued his journey by train to Switzerland for a hectic series of meetings. Everywhere he went he sought to engender faith and hope among his listeners.

In the fall of 1945 the Church was sending relief supplies to Europe. Since they were sent through the regular mail, only small packages were accepted, and the cost was prohibitive; nevertheless, by January 1946 the Church had shipped thirteen thousand of these packages. Many more were mailed by individual members of the Church. In the meantime the Church sought means of shipping larger quantities. This required the cooperation of government officials. Consequently, President George Albert Smith, together with Elders John A. Widtsoe and David O. McKay, went to Washington, D.C., where they spent a considerable amount of time conferring with ambassadors and other officials of some of the foreign nations. President Smith later described his twenty-minute interview on 3 November with President Harry S. Truman at the White House:

" 'I have just come to ascertain from you, Mr. President, what your attitude will be if the Latter-day Saints are prepared to ship food and clothing and bedding to Europe.'

"He smiled and looked at me, and said: 'Well, what do you want to ship it over there for? Their money isn't any good.'

"I said: 'We don't want their money.' He looked at me and asked: 'You don't mean you are going to give it to them?'

"I said: 'Of course, we would give it to them. They are our brothers and sisters and are in distress. God has blessed us with a surplus, and we will be glad to send it if we can have the co-operation of the government.'

"He said: 'You are on the right track,' and added, 'we will be glad to help you in any way we can.' "[2]

On 14 January 1946 the First Presidency announced that Elder Ezra Taft Benson, a member of the Quorum of the Twelve who had extensive experience in national agricultural organizations, was assigned to reopen the missions in Europe and attend to the spiritual and temporal needs of those Saints. The First Presidency promised, "Your influence [will] be felt for good by all you come in contact with, and . . . you and they [will] be made to feel that there is a power and spirit accompanying you not of man."[3] Events would amply demonstrate the prophetic nature of this promise.

Elder Benson was accompanied by Frederick W. Babbel, who had served in the Swiss-German Mission just before the outbreak of the war. They left Salt Lake City on 29 January 1946 for England. During this great mission they frequently referred to a scriptural promise, which they regarded as being fulfilled in their behalf: "And they shall go forth and none shall stay them, for I the Lord have commanded them" (D&C 1:5). Elder Benson related in general conference, "Barriers have melted away. Problems that seemed impossible to solve have been solved, and the work in large measure has been accomplished through the blessings of the Lord." Two days after arriving in London, they secured ideal facilities for their headquarters, despite a severe housing shortage.[4]

Elder Ezra Taft Benson became the first civilian American authorized to travel throughout all four occupied zones of Germany. His travels were often characterized by an amazing series of events enabling him to meet his demanding schedule. He and his associates accepted these circumstances as manifestations of divine intervention. Typical were these experiences as he traveled with LDS chaplain Howard S. Badger from Paris to the Hague. Railway officials in Paris advised him that there would be a day's delay because Holland could only be entered through the eastern border rather than through a more direct route. Elder Benson noticed a train preparing to leave and asked the stationmaster where it was going. He was told it was going to Antwerp, Belgium.

"I told him we would take that train and he assured me that we would lose an extra day because all connections between Antwerp and Holland had been cut off as a result of the war.

"But I felt impressed to board that train in spite of his protestations. . . .

"When we arrived at Antwerp, . . . the stationmaster was very upset and advised us that we would have to back-track somewhat and lose an extra day. Again I saw another train getting ready to leave and inquired where it was

Frederick W. Babbel and Elder Ezra Taft Benson traveling abroad during a snowstorm.

going. We were advised that this was a local shuttle-service which stopped at the Dutch border where the large bridge across the Maas river still lay in ruins. I felt impressed that we should board that train in spite of the station-master's protests.

"When we reached the Maas river, we all had to pile out. As we stood picking up our luggage, we noticed an American army truck approaching us. Brother Badger flagged it down and, upon learning that there was a pontoon bridge nearby, he persuaded them to take us into Holland. When we arrived at the first little village on the Dutch side, we were pleasantly surprised to find this local shuttle-service waiting to take us into The Hague."[5]

One of Elder Benson's early visits was to Karlsruhe, a key German city on the Rhine River. Upon inquiring where the Latter-day Saints might be meeting, Frederick W. Babbel recounted that the group was directed to an area of nearly demolished buildings.

"Parking our car near massive heaps of twisted steel and concrete, we climbed over several large piles of rubble and threaded our way between the naked blasted walls in the general direction which had been pointed out to us. As we viewed the desolation on all sides of us, our task seemed hopeless. Then we heard the distant strains of 'Come, Come Ye Saints' being sung in German. . . .

Elder Ezra Taft Benson observing the destruction of war–torn Europe

"We hurried in the direction of the sound of the singing and arrived at a badly scarred building which still had several usable rooms. In one of the rooms we found 260 joyous saints still in conference, although it was already long past their dismissal time. . . .

"With tears of gratitude streaming down our cheeks, we went as quickly as possible to the improvised stand. Never have I seen President Benson so deeply and visibly moved as on that occasion."[6]

Elder Benson later described his feelings during the meeting in this way: "The Saints had been in session for some two hours waiting for us, hoping that we would come because the word had reached them that we might be there for the conference. And then for the first time in my life I saw almost an entire audience in tears as we walked up onto the platform, and they realized that at last, after six or seven long years, representatives from Zion, as they put it, had finally come back to them. Then as the meeting closed, prolonged at their request, they insisted we go to the door and shake hands with each one of them as he left the bombed-out building. And we noted that many of them, after they had passed through the line went back and came through the second and third time, so happy were they to grasp our hands. As I looked into their upturned faces, pale, thin, many of these Saints dressed in rags, some of them barefooted, I could see the light of faith in their eyes as they bore testimony to the divinity of this great latter-day work, and expressed their gratitude for the blessings of the Lord."[7]

Elder Benson felt a sense of urgency to visit the scattered Saints in what had been East Prussia (a part of Germany) but now was Polish territory. Repeated visits to the Polish embassy in London, however, failed to secure the needed visas to Warsaw. Brother Babbel reported:

"After a few moments of soul-searching reflection, Elder Benson said quietly but firmly, 'Let me pray about it.'

"Some two or three hours after President Benson had retired to his room to pray, he stood in my doorway and said with a smile on his face, 'Pack your bags. We are leaving for Poland in the morning!'

"At first I could scarcely believe my eyes. He stood there enveloped in a beautiful glow of radiant light. His countenance shone as I imagine the Prophet Joseph's countenance shone when he was filled with the Spirit of the Lord."[8]

After flying to Berlin, Elder Benson obtained the necessary clearances for his party to go to Poland, although they had been definitely told that the Polish Military Mission in Berlin had no authority to issue them visas without first consulting with Warsaw, a fourteen-day process. Upon arriving in Poland, Elder Benson's party drove to the small town of Zelbak where a German branch of the Church had been located. Not a sign of life was visible upon the streets as they entered the village. They asked the only woman in sight where they might find the branch president. Elder Babbel again recalled:

"We had spotted the woman hiding behind a large tree. Her expression was one of fear as we stopped, but upon learning who we were she greeted us with tears of gratitude and joy. . . .

". . . Within minutes the cry went from house to house, 'The brethren are here! The brethren are here!' Soon we found ourselves surrounded by about fifty of the happiest people we had ever seen.

"Having seen our strange jeep approaching with what they feared to be Russian or Polish soldiers, they had abandoned the streets as if by magic. Likewise, when they learned of our true identity and mission, the village became alive with joyous women and children—women and children, because only two of our former twenty-nine priesthood holders remained.

"That morning in fast and testimony meeting over one hundred saints had assembled together to bear their testimonies and to petition Almighty God in song, in fasting and prayer, to be merciful to them and let the elders again come to visit them. Our sudden and unheralded arrival, after almost complete isolation from Church and mission headquarters since early 1943, was the long-awaited answer, so wonderful that they could scarcely believe their good fortune."[9]

Elder Benson found the European Saints eager to move forward again in promoting the Lord's work. Nevertheless, substantial problems had to be overcome before Church programs could be reimplemented. Many branches could not be fully organized because so many of their priesthood leaders were lost during the war. Furthermore, when meetinghouses and homes were destroyed, the Saints lost not only material possessions, but items of spiritual importance as well. In some branches, for example, not even copies of the scriptures remained. Nevertheless, Elder Benson reported, "We found that our members had carried on in a marvelous way. Their faith was strong, their devotion greater, and their loyalty unsurpassed."[10]

One of Elder Benson's most important assignments was to supply desperately needed food and clothing for the Saints in Europe. In Germany, where the needs were particularly serious, members had already exhibited courage, faith, and resourcefulness in meeting the emergency. During the last months of the war, they had gathered clothing, hidden it in safe places, and shared it cooperatively. Richard Ranglack, the mission president in Berlin, compared these German members to the early Latter-day Saints who were driven closer together by the difficulties they suffered.[11]

As the war ended, Dutch Saints planted potatoes wherever they could obtain land. They shared their harvest with their brothers and sisters in Germany even though their nations had recently been enemies. By mid-March, Elder Benson had made the necessary arrangements with government and military authorities in Europe to have additional relief supplies sent from America.

To supplement the supplies already in storage in the United States, the Church had launched drives for used clothing and other goods. President George Albert Smith took the lead in demonstrating his love and concern for the suffering Saints in Europe. He donated at least two suits fresh from the cleaners and several shirts still in their wrappings from the laundry. During a visit to Welfare Square to inspect the results of these clothing drives, he took off his topcoat and laid it on one of the piles of clothing being prepared for shipment to Europe. Despite the protests of his associates he insisted on returning to the office without his coat.[12]

Military and other officials in Europe were amazed at the speed with which the shipments arrived from the Church in America. European Church leaders openly wept for joy and gratitude as they examined clothing and felt the sacks of grain when visiting the storehouses where the welfare goods arrived. In all, some ninety-three railroad carloads of supplies were sent.

Elder Benson was also instrumental in extending missionary work to Finland. On 16 July 1946, atop a beautiful hill near Larsmo, Finland, he dedicated and blessed that land that it might be receptive to the gospel. The following day, a surprising 245 persons attended a public meeting in Helsinki and manifested genuine interest.[13] A separate Finnish mission was organized the following year.

Elder Benson returned home in December 1946 having traveled more than sixty thousand miles during his ten-month assignment in Europe. By this time newly called presidents were once again directing the missions there.

Matthew Cowley (1897–1953) was known as the Apostle of the Polynesians. As a young missionary in New Zealand, he learned the Maori language and translated the Doctrine and Covenants and Pearl of Great Price into that language.

REOPENING THE PACIFIC

Reopening missionary work in the Pacific was not as difficult as it was in Europe. Although missionaries had been withdrawn, except from Hawaii, mission presidents had remained in their assigned countries. Furthermore, most of these areas were never in actual combat zones. Following the end of the hostilities missionaries were again assigned there without difficulty.

The appointment of Elder Matthew Cowley as president of the Pacific Mission was announced by the First Presidency in late 1946. Prior to this Elder Cowley had presided for eight years over the New Zealand Mission, including the war period, and had been called to the Quorum of the Twelve almost immediately following his release from his mission assignment. He fulfilled a function to the missions of the Pacific similar to that of Elder Benson in Europe. During the next three years Elder Cowley traveled widely in the Pacific and had many remarkable experiences. On one occasion, for example, he gave blessings to fifty people. On another day he blessed seventy-six people, many of whom got in line as early as 5 A.M.

Elder Cowley noted in his journal, "This seemed the usual thing. . . .

"And they are made well, such is their faith. . . . I know that when I lay my hands upon their heads that they are made whole. It is not my faith. I just have faith in their faith."[14] Elder Cowley's great love for the peoples of the Pacific, his deep faith in the gospel of Jesus Christ, and his enthusiastic leadership helped provide the impetus for Church growth throughout the area.

The Church faced a particularly great challenge in Japan. The mission there had been closed since 1924. By 1945 only about fifty members remained in the Land of the Rising Sun, but Latter-day Saint servicemen among the American occupation forces made an important contribution to the future of the Church in Japan. Many were anxious to bless the Japanese people with the spirit and message of the gospel. When three Mormon soldiers were offered a cup of tea in a curio shop in the village of Narumi, they declined and took the opportunity to explain the Church's teachings concerning the sanctity of the body. This led to further gospel conversations with one of the people there, and soon Tatsui Sato and his family became the first postwar converts baptized in Japan. Members of this family became stalwarts in the gospel. Brother Sato served as the Church's chief translator in Japan. The young serviceman who baptized Mrs. Sato was Boyd K. Packer, a future member of the Quorum of the Twelve Apostles.[15] Other convert baptisms followed, and thus foundations were laid for the eventual reopening of the Japanese Mission.

In 1947 the First Presidency called Edward L. Clissold, who had served as a military officer in Japan with the Allied occupation forces, to return and open the mission there. Upon his arrival, he found the climate far more conducive to successful missionary work than in former decades. There was a spiritual void that needed to be filled, and many people actively sought for meaning in life. The first five missionaries assigned to Japan were former servicemen who returned to share the gospel with the nation which had so recently been their enemy. By 1949 there were 135 Church members in Japan.

The years following the close of World War II were years of continued growth in various areas of North America where Latter-day Saints sought employment during the war. Furthermore, the Church reached a significant milestone in 1947 when membership passed the one million mark. The postwar years were also a period of revitalization for the Church's varied programs and activities.

POSTWAR REVIVAL IN CHURCH ACTIVITIES

Missionary work and the construction of Church buildings were undoubtedly the activities most hampered by wartime restrictions. With the ending of hostilities, however, these and other programs were not only revived, they were expanded in order to better meet the needs of the Saints. As wartime restrictions on calling missionaries were lifted, many young men who had been forced to postpone their missions accepted the opportunity to serve. The rapid influx of missionaries pushed their numbers to new highs. From an average of only 477 missionaries serving in 1945, the number soared to 2,244 a year later. As before the war, most of the missionaries were young elders. This meant that there were many new missionaries serving in the field who lacked experience in teaching the gospel and could profit from some help and direction.

The most widely circulated postwar proselyting outline was prepared by Richard L. Anderson in the Northwestern States Mission. He built on methods he had worked out while serving as a stake missionary when he was in the military. According to his plan, the missionary's goal was not merely to hand out tracts, but to be invited into homes where the gospel message could be presented. Doctrinal discussions stressed a careful study of the scriptures and were arranged in a logical sequence leading to conversion. As these improved methods were adopted throughout the mission, the results were apparent. In 1949 the Northwestern States Mission had more than one thousand convert baptisms in a single year.

As the pace of missionary work picked up, the administrative load of mission presidents increased. Therefore, in 1947 the General Authorities directed mission presidents around the world to call counselors from among the missionaries and local Melchizedek Priesthood bearers. Elder Spencer W. Kimball later declared that this decision to appoint counselors had been a revelation to the Presidency of the Church.[16]

While mission organization was being strengthened and proselyting missionaries were refining their methods of teaching the gospel, the Church also took advantage of other means to share its message with the world. With the end of wartime gasoline rationing and the resulting upsurge in travel, Temple Square became a tremendous missionary tool. In 1948 the number of visitors to Temple Square topped the one million mark for the first time.[17] That same year the annual Hill Cumorah pageant, "America's Witness for Christ," was resumed as a missionary tool that presented the story of the Book of Mormon and the restoration of the gospel.

Also during these postwar years the Church became increasingly involved in motion picture production. New Latter-day Saint films were produced during the late 1940s about Church historic sites, Temple Square, and the welfare program. Likewise, as television developed during the postwar years, the Church was quick to make use of it.[18] The October 1949 general conference was the first to be telecast.[19]

The shortage of critical materials had almost halted the Church building program during the war. As supplies once again became available, the Church embarked on an ambitious chapel-building program. By 1949, two hundred local meetinghouses were completed, and the total reached nine hundred only three years later. In the mid-1950s, more than half of all Latter-day Saint buildings in use had been constructed since the end of World War II. Expenditures for these building projects accounted for more than half of the appropriations from general Church funds during these years.

In 1937, President Heber J. Grant announced plans to build a temple in Idaho Falls, Idaho, and construction began two years later. On 19 October 1941 the capstone was laid, and from the outside the structure appeared to be completed. Less than two months later, however, the attack on Pearl Harbor propelled the United States into war, and the temple's completion was delayed as building materials suddenly became scarce. By mid-1945 the Idaho Falls Temple was finally ready for dedication. In his dedicatory prayer, President George Albert Smith expressed gratitude for the cessation of war and prayed that the peoples of the world might be inclined to live the gospel of Jesus Christ, thereby making peace permanent.

The microfilming of vital records for genealogical purposes, interrupted by the war, resumed even before the conflict ended. In March 1945 the Church began microfilming 365 English parish registers. During 1947, Archibald F. Bennett, secretary of the Genealogical Society, spent four months in Europe conferring with government and religious officials, where he obtained permission for the society to microfilm in England, Scotland, Wales, Denmark, Norway, Sweden, Holland, Germany, Finland, Switzerland, northern Italy, and France. In the wake of war most archivists eagerly cooperated with the microfilmers to ensure that a copy of their records would be preserved in case the originals were destroyed. The society also presented each library or church with a copy of the material microfilmed, allowing the public to have access to the information without handling fragile originals.

By early 1950 twenty-two full-time microfilmers were at work in the United States and several European countries. As copies of these vital records became available through the Church's genealogical library, the Saints were better able to conduct the research necessary to identify those people whom temple ordinances could be performed for.

Postwar social trends placed stress on the family and caused Church leaders to give added attention to the home. The end of the war witnessed a sharp increase in the number of marriages, followed by a postwar baby boom. There were more new families and new parents than at any previous time in the Church's history. Unfortunately, however, the rate of divorces in the United States almost doubled between 1940 and 1950. Therefore the Church gave considerable attention to the home and family during the postwar years. In 1946 several Church organizations inaugurated programs to strengthen families and promote a regular "family hour."

The uprooting of families and other wartime pressures posed significant challenges for the youth of the Church, causing General Authorities to instruct local leaders to look out for their welfare. To provide wholesome recreational activities for the youth, the Young Men's and Young Women's Mutual Improvement Associations sponsored road shows and other dramatic presentations, speech contests, and music festivals. Hundreds of colorfully costumed dancers filled football fields in regional dance festivals. Ward softball and basketball teams played for stake, region, and finally Churchwide championships; these Church-sponsored activities were thought to be the largest athletic leagues in the world. The varied programs blessed the Church's youth and attracted widespread attention and praise.

Church leaders encouraged the Saints to make spiritual growth a priority in their homes. They emphasized honoring Sunday as a holy day of worship. On Sunday morning men and boys attended an hour-long priesthood meeting. Afterward the entire family went to Sunday School; the half-hour "opening exercises" included two-and-a-half–minute talks given by two young people of the ward. The congregation would then have a ten-minute hymn practice followed by nearly an hour of class instruction from the scriptures and other related gospel topics. Families again returned later in the afternoon or evening for sacrament meeting. This meeting also lasted an hour and a half and featured inspirational music, often by the ward choir, and talks on religious subjects given by both the youth and adult members of the Church. On one or more Sunday evenings during the month, youth and adult groups conducted "firesides," informal discussions followed by refreshments. The Saints' Church activity increased rapidly during the postwar years.

During the postwar years the Church also continued efforts to enhance the health care of its members. Hospitals in Salt Lake City and Ogden were renovated and enlarged, and the Church cooperated with rural communities in Utah, Idaho, and Wyoming to open and operate small hospitals. Construction began in 1949 for the 1.25-million-dollar Primary Children's Hospital in Salt Lake City, which was to replace the small facility being used

On President Heber J. Grant's eighty-second birthday, 22 November 1938, he received a copper box filled with one thousand silver dollars to give to his favorite charity. President Grant had the silver dollars placed in paperweights and sold to raise money for the construction of the new Primary Children's Hospital.

The Primary Children's Hospital was completed in 1952 and was dedicated by President David O. McKay.

on North Temple. This modern facility would provide care to children of all religions and races. Care was given free to families unable to pay.

CONCERN FOR THE LAMANITES

The 1940s brought a significant expansion of Church programs for the American Indians and related groups identified as descendants of the Book of Mormon peoples. Twentieth century missionary work among the native Americans began in 1936, when the First Presidency directed the Snowflake Stake in northeastern Arizona to open formal missionary work among the Navajos, Hopis, and Zunis. Soon other stakes became similarly involved.

These efforts received a significant boost in November 1942 when George Jumbo, a Navajo Latter-day Saint, went to Salt Lake City for back surgery. Before returning home, his wife Mary expressed the desire to meet President Heber J. Grant. Arrangements were made, and Mary stood before him and "pled with the President for missionaries to be sent amongst her people." President Grant, with tears running down his cheeks, turned to Elder George Albert Smith of the Quorum of the Twelve and said, " 'With all of your great responsibilities as the President of the Council of the Twelve would you please accept one more assignment and get this missionary work started amongst those people . . . and will you please see to it that it gets started on a permanent basis and that it will grow and increase instead of diminishing and fading away.' "[20] Early the following year the Navajo-Zuni Mission was organized. Missionaries were soon sent to other tribes, reaching Indians throughout the United States and Canada.

Beginning in 1945 another group of Lamanites was blessed in quite a different way. Many Spanish-speaking members did not understand the full meaning of the temple ceremonies as presented in English. To assist these members, the Arizona Temple presented the ordinances in Spanish for the first time. At a special Lamanite conference in Mesa early in November 1945, about two hundred people gathered, some coming from as far as Mexico City. Most of these Saints made a substantial economic sacrifice to travel the long distances to Mesa; some even gave up jobs. President David O. McKay,

Second Counselor in the First Presidency, congratulated those who had come. The history-making Spanish-speaking endowment sessions commenced two days later.[21] Those who attended the Lamanite conference discovered that the Church included more than just the small branch where they worshiped each week. During succeeding years the Lamanite conference and Spanish-speaking temple sessions at the Arizona Temple became eagerly anticipated annual events.

In 1946, President George Albert Smith called Elder Spencer W. Kimball to give special attention and leadership to the Lamanite people. Elder Kimball reflected:

"I do not know when I began to love the children of Lehi. . . . It may have come from my patriarchal blessing which was given to me by Patriarch Samuel Claridge, when I was nine years of age. One line of the blessing reads:

" 'You will preach the gospel to many people, but more especially to the Lamanites. . . .'

". . . and now, forty-two years after the promise, President George Albert Smith called me to this mission, and my blessing was fulfilled."[22]

While touring the Mexican Mission in 1947, Elder Kimball envisioned a glorious future for the Lamanite people, which he spoke of at the Lamanite conference in Mesa during November of that year. He saw them not as the servants of others, but as the owners of banks and businesses. He envisioned them as construction engineers, political leaders, lawyers, and doctors. As newspaper publishers and as authors of books or articles, he anticipated that they would have great influence. Elder Kimball stated, "I saw the Church growing in rapid strides and I saw wards and stakes organized. I saw stakes by the hundreds.

"I saw a temple and expect to see it filled with men and women."[23]

Thirty years later President Kimball presided over the area conference in Mexico City, where he again told the people of his 1947 vision and remarked that he could see it was well on its way to fulfillment.[24]

One of the Indians' most critical needs was for education. A unique program to help meet this need had its beginning in central Utah during the late 1940s. Golden R. Buchanan was a member of the Sevier Stake presidency in Richfield, Utah. During the autumn of 1947 he observed the deplorable condition of some migrant Indian agricultural workers in the area. Speaking at a stake conference he admonished the Saints to take better care of their Lamanite brethren.

Shortly afterward a member from a neighboring town came to President Buchanan and told him of a teenage Indian girl named Helen John who did not want to return to the reservation with her family but was determined to remain and go to school. She pleaded with her Latter-day Saint employers, " 'If you'll let me pitch my tent out back of your house, I promise I won't be any bother to you. I'll take care of myself, but I would like to live where I can go to school with your girls.' " President Buchanan was impressed with the idea. He envisioned that "if a program of this sort were undertaken by the Church that literally hundreds of Indian children would have the privilege of living in LDS homes where they not only could be taught in school but they could be taught the principles of the gospel." He outlined his ideas in a letter to Elder Spencer W. Kimball. Elder Kimball personally invited the Buchanans to take Helen into their home. Several other Indian youth were also placed in other homes in the area.

From these beginnings the program grew. It became an official Church-sponsored activity in the 1950s. Eventually, as many as five thousand students a year were placed in Latter-day Saint homes, especially throughout the western United States and Canada.

THE PIONEER CENTENNIAL

In the midst of the postwar revival of Church activity, the celebration of the pioneer centennial in 1947 focused the Saints' attention on their heritage. President George Albert Smith headed the civic committee planning appropriate observances. Few Church leaders, if any, excelled President Smith's zeal in commemorating the achievements of the past. During the spring and summer, dozens of musical performances, art exhibits, sporting events, and dramatic productions marked the occasion. The pageant, "Message of the Ages," which had been so popular during the 1930 centennial, was again staged in the Salt Lake Tabernacle. Fourteen hundred people were involved in the production, and a total of 135,000 people witnessed the twenty-five performances.

A new musical production, "Promised Valley," was presented in the University of Utah stadium for two weeks with more than 85,000 people attending. Featuring original music by Crawford Gates, a noted Latter-day Saint composer, this production depicted the frustrations and dedication of the early pioneers. It was presented throughout the Church by local MIA groups and later became a popular summer attraction in Salt Lake City. A group driving seventy-two automobiles outfitted with canvas covers and plywood oxen to look like covered wagons reenacted the original pioneer trek from Nauvoo to the Salt Lake Valley.

The centennial celebration climaxed on 24 July, exactly one hundred years from the day the first pioneer company entered the Salt Lake Valley. A gigantic "Days of 47" parade included numerous floats honoring these early founders, and the United States post office issued a commemorative stamp in memory of the pioneers. The highlight of the celebration was President George Albert Smith's dedication of the sixty–foot–high "This Is the Place" monument near the mouth of Emigration Canyon east of Salt Lake City. The goodwill developing between the Saints and other people on this occasion was symbolized by President Smith's picture on the cover of *Time* magazine.

"This Is the Place" monument

Reflecting on the significance of the pioneer centennial, the First Presidency declared: "As that small group of Pioneers looked upon what appeared to be a sterile desert, so today the Church faces a world lying in moral lethargy and spiritual decline. A sense of responsibility to build up the Kingdom of God . . . should be and is in the Church today." The Presidency compared the physical dangers faced by the pioneers with the temptations confronting the Church, particularly the youth, in the twentieth century and charged the Saints to be as prepared to meet these challenges as their forebears were.[25]

The midpoint of the twentieth century was reached with the end of 1950. Just over three months later, President George Albert Smith died and a new leader was sustained. Both of these milestones provided occasion for the Latter-day Saints to reflect on the Church's status—what had been

The first half of the twentieth century was a period of substantial growth for the Church. Membership passed the one million mark only three years before mid-century. At the general conference held in April 1950, President George Albert Smith shared his feelings about this growth: "The Church has increased during the past year more than any other year since it was organized. . . . How happy we should be, not that we have increased in numbers in the organization that we belong to, but that more of our Father's children, more of his sons and daughters, have been brought to an understanding of the truth."[26]

ENDNOTES

1. George Albert Smith, "After Eighty Years," *Improvement Era*, Apr. 1950, p. 263.

2. In Conference Report, Oct. 1947, pp. 5–6; see also "President Smith in East on Mission of Mercy," *Church News*, 10 Nov. 1945, p. 1; "President Smith Returns from Successful Trip to Capital," *Church News*, 17 Nov. 1945, p. 1.

3. In Frederick W. Babbel, *On Wings of Faith* (Salt Lake City: Bookcraft, 1972), p. 46.

4. In Conference Report, Apr. 1947, p. 153.

5. In Babbel, *On Wings of Faith*, pp. 7–8.

6. Babbel, *On Wings of Faith*, p. 36.

7. In Conference Report, Apr. 1947, p. 154.

8. Babbel, *On Wings of Faith*, p. 132.

9. Babbel, *On Wings of Faith*, pp. 148–49.

10. In Conference Report, Apr. 1947, p. 154; see also Babbel, *On Wings of Faith*, pp. 25–26.

11. See "Reports Tell of Saints in Europe," *Church News*, 24 Nov. 1945, pp. 5, 9.

12. See Joseph Anderson, *Prophets I Have Known* (Salt Lake City: Deseret Book Co., 1973), p. 103.

13. See Babbel, *On Wings of Faith*, pp. 126–28.

14. In Henry A. Smith, *Matthew Cowley: Man of Faith* (Salt Lake City: Bookcraft, 1954), p. 160.

15. See Harrison T. Price, " 'A Cup of Tea,'" *Improvement Era*, Mar. 1962, pp. 161, 184, 186; Spencer J. Palmer, *The Church Encounters Asia* (Salt Lake City: Deseret Book Co., 1970), pp. 65–69; Boyd K. Packer, in Conference Report, Apr. 1975, p. 155; or *Ensign*, May 1975, p. 104.

16. See "Mission Heads Will Select Two Counselors to Form Presidency," *Church News*, 12 Apr. 1947, p. 1; Spencer W. Kimball, in James R. Clark, comp., *Messages of the First Presidency of The Church of Jesus Christ of Latter-day Saints*, 6 vols. (Salt Lake City: Bookcraft, 1965–75), 6:256–58.

17. See Melvin Kay Johnson, "A History of the Temple Square Mission of The Church of Jesus Christ of Latter-day Saints to 1970," Master's thesis, Brigham Young University, 1971, pp. 50–51.

18. See David Kent Jacobs, "The History of Motion Pictures Produced by The Church of Jesus Christ of Latter-day Saints," Master's thesis, Brigham Young University, 1967, pp. 69–99.

19. See "Telecast Sessions Make New History," *Church News*, 9 Oct. 1949, pp. 12–13.

20. Ralph William Evans Oral Dictation, LDS Historical Department, Salt Lake City, p. 5.

21. See "200 Lamanites Gather in History-Making Conference, Temple Sessions," *Church News*, 10 Nov. 1945, p. 1.

22. In Conference Report, Apr. 1947, pp. 144–45.

23. "Emotional Farewell in Mexico," *Church News*, 19 Feb. 1977, p. 3; see also Spencer W. Kimball, "Hope Sees a Star for the Sons of Lehi," *Church News*, 20 Dec. 1947, p. 9.

24. See Richard O. Cowan, *The Church in the Twentieth Century* (Salt Lake City: Bookcraft, 1985), p. 224.

25. "A Centennial Message from the First Presidency," *Improvement Era*, July 1947, p. 422.

26. In Conference Report, Apr. 1950, p. 6.

GROWTH INTO A WORLDWIDE CHURCH

PRESIDENT GEORGE ALBERT SMITH died on his eighty-first birthday, Wednesday, 4 April 1951, just two days before the scheduled opening of general conference. The Saturday sessions of conference were canceled for President Smith's funeral. The conference had been scheduled to conclude on Sunday, but a special solemn assembly session was convened on Monday, 9 April, at which David O. McKay was sustained as the ninth President of the Church.

As he accepted this high and holy office, President McKay acknowledged, "No one can preside over this Church without first being in tune with the head of the Church, our Lord and Savior, Jesus Christ. He is our head. This is his Church. Without his divine guidance and constant inspiration, we cannot succeed. With his guidance, with his inspiration, we cannot fail."[1]

President McKay's seventy-eight years of unusually rich experiences prepared him well for his calling as President of the Church. He was born in September 1873, when Brigham Young still served as President of the Church. The gold spike completing the first American transcontinental railroad had been driven only four years before his birth, and yet he lived to watch the first man land on the moon. In 1897 he was called as a missionary to the British Isles. At an unusually spiritual missionary conference two years later in Glasgow, Scotland, James L. McMurrin, counselor in the mission presidency, turned to Elder McKay and said, "If you will keep the faith you will yet sit in the leading councils of the church."[2]

In April 1906, at the age of thirty-two, David O. McKay was called to the Council of the Twelve, and in October of the same year he became a member of the general Sunday School presidency. During the next three decades he also served as commissioner of Church education and as chairman of the General Priesthood Committee and other committees assigned to correlate various Church programs. His 1920–21 world tour to assess conditions in the Church's missions and his two years of presidency over the European Mission substantially broadened his horizons. In 1934 he became a member of the First Presidency, serving as a counselor to both Heber J. Grant and George Albert Smith. Thus, President David O. McKay was well prepared to lead the Church during an era of rapid expansion.

President David O. McKay (1873–
1970) served in the Quorum of the
Twelve or the First Presidency for a
combined total of sixty-three years and
nine months. His service as an Apostle in
this dispensation was longer than that of
any other man who has held this office.

What E'er Thou Art Act Well Thy Part.
This stone was part of a building in
Stirling, Scotland. Its message inspired
President McKay when he first saw it as
a missionary in 1898:
   "That was a message to me that
morning to act my part well as a
missionary of The Church of Jesus
Christ of Latter-day Saints. It is merely
another way of saying . . . 'Not every
one that saith unto me, Lord, Lord, shall
enter into the kingdom of Heaven, but
he that doeth the will of my Father which
is in heaven.' (Matthew 7:21.)"[3]
   The stone was acquired by the
Church in 1965 and kept at the mission
home in Scotland until 1970, when it
was taken to Salt Lake City. It is now on
display at the Museum of Church
History and Art located next to Temple
Square.

AN ERA OF UNPRECEDENTED GROWTH AND CHALLENGES

By 1950 the Church was 120 years old, and membership had reached approximately 1.1 million. During the next twenty years the number of Latter-day Saints almost tripled, reaching more than 2.9 million. Taking into account those who had died during this period, nearly three-fourths of all Church members living at the beginning of 1970 had probably known no other president than David O. McKay. During the 1950–60s Church membership increased about twice as fast as it had in earlier decades. The Church was not only becoming strong numerically, its members were more widely distributed throughout the world. This came about through increased missionary success worldwide and through Church leaders' urging the Saints to remain in their own lands and build up the kingdom.

As the Church expanded into more areas of the world, its members increasingly faced a diversity of challenges and opportunities. Gospel principles had to be understood and applied by Saints who lived in many different environments and cultures. In some parts of Europe, the aftermath of war and slowly increasing prosperity brought religious apathy. Some countries, which required their citizens to pay taxes to support established state churches, reported attendance of less than 5 percent at their Sunday services. High taxes and other economic pressures made having more than one or two children a real sacrifice and required many mothers to work outside of the home. Lax moral standards and liberal laws on pornography also threatened to undermine strong families. Among some Europeans, drinking of alcoholic beverages was an accepted part of life. Finally, because so many diverse languages are spoken by peoples of the world, Church conferences, temple sessions, and other activities generally needed to be multilingual.

The Polynesians of the South Pacific have been characterized as some of the most lovable people on earth. Their spirituality was evidenced by remarkable healings and inspiring manifestations of the gift of tongues. Traditions describe how their forebears sailed thousands of miles in primitive craft from the Americas to the South Pacific. Speaking at an area conference in New Zealand, President Spencer W. Kimball affirmed that the Maori's origin is recorded in the Book of Mormon.[4] Hence, Latter-day Saints in Polynesia came to identify themselves with the Book of Mormon people. The importance of families to the Polynesians is evidenced by elaborate genealogies memorized and recited or intricately carved in wood. The Church flourished among these people.

Nowhere outside of Utah was there a higher ratio of Church members among the total population. In 1970 the ratio was 13 percent in Samoa and approximately 20 percent in Tonga, as compared to only 1 percent in the United States as a whole. Nevertheless, life in this tropical paradise was not always easy. In some areas dependence on a single crop provided only a meager living. Latter-day Saint missionaries sometimes had to overcome opposition from governments strongly influenced by European missionary societies. Transportation was a practical challenge Church leaders faced as they visited local units on separate islands.

The Saints in Latin America faced a different set of challenges. Perhaps nowhere else is a single religion so pervasive throughout the culture, as evidenced in place names and holidays and other aspects of everyday life. Conversion to the restored gospel represented more of a change for people here than in other areas. Church members in Latin America, especially in Mexico, Central America, and Western South America, regarded themselves as being among the descendants of the Nephites and Lamanites described in the Book of Mormon and hence as heirs to the great promises contained there (see 2 Nephi 30:6). In no other area was there greater Church growth during the third quarter of the twentieth century. Church membership in Latin America skyrocketed from less than nine thousand members in 1950 to over two hundred thousand by 1970.

North American missionaries carrying the gospel to Asia felt they were entering a different world. Christians represented only a very small minority, and not even the familiar western alphabet was used. Despite the cultural differences, the gospel took root in several of the nations of Asia, and the Church began to experience rapid growth there. The Latter-day Saint emphasis on the importance of families struck a responsive chord in the hearts of many whose families had for generations revered their ancestors.

Even though the Church was growing rapidly in many parts of the world, some forces threatened to block this progress. In 1950 international tensions led to the closing of missions in the Near East and in Czechoslovakia. The 1949 Communist takeover in China and the 1950 outbreak of the Korean War also led to the temporary closing of the Chinese Mission in Hong Kong.

The impact of the Korean War was not limited to the Far East, however. As the United States assumed a major role in the United Nations peace-keeping force, young men were again being drafted. This meant that fewer elders were available for missionary service. In contrast to the 3,015 missionaries called by the First Presidency in 1950, only 872 received mission calls two years later.

In the midst of the Church's rapid growth, President McKay felt the need to stress the vital importance of spiritual as well as numerical growth. He was convinced that "man's chief concern in life should not be the acquiring of gold, or of fame, or of material possessions. It should not be development of physical powers, nor of intellectual strength, but his aim, the highest in life, should be the development of a Christ-like character."[5]

He believed that in order to live on this loftier plane, man must overcome the worldly or carnal aspects of his character. "The world needs to be saved, first, from the dominating influence of animal instincts, of passions, of appetites." Selfishness, he believed, was a major cause of man's ills.[6]

President McKay insisted, "The development of our spiritual nature should concern us most. Spirituality is the highest acquisition of the soul, the divine in man; 'the supreme, crowning gift that makes him king of all created things.' It is the consciousness of victory over self and of communion with the infinite. It is spirituality alone which really gives one the best in life."[7]

PRESIDENT OF A WORLDWIDE CHURCH

David O. McKay became the most widely traveled President in the history of the Church. In 1952 he visited the missions in Britain and on the European continent. The following year he returned to Europe to dedicate sites for the first temples outside of North America or Hawaii. In 1954 he stopped briefly in London on the first leg of a thirty-seven-thousand-mile tour that took him to South Africa and Latin America. On this trip he became the first General Authority ever to visit South Africa (the one area he had not visited during his 1921 tour) and the first President of the Church ever to be in South America.

In 1955 he traveled throughout the South Pacific, returning to places where he had enjoyed sacred experiences some thirty-four years earlier. While on this trip he announced plans to construct a temple in New Zealand—a further step in making the blessings of the house of the Lord available to the Saints in various parts of the world. A few months later he was in Europe for the fourth time in four years, this time to dedicate the

By 1960 there were 319 stakes in the Church. Seven of these stakes had been organized outside of North America and Hawaii.

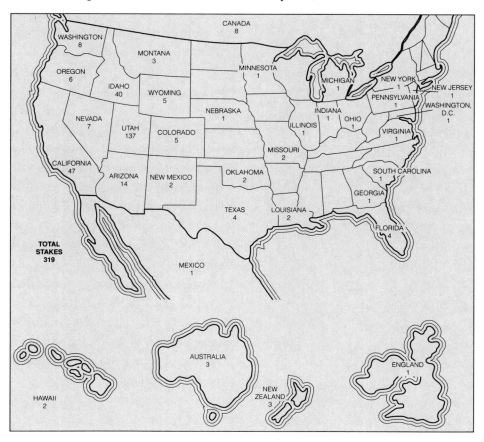

Swiss Temple. In 1958 he returned to the Pacific to dedicate the New Zealand Temple. While in that country, he also organized the Auckland Stake, the first outside of North America or Hawaii, and a further evidence of the Church's international growth. Later that same year he returned to England to dedicate the London Temple.

Everywhere President McKay went he was greeted with love and respect. He was the first living prophet most of the Saints had ever seen in person. At airport after airport they welcomed him with tear-filled eyes and choked voices as they sang the familiar strains of "We Thank Thee, O God, for a Prophet."

President McKay often felt the reality of divine blessings and guidance as he traveled. In 1955, for example, his flight was delayed because of warnings that a hurricane was headed toward Fiji, his next stop. By the time the plane reached the area, however, it was able to land safely. Officials in Fiji were puzzled as to why the hurricane "had suddenly reversed its course at the same time of his arrival at Suva and President McKay remarked that something very unusual had happened."[8] Heavy tropical rains delayed the Prophet's departure from Fiji.

Until he unexpectedly met two elders, President McKay was not aware that only three months earlier Latter-day Saint missionaries had been assigned in the area. He arranged to meet the following day, which was Sunday, with the small group of Saints living in Suva. They met at the home of Cecil B. Smith, who, all alone, had kept this little flock of Saints together for many years. As Brother Smith welcomed God's prophet to his home and to their meeting "he broke down and wept tears of joy and thanksgiving. . . .

"The congregation sung so sweetly, 'We Thank Thee O God for a Prophet.' . . . With tears of joy in their eyes they said every word as if it were a prayer. . . .

"In his remarks President McKay declared this was a significant meeting. He explained we had not intended to remain in Suva over Sunday because our schedule called for us to be somewhere between Suva and Tonga but we were delayed a day because of the hurricane warnings. He explained we were not aware there were Church members in Suva.

". . . He explained that circumstances have provided that they were here today to preach the Gospel in Suva and commence the building up of the Kingdom of God. 'Surely,' he said, 'God has had a hand in changing our schedule so that we can be with you members of the Church.' "[9]

President McKay's travels were a source of inspiration to more than just those scattered Saints he visited. The *Church News* carried day-by-day accounts of his experiences, and they were followed with great interest. Even those in the strong central areas of the Church found their faith strengthened as they read about the faith and gratitude manifested by their fellow Saints in far-flung countries.

The first worldwide seminar for all mission presidents convened in Salt Lake City on 25 June 1961 and lasted ten days. Fifty-one out of sixty-two mission presidents attended. The eleven not attending had been released but not replaced.

"EVERY MEMBER A MISSIONARY"

President David O. McKay recognized that effective missionary work was the key to the Church's continued growth. The first proselyting plan officially published by the Church appeared in 1952. Missionary presentations were condensed into six discussions featuring a logical presentation of gospel principles bolstered by scripture reading, testimony bearing, and sincere prayer. In 1961 Church leaders convened the first worldwide seminar for mission presidents. Under the leadership of the General Authorities the mission presidents pooled their experience to further refine proselyting methods.

Using the slogan "Every Member a Missionary," President McKay stressed the Saints' role in finding and fellowshipping potential converts.[10] He admonished Church members to lead exemplary lives that would win the respect of others and open the way for gospel discussions. The Saints were encouraged to invite nonmember friends into their homes to hear the missionaries' message. This enabled missionaries to use their time more effectively in teaching rather than in looking for people to teach. Furthermore the families who introduced their friends to the missionaries could also fellowship them as they became converted to the gospel, helping them make the transition from one way of life and circle of friends to another.

During these years the Church continued to refine its orientation for outgoing missionaries. A significant step came in 1961. Elders were experiencing lengthy delays in obtaining visas to enter Argentina and Mexico, so a special language training program was set up for them at Brigham Young University. Instruction focused on conversation; the "live your language" program encouraged missionaries to speak only in the tongue they were learning. There was also opportunity to practice the proselyting discussions with native speakers posing as contacts. Furthermore, the elders and sisters adhered to standards of missionary life and conduct and developed proper habits and attitudes even before reaching the mission field. Because of the program's success, it was officially organized in 1963 as the Language Training Mission. Instruction in numerous other languages was added during subsequent years.

To supplement the personal contacts of proselyting missionaries, the Church employed a variety of other methods, including the mass media, to present its message to the world. Visitors' centers and broadcasting media played an increasingly important part in improving public understanding of the Church and its members.

As the volume of travel increased following World War II, the annual number of visitors to Temple Square soared past the million mark. In 1966 the Church built a more spacious visitors' center on Temple Square, equipped with dioramas and other displays designed to explain various facets of the gospel.

In light of the success on Temple Square, the Church continued its program of opening visitors' centers at other historic sites, such as Joseph Smith's birthplace in Vermont; the Sacred Grove and Hill Cumorah in New York state; Independence, Missouri; and Nauvoo, Illinois. Because of the continuing positive response to the Hill Cumorah pageant, additional pageants at Independence, Nauvoo, the Manti Temple, and other locations became another important means of sharing the gospel message with the public.

The restoration of the old Mormon city of Nauvoo began during the 1960s. This ambitious project was patterned after the very successful restoration of the American colonial city of Williamsburg, Virginia. The Nauvoo Temple site was landscaped with a row of stones in the lawn indicating where the original structure had stood. Missionary guides escorted visitors through homes and shops restored to their 1840s appearance and functions. The objective was to depict interesting facets of Nauvoo life in the 1840s when Nauvoo was one of the largest cities in the state of Illinois. Also, more importantly, its purpose was to communicate the faith of the Saints who sacrificed to build the city and then were forced to leave it in the face of religious persecution.

The Church also took advantage of opportunities to share the gospel with the public at fairs and expositions. More than three million people visited the Mormon pavilion at the New York World's Fair during 1964–65. For this exhibit the BYU Motion Picture Studio produced a new film entitled "Man's Search for Happiness" depicting the Latter-day Saint concept of life before and after mortality. Experience with displays and methods of presentation at the fair enabled the Church to transform its visitors' centers into more effective tools for teaching the gospel.

As television was perfected during the years immediately following World War II, the Church quickly made use of it. As early as April 1948, sessions of general conference were being carried from the Tabernacle by closed circuit television to other buildings on Temple Square. In October 1949 the conference was broadcast for the first time beyond Temple Square. Television coverage of conference was extended to California by the late 1950s, and in 1962 sessions were carried from coast to coast for the first time. The Church paid to get the conference broadcast to the local stations, many of which in turn donated air time as part of their public service commitment.

Beginning in 1952 the priesthood session of general conference was transmitted by closed circuit direct wire to selected stake centers and other Church buildings. In time, well over a thousand groups of priesthood bearers throughout the United States and Canada as well as in Australia, New Zealand, and several other countries had the privilege of simultaneously hearing these conference sessions. Still another broadcast medium was employed in 1962 when shortwave radio carried general conference sessions in English to Europe and Africa and in Spanish to Latin America.

Over the years the Church developed materials to be used by the media. For example, the Radio, Publicity, and Mission Literature Committee distributed radio programs, filmstrips, and literature. As demands increased, a division of responsibility was effected in 1957 when the Church Information Service came into being to handle nonmember contacts. The primary objective was to promote missionary work by projecting a positive image of the principles and activities of the Church. It maintained a photo library; coordinated publicity for such special events as conferences and temple dedications; and prepared feature articles on such phases of Church activity as the welfare plan, family home evening, or youth activities. It also provided posters, displays, and support for open houses conducted in local chapels.

A hosting service introduced important visitors to Church headquarters, including government and business officials, heads of other churches, artists, and entertainers. The groups were taken to such points of interest as Temple Square and Welfare Square. These visitors often appreciated being entertained in individual Latter-day Saint homes as well as attending church services in local wards.

EXPANDED OPPORTUNITIES FOR EDUCATION PROVIDED WORLDWIDE

The basic character of the Church's educational program had been established in the 1930s, placing the emphasis on part-time religious education to help supplement the instruction available in the public schools.

From then on growth, especially following World War II, has been a major focus of the Church in education. Enrollment in the Church's various educational programs increased approximately five-fold during the two decades when David O. McKay presided over the Church. President McKay's background and personal commitment to education suited him well to lead the Saints during this era of phenomenal growth.

In 1953, President McKay directed the formation of a unified Church Educational System including schools, seminaries, and institutes of religion worldwide. Surging enrollments following the close of World War II created great pressures on the Church's educational programs. Furthermore, in 1950 the First Presidency affirmed that they wanted Brigham Young University to become "the greatest educational institution in the world."[11]

BYU therefore launched an unprecedented building program. The capacity of on-campus student housing was tripled; other facilities, including a motion picture studio, student center, and new stadium, were added. Major new academic buildings were constructed. Ernest L. Wilkinson, president of BYU at the time, took steps to see that academic progress kept pace with physical growth. In 1960, BYU offered a doctorate program for the first time. In the same year the university also launched an honors program, which allowed more serious students to enjoy small classes with some of the university's most outstanding faculty members.

Student Enrollment in Church Educational Programs

	1900	1910	1920	1930	1940	1950	1955	1960	1965	1970	1975	1980	1985
Seminaries			2,980	27,075	26,128	28,677	38,285	62,253	103,500	132,053	174,010	199,317	225,709
Institutes				321	3,352	4,309	5,558	10,270	30,052	44,005	73,643	124,939	127,470
BYU	40	111	438	1,448	2,715	5,429	9,440	11,555	21,286	25,950	25,950	27,772	26,894
Other Church Schools									12,076	17,459	15,659	27,449	18,664

The church activity of students was also a source of concern. Some students became careless in their church attendance while away from home. Wards adjacent to college campuses became overcrowded by the attendance of active college-age students. As early as 1947 two branches were formed to meet the needs of both the married and single students at Brigham Young University. At first these units were considered experimental, but they soon demonstrated their success by setting the highest attendance record in the East Provo Stake. As enrollment at the university grew, the first student stake in the Church was organized at BYU in 1956. This made a unique and significant contribution to life at BYU and to the students' personal development.

Soon student wards and stakes were organized on many other campuses, wherever numbers were sufficient. Typically the bishop was a faculty member or an adult from the community, but students filled most other ward positions. Students thus gained experience as quorum and auxiliary leaders, teachers, and clerks. Mature students even had the opportunity to serve as counselors in bishoprics or as members of the stake high council. In contrast to campuses of most major universities, which were almost deserted on Sundays except for the handful attending chapel services, at Brigham Young University and Ricks College the buildings where student wards met were as crowded on Sunday as on weekdays. President Wilkinson, reflecting on his two decades of leadership at BYU, declared that the organization of these student stakes and wards was "the most satisfying accomplishment during the time I have been here."[12]

Significant progress was also being made in Church educational programs for part-time religious education. Seminaries and institutes were being started throughout the United States and around the world to meet the needs of high school and college students.

Adaptations in the seminary program made possible rapid growth in the number of high school students enrolled. Originally all seminaries were the "released-time" variety, with students attending classes in a seminary building near a high school. As the Latter-day Saints spread beyond the Intermountain stakes, however, this arrangement was not possible. Therefore early-morning and home-study programs were developed to meet the needs of Church members.

Early-morning seminary classes were inaugurated in Salt Lake City and Pocatello, Idaho, in 1929; however, the program in Pocatello was discontinued after only one year. The need existed in other areas. As early as 1941 the institute director in southern California reported that five high schools in the Los Angeles area had more than one hundred Latter-day Saint students, and that several others approached that number. Wartime restrictions, however, precluded any new programs being developed at that time. In 1950 the eleven Los Angeles area stake presidents unanimously urged that early-morning seminaries be started at once.

Formidable obstacles had to be overcome: many classes had to serve more than one high school. Differences in school schedules meant that seminary could only be held at 7 A.M. or even earlier. Almost no chapels were located within walking distance of the high schools, so car pools or other transportation had to be arranged. In September 1950, six pilot classes were inaugurated, and their success led to the addition of seven more classes that same school year. Despite the difficulties, the 461 southern California seminary students registered had an average attendance of 88 percent that first year.

Three years later there were fifty-nine classes, with an average attendance of 92 percent. This record was a tribute to the devotion of the students and their parents who were willing to get up as early as 5:00 A.M. to support a religion class before school. During the next quarter century, early-morning classes made seminary instruction available to Latter-day Saint students in many parts of the world, especially in centers of Church population in the United States and Canada outside the Intermountain area.

Home-study seminaries were established where there were not enough students to make a regular daily class possible. These were started as a pilot project in the Midwest during the 1966–67 school year. The young people studied their seminary lessons at home during the week and met Sunday with a volunteer teacher to go over the material. About once each month all the students from a district gathered at a central location under the direction of a full-time seminary coordinator. During the morning they reviewed the highlights of their past month's study. In the afternoon they enjoyed social or recreational activities conducted by Mutual leaders, while the volunteer teachers received a preview of the coming month's lessons from the seminary coordinator. Home-study seminary programs have made seminary instruction available to Latter-day Saints everywhere. A similar home-study institute course for college students was inaugurated in 1972.

In the Pacific and in Latin America, two areas of particularly rapid Church growth, public education was not widely available. Church leaders were concerned that a substantial portion of the Saints lacked the opportunity for even an elementary education. In these areas, therefore, the Church returned to the practice of nineteenth-century pioneer times and established schools to teach the basics of secular education along with religious instruction.

During the early twentieth century, several of the Pacific missions had conducted schools for the benefit of Latter-day Saint children. These were usually small, but an outstanding example was the Maori Agricultural College in New Zealand. Full-time missionaries were called on to act as teachers in these schools. Church growth after World War II heightened the need for expansion of these schools. During the early 1950s the Church opened the Liahona College in Tonga, the Pesega and Mapusaga high schools in Samoa, the Church College of New Zealand near Hamilton, and several elementary schools in these countries. Even though two of these schools were called colleges, they included work only to the high school level. Buildings for these badly–needed schools were constructed through the building missionary program, which had its beginning at this time in the South Pacific. Throughout the 1950s and early 1960s, hundreds of labor missionaries were called to help build chapels, schools, and other Church-sponsored projects. The program of using labor missionaries to construct church buildings was stopped when it was no longer cost effective.

The Church College of Hawaii, a two-year institution of higher education at Laie, opened in 1955. In 1957 it became a four-year institution. The school came to serve about a thousand students, most coming from the Pacific Islands. Emphasis on teacher education made it possible for many Polynesian young people to return to their homelands and become faculty members in the Church schools there. In 1958, President David O. McKay dedicated a complex of new buildings on the Church College of Hawaii campus. A 33–foot mosaic on the facade of the administration building depicted the flag-raising ceremony that had prompted Elder McKay to prophesy some thirty-seven years earlier that Laie would one day become the educational center for the Saints in the Pacific.

In 1963 the Church opened the Polynesian Cultural Center adjacent to the college campus. This center not only helped to preserve and share the unique cultures of several Pacific peoples, but it also became a very popular tourist attraction, which created goodwill for the Church and provided meaningful employment for a large number of Polynesian students at the Church College of Hawaii. In 1974 the Church College of Hawaii was renamed the Hawaii Campus of Brigham Young University, emphasizing subjects which could be taught more advantageously in the Pacific setting than on BYU's main Provo campus.

The expansion of the Church's educational program in Latin America also came between 1950 and 1975. The Juarez Academy in the Mormon colonies of northern Mexico was started in 1897. Beginning in 1960, however, with the encouragement of President David O. McKay, a system of forty elementary and secondary schools was established to meet the educational needs of the Saints in various parts of Mexico. Over two thousand students, many at the college level, attended the Church's school Benemerito de las Americas, near Mexico City. Here again, emphasis was on teacher training.

As in the Pacific, these schools made a significant contribution to Latter-day Saint activity as a whole since a sizable number of local Church leaders were graduates from them. For a time, the Church also operated a few schools in Chile, Peru, Bolivia, and Paraguay.

An especially important contribution was made by the Church's literacy program. In some developing areas, people who did not know how to read or write were being called as leaders and teachers. Under the direction of Brigham Young University, a simple plan was developed to teach these basic skills. In Bolivia, for example, Spanish-speaking members received fifteen hours of individual instruction teaching them how to read. After they completed this course, an additional four hours of training prepared these people to teach others. In this way hundreds of Latter-day Saints were enabled to read the scriptures, as well as handbooks, lesson manuals, and other Church literature. Many were able to obtain better employment, and their self-esteem received a substantial boost. One branch president commented that before he had learned to read, opportunities had been like a closed book for him; now his life was rich and full like an open book.

ENDNOTES

1. In Conference Report, Apr. 1951, p. 157.

2. In Francis M. Gibbons, *David O. McKay: Apostle to the World, Prophet of God* (Salt Lake City: Deseret Book Co., 1986) p. 50.

3. David O. McKay, "Ye Shall Know Them by Their Fruits," address delivered at the dedicatory services of the Sauniatu Church edifice in Sauniatu, Upolu, Samoa, 15 Jan. 1955, Addresses and papers, 1906–70, LDS Historical Department, Salt Lake City, p. 3.

4. See New Zealand Area Conference 1976, p. 3.

5. Jeanette McKay Morrell, *Highlights in the Life of President David O. McKay* (Salt Lake City: Deseret Book Co., 1966), p. 240; see also Conference Report, Oct. 1953, p. 10.

6. David O. McKay, "The World Needs to be Saved from Dominating Animal Instincts," *Instructor*, June 1962, pp. 181–82.

7. In Conference Report, Oct. 1936, p. 103.

8. "Hawaiian and Fiji Islands Members Greet Church Leaders," *Church News*, 22 Jan. 1955, p. 2.

9. "South Sea Islands Members Pay Devotions to Leader," *Church News*, 29 Jan. 1955, p. 2.

10. See Conference Report, Apr. 1959, p. 122.

11. See Ernest L. Wilkinson and W. Cleon Skousen, *Brigham Young University: A School of Destiny* (Provo: Brigham Young University Press, 1976), p. 433.

12. *Decades of Distinction: 1951–1971*, Brigham Young University Speeches of the Year (Provo, 9 Mar. 1971), p. 7.

AN ERA OF CORRELATION AND CONSOLIDATION

OVER THE YEARS the General Authorities have taken steps to ensure that the Church and its programs were perfecting the Saints and preparing a people worthy to establish Zion on earth. Their concerns became more urgent as the Church membership doubled in just a decade and a half and passed the two million mark in 1963. Church leaders became increasingly convinced that the varied organizations had to work harmoniously together under the direction of the priesthood, that families had to be strengthened, and that administration needed to be streamlined in order to more adequately meet the complex needs of the Saints. Hence the Church's unprecedented growth during the 1950s set the stage for the emphasis on correlation and consolidation that characterized the 1960s and early 1970s. To this end they conducted periodic reviews to be sure that all Church organizations and their activities were properly correlated.

EMPHASIS ON PRIESTHOOD CORRELATION

A thorough correlation effort began in 1960 when the First Presidency directed the General Priesthood Committee under Elder Harold B. Lee of the Quorum of the Twelve to conduct "an exhaustive, prayerful study and consideration" of all programs and curriculum in the light of the Church's ultimate objectives "so that the Church might reap the maximum harvest from the devotion of the faith, intelligence, skill and knowledge of our various Auxiliary Organizations and Priesthood Committees."[1] Elder Lee and his committee recognized that more was needed than simply ensuring that all gospel topics were being treated adequately in the Church's curriculum. They realized that an organization was needed at the general Church level to correlate the teaching of doctrines in the varied priesthood auxiliary quorums and organizations.

At the fall general conference in 1961, Elder Lee outlined the basic principles that would guide what came to be known as priesthood correlation. He quoted Paul's comparison of the Church to a perfectly functioning human body (see 1 Corinthians 12:14–28) and then quoted from a modern revelation, which declared: "Let every man stand in his own office, and labor in his own calling; and let not the head say unto the feet it hath no need of the feet; for without the feet how shall the body be able to stand? Also the body hath need of every member" (D&C 84:109–10).

Elder Lee stressed, "Each organization was to have its specific function, and it was not to usurp the field of the other, which would be like the eye saying to the hand, 'I have no need of thee.' " He also reemphasized the First Presidency's 1940 declaration, "The home was the basis of a righteous life and that no other instrumentality can take its place nor fulfil its essential functions and that the utmost the auxiliaries can do is to aid the home in its problems, giving special aid and succor where such is necessary." Church leaders often referred to the family as the central unit in Church organization.

At this time Elder Lee announced the formation of an all-Church coordinating council consisting of certain General Authorities and executives of various Church organizations. This council's purpose was to formulate policies governing the planning and operation of all Church programs. Under this council's direction, separate committees for children, youth, and adults were to write courses of study and coordinate activities for their respective age groups. The various auxiliary organizations would then carry out the programs prepared by these three committees. Under the direction of the Church coordinating council, four general priesthood committees gave direction and emphasis to the home teaching, genealogy and temple, missionary, and welfare programs Churchwide. Elder Lee further explained, "In the adoption of such a program, we may possibly and hopefully look forward to the consolidation and simplification of church curricula, church publications, church buildings, church meetings, and many other important aspects of the Lord's work."[2]

In 1962, Elder Richard L. Evans, a member of the Twelve working with the correlation effort, explained the intent:

"That the gospel be taught as completely as possible at least three times during these three age levels of life: children, youth, and adults.

"Within these major groupings there will be many minor groupings, taking into account school associations, social interests, priesthood ages, missions, marriage, and other factors. . . .

"The basic program for the various age groups will be made flexible enough to meet the varying needs and circumstances of individuals and of wards and stakes and branches and missions."[3]

Although significant strides had been taken in coordinating the planning of programs at the general level, more needed to be done among the wards and stakes. The first steps were taken in 1964. In weekly meetings of the ward priesthood executive committee, the bishopric and Melchizedek Priesthood leaders gave direction to coordinate all ward activities. Monthly ward council meetings also included auxiliary and other leaders; here they could correlate schedules and activities and, most importantly, discuss how the ward's programs could best meet the needs of individual members and families. Similar organizations were implemented at the stake level three years later.

A key step in priesthood correlation at the local level was the inauguration of home teaching in 1964. Home teachers became the major means to bring the varied Church programs to the family. They replaced contacts formerly made separately by ward teachers, representatives of priesthood quorums, or members of auxiliary classes. The home teachers' regular visits, made at least monthly, provided a channel for two-way communication between the family and the ward priesthood leaders.

A new Melchizedek Priesthood handbook published in 1964 affirmed that the Church had three major objectives:

"1. Perfect the Saints—To keep the members of the Church in the way of their full duty and to help them to walk uprightly before the Lord.

"2. Missionary Work—To teach the Gospel to those who have not yet heard it or accepted it.

"3. Temple Work—To have every member worthy to go to the temple for his own endowments and have his family sealed to him. Also to perform genealogical research and vicarious temple ordinances so that the worthy dead may participate in the blessings of the gospel."[4]

Further steps to correlate Church activities continued. An important improvement came in 1967 with the adoption of a uniform Church year. Previously some Church organizations had commenced their lesson work at the beginning of the local school year, while others had operated on a calendar year. Now all priesthood and auxiliary organizations began their courses of instruction at the same time. Furthermore, age groupings were standardized from one organization to another. This enabled teachers in various ward organizations to work more closely to meet the needs of any given group of young people.

During the 1960s young Latter-day Saints in many parts of the world became increasingly active in sharing the gospel with their friends, and youth missionary committees were formed. In 1967 the scope of these committees was expanded to form bishop's youth councils, which brought youth and adult leaders together monthly in each ward to consider the needs of the youth and to coordinate activities. In addition, collections of teaching aids formerly maintained by each organization were consolidated into a single meetinghouse library. Similarly, separate teacher training programs sponsored by each auxiliary were combined under a single ward teacher development director.

STRENGTHENING THE FAMILY

One of the most important thrusts of priesthood correlation was to strengthen Latter-day Saint families. Church leaders gave renewed emphasis to family home evenings. Beginning in 1965 the Church published manuals with weekly lessons to be used by families around the world. While instruction in priesthood and auxiliary classes presented gospel principles, the activities in the home focused on the practical everyday application of those principles. In addition to the Church's home evening manuals, various organizations issued suggestions for family activities. The Relief Society provided specific helps for mothers, and Melchizedek Priesthood quorums conducted training for fathers.

Elder Harold B. Lee testified that this program was inspired: "My mind has been filled with the realization that in 1964 and the year just preceding, we have been receiving as pertinent and important divine direction as has ever been given to the Church in any similar period in its history through the prophet and leader who now presides as the President of this Church."[5]

In the preface to the first family home evening manual, President David O. McKay declared, "The problems of these difficult times cannot better be solved in any other place, by any other agency, by any other means, than by love and righteousness, and precept and example, and devotion to duty in the home."[6]

A later manual contained this promise: "Families who prayerfully prepare and constantly hold their weekly Home Evenings, and who work together during the week to apply the lessons in their lives, will be blessed. There will be better feelings between husband and wife, between parents and children, and among children. In such homes the Spirit of the Lord will be made manifest."[7]

Encouraged by such promises, Latter-day Saint parents around the world gratefully implemented this new program. Whether the family home evening was held in a New York City apartment, a Navajo hogan, or in a Polynesian thatched home, there were usually certain common elements: family members took turns conducting the program, offering prayers, leading the singing, and presenting the lesson. Families often combined these elements of their home evenings with special recreational activities and almost always served refreshments. In 1970 Church leaders announced that Monday evenings were set aside for these family gatherings and that no other Church activities were to be held on that night.

Even missionary work was affected by the Church's emphasis on the family. Wholesome family relationships were the theme of a series of brief announcements the Church produced for radio and television. Many of these "Homefront" messages earned awards for excellence from religious and broadcasting groups. Showing families how to conduct home evenings was an effective way for missionaries to introduce nonmembers to the gospel. Following this initial contact, missionaries frequently were invited back to present their regular proselyting discussions.

President David O. McKay often endorsed the importance of the family. In an oft-quoted declaration he affirmed, "No other success can compensate for failure in the home.[8] . . . The poorest shack of a home in which love prevails over a united family is of greater value to God and future humanity than the richest bank on earth. In such a home God can work miracles and will work miracles. . . . Pure hearts in a pure home are always in whispering

This is one of the series of the Homefront messages, "I'll Always Make Time for You," produced by the Church:

I'll always make time for you.
Cause there's nothin' that I'd rather do.
Than to sit down beside you and hear all about you.
No, there's nothin' that I'd rather do.
I promise, I'll always be there for you.
No, there's nothin' that you and I can't get through.
As long as we sit down together and hear out each other.
Oh, I'll always make time for you.

Families grow closer
One conversation at a time.

distance of heaven."⁹ Following President McKay's death early in 1970, his successors continued his emphasis on priesthood correlation and the family.

PRESIDENTS JOSEPH FIELDING SMITH AND HAROLD B. LEE

During the early 1970s the Church was led by two outstanding latter-day prophets. Joseph Fielding Smith served as President of the Church for two and a half years, and Harold B. Lee occupied the office for eighteen months. In each case these brief presidencies were the culmination of long and significant service to the Church.

Joseph Fielding Smith, who became President of the Church in the late twentieth century, was born in 1876—one year before the death of Brigham Young. Varied experiences and assignments during his long life had prepared him well to make a substantial contribution to the progress of God's work on earth. In 1910 he was sustained as a member of the Council of the Twelve and was ordained an Apostle by his father, President Joseph F. Smith. Joseph Fielding Smith served in the Quorum for sixty years, longer than any other member. Elder Smith was also appointed as Church historian and recorder in 1921, a position he held until he was sustained as President of the Church a half century later.

As with several other Church presidents, Joseph Fielding Smith made some of his greatest contributions to the Church in the years preceding his service as Church president. His entire apostolic ministry was characterized by his notable defense of the teachings and the doctrines of the Prophet Joseph Smith and the message of the Restoration.

Joseph Fielding Smith received his patriarchal blessing from Patriarch Joseph D. Smith in 1913. In his blessing he was promised that he would never be confounded as he defended the divinity of the Prophet Joseph Smith's mission: "You have been blessed with ability to comprehend, to analyze, and defend the principles of truth above many of your fellows, and the time will come when the accumulative evidence that you have gathered will stand as a wall of defense against those who are seeking and will seek to destroy the evidence of the divinity of the mission of the Prophet Joseph; and in this defense you will never be confounded."¹⁰

Joseph Fielding Smith (1876–1972).
Soon after President Smith was called as
President of the Church, Elder Bruce R.
McConkie said, "Our new president is a
doctrinal teacher, a theologian, a scriptorian, a preacher of righteousness in the
full and true sense of the word."[11]

Consider the impact just one of his more than two dozen books—*Teachings of the Prophet Joseph Smith*—has had on doctrinal understanding and clarity in the Church. Joseph Fielding Smith's journal explained that the book was compiled because many Church teachers had "accepted too readily the views of uninspired educators."[12] Since its first printing, *Teachings of the Prophet Joseph Smith* has been a basic reference for doctrinal interpretation, Church policy, and Church government.

In vindication of what he had written and said during his five decades as an Apostle, President Joseph Fielding Smith declared in his first message as Church president:

"All my days I have studied the scriptures and have sought the guidance of the Spirit of the Lord in coming to an understanding of their true meaning. The Lord has been good to me, and I rejoice in the knowledge he has given me and in the privilege that has been and is mine to teach his saving principles.

". . . What I have taught and written in the past I would teach and write again under the same circumstances."[13]

In the two and one-half years of his administration, President Smith continued to proclaim the basic principles of the Restoration as revealed to the Prophet Joseph Smith. His administration emphasized and interpreted the timeless teachings and doctrines of the Prophet Joseph Smith to an expanding international Church in the 1970s. A few passages excerpted from his message as Church president illustrate how President Smith emphasized and interpreted the teachings of the Prophet Joseph Smith to the Church.

"God is our Father. . . . He is omnipotent and omniscient; he has all power and all wisdom. . . .

These books written by Joseph Fielding Smith are representative of twenty-five he wrote.

". . . I am grateful that we know he is an infinite and eternal being who knows all things and has all power and whose progression consists not in gaining more knowledge or power, not in further perfecting his godly attributes, but in the increase and multiplying of his kingdoms. This also is what the Prophet taught."[14]

"The Prophet Joseph Smith taught that man is saved no faster than he gains knowledge of Jesus Christ and the saving truths of the gospel, and that no man can be saved in ignorance of these things."[15]

President Smith assumed the reins of leadership at the advanced age of ninety-three. With the help of his two able counselors, Harold B. Lee and N. Eldon Tanner, President Smith directed the implementation of a variety of improvements in Church activities and programs. He traveled widely, conducted conferences, dedicated buildings, and in other ways strengthened the Church and its members. After serving as President of the Church for nearly thirty months, Joseph Fielding Smith died peacefully just two weeks before his ninety-sixth birthday.

Following President Smith's death, Harold B. Lee was sustained as the eleventh President of the Church. Like his predecessor, President Lee had already made significant contributions that had had a far-reaching impact on the Church and its programs. Perhaps best known were his roles in the innovative projects that influenced the welfare plan he later helped to introduce throughout the Church and his leadership in the development of the priesthood correlation program. During the late 1930s he traveled extensively, instructing stake leaders in the new program.

Elder Lee was sustained as a member of the Quorum of the Twelve Apostles in April 1941. After World War II broke out, he was named as the first chairman of the Church Servicemen's Committee in October 1942. By 1960 he had become chairman of the General Priesthood Committee. It was in that capacity he received the assignment to conduct an exhaustive study of Church curriculum and programs. During the next several years, he reported in general conferences on the progress of priesthood correlation and the introduction of such key activities as home teaching, priesthood executive committees, ward correlation councils, and family home evenings. All these experiences provided Harold B. Lee with a rich background for his service as President of the Church.

At a press conference on the occasion of his assuming the leadership of the Church, President Lee declared, "The safety of the church lies in the members keeping the commandments. There is nothing more important that I could say. As they keep the commandments, blessings will come."[16] President Lee led the Church for only a year and a half before he died unexpectedly on 26 December 1973. Though brief, his administration continued the important trends that had been inaugurated by his predecessors, particularly in terms of consolidating and streamlining Church programs in the midst of continued rapid growth.

Harold B. Lee (1899–1973)

CONSOLIDATION DURING THE EARLY 1970s

During the four years that Joseph Fielding Smith and Harold B. Lee led the Church, the membership climbed from 2.8 to 3.3 million. Early in 1970, on the day President David O. McKay died, the five hundredth stake was organized. During that same year sixty-four stakes were formed (the previous record for one year had been twenty-nine). These included stakes in Tokyo, Japan, the first in Asia; Johannesburg, South Africa, the first in Africa; and Lima, Peru, the first on the west coast of South America. Efforts to sustain this growth through sharing the gospel also continued. Over six million people visited the Church's pavilion at "Expo '70" in Osaka, Japan. This made the Church's programs and teachings more widely known than ever before in Japan and other countries of east Asia. In 1972 the Church opened a visitors' center in San Diego where the Mormon Battalion had concluded its epic march. The Church also opened a public relations office in New York City. The following year a complex of restored buildings was dedicated in Nauvoo, and Japanese language tours were inaugurated at the Hawaii Temple visitors' center.

Yet the early 1970s were not only an era of growth and expansion. These years also witnessed a consolidation of administrative responsibilities at Church headquarters, a continuing effort to improve the Church's varied programs, and an intensified desire to help each individual member cope with the mounting challenges of the modern world.

Some important reorganizations at Church headquarters grouped related agencies and activities into several large departments. One of the departments consolidated responsibilities for writing, editing, and translating magazines, lesson manuals, and other instructional materials. The Public Communications Department coordinated broadcasting, visitors' centers, and other public relations activities. Real estate, construction, and building maintenance became responsibilities of the Physical Facilities Department. The Historical Department was given the responsibility to gather and preserve records and make them available for research. A tangible consolidation of Church administration came with the construction of a twenty-eight-story office building just north of the Church Administration Building in Salt Lake City. When this facility opened in 1972, offices previously located in rented space in a dozen downtown buildings were housed under one roof.

In the spirit of correlation and consolidation, several formerly separate Church activities were combined. For example, the Aaronic Priesthood youth and programs for the Young Men's Mutual Improvement Association were combined; quorum advisers became the ward Young Men's presidency. A similar streamlining reduced the number of officers and teachers in the Young Women's MIA. Beginning in 1971 the Church published only three magazines in English: the *Ensign* for adults, the *New Era* for youth, and the

Friend for children. Auxiliary and other Church organizations had previously issued their own magazines. Now a single staff under the direction of the General Authorities was set up to handle production and circulation.

Changes during this period often involved abandoning the traditional names of Church programs. After ninety-nine years, the title "Deseret Sunday School Union" was replaced by the designation "Sunday School of The Church of Jesus Christ of Latter-day Saints." Other names that were discontinued during these years included Trail Builders (nine- to eleven-year-old boys in Primary), M Men and Gleaners (young single adults), and even the name Mutual Improvement Association or MIA itself. The shift from senior Aaronic to prospective elder, for older male members who had not yet received the Melchizedek Priesthood, represented a new emphasis for this program. The former title seemed to reflect a man's past failure to advance beyond the lesser priesthood, while the new name reflected hope for future progress. Giving the elders quorum responsibility for reactivating these men placed them in the mainstream of priesthood activity and associations. Recently returned missionaries, usually members of the elders quorums, could employ the same skills in working with their inactive brethren that they had used in teaching nonmembers.[17]

President Joseph Fielding Smith's interest in gospel scholarship was reflected in another refinement of Church activity. In 1972, the adult Gospel Doctrine class in Sunday School began a systematic study of the standard works. Up to this time a variety of manuals had been prepared for this class, but beginning in 1972 the scriptures themselves became the sole text. The Old Testament, the New Testament, the Book of Mormon, and the Doctrine and Covenants were studied in rotation, two years (later only one) being spent on each. The Pearl of Great Price was studied in conjunction with relevant sections of the other standard works. Church leaders anticipated a spiritual resurgence as a result of the Saints' added contact with the scriptures.

Under the leadership of Presidents Smith and Lee, the momentum in temple activity continued. In 1972 the Ogden and Provo temples were dedicated. With their use of technological advances and locations in areas with large populations of Church members, these immediately became the most productive temples in terms of the number of ordinances performed. Construction of the Washington D.C. Temple, the largest ever built by the Church, was commenced in 1971. The extensive remodeling of five existing temples was also announced. Permission was granted to submit names for temple ordinances individually rather than only as family groups, which sparked an upsurge in genealogical and temple activity.

GUIDELINES FOR CHURCH EDUCATION

Consistent with the objective of consolidating related activities, the Church streamlined its Church Educational System. In 1970, Neal A.

The site for the Washington D.C. Temple was dedicated in 1968 by President Hugh B. Brown of the First Presidency. President Spencer W. Kimball dedicated the completed temple in November 1974.

Maxwell, an administrator at the University of Utah, was called as commissioner of education. He and his staff gave thorough consideration to the Church's efforts in education and issued a report in 1971 that identified three major principles.

(1) "Literacy and basic education are gospel needs. . . . Education is often not only the key to the individual member's economic future, but also to his opportunities for self-realization, for full Church service and for contributing to the world around him." To meet this need, the Church operated seventy-five elementary and secondary schools in Latin America and the South Pacific. Without them, members in these areas would almost totally have been left without any opportunity for education. Later, however, as local governments began providing more public education, some of these Church schools were closed.

(2) "Church programs will not duplicate otherwise available opportunities especially in higher education." The commissioner pointed out that post-high school education was within reach of a majority of Church members. "Of the more than 200,000 members . . . enrolled in colleges and universities, only 32,000 of them are in a Church school. However, 50,000 LDS college students on 321 other campuses are enrolled in LDS institutes of religion to receive instruction in religion and enjoy social and cultural opportunities."

(3) "Ultimately, all high school and college-age Latter-day Saints should have access to weekday religious education, in tandem with secular education. The greatest impact, in terms of numbers of individuals served by Church educational programs, comes from seminary and institute programs which enroll 190,000 students," the commissioner concluded.[18]

Formation of the Latter-day Saint Student Association (LDSSA), beginning in 1966 on campuses in Utah and southern California, was a specific example of how correlation applied to the Church's educational program. Under the direction of priesthood leaders, LDSSA coordinated the efforts of student wards or branches, as well as institutes of religion and Church-related social organizations. Rather than competing, these programs were to function unitedly in promoting the students' spiritual and intellectual development. LDSSA also sponsored activities of its own and sometimes provided an official link between Church programs and student organizations on campus.

The 1969 international convention of LDSSA, held at the University of Utah institute, was a memorable spiritual experience for the over three hundred students in attendance. Church leaders wanted to strengthen these carefully chosen student leaders from campuses throughout the United States and Canada so that they might be beacon lights in an era of general unrest and confusion among college students. Elder Harold B. Lee was the featured speaker at the convention.

"He related personal experiences of true modern miracles which had occurred to him. . . .

"Then, considerably more than midway in his sermon of one hour and fifteen minutes, the mood changed. . . .

". . . Elder Lee concluded his sermon with considerable emotion, firmly and fervently witnessing to the truth of his convictions as they had been expressed, and bearing personal, heartfelt testimony that God lives. He told of how he had come to know this truth as one of His special witnesses on the earth. Everyone there knew that he knew!" For some time following the closing prayer, everyone remained seated in silence, nobody wanting to break the spirit of the occasion. Elder Marion D. Hanks, who had conducted the meeting, then went with Elder and Sister Lee to the foyer. "Elder and Sister Lee shook hands with an absolutely mute and generally tearful group of young people as they filed by."[19]

MEETING NEW CHALLENGES

The decades following World War II brought a general disintegration of institutions and traditions that in earlier years had provided social stability and security. Crime rates increased. The growing number of divorces broke up more families. More people were living in urban areas rather than rural environments. City life typically was hectic with an array of attractions pulling family members in many directions. Although the gospel offered defenses against these social problems, Latter-day Saints were not immune. President Harold B. Lee was concerned about these difficulties and stressed the need of blessing each member with the full program of the Church. Some of the greatest challenges for members were in the areas of emotional well-being and physical health. To meet these challenges the Church established social service and health programs.

Over the years the Church established three programs to meet specific social challenges: The Relief Society social welfare department served as an adoption agency and provided foster homes for disadvantaged children. Since the mid-1950s the Indian student placement program helped thousands of children gain a better education. The youth guidance program provided counseling, foster care, and day camps to youth in need. All three of these programs were required by law to employ licensed professional social workers. In 1969 they were unified to form the new Social Services department.

From this beginning, the program expanded to provide a wide variety of services. Special foster homes assisted unwed mothers, and Church leaders encouraged them to marry where appropriate. The Church's adoption agency helped provide children for childless couples and found Latter-day Saint homes for children needing adoption. Services to Church members in prison and their families included counseling and rehabilitation; special home evenings were arranged for inmates. In working with members who had drug or alcohol problems, Church Social Services coordinated with public agencies and also provided instruction for local Church leaders. In areas where Church membership was more concentrated, particularly in the western United States and Canada, the Church established social service agencies. These employed professionally trained and licensed personnel, and operated in accordance with government regulations.[20]

Since its earliest years the Church had stressed the importance of physical health, the Word of Wisdom being a well-known example. By the second half of the twentieth century the number of hospitals operated by the Church in Utah, Idaho, and Wyoming reached fifteen. The early 1970s, however, brought a new and broader emphasis in the Church's health program.

In 1971 the Church called its first health missionaries. In addition to doing regular proselyting, they provided specialized instruction in health principles, nutrition, and sanitation. While other governmental and religious agencies typically sponsored clinics where doctors could treat relatively few, the Church's health missionaries stressed prevention of illness through education and thus were able to serve thousands. These missionaries worked through the regular Church organizations. Using posters and other teaching aids, they taught Primary children the importance of washing before eating, and instructed Relief Society women in methods of preserving and preparing wholesome foods. In later years they received broadened assignments and were called welfare services missionaries or missionaries with special assignments.

The new emphasis in the Church's health program was reflected in the 1974 decision to give up ownership of its hospitals. The First Presidency declared, "The growing worldwide responsibility of the church makes it difficult to justify provision of curative services in a single, affluent, geographical locality." Instead, the Church put its resources into improving the health of members throughout the world by education. An independent corporation, Intermountain Health Care, Inc., was set up to own and operate the hospitals formerly belonging to the Church.[21]

In 1973 the General Welfare Program, Health Services, and Social Services were brought together to form the new Welfare Services department under the supervision of the Presiding Bishopric. This was done to "unify activities in meeting the total needs of the whole man."[22]

Over the years the Church has published literature in braille or in recorded form for Church members who are blind. A continuing concern for meeting the unique needs of handicapped members has continued and expanded. Special education seminaries are provided for those with learning disabilities. Bishops have received instructions on how to involve handicapped members more fully in Church activities. Sighted companions have been invited to help blind teachers prepare lessons. Home teachers can help members in wheelchairs get to Church. Young people have learned sign language and interpreted Church services for deaf friends. The number of special branches for the deaf has expanded throughout the United States. A

Mary Jane Pulley (1900–) began her work at the training school for handicapped people in American Fork, Utah, in 1957. In 1967 she was called to organize a seminary at the school. It was the first seminary for the handicapped in the Church.

conference in 1972 considered how the Church could better meet the needs of deaf Latter-day Saints. A film was produced to show how priesthood ordinances can be performed without the use of speech, and a dictionary was compiled to standardize signs used to interpret unique gospel or Church-related terms to the deaf.[23]

The early 1970s was an era of growing minority consciousness. Ethnic groups became increasingly proud of their unique heritages. The Church took steps to meet the particular needs of these groups. In 1970 the name of the Indian committee was changed to Committee for Lamanites and Other Cultures to reflect a broader scope. This committee did not administer programs of its own but rather coordinated efforts of existing Church organizations in behalf of various minority groups. The committee considered different ways gospel principles could be taught more effectively in terms of the understanding of the various cultural groups. It also sought to "glean from and preserve those contributions of the various cultural groups which might benefit other members of the Church."[24]

In 1972, President Harold B. Lee and his counselors instructed local priesthood leaders to assume the responsibility for adequately meeting the needs of minority groups residing within their boundaries. Special attention was given to those not speaking the language of the majority. As a result, translation facilities, classes taught in the minority language, or even separate branches or wards were provided. Although particular needs were to be met, the basic goal was to involve minority members as fully as possible in the mainstream of Church activity.

Another group with unique needs was the growing number of single adults in the Church. Traditional couple-oriented activities did not adequately meet the needs of these individuals. A branch for single adults was started in August 1973 in Salt Lake City. Later wards were organized to meet the needs of single adults. The Church also enhanced its activities for singles through programs sponsored by the Melchizedek Priesthood and the Relief Society.

The formation of social, health, and related programs in the twentieth century illustrates how, under inspired direction, the Church is able to respond to new needs as they arise.

LINES OF COMMUNICATION WORLDWIDE

During these years when existing activities were being refined and correlated and when others were emerging in response to new needs, the General Authorities keenly felt the need to enhance channels of communication in order to strengthen the Saints and their leaders worldwide. This was accomplished in at least three distinctive ways.

In 1936 regions had been formed to coordinate the efforts of several stakes in operating welfare projects. In 1964 the scope of these regions was broadened to include all priesthood-sponsored activities. Three years later the First Presidency announced the appointment of Regional Representatives, experienced men who would give greater guidance and direction to stake leaders.[25] Under the direction of the General Authorities they conducted instruction meetings in their assigned regions to introduce or emphasize the Church's programs and activities. Originally sixty-nine Regional Representatives were called. In subsequent years the number and duties of these men were greatly expanded.

Area conferences, begun in 1971, became a second means of enhancing communications with Church members worldwide. The first of these conferences convened in Manchester, England, in August of that year. The news media provided extensive coverage as time for the conference drew near. Lengthy articles in such noted British papers as the *Guardian, Times*, and *Sunday Telegraph* traced the Church's progress in Britain and commented favorably on such principles as the Word of Wisdom and latter-day prophecy.

The first area conference of the Church was held in England in August 1971 under the direction of President Joseph Fielding Smith. Fourteen General Authorities attended the conference and participated in the various sessions. Elder Howard W. Hunter is pictured speaking from the podium.

Courtesy of Deseret News

The Mormons were also the subject of a fifty-five minute documentary aired on BBC television. Principal meetings convened in the Belle Vue Exhibition Center in King's Hall, which took on the appearance of the Salt Lake Tabernacle as the Brethren were seated in high-backed red chairs on the stand. From twelve to fourteen thousand people attended general sessions, a number approximately equal to one-fifth of the Church's total membership in Britain. Addressing this vast throng, President Joseph Fielding Smith asserted:

"We are members of a world church, a church that has the plan of life and salvation, a church set up by the Lord himself in these last days to carry his message of salvation to all his children in all the earth.

"The day is long since past when informed people think of us as a peculiar group in the tops of the Rocky Mountains in America. . . .

"But now we are coming of age as a church and as a people."[26]

Speaking in the concluding session Sunday afternoon, Regional Representative Derek A. Cuthbert, who had coordinated local arrangements for the conference, said, "There is no longer a need for British Church members to leave their homeland to partake of the blessings of Church membership."[27]

As the conference ended, the entire congregation stood as President Joseph Fielding Smith prepared to leave the stand. Nobody moved, and conversations were in subdued tones. "It was as though they did not want to leave the spirit that had prevailed in the meeting. There was a sacred air about King's Hall and as a testimony to the spirit the audience burst into spontaneous singing of 'We Thank Thee O God for a Prophet.' " Then they sang "God Be with You Till We Meet Again."[28]

A similar area conference convened in Mexico City the following year, only one month after Harold B. Lee became President of the Church. At great sacrifice, Saints traveled as far as three thousand miles to be present. A group from Tijuana, Mexico, journeyed fifty-three hours by bus; they took turns standing because there were ten more people on board than seats. The "Folklorico" cultural program Friday evening featured talented musicians and dancers from throughout Mexico and Central America. On Saturday evening, President Lee spoke to Aaronic Priesthood, Young Women, Relief Society, and Melchizedek Priesthood groups convened simultaneously at several locations around Mexico City. President Lee rotated to each meeting, where he spoke and inspired those in attendance. The Tabernacle Choir presented its regular Sunday morning broadcast from the national auditorium in Chapultepec Park. The choir brought tears of appreciation to the eyes of many as it presented several of its numbers in Spanish. During the morning session, the new First Presidency, with all three members present, was sustained for the first time in an area general conference.

At this conference, Elder Bruce R. McConkie clearly enunciated the updated understanding of the principle of the gathering: "The place of gathering for the Mexican Saints is in Mexico; the place of gathering for the Guatemalan Saints is in Guatemala; the place of gathering for the Brazilian Saints is in Brazil; and so it goes throughout the length and breadth of the whole earth. Japan is for the Japanese; Korea is for the Koreans; Australia is for the Australians; every nation is the gathering place for its own people."[29]

In succeeding years similar area conferences were held in Germany, Sweden, and in other parts of the world. The Saints in these areas were similarly edified and uplifted.

The International Mission, organized in 1972, became a third means of keeping in touch with Church members throughout the world, particularly with those who did not live within the boundaries of an organized stake or mission. Thousands of Latter-day Saints lived in such scattered locations as Tanzania, Zambia, Morocco, Guiana, New Guinea, Hungary, and the Soviet Union. Typically they were diplomatic or foreign service envoys, representatives of major business corporations, or advisers for agricultural or other developmental projects. Sometimes these individuals were accompanied by their families; others were alone. While most came from the United States or Canada, some were from England, France, Germany, Scandinavia, and many other parts of the world.

Wherever they lived, these Saints generally valued Church membership and activity. Elder Bernard P. Brockbank, the International Mission's first president, explained:

"The organization of this mission was wisdom in that the member need not feel alone. He or she has someone to contact for supplies, to have questions answered, for counseling or just to keep in contact with the Church. . . .

". . . wherever he is, . . . the Church is as close as the nearest mailbox."[30]

Primarily by means of correspondence, the International Mission facilitated the ordering of Church supplies, maintained membership records, received and issued receipts for tithes and other donations, and coordinated interviews for priesthood advancement and temple recommends. Subsequently, the International Mission also played a key role in opening new areas of the world for gospel teaching and Church activity. With these lines of communication in place, and with its programs more perfectly correlated, the Church was ready to lengthen its stride in fulfilling its global mission.

ENDNOTES

1. Harold B. Lee, in Conference Report, Apr. 1963, p. 83.

2. In Conference Report, Sept. 1961, pp. 77, 79, 81.

3. In Conference Report, Oct. 1962, pp. 74, 76.

4. *Melchizedek Priesthood Handbook*, 1964, pp. 18–19.

5. In Conference Report, Oct. 1964, p. 137.

6. *Family Home Evening Manual*, 1965, p. iii.

7. *Family Home Evening Manual*, 1967, pp. iii–iv.

8. David O. McKay first used this thought in general conference April 1935 (p. 116). He was quoting J. E. McCulloch, *Home: The Savior of Civilization* (Washington, D.C.: Southern Cooperative League, 1924), p. 42.

9. In Conference Report, Apr. 1935, p. 116.

10. Joseph Fielding Smith, Jr., and John J. Stewart, *The Life of Joseph Fielding Smith* (Salt Lake City: Deseret Book Co., 1972), p. 195.

11. "Joseph Fielding Smith—Our New President," *Instructor*, Mar. 1970, p. 78.

12. In Smith and Stewart, *Life of Joseph Fielding Smith*, p. 212.

13. In Conference Report, Oct. 1970, p. 5.

14. Joseph Fielding Smith, "The Most Important Knowledge," *Ensign*, May 1971, p. 3.

15. Cited in Joseph Fielding Smith Scrapbooks, 1970–72, address delivered at Southern Utah State College, 28 May 1971, LDS Historical Department, Salt Lake City, p. 5.

16. In "Presidency Meets the Press," *Church News*, 15 July 1972, p. 3.

17. See "Elders Presidency Magnified," *Church News*, 29 Jan. 1972, p. 3.

18. "Seek Learning Even By Study and By Faith," report for 1971 from Commissioner of Education of The Church of Jesus Christ of Latter-day Saints, p. 1.

19. L. Brent Goates, *Harold B. Lee, Prophet*

and Seer (Salt Lake City: Bookcraft, 1985), pp. 394, 396.

20. See Marvin J. Ashton, "The Church Focuses on Social and Emotional Problems," *Ensign*, Jan. 1971, pp. 30–31; "Help Available Here," *Ensign*, Dec. 1973, pp. 54–56.

21. "Church Divests Self of Hospitals," *Church News*, 14 Sept. 1974, p. 3.

22. "Three Welfare Units Joined," *Church News*, 7 Apr. 1973, p. 4.

23. See "Needs Identified at Seminar for LDS Deaf," *Church News*, 19 Aug. 1972, pp. 7, 12.

24. "New Name, More Duties Given Church Indian Committee," *Church News*, 27 June 1970, p. 6.

25. See Conference Report, Oct. 1967, pp. 25–26.

26. In Manchester England Area Conference 1971, p. 5.

27. "No Longer Need to Leave Homeland, Members Told," *Church News*, 4 Sept. 1971, p. 13.

28. "Prophet Leads Conference; British Saints Rejoice," *Church News*, 4 Sept. 1971, p. 3.

29. In Mexico and Central America Area Conference 1972, p. 45.

30. "Unique Mission Serves World," *Church News*, 1 Feb. 1975, p. 3.

THE CHURCH LENGTHENS ITS STRIDE

Spencer W. Kimball (1895–1985)

FOLLOWING THE UNEXPECTED death of President Harold B. Lee on 26 December 1973, Spencer W. Kimball became the twelfth President of the Church. He humbly announced, "We will, in large measure, carry forward the same program, which we have helped in a small way to make and give it greater emphasis to carry forward the work as much as our talents and abilities will permit."[1] Despite this modest declaration, President Kimball's administration would be noted for numerous and far-reaching innovations.

PREPARATION OF A PROPHET

Spencer W. Kimball was born in Salt Lake City on 28 March 1895. When he was only three years old his family moved to southeastern Arizona, where he lived until his call as a General Authority. From his parents, Spencer learned the importance of tithe paying and obedience. He demonstrated an early interest in spiritual things—memorizing the Articles of Faith while milking the cows, reading the scriptures by the light of a coal oil lamp, and maintaining a nearly perfect attendance record at Church meetings. As a boy he also set a pattern of hard work, pitching hay alongside the men, using a special short-handled fork his father provided. Spencer suffered facial paralysis, which was overcome by a priesthood blessing. He drowned while swimming in a canal, but was successfully revived. His mother died when he was only eleven years old. Such experiences taught him important lessons of patience, courage, and faith.

Following service in the Central States Mission, he married Camilla Eyring, and they became the parents of four children. As a banker and businessman, he soon became a community leader. He was twenty-three years old when he was called to be a stake clerk, and he became a counselor in the stake presidency just a few years later. When the new Mount Graham Stake was created in 1938, he became its first president. He was serving in this capacity when his call to the apostleship came five years later.

A phone call from Salt Lake City in 1943 completely changed Spencer W. Kimball's life. President J. Reuben Clark, Jr., phoned to notify him of his call to the Quorum of the Twelve. Elder Kimball recalled, "I sensed immediately my inability and limitations and I cried back, 'Not me, Brother Clark! You can't mean that!' " For the next several weeks he settled his affairs, taking steps to ensure that no one felt he had dealt with him or her unfairly.

Elder Kimball continued, "I remember reading that Jacob wrestled all night, 'until the breaking of the day,' for a blessing; and I want to tell you that for eighty-five nights I have gone through that experience, wrestling for a blessing. Eighty-five times, the breaking of the day has found me on my knees praying to the Lord to help me and strengthen me and make me equal to this great responsibility that has come to me."[2]

As a member of the Twelve, Elder Kimball's influence was quickly felt throughout the Church. He became an important member of the committee that prayerfully considered how the tithing funds of the Church should be spent. His appointment as chairman of the Church's Indian committee was particularly close to his heart because of his long-standing interest in the Indian people. His masterful discourses had a powerful impact on the Latter-day Saints. Using vivid imagery, he effectively taught the Saints the importance of personal purity and pleaded with them to carry out the Church's responsibilities toward the various groups identified as Lamanites.

Serious health problems plagued Elder Kimball. In 1957 throat cancer threatened to rob him of his voice. He agonized, "Shall I ever speak at another temple dedication? Shall I ever preach again?" Following much prayer and fasting, however, the needed operation proved to be less radical than expected. Nevertheless, Elder Kimball lost most of his vocal cords. As he learned to speak again, he continued to ask himself, "Will my gruff fringe voice be an affront to the people?"[3] It was not long, however, until the Saints came to respect and heed and love Elder Kimball's "new voice."

Then in 1972 a problem with his heart recurred, and he underwent a particularly complicated open-heart operation. With the faith of many people and through the outstanding skill of a devoted Latter-day Saint surgeon, Dr. Russell M. Nelson, Elder Kimball's life once again was spared. Just prior to the surgery, the First Presidency blessed Dr. Nelson. "They blessed me that the operation would be performed without error, that all would go well, . . . for I had been raised up by the Lord to perform this operation." It went flawlessly. As Elder Kimball's heart resumed beating with power and vigor, Dr. Nelson recalled, "The Spirit told me that I had just operated upon a man who would become president of the Church."[4] Despite physical difficulties, Elder Kimball set a legendary example of long hours of selfless and devoted service in building up the kingdom of God. A motto prominently displayed on his desk proclaimed simply "Do It." These experiences helped prepare Spencer W. Kimball to lead the Church when the call came.

CHALLENGE TO LENGTHEN OUR STRIDE

As Spencer W. Kimball assumed the presidency of the Church, he chose to retain the same counselors who had served with his predecessor. This meant that N. Eldon Tanner, First Counselor, had served as a counselor to four Presidents of the Church, a record not exceeded in Church history.

President Tanner not only provided inspired counsel to the Saints and capable administrative leadership to the Church, but he also reached out to bless the community as a whole. Non-Latter-day Saint businessmen and educational leaders in Salt Lake City honored him for his selfless and effective community service. President Kimball's second counselor, President Marion G. Romney, had served as a General Authority longer than anyone else in the First Presidency, having been named as one of the original Assistants to the Twelve in 1941—two years before President Kimball had been called to the Twelve. For more than three decades his powerful leadership and scripture-centered teachings had motivated the Saints to improve both their spiritual and temporal welfare.

At the Regional Representatives' seminar in April 1974, Elder W. Grant Bangerter remembered that President Kimball had not spoken very long when "we became alert to an astonishing spiritual presence, . . . different from any of our previous meetings. It was as if, spiritually speaking, our hair began to stand on end. . . . President Kimball was opening spiritual windows and . . . inviting us to view with him the destiny of the gospel and the vision of its ministry."[5]

In 1974 President Kimball spoke for forty-five minutes to the Regional Representatives, delivering what became one of his most oft-quoted discourses and set the pace for his administration:

"It seems to me that the Lord chose his words when he said [the gospel must go to] 'every nation,' 'every land,' 'uttermost bounds of the earth,' 'every tongue,' 'every people,' 'every soul,' 'all the world,' 'many lands.'

"Surely there is significance in these words!

". . . A universal command!

"My brethren, I wonder if we are doing all we can. Are we complacent in our approach to teaching all the world? . . . Are we prepared to lengthen our stride? To enlarge our vision? . . .

"I believe the Lord can do anything he sets his mind to do.

"But I can see no good reason why the Lord would open doors that we are not prepared to enter. Why should he break down the Iron Curtain or the Bamboo Curtain or any other curtain if we are still unprepared to enter?

"I believe we have men who could help the apostles to open these doors—statesmen, able and trustworthy—but, when we are ready for them. . . .

"A year ago now I was in Japan and Korea, and . . . I seemed to envision a great movement when there would be thousands of local men prepared and anxious and strong to go abroad. . . . I seemed to envision again Mexican youth and Latins from Central and South America in great numbers qualifying themselves for missionary service within their own country and then finally in other lands until the army of the Lord's missionaries would cover the earth as the waters cover the mighty deep."[6]

When President Kimball concluded his address, President Ezra Taft Benson, who was conducting the seminar, echoed the feelings of all present as he declared in a voice filled with emotion, "Truly, there is a prophet in Israel."[7]

REACHING OUT WORLDWIDE

In order to promote this worldwide expansion of the gospel, the First Presidency called David M. Kennedy to be a special consultant on diplomatic affairs. Brother Kennedy, who had served in a stake presidency in Chicago, had ample secular background for this significant assignment. He had been chairman of the board and chief executive officer of one of the United States banks most heavily engaged in international business. He had also served as United States secretary of the treasury, ambassador to the North Atlantic Treaty Organization, and ambassador at large for the United States. In succeeding years he played a key role working with governments of many nations in order to resolve problems that had hindered the Church's activities there.[8] He was instrumental in arranging for mature couples to serve as special representatives of the Church in countries where traditional missionary work was not yet possible. One of his outstanding achievements in 1977 was securing legal status and official recognition for the Church in Poland. This opened the way for a visit by President Kimball to Warsaw, where he "dedicated the land of Poland and blessed its people that the work of the Lord might go forth."[9]

During these same years, others were involved in negotiations with the government of Israel that led to the Church developing the five-acre Orson Hyde Memorial Garden on the western slope of the Mount of Olives, overlooking the old city of Jerusalem.[10]

President Kimball emphasized the importance of every young man being worthy and prepared to serve a mission. In 1976 the Church's Language Training Mission moved into a new multi-building complex near the campus

President Spencer W. Kimball dedicated Poland for the preaching of the gospel while in Warsaw 24 August 1977.

The Orson Hyde Memorial Garden was dedicated 24 October 1979 by President Spencer W. Kimball in honor of Orson Hyde, who had ascended the Mount of Olives on 24 October 1841 and offered a dedicatory prayer, asking that Israel might be gathered home to their inheritance. The sign identified the location prior to construction.

Map of Jerusalem

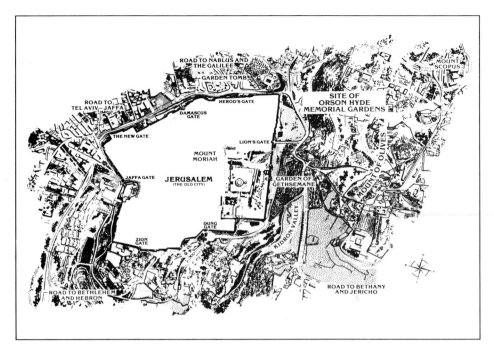

of Brigham Young University. In 1978 the Salt Lake City mission home was closed, and English-speaking missionaries, primarily from the United States and Canada, began to receive instruction at this new facility, which was renamed the Missionary Training Center. Since 1978 other training centers have been established in Brazil, Chile, Mexico, New Zealand, England, Japan, and other countries in order to enhance the preparation of local young men and women called to serve in these areas.

Latter-day Saint performing groups from various college campuses became another effective means of building goodwill toward the Church. In 1978 a group from BYU presented music and dance variety shows in Poland and in the Soviet Union. Before their tour, the performers spent several weeks studying the cultures and languages of the peoples they would visit so that they could announce their numbers in the local language and greet audience members individually following the performances. They were eager to communicate the spirit of the gospel by setting a good example and by radiating love. In both countries the performers were well received and their performances were taped for later release on nationwide television. The following year, another group made similar preparations for a tour of mainland China. Here again their presentations in the most prestigious concert halls of the country, as well as impromptu performances in factories, were highly appreciated. Additional tours in succeeding years continued to spread goodwill throughout the world.[11]

BYU sports teams also helped make friends for the Church. In the fall of 1984 the BYU Cougars were the only undefeated major college football team in the United States, and at the end of the football season they were ranked number one in the nation by both the coaches and sportswriters. Numerous articles in national publications presented favorable views of the BYU players, their school, and their religion.

The Church's worldwide nature was reflected in the increasingly international make-up of the General Authorities. Among those called to the First Quorum of the Seventy through President Spencer W. Kimball were five Europeans, Elders Charles A. Didier from Belgium, Jacob de Jager from the Netherlands, F. Enzio Busche from Germany, Derek A. Cuthbert from England, and Hans B. Ringger from Switzerland; the first of oriental ancestry, Elder Adney Y. Komatsu; the first from Asia, Elder Yoshihiko Kikuchi; and two from South America, Elders Angel Abrea and Helio R. Camargo. These leaders brought to the presiding councils of the Church a firsthand awareness of international challenges and opportunities facing the Church in their areas.

THE PRIESTHOOD EXTENDED TO ALL RACES

Perhaps few events have had a greater impact on the worldwide spread of the gospel than did the 1978 revelation received through President Spencer W. Kimball extending the priesthood to worthy males of all races. For some time, the General Authorities had discussed this topic at length in their regular temple meetings. In addition, President Kimball went frequently to the temple, especially on Saturdays and Sundays when he could be there alone, to plead for guidance. "I wanted to be sure," he explained.[12]

On 1 June 1978 nearly all of the General Authorities gathered, fasting as was their custom, for their regular monthly meeting in the temple. After this three-hour session, President Kimball invited his counselors and the Twelve to remain with him. When the First Presidency and the Twelve were alone, he again brought up the possibility of conferring the priesthood upon worthy brethren of all races. He expressed the hope that there might be a clear answer received one way or the other. Elder Bruce R. McConkie recalled, "At this point President Kimball asked the brethren if any of them desired to express their feelings and views as to the matter in hand. We all did so, freely and fluently and at considerable length, each person stating his views and manifesting the feelings of his heart. There was a marvelous outpouring of unity, oneness, and agreement in the council."[13]

After a two-hour discussion, President Kimball asked the group to unite in formal prayer and modestly suggested that he act as voice. He recalled:

"I told the Lord if it wasn't right, if He didn't want this change to come in the Church that I would be true to it all the rest of my life, and I'd fight the world against it if that's what He wanted.

". . . I had a great deal to fight, of course, myself largely, because I had grown up with this thought that Negroes should not have the priesthood and I was prepared to go all the rest of my life till my death and fight for it and defend it as it was. But this revelation and assurance came to me so clearly that there was no question about it."[14]

Elder McConkie of the Twelve added this description of what happened: "It was during this prayer that the revelation came. The Spirit of the Lord rested mightily upon us all; we felt something akin to what happened on the day of Pentecost and at the dedication of the Kirtland Temple. From the midst of eternity, the voice of God, conveyed by the power of the Spirit, spoke to his prophet. . . . And we all heard the same voice, received the same message, and became personal witnesses that the word received was the mind and will and voice of the Lord."[15]

Faithful black Latter-day Saints rejoiced as they received the long-hoped-for ordination to the priesthood, mission calls, calls to serve in priesthood leadership roles, and, of course, the eternal blessings of the temple. In November 1978, just five months after the revelation came, the First Presidency called two experienced couples to open missionary work in the black African nations of Nigeria and Ghana. Later mission efforts expanded to other parts of Africa and among the blacks in northern Brazil and the Caribbean.

WARNING VOICE

As the prophet of the Lord, Spencer W. Kimball increasingly felt compelled to raise a warning voice on a wide variety of subjects. In his first two general conferences as President of the Church, for example, he reaffirmed the Saints' political responsibilities to elect wise leaders and to obey constitutional law. He challenged the Saints to clean up and repair their homes and farms and urged them to plant gardens, store food (in areas where it was legal), and avoid waste. He also reminded them of the virtues of work, industry, and thrift. He urged the Saints to keep the Sabbath holy and refrain from taking the name of the Lord in vain. He counseled against the use of playing cards. He also warned the Saints to have nothing to do with apostate groups.

Many of President Kimball's teachings were centered in the family. He encouraged all young Latter-day Saints to marry and have children. He said, "We call upon all people to accept normal marriage as a basis for true happiness." He lamented the growing number of divorces and believed that selfishness was a major cause of family break-ups. He regarded abortion as a related evil. "Certainly the terrible sin of premeditated abortion would be hard to justify. . . . We place it high on the list of sins against which we strongly warn the people."

He declared that "the Church has consistently opposed the improper and harmful use of drugs or similar substances under circumstances which would result in addiction, physical or mental impairment or in lowering moral standards."

President Kimball saw immoral or improper use of the body as a major threat to family happiness: "The human body is the sacred home of the spirit child of God, and unwarranted tampering with or defilement of this sacred tabernacle can bring only remorse and regret. We urge: stay clean, uncontaminated, undefiled." The President also spoke out against the sin of homosexuality, "unisex" attempts to blur the distinction between masculine and feminine, and the practice of couples living together without marriage. Although President Kimball vigorously denounced such evils, he also offered hope to those who had become ensnared in them. This was the prime message of his widely read book, *The Miracle of Forgiveness*, published a few years earlier.

President Kimball particularly stressed the importance of the mother's role: " 'Motherhood is near to Divinity. It is the highest, holiest service to be assumed by mankind. It places her who honors its holy calling and service next to the angels.' "[16] President Kimball emphasized the responsibility of parents to teach the gospel of Jesus Christ to their children, including such virtues as honor, integrity, and honesty. "The home is the teaching situation. Every father should talk to his son, every mother to her daughter. Then it would leave them totally without excuse should they ignore the counsel they have received."[17]

Few family-related issues generated more discussions both in and out of the Church, especially in America, than did the proposed Equal Rights Amendment, which sought to provide that equal treatment under the law not be denied or abridged on account of gender. At first these provisions seemed wholly commendable, but further analysis raised some concerns. In 1976, though reaffirming the Church's commitment to equal opportunities for women, the First Presidency opposed passage of the proposed amendment.

"It would strike at the family, humankind's basic institution. . . .

"Passage of ERA, some legal authorities contend, could nullify many accumulated benefits to women in present statutes."[18] The Presidency also feared that the amendment would undermine the unique status of women. Although this stand was approved by the vast majority of Latter-day Saints, a small but vocal minority saw it as a threat to women's rights, refused to accept it, and even mounted disruptive demonstrations at general conferences. In various areas of the United States, groups of Latter-day Saints organized to work with legislators and in other ways mobilized public opinion to defeat the amendment.

The Equal Rights Amendment was not ratified by the 1981 deadline, but attention continued to be focused on the role of women. Articles in national periodicals increasingly lauded women who found fulfillment in careers outside the home, and described traditional homemaking as demeaning drudgery. Church leaders were aware of the pressures such attitudes placed on Latter-day Saint women. Therefore, in 1978 the Church inaugurated annual meetings for women, preceding the fall general conferences. Like the priesthood sessions for men, these gatherings in the Salt Lake Tabernacle were carried by closed circuit to hundreds of meetinghouses throughout the United States and in other countries. Speaking at the first of these sessions, President Spencer W. Kimball urged women to have programs of self-improvement and to reach for new levels of achievement and self-fulfillment. He said:

"We want our sisters to be scholars of the scriptures as well as our men. . . .

". . . Let there be no question in your mind about your value as an individual. . . .

"Much is said about the drudgery and confinement of the woman's role. This is not so. . . . There is divinity in each new life, challenge in raising each child. Marriage is a partnership. Please be a contributing and full partner."[19] Because many women would face the challenge of earning a living for themselves or for their families, Church leaders encouraged them to obtain education, while not losing sight of their primary role as mothers in the home.

More than twenty thousand Church members gathered for the dedication of the Relief Society Monument to Women at Nauvoo, Illinois, in 1978. Thirteen bronze statues stand in a two-acre park. "The statues represent various spheres of a woman's circle of influence. . . .

"President Kimball commented upon the statuary garden and said, 'As we walk through the garden, we are reminded of the great, powerful influence of women upon the world.' "[20]

The Relief Society Monument to Women, consisting of thirteen life-size statues, is situated in a beautiful garden directly behind the visitors' center of The Church of Jesus Christ of Latter-day Saints in Nauvoo, Illinois. The monument was dedicated on 28–30 June 1978.

THE STANDARD WORKS

Under President Spencer W. Kimball's leadership, three new items were added to the scriptural canon—the first additions to the standard works in nearly three-quarters of a century.

Two of these additions, which became sections 137 and 138 of the Doctrine and Covenants, shed light on the subject of life after death. Concerning their importance, Elder Bruce R. McConkie declared: "Their contents have been known; their provisions have been in force; their principles have been widely taught. But now, at this hour, with their addition to the formal scriptures of the saints, they become a new commandment—they become a new divine pronouncement both to say and to do all that is required in the soul-expanding doctrine of salvation for the dead."[21]

These items explained in greater detail the doctrinal foundations of vicarious work for the dead. Hence their addition to the canon of scripture fittingly anticipated the era of unprecedented temple construction with resulting increase in temple activity, which would characterize the final years of President Kimball's administration.

The issuing of new editions of the scriptures was the second major scripture-related development of President Kimball's administration. In 1979 a new edition of the King James Bible was published. Although the biblical text itself was not changed, this new edition featured an improved footnote system, excerpts from the Joseph Smith Translation, cross-references to related passages in the other standard works, more meaningful chapter headings, a 598-page Topical Guide and concordance, a 194-page dictionary section reflecting unique understanding available through latter-day revelation, and a gazetteer and maps. Two years later a new edition of the triple combination—the Book of Mormon, the Doctrine and Covenants, and the Pearl of Great Price—became a companion to the new edition of the Bible. It contained many of the same improvements.

Elder Boyd K. Packer said of the new scriptures: "The stick or record of Judah—the Old Testament and the New Testament—and the stick or record of Ephraim—the Book of Mormon, which is another testament of Jesus Christ—are now woven together in such a way that as you pore over one you are drawn to the other; as you learn from one you are enlightened by the other. They are indeed one in our hands. Ezekiel's prophecy now stands fulfilled."[22]

On 15 October 1982, Max Chopnick, vice president of the Laymen's National Bible Committee, presented to the Church an award for outstanding service to the Bible cause. The award was accepted by President Gordon B. Hinckley.

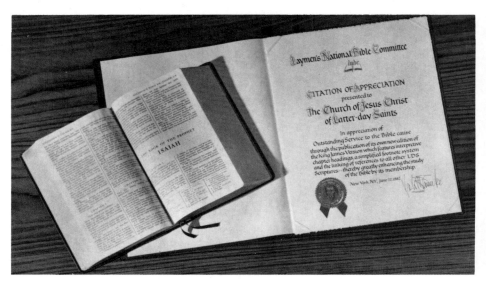

These publications were the result of at least a decade of intense effort. A committee consisting of Elders Thomas S. Monson, Boyd K. Packer, and Bruce R. McConkie gave constant direction to the project. Elders Marvin J. Ashton and Howard W. Hunter also served for a time. They were assisted by a task committee made up of three members of the BYU religion faculty, who in turn were assisted by hundreds of volunteers. Those who worked on this project testified that at key points the right person was available to provide expertise and enable the work to move forward. Elder Packer regarded these new editions of the scriptures with their improved study aids as extremely important:

"With the passing of years, these scriptures will produce successive generations of faithful Christians who know the Lord Jesus Christ and are disposed to obey His will.

". . . They will develop a gospel scholarship beyond that which their forebears could achieve. . . .

"As the generations roll on, this will be regarded, in the perspective of history, as the crowning achievement in the administration of President Spencer W. Kimball. . . .

"These references from the four volumes of scripture constitute the most comprehensive compilation of scriptural information on the mission and teachings of the Lord Jesus Christ that has ever been assembled in the history of the world."[23]

With the continued expansion of the Church, President Kimball and other Church leaders increasingly took measures to meet the needs of the Saints worldwide.

ENDNOTES

1. "First Presidency Meets with News Media," *Church News,* 5 Jan. 1974, p. 14.

2. In Conference Report, Oct. 1943, pp. 15–16.

3. Spencer W. Kimball, *One Silent Sleepless Night* (Salt Lake City: Bookcraft, 1975), pp. 35, 51.

4. Russell Marion Nelson, *From Heart to Heart* (Salt Lake City: Russell M. Nelson, 1979), pp. 164–65.

5. In Conference Report, Oct. 1977, p. 38; or *Ensign,* Nov. 1977, p. 26.

6. Spencer W. Kimball, " 'When the World Will Be Converted,' " *Ensign,* Oct. 1974, pp. 5, 7, 14.

7. In W. Grant Bangerter, Conference Report, Oct. 1977, p. 39; or *Ensign,* Nov. 1977, p. 27.

8. See "Diplomatic Affairs Consultant Appointed," *Church News,* 13 Apr. 1974, p. 17.

9. "Poland Dedicated by President Kimball," *Church News,* 17 Sept. 1977, p. 3.

10. See "Gardens to Blossom in Israel," *Church News,* 29 Oct. 1977, p. 3.

11. See "Performers Tour Russia," *Church News,* 15 July 1978, p. 5; "Y Students a Success in China," *Church News,* 11 Aug. 1979, p. 9.

12. See " 'News' Interviews Prophet," *Church News,* 6 Jan. 1979, p. 4.

13. Bruce R. McConkie, "The New Revelation on Priesthood," *Priesthood* (Salt Lake City: Deseret Book Co., 1981), p. 27.

14. " 'News' Interviews Prophet," p. 4.

15. McConkie, "New Revelation on Priesthood," p. 128.

16. In Conference Report, Apr. 1974, pp. 7–9; or *Ensign,* May 1974, pp. 6–8.

17. In Conference Report, Oct. 1974, p. 8; or *Ensign,* Nov. 1974, p. 7.

18. "First Presidency Opposes ERA," *Church News*, 30 Oct. 1976, p. 2.

19. "Women Urged to 'Reach for Stars,' " *Church News*, 23 Sept. 1978, pp. 3, 10.

20. "Nauvoo Park Honors Women," *Church News*, 8 Jul. 1978, p. 3.

21. Bruce R. McConkie, "A New Commandment," *Ensign*, Aug. 1976, p. 8.

22. In Conference Report, Oct. 1982, p. 75; or *Ensign*, Nov. 1982, p. 53.

23. In Conference Report, Oct. 1982, pp. 75–76; or *Ensign*, Nov. 1982, p. 53.

MEETING THE NEEDS OF A WORLDWIDE CHURCH

CHURCH MEMBERSHIP HAD reached 3,321,556 by the time Spencer W. Kimball became president at the end of 1973.[1] This growth accelerated under President Kimball's leadership. By the early 1980s over a quarter of a million new members were being added each year, and in 1982 Church membership passed the five million mark. Such growth within a single decade posed great challenges: How could the General Authorities effectively keep in touch with rapidly expanding numbers of Saints throughout the world? How could Church activities most adequately meet the needs of members living in widely varying circumstances? How could blessings of the temple be placed within their reach? These and similar questions required actions and solutions.

FIRST QUORUM OF THE SEVENTY ORGANIZED AS A GOVERNING CHURCH QUORUM

As growth in Church membership accelerated, there was a corresponding increase in the number of stakes and missions. This meant that there were more stake conferences for the General Authorities to attend and more missions for them to supervise. To meet the challenge of Church expansion, five high priests had been called in 1941 to serve as Assistants to the Twelve. With the Church's continued growth, additional Brethren were called. By 1975 the number of Assistants to the Twelve had reached twenty-three. During these decades added responsibilities were also given to the seven General Authorities who constituted the First Council of the Seventy. In 1961 President David O. McKay announced that these Seventies were to be ordained to the office of high priest because as General Authorities their duties increasingly included such responsibilities as ordaining high priests and setting apart stake presidents.[2] Nevertheless, for the time being, the practice continued of calling into the First Council only those who were currently members of stake seventies quorums.

In 1975, President Spencer W. Kimball announced that the time had come to begin organizing the First Quorum of the Seventy as a General Authorities quorum and that, in addition to the seven presidents, three men were being called to this quorum "to assist in the carrying forth of work of the Lord, especially in the missionary area."[3] All three were Seventies at the time of their call. In the April 1976 general conference, four more were added, three being high priests and one an elder at the time. The First Presidency stated that members of the First Quorum of the Seventy were to have the same authority as Assistants to the Twelve.

At the October 1976 general conference, President Kimball announced a consolidation of Church leadership at the general level. He disclosed that the First Presidency "felt inspired to call all of the Assistants to the Twelve into the First Quorum of the Seventy. . . .

". . . these changes . . . bring to thirty-nine the total number in the First Quorum of the Seventy. . . .

"With this move, the three governing quorums of the Church defined by the revelations,—the First Presidency, the Quorum of the Twelve, and the First Quorum of the Seventy,—have been set in their places as revealed by the Lord. This will make it possible to handle efficiently the present heavy workload and to prepare for the increasing expansion and acceleration of the work, anticipating the day when the Lord will return to take direct charge of His church and kingdom"[4] (see also D&C 107:28). At each of the next several general conferences, more members were added to the First Quorum of the Seventy, which assumed an important role in Church administration.

KEEPING IN TOUCH WITH THE SAINTS THROUGHOUT THE WORLD

While the Seventies were providing needed help at Church headquarters, steps were also being taken to strengthen links with the Church's far-flung local units. This involved two new intermediate levels of administration.

Beginning in 1936, stakes had been grouped into regions in order to coordinate welfare production projects. The functions of these regions were broadened during the 1960s, and Regional Representatives were appointed to supervise these increasingly important units under the direction of the General Authorities. During the 1960s missions were also grouped into areas and placed under the personal supervision of a General Authority. By 1966 eleven of the Brethren were living outside the United States and serving as resident General Authority supervisors.

A key development came in 1984 when the world was divided into thirteen broad areas, each to be headed by an Area Presidency consisting of three members of the First Quorum of the Seventy. This change brought new strength to Church government at the area level by providing the knowledge and experience of the three General Authority members of the presidency in reaching decisions in light of the varying needs and circumstances of the Saints in different parts of the world. President Gordon B. Hinckley, Second Counselor to President Spencer W. Kimball, "emphasized that the Church's growth requires flexibility in administration as the Church pursues its unchanging divine mandate."[5]

The General Authorities were also responsible for administering the numerous and diverse departments and committees at Church headquarters. In 1977, the First Presidency announced a delineation between the responsibility of the Presiding Bishopric for temporal affairs on one hand, and that of the Twelve and Seventy for ecclesiastical and spiritual affairs on the other. Members of the First Quorum of the Seventy received major responsibility for the day-to-day administration of the missionary, temple, and genealogical programs of the Church as well as for the various departments that directed the work of the priesthood quorums and auxiliaries. As the Seventies assumed this responsibility, the Twelve were free to give broader attention to the needs of the Church worldwide.

General conference provided another important link between the General Authorities and the Saints around the world. Bringing local leaders to Church headquarters, however, posed an increasingly heavy financial burden on the Church, and the throngs who had traveled long distances to hear the messages of Church leaders found it more and more difficult to obtain seating in the Salt Lake Tabernacle. Hence, area conferences, which had been inaugurated in 1971, were increased in frequency. Typically these gatherings convened in large auditoriums or sports arenas in the local areas.

Thousands of members traveled from a broad area to attend, often coming from small branches. They gained strength from being part of such a large group and received a spiritual boost from being in the presence of their inspired leaders. Nevertheless, as the Church continued to grow, even conferences at this level became impractical. By the mid-1980s regional or multi-regional conferences became more common and were still attended by a small delegation of General Authorities.

In 1975, President Kimball announced that auxiliary conferences at Church headquarters were being discontinued. They had been held annually by the Relief Society, Young Men and Young Women, and the Sunday School. Instructions to local leaders would now be given in regional meetings.

Similarly, beginning in 1977 general conference was shortened from three days to two. General sessions were scheduled for the first weekend of April and October, respectively. This meant that the spring conferences would no longer necessarily include 6 April, the anniversary of the Church's organization and a traditional general conference date. Limiting the general sessions to the weekends facilitated attendance for stake presidents and others who could not leave employment responsibilities on weekdays. The General Authorities regularly conduct seminars for Regional Representatives on the Friday immediately preceding the general conference weekend.

On a more local level, beginning in 1979 the number of conferences held annually in each stake was reduced from four to two. This was done "to ease the burdens of time, travel and money upon members of the Church."[6] By the mid-1980s members of the Quorum of the Twelve increasingly attended regional or multiregional stake conferences rather than individual stake conferences.

ACTIVITIES STREAMLINED

Church leaders continued to take steps to ensure that the objectives of the Church were met without undue demands on the time or finances of the Saints. A more energy-efficient and therefore more economical design was adopted for meetinghouses. General Authorities also cautioned local leaders not to sponsor youth trips or other elaborate activities that would unduly tax member resources. The Young Men and Young Women organizations had heretofore called music, drama, speech, and sports directors on an on-going basis. In 1977 these persons were released, and a single three-member activities committee was instituted to coordinate all such activities for the entire ward. The purpose of this committee was "to encourage appropriate arts and cultural and recreational activities in the Church." Individuals with special talents were called on a temporary basis to promote specific events, which ranged from fitness contests to musical or theatrical productions for the overall development of the Saints.[7]

Many Latter-day Saints throughout the world found themselves as part of a small group consisting of only two or three families and isolated from other Church members. Obviously these members could not conduct the full programs of a large, fully organized ward. In 1978, therefore, the Church inaugurated a small unit or basic unit program. This program also served Church units in emerging or developing areas of the world, which needed to begin simply and progress through various stages of development. A special handbook explained which officers should be called and which activities conducted at each level of development. A guide for families indicated which meetings should be held if the family were isolated and completely on its own. Such families typically held Church meetings in their own homes, with all family members taking turns speaking and accepting other assignments.

In Portugal, a father and his deacon son regularly held priesthood meetings. A family in East Africa taught their small children to leave the living room and return reverently to the "chapel" a few minutes later. Such isolated Saints gained a strong appreciation for fellowship with other Church members.

Soon after arriving at a new assignment in North Africa, a mother picking up some groceries noticed another North American couple in the store, and they casually exchanged greetings. She recounted, "Just then our son walked up wearing one of his brothers BYU tee shirts. The woman then said, 'Brigham Young University, do you folks happen to be LDS?'

"I told her yes. She said, 'So are we.' I had an instant flood of tears as we embraced, shook hands and all talked at once. We had just experienced a Mormon miracle of instant love and friendship for complete strangers."[8]

Church programs and materials were developed for these isolated groups. Even in areas with fully organized stakes, the simplified program was adopted for small groups of members isolated from the majority by language barriers. Similarly, *Gospel Principles,* one of six manuals specifically developed for use in small units, became popular among Latter-day Saints generally as an excellent compendium of doctrinal teachings. Furthermore, the Church's favorable experience with an abbreviated program for these scattered units provided a precedent for solving the problem of soaring travel and heating costs in the wake of a worldwide energy shortage.

For decades priesthood and Sunday School meetings were held on Sunday mornings, and sacrament meeting was held during the afternoon or evening. Relief Society meeting for women, Primary activities for children, and Mutual Improvement Association instruction and activities for youth were held during the week. In 1980 the basic ward meetings—priesthood, Relief Society, Young Women, Primary, Sunday School, and sacrament meeting—were restructured and consolidated to fit into a single three-hour block on Sunday morning or afternoon. Such long-standing traditions as the Sunday School's half-hour opening exercises were discontinued. The Junior Sunday School was amalgamated into the Primary Association as part of the consolidation. Only a youth activity night, monthly Relief Society home-making meeting, and an occasional activity continued to be held during the week.

This plan reduced the amount of travel required to attend Church meetings and cut the number of days buildings needed to be heated or cooled. This new plan had obvious energy saving advantages, an important consideration at that time. The First Presidency explained, however, that the more enduring consideration was to give families more time for scripture study and other activities at home. The Saints were also encouraged to reach out and become more involved in community service.[9]

GROWTH IN TEMPLE ACTIVITY

The 1970s were only the beginning of an unprecedented era in temple construction and activity. The Washington D.C. Temple was dedicated by President Kimball in 1974. Not only did it include six lecture rooms for presenting the endowment, but it was the second twentieth-century temple to have a large priesthood assembly room on an upper floor, the other being the Los Angeles Temple. A year earlier, the Arizona and St. George temples had closed for renovation. They were redesigned to present the endowment through the use of motion picture equipment. The rebuilding was so extensive that in 1975 these two temples were reopened for public open houses and then rededicated, the first time this had ever been done. The Hawaii and Logan temples were similarly remodeled and rededicated later in the decade.

The year 1975 also brought the announcement of three new temples to be built at Sao Paulo, Brazil, the first in South America; Tokyo, Japan, the first in

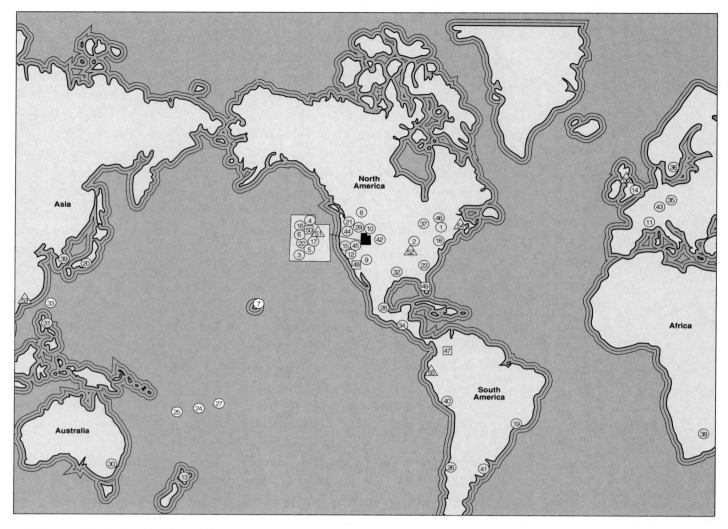

The location of temples throughout the world listed chronologically by their original dedication date.

1. Kirtland Temple
   27 March 1836
2. Nauvoo Temple
   30 April 1846
3. St. George Temple
   6 April 1877
4. Logan Temple
   17 May 1884
5. Manti Temple
   17 May 1888
6. Salt Lake Temple
   6 April 1893
7. Hawaii Temple
   27 November 1919
8. Alberta Temple
   26 August 1923
9. Arizona Temple
   23 October 1923
10. Idaho Falls Temple
    23 September 1945
11. Swiss Temple
    11 September 1955
12. Los Angeles Temple
    11 March 1956
13. New Zealand Temple
    20 April 1958
14. London Temple
    7 September 1958

Asia; and Seattle, Washington, the first in the Pacific Northwest. Latter-day Saints in these areas were full of gratitude as building of the long awaited temples came closer.

"A wave of emotion swept through the Area General Conference in Brazil as President Spencer W. Kimball announced March 1 that a temple would be built in Sao Paulo.

" 'I have an important announcement,' he said, making it the first order of business, even before the opening prayer. . . .

" 'A temple will be built in Brazil,' he said.

"A gasp could be heard across the congregation.

" 'It will be built in Sao Paulo,' the president continued.

"By now tears filled the eyes of many. They openly wept for joy."[10]

The pace of temple construction increased as the 1970s drew to a close. Plans for the Mexico City Temple were announced in 1977, and the following year Church leaders disclosed that the Jordan River Temple would be built in the southern part of the Salt Lake Valley. The year 1980 brought the unprecedented announcement of seven new temples all at once. They were

15. Oakland Temple
17 November 1964

16. Ogden Temple
18 January 1972

17. Provo Temple
9 February 1972

18. Washington D.C. Temple
19 November 1974

19. Sao Paulo Temple
30 October 1978

20. Tokyo Temple
27 October 1980

21. Seattle Temple
17 November 1980

22. Jordan River Temple
16 November 1981

23. Atlanta Georgia Temple
1 June 1983

24. Apia Samoa Temple
5 August 1983

25. Nuku 'alofa Tonga Temple
8 August 1983

26. Santiago Chile Temple
15 September 1983

27. Papeete Tahiti Temple
27 October 1983

28. Mexico City Temple
2 December 1983

29. Boise Idaho Temple
25 May 1984

30. Sydney Australia Temple
20 September 1984

31. Manila Philippines Temple
25 September 1984

32. Dallas Texas Temple
19 October 1984

33. Taipei Taiwan Temple
17 November 1984

34. Guatemala City Temple
14 December 1984

35. Freiburg Germany Temple
29 June 1985

36. Stockholm Sweden Temple
2 July 1985

37. Chicago Illinois Temple
9 August 1985

38. Johannesburg South Africa Temple
24 August 1985

39. Seoul Korea Temple
14 December 1985

40. Lima Peru Temple
10 January 1986

41. Buenos Aires Argentina Temple
17 January 1986

42. Denver Colorado Temple
24 October 1986

43. Frankfurt Germany Temple
28 August 1987

44. Portland Oregon Temple
19 August 1989

45. Las Vegas Nevada Temple
16 December 1989

46. Toronto Ontario Temple
25 August 1990

□ Under Construction
47. Bogota Colombia Temple
48. San Diego California Temple
49. Orlando Florida Temple
50. Bountiful Utah Temple

△ Announced
51. Utah County (no official name yet)
52. St. Louis Missouri Temple
53. Hong Kong Temple
54. Hartford Connecticut Temple
55. Guayaquil Ecuador Temple
56. Preston England Temple

Latter-day Saints plan to build many temples in the future. We believe temple work will be one of the most important things done in the Millennium (see Spencer W. Kimball, in Conference Report, Mar.–Apr. 1979, pp. 3–8 or Ensign, May 1979, pp.4–7).

to be built in Atlanta, Georgia, the first in the southeastern United States; Argentina; Chile; Australia; Tonga; Tahiti; and Western Samoa. President Spencer W. Kimball declared:

"There now begins the most intensive period of temple building in the history of the Church. . . .

"We look to the day, when the sacred ordinances of the Church, performed in the temples, will be available to all members of the Church in convenient locations around the globe."[11]

Consistent with this expectation, Church leaders in the early 1980s announced plans to construct yet more temples, including one in South Africa and another in the German Democratic Republic, East Germany.

Six temples, an unprecedented number, were dedicated during 1983. By mid-1984 there were twenty-one additional temples either being planned or under construction. Completion of these new temples would bring the total to forty-seven, compared to only fifteen in service when President Kimball began his administration. The previous record had been three temples being built at once—when the Salt Lake, Logan, and Manti temples were under construction during the 1880s. Furthermore, for the first time in the Church's history, temples would be located on every continent.

For years many families had sacrificed most of their material possessions in order to make the once-in-a-lifetime trip to the nearest, yet often distant temple. Almost a full year's wages were required for a Tahitian family to travel to the New Zealand Temple. A shoemaker in Costa Rica had to sell his automobile and his entire stock of shoes in order to take his wife and seven children to the Arizona Temple so that their family might be sealed for eternity; during the eight-thousand-mile round trip their group had to sleep in chapel cultural halls each night and change buses every time they crossed into a new country. These and other Saints in similar circumstances were willing to make such sacrifices because of their burning desire to receive the sacred blessings available only in temples.

In some countries, such as Korea, government restriction on travel prevented couples from leaving the country at the same time, making it impossible for them to be sealed. In other cases, parents with limited funds had to make the painful decision as to which of their children they would take with them to the temple to be sealed. As the new temples began to dot the earth, such sacrifices were alleviated.

The expansion in temple building was accompanied by significant improvements in methods of gathering genealogical information. The computer became an indispensable tool in genealogical research. In 1961, when more names were needed for temple work, Genealogical Society employees extracted vital information from selected parish and civil records. The computer then quickly alphabetized and printed these names. Beginning in 1969 Church members were permitted to submit individual names for computer processing rather than having to first group them into families. This greater freedom allowed the Saints to accelerate their genealogical activity, so thousands of more names were added each year to the Church's growing computerized International Genealogical Index.

By the mid-1970s more than three million endowments for the dead were being performed annually, but less than one million names were being supplied by the Latter-day Saints' own genealogical research. The difference was being made up through the records tabulation program by staff members of the Genealogical Department at Church headquarters. General Authorities felt the need to increase the amount of temple work, but they felt a greater need to expand the Saints' role in providing names for temple ordinances. President Spencer W. Kimball declared:

"I feel the same sense of urgency about temple work for the dead as I do about the missionary work for the living, since they are basically one and the same. I have told my brethren of the General Authorities that this work for the dead is constantly on my mind.

"The First Presidency and the Council of the Twelve recently gave careful consideration as to how we can lengthen our stride in this tremendously important responsibility. We announce a twofold emphasis.

"First, all members should write a personal history and participate in a family organization. Also, we want to emphasize again and place squarely upon the shoulders of these individuals and their families the obligation to complete the four-generation program. . . .

"Secondly, we are introducing a Church-wide program of extracting names from genealogical records. Church members may now render second-mile service through participating in this regard in extracting these names in this program supervised by the priesthood leaders at the local level."[12]

Hence, rather than several individual members searching endless hours in the same records, volunteers would extract all names from the original record. These names would then be alphabetized by the computer for easy reference. The Saints' involvement in this extraction program would help achieve the goal of each temple district supplying its own names for temple ordinance work. To this end, temple service centers were established in conjunction with the São Paulo, Tokyo, and Mexico City temples to expedite the local processing of names for temple work.

SPENCER, THE BELOVED

Even though his relatively poor health had led some people to predict that Spencer W. Kimball's presidency would not bring many significant accomplishments, his twelve years as president were filled with developments that would have a far-reaching impact. The privilege of holding the priesthood was extended to all races. New editions of the scriptures included important study aids and additions to the scriptural canon. The First Quorum of the Seventy took its revealed place in Church administration.

Gordon B. Hinckley (1910–) was called as an Assistant to the Twelve Apostles in April 1958. Three years later he was called to the Quorum of the Twelve Apostles, and in July 1981 he was called to serve as a counselor to President Spencer W. Kimball in the First Presidency of the Church.

The pattern of Church meetings was streamlined. Temples in unprecedented numbers provided the highest gospel blessings to Latter-day Saints around the world.

President Kimball's personal life matched the Church's rapid pace. The tempo of his life slowed, however, as his health declined. During this time President Kimball had been inspired to call Elder Gordon B. Hinckley as an additional counselor in the First Presidency. For over four decades President Hinckley had held major responsibility for directing the missionary program and other Church activities. He became an Assistant to the Twelve in 1958 and was chosen as a member of the Quorum of the Twelve Apostles three years later. His appointment to the First Presidency assumed greater importance when President N. Eldon Tanner became ill and died in 1982, and President Marion G. Romney also became seriously ill and incapacitated. Under these circumstances President Kimball increasingly delegated responsibility for the day-to-day functions of the Church to President Hinckley.

Since this was a period when many temples were completed, President Hinckley traveled to far-flung places to dedicate them. As a counselor in the First Presidency, he dedicated eighteen temples, more than any other person in the history of the Church had done. In this labor, President Hinckley was merely continuing the selfless service of his lengthy ministry. Elder Boyd K. Packer declared of him: "No man of this generation has traveled so many miles, to so many places, with so single a purpose—to preach the gospel, to minister to the Saints, to see to the redemption of the dead."[13]

Spencer W. Kimball died 5 November 1985, following a lengthy illness, and was deeply missed by the millions who had so gratefully sustained him as prophet, seer, and revelator. Speaking of President Kimball, President Hinckley declared: "For forty-two years he served as Apostle and prophet. His moving example of sincere humility, his outreaching love for people, his quiet and earnest declarations of faith have touched all of us. The majesty of his life was found in its simplicity. There was never any of the ostentatious, the boastful, the proud evident in his character. Yet there was an excellence that shone like gold. He was a man from whose life the husk of mediocrity had been winnowed by the hand of God. I loved him with that love which men in the service of the Lord come to feel and know."[14]

In like spirit, Elder Neal A. Maxwell affirmed, "It is not only appropriate but necessary to use some superlatives to describe the ministry of President Spencer Woolley Kimball. . . . His many accomplishments already vie with each other for preeminence in our memories. . . .

". . . There is a special and discernible dimension of affection for and identification with President Kimball." Hence, he believed, this prophet might truly be remembered as Spencer, the beloved.[15]

ENDNOTES

1. See Conference Report, Apr. 1974, p. 27; or *Ensign*, May 1974, p. 20.

2. See Conference Report, Oct. 1961, p. 90.

3. In Conference Report, Oct. 1975, p. 3; or *Ensign*, Nov. 1975, p. 4.

4. In Conference Report, Oct. 1976, p. 10; or *Ensign*, Nov. 1976, p. 9.

5. "Area Presidencies Called as Church Modifies Geographical Administration," *Ensign*, Aug. 1984, p. 75.

6. In "Stake Conferences to Be Semi-annual," *Church News*, 1 Apr. 1978, p. 4.

7. "New Activities Committee," *Church News*, 28 May 1977, pp. 8–9.

8. "Unique Mission Serves World," *Church News*, 1 Feb. 1975, p. 12; see also "Mission Organized to Aid 'Unattached,' " *Church News*, 16 Dec. 1972, pp. 4, 6; "Church Family Style in Tanzanian Home," *Church News*, 22 Feb. 1975, p. 6.

9. See "Meeting Schedule Approved," *Church News*, 2 Feb. 1980, p. 3.

10. "Area Conference in Brazil," *Church News*, 8 Mar. 1975, p. 3.

11. In Jay M. Todd, "Report of the Regional Representatives' Seminar," *Ensign*, May 1980, p. 99.

12. In Conference Report, Apr. 1978, p. 4; or *Ensign*, May 1978, p. 4; see also *Church News*, 22 Apr. 1978, p. 3.

13. Boyd K. Packer, "President Gordon B. Hinckley, First Counselor," *Ensign*, Feb. 1986, p. 7.

14. In Conference Report, Apr. 1986, p. 61; or *Ensign*, May 1986, p. 46.

15. Neal A. Maxwell, "Spencer, the Beloved: Leader—Servant," *Ensign*, Dec. 1985, p. 8.

A PERIOD OF CHALLENGE AND GROWTH

President Ezra Taft Benson (1899–)

FOLLOWING THE PATTERN of nearly a hundred years, the Quorum of the Twelve met the day after the funeral of President Spencer W. Kimball and sustained the senior Apostle, Ezra Taft Benson, to preside over the Church.

President Benson at age eighty-six was ordained President of the Church—forty-two years after he became an Apostle. He called Gordon B. Hinckley and Thomas S. Monson as his counselors. At age fifty-eight, President Monson was the youngest man to be called to the First Presidency in over a hundred years. When the new First Presidency was announced, President Benson emphasized that the major purpose of the Church was to bring people to Jesus Christ. He declared, "My heart has been filled with an overwhelming love and compassion for all members of the Church and our Heavenly Father's children everywhere. I love all our Father's children of every color, creed, and political persuasion."[1]

THE PREPARATION OF A PROPHET

Ezra Taft Benson was born in the farming community of Whitney, Idaho, in 1899, the first of eleven children. He bore the same name as his great grandfather, who served in the Quorum of the Twelve from 1846 to 1869. "T," as he was known, began farm work at age four, and at age fourteen he shouldered increased responsibility when his father began a full-time mission. Later he attended Utah State Agricultural College in Logan, Utah, where he met his future wife, Flora Amussen. They married after both had returned from missions. He went on a mission to Great Britain, and she went to the Hawaiian Islands.

Ezra Taft Benson graduated with honors from Brigham Young University, and earned a master's degree in agricultural economics from Iowa State University. After returning to Idaho, Ezra Taft Benson came to be highly respected as a county agriculture agent and later as an extension economist in the state capital in Boise, Idaho. In 1939 he moved to Washington, D.C., as executive secretary of the National Council of Farmer Cooperatives. He also served as stake president in both Boise and Washington, D.C.

Elder Benson's labors as a member of the Quorum of the Twelve for over forty years were illustrious. He was called to the Twelve along with Spencer W. Kimball. When they became General Authorities in October

1943, the Church had only 837,000 members and 146 stakes. In 1946, Elder Benson went as a mission president to war-torn Europe, where he succeeded in reestablishing contact with the European Saints, providing needed welfare supplies to the stricken members, and resuming missionary work. This was a particularly memorable experience for Elder Benson to express the compassion he feels for others, which he is often recognized for.

In 1952 the President-elect of the United States, Dwight D. Eisenhower, asked Church authorities if it would be possible for Elder Benson to become Secretary of Agriculture in his cabinet. President David O. McKay encouraged Elder Benson to accept the appointment and subsequently blessed him that he would have clear vision to see the needs of the nation and to be fearless in defense of the Constitution against subversive elements threatening the nation's freedoms. For the next eight years, which he described as a "cross fire," Elder Benson served in the United States presidential cabinet. He traveled over eight hundred thousand miles in forty-four countries, making many friends for the Church with his example of devoutness and integrity. Later he wrote a book, which he entitled *Cross Fire*, recounting those political years and his many opportunities and experiences.

Returning to full-time Church service in 1961, Elder Benson was in constant demand as a speaker. During the mid-1960s he again presided over the European Mission, and later in the decade he presided over the missions in Asia. In 1973 he was sustained as President of the Twelve and served in that capacity for twelve years. Elder Mark E. Petersen, a close colleague in that council, described Elder Benson's leadership:

"He has led the quorum with great efficiency, constant inspiration, and a never-ceasing flow of love for his Brethren. Their well being has been a constant concern. Always he has kept their best interests in mind, together with 'what is best for the Kingdom,' as he has assigned them to their responsibilities in various parts of the world.

"Abiding harmony characterized his administration in the Twelve."[2]

In 1983, President Benson completed his book *Come unto Christ*, which emphasized such themes as "Walk in His Steps," "What Would Jesus Do?" "What Manner of Men Ought We to Be?" "Lead Your Children to Christ," "Preach the Gospel to Every Nation," and "Feed My Sheep," thus foreshadowing some of his principal teachings as prophet of God.[3]

COME UNTO CHRIST

Though the Church has always reached out to its disaffected members, President Benson issued a special plea to come back to Christ. This is a determined, continuing effort to bring the lost sheep back to the fold. In their Christmas message of 1985, the First Presidency wrote, "We are aware of some who are inactive, of others who have become critical and are prone to find fault, and of those who have been disfellowshipped or excommunicated because of serious transgressions. To all such we reach out in love. . . . Come back. Come back and feast at the table of the Lord, and taste again the sweet and satisfying fruits of fellowship with the saints."[4]

Part of this appeal was to those who had left the Church over some disagreement with the doctrines or practices and had in some instances joined anti-Mormon movements. Since the mid-1970s such groups have grown in size and intensity. But instead of arguing and attacking in the public press, as the opponents of the Church were prone to do, Church leaders encouraged the Saints to pray for their enemies and to help return them to the truth through love.

THE BOOK OF MORMON, KEYSTONE OF OUR RELIGION

President Benson counseled the Latter-day Saints to read and use the Book of Mormon as the chief means to come unto Christ. In nearly every address he has given as prophet, he reemphasized the importance of the Book of Mormon, quoting Joseph Smith's statement: "I told the brethren that the Book of Mormon was the most correct of any book on earth, and the keystone of our religion, and a man would get nearer to God by abiding by its precepts, than by any other book."[5] President Benson explained that the Church was still under the condemnation pronounced by the Lord in 1831 for not using the Book of Mormon as they should (see D&C 84:54–57). President Benson declared, "Now we not only need to *say* more about the Book of Mormon, but we need to *do* more with it. . . .

". . . The Book of Mormon has not been, nor is it yet, the center of our personal study, family teaching, preaching, and missionary work. Of this we must repent."[6]

The response to President Benson's plea was immediate and ongoing. The prophet received numerous letters from Saints, both old and young, who accepted the challenge to read and study the Book of Mormon. The number of copies of the Book of Mormon distributed during the year 1986 doubled from the previous year, reaching a total of 2,911,916, 15 percent of which included members's photos and testimonies provided through the family-to-family Book of Mormon program.[7] President Benson and his family led the way in personalizing "dozens of copies of the Book of Mormon each month."[8] In the April 1987 general conference, he called upon the Lord to bless the Saints with an "increased desire to flood the earth with the Book of Mormon."[9]

DEALING WITH CURRENT ISSUES

As previous Church Presidencies had done, the First Presidency gave inspired counsel and leadership on numerous current issues.

During the early 1980s a severe drought hit much of northeastern Africa, causing the malnutrition and death of millions of people in several countries. Elder M. Russell Ballard, of the First Quorum of the Seventy, and Glenn L. Pace, managing director of Welfare Services, went on assignment to Africa in March 1985 to inspect conditions and see what the Church might do to assist the multitudes of hungry people. Participating in the national day of fasting in America on 24 November 1985, members of the Church contributed $3.8 million. Proceeds of the fast combined with those of a similar fast the previous January raised the donations of Church members to more than $10 million. Early in January 1986, President Ezra Taft Benson traveled to Washington, D.C., to install a new temple presidency and create a new stake. While in the nation's capital, he met with President Ronald Reagan and reported on the contributions of the Saints to the stricken people in Africa.[10]

Throughout the 1980s the Church pressed forward with its project of creating the Brigham Young University Jerusalem Center. Opposition to this large educational center arose from orthodox Jewish groups who feared the Latter-day Saints were planning to use the center as a base for proselyting. Members of the First Presidency and the Twelve, as well as BYU President Jeffrey R. Holland, met repeatedly with government, religious, and educational leaders in Israel and the United States who had influence with the Israelis. They assured all concerned parties that the Jerusalem Center would participate only in educational activities and that BYU students would be committed to not engage in any form of missionary work during their stay in Israel.

The Jerusalem Center is located on a five-acre site on Mount Scopus. The center is used by Brigham Young University for its study abroad programs. The center was first occupied in March 1987. It was dedicated in May 1989 by President Howard W. Hunter, President of the Quorum of the Twelve.

Throughout his ministry President Benson has spoken and written frequently on family solidarity and the ways individual family members could fulfill their God-given responsibilities even in the midst of wickedness. In the October 1985 general conference, a few weeks before the death of

President Spencer W. Kimball, President Benson urged the men of the Church to magnify their calling as fathers, using the example of righteous fathers in the Book of Mormon as their guide. As President of the Church, Ezra Taft Benson delivered in sequence pointed messages to the young men, the young women, and the mothers of the Church, and he spoke again in October 1987 to the fathers of the Church.

"You are to be the royal army of the Lord in the last days," he told the young men in the priesthood session of the April 1986 general conference. The prophet urged them to draw close to their mothers and to obey their fathers, emulating their manly qualities. He pleaded with them to daily read and ponder the scriptures, especially the Book of Mormon. He counseled them that every young man should obtain his patriarchal blessing, attend his meetings, participate in Scouting, attend seminary, and in any other righteous way prepare for missionary service. "The Lord wants every young man to serve a full-time mission. Currently, only a fifth of the eligible young men in the Church are serving full-time missions. This is not pleasing to the Lord. We can do better. We *must* do better."[11]

Six months later, President Benson gave similar counsel to the young women stating, "Give me a young woman who loves home and family, who reads and ponders the scriptures daily, who has a burning testimony of the Book of Mormon. . . . Give me a young woman who is virtuous and who has maintained her personal purity, who will not settle for less than a temple marriage, and I will give you a young woman who will perform miracles for the Lord now and throughout eternity."[12] On numerous other occasions, President Benson spoke to large groups of young people, conveying his love to them and urging them to utilize the Book of Mormon and live honorable and virtuous lives.

On 22 February 1987, President Benson addressed the mothers in Zion in a fireside for parents broadcast over the Church's satellite network. He affirmed, "There is no more noble work than that of a good and God-fearing mother. . . .

"Young mothers and fathers, with all my heart I counsel you not to postpone having your children, being co-creators with our Father in Heaven." He explained that the Lord's way of rearing children was far different than the world's way. Recognizing that circumstances required some sisters to work outside the home, the prophet nevertheless reaffirmed that women in the Church rightfully " 'have claim on their husbands for their maintenance.' . . . The counsel of the Church has always been for mothers to spend their full time in the home in rearing and caring for their children." In addition, President Benson encouraged mothers to spend effective time with their children.[13] The Church also published *A Parent's Guide* designed to help parents in teaching moral values and responsibilities to their children.

President Gordon B. Hinckley of the First Presidency addressed the major topic of AIDS (Acquired Immune Deficiency Syndrome) in a priesthood conference address:

AIDS is "a plague of fearsome dimensions. . . .

"We, with others, hope that discoveries will make possible both prevention and healing from this dread affliction. But regardless of such discoveries, the observance of one clearly understandable and divinely given rule would do more than all else to check this epidemic. That is chastity before marriage and total fidelity after marriage. . . .

". . . Our concern for the bitter fruit of sin is coupled with Christ-like sympathy for its victims, innocent or culpable."[14]

The First Presidency also spoke out on another moral issue of the day—public lotteries. A majority of states in the United States as well as several other countries had either legalized lotteries or were considering doing so. The Brethren hastened to urge members of the Church to oppose public lotteries in their respective localities. President Thomas S. Monson explained, "All too often lotteries only add to the problems of the financially disadvantaged by taking money from them and giving nothing of value in return. The poor and the elderly become victims of the inducements that are held out to purchase lottery tickets."[15]

A most unusual public issue affecting the Church was the Mark Hofmann bombing case in Salt Lake City in October 1985. Beginning in 1980, Mr. Hofmann had sold, donated, or traded several documents allegedly connected with historical events to the Church. Some of them received considerable public acclaim, such as the Anthon Transcript, allegedly the document Martin Harris had shown Charles Anthon, and the Martin Harris letter to William W. Phelps, which cast Joseph Smith in a role heavily involved in folk magic and treasure seeking. In October 1985 homemade bombs tragically killed Steven F. Christensen, a bishop and documents collector, and Kathleen Sheets, wife of Christensen's former business partner, J. Gary Sheets. A third bomb severely injured Mark Hofmann a day later.

After over a year of uproar in the press concerning the documents, document dealing, and responsibility for the bombings, Hofmann, who had been indicted for the bombings, confessed to the murders as part of a plea bargain arrangement and was sent to the Utah State Penitentiary. Hofmann also confessed that he had forged documents connected with LDS Church history. Elder Dallin H. Oaks explained, "These forgeries and their associated lies grew out of their author's deliberate attempt to rewrite the early history of The Church of Jesus Christ of Latter-day Saints."[16]

From the beginning, Church leaders had expressed caution about the documents. "President Gordon B. Hinckley repeatedly cautioned that the Church did not know whether these documents were authentic."[17]

Elder Dallin H. Oaks also stated: "The news media are particularly susceptible to conveying erroneous information about facts, including historical developments that are based on what I have called scientific uncertainties. This susceptibility obviously applies to newly discovered documents whose authenticity turns on an evaluation of handwriting, paper, ink, and so on. As readers we should be skeptical about the authenticity of such documents, especially when we are unsure where they were found, or who had custody of them for 150 years. Newly found, historically important documents can be extremely valuable, so there is a powerful incentive for those who own them to advocate and support their authenticity. The recent spectacular fraud involving the so-called Hitler diaries reminds us of this and should convince us to be cautious."[18]

At the conclusion of the Hofmann trial, the Church's Public Communications department issued a statement which included the following:

"We extend again our heartfelt sympathies to the families and associates of all whose lives have been so deeply affected by the bombings and related events of the past months. It is our hope that the healing process may now be hastened for those who have suffered these tragedies. . . .

"Like other document collectors throughout the nation, the church has relied on competent authorities in document acquisition and with the others has been a victim of the fraudulent activities which have now been acknowledged in the courtroom."[19]

PRIESTHOOD CHANGES AND NEW DIRECTION

In October 1986, President Ezra Taft Benson announced that seventies quorums in the stakes would be discontinued. Stake seventies were instructed to join with their ward elders quorum, and stake presidents were instructed to "determine who among such brethren should be ordained to the office of high priest."[20] Until this time, many members had felt that only seventies needed to be concerned with missionary work. With the new policy, new instructions were given to upgrade the stake missionary force and to involve all members of the Church in the missionary program. These changes were made "to provide a renewed impetus in missionary work throughout the stakes of the Church."[21] With the dissolving of all stake seventies quorums, the only quorum of seventy that would continue to function in the Church is the First Quorum of the Seventy, the third presiding quorum over the Church.

Church leaders continued to promote the need for more missionaries. Priesthood leaders were charged to pray about each single elder and older couple and then extend a call to them from the Lord to participate in missionary service. The Brethren also encouraged the calling of highly motivated adult leaders to increase the percentage of young men prepared to enter the mission field at the proper age.

A greater emphasis was also placed on ensuring that new converts received the help they needed. Missionaries, particularly stake missionaries, were assigned to continue visiting new members of the Church for several weeks until they had received appropriate Church callings and adult males had received the Aaronic Priesthood. Ward mission leaders utilized a new convert baptism checklist in priesthood executive committee meetings and ward council meetings to coordinate fellowshipping activities for new converts.

Bishops were given greater responsibility in coordinating reactivation efforts. Elder Marvin J. Ashton of the Twelve urged, "The Bishop must get out of the chair in his office and seek the lost sheep."[22] Bishops were charged to hold priesthood executive committee meetings and the ward council meetings weekly. "These meetings should focus on people more than on programs, calendaring and activities. This requires less emphasis on 'administering' and more emphasis on 'ministering.' " Bishops were also encouraged to use ward priesthood meetings as required to train their fellow priesthood holders in their duties to be shepherds of the flock.[23]

The program of home teaching, which had been upgraded from "ward teaching" in 1964 during the great correlation era of the Church, received new emphasis as the best means of reaching less-active members. High priests, who had gained maturity through many years of service in the Church, were called, where appropriate, to fellowship prospective and inactive elders and their families through home teaching. In his charge to home teachers, President Benson declared:

"Do not settle for mediocrity in this great priesthood program of home teaching. Be an excellent home teacher in every facet of the work. Be a real shepherd of your flock. . . .

"Remember, both the quality and quantity of home teaching are essential in being an effective home teacher."[24]

Church leaders also recognized that genealogy was considered difficult by most members of the Church. Elder James E. Faust of the Quorum of the Twelve explained, "We are trying to simplify and demystify the seeking and finding of our ancestors. We are also hoping to make it easier for everyone with little training to find his or her own forefathers and receive the temple ordinances in their behalf."[25] Simpler family group sheets, pedigree charts, and name submission procedures were implemented to assist in this objective. In 1987 the Church changed the name Genealogy to Family History. Ward consultants were called to go to the Saints' homes and help in family history work. A new motto arose: Take an ancestor to the temple. A new booklet, entitled *Come unto Christ through Temple Ordinances and Covenants*, was produced to be used by ward family history classes. This replaced *From You to Your Ancestors*. The new booklet provided information to help members "prepare to receive their own endowments and sealings." It also provided an "overview of the simplified family history resources available."[26]

Charles Ora Card (1839–1906) crossed the plains from Nauvoo to Utah when he was sixteen years old. He helped settle Logan, Utah, where he later superintended the construction of the tabernacle and temple in Logan. He then went on to Canada, where his influence is greatly found.

ANNIVERSARY CELEBRATIONS

In 1987 the Church celebrated four anniversaries that pertained to the restoration of the gospel and the charge to take it to all the world. The first of these was in recognition of the pioneering efforts of the early Saints who settled along Lee's Creek, Alberta Province, Canada, to found the city of Cardston. In 1886, Charles Ora Card, president of the Cache Stake, was commissioned by President John Taylor to find a place of refuge and asylum to the north. In 1886, Brother Card went into Canada, returned and reported favorably on the prospects, and then went back to Canada to make a permanent settlement in the early spring of 1887. By May the first sod had been turned and crops planted.

In an attempt to understand the contribution of the early Latter-day Saint settlers in Western Canada, the University of Alberta sponsored a three-day conference entitled "The Mormon Presence in Canada." The conference, meeting 6–9 May 1987, was addressed by participants from both without and within the Church. On 1 August, President Ezra Taft Benson was honored as grand marshal of the Cardston centennial parade. The following day the prophet spoke to seven thousand people on the grounds of the beautiful Alberta Temple.

The commemoration of the anniversary of the opening of missionary work in the British Isles received wide media attention both in the United States and in Great Britain. President Gordon B. Hinckley gave the keynote address early in the year at a special BYU symposium on this event. In his address he described how in mid-July 1837, Elder Heber C. Kimball had arrived at the docks in Liverpool, England, and enthusiastically jumped the final six feet to shore. Three days later, Elder Kimball was in nearby Preston where a wonderful harvest of souls commenced, a harvest that has had an astonishing effect upon the history of the Church from those days to the present. Nearly 100,000 converts over the years have immigrated from Britain to gather with the Church in America. The British Isles have 140,000 members in four hundred wards and branches.

To focus upon the work of the early British missionaries and members, the Church sponsored a series of important events. Prior to a weekend of area conferences, the Church hosted an anniversary banquet for four hundred guests at London's prestigious Savoy Hotel. In attendance were General Authorities, local Church leadership, and well-known LDS sports and entertainment personalities. British political and business leaders, including former Prime Minister Edward Heath, paid public recognition to the importance of the Latter-day Saint movement. A special greeting from United States President Ronald Reagan was shown on video. On 26 July, area conferences were held in six different locations in England, Ireland, northern Ireland, Wales, and Scotland with over thirty-five thousand people in attendance. In addition, eight markers drawing attention to important Church historical sites were dedicated throughout Britain. The combination of meetings, historical conventions, and extensive coverage in the Church and public media increased Church members' awareness of the struggle and success of these early missionaries.

From 24 July through 1 August, the Hill Cumorah pageant was held at the Hill Cumorah in the Palmyra, New York, area. It was the fiftieth annual run of this production, which has attracted hundreds of thousands of visitors since its inception in 1937 when Eastern States mission president Don B. Colton organized a committee to produce a pageant. The first pageant was called "America's Witness for Christ" and had a cast of about seventy. Fifty years later the pageant includes a six hundred member cast and a crew of fifty. During 1987 about one hundred thousand people attended the pageant. Approximately 60 percent of them were nonmembers.[27]

During 1987 Latter-day Saints in the United States joined with fellow citizens to celebrate the bicentennial observance of the nation's Constitution. Inasmuch as the Doctrine and Covenants affirms the inspired origin of the principles written into the Constitution (see D&C 98:6, 101:80, 109:54), Church leaders promoted active participation in this national commemoration. The First Presidency called Elder L. Tom Perry, of the Quorum of the Twelve, and Elders Robert L. Backman and Hugh W. Pinnock, both of the presidency of the First Quorum of the Seventy, to serve as a committee in organizing the Church's participation in the bicentennial event.[28] President Benson took several opportunities to speak and write about his love for the Constitution and urged a careful study of it. To implement this, a special packet with three home evening lessons on the subject of the Constitution was given to U.S. Church members.

In further support of the bicentennial celebrations, Church choruses participated in several major public events. In July 1987 the 350-voice Mormon Youth Symphony and Chorus represented the state of Utah with a series of five well-attended concerts in the eastern United States. Their concert was also presented to a capacity audience in the Salt Lake Tabernacle on 17 September with a greeting by Utah's governor, Norman H. Bangerter. The Mormon Tabernacle Choir sang at the nationally televised "We the People, 200 Constitution Gala" broadcast from Convention Hall in Philadelphia on 17 September. That morning, as the Constitution Parade began, the choir sang the national anthem in front of Independence Hall. Many wards and stakes produced musicals, skits, and dramas reflecting the priceless values found in the Constitution.

The administration of President Ezra Taft Benson has been marked by a renewal of spiritual vigor in the families and congregations of the Saints as they strive to use the Book of Mormon more effectively in understanding and fulfilling their roles upon the earth. It has been a period of challenge and growth as well as a time of reflection on the great events that have transpired in this dispensation and have so greatly affected the lives of the Latter-day Saints.

ENDNOTES

1. Don L. Searle, "President Ezra Taft Benson Ordained Thirteenth President of the Church," *Ensign*, Dec. 1985, p. 5.

2. Mark E. Petersen "President Ezra Taft Benson," *Ensign*, Jan. 1986, pp. 4–5.

3. See Ezra Taft Benson, *Come unto Christ* (Salt Lake City: Deseret Book Co., 1983).

4. "An Invitation to Come Back," *Church News*, 22 Dec. 1985, p. 3.

5. *History of the Church*, 4:461; see also Book of Mormon introduction.

6. In Conference Report, Apr. 1986, p. 4; or *Ensign*, May 1986, p. 5.

7. See "Missionaries Number 33,000," *Church News*, 14 Mar. 1987, p. 3.

8. *Deseret News 1987 Church Almanac* (Salt Lake City: Deseret News, 1986), p. 134.

9. In Conference Report, Apr. 1987, p. 108; or *Ensign*, May 1987, p. 85; see also Conference Report, Oct. 1988, pp. 3–5; or *Ensign*, Nov. 1988, pp. 4–6.

10. See "Day of Fasting for Africa Yields $6 Million in Aid," *Church News*, 14 Apr. 1985, p. 19; "Prophet Is 'At Home' in Capital," *Church News*, 12 Jan. 1986, p. 3.

11. In Conference Report, Apr. 1986, pp. 55, 57; or *Ensign*, May 1986, pp. 43–44.

12. "To the Young Women of the Church," *Ensign*, Nov. 1986, p. 84.

13. *To the Mothers in Zion* (pamphlet, 1987), pp. 1–3, 5, 8.

14. In Conference Report, Apr. 1987, pp. 57–58; or *Ensign*, May 1987, pp. 46–47.

15. In "Church Opposes Government-sponsored Gambling," *Ensign*, Nov. 1986, pp. 104–5.

16. Dallin H. Oaks, "Recent Events Involving Church History and Forged Documents," *Ensign*, Oct. 1987, p. 63. Scores of fraudulent documents were either produced or altered by Mark Hofmann. Some documents, such as the McLellin collection, never even existed. The following documents are among those known to have been forged:

Charles Anthon transcript

Joseph Smith III blessing, dated 17 Jan. 1844

White notes—Early handwritten currency carrying the signatures of three Brethren, dated 1849

Lucy Mack Smith letter, dated 23 Jan. 1829

David Whitmer letter to Walter Conrad, dated 13 Jan. 1873

Joseph Smith letter to Josiah Stowell, dated 18 June 1825

Martin Harris letter to W. W. Phelps, dated 23 Oct. 1830

E. B. Grandin Book of Mormon contract, dated 17 Aug. 1829

Peter and David Whitmer letter to Bithel Todd, dated 12 Aug. 1828

Joseph Smith letter to Jonathan Dunham, dated 27 June 1844

Solomon Spaulding-Sidney Rigdon land deed, dated 1822

Joseph Smith letter to Hyrum Smith, dated May 1838

17. Oaks, "Recent Events Involving Church History," p. 69.

18. Dallin H. Oaks, "Reading Church History," in Doctrine and Covenants and Church History *Symposium Speeches* (Salt Lake City: The Church of Jesus Christ of Latter-day Saints, 1985, p. 1; see also Oaks, "Recent Events Involving Church History," p. 69.

19. In "LDS Leaders Offer Sympathies and Hope for a Swift Healing," *Deseret News*, 24 Jan. 1987, p. A-3.

20. In Conference Report, Oct. 1986, p. 64; or *Ensign*, Nov. 1986, p. 97.

21. "Stake Seventies Quorums Discontinued," *Ensign*, Nov. 1986, p. 97.

22. "LDS Leaders Stress Missionary Work, Present New Home-teaching Guidelines," *Deseret News*, 4 Apr. 1987, p. A-2.

23. "Come unto Christ," *Church News*, 11 Apr. 1987, p. 5; see also "Key Concepts to Help Leaders," *Church News*, 4 July 1987, p. 9.

24. In Conference Report, Apr. 1987, pp. 62–63; or *Ensign*, May 1987, p. 51.

25. In "Church Bears Glad Tidings," *Church News*, 4 July 1987, p. 10.

26. "Department Clarifies Use of New Booklet," *Church News*, 26 Sept. 1987, p. 4.

27. See "Hill Cumorah Spectacular Celebrates Its Fiftieth Year," *Church News*, 25 July 1987, pp. 6–7.

28. See "Committee to Guide Church's Constitutional Celebration," *Church News*, 16 May 1987, p. 3.

CHAPTER FORTY-SEVEN

THE DESTINY OF THE CHURCH

W HILE THE PROPHET JOSEPH SMITH and Oliver Cowdery were translating the Book of Mormon, the Lord, in a revelation to them, tenderly referred to his restored kingdom as a "little flock" (D&C 6:34). Continuing, he told them to fear not, for "earth and hell" combined would not prevail against his church. Thus, from the Church's very beginning, prophetic knowledge of its eventual success has provided hope, encouragement, and optimism to the Latter-day Saints. Often the Lord and his prophets have used the metaphor of "a stone which is cut out of the mountain without hands [and] shall roll forth until it has filled the whole earth," to describe the Church's destiny (D&C 65:2).

THE LITTLE STONE

At the request of John Wentworth, editor and proprietor of the *Chicago Democrat*, the Prophet Joseph Smith wrote a brief history of the Latter-day Saints. The article was published in the *Times and Seasons* on 1 March 1842. This provided the Prophet with an opportunity to reflect upon the early history of his life and that of the Church and to prophesy regarding the destiny of the restored gospel. He declared:

"Persecution has not stopped the progress of truth, but has only added fuel to the flame. . . . Proud of the cause which they have espoused, . . . have the Elders of this Church gone forth, and planted the Gospel in almost every state in the Union; it has penetrated our cities, it has spread over our villages, and caused thousands . . . to obey its divine mandates. . . . It has also spread into England, Ireland, Scotland, and Wales . . . ; there are numbers now joining in every land.

". . . no unhallowed hand can stop the work from progressing; persecutions may rage, mobs may combine, armies may assemble, calumny may defame, but the truth of God will go forth boldly, nobly, and independent, till it has penetrated every continent, visited every clime, swept every country, and sounded in every ear, till the purposes of God shall be accomplished, and the Great Jehovah shall say the work is done."[1]

After the martyrdom of the Prophet Joseph Smith and the expulsion from Nauvoo, the Church moved on again to begin anew in the Salt Lake Valley under the leadership of Brigham Young. While President Young traveled back to Winter Quarters, the few Saints in the Salt Lake Valley met in conference in October 1847. The small group assembled in the village of Salt Lake was in sharp contrast to the thousands of Church members still in Winter Quarters and in Great Britain.

John Young, brother of the prophet, nine years later said of that gathering: "So I walked down to where they were holding conference, and I found them by the side of a haystack. There was Father John Smith [whom Brigham Young had left in charge] and a little handful of men that might have been covered with a small tent, and they were holding the semiannual conference of The Church of Jesus Christ of Latter-day Saints."[2]

Elder Orson Pratt provided, in an early sermon delivered in the Great Basin, a scriptural foundation for having been led to such a remote place.[3] He quoted Isaiah's prophecy that "the Lord's house [would] be established in the top of the mountains" (Isaiah 2:2).

President Young described his feelings regarding the Church and its destiny in a letter to Elder Orson Hyde, who was presiding over the Saints in Kanesville: "We feel no fear. We are in the hands of our Heavenly Father, that God of Abraham and Joseph who guided us to this land, who fed the poor Saints on the plains with quails, who gave his people strength to labour without bread, who sent the gulls of the deep as Saviours to preserve the Golden Wheat for bread for his people and who preserved his Saints from the wrath of their enemies, delivering them. . . . We live in this light, are guided by his wisdom, protected by his strength."[4]

Over a century later in the April 1976 general conference of the Church, President Spencer W. Kimball bore testimony that he knew the Church was the little stone that was cut out of a mountain without hands. He also bore witness that it would fill the earth as prophesied, and that life eternal was promised to those who would accept and abide by its precepts.[5] In the April 1979 conference he spoke of temples dotting the United States and other lands "from end to end," of significant increases in the number of missions and missionaries, and of an upsurge in spirituality. He spoke of a readiness in the Latter-day Saints to accomplish things which could not have been done in the past.[6] In the October general conference of that same year, he spoke of the challenges facing us, "There are great challenges ahead of us, giant opportunities to be met. I welcome that exciting prospect and feel to say to the Lord humbly, 'Give me this mountain,' give me these challenges." He compared them to the things Caleb and Joshua faced upon entering the promised land.[7]

THE CHURCH MOVES ON

President Joseph F. Smith once said: "It has not been by the wisdom of man that this people have been directed in their course until the present; it has been by the wisdom of Him who is above man and whose knowledge is greater than that of man, and whose power is above the power of man. . . . The hand of the Lord may not be visible to all. There may be many who can not discern the workings of God's will in the progress and development of this great latter-day work, but there are those who see in every hour and in every moment of the existence of the Church, from its beginning until now, the overruling, almighty hand of Him who sent His Only Begotten Son to the world to become a sacrifice for the sin of the world."[8]

Because the hand of God will always guide the Church, Elder G. Homer Durham was able to declare in the April 1982 general conference, "There *is* a great Church history behind us. There is an even greater Church history ahead of us for every member, every unit of the Church. That history is being made every day, some way, in Korea, in the Philippines, in the Andes, and in every stake."[9]

In a sermon delivered in the October 1984 general conference, Elder Bruce R. McConkie likened the restored Church to a great caravan that has been prepared, organized, and is traveling along its appointed course. The oxen, he declared, are strong, and the teamsters (Church leaders) are wise. While he believed that the caravan would yet encounter storms along the way, that floods would wash away some of the bridges, and that there remained deserts yet to cross and rivers to ford, the caravan would move on. Ahead, Elder McConkie saw the celestial city, the eternal Zion of the Great Jehovah. There, he prophesied, the caravan and those who remain faithful within its wagons will find food, drink, and rest.[10]

Elder Neal A. Maxwell has reminded us, "The Church will be much larger in the latter days than it now is, as we learn from prophecy. (D&C 105:31.) Nevertheless, the Church's 'dominions upon the face of the earth' will still be comparatively small. Its members will be 'scattered upon all the face of the earth.' "[11] Like the leaven in a loaf, the Church will greatly influence world events.

President Gordon B. Hinckley in his April 1987 conference address told the Saints, "There was never a brighter day than today in the history of The Church of Jesus Christ of Latter-day Saints." While he marveled at the growth and expansion of the Church, he concluded his talk by saying that "what we see today is but the scratching of the surface of far greater things yet to come."[12]

With such a destiny and such greater things in mind, President Ezra Taft Benson said: " 'Shall we not,' as the Prophet Joseph Smith declared, 'go on in so great a cause? Go forward and not backward. Courage, . . . and on, on to the victory! Let your hearts rejoice, and be exceedingly glad. Let the earth break forth into singing. Let the dead speak forth anthems of eternal praise to the King Immanuel, who hath ordained, before the world was, that which would enable us to redeem them out of their prison; for the prisoners shall go free.' "[13]

President Benson also told Church members that there is much left to do before the Church can safely rest. The hearts of the world's leaders must be softened so that the gospel can be proclaimed in their lands. False ideologies must be successfully combatted and overcome, and the Church's message of joy and salvation must be presented to all of the earth's inhabitants.[14]

The same testimony Joseph Smith first bore to his neighbors in upper-state New York may be heard in many languages, declaring that God lives, that Jesus is the Christ, that his ancient gospel has been restored, and that the Church of Jesus Christ is again available to all mankind.

The little stone, we are assured, is destined to grow ever larger. It is even now rolling forth with greater speed, as thousands are drawn into the Church and, while momentary setbacks and persecution may slightly slow its progress from time to time, the gospel will triumph, and one glorious day truth will prevail throughout the earth.

ENDNOTES

1. *History of the Church,* 4:540.

2. In "Conference: An Enduring Tradition for 155 Years," *Church News,* 6 Oct. 1985, p. 7.

3. See Breck England, *The Life and Thought of Orson Pratt* (Salt Lake City: University of Utah Press, 1985), p. 134.

4. Letter from Brigham Young to Orson Hyde, 28 July 1850, LDS Historical Department, Salt Lake City.

5. See Conference Report, Apr. 1976, pp. 9–12; or *Ensign,* May 1976, pp. 7–9.

6. In Conference Report, Apr. 1979, p. 3; or *Ensign,* May 1979, p. 4.

7. In Conference Report, Oct. 1979, p. 115; or *Ensign,* Nov. 1979, p. 79.

8. In Conference Report, Apr. 1904, p. 2.

9. In Conference Report, Apr. 1982, pp. 95–96; or *Ensign,* May 1982, p. 68.

10. See Conference Report, Oct. 1984, p. 105; or *Ensign,* Nov. 1984, p. 85.

11. Neal A. Maxwell, *Meek and Lowly* (Salt Lake City: Deseret Book Co., 1987), pp. 62–63.

12. In Conference Report, Apr. 1987, pp. 65, 69; or *Ensign,* May 1987, pp. 52, 59.

13. In Conference Report, Oct. 1978, p. 43; or *Ensign,* Nov. 1978, p. 32.

14. See Conference Report, Apr. 1985, p. 6; or *Ensign,* May 1985, p. 6.

MEMBERS OF THE QUORUM
OF THE TWELVE APOSTLES
IN THE DISPENSATION OF THE FULNESS OF TIMES

Thomas Baldwin Marsh
Born: 1 November 1800
Ordained an Apostle: 26 April 1835
Died: January 1866

David Wyman Patten
Born: 14 November 1799
Ordained an Apostle: 15 February 1835
Died: 25 October 1838

Brigham Young
Born: 1 June 1801
Ordained an Apostle: 14 February 1835
Died: 29 August 1877

Heber Chase Kimball
Born: 14 June 1801
Ordained an Apostle: 14 February 1835
Died: 22 June 1868

Orson Hyde
Born: 8 January 1805
Ordained an Apostle: 15 February 1835
Died: 28 November 1878

William E. McLellin
Born: 18 January 1806
Ordained an Apostle: 15 February 1835
Died: 24 April 1883

Parley Parker Pratt
Born: 12 April 1807
Ordained an Apostle: 21 February 1835
Died: 13 May 1857

Luke S. Johnson
Born: 3 November 1807
Ordained an Apostle: 15 February 1835
Died: 9 December 1861

William Smith
Born: 13 March 1811
Ordained an Apostle: 15 February 1835
Died: 13 November 1893

Orson Pratt
Born: 19 September 1811
Ordained an Apostle: 26 April 1835
Died: 3 October 1881

John Farnham Boynton
Born: 20 September 1811
Ordained an Apostle: 15 February 1835
Died: 20 October 1890

Lyman Eugene Johnson
Born: 24 October 1811
Ordained an Apostle: 14 February 1835
Died: 20 December 1856

John Edward Page
Born: 25 February 1799
Ordained an Apostle: 19 December 1838
Died: 14 October 1867

John Taylor
Born: 1 November 1808
Ordained an Apostle: 19 December 1838
Died: 25 July 1887

Wilford Woodruff
Born: 1 March 1807
Ordained an Apostle: 26 April 1839
Died: 2 September 1898

George Albert Smith
Born: 26 June 1817
Ordained an Apostle: 26 April 1839
Died: 1 September 1875

Willard Richards
Born: 24 June 1804
Ordained an Apostle: 14 April 1840
Died: 11 March 1854

Lyman Wight
Born: 9 May 1796
Ordained an Apostle: 8 April 1841
Died: 31 March 1858

Amasa Mason Lyman
Born: 30 March 1813
Ordained an Apostle: 20 August 1842
Died: 4 February 1877

Ezra Taft Benson
Born: 22 February 1811
Ordained an Apostle: 16 July 1846
Died: 3 September 1869

Charles Coulson Rich
Born: 21 August 1809
Ordained an Apostle: 12 February 1849
Died: 17 November 1883

Lorenzo Snow
Born: 3 April 1814
Ordained an Apostle: 12 February 1849
Died: 10 October 1901

Erastus Snow
Born: 9 November 1818
Ordained an Apostle: 12 February 1849
Died: 27 May 1888

Franklin Dewey Richards
Born: 2 April 1821
Ordained an Apostle: 12 February 1849
Died: 9 December 1899

George Quayle Cannon
Born: 11 January 1827
Ordained an Apostle: 26 August 1860
Died: 12 April 1901

Joseph Fielding Smith
Born: 13 November 1838
Ordained an Apostle: 1 July 1866
Died: 19 November 1918

Brigham Young, Jr.
Born: 18 December 1836
Ordained an Apostle: 4 February 1864
Died: 11 April 1903

Albert Carrington
Born: 8 January 1813
Ordained an Apostle: 3 July 1870
Died: 19 September 1889

Moses Thatcher
Born: 2 February 1842
Ordained an Apostle: 9 April 1879
Died: 21 August 1909

Francis Marion Lyman
Born: 12 January 1840
Ordained an Apostle: 27 October 1880
Died: 18 November 1916

John Henry Smith
Born: 18 September 1848
Ordained an Apostle: 27 October 1880
Died: 13 October 1911

George Teasdale
Born: 8 December 1831
Ordained an Apostle: 16 October 1882
Died: 9 June 1907

Heber Jeddy Grant
Born: 22 November 1856
Ordained an Apostle: 16 October 1882
Died: 14 May 1945

John Whittaker Taylor
Born: 15 May 1858
Ordained an Apostle: 9 April 1884
Died: 10 October 1916

Marriner Wood Merrill
Born: 25 September 1832
Ordained an Apostle: 7 October 1889
Died: 6 February 1906

Anthon Henrik Lund
Born: 15 May 1844
Ordained an Apostle: 7 October 1889
Died: 2 March 1921

Abraham Hoagland Cannon
Born: 12 March 1859
Ordained an Apostle: 7 October 1889
Died: 19 July 1896

Matthias Foss Cowley
Born: 25 August 1858
Ordained an Apostle: 7 October 1897
Died: 16 June 1940

Abraham Owen Woodruff
Born: 23 November 1872
Ordained an Apostle: 7 October 1897
Died: 20 June 1904

Rudger Clawson
Born: 12 March 1857
Ordained an Apostle: 10 October 1898
Died: 21 June 1943

Reed Smoot
Born: 10 January 1862
Ordained an Apostle: 8 April 1900
Died: 9 February 1941

Hyrum Mack Smith
Born: 21 March 1872
Ordained an Apostle: 24 October 1901
Died: 23 January 1918

George Albert Smith
Born: 4 April 1870
Ordained an Apostle: 8 October 1903
Died: 4 April 1951

Charles William Penrose
Born: 4 February 1832
Ordained an Apostle: 7 July 1904
Died: 16 May 1925

George Franklin Richards
Born: 23 February 1861
Ordained an Apostle: 9 April 1906
Died: 8 August 1950

Orson Ferguson Whitney
Born: 1 July 1855
Ordained an Apostle: 9 April 1906
Died: 16 May 1931

David Oman McKay
Born: 8 September 1873
Ordained an Apostle: 9 April 1906
Died: 18 January 1970

Anthony Woodward Ivins
Born: 16 September 1852
Ordained an Apostle: 6 October 1907
Died: 23 September 1934

Joseph Fielding Smith
Born: 19 July 1876
Ordained an Apostle: 7 April 1910
Died: 2 July 1972

James Edward Talmage
Born: 21 September 1862
Ordained an Apostle: 8 December 1911
Died: 27 July 1933

Stephen L Richards
Born: 18 June 1879
Ordained an Apostle: 18 January 1917
Died: 19 May 1959

Richard Roswell Lyman
Born: 23 November 1870
Ordained an Apostle: 7 April 1918
Died: 31 December 1963

Melvin Joseph Ballard
Born: 9 February 1873
Ordained an Apostle: 7 January 1919
Died: 30 July 1939

John Andreas Widtsoe
Born: 31 January 1872
Ordained an Apostle: 17 March 1921
Died: 29 November 1952

Joseph Francis Merrill
Born: 24 August 1868
Ordained an Apostle: 8 October 1931
Died: 3 February 1952

Charles Albert Callis
Born: 4 May 1865
Ordained an Apostle: 12 October 1933
Died: 21 January 1947

Joshua Reuben Clark, Jr.
Born: 1 September 1871
Ordained an Apostle: 11 October 1934
Died: 6 October 1961

Alonzo Arza Hinckley
Born: 23 April 1870
Ordained an Apostle: 11 October 1934
Died: 22 December 1936

Albert Ernest Bowen
Born: 31 October 1875
Ordained an Apostle: 8 April 1937
Died: 15 July 1953

Sylvester Quayle Cannon
Born: 10 June 1877
Ordained an Apostle: 14 April 1938
Died: 29 May 1943

Harold Bingham Lee
Born: 28 March 1899
Ordained an Apostle: 10 April 1941
Died: 26 December 1973

Spencer Woolley Kimball
Born: 28 March 1895
Ordained an Apostle: 7 October 1943
Died: 5 November 1985

Ezra Taft Benson
Born: 4 August 1899
Ordained an Apostle: 7 October 1943

Mark Edward Petersen
Born: 7 November 1900
Ordained an Apostle: 20 April 1944
Died: 11 January 1984

Matthew Cowley
Born: 2 August 1897
Ordained an Apostle: 11 October 1945
Died: 13 December 1953

Henry Dinwoodey Moyle
Born: 22 April 1889
Ordained an Apostle: 10 April 1947
Died: 18 September 1963

Delbert Leon Stapley
Born: 11 December 1896
Ordained an Apostle: 5 October 1950
Died: 19 August 1978

Marion George Romney
Born: 19 September 1897
Ordained an Apostle: 11 October 1951
Died: 20 May 1988

LeGrand Richards
Born: 6 February 1886
Ordained an Apostle: 10 April 1952
Died: 11 January 1983

Adam Samuel Bennion
Born: 2 December 1886
Ordained an Apostle: 9 April 1953
Died: 11 February 1958

Richard Louis Evans
Born: 23 March 1906
Ordained an Apostle: 8 October 1953
Died: 1 November 1971

George Quayle Morris
Born: 20 February 1874
Ordained an Apostle: 8 April 1954
Died: 23 April 1962

Hugh Brown Brown
Born: 24 October 1883
Ordained an Apostle: 10 April 1958
Died: 2 December 1975

Howard William Hunter
Born: 14 November 1907
Ordained an Apostle: 15 October 1959

Gordon Bitner Hinckley
Born: 23 June 1910
Ordained an Apostle: 5 October 1961

Nathan Eldon Tanner
Born: 9 May 1898
Ordained an Apostle: 11 October 1962
Died: 27 November 1982

Thomas Spencer Monson
Born: 21 August 1927
Ordained an Apostle: 10 October 1963

Boyd Kenneth Packer
Born: 10 September 1924
Ordained an Apostle: 9 April 1970

Marvin Jeremy Ashton
Born: 6 May 1915
Ordained an Apostle: 2 December 1971

Bruce Redd McConkie
Born: 29 July 1915
Ordained an Apostle: 12 October 1972
Died: 19 April 1985

Lowell Tom Perry
Born: 5 August 1922
Ordained an Apostle: 11 April 1974

David Bruce Haight
Born: 2 September 1906
Ordained an Apostle: 8 January 1976

James Esdras Faust
Born: 31 July 1920
Ordained an Apostle: 1 October 1978

Neal Ash Maxwell
Born: 6 July 1926
Ordained an Apostle: 23 July 1981

Russell Marion Nelson
Born: 9 September 1924
Ordained an Apostle: 7 April 1984

Dallin Harris Oaks
Born: 12 August 1932
Ordained an Apostle: 3 May 1984

Melvin Russell Ballard, Jr.
Born: 8 October 1928
Ordained an Apostle: 10 October 1985

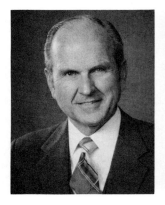  

Joseph Bitner Wirthlin
Born: 11 June 1917
Ordained an Apostle: 9 October 1986

Richard Gordon Scott
Born: 7 November 1928
Ordained an Apostle: 6 October 1988

INDEX